The St. Martin's
Guide to Teaching Writing

The St. Martin's Guide to Teaching Writing

Sixth Edition

CHERYL GLENN
PENNSYLVANIA STATE UNIVERSITY

MELISSA A. GOLDTHWAITE
SAINT JOSEPH'S UNIVERSITY

BEDFORD / ST. MARTIN'S
Boston ◆ New York

For Bedford/St. Martin's

Developmental Editor: Nathan Odell
Production Editor: Diana P. George
Production Supervisor: Andrew Ensor
Senior Marketing Manager: John Swanson
Art Director: Lucy Krikorian
Cover Design: Donna L. Dennison
Composition: Stratford/TexTech
Printing and Binding: Haddon Craftsmen, Inc., an R. R. Donnelley & Sons Company

President: Joan E. Feinberg
Editorial Director: Denise B. Wydra
Editor in Chief: Karen Henry
Director of Development: Erica T. Appel
Director of Marketing: Karen Melton Soeltz
Director of Editing, Design, and Production: Marcia Cohen
Managing Editor: Shuli Traub

Library of Congress Control Number: 2007920785

Manufactured in the United States of America.

2   1   0   9   8   7
f   e   d   c   b

For information, write: Bedford/ St. Martin's, 75 Arlington Street, Boston, MA 02116   (617-399-4000)

ISBN-10: 0-312-45133-4
ISBN-13: 978-0-312-45133-2

Acknowledgments

Acknowledgments and copyrights appear at the back of the book on pages 534–35, which constitute an extension of the copyright page.

Preface

There it is in black and white. You've been assigned to teach a college writing course: first-year composition. Sentences, paragraphs, essays. "Me—teach writing? I never took a writing course in my life, except freshman English, which I barely remember. What am I going to do?" This book was written to help you plan your writing classes and help you teach your students to become better writers. The theories, techniques, and methods discussed in the following chapters are based on our own teaching practice; they have been classroom-tested and as a whole represent the greater part of our current knowledge—both theory and practice—about teaching writing.

The St. Martin's Guide to Teaching Writing, Sixth Edition, is informed by a three-part thesis. First, writing is teachable; it is an art that can be learned, rather than a mysterious ability that one either has or does not have. Second, students learn to write from continual trial-and-error writing and almost never profit from lectures, from teacher-centered classes, or from studying and memorizing isolated rules. Third, the theories and methods included here should represent strategies that work in the classroom. Therefore, this book is not a complete introduction to composition studies; some important composition and education theories are not covered here because they don't immediately lend themselves to classroom use.

This book is divided into three parts: "Classroom Issues," "Rhetorical Practices," and "An Anthology of Essays." If you're teaching writing for the first time, Part I offers you the nuts and bolts of teaching composition, with chapters ranging from "Preparing for the Course" (Chapter 1) to "Evaluating Student Essays" (Chapter 5). This part will help you prepare for, set up, and teach your first writing course. In this edition, we have provided additional attention to the ways changes in technology affect classroom practices, from information on teaching in wired, wireless, and hybrid classrooms to assignments for analyzing and creating visual, oral, and electronic texts (including a new sample syllabus that focuses on visual rhetoric). We have also expanded coverage of teaching multilingual writers, including a section on cultural differences in peer response groups.

If you're a more experienced teacher, you may want to begin with Part II, on the theoretical background of the composition process and its application. Also covered here are the traditional canons of rhetoric—not only invention, arrangement, and style, but also new chapters on memory and delivery. Each of the chapters in Part II consists of an introduction followed by discussions of specific theories and classroom activities. These activities have been successful for us and for other teachers. We hope they work for you—and that you will help to improve them.

Part III includes a collection of essays, four of which are new to this edition, that explicitly attempt to link theory and practice with society at large. All of the essays interanimate one another, fusing classroom issues with social ones. We start with readings that concentrate on classroom practices and pressures and then move to essays that interrogate social conditions and expectations. Not surprisingly, the selections converge in rich and complex ways: the essays toward the end of Part III inform those at the beginning, and those at the beginning provide concrete illustrations of classroom practices that grow from and need to be revised by the exigencies explored in the later essays. Although we've loosely categorized the essays, we see them as richly overlapping in terms of their application to writing courses—both first-year writing and basic writing—based in contemporary essays, literature, and student writing. We believe these issues and topics will inform and vitalize your teaching, writing, and research, whether your work takes place at a two-year college, four-year college, or research university. We hope these essays will lead you to conduct research in your own classrooms.

ACKNOWLEDGMENTS

Many people have helped us write this book. We're especially grateful to Andrea Lunsford, who updated Chapter 11, "Invitation to Further Study," and whose work helped shape Chapter 10, "Teaching Delivery." We can think of no one better suited to host the dynamic conversation that continues to shape and reshape our field.

At Bedford/St. Martin's we wish to thank Nancy Perry, Nathan Odell, and Stephanie Butler, whose editorial support made this revision possible. Special thanks go to the reviewers for this edition: Cynthia Cox, Belmont University; Barb Blakely Duffelmeyer, Iowa State University; Jessica Enoch, University of New Hampshire; Marti Singer, Georgia State University; and Patricia Webb, Arizona State University. Throughout the text, we rely on the expertise and materials of many successful teachers. We're grateful to the teachers who allowed us to quote them in our epigraphs for each chapter: Rosalyn Collings, Jessica Enoch, Keith Gibson, Amy Hodges Hamilton, Jay Jordan, Lindsay Lightner, Lisa Schifano, Steve Schneider, Steve Thomas, and Scott Wible. We also thank the teacher-researchers whose work constitutes Part III of this book for their kind permission to reprint their articles. As the preceding paragraph suggests, teaching writing is always collaborative—and this book is no exception.

More than twenty years ago, not long after they had become friends, Cheryl Glenn and Bob Connors sat together and worked out a plan for this book, never expecting that the book would make its way into the twenty-first century without Bob. Even though there are few teaching methods that can really be said to belong to any one person, Bob's intellectual and pedagogical influence on this project remain easily identifiable, even within this large and far-flung community we refer to as composition studies. We dedicate this sixth edition of the *Guide to Teaching Writing* to the memory of Bob, teacher, scholar, researcher, and writer extraordinaire. His influence on this project and on our field remains immeasurable.

Thus it is that we're all in this together, and one of the most satisfying parts of teaching writing is the way we all help one another out. We want to welcome you to our community, and we hope this book helps you get ready for your first—or your twenty-first—adventure in the writing classroom.

Cheryl Glenn
Melissa A. Goldthwaite

Contents

The St. Martin's
Guide to Teaching Writing

I

Classroom Issues

1

Preparing for the Course

Before my first teaching job, a veteran teacher had told me, "Have the first day of class planned to the last detail. Script out everything you're going to do and say, so that at least you won't have to worry about that." So before the semester began, I visited the first college classroom in which I would teach and tried to imagine the twenty-four close-spaced desks full of freshmen. I hope they'll be more nervous than I will, I thought. I practiced my opening lines out loud: "Good morning; is everyone here for section 89 of English 15?" And then it struck me that it wasn't really the first day of class that I was anxious about; it was the second day. The first day is vital, of course, but it's on the second day that the real work takes place. The students will have read and written and prepared, and I will have to respond and start teaching, unscripted save for my syllabus and lesson plans. It was then that I thought, Wow. I hope I know what I'm doing.

–LINDSAY LIGHTNER

FINDING OUT ABOUT THE COURSE

The first thing any new teacher must do is gather information. You have been assigned to teach a writing course, but writing courses, even first-year (FY) writing courses, come in many varieties. Before you can make intelligent and useful plans, you'll want to find out some of the definitions and vital statistics concerning your course. Such information may be presented in the form of an orientation session for new teachers. Indeed, some departments organize special colloquia for new teaching assistants, and new instructors are usually welcome to sit in. Such an introduction will provide you with all the information you need. If your program does not offer an orientation session, the writing program administrator (WPA) or the chair of the department can undoubtedly answer most of the questions raised here. Some of your most important questions concerning unwritten practices may be answered by experienced teachers; at many schools, their wisdom is a vital element of the program. But your WPA is the most reliable source for official departmental policy.

The first details you should find out about are the number of credit hours the course carries and the number of times the class meets each week. A three-credit course that meets three hours a week provides far less time for reading and writing than, say, a five-credit, five-hour course; students willing to write ten essays and fifty journal entries for five credits may object to doing the same amount of work for three credits. As you plan your syllabus, adjust the number of writing assignments according to the number of credit hours.

Second, ask how many sections you will be teaching and how many students you should expect to have in each class. The National Council of Teachers of

English (NCTE) recommends that each graduate student teach only one under-graduate section each term and that the maximum number of students in a class be twenty (or fifteen in a basic writing course). Most English departments try to adhere to these recommendations, keeping the numbers within reason-able limits (from twenty to twenty-five students). Of course, the fewer students you have, the fewer papers you'll be reading and evaluating, the fewer confer-ences you'll be conducting, and the more time you will be able to devote to each student and your class preparation. If you are willing to teach at 8:00 A.M. or 5:00 P.M., you may get a smaller class than if you teach at a more popular time slot, such as late morning or early afternoon. Nonetheless, you should count on having the maximum allowable number of students in your class. Information about your student load will help you organize assignments and plan a syllabus.

Third, find out whether there is a standardized departmental structure for the course. The structure of composition courses is shaped by pedagogical goals and curricular concerns. You'll need to find out how many composition courses students are required to take at your school. Some schools, for instance, have one term devoted to learning various rhetorical methods (such as narration, description, and argument) and another term devoted to study-ing literature and composition or writing research papers. Other programs require just one composition course and expect students to gain experience writing personal essays and arguments.

The structure of composition courses varies widely: Knowing early on what your department expects and how the curriculum is shaped will help you plan the appropriate course. Many departments have official policies that new teachers must follow, and such policies and standards will inform your own course arrangement. For instance: Must students write and submit a certain number of essays? Must they keep journals or reading logs? Is there an official policy with regard to revisions? peer evaluation? teacher conferences? evalua-tion and grading? Is an exit exam required?

Finally, make inquiries about the academic level of the students you will be teaching. If your college or university has open admissions, then the range of your students' abilities will probably be wide. Some FY students may be basic writers with reading and writing abilities far below the average, whereas other students may be strong writers, accomplished and sophisticated products of hard-driving college-prep programs. Naturally, you must gear your prepara-tion — from textbook selection to syllabus design — to the abilities of your stu-dents. If you are teaching at an open-admissions school, find out whether incoming students write English placement essays and whether the school has a basic writing (BW) program, an English as a second language (ESL) program, and a writing center (WC). You will also want to know whether there are differ-ent levels of FY courses — an honors section, perhaps, or special-interest sec-tions — or whether all FY students are placed in the same course. Try to find out whether students from all years and levels can be placed in FY English; if that is the case, then you may have some more experienced students in your class.

Try at this point to find out all you can about the backgrounds of the students you are likely to encounter. Until fairly recently, teachers of writing have treated all students as if they were very much alike, but that convenient fiction is no longer feasible to maintain. Our students have different mother tongues and different levels of fluency in edited American English (also called standardized English); they come from different socioeconomic classes and different sectors of society. And now more than ever before, there is a huge range in their ages and life experiences. The entrance of such a diverse student body into the academy has made us aware of our past inattention to these differences and of how we had neglected to devise curricula that addressed the differences and the political (or apolitical) agendas of our institutions. Find out what you can about your students' gender, ethnicity, age, and so on. You'll find that planning a course aimed mainly at Euro-American eighteen-year-old, able-bodied students from suburban high schools is very different from planning one for a group that includes urban minorities, recent immigrants, students with disabilities, and returning or part-time students. Especially if your course meets in the late afternoon or evening — that is, after the workday — be prepared for more diversity in your students and, correspondingly, more diverse demands on you. (See the scholarship by Brueggemann et al.; Bruch and Marback; Davis; Redd; Richardson; and Trainor cited at the end of this chapter; see also the article by Leki, starting on p. 330.)

If your school has a BW or an ESL program, you might want to find out its entrance and exit requirements and its relation to the standard FY writing course. Also try to find out about other writing programs on campus — not only to get a better picture of the entire writing program, but also so you will know where to send your students for help. You may be surprised at the number of support systems your school offers. Some schools have writing centers that will work with students at any stage in the writing process and will send representatives into classrooms to give mini-lessons on such topics as process writing, writer's block, and essay exams. In addition, some schools have reading centers, where reading and comprehension problems can be diagnosed and helped. Often affiliated with the communications department, the College of Education, or the College of Allied Medicine may be a learning disabilities center, where dyslexia, dysgraphia, and attention deficit disorder (ADD) can be diagnosed and treated. If you have a student who is physically disabled, you may also find yourself needing to make contact with the disability services office. By asking questions and talking with representatives of the various academic support programs on your campus, you will be much better prepared to guide your students through their writing course. When they have problems you cannot solve, you will be ready to send them to the specialists who can help.

At times, a student might exhibit behavioral or emotional issues that disrupt schoolwork or even the classroom. Your school likely offers psychological support to these students. If such a student acts out in class in a way that might be dangerous, immediately call campus security. Such situations are rare. It is not rare, however, for students to need counseling or support for substance-abuse problems, eating disorders, or other psychological issues — especially when such issues interfere with the student's ability to focus on schoolwork. Many teachers talk to and listen to students in crisis, but often these students will need professional help; in these cases, refer the student to the campus counseling center.

CHOOSING THE TEXTBOOKS

After you have discovered all you can about the nature of the courses you are to teach and the kinds of students you can expect, the next step is to investigate your textbook options. Since the textbook you use will underpin a number of important elements in your course, you will undoubtedly want to make use of it in as well-informed a manner as possible. Many writing programs require that all teachers use certain texts for a certain period; others specify a primary text and allow teachers to choose the supplementary ones; and still others allow teachers to choose from a list of approved texts. The freedom you have in choosing textbooks will depend on your school and its program as well as on the needs and interests of your students. In general, you may choose from among three types of textbooks: (1) rhetorics or general textbooks, which explain the step-by-step techniques of writing and can include argument, research, online writing, and readings; (2) readers or anthologies, which provide selections of readings, usually accompanied by explanations, discussion questions, and suggestions for writing; and (3) handbooks, which give guidance about the writing process, style, grammar, punctuation, and documentation. Some textbooks combine two or more of these purposes.

Begin your consideration of textbooks by finding out which ones have been used with success and examining those texts carefully. Most departments that allow teachers some freedom in textbook selection maintain a small library of texts for teachers to examine. In order to make sense of the books you find there, you may wish to do some background reading on textbooks; several review articles and bibliographies provide an overview of the world of textbooks. To learn more about composition textbooks, see the CCCC *Bibliography of Rhetoric and Composition* for current essays on and abstracts of textbooks. In addition, *Composition Studies* and the *Journal of Teaching Writing* often carry textbook reviews. Publishers' brochures, catalogs, and Web sites are another source of information about the textbooks they offer. Book fairs, if your department or school organizes them, provide opportunities to see and compare a range of texts from different publishers. Through publishers' Web sites and book fairs you can get in touch with representatives who can help advise you about the texts available from particular presses. If you're seriously considering the adoption of a text, most publishers will provide a free or low-cost examination copy.

When examining textbooks, keep in mind the question of structure: How much do you want the structure of the textbook(s) to inform the structure of the course? If the textbook's order of topics is invention, organization, diction, style, and paragraphs, will you design your course around that structure and plan to spend a week or two weeks on each chapter? Or will you structure your course differently and organize textbook readings according to a theme, a rhetorical method, types of argument, or some other plan? Perhaps you will find a book whose organization or thematic schema is congenial to you; however, you may decide to reorder the topics or to use only certain sections of a book. Many publishers also allow instructors to create custom textbooks. This option provides freedom for the instructor to choose both the content and structure of the text.

Talking with experienced teachers in your program about textbooks can be helpful at this point. Get several teachers' opinions about a book before you make your choice, and don't decide hastily. Remember, for the next ten to fifteen weeks, you — and your students — will be living with your decision (or the decisions of a textbook selection committee). Make sure you're comfortable with the texts you use and with your plan for teaching from them.

Finally, be aware that there is no substitute for personal experience with a textbook. After teaching from a text, you may or may not want to continue to use it. Have your students evaluate each textbook; their responses will make your future choices easier. In any case, choose your first text carefully.

COMPUTERIZED LEARNING TECHNOLOGIES

Whether you teach at a school that has computer-supported classrooms or you simply use email to contact your students, you can use various technologies to support your pedagogical goals. Depending on the resources and support your school offers, you may be able to make such technologies a significant part of your classroom. Some schools offer online writing labs (OWLs) where students can send a draft and receive an online response to their writing. Many schools provide computer-supported classrooms and specialized software. Talk with your WPA about the technology and support your school offers. The following section provides an overview of some of the specific technologies writing teachers have found useful both inside and outside of the classroom. Keep in mind that the quickest way to learn how to incorporate these technologies into your own class is to sit in on the class of an experienced teacher. (See the scholarship by Doheny-Farina; Gurak; Handa; Hawisher and C. Selfe; and R. Selfe cited at the end of this chapter; also see chapter 3, which includes a section on teaching in wired or wireless classrooms.)

In a computer-supported classroom, each student and teacher has a computer on which to compose, respond to, and revise drafts. Students then trade drafts electronically — often through email. Many computer-supported classrooms connect students with each other and their teacher through a local area network (LAN), which links individual computers via a central server. Using a LAN, students and teachers can save their work on the central server, allowing for the easy sharing of drafts and evaluations digitally, rather than through hard copies.

Some colleges and universities use LAN-based writing software packages, such as Daedalus Integrated Writing Environment (daedalus.com/products_diwe_overview.asp). Such programs allow students to create drafts on a word-processing component and then to share drafts and comment on them through work groups and (computer-to-computer) linked conferences. In addition, some of the packages include invention and response heuristics, spelling and grammar checkers, bibliography generators, and even grading modules. The new generation of these programs — for example, Bedford/St. Martin's *Comment*, which is used primarily for responding — are Web-based rather than LAN-based, which makes them accessible beyond the computer classroom (comment.bedfordstmartins.com).

Increasingly, schools are providing a Web-based software package, such as WebCT/Blackboard, which allows teachers to manage course materials online. WebCT/Blackboard provides an area for announcements, updates, and reminders; a space for course information, including the syllabus; staff information, where you can post your contact information and office hours; an area for course documents, where you can post additional readings or lecture notes; a communications section, where you can mount online discussions, chat, or email links; and other spaces for external links or various tools. Even without Blackboard or a similar software program, however, you can most likely put your syllabus online and use other Web-based programs for pedagogical purposes. Edutech (edutech.ch/lms/ev2.php) offers reviews of some popular services.

Even if you don't have access to a fully equipped computer-supported classroom, you'll probably have access to email through your college or university, so some part of your class work can be conducted online. There are obviously problems inherent in attempting to make complex connections through email, especially if some of your students do not have easy access to the Internet or the time to use it. Students who are working full-time and do not have a home computer may not be able to take advantage of email, for instance. Even so, email allows you to communicate easily with your students away from class, allows students to share drafts with each other, and allows them to send drafts to you for comment.

Many teachers also use Web-based discussion pages for conversation outside of class. A Web-based discussion page is a kind of private electronic bulletin board that allows you and your students to post messages and receive responses on the same thread or to start new threads. An advantage of Web-based discussion is that the discussion is stored and archived on the Web and can be accessed from any place you or your students have an Internet connection. If your school does not provide a Web-based discussion page for you, you can set one up yourself at http://www.free-forums.com.

Other technological support for your pedagogy might include using online textbooks or supplementing printed texts with online journal articles. Many presses that sell composition textbooks, including Bedford/St. Martin's (customreader.bedfordstmartins.com), also allow you to create your own custom reader online by choosing from a substantial list of readings. In addition, many textbooks have companion Web sites that offer support and information for both teachers and students, including interactive exercises, sample assignments, and model student essays. In addition to book-specific sites, many publishers also provide helpful general resources for teachers and students.

LINKS TO COMMUNITY SERVICE

The past fifteen years have seen burgeoning interest in the idea of service learning — an educational concept based on combining standard classroom work with the movement of students out into the community, where they engage in various kinds of community service as part of the course activity. Service learning has gained considerable momentum as a result of the power of Mike Rose's *Lives on the Boundary,* a book that movingly details the struggle for literacy that underprepared students must engage in. Community service by college students is a particularly promising concept in writing courses, which are always involved with seeking meaningful issues for students to write about. A number of respected writing programs at both state and private schools have incorporated community service as an important part of some of their first-year courses. (See Adler-Kassner, Crooks, and Watters; Franco; Hellman; Herzberg; Huckin; Peck, Flower, and Higgins; and Schutz and Gere cited at the end of this chapter.)

Service learning in the writing class usually means asking students to involve themselves either in a community literacy outreach program or in writing for businesses, civic groups, or other organizations. Literacy outreach activities can include working in a variety of off-campus educational settings ranging from public schools to homeless shelters, community centers, social-service offices, public libraries, and the Internet. Students involved in service learning may work with schoolchildren, welfare clients, adults struggling with literacy issues, single parents, or second-language speakers trying to improve their English. Some may gain experience writing grants and Web sites. The placements students seek will depend largely on your pedagogical goals and the kinds of learning and writing experiences that will best meet those goals. Placements can also be influenced by students' interests and available service sites.

A writing program that has a vital service-learning component can be exciting for both teacher and students because it invests the whole course with an identifiable purpose and gives every student experiences to detail in writing. Writing assignments suggest themselves almost automatically, and involvement in the literacy struggles of others helps students recognize how those struggles appear in their own lives. When service learning works, as Bruce Herzberg says, students' writing shows "a sense of life as a communal project, an understanding of the way that social institutions affect our lives, and a sense that our responsibility for social justice includes but also carries on beyond personal acts of charity" (317). Working with people who are less educated and often less fortunate can be a true revelation for first-year college students, many of whom have never been discriminated against. Especially in schools with a multicultural population, service learning and service-related values can help define what a writing program is about.

If your program has a service-learning component, you will probably need to ask your WPA about working within it. Even writing programs that include community service as important parts of their work may not ask or even allow first-time teachers to take part in the service component, preferring to work with more experienced teachers. Speak with your WPA about making service-learning connections for your students. If your program does not have a service-learning component, perhaps you can work up some interest in starting one. However, we cannot advise that you try doing service learning alone, especially not as a new teacher. Successful community service requires tight and effective coordination between a teacher or program and community organizations, and experience shows that firm relations between the agency and writing program must be established *before* the program begins in order for it to be effective. Some shelters or community centers will accept any sort of tutoring or teaching, even if it is only short-term, but many ask that tutors agree to work with their clients over longer terms. Service learning is best accomplished in the context of a program that believes in and has committed to it. So if you feel drawn to trying service learning as part of your course, plan to get involved for the long haul.

Many schools have a service-learning center or office that helps teachers from a variety of disciplines develop service-learning classes. The center can provide valuable resources, such as individual teacher consultations, development workshops, information on curriculum development grants, contacts with community-based organizations, assistance in identifying placements compatible with your pedagogical objectives, and service-learning research materials. The center's experienced staff can help you set up your class in ways that will avoid potential problems. (For online service-learning resources, see the Web sites for Campus Compact, ABCD Books, National Service-Learning Clearinghouse, and The Big Dummy's Guide to Service Learning, listed at the end of this chapter.)

CREATING A SYLLABUS

Writing the syllabus is your next major task. The syllabus provides an overview of, and a plan for, the entire course: the forms your classes will take, the sorts of writing assignments you will require, the order of the material you plan to teach, and so forth. After you have read through this book, talked with your colleagues, and carefully looked over your chosen texts, you should be ready to make a rough draft of your plan. Formalized, this draft will be the basis for the central document of your course, the syllabus.

The syllabus for college courses originated as a list of the books for which every student was to be held responsible. Now, a syllabus is more encompassing. For all intents and purposes, the syllabus for a FY writing course is a contract between teacher and student that states the responsibilities of the teacher and the students as well as the standards for the course. Everyone concerned, from your department administrators to the parents of incoming students, may want to know your exact plans and expectations. Such a written contract has other uses: for instance, it shows a student who feels ill-used or wants special privileges your position on the issue in question, whether it is your attendance policy or your due-date policy. To protect yourself and your students from potential misunderstanding, a detailed syllabus that clearly spells out your purposes and policies is best.

The syllabus also informs the structure of the class, explaining what the course will cover, when it will be covered, and what your qualitative and quantitative expectations are. In other words, the syllabus saves you from having to repeat explanations of course policies, goals, and dates. It is also the first written expression of your personality that you will present to your students. Although many elements of the syllabus will be constructed by the requirements of your program, writing it also gives you a chance to reflect philosophically on what you are asking of your students and why you are asking it. What does it mean that you are asking for six 5-page essays rather than three 10-page essays? Why are you (or your department) refusing to allow more than three absences? What do you want students to gain from using an anthology? a handbook? Your syllabus asks you to answer those questions in a practical way.

Syllabi for writing courses usually need to be detailed for a number of reasons, not the least of which is that few students have developed a set of expectations and intentions for composition courses. But just as important is the fact that students deserve to see their assignments written out. If you write out the assignments, you take the time to explain what it is you want your students to do and be able to do. By following the outline presented here, you should be able to create a syllabus that fills all your major needs and answers all your students' major questions. This outline will not lead you to produce an exhaustive syllabus, but it is a good model for first-time teachers because of its simplicity and schematic development. Keep in mind that although few teachers adhere unconditionally to their syllabi, fewer still depart from them seriously. (See the two sample syllabi, starting on page 14.)

1. *Your name, the course number, your office address, classroom location, your office hours, your email address, and your office telephone number.* Office hours are those periods when you must be in your office so that students may drop by without an appointment. If your department does not require a minimum number of office hours, a rule of thumb is that you should schedule as many office hours as your course has contact hours — hours you are in the classroom with your students. For example, if your class meets five hours a week, set aside five hours a week for your office hours. (In a conferencing system, these would include hours spent in conference. See pp. 75–78 for more information on conferences.) Although teachers can generally choose their office hours, immediately before or after class can be the most convenient times for teachers as well as students. Try to schedule office hours on two successive days so that students who come in only on Mondays, Wednesdays, and Fridays or only on Tuesdays and Thursdays have a chance of seeing you.

2. *Information about the textbooks.* This includes the author, title, edition, and publication information for each text. If you wish students to purchase any supplementary materials (course packets, for example), purchasing details should be included.

3. *Course policy.* Include in this section your policies on the following:
   a. Attendance — how many absences you allow and what you will do if that number is exceeded. You'll need to see whether the department has a policy on this before making your own.
   b. Tardiness — what you will do about students who consistently come to class late.
   c. Participation — how much, if any, of the final course grade will depend on classroom participation.
   d. Late papers — whether and under what conditions you will accept written assignments after their due dates.
   e. Style of papers — what you will demand by way of the physical format for graded assignments: what format they must use for citing sources (usually MLA), whether papers must be word-processed, whether they must be single- or double-spaced, and so forth.
   f. Reminders — include a statement asking students to turn off cell phones and pagers before entering the classroom.

4. *Course requirements.* Discuss the following features of written work:
   a. The number and length of essays to be submitted for grading; your policy on revision.
   b. The requirements for keeping a journal, an explanation of the journal policy, and how or whether the journal will be applied to the final grade (optional).
   c. Any explanation of a policy on ungraded homework, in-class writing assignments, drafts, and so forth and how or whether ungraded work will apply to the final grade.

5. *Grading procedures.* Here you set forth the procedures you will follow in evaluating and grading written work. You do not have to discuss the standards that will be applied; you may merely detail how you will deal with assignments in order to arrive at final grades. Include a listing of the percentage value of each piece of written work as it applies to the final grade and, if you are using a revision option, a detailed review of how it works. The statement needs to be spelled out in detail; otherwise, students may be confused and may not do the required amount of work.

6. *Grading standards.* This section is optional; many teachers do not like to spell out the standards they will use in any quantitative or prescriptive way. Nevertheless, many departments have created grading standards that must be used by all teachers, and they may require that these standards be published in the syllabus. If a section on grading standards is included, it can contain the following:
   a. Standards of content — the levels of semantic and organizational expertise (a clear thesis, support of assertions, coherently developed

paragraphs and arguments, and so forth) that must be apparent in a passing essay.

   b. Standards of form — the impact of serious syntactic errors (sentence fragments, comma splices, run-ons, and so forth) and of lesser errors (in spelling, punctuation, and usage) in "acceptable" essays.

7. *Meetings.* Specify how many days per week the course will meet, on which days, and any special information about specific events — for instance, workshop meetings, in-class writing assignments, or regular due dates that will always fall on the same day of the week.

8. *Course calendar.* Course calendars may be simple or complex. The only essential element is a listing of the due dates for written assignments and, if a journal is part of the syllabus, journal reviews. The calendar can also contain detailed information on reading to be done, skills to be worked on, goals to be met, and a host of other information. Whether you choose to include this more detailed material will depend on the degree to which you want to structure your course beforehand.

9. *Course goals.* Whether this is a departmental statement that must be included in the syllabus or a personal definition of your objectives for the course, some statement of goals should be included. It should mention the number of graded assignments, the basic skills that will be expected of each student by the end of the course, the importance of student participation, and the level of competency in writing each student will need to demonstrate in order to pass the course. You can also include a personal message about the course and its expectations.

10. *Additional information and resources.* Your department may designate a director of writing or an ombudsperson for handling students' questions and complaints. If so, you may be required to list the pertinent information on your syllabus: names, office numbers, office hours, official capacity, policy on confidentiality, and so forth. In this section, you can also list additional resources for students, including information on the writing center, the office of disability services, the study skills center, and other resources available at your school. You should make clear in this section that you will make reasonable accommodations for students with diagnosed disabilities.

The preceding ten points comprise the essential elements of a composition syllabus. Other sections can be added, of course, but these are the ones needed for your protection and for your students' understanding of the course.

To have your syllabus ready for distribution on the first day of class, avoid the inevitable rush and get your photocopying done as early as possible. Make more copies than there are students on your roster; a rule of thumb is to increase the number by one-third: if you have twenty-four students on your roster, make thirty-two copies of the syllabus. Students who drop the class will carry off their copies, and students who join the class late will need copies; others will lose theirs and ask for new ones.

SAMPLE SYLLABI

Following are two sample syllabi for FY writing. The first one, written by Jessica Enoch for a FY writing class at the University of New Hampshire, uses a rhetorically arranged reader and a handbook. It includes all the basic information — plus much more: resources, information on plagiarism, and a course schedule. The second syllabus, prepared by Alyssa O'Brien for a FY writing class at Stanford University, uses a text that focuses on visual rhetoric and recommends a handbook. In addition to a course description and schedule, O'Brien's syllabus provides assignments as well as suggestions that will guide students in their use of technology for her class. We have abridged these syllabi but left much of the important information that will give you ideas for preparing your own syllabi.

Sample Syllabus 1   **USING A RHETORICALLY ARRANGED READER AND HANDBOOK**

Part I: Course Description and Policies

Instructor: Office Hours:

Email: Office:

Office phone:

The ability to articulate ideas, communicate thoughts, and share concerns is vital to participation in communal, academic, and civic discussions. Whenever a person engages in such discussions, he or she *must* possess those literacy skills (the skills to read, write, and think critically) that enable him or her to share ideas, voice concerns, or articulate arguments. In English 401 this semester, you will fine-tune your literacy skills so that you too are able to enter these kinds of discussions and communicate your ideas to an audience. You already, of course, possess those literacy skills that enable you to enter into conversations. Every day you communicate your ideas to various audiences: You are always speaking, listening, reading, and writing to friends, family, community members, classmates, teachers, and work colleagues. Thus, the idea behind this course is not something new. What this course will give you, though, is the opportunity to build on those literacy skills that you already have so that you can improve your ability to communicate your ideas and concerns in a variety of settings and situations.

Over the course of the semester you will enhance your literacy skills in a variety of ways. In your first major assignment, you will reflect on what it means to be literate both inside and outside the educational setting, and you will explain to an audience how you became literate and what this literacy means to you. In your second major assignment, you will analyze a public issue of your choice (such as debates over Title IX, the draft, Native American mascots, or vegetarianism), and you will analyze the various positions people take inside this debate to see how stakeholders are or are not communicating with one another. Finally, in your third and last assignment for the semester, you will enter into the conversation you studied in essay #2 by proposing a solution, clarifying a point of concern, or calling attention to ideas that are being ignored. Here, you will intervene in the debate and make your voice heard.

Thus, the concept at the heart of this course is participation. The goal of the course is for you to recognize those conversations that mean something to you and then to enter into those conversations with thoughtful arguments and suggestions. The skills you learn in this course will no doubt enable you to become a more effective writer and engaged student in your other classes here at UNH, but, even more importantly, this course should help you to become an active participant inside the various academic, social, cultural, and civic communities to which you belong.

Required Texts:

Glenn, Cheryl. *Making Sense: A Real-World Rhetorical Reader.* 2nd ed. Boston: Bedford/St. Martin's, 2005.

Lunsford, Andrea A. *The St. Martin's Handbook.* 6th ed. Boston: Bedford/ St. Martin's, 2008.

Requirements:

You will be expected to:

1. Attend all class meetings, prepared (see attendance policy).
2. Participate in class discussions.
3. Participate in in-class writing exercises; participate in draft workshops and group work (a draft for workshop must be a complete draft: it must

have a beginning, middle, and end and be ready to share); compose and submit on time (at least) 17 Statements of Understanding (SUs) and one annotated bibliography.

4. Attend three campus events to assess community concerns and compose a SU that describes and assesses each event you attended.

5. Propose, draft, write, and revise three essays of various lengths and purposes (submit each essay in a folder, along with any rough draft[s], revisions of your proposals/thesis statements, peer review comments from draft workshops, and other materials and notes that represent the various stages of your work, including notes, photocopies, or printouts from any sources you have used); submit all work **on time** (on the hour/day it is due; late papers will normally be docked one letter grade per day, unless you get my approval for an extension before the due date); submit, at the end of term, a one-folder portfolio of all your written work for this course: proposals, drafts, and revisions of papers; group work and peer review; in-class writing, short exercises. (If you would like to have your portfolio returned, please submit a self-addressed large envelope with plenty of postage.)

Please note: Passing the course requires **timely completion** of all of the assignments, long and short, in-class and out-of-class.

Attendance:

As noted above, regular attendance is required. You are permitted a total of three absences over the course of the semester. If you miss a fourth class, your final grade will drop by one letter grade. For example, if you were going to earn a B in the class, after four absences you would now earn a C.

If you miss five classes over the course of the semester, you will fail the class.

It is your responsibility to get the assignments, class notes, and course changes from a classmate if you do miss a class. It is also your responsibility to keep track of and complete the missing work.

In-class work cannot be made up. If you miss class on the day a written assignment is due, make arrangements to send it along with a classmate.

Grades:

To pass this course, you must complete *all* of the major and short assignments. Your attendance and class participation will also affect your final grade for the course.

Statements of Understanding	15%
Attendance/Class Participation	10
Campus Event SUs	5
Literacy Narrative *or* Cultural Literacy Narrative	20
Annotated Bibliography	5
Issue Analysis	20
Engaging the Issue (Persuasive Essay)	25

If you have any questions about a grade, please see me in office hours, and I will be happy to discuss your grade with you.

Office Conferences:

Think of my office as an extension of the classroom, and use my office hours to discuss any aspect of your reading or writing. Come to office hours with questions concerning writing techniques or strategies, essays you're working on, ideas you wish to develop, strategies you'd like to try, and so on.

We will meet in office hours on a regular basis, but you may stop by my office during open office hours whenever you need to. During our regular visits, which will occur once every two weeks or so, I will meet with you individually or in small groups. These scheduled meetings are **mandatory**. If you cannot attend a scheduled meeting, please email or call me at least 2 hours before our planned time. If you miss a meeting without contacting me first, I will count it as one of your three class absences.

Writing Center:

The Writing Center is an invaluable resource for all kinds of writers at UNH. The Writing Center is not only for those who feel they "need help" with their writing. Although you will definitely "get help" at the Writing Center, you should see it as a place to share ideas, work through concepts, and fine-tune your writing. Please visit the Writing Center by appointment or by dropping in.

Contact Information: www.unh.edu/writing; 862–3272; 7 Hamilton Smith Hall

Access:

If you are a student with a disability, I am more than willing to accommodate you in any way I can. Please see me and consult this website: (http://www.unh.edu/access/prospective.html), so that we can begin to work together.

Essay Format:

Your papers should be typed, printed in dark ink, and *double-spaced,* with one-inch margins. Place your name, the date, and my name in the upper left-hand corner of the first page. Double space, and then center your title, which should be neither underlined nor quoted. Double space again and begin typing your essay, numbering all the pages except page 1.

Fasten the pages with a paper clip.

Place in a simple file folder.

Plagiarism:

Plagiarism is the act of passing off someone else's work as your own.

- Sometimes plagiarism is simple dishonesty.
- People who buy, borrow, or steal a paper to turn in as their own work know they are plagiarizing.
- Those who copy word-for-word — or who change a word here and there while copying — without enclosing the copied passage in quotation marks and identifying the author should know that they are plagiarizing.

But plagiarism can be more complicated in act and intent.

- Paraphrasing, which is stating someone else's ideas, can be a useful way to support your own ideas, but it can lead to unintentional plagiarism.
- Jotting down notes and ideas from sources and thoughtlessly using them without proper attributions to the authors or titles of those sources may result in a paper that is only a mosaic of your words and those of others that appear, nonetheless, to be yours.
- Another innocent way to plagiarize is to allow your fellow students and friends — those outside your peer-review group — to give you too much

rhetorical help or do too much editing and proofreading of your work. If you think you have received substantial help in any way from people whose names will not appear as authors of the paper, acknowledge that help in a short sentence at the end of the paper or in your list of works cited.

- If you are not sure how much help is too much, talk with me, so that we can decide what kind of outside-of-class help (and how much) is proper, and how to give credit where credit is due.

- As they are drafting their work, conscientious writers keep careful track of when they use ideas and words from sources.

- They diligently try to distinguish between their own ideas, those of others, and common knowledge.

- They try to identify any parts of their work that comes from an identifiable source and then document their use of that source in accordance with established academic or professional conventions, such as a parenthetical citation and a works cited list.

- If you are in doubt about what needs documenting, talk with your instructor. When thinking about plagiarism, it is hard to avoid talking about ideas as if they were objects like tables and chairs. Of course they are not.

- You should not feel that you are under pressure to invent new ideas — which is probably impossible.

- So-called original writing consists of thinking through ideas and expressing them in your own way.

- The result may not be new, but if honestly done, it may well be interesting and worthwhile reading.

- Print or electronic sources, as well as other people, may add good ideas to your own thoughts.

- When they do so in identifiable and specific ways, give them the credit they deserve.

Part II: Course Schedule

Making Sense: MS
St. Martin's Handbook: SMH

Date	Topics Under Discussion	Reading Due	Writing Due
Week 1			
M	Course Introductions; Discuss Syllabus; Discuss Essay #1 Options 1 & 2: Literacy Narrative and Cultural Literacy Narrative; What Is Literacy?		
W	Literacy/Rhetorical Situations	*MS:* Ch. 1, "Introduction," pp. 1–20	SU #1
F	Literacy Narrative	*MS:* Ch. 3, "Narration," pp. 131–150; Malcolm X, "Prison Studies," pp. 151–154	SU #2
Week 2			
M	Labor Day — No Classes		
W	Literacy Narrative	*MS:* Angelou, "Finishing School," pp. 175–180; Sedaris, "Me Talk Pretty One Day," pp. 157–163	SU #3
F	Cultural/Literacy Narrative	*MS:* Ch. 4, "Exemplification," pp. 203–221; Kozol, "The Human	SU #4

Date	Topics Under Discussion	Reading Due	Writing Due
		Cost of an Illiterate Society," pp. 254–262	
Week 3			
M	Cultural Literacy Narrative; Discuss Proposals	*MS:* Ch. 2, "Description," pp. 47–61; Borich, "What Kind of King," pp. 107–118	SU #5
W	Cultural Literacy Narrative; Review Proposals	*MS:* Drayer, "Bedside Terror," pp. 169–174; Orlean, "The American Man, Age Ten"	Draft Proposals
F	Cultural Literacy Narrative; Rhetorical Situations	Handout, "Punk Literacy"; *MS:* Ch. 1: Intro., pp. 20–44	Group #1 Essays in (3 pages)
Week 4			
M	Preparing Your Draft: Narration, Description, and Exemplification; Bring Drafts to Class	*SMH:* Ch. 7, "Developing Paragraphs," pp. 110–138	Group #2 Essays in (3 pages)
W	Draft Workshop; Style, "The Comma"	*SMH:* Ch. 46, "Commas," pp. 710–726	Draft Essays; Comma, *SMH* Ex. 46.1 (p. 711) & Ex. 46.2 (p. 712)

Date	Topics Under Discussion	Reading Due	Writing Due
F	Preparing Your Draft/ Creating a Professional Ethos; Style: The Comma; Introduce Essay #2	*SMH:* Ch. 4, "Reviewing, Revising, and Editing," pp. 81–109	Draft Essays; Comma, *SMH* Ex. 46.3 (p. 717)
Week 5			
M	Essay #1 Due; Issues of Concern Today		Bring to Class Your Designated News Item
W	What's Analysis?; Style: Semicolon	*SMH:* Ch. 11, "Analyzing Arguments," pp. 146–167; Semicolons, pp. 727–731	Semicolon, *SMH* Ex. 47.2 (p. 729)
F	Vegetarianism: What's the Issue?	*MS:* Casebook, pp. 674–706	SU #6
Week 6			
M	The Draft: What's the Issue?	*MS:* Casebook, pp. 709–728	SU #7
W	College Athletics: What's the Issue?; Discuss Proposals	*MS:* Casebook, pp. 654–669	SU #8
F	What's the Issue for You?; Proposals Due; Discuss Annotated Bibliography		Draft Proposals SU #9

Date	Topics Under Discussion	Reading Due	Writing Due
Week 7			
M	Fall Break— No Classes		
W	Reading the Web	**Bring to class your *SMH* and two Web resources relevant to your essay**	Draft Annotated Bibliography
F	Evaluating Text-Based Sources: Bring 5 text sources to class; MLA bibliographic style	*SMH:* Ch. 14, "Evaluating Sources and Taking Notes," pp. 249–269	Draft Annotated Bibliography
Week 8			
M	Considering Audience and Using Comparison and Contrast to Inform Annotated Bibliography Due	*MS:* Ch. 6, "Comparison and Contrast," pp. 351–370	Draft Annotated Bibliography
W	Planning and Arranging	*MS:* Costas, "Ali and Jordan," pp. 383–387; Tannen, "Cross-Talk," pp. 371–377	SU #10

Date	Topics Under Discussion	Reading Due	Writing Due
F	Paraphrasing, Quoting, and Summarizing	*SMH:* Ch. 15, "Integrating Sources into Your Writing," pp. 270–280; Ch. 16, "Acknowledging Sources and Avoiding Plagiarism," pp. 281–287 **Bring one of your sources to class**	Group #1 Essays in (3 pages)
Week 9			
M	Creating Your Ethos; Style: Pronouns	*SMH:* Ch. 27, "Language that Builds Common Ground," pp. 511–518	Group #2 Essays in (3 pages); *SMH* Ex. 34.4 (p. 634)
W	Draft Workshop		Draft Essay #2
F	Preparing Your Essay; Introduce Essay #3	Editing for Clear Pronoun Reference (*SMH,* p. 634), Commas (*SMH,* p. 725), Semicolons (*SMH,* p. 730)	Draft Essay #2
Week 10			
M	Essay #2 Due; Where Do We Go From Here?		

Date	Topics Under Discussion	Reading Due	Writing Due
W	Engaging the Issue through Cause and Consequence Analysis	*MS:* Ch. 8, "Cause and Consequence Analysis," pp. 483–503	SU #11
F	Engaging the Issue through Cause and Consequence Analysis	*MS:* Sylves, "Credit Card Debt," pp. 509–517	SU #12
Week 11			
M	Engaging the Issue through Definition	*MS:* Ch. 9, "Definition," pp. 571–590; Dyson, "The Public Obligations," pp. 615–621	SU #13
W	Engaging the Issue through Process Analysis	*MS:* Ch. 7, "Process Analysis," pp. 429–444; Gladwell, "The Trouble with Fries," pp. 471–476	SU #14
F	Veterans Day University Holiday		
Week 12			
M	Engaging the Issue by Proposing a Solution/Discuss Proposals	*MS:* Swift, "A Modest Proposal," pp. 753–761	SU #15
W	Proposals Due/ Revisit Research	**Bring to class three additional research sources**	Draft Proposals

Date	Topics Under Discussion	Reading Due	Writing Due
F	Audience Analysis; Style: Parallelism	*SMH:* Ch. 37, "Parallelism," pp. 651–655	SU #16
Week 13			
M	Using Visual Arguments; Style: Parallelism	*SMH:* Ch. 10, "Thinking Critically about Visuals," pp. 168–176; **Bring to class three possible visuals**	*SMH* Ex. 37.1 (p. 653) & 37.2 (p. 653)
W	Discuss Visual Arguments		
F	Thanksgiving Break— No Class		
Week 14			
M	Constructing Arguments	*SMH:* Ch. 11 "Constructing Arguments," pp. 177–210	SU #17
W	Remembering Exemplification, Narration, and Description; Style: Creating Memorable Prose	*SMH:* Ch. 45, "Memorable Prose," pp. 701–708	Group #1 Drafts in (complete draft); *SMH* Ex. 45.1 & Ex. 45.2 (pp. 703–704)

Date	Topics Under Discussion	Reading Due	Writing Due
F	Catch-Up Day/ Creating a Strong Introduction and Conclusion		Group #2 Drafts in (complete draft)
Week 15			
M	Draft Workshop		Draft Essay #3
W	Preparing the Draft	Points for Editing: Comma, Semicolon, Parallelism, etc.	Draft Essay #3
F	Last Day of Class; Essay #3 Due		

Sample Syllabus 2   **VISUAL PERSUASION: THE RHETORIC OF IMAGES**

Instructor: Office Hours:

Email: Office:

Office phone:

What is this course about in a nutshell?

Effective writing, researching, and rhetorical analysis of the materials that interest you in the world around us!

What is the official course description to make such a grand claim possible?

How does a political cartoon about U.S. relations with China convince readers to view international diplomacy in a certain way? How do newspaper photographs from Iraq filter "reality" into media representations that tell only part of the story? How do propaganda posters from World War I vilify international leaders for nationalist reasons? This course will address such questions while teaching you how to write powerful, effective essays that examine how visual images shape attitudes toward issues of interest to you. As we analyze the rhetorical strategies in a range of political cartoons and advertisements, you'll write an essay exploring the power of visual rhetoric in a text of your choice. You might examine the rhetorical strategies of tobacco and Truth.com campaigns, the reliance on racial stereotypes in movie trailers, or the images of utopian worlds in technology ads. Then, after studying Susan Sontag's essay on war photography and Nora Ephron's essay on sensationalist photojournalism — both of which present arguments on the ethics of media coverage — you'll write your own argumentative essay exploring the contexts of a potential research area. As you turn to the research-based argument, we'll travel to the Hoover Archives for a lesson on propaganda posters, visit the Cantor Museum for an "Insider's Glimpse" of how curators work with research materials, and learn how to use the database resources in Green Library. The main project of the course will be your own research-based argument on how visual texts have shaped the contours of a contemporary issue. For example, how does the AIDS red-ribbon campaign target different audiences in the United States and internationally? How did Monsanto change its Web site to alter public opinion on genetically modified foods? How did financial analysts in the 1990s use strategic visual graphs to sway investors? You can choose an issue in politics, medicine, technology, advertising, or even explore the persuasive power of visuals to define sports culture, film, or pre-Raphaelite poetry. We'll end the term with a class exhibition showcasing your research. This course will introduce you to many of Stanford's research resources and will be taught in a computer classroom.

What texts are required?

Required: *Envision: Persuasive Writing in a Visual World,* by Christine Alfano and Alyssa O'Brien (Longman 2005).

Recommended: *The St. Martin's Handbook,* by Andrea A. Lunsford, 6th ed. (Bedford/St. Martin's, 2008).

Binder for Your Visual Rhetoric Portfolio. As a writer beginning a rigorous program of university research and writing, you will find yourself producing lots of writing in various forms that should be carefully collected in a portfolio; I will need to read through all this work at the end of the quarter, and, therefore, you should assemble all your writing in the portfolio throughout the term, adding materials as we move from assignment to assignment, and extracting materials to submit to me on due dates. When you submit materials to me, please include all your drafts and brainstorming ideas and, importantly, enclose everything in a clearly labeled folder. When you come to class or, especially, to conferences with me, bring your portfolio in progress so that we can refer back to previous work if we need to do so. The careful packaging of this binder is worth part of your grade; in it will be all your assignments as well as the opening introduction, the visual rhetoric narrative, your What's Cool leadership notes, and the Closing Preface in which you reflect on your intellectual development and progress at university research. Most of all, this package will be a treasure for you to look back upon, a marketing tool for you to use in securing a job, or a source of personal pride at achieving your goals. It will be, in essence, the book of your writing achievements.

What technology components are required for this course?

Access to and Regular Use of http://coursework.stanford.edu: You should use Coursework regularly to access lists of resources, posted examples from class lectures and activities, and important announcements.

Regular Postings through Coursework to Course Forum, our Class E-Discussion Site: I have set up CourseForum, a Stanford-designed online bulletin board environment, in order to provide a space for you to share and store documents draft-by-draft, from idea to final revision; to post peer-review comments for the writers in our class community; reply to messages in virtual conversation; load materials for discussion and presentation on What's Cool days or just to show in class!

That is, while you will be responsible for posting all of your assignments on CourseForum as you complete them, you should also use this space as a repository for work in progress, drafts, announcements of interest to the class, and sharing of materials you find relevant to our work together. It's your space, so do make the most of it! Note that you need to go into Coursework first and register for this PWR course; then you can access CourseForum using your SUnet ID.

<u>What are some strategies for effective computing in this course?</u>

Macintosh users should be sure to include the .doc extension on all documents posted to the class; alternately, they can save attachments as .rtf documents (rich text format) or .pdfs to allow viewing across different computer platforms.

All students should routinely back up their work, using CDs and their personal Leland space in addition to CourseForum.

Make friends with your RCC and become familiar with Stanford's many computing resources to help you in today's technology age!

<u>What are the major assignments for this class?</u>

Assignment 1: Rhetorical Analysis: 4 pages, double-spaced, plus a complete Works Cited list in MLA format.

The first assignment is a 4-page rhetorical analysis exploring the power of visual rhetoric in the text of your choice. This can be anything in the visual world across many disciplines and areas of contemporary culture — from covers of scientific journals to photojournalism, from political cartoons to cross-cultural advertisements. You will need to use our terms of rhetorical analysis (pathos, logos, ethos, kairos, audience, purpose, etc.) as a way to become familiar with this discipline-specific way of looking at and writing about texts, and you should cite relevant passages from *Envision* to help you get used to acknowledging sources that give you ideas about how to write about a subject.

Assignment 2: Contextual Analysis as FAMS (Feature Article Multiple Sides) Project: 4 pages, single-spaced, plus inserted article of choice and a complete Works Cited list in MLA format.

Next, after we read several compelling essays on the power of images, you'll write an argumentative essay exploring a potential research area and the importance of context. You'll compose this essay as a feature article exploring multiple sides of a potential research area. This assignment requires you to find an article related to your topic, compose an introductory frame, insert the article, write two response arguments that use visual rhetoric as part of the argumentative strategy, and then compose a closing frame that analyzes the context and rhetorical strategies of your arguments. We'll look at many models of past student projects that have taken creative approaches and designed innovative magazine or electronic formats for this assignment.

Assignment 3: Research-Based Argument: 12 pages, double-spaced (count does not include images which need to be inserted), plus an Annotated Works Cited list in MLA format.

Building on your previous project, you will expand your research sources from one article to at least 3 scholarly articles, 3 scholarly books, and 3 Web site articles for the research-based argument, a 12-page paper on how visual rhetoric has shaped the contours of a debate of your choosing. We'll approach the assignment through a series of library workshops, field trips, and collaborative class activities, as well as through a number of shorter writing assignments. By the end of it all, you'll have mastered the process of research and argumentation while also implementing your expertise with visual rhetoric in crafting your paper. You'll also have the chance to design a professional cover page that includes a "bio," an "abstract," and an appropriate image for the paper.

Creative Visual Project and Closing Preface

The last week of classes will be devoted to a celebration and sharing of your work through a class exhibit of visual rhetoric projects. You'll create a creative visual version of your argument and make a creative take-away to give to everyone in the class. This creative visual project will become the back cover to your Writer's Portfolio. As you submit your portfolio at the end of the quarter, you'll have a chance to write a "Preface" to your now-complete book of PWR 1 achievements in which you reflect on your writing and the ways in which you've reached the goals you set at the beginning of the quarter. You'll be able to look back on how you've learned to understand and harness visual rhetoric in order to analyze, utilize, and produce persuasive visual texts of your own. As you compile your portfolio, you should include any final revisions (with their cover letters) as well as the a print-out of your course introduction post, your visual rhetoric narrative post, your What's Cool leadership notes, and the Closing Preface, then submit your entire quarter portfolio for my reading pleasure and final assessment.

How does the work add up? How do grades work?

Assignment Description and Components	Points That Add Up to 100
Assignment 1: Rhetorical Analysis	15
Assignment 2: Contextual Analysis (FAMS)	20

Assignment 3: Research-Based Argument Project	45
Library Topic Form and Research Freewrite	included above
Dialogue of Sources	included above
Outlines and Drafts	included above
Annotated Bibliography	included above
Final Revision	included above
Peer Review throughout the Project	included above
Assignment 4: Creative Visual Rhetoric and Portfolio	15
Includes Introduction, Visual Rhetoric Narrative, What's Cool Leadership Notes (5 pts.), Closing Preface	
Also: Attendance, Alertness, Attitude, and Engagement	5

What's the schedule for this course?

Here, you'll find a detailed description of the reading, writing, and in-class activities planned for each class meeting. Please come to class fully prepared to participate by having completed the reading and the writing listed for that day.

Remember, if you are absent, it is your responsibility to: (1) Contact someone from the class to get the notes and (2) Email me to let me know how you propose to make up the work and catch up with all of us. Thanks.

Week One: Introduction — Writing in a Visual World: Introducing Visual Rhetoric in PWR

W   What Is PWR? What Is Visual Rhetoric? **Overview and Introductions**

F   Getting Started; Building Community; Beginning Your Research Log

Reading due today: Envision, preface; syllabus and course handouts; explore "Library Page for PWR Students."

Writing due today: (1) Complete student info./goals sheet; (2) Create a Portfolio Cover and bring it to class; (3) Post on CourseForum an introduction for yourself in which you attach and explain some visual rhetoric that you might want to focus on for your research project (be sure to include the source!).

In class: Share these responses; plasma-screen exploration work; pick "What's Cool" presentation dates.

**Week Two: Visual Rhetoric Focus — Political Cartoons, Advertisements,
Photographs Writing Focus — Developing Rhetorical Analysis Skills; Thesis
Statements**

M   **Images and Words as Persuasive Texts; Focus on Political Cartoons**

        <u>Reading due today</u>: *Envision,* Ch. 1.

        <u>Writing due today</u>: Compose "Narrative of Visual Rhetoric," from *Envision,*
        Ch. 1, p. 7; post on CourseForum and be sure to include visual rhetoric of
        choice; print a copy to hand in to me.

        <u>In class</u>: Share these responses; conduct plasma-screen work with
        international cartoons.

        <u>What's Cool Leaders</u>: _____ and _____.

W   **Rhetorical Appeals (Pathos, Logos, and Ethos) Applied to Advertisements**

        <u>Reading due</u>: *Envision,* Ch. 2.

        <u>Writing due</u>: Select ad of choice; write one paragraph about what rhetorical
        appeals it uses (post on CourseForum and prepare to bring up on plasma
        screens in class); see *Envision* p. 54, option 1 or 2.

        <u>In class</u>: Go over Ch. 2, appeals; and discuss your cartoons.

        <u>What's Cool Leaders</u>: _____ and _____.

F   **Your Visual Rhetoric Choice; Workshop on Thesis**

        <u>Reading due</u>: *Envision,* Ch. 3.

        <u>Writing due</u>: Select cartoon, ad, or photograph of choice; work through
        Envision, pp. 62–66, for your visual text, then write one paragraph with a
        thesis — what is the rhetorical argument of this text? (post both the working
        questions and the paragraph on CourseForum and prepare to bring up on
        plasma screens in class).

        <u>What's Cool Leaders</u>: _____ and _____.

**Week Three: Visual Rhetoric Focus — More on Advertisements and Photographs
Writing Focus — Writing, Revision, and Peer-Review Strategies; Spotlight
on Titles**

M   **No class; Martin Luther King Jr. Day — Do something in memory
    of his vision!**

W   **Assignment #1 Rhetorical Analysis Drafts; Workshop on Titles**

        <u>Reading due</u>: *Envision,* Ch. 3.

<u>Writing due</u>: Assignment #1 Rhetorical Analysis drafts (4 pages, double-spaced, plus Works Cited page); post on CourseForum by 9 A.M. Wednesday; make sure you have a title and page numbers; bring in one print copy. Either before or after your draft, complete the Prewriting Checklist appropriate for your medium; in your title for the checklist, tell me which chapter it's from (give complete source), and if you chose "before" or "after." Post and print this step of your work in progress as well.

<u>In class</u>: Begin peer review in class; talk about thesis statements; Workshop on Titles.

F   **Peer Review; Looking at More Ads**

<u>Reading due</u>: Read carefully peer papers on CourseForum.

<u>Writing due</u>: Peer-review responses of Rhetorical Analysis; post on CourseForum; print for your peers.

<u>In class</u>: Peer review; Guest Speaker visits to talk about ads and photography.

<u>What's Cool Leader</u>: Guest speaker today.

Week Four: Visual Rhetoric Focus — Magazines, More on Photographs, Some PhotoDrama

Writing Focus — Contextual Analysis, Developing Argument, Visual Persuasion in Action

M   **Putting Writing in Context: Initial Visit to Green Library**

<u>Reading due</u>: Green, virtual tour; http://www-sul.stanford.edu/depts/green/greentourphoto.html.

<u>Writing due</u>: Revision of Rhetorical Analysis (include all brainstorming notes, prewriting checklists, drafts, and peer reviews; post your final revision on CourseForum with a new date; put hard copies in a folder to hand in).

<u>In class</u>: Field Trip: Meet in Rose Garden in front of Green Library.

W   **Photos, Personas, and the Ethics of Representation**

<u>Reading due</u>: *Envision*, Ch. 3; focus in on Ephron "The Boston Photographs"; read Susan Sontag "Looking at War" and "This PG-Rated War" (through *Envision* online).

<u>Writing due</u>: Post one paragraph in response to two of the articles (pick two).

In class: Look at photos online; Explore Photo-essays on War.

What's Cool Leaders: _____ and _____.

F   **Assignment #2 Contextual Analysis Plan; Frames of Persuasion**

Reading due: Locate, copy/scan/post and print the article for your
individual FAMS project.

Writing due: Plan for FAMS Contextual Essay project (post introduction
frame plus outline for the rest on CourseForum); post potential images
(photos, cartoons, ads, altered texts) for group analysis in class.

In class: Discuss plans for FAMS; watch part of *Twilight Los Angeles*.

**Conferences Thursday and Friday (Rhetorical Analysis returned;
Contextual Analysis Projects and Research Ideas discussed)**

**Week Five: Visual Rhetoric Focus — Magazine Projects and Propaganda Posters
Writing Focus — Integrating Sources, Visual Evidence, New Revision Strategies,
Research Plans**

M   **Assignment #2 Contextual Analysis complete draft due; Peer Review
of FAMS**

Reading due: *Envision*, Ch. 3.

Writing due: Assignment #2 Contextual Analysis drafts (4 pages, single-
spaced, plus article, plus Works Cited page); post on CourseForum by 9 A.M.
Monday; make sure you have chosen a magazine, created an introduction
page, inserted the article, written two response articles with images,
written a conclusion page, and crafted a complete works cited page.
Bring in one print copy as backup for in-class peer review.

In class: Begin peer review in class; Workshop on integrating sources and
visual evidence.

W   **Peer Review; Working on Visual Integration and Argument
as Conversation**

Reading due: Read carefully peer papers on CourseForum.

Writing due: Peer-review responses of Contextual Analysis; post on
CourseForum.

In class: Peer review; Work on plasma screens at revising projects; Look
ahead to Research Project.

F   **Transition to Research Plans: Visit to Hoover Archives**

Reading due: *Envision,* Ch. 4; Explore Hoover Web site.

Writing due: Revision of Contextual Essay in folder.

In class: Field Trip: Meet on Steps of Hoover Tower for tour and workshop in Hoover.

What's Cool Leader: Curator of the Hoover Archives.

Week Six: Visual Rhetoric Focus — Propaganda Posters, Journal Covers, Web sites, and Libraries

Writing Focus — Research Proposals, Research Logs, Developing Research Skills

M   **Moving into Library Research; Propaganda Exploration Session**

Reading due: *Envision,* Ch. 4; SKIL tutorial.

Writing due: Library Topic Form (post on CourseForum and bring two print copies to class).

In class: Share research ideas; go over propaganda, historical and contemporary.

What's Cool Leaders: _____ and _____.

W   **Resources for Research: Searches, SKIL, Iliad**

Reading due: *Envision,* Ch. 5; explore "Library Page for PWR Students"; continue SKIL tutorial.

Writing due: Three-paragraph freewrite of research proposal from *Envision,* pp. 110–11 (post on CourseForum).

In class: Brainstorming approaches to research; exploring the Iliad database.

What's Cool Leaders: _____ and _____.

F   **Visit to Green Library for Databases Workshop**

Reading due: *Envision,* Ch. 5; Finish SKIL tutorial for today and take the final SKIL exam.

Writing due: Proposal Timeline due (post on CourseForum); copy results of SKIL and post on CourseForum.

In class: Field Trip: Meet at Green Library's east entrance (by red fountain).

What's Cool Leader: Librarian to show us the Socrates and databases resources.

Conferences Tuesday through Thursday (Contextual Analysis returned; Research Plans discussed)

Week Seven: Visual Rhetoric Focus — Web sites, Icebergs of Research, Museums as Exhibition Research Spaces
Writing Focus — Bibliographies, Dialogue of Sources, Research Logs in Progress

M   **Debrief after your own Scavenger Hunt in and through Green Library**

<u>Reading due</u>: Socrates and Database searching; *Envision,* Ch. 5; also Ch. 6, pp. 174–75 on Avoiding Plagiarism.

<u>Writing due</u>: Bring to class 3–5 hard-copy sources (books or articles) plus 3 database sources (not Internet sources), posted on CourseForum or printed out.

<u>In class</u>: Workshop on using these sources without plagiarism.

<u>What's Cool Leaders</u>: _____ and _____.

W   **Work in Progress; Workshop with Inspiration**

<u>Reading due</u>: *Your research sources.*

<u>Writing due</u>: Post Preliminary Bibliography (list your sources; see *Envision,* p. 158, option 1) on CourseForum.

<u>In class</u>: Map your iceberg of research.

F   **Conversations in Research; Visit to Cantor Center Museum for "Insider's Glimpse"**

<u>Reading due</u>: *Your research sources;* Review *Envision,* Ch. 5.

<u>Writing due</u>: Installment for Research Log: Annotated Bibliography or Dialogue of Sources with at least 5 sources (see *Envision,* pp. 152–56; 158, option 2); post on CourseForum.

<u>In class</u>: Field Trip: Meet at Rodin Garden outside Museum.

<u>What's Cool Leaders</u>: Cantor Museum curators talk to us about research, writing, and Museum exhibitions.

Week Eight: Visual Rhetoric Focus — Film, Trailers, and Documentary Texts
Writing Focus — Creating Visual Maps and Developing Detailed Outlines

M   **No Class: Washington's Birthday — Look up something historical!**

W   **Looking to Film for Strategies of Arrangement**

<u>Reading due</u>: *Envision,* Ch. 6; *your own research reading should be **done** by now*

<u>Writing due</u>: Post link to interesting film trailers or documentaries; one-paragraph response to Creative practice, p. 177.

In class: Using inspiration to shape ideas into maps and charts; Creative practice, p. 165.

What's Cool Leaders: _____ and _____.

F   **Film Trailers as Organizational Tools; Moving into Outlines**

Reading due: *Envision,* Ch. 6; *Frontline*'s The Merchants of Cool (through *Envision* Online).

Writing due: Detailed Outline (integrate images and use argumentative headings) with Trial Introduction and Conclusion paragraphs posted on CourseForum (see *Envision,* p. 194, option 2).

In class: Peer review of outlines; revising headings and sections.

What's Cool Leaders: _____ and _____.

Week Nine: Visual Rhetoric Focus — Writing Visually (Integrating Words and Images Effectively)

Writing Focus — Drafting Introductions, Conclusions, Drafts, Avoiding Plagiarism, Cover Bio and Abstract

M   **"How I Write" Discussion on Draft I *aka "SFD"*; Spotlight on Introduction and Conclusion Strategies**

Reading due: *Envision,* Ch. 6; Boothe essays (pick 2); suggestions: Yieh, Rinder, Chung, Adamson.

Writing due: Full Draft I; post paragraph assessment of two of the Boothe essays.

In class: Discuss SFD writing process and concerns; Introduction/Conclusion workshop using Boothe essays.

What's Cool Leaders: _____ and _____.

W   **Workshop on Integrating Sources and Avoiding Plagiarism, Again**

Reading due: Read carefully Peer Papers; "Doris Kearns Goodwin" through *Envision* online; review Ch. 6, pp. 177–85.

Writing due: Peer-Review Responses; post on CourseForum (use Checklists through *Envision* online).

In class: Peer-review session.

What's Cool Leaders: _____ and _____.

F   **Draft II due plus development of Bio and Cover page; brainstorm for Creative Project**

Reading due: *Envision,* final checklist through *Envision* online; *Envision,* Ch. 7, pp. 226–27 and Ch. 8, pp. 232–244.

Writing due: Full Draft II; plus Cover page with Abstract and Bio (*Envision,* p. 195, option 3).

In class: Brainstorm ideas for visual project; Peer Groups meet in class to review Draft II.

What's Cool Leaders: _____ and _____.

Conferences Tuesday through Friday (Drafts discussed)

Week Ten: Visual Rhetoric Focus — Your Research as Visual Arguments for Class Exhibit

Writing Focus — Peer Review, Completing PWR, Crafting Visual Arguments, Submission of Portfolios, Party!

M   **Peer Review Draft II and Creative Projects**

Reading due: Read through peer-group papers carefully.

Writing due: Complete peer-review forms and provide e-comments; Post drafts of Visual Rhetoric Op-Ad Projects.

In class: Double peer-review session of Drafts and Cover Pages; Visual Arguments for Showcase.

W   **Visual Rhetoric Exhibition of Research**

Reading due: *Envision,* Ch. 7–9 (browse for ideas).

Writing due: Creative Visual Project plus takeaway for class.

In class: Visual Project exhibition and celebration.

F   **Visual Rhetoric Exhibition continued; Celebration of your work!**

Reading due: Your work for the quarter!

Writing due: **Final** Revision of Research Paper (Post on CourseForum in order to get full credit) plus Visrhet Portfolio with Back Cover (put in Creative Visual Project); also, written "Preface" for the Portfolio — (use *Envision,* p. 195, option 3, to get started, but also reflect on your goals; follow format of *Envision* "Preface").

In class: Closing celebration: Food, Fun, Showcase of your work, celebrating the end of the journey!

WORKS CITED

Adler-Kassner, Linda, Robert Crooks, and Ann Watters, eds. *Writing the Community: Concepts and Models for Service-Learning in Composition.* Washington, DC: American Association for Higher Education, 1997.

Bruch, Patrick, and Richard Marback. "Race, Literacy, and the Value of Rights Rhetoric in Composition Studies." *CCC* 53 (June 2002): 651–74.

Brueggemann, Brenda Jo, et al. "Becoming Visible: Lessons in Disability." *CCC* 52 (2001): 368–98.

CCCC Bibliography of Rhetoric and Composition. 10 vols. Carbondale: Southern Illinois UP, 1987–1996.

Davis, Lennard. *The Disabilities Studies Reader.* New York: Routledge, 1997.

Doheny-Farina, Stephen. *The Wired Neighborhood.* New Haven: Yale UP, 1996.

Franco, Robert W. "Integrating Service into a Multicultural Writing Curriculum." *New Directions for Community Colleges* 24 (1996): 83–90.

Glenn, Cheryl. *Making Sense: A Real-World Rhetorical Reader,* 2nd ed. Boston: Bedford/ St. Martin's, 2005.

Gurak, Laura J. *Persuasion and Privacy in Cyberspace: The Online Protest over Lotus Marketplace and the Clipper Chip.* New Haven: Yale UP, 1997.

Handa, Carolyn, ed. *Computers and Community: Teaching Composition in the Twenty-first Century.* Portsmouth: Boynton/Cook, 1990.

Hawisher, Gail E., and Cynthia L. Selfe, eds. *Passions, Pedagogies, and Twenty-first Century Technologies.* Logan: Utah State UP and NCTE, 1999.

Hellman, Shawn. "Distant Service Learning in First-Year Composition: A Grant Writing Unit." *Teaching English in the Two-Year College* 28.1 (Sept. 2000): 11–20.

Herzberg, Bruce. "Community Service and Critical Teaching." *CCC* 45 (1994): 307–19.

Horner, Bruce. "Discoursing Basic Writing." *CCC* 47 (1996): 199–222.

Huckin, Thomas N. "Technical Writing and Community Service." *Journal of Business and Technical Communication* 11 (Jan. 1997): 49–59.

Lunsford, Andrea. *The St. Martin's Handbook.* 6th ed. Boston: Bedford/St. Martin's, 2008.

Peck, Wayne Campbell, Linda Flower, and Lorraine Higgins. "Community Literacy." *CCC* 46 (May 1995): 199–220.

Redd, Teresa M. "A Cultural Perspective: Teaching Composition at a Historically Black University." *Strategies for Teaching First-Year Composition.* Ed. Duane Roen et al. Urbana: NCTE, 2002. 21–34.

Richardson, Elaine. " 'To Protect and Serve': African American Female Literacies." *CCC* 52 (June 2002): 675–704.

Rose, Mike. *Lives on the Boundary.* New York: Free, 1989.

Schutz, Aaron, and Anne Ruggles Gere. "Service Learning and English Studies: Rethinking 'Public' Service." *CE 60* (Feb. 1998): 129–48.

Selfe, Richard. *Sustainable Computer Environments: Cultures of Support in English Studies and Language Arts.* Cresskill: Hampton P, 2005.

Trainor, Jennifer Seibel. "Critical Pedagogy's 'Other': Constructions of Whiteness in Education for Social Change." *CCC* 53 (June 2002): 631–50.

White, Linda Feldmeier. "Learning Disability, Pedagogies, and Public Discourse." *CCC* 53 (June 2002): 705–38.

Useful Web Sites

ABCD Books
www.abcdbooks.org

The Big Dummy's Guide to Service Learning
www.fiu.edu/~time4chg/Library/bigdummy.html

Campus Compact
http://www.compact.org/resources

Comment
http://comment.bedfordstmartins.com/

Daedalus Integrated Writing Environment: Overview
http://www.daedalus.com/products_diwe_overview.asp

National Service-Learning Clearinghouse
www.servicelearning.org

2

The First Few Days of Classes

On the first few days of classes, I want to show my students, through my tone, composure, and energy, that I am both a compassionate, fun person and an instructor who understands writing and wants to share this enthusiasm for the subject matter. While the students describe their hometowns and discuss their favorite musicians during first-day introductions, I am immediately trying to connect those personal interests with the names and the faces. I also work to create a classroom community where I impart my sense of responsibility to the class as well as the students' responsibility to their peers as I cover the course objectives and class policies. Ultimately, though, I want to use these first few days of classes to create a productive energy level in the classroom, so early on I get students working together and trying to feel comfortable handling their responsibilities for a successful, fun semester.

–Scott Wible

THE FIRST CLASS

Although you may begin to feel anxious as the time approaches for you to walk into your first class meeting, know that the nervousness you feel is natural and that every good teacher feels something of it on the first day of every new class. Even if you're a new teacher, teaching a subject that you've never taught before, your education, experience, and training have prepared you for this moment. You've seen effective teachers and communicators, and no matter what area of English studies you specialize in — rhetoric and composition, literature, creative writing, or film — you know a lot about good writing and strong reading strategies. You've also likely had experience speaking or performing in front of groups of people. Remember that the teaching act is a performance in the full sense of that word. The teacher is instructor, coordinator, actor, facilitator, announcer, pedagogue, and ringmaster, working to provide an environment where students can participate fully and actively.

Teaching style, the way you carry off your performance, is determined partly by conscious decisions that you make and partly by personality factors over which you have little control. It is difficult to control completely the manner and tone with which you naturally address the class as a whole, the way you react to individual students on an intuitive level, the quick responses you make to classroom situations as they come up, and the general public self you exhibit in front of the class. You cannot change who you are, nor should you try.

This is not to say, however, that teachers have no control at all over how they appear. Although your essential style may not be amenable to change, you can consciously modify other variables. You can control what the class does with its time, the order in which you present material, the sorts of skills you will concentrate on — all the content-oriented material that is at the heart of every class. You can also make an effort to control those aspects of your style that you want specifically to change or suppress. If your personality tends toward sarcasm or intimidation (intentionally or not), you can carefully and consciously reconsider your comments so that they convey encouragement; if you tend toward too much modesty or passivity, you can work toward speaking up more and taking a more active approach.

As you think about your own teaching persona, consider both what makes you feel most comfortable and what helps you facilitate classroom interactions. Many younger, female teachers find it helpful to establish authority by wearing professional clothing — especially toward the beginning of the term and when handing back graded essays. Others do well with establishing a more informal persona. Anne Curzan and Lisa Damour, in *First Day to Final Grade,* provide (in addition to other practical advice) lists of pros and cons for dressing up or dressing more casually. They note that while dressing up can make you look and feel more professional, helping you establish your authority, it can also be expensive, be less comfortable, and create distance between you and your students (14). Finding an appropriate and comfortable balance is key.

There are many questions you'll need to answer for yourself: what you will wear; what you'll have your students call you; whether you'll stand up in front of students behind a podium, move around the classroom, or sit among the students in a circle. Whatever configuration you decide on (the shape and size of the classroom will limit your options), make sure you're in a position to make eye contact with every student. The class will have a personality of its own, and your persona will likely be shaped in part by your level of comfort, but your persona — the choices you make in presenting yourself and interacting with others — will also shape the feel of the classroom.

More important than anything else, you should try to evince the two most important traits of a good teacher: humanity and competence. If students believe you to be kind and to know your stuff, they will, for the most part, be receptive. Humanity and competence, however, cannot be demonstrated in one day. They show themselves over time, not by how many jokes you tell or how hard you grade, but by the total picture of who you are and how you feel about your students, their successes, and their trials as beginning writers. If you are humane and know your subject, you and your students will, over time, build a common ethos based on mutual respect and trust. (For further reading on college-level teaching, see Anson et al.; Boothman; Brookfield and Preskill; Curzan and Damour; Haswell and Lu; and Tremmel, cited at the end of this chapter.)

Bureaucratic Tasks (10 minutes)

On the first day of classes, teachers often do little more than distribute syllabi and show the texts; writing teachers, however, have a good deal to get done on the first day. You'll likely spend the first ten minutes of the first class in an undemanding routine. Put your materials on the front desk, and greet the students present. Students will continue to come in, even well into the class hour. (For further reading on getting started, see Haswell and Lu, Chapter 2, "Beginnings"; and Curzan and Damour, Chapter 2, "The First Day of the Term.")

Write your name, office number, and office hours on the blackboard, and then arrange your books, notes, and handouts so they are within easy reach. Look up every few seconds, trying to maintain eye contact with the students — it is natural to avoid their eyes until you speak to them in an official capacity, but eye contact establishes a friendly connection. Since you will probably want to begin teaching while standing up, check to see that the classroom has a lectern that you can use, or set up your satchel or briefcase so that it will hold your papers.

Your students are learning their way around campus, so some of them will almost certainly continue to drift in during the first fifteen minutes. Give most of the stragglers a chance to come in before you call the roll. Introduce yourself, the course, and your office number and hours. These first few announcements, routine though they are, are the most difficult. Speak slowly, and remember that you have everything planned, that you are in your element, that you will perform well. Meet the students' eyes as you speak, and try to develop the ability to take in large groups of students as you move your gaze about the classroom. You may be surprised at how young some of them look. This may be their first day in college, and depending on the time of day, you may be their first college teacher. If you feel nervous, remember that your students probably feel the same way.

Describe the add-drop policy of your college or university. There may be specific school or departmental policies you are expected to announce; it usually pays to repeat the add-drop policy at least once. Finally, call the names on your class roster, marking absences. You will want your students to raise their hands if present and to tell you if you have mispronounced their names or if they have a nickname they would prefer you to use. Note the preferred name and pronunciation on your roster, and try to make eye contact with each student as you call the roll. Attempt to connect names with faces as soon as possible.

After you have called the roll, ask for a show of hands of those whose names you did not call. There will always be a few, usually students who have registered late or who have shown up hoping they can add the class. Now is the time to announce that after class, you will talk to those students who wish to add or drop the course. After class, then, you can attend to them and decide whether you can handle more students in your class. Often there is a maximum number of students established by the department, and only the director of the writing program, the department chair, an advisor, or scheduler can give permission for an overload. If the ultimate decision about accepting more students is yours, keep in mind that each student whom you accept over the limit means that less of your time and energy will be available for the rest of the students. If the decision is not yours, do not make it. Send the student to the appropriate person.

The Syllabus (15–20 minutes)

Hand out copies of the syllabus. After every student has one, read through the important parts of it aloud. On this first reading, stress the textbooks — display your copies in class so students will know what to look for at the bookstore — and discuss attendance and lateness policies, the form for written assignments (typed or handwritten, double-spaced or single-spaced, and so forth), the number and length of required essays, and the policy on keeping a journal or writing log. If you are using a revision policy, go over it in detail, giving examples of how it should be used. During this initial explanation of the syllabus, you will actually start to teach students what revision is. Some students will initially think of revision as punishment or as simply editing for a cleaner copy. There is inevitably confusion about the revision policy and how it works (and you will be explaining revision for the first few weeks of the course). Go over the calendar of due dates, and mention the grading standards you will be applying.

It is important, as you explain the syllabus, not to back away from or undercut any of the policies it states. Sometimes you will sound harsh to yourself as you explain the penalties for absence, lateness, or failure to do work on time, but do not apologize. You will find that it is far simpler to ease up on harshly stated policies than to tighten up lax policies. After you have gone through it, ask whether there are any questions about the syllabus. Finally, you will want to tell students about the diagnostic essay that you have scheduled for the second day of class.

Introductions (15–20 minutes)

Next, you might try to get to know some basic information about your students. Hand out index cards and ask students to provide specific information:

1. Name
2. Email address (and how often they check email)
3. Phone number (and whether they wish to be included on any contact list you'll be making and if there are other specific instructions, such as a time after which it is too late to call students who work night shifts or have small children)
4. Any other information you need about students (such as their major, goals for the class, interests, favorite authors, and so on)

You can keep these index cards in a file, referring to them if you need to contact a student outside of class. The answers to the final question will help you get to know your students better and learn about what is important to them.

After you've collected the index cards, have students introduce themselves to the class. You can do these introductions in any number of ways. For instance, you could have students pair up and introduce themselves to each other and then have one partner introduce the other to the class. You could give the students a prompt: "The most interesting thing I've ever done is…" or "Writing for me is like.…" Their answers to prompts or how they introduce themselves or each other will help you begin to connect faces with names. If you give students a prompt—such as "I'm the one who…"—to use as an introduction, be prepared to introduce yourself in the same way. During these introductions, students will see glimpses of your personality, and you will see glimpses of theirs. Through this process, you will begin to develop an environment in which students feel comfortable speaking and listening to each other.

Dismissal (5–15 minutes)

Before dismissing the class, ask your students to write down any questions about course policies that they want to talk about during the next class. Make your assignments, including the reading of the syllabus. If there are no final questions, dismiss the class.

You will undoubtedly be surrounded by a post-class swirl of students wishing to talk to you—students who only a moment ago had no questions. Some will want to add the course: Tell them whether they have a chance, and send them to the appropriate office. Some will have completed add or change-of-section forms: Add those students' names to your roster. Some will have questions that they were too shy to ask in class: Speak to them. As you resolve each situation, the crowd will diminish, and eventually the last petitioner will leave. You will be alone. This first day of class is over.

THE SECOND CLASS

Bureaucratic Tasks (10 minutes)

On the second day of class, there are still some bureaucratic tasks to be cleared away—you will need to call the roll again (make eye contact, and see whether you can begin to remember students' names), and perhaps you will want to make a short speech about the add-drop policy. If new students have joined the class, as will probably happen on the second and third days, give them copies of the syllabus and ask them to speak to you after class. Ask the class for the questions they wrote down about the syllabus and course policies; answer their questions, clearing up any confusion.

Diagnostic Essay (30–40 minutes)

Because you want to determine as soon as possible your students' strengths and weaknesses as writers, you will want to assign the diagnostic essay (sometimes called a "placement essay") today. If your school offers a BW or an ESL program, the diagnostic essay serves to alert you to students who might best be helped by one of these other programs. If your school has a writing center, learning disabilities center, office of disabilities services, or center for language acquisition, you have backup resources. Writers are helped most when they receive an evaluation early, and the diagnostic essay allows you to gauge immediately the level of writing each student is capable of and to calculate your own pace in teaching each student and the class as a whole.

This exercise gives you an idea of how prepared your students are as writers. Ask students to take out paper and pen and to write for twenty to thirty minutes on a topic that allows for narrative or descriptive responses. (You can bring paper with you and pass it out if you object to the appearance of paper torn from notebooks.) The best topics for the diagnostic essay are those that (1) can be answered in a relatively short essay and (2) ask students to rely on their own experiences. Master diagnostician Edward White offers the following option in his *Teaching and Assessing Writing:*

> Describe as clearly as you can a person you knew well when you were a child. Your object is to use enough detail so that we as readers can picture him or her clearly from the child's perspective and, at the same time, to make us understand from the tone of your description the way you felt about the person you describe. (252)

Here are two other options.

1. In a short essay, discuss the reasons why your best (or worst) high school teacher was effective (or ineffective).
2. In a short essay, discuss the best, most worthwhile, and most valid advice you have received about adjusting to college life so far. What advice stands out most to you in your first week?

Introduce the diagnostic essay to the class for what it is — an exercise that will give you an idea of how well students are writing now. Stress that the essay will not be given a letter grade and will have no effect on the final class grade. But remind students that you will be looking at form and content, at their ability to organize a piece of writing and develop it with specific examples. Explain the methods of rhetorical development you want them to use. If you want students, for example, to write a descriptive essay, provide examples that help illustrate the difference between general assertion and specific, sensory detail.

Ask students to try to write as finished a piece of work as possible in the time allowed. Make certain that they put their names on the essays and that they note whether they have already taken BW or ESL courses. Write the diagnostic assignment on the board, and then give the class the rest of the hour to think and write. Announce the amount of time remaining once or twice so that no one runs short of time. At the end of class, collect the essays.

Dismissal (5–10 minutes)

After you collect the essays, explain that you will talk more about the diagnostic essays next time and remind students of the reading they must do before the next class. Ask students if they have any questions. Once you have answered their questions, dismiss the class, but ask new students to stay for a few minutes to discuss the syllabus with you.

After the Second Class

You will have several tasks to accomplish after class or that evening, the most important of which are marking and evaluating the diagnostic essays. The range of writing skills evidenced by these essays may be wide, and in some essays, you'll find many formal usage errors and mechanical problems. As Mina Shaughnessy points out, some teachers of underprepared or differently prepared students initially cannot help feeling that their students might be deficient in some organic sense; certain pervasive error patterns are so severe and look so damaging on a paper that they can be shocking (2–3). This problem is particularly likely if you are teaching at a two-year or an open-admissions college without a BW or ESL program. Even large numbers of errors, however, usually fall into just a few patterns. (For more on patterns of nonstandardized English in students' writing, see Ball; Belcher and Connor; Connors and Lunsford; Delpit and Dowdy; Fox; Gilyard; Li; Schroeder, Fox, and Bizzell; Shaughnessy; Silva and Matsuda; and Smitherman, "Talkin and Testifyin," cited at the end of this chapter.)

Having prepared yourself, plunge into the pile of essays. Keep in mind that students had only twenty to thirty minutes to write these pieces and no advance knowledge of the prompt. Since good writing generally takes time and revision, it's best not to expect beautifully crafted prose or flawless standardized English, but you may be surprised by how well some of your students write already. Most of the essays will be short — two or three pages in length. Aside from some nearly illegible handwriting and inventive spellings, most essays should be readable. It is a good idea to scan each essay quickly, trying to get a sense of the writing as a purposeful whole. Then, in a second reading, mark the essay, looking for the following three specific areas of skill (listed here in order of importance):

1. Knowledge of and ability to use paragraph form, specific details and examples, and a well-supported and well-developed controlling idea.
2. Ability to write a variety of grammatically correct (according to standardized English) and interesting sentences.
3. Ability to use language — including grammar, usage, punctuation, and spelling — in a relatively standardized fashion.

To get a sense of how these three skills are demonstrated in an essay, you may have to read the essay two or three times — but since each one is not very long, this task is not as time-consuming as it sounds. By the time you reach the bottom of the pile, you should be spending about ten minutes on each diagnostic essay, noting the mechanical problems and writing a short comment at the end. Whether or not you decide to use some form of portfolio evaluation, you may want to create a computer file in which to keep semester-long records, noting the progress of each student's writing. (See Chapter 5, "Evaluating Student Essays," for a detailed discussion of portfolio evaluation.) With such a record, you can chart each student's strengths and weaknesses as they appear in each major piece of writing. The first entry would cover the diagnostic exercise. Note whether the student grasps organization, can use sentences, has control of usage, and so forth. A short, three- to five-sentence description of each student's writing strengths and weaknesses, consulted and added to as you evaluate each new writing assignment, can be of great help in setting individualized goals for students and in discovering the particular kind of practice writing each student needs. These notes on students' progress will also help you when you confer individually with students.

As you read the diagnostic essays, look especially for patterns of divergence from standardized English — a continual inability to use commas correctly, a continual confusion about verb endings, a continual tendency to begin fragments with relative pronouns. Chart such patterns carefully, for they will be your concern in the future, and they can provide important information for tutors at the campus writing center, learning disabilities center, or center for language acquisition.

The diagnostic essays and the way you respond to them will shape your students' perceptions of you as much as your classroom attitude will. As always in grading and evaluating, take the time to consider how students will feel upon reading your comments. Will they come away thinking they have problems they can deal with, or will they be overwhelmed? Try to balance critique with encouragement; find something to praise, and treat errors and problems as signposts pointing to needed work, not as dead-end signs. (Before you write detailed comments, you may want to read "Responding to Student Writing" in Anson et al.; "Grading" in Curzan and Damour; and "The Writing" in Haswell and Lu, cited at the end of this chapter.)

Before the next class, you must decide whether any of your students might benefit from switching to another course or working with a tutor at the writing center. If you feel that a particular student should be enrolled in the BW or ESL program instead of FY writing, now is the time to make the necessary arrangements through either the director of composition or the director of one of these other programs. Do not feel you are betraying a student by recommending BW or ESL; you want your students to thrive under your guidance, not merely survive.

If you think a student would benefit from the services of the writing center, learning disabilities center, office of disability services, or center for language acquisition, you might talk with a consultant at the appropriate center to find out how the student can enroll and how you can work with the writing tutor to best help the student.

For students with especially good writing skills, the diagnostic essay may provide pleasant news: some schools exempt strong writers from FY writing courses or place them in honors sections. If that is the case at your school, make the necessary arrangements. Often, though, placement has already been determined by an earlier diagnostic essay or by a student's experience in high school. If this is the case, don't worry: Even already strong writers can become better writers, and many of these students will be a pleasure to work with, contributing much to the class.

If you have concerns about the level of a specific student's writing and whether that student might be underprepared or overprepared for your class, write a note requesting a meeting after class. Often, in talking with students, you can learn more about their level of preparation. Sometimes, too, you may discover unusual circumstances that affected their performance on the diagnostic essay.

After you have read the diagnostics, marked them, and recorded the marks and your comments, you can put them aside and turn to the other task of the evening: planning the next class. The third class will be your first real class, the first class that demands a prepared lesson plan. Be certain that you know what you want to introduce and accomplish.

THE THIRD CLASS

Before the third day of class, you need to prepare a lesson plan that includes your objective for the class as well as planned activities that will help you achieve that objective. You will also need to reserve class time for discussing the diagnostic essays that you will be handing back to students.

Begin by taking attendance, and then announce that you will talk about the diagnostic essays at the end of the class. This is a good way to introduce the policy of not returning assignments until the end of a period. Such a policy keeps attention on the day's lesson and keeps students' reactions to their grades and your comments from coloring the class period.

As you begin your first day of actual teaching, introduce and state the goals of the first lesson. You may decide to connect the work you begin today with the first writing assignment. No matter what your objectives are, however, remember that you are there to lead the class, not to do all of the work. Early in the course, get students talking—to you, in pairs or small groups, and in whole-class discussions. The more comfortable students are with class discussions and group work, the more comfortable they will be with peer response and whole-class workshops on their writing. (See Chapter 3, "Everyday Activities," for detailed information on leading class discussions, peer response, and workshops.)

Fifteen minutes or so before the end of class, make your assignments for reading and homework, and return the diagnostic essays. Before you dismiss the class, ask students to read over the comments you've written on their essays, and ask those who need to talk with you after class to do so. Since some students will have to get to their next class, dismiss your students at least ten minutes early so you'll have time to spend with those who need to talk with you.

Students whose writing is so advanced that they may be exempted from your course should be congratulated, and arrangements should be made for their transferrals. Students who need to work at one of the support-services centers on campus while they take your course should be encouraged to schedule an appointment with a representative of that center and to take their diagnostic essay with them to that appointment. Students who will not be able to do the level of work required in your course should be moved to the BW or ESL program. (You should speak to these students privately. Ask them to come back to your office during the remaining class time, and explain the situation to them there.)

LESSON PLANS

Leading a class of college-level writers may at first seem like a daunting prospect. You may have heard composition referred to as a contentless course, and many new teachers fear the prospect of running out of material. Therefore, it is best to prepare your classroom time for the first two weeks with extra thoroughness. Carefully think through the structure for each class; it is always better to carry some of your lesson plan over to the next class than to take the chance of coming to the end of your prepared notes with half an hour of class time left. At first, it might be difficult to gauge how long an activity or discussion will take, and sometimes a discussion will lead the class in a new, productive direction, causing you to discard part of your plan. Even so, it's always best to be prepared and go from there.

With experience, you will find that the classroom offers more teaching possibilities than you can take advantage of; by dipping into the following chapters you can get a quick idea of some options. As you'll see, teaching writing is so activity-oriented that with a little preparation, you'll never run out of material.

When drawing up plans for a class, always make sure you note the goal or purpose for each assignment and activity. The amount of other material you include in a lesson plan is up to you. Some teachers, at the beginning of their careers, prepare full paragraphs and detailed notes, whereas experienced teachers often work from notes made up only of key words. Make certain that you add to your notes cross-references to pages in the textbook or reader you are using.

You're an experienced teacher by now and starting to get used to the role. Enjoy it, but don't allow yourself to get too comfortable. There's still plenty left to learn.

Example 2.1 **SAMPLE LESSON PLAN: INQUIRY ACTIVITY**

Inquiry Activity 1

Day 6 [Day 5 was "responding to the visual" in terms of "The Deer at Providencia."]

- Before class, look over the rough drafts; see what problems and successes students have had, making brief comments on their drafts where appropriate. Select one or two examples from students' writing for class discussion, asking the students ahead of time for permission to use passages from their drafts.
- Have students read the sample description(s). Ask the other students to identify the dominant impression they get from the written description. Ask them to identify the features of the writing that make it easy or difficult to connect the visual with the essay. Discuss. (15–20 minutes)
- Look at the visual again. Discuss how each student's essay could be improved in terms of emphasizing the main point of Dillard's essay, particularly in terms of the accompanying visual. As a part of the discussion, examine the roles that establishing a purpose, establishing an audience, conveying a quality or an atmosphere, including sensory details, and organizing descriptions play in descriptive writing. (15–20 minutes)
- Have students begin revising their drafts. (25–30 minutes)
- Collect the revised drafts, remind students of assignment for next class. (3–5 minutes)
- After class, make brief comments on drafts, especially on their use of details to picture and support the dominant impression. Assign each draft a check, a check plus, or a check minus.

Example 2.2 **SAMPLE LESSON PLAN: OBJECTIVE SUMMARY WRITING**

Before class, assign "On Eating Meat" by Andy Kerr (Glenn 674–81). After having read the essay, students should be prepared to write an objective summary of it, and, to that end, they should have read it carefully in order to gather information for their writing assignment. When you assign the essay, ask students to consider the following as they read: (1) the title of the piece, (2) what they already know about the topic, and (3) the main point of the essay. Also, as they read, they should mark places in the text that are confusing to them, that identify key points and terms, and that they question.

In class, ask students to identify in writing (1) the central issue of the essay, (2) the writer's point of view, (3) the organization of the essay and its connection to the purpose of the essay, and (4) the assumptions on which the writer's views are based.

- Encourage students to compare their responses and to talk among themselves about "On Eating Meat." After they have compared notes for five minutes or so, ask them each to write an objective summary of the essay. Students should aim to write an objective summary that:
  1. is one-third the length of the original essay.
  2. foregrounds the main idea (the thesis statement),
     a. includes key words and phrases.
     b. mentions the supports for the author's main point or argument.
  3. is in their own words, avoiding plagiarism.
  4. follows the author's pattern of organization.
  5. uses only the information in the original essay.
  6. avoids coloring the information with personal opinion.
  7. lists the source of the original essay.
- Remind students that an objective summary conveys information, not opinion.

Examples 2.1 and 2.2 show two kinds of daily lesson plans based on Cheryl Glenn's *Making Sense*. Example 2.1 outlines an inquiry activity, which asks students first to respond to a photograph of a badly burned student, wrapped in bandages, and then to draft an essay explaining how the visual enhances the accompanying essay, Annie Dillard's "The Deer of Providencia." Students are asked to bring their drafts to class for peer review and then to begin revising them. Notice how the teacher describes her objective in the first sentence: "Look over the rough drafts; see what problems and successes students have had, making brief comments on their drafts where appropriate." Her objective drives her carefully ordered and carefully timed classroom activities. Example 2.2 is based on an assigned reading, "On Eating Meat" by Andy Kerr. If, like this teacher, you are using a rhetorically arranged reader, you will naturally want to draft lesson plans that incorporate material from your textbook. In preparation for an upcoming writing assignment, this teacher wants his students to master the art of writing objective summaries, starting with a summary of "On Eating Meat." But before students begin writing, the teacher wants to talk about the genre of summary and the trouble students might encounter with the word *objective*. So he outlines important points he wants to hear students talk about: the central issue of the essay, the writer's point of view, how the progression of the essay relates to its purpose, and the assumptions on which a writer's views are based.

Then the class turns to another essay and talks through the same points, discussing the problems with any claim to objectivity. Only toward the end of class does the teacher specify the practical elements of the assignment, saying, perhaps, "Use only the information in the essay. Try hard not to color your summary with your opinions or with extra information. An objective summary means you are conveying information and not opinion."

Until you know how effective your examples will be and how much time you will devote to each item on your lesson plan, for every concept you introduce and exemplify (plagiarism, for instance), you should have two or three other examples in your notes and ready to use. It's always better to be slightly over-prepared with examples.

While working out your classroom strategies and preparing your lesson plans, you may wish to annotate your textbooks, noting material you plan to key to class work. Annotating your textbook is a way of inhabiting it; underline and mark in it, if doing so will make your teaching life easier. Textbooks are a raw material, and they may be with you for years. Make sure they serve you and save you from repetitious work in the future. Annotate any part of the rhetoric that you feel may need more explanation, and mark the exercises you plan to use. If any exercises fail, note the problem and the potential reasons for it. Your marks need be no more than checks or underlines, so long as they are meaningful to you. You should be able to open the book to a page and know immediately what you wish to accomplish with it.

WORKS CITED

Anson, Chris M., et al. *Scenarios for Teaching Writing.* Urbana: NCTE, 1993.

Ball, Arnetha. "Cultural Preference and the Expository Writing of African-American Adolescents." *Written Communication* 9 (1992): 501–32.

Belcher, Diane, and Ulla Connor, eds. *Reflections on Multiliterate Lives.* Clevedon, UK: Multilingual Matters, 2001.

Boothman, Nicholas. *How to Make People Like You in 90 Seconds or Less.* New York: Workman, 2000.

Brookfield, Stephen D., and Stephen Preskill. *Discussion as a Way of Teaching.* San Francisco: Jossey-Bass, 1999.

Connors, Robert J., and Andrea A. Lunsford. "Frequency of Formal Errors in Current College Writing, or Ma and Pa Kettle Do Research." *College Composition and Communication* 39 (December 1988): 395–409.

Curzan, Anne, and Lisa Damour. *First Day to Final Grade: A Graduate Student's Guide to Teaching.* Ann Arbor: U of Michigan P, 2000.

Delpit, Lisa, and Joanne Kilgour Dowdy, eds. *The Skin That We Speak.* New York: Norton, York, 2003.

Fox, Helen. *Listening to the World.* Urbana: NCTE, 1994.

Gilyard, Keith. *Voices of the Self: A Study of Language Competence.* Detroit: Wayne State UP, 1991.

Haswell, Richard H., and Min-Zhan Lu. *CompTales.* New York: Longman, 2000.

Li, Xiao-Ming. *"Good Writing" in Cross-Cultural Context.* Albany: State U of New York P, 1996.

Schroeder, Christopher, Helen Fox, and Patricia Bizzell, eds. *AltDis: Alternative Discourses and the Academy.* Portsmouth: Boynton/Cook, 2002.

Shaughnessy, Mina. *Errors and Expectations: A Guide for the Teacher of Basic Writing.* New York: Oxford UP, 1977.

Silva, Tony, and Paul Kei Matsuda, eds. *On Second Language Writing.* Mahwah: Lawrence Erlbaum, 2001.

Smitherman, Geneva. *Talkin and Testifyin: The Language of Black America.* Detroit: Wayne State UP, 1986.

———. *Talkin That Talk: Language, Culture, and Education in African America.* New York: Routledge, 2000.

Tremmel, Robert. *Zen and the Practice of Teaching English.* Portsmouth: Boynton/Cook, 1999.

White, Edward M. *Teaching and Assessing Writing.* 2nd ed. San Francisco: Jossey-Bass, 1994.

3

Everyday Activities

> *The question I wrestle with constantly is not so much what to teach as how to teach it. If writing is its own apprenticeship, if the only way to learn to write is to actually write (which both my own experience and composition theorists tell me), then how can I structure my class in a way that foregrounds writing? How can I orient classroom discussions in a way that they enhance, rather than detract from, our focus on writing? How can I use peer workshops to help my students appreciate their tacit obligations to their audience to make their writing clear? And how can I use student conferences more effectively to teach students about their writing?*
>
> –ROSALYN COLLINGS

CLASSROOM ORDER AND GROUP ETHOS

The primary management issue you will deal with as a teacher is that of classroom order. *Order,* of course, is a relative term; very often an orderly writing class is abuzz with discussions of rhetorical choices, editing, language diversity, and correctness. Order does not mean silence. It does, though, signify students' being "on task," engaged in a progression of meaningful activities. It's your responsibility not to let that progression be disrupted. Whether students are taking part in a class-wide discussion, listening to your explanation, or working in small groups, certain protocols should be observed. One of your functions is to demonstrate these protocols to make the progression of activities possible. But students also need to take some responsibility for meaningful progress in class.

In the best of all teaching situations, the class members develop a group ethos, a feeling that they're all in it together, depending on one another for support and direction. When you use class discussions as a way to help students talk with and listen to one another and not just to you; when you set aside class time for group work and peer editing; when you encourage students to call, visit, and email one another about their assignments and their writing; and when you expect and demand that students are respectful of one another regardless of race, class, clan, religion, ethnicity, sexual orientation, physical ability, appearance, and gender, you can feel fairly confident that your class will develop a positive group identity. Still, even the best, most experienced teachers can teach two sections of the same course, using the same materials in the same ways, and still find that one group has coalesced better than the other. Unless you're teaching ESL, basic writing, or honors sections of FYW, your class will be composed of a random grouping of students. But as soon as your students meet and begin to know each other and you, the class will develop subgroup personalities and then a class personality.

It is important for any teacher to know and recognize the subgroup personalities in a class. Most FY writing classes have pleasant and flexible group dynamics, and your main task will be to keep willing (and sometimes overawed) students working productively. All teachers are familiar with the hardworking, enthusiastic group at the front of the class, whose hands go up before you finish posing questions. Most of the material in this book is based on the premise of such a student attitude. When students are working together with mutual respect and on task, a classroom feels taut, sometimes even exhilarating. Though it's difficult to describe, you will know when the class is coming together productively by the atmosphere of satisfaction and achievement that fill the room.

However, in some classes you may have a back-of-the-class group, whose responses are less apt to be raised hands than whispers or snickers. In this case, you'll want to strive even harder to establish a sense of inclusivity for your entire class, including the group in the back. The worst thing you can do is get angry or exclude those back-sitters. The best thing to do is to ask them direct questions, to watch for a flicker of interest or knowledge, to invite them to speak to you and the others as often as possible, and to ask about their absences. Inclusivity is one of the most important reasons to stress attendance: Your class needs everyone, every day. Your class ethos might also benefit from some rearranging: On occasion, you can ask those front-sitters to take seats in the back so that there's a kind of seat rotation. As your class begins to witness your inclusive practices, they will come to believe that they have something to learn from everyone — and that everyone in the class (including and especially the teacher) has something to learn from them. Each student must feel like a necessary and important part of the class, of class discussion, of deliberations on assignments and due dates, of group work. As you read further in *The St. Martin's Guide to Teaching Writing*, you'll see that we offer you a number of ways to facilitate positive group dynamics in your class. (For further study of classroom dynamics, see Anson et al., Chapter 5, "Managing Discourse in Classes, Conferences, and Small Groups"; Curzan and Damour, Chapter 4, "Running a Discussion"; and Brookfield and Preskill, cited at the end of this chapter.)

Rare is the problem with classroom order that cannot be solved by talking to the right person — in private. College students are anxious to prove their maturity and usually will not continue behavior that they have been made to understand is undesirable, particularly if they realize that their peers also disapprove. If one or two students continually skip or disrupt class, speak to them after class separately, stressing the importance of their participation. In most cases — and particularly if they don't feel humiliated — FY students are willing to act as productive members of the class. If you provide such students with a series of classroom opportunities to demonstrate their improved attitude, they will nearly always help you and the rest of the class out by becoming more cooperative.

You may find, however, that some students do not respond to subtlety or to the personal approach. Occasionally, a student will test a teacher's authority, often in cases when a teacher is less experienced, female, and/or young. Differences in race, sexual orientation, or physical ability — depending on the backgrounds and expectations of the students — can also affect classroom interactions. While on most days, all will go well, in cases of serious classroom disruptions, you should make yourself aware of what sorts of backup you have from your department and university. Some students have become accustomed to acting out, have learned to deflect reprimands, and show little respect for others. Find out from your WPA, if necessary, how your program wishes you to handle such disruptive students. You may need to ask the student to speak to the WPA directly, or you may simply need to tell the student to leave the class. If you choose to talk with a disruptive student in private, be sure to leave your office door open and, whenever possible, have a trusted colleague within listening distance. Your safety is important. It is also important that such disciplinary issues not disrupt your class any more than is necessary. If a student is resistant or becomes confrontational in class, it's best to dismiss the whole class for that day and go directly to your WPA for help. It is very rare for student defiance to reach such a level, but if it does, don't try to handle it alone. If necessary, call campus security. In less severe cases, seek immediate assistance from your program or department head, and if the disruptive behavior continues, get the student out of your class. You owe it to the other students in the class — as well as to yourself.

CLASSROOM ROUTINES

Most new teachers of writing are used to the classroom routines they grew up with — lecture by the teacher or teacher-directed classroom discussion. These are the routines we know best, and we all are tempted to rely on them in writing classes as completely as we have in literature classes. Unfortunately, however, they cannot be used successfully as the only methods of classroom instruction in a writing course; in fact, they cannot even hold center stage. The writing teacher must use a much larger array of classroom activities that bring students' writing — not their talking, listening, or note-taking — to center stage.

Limiting Lectures

An old standby of classroom routines, one with which most new teachers are familiar, is the lecture. Many of us admire teachers who deliver brilliant lectures in literature courses. Lectures in writing classes, however, are not as likely to be brilliant, though they can be engaging. They must consist of the application of abstract rhetorical principles; and as the thesis of this book suggests, students simply do not learn to write — or to control any art — by studying abstract principles. As the philosopher Michael Polanyi writes,

> The aim of a skillful performance is achieved by the observance of a set of rules which are not known as such to the person following them.... Rules of art can be useful, but they do not determine the practice of art; they are maxims, which can

serve as a guide to an art only if they can be integrated into the practical knowledge of the art. (49–50)

In this case, the "practical knowledge" of writing cannot be gained by listening to lectures on the rules and protocols of writing; it can be gained only by actually writing and performing writing-based activities.

We're not suggesting that you cannot tell your students anything about writing or that explaining material to students is somehow invalid; after all, the very act of teaching is predicated, as rhetorician Richard Weaver says, on the idea that one person can know more about a specific subject than another and that knowledge or skill can be transmitted. Your explanations will be validated by students' writing or their writing-based activities. After explaining, exemplifying, and pointing out the major components of a skill, you'll want to set up a learning situation that allows students to practice the skill—and the sooner the better. Only in this way are "lectures" in a writing class truly beneficial.

Leading Effective Class Discussions

Classroom discussion is probably the teaching method most congenial to new writing teachers. Teachers do not "lead" the class in any authoritarian way; instead, they guide the discussion, and everyone in class has a chance to contribute. Inexperienced teachers of composition usually envision themselves using classroom discussions, but the essential component of discussion—content—is much more complex in a composition course than in other courses. History, biology, and psychology courses are all about "knowing that," but composition courses are concerned not only with "knowing that" but also with "knowing how." Therefore, the content of a composition class is often practical as well as theoretical. The theory is best discussed in practical terms, as it applies to a student's piece of writing or to an article, essay, short story, or poem.

This is the hard truth about discussion in writing classes: "knowing how" cannot be practiced without "knowing that," and emphasizing one at the expense of the other risks turning discussion into talk for its own sake. If the content of essays is discussed, it should be applicable to the content of the students' own writing. Students aren't usually interested in talking about sentence fragments or three-part organization unless the fragments and the organization are in their own writing. Therefore, to be useful and interesting, classroom discussions must be carefully planned and directed. You can, of course, assign essays or short stories and then spend the class time discussing them—but such use of class time is more appropriate to a course in creative nonfiction or literary appreciation than to a writing course, unless you manage to connect the reading of the literature to issues that students can work on in their own writing.

Discussion plays two important roles in the writing classroom. The first is relatively traditional: Classroom discussion of an object, idea, or situation is a prewriting activity that can give students ideas about content that they might wish to use in their writing. Fifteen minutes of discussion on different kinds of computers, for instance, might allow students access to ideas for their own essays about using computers in college. Such discussion needs to be limited and carefully directed, however, because it can easily take up more class time than it is worth. (In other words, such discussion should not be used in place of the invention activities described in Chapter 6, "Teaching Invention," but as a supplement to them.)

The second valid use of discussion in a composition course involves classroom conversations about different stylistic and organizational options available in the construction of sentences and paragraphs. (See also the descriptions of classroom discussion in Chapters 6–10, on teaching specific features of good writing.) Such discussion can be a valuable element in helping students make formal and stylistic choices about their writing. Any discussion of form, however, must focus on concrete examples of stylistic choices; otherwise, students may try to engage in arguments over abstract concepts but will not be able to apply their ideas to their work. Examples printed on handouts, drawn on a chalkboard, or projected on an overhead or computer screen often successfully supplement this kind of discussion by making the concepts concrete.

So how *do* you lead successful discussions? Important keys are knowing exactly what you wish students to gain from a discussion and having quick access to the specific materials in the reading that will apply to your purpose. For this reason, you must know the reading materials very well and have marked and labeled in your copy each line, sentence, and paragraph that you may need to call to the class's attention. If, for instance, you want to point out how the author of an essay moves from narration into argument smoothly, you must underline at least two or three examples of exactly where such a movement occurs. If you want to uncover the structure of an explanatory organization hidden by expert transitions, you need to write notes in your copy that allow you to demonstrate it. You will never regret making good directive notes in your teacher's copy; even if you have an excellent memory, notes allow you to have quick access to what you want to exemplify and thus to avoid what feels like the endless gaze of all your students while you search page after page for your lost example.

Once you have determined what you want the class discussion to accomplish and have prepared your own copy of the readings, you can look over the apparatus that usually follows most readings in anthology textbooks. These questions and issues developed by the textbook's author or editor may serve your purposes, but most often the apparatus will be only partially useful. You know what you need from the text, and the book does not, so feel free to ignore the apparatus. If you find helpful materials, mark them.

Leading classroom discussion itself is a complicated skill that improves with practice. It consists of orchestrating a few sub-skills that move within the discourse triangle of text, students, and teacher. You must be able to frame questions that are concrete enough to be answered by a good reader but not so simple that they are condescending. You must be able to sequence those questions so that potential answers will continue toward the issue you want to explore. You must be able to build verbally on the answers students give so as to move the discussion along in fruitful directions or to move it back from tangents to task. And you must be able to read the tenor of the group as you go along in order to encourage some students, calm the ardor of some, start others from passivity or silence, and draw still others out. In the ideal discussion, every student participates, and though teachers seldom achieve that ideal, they always try to approach it.

One way to make sure students will have something to say about an important point of discussion is to give them time to write about the issue before you discuss it as a class. Beginning the class session with a short in-class writing, telling students one class period earlier what they'll be discussing in the next class so they can take notes, or starting the conversation as a Web-based discussion are all ways of making sure students have something to say. Some students are understandably nervous about speaking on the spot; but if they've expressed their ideas in writing, they have a starting place. If conversation begins to lull, you can ask a quiet student, "What did you write about?" Or you can ask the class, "Did anyone take a similar or different position from John on this issue?"

Stephen D. Brookfield and Stephen Preskill, in *Discussion as a Way of Teaching*, offer several types of questions that help keep class discussions moving. Questions that ask for more evidence encourage students to consider the sources for their interpretations and opinions. Questions that ask for clarification help students refine their ideas by expressing them in different ways or by providing additional examples to explain their points. Brookfield and Preskill also discuss hypothetical questions, which "ask students to consider how changing the circumstances of a case might alter the outcome" (89). Related to hypothetical questions are cause-effect questions. You can ask, for example, "What would be the effect of ending this essay where it begins, or moving this section over here?" Particularly useful in composition classes are open questions and linking or extension questions. Open questions, Brookfield and Preskill note, often begin with *how* or *why* and draw on students' problem-solving abilities (88). Instead of asking questions that elicit a yes/no answer or that encourage only one student to respond, try beginning a question with "Why do you think...." This question format encourages more than one response because it assumes that students might actually have different thoughts on an issue. Open questions then can be extended by linking questions, such as "Is there any connection between what you said and what Susan said earlier?"

One of the most demanding skills involved in leading class discussions is learning to cultivate your own silence. There will be times when you can choose a hand from a number of enthusiastic hands, but there will also be times when all eyes are cast downward and you must call on students by name to get any response. Don't expect that a lack of immediate response to a question means you must answer it yourself; let the silence build for five or ten seconds, and then ask the question in a different way rather than answering it yourself. (As a colleague of ours says of post-question silences, "Keep quiet. They'll crack before you will.") If students are still quiet, point them to a particular place in the text you're discussing and give them a chance to write an answer to the question you have asked. Providing time for writing helps students compose their thoughts and reaffirms the important role that writing plays in learning. Finally, you will need to acquire the skill of knowing when you have achieved all you can achieve from discussing a text, and how to recap the main points through summary and synthesis questions and then move on.

Example 3.1   **DISCUSSION ACTIVITIES**

1. <u>Collaborative Talking</u>: Allow students to help one another out with their class participation. If student #1 raises an issue that she doesn't fully understand, encourage student #2 to amend or address her thoughts. If student #2 almost nails the issue, encourage student #3 to do the final nailing. In other words, let them help one another out. (This procedure is particularly important if you expect them to respond to one another's writing; if they trust and respond to one another in class, they'll do the same out of class.)

2. <u>Believers and Doubters</u>: Assign early on in the term a "believer" and a "doubter" for each reading assignment. Expect the believer to start off the discussion by very briefly (2–3 minutes) explaining the main points the author wants to make. Then the doubter can offer one or two compelling questions (doubts) about the author's argument. Class discussion follows. Make sure that each student has the opportunity to play both roles during the term.

In-Class Writing

In-class writing activities can take a number of different forms, but they all have one thing in common: they involve students in practicing the skills of planning, writing, revising, and editing. Most of the classroom material in the following chapters is based on this sort of in-class activity approach, according to which students may work alone, with one other student, or in a group. At first, the writing-centered classroom may seem appallingly disorienting, accustomed as we are to the teacher-centered atmosphere — especially in literature, history, and political science classes — of our own education. It may take you some time to get used to the meaningful chaos of a writing classroom, but as you do, you will begin to see how discoveries take place within the busy buzz.

In-class writing assignments, an important part of the writing-centered classroom, can take the form of writing short essays based on the instructions of the teacher, freewriting in response to a prompt, practicing sentence or paragraph patterns, or editing drafts according to specific guidelines. What use you make of writing-based activities will depend on the skills you are trying to teach. Example 3.2 provides some activities that can be used with excellent results.

Example 3.2 **IN-CLASS WRITING ACTIVITIES**

1. Opening: Pose a question that allows students to synthesize or explore the topic at hand. Give them five minutes to write. Ask them to read aloud their responses and encourage them to respond to one another.

2. Middle: If students seem uninterested or perplexed (or bored), stop talking for a minute and ask them to focus their thoughts. If you can pose a question that forces them to assimilate the reading assignment or problem at hand, you're on your way to getting the class back on track. For instance, "What prior knowledge does this writer expect from you?" or "What was the hardest thing to understand about today's reading?" "What's your biggest doubt about today's lesson? And what information could assuage that doubt?" "What does this reading make you think about?" "Describe this scene/setting/problem from a minor character's/the object's/the experimentation subject's point of view."

3. Closing: Near the end of class, ask students to write out (1) what they learned in class today that they didn't know before they walked in, and (2) how today's learning connects with yesterday's — or will connect with tomorrow's.

Teaching in Wired, Wireless, and Hybrid Classrooms

Teaching in a computer-supported classroom provides for a class routine different from the one in a traditional classroom. Most writing courses in computer-supported classrooms are structured so that class time is spent writing, workshopping, conferring, and revising onscreen, so such classrooms are often quiet. The traditional buzz of classroom talk is much less often heard in an environment where students' comments are usually text-specific and written rather than spoken. In addition, students work on each other's drafts much more consistently and seriously than non-linked environments allow, and therefore such work seems and feels much more socially constructed. Depending on the software package being used, interaction with a text can involve one other person, a small group, or the whole class, and the teacher can choose to play various roles. This is a fascinating and quickly developing part of composition teaching; if you are interested in computer-supported teaching and your program does not offer it or have access to computer-supported classrooms, you may wish to speak to your WPA about future plans and possibilities and indicate your interest.

If you are teaching for the first time in a computer-supported classroom, try to focus on one or two technologies that will best support your pedagogical goals and can be supported by your technological expertise. If you try to do too much in one term, to learn and teach too many technologies, you're likely to get overwhelmed — as will your students. The first time you teach in a computer-supported classroom, for instance, try to learn all you can about word-processing features, in particular the "track changes" and "comment" features of Word for peer response. Or use word processing for in-class writing and start a Web-based discussion page. The next term, once you're more comfortable, add a technology or two: teach online research and create a collaborative course Web site. If you add one technology at a time, you'll have time to learn what works and what doesn't and will spend less class time trying to deal with the inevitable problems caused by trying to do too much.

As an alternative to traditional class discussion, for example, Web-based discussion can be used for a variety of purposes, including posting announcements, allowing students to serve as resources for each other, and preceding or extending classroom conversation. Web-based discussion works best when all students in your class can log on several times a week or at least once before each class meeting. Preceding a class meeting, you can provide a prompt or other guidance on what students should focus on in the reading or ask students to post questions about the reading that can be discussed online and then in class. If a conversation begins online, you can use the online postings as a starting point for classroom discussion, drawing those who have posted into the conversation ("As Katie mentioned in the Web-based discussion.... Katie, can you explain that idea further?"). Likewise, Web-based discussion works well for extending classroom discussion, for making connections or additions after the class period is over. Sometimes you and your students will leave class and think, "I wish I had said...." Web-based discussions allow you to fulfill that wish. You can encourage frequent access by requiring a certain number of weekly posts, asking each student to start one thread and respond to one thread each week, for instance. Some students will do so more often on their own. Your WPA may be able to point you to the person who can help you set up a Web-based discussion page that is password protected and reserved for your class only.

You don't need to teach exclusively in a computer-supported classroom in order to make effective use of technology. Some writing programs will allow you to set up one or two class meetings in a computer lab in order to teach specific research skills or participate in real-time chat sessions. In addition, since some of your students will have access to computers — in an on-campus lab, at home, or in their dorm rooms — you can set up a Web-based discussion site or course Web site to support the work you're doing in an otherwise traditional classroom.

Remember, you don't have to do everything, and the computers don't have to be — and shouldn't be — the focus of the class. If you're not asking students to use outside sources for their papers, don't teach online research. The technology should support — not determine — your pedagogical goals. Just because computers can be used for peer response doesn't mean they *have* to be: you can have students print out their papers and talk face to face.

Since you're in the class to teach writing, not technology, you'll need to take a few steps to prevent the technology from taking the focus away from your goals. If you ask students to do an assignment that involves computers, be sure to prepare a written handout beforehand that takes them through the process step by step. Although some students will know far more than you do about technology, many will know far less. Written handouts help students follow along — and they keep you from having to run around the room, answering the same questions repeatedly. Also, experienced classmates can be an excellent resource for students who have less familiarity with computers. When asking students to work in small groups, make sure at least one student has a good deal of experience with the technology. And if you're assigning computer work as homework, remember that not all students will have easy or reliable access to a computer or the Internet.

Even when technology supports your pedagogical goals, remember that it sometimes fails, and you'll need to have a plan to fall back on. You may have prepared an elaborate PowerPoint presentation on invention techniques, but if the digital projector breaks down, you'll need a backup plan. Printers jam, networks go down, and computers freeze. At such times you can gracefully turn to something else, rather than spending twenty minutes trying to fix a fitful computer. When computers become distracting — through the interruption of instant messaging, the lure of surfing the Net, or the droning buzz and hum of the machines — you can always turn them off.

Example 3.3   **CONSIDERING STUDENTS' TECHNOLOGICAL
                  LITERACY: A WRITING ACTIVITY**

Drawing on the work of Gail Hawisher, Dickie Selfe, Karla Kitalong, and Tracy Bridgeford, Cynthia Selfe provides a technological literacy activity in *Writing New Media*. This activity, simplified and excerpted here, encourages students to consider the literacy practices and values they bring with them to the composition classroom (59). Here are just a few of the questions Selfe asks students to answer in writing (for the full activity, see pp. 59–62 in *Writing New Media,* cited at the end of this chapter):

Early Literacy Development

- What stories can you tell about when, where, how you first came in contact with computers? (including mainframe computers, personal computers, computer games)
- What stories can you tell about when, where, how you first learned to use computers to read or write? To speak or listen to others? To view/interact with/compose texts? Where did this take place? Did anyone help or encourage you?

Current Literacy

- Do you (or your family) own a computer(s) now?
- What specific kinds of reading and writing, speaking and listening, viewing/interacting and composition do you do now in computer environments at home? At school? Elsewhere?
- What are your favorite kinds of projects/activities in online environments? Please explain. (Wysocki et al. 59–61)

Asking students to write in answer to these and other related questions and to share their responses with you and their classmates can help you gauge their level of comfort and expertise with computers and other forms of technology. Such knowledge, then, will help you structure additional classroom activities that draw on what students already know in order to help them become better writers.

COLLABORATION: WORKSHOPS AND PEER RESPONSE

Students need guidance for their collaborations to be beneficial. A composition teacher, for example, cannot simply assign students to peer-response groups and expect them to function successfully. To ask one student to read another's essay and respond to it is to invite the disappointment of noncommittal comments such as "I really liked it" and "It flows really well." Given the traditional emphasis on individual effort and the enforcement of student passivity in many secondary school classrooms, FY writers are often unprepared and initially ill at ease when placed in collaborative learning situations. For collaborative learning to succeed, then, it must be gradually cultivated and always supported.

Even before doing whole-class workshops or establishing peer-response groups, you can organize collaborative activities that help students become more comfortable working with each other. For example, you might ask your students to select a satisfying passage (of fifty to one hundred words) from one of their essays and to read it aloud to two other students. Because the intended audience in the traditional classroom has usually been the teacher, this practice may seem unusual to many students. The students who are to listen should be instructed to offer no comments at first, for they will best learn to practice effective listening by suppressing both vacuous praise and harsh criticism.

After this simple shared reading, Peter Elbow and Pat Belanoff suggest that the listeners (the response group) employ the "sayback" technique: After listening to the draft, the response group tries to restate the effect of the text on the audience in the form of a question. Responses like "Do you mean...?" and "Are you trying to show...?" serve as invitations for the writer to continue developing or even inventing ideas (13). When the writer replies, "Yes, I was trying to explain..." and expresses the text's ideas with newfound clarity, then a more conversational model of writing has been enacted.

In *Sharing and Responding*, Elbow and Belanoff offer several more demanding response techniques. Descriptive responding consists of "pointing" to memorable or striking features of a text; then "summarizing" the piece, focusing on the main meaning and suggesting ideas "almost said" but undeveloped or even unstated; and then locating the "center of gravity," the point or idea most important to the piece (15-16). For more persuasive or argumentative writing, analytic responding involves noticing how the writer initially gets the reader "listening" and interested in the subject; identifying the main claim, the reasons provided, and additional or counter-supports; and considering the tone of the text, the intended audience, and the assumed attitude of the audience. Both response techniques are designed to encourage peer comments on broader issues of form and style and the content of the text, rather than a premature concentration on mechanical correctness; consequently, peer response should not be confused with peer editing, which involves proofreading.

Many kinds of collaborative activities are possible, such as submitting a student's draft for comments by the entire class (workshopping) and having the class respond in small groups during class, at conferences, outside class at mutually convenient times, or online — and each variation can be valuable for helping students work together.

Workshops and peer-response groups allow writers control over their work but give them the benefit of several readers' responses. Sometimes the peer reviewers align their judgments, sometimes not; but whatever the situation may be, the writers will want to choose among the possibilities for revision (ideas they might not have generated on their own) to revise accordingly. Workshops and peer-response sessions allow writers to see their work through the eyes of their readers and help them gain distance so they can improve their ability to evaluate their writing on their own.

Whole-Class Workshops

The whole class can act as an effective workshop group. Before setting up small groups, some teachers prefer to run several whole-class workshops in order to train students in the process and to get to know them as readers. In whole-class sessions, you will provide guidance on tasks through your questions and comments. The following techniques can help make whole-class workshops positive learning experiences:

1. Present strong student-generated work so the class can easily recognize its strengths. Readers will learn the techniques that work for their peers; writers will gain confidence from well-deserved praise and from recognizing what in their drafts is working. (Be sure to ask for permission ahead of time before using a student's text as your example.)

2. A day or two ahead of time, hand out copies of the essay to be discussed to give students a chance to read it at their own pace. Ask them to write comments in the margins as they read, indicating points of strength and confusion. Finally, have them write a note to the writer, giving their reaction to the overall content, describing the work's strengths, and offering one or two specific suggestions for improvement. Ask them to sign their name to their comments.

3. Begin the workshop by asking the writer or another class member to read aloud from the draft. This practice helps students focus on the essay and remember it. Readers should then be prepared to ask about the background of the piece: "How long have you been working on this?" "What are your concerns?" "Do you already have plans for revision?" After learning about the background, readers can comment on the positive features of the draft: what worked and what they admired. After establishing the strengths, readers can then move on to discussing what needs to be strengthened in the draft — and specific ways to build those strengths. Ask the writer to take notes on what her classmates are saying rather than to try to defend her work. After listening to the comments of her classmates, the writer should be allowed to ask for specific advice or clarification of what a reader has said. In this process, all students will get some idea about the kind of feedback that is helpful.

4. At the end of the workshop, you should recap some of the strengths that were mentioned and point to two or three elements that the writer can work on in revision, summarizing those comments that seem most salient. You should then have readers hand the writer their signed comments. Let the class know that after the writer reads their comments, you will also read them (in order to record students' progress as readers).

Peer-Response Groups

If you use whole-class workshops as a training ground for talking constructively about writing, then your students may be able to move directly into peer-
response groups without much further preparation. However, many teachers
prefer to use peer-response groups from the start because beginning writers,
whose self-confidence may not be high, tend to be more comfortable in smaller
groups. In addition, with several peer-response groups meeting simultaneously,
more essays can be discussed in a given period of time. A final advantage of
small peer-response groups is that they often evolve into support groups, especially when their members make contact outside the scheduled meetings, either
in person or electronically. Many peer-response groups become familiar, intimate, and trustworthy groups for all involved and survive long after the FY
writing class itself, especially if you've encouraged students to swap names,
email addresses, and phone numbers so they have easy access to one another.

Small groups meet during class to accomplish specific tasks: discussion of
an essay topic, analysis of an upcoming assignment, editorial work on one
another's drafts, advice about one another's problem areas, division of a
research project, and other mutual-aid endeavors. The expertise of group members usually evolves over the course of the term as students become better readers, questioners, and revisers — especially if you initially help them understand
what exactly they are expected to do for one another.

Should you assign students to peer-response groups, or should they form
their own? How many students should there be in a group? Should membership rotate or remain intact week after week? Should groups deal with one
essay in depth during a session, or should each student receive feedback each
time? Should you drop in on the groups (even those held outside of class), participate actively, or stay away? The answers to these and similar questions will
depend on you, your students, the dynamics of your class and the groups, and
the task at hand. The answers will also change as the term progresses and the
class changes, but some general guidelines are provided here.

The size of the groups — and they should be created by the second week, if
possible — depends on the amount of time you have and the complexity of the
tasks to be accomplished. After all, the more group members, the longer it will
take the group to go through the written work. Asking a group of three people
to share thesis ideas in twenty minutes is realistic; asking a group of six is not.
Keep in mind that groups seem to work best (more inclusively) when there are
no more than four students in each — and when the group is balanced in terms
of writing ability, race, age, personality, and gender. The best writing groups are
usually made up of students who don't know one another well enough initially
to talk about anything but the writing assignment. In fact, by waiting until the
second week of class to form groups, you will have had the opportunity to see
who is friends with whom and then assign friends to different groups.

Assigning tasks to small groups early in the term shows students what kinds
of activities might be useful, gives groups a shared set of goals and objectives,

and builds camaraderie. Later in the semester little instruction is needed if students are already used to working in groups: Students who are working well in their groups will respond naturally and in a variety of useful and supportive ways to one another's needs.

Membership in groups can be rotated purposely during the term to allow students to make contact with new peers, but some rotation will occur naturally if you move students around to replace absentees. How often you want to reconstitute your groups is up to you, of course. Rotating the makeup of groups every three weeks or so allows members a chance to move beyond introductions and to trust one another, but not to become so predictable in their behaviors as to be unhelpful. Often, though, a group will work so well that the students will ask to remain together. Most teachers will respect such a request.

Tasks for Peer-Response Groups

The ideal peer-response group — a number of motivated students who know how, and are willing, to talk about writing in progress — responds to the questions of the writer honestly, tactfully, specifically, and more successfully than a teacher could alone. Initially, students may be hesitant to critique one another's work because they don't know how to do so constructively or because they think they're supposed to criticize. Therefore, the tasks you assign must model appropriate reading and evaluation. By seeing different stages in one another's essays, students will develop a sense of the plasticity of prose and how changes can help. Finally, peer judgments make the teacher's evaluation seem less arbitrary. Once students learn these lessons and techniques and know what is expected, all you have to say is, "Writing groups, one hour, go to it," and they will.

In the beginning, though, you will want to offer detailed instructions, which may change from session to session as you train students to take on increasingly sophisticated tasks. For example, the first workshop might be a simple exercise in reading aloud: each group member reading a draft to the others, who simply listen, concentrating on the work. Through reading aloud, writers gain distance: they hear strengths and weaknesses they hadn't noticed before; they hear the draft with new objectivity, as though someone else had written it. Just as important, group members get to know what others are working on, gain a sense of how their work compares, and learn to give the most useful advice.

In subsequent sessions, the groups might be asked to work on the following tasks:

1. Without rereading, recall the most memorable points. ("This is what struck me as I listened/read.")
2. Jot down ideas or questions you want to raise.
3. Summarize the writer's point. ("This is what I think you're trying to say.")
4. Respond honestly and thoroughly to the writer's specific questions.
5. Talk through ideas for essays.

Although peer-response groups are capable of performing many tasks, their primary use lies in providing advice about revising and practice in editing. Several days or a week before a written assignment is due, have students meet in groups to discuss rough drafts of the assignment. Have them pass around and respond to their peers' writing. Better than having two students trade drafts, the system of peer-response-group revision allows each draft to be considered by at least two readers. Problems not spotted by one member of the group are usually caught by others, and every writer may hear a variety of responses to a piece of writing. In addition, better writers get the opportunity to assist poorer ones, weaker writers witness the behaviors of stronger writers, and all students get an idea of how others approach an assignment.

Example 3.4   **HOW TO RESPOND IN HELPFUL WAYS TO A PEER'S DRAFT**

Keep this list of questions by your side as you're reviewing your classmate's draft — or your own. Please know that these questions are suggestions or ideas to help you think of encouraging, truly helpful ways of responding. Responding does *not* mean criticizing — it means helping your classmate do his or her best work. In addition, by answering these questions about your peer's draft, you'll improve drastically and quickly your ability to answer the same questions about your own draft.

1. <u>The Assignment</u>. Does the draft carry out the assignment? How might the writer better fulfill the assignment?

2. <u>The Title and Introduction</u>. Does the title tell the reader what the draft is about? Does it catch the reader's interest? What does the opening accomplish in terms of hooking the reader's interest, establishing common ground, and establishing the writer's ethos? How else might the writer begin?

3. <u>The Thesis and Purpose</u>. Paraphrase the thesis as a promise: "In this essay, I will. . . ." Does the draft fulfill that promise? Why, or why not? What is the writer's purpose? How does the draft fulfill (or not fulfill) that purpose?

4. <u>The Audience</u>. Who is the audience? How does the draft establish goodwill with the audience? How does it capture the interest of the audience? What values does the audience hold that are different from the writer's?

5. The Exigence. What is the situation (or context) that calls for this writer's rhetorical transaction?

6. The Rhetorical Stance. Where does the writer stand on issues involved with this topic? What words or phrases in the draft indicate the values the writer holds with regard to this topic? How does the writer identify her cause with the interests (or different values) of her audience?

7. The Supporting Points. List the main points, in order. Number them in order of interest to *you*. Which of them could be explained or supported more fully? What evidence, examples, or details might do the trick? Which of the supporting points could be de-emphasized or eliminated?

8. The Paragraphs. Which paragraphs are clearest? best developed? Which paragraphs need further development? What kinds of information might help?

9. The Organization. How is the draft organized — chronologically, spatially, emphatically, or in some other way? Given the organizational pattern, could the main points be presented in a more effective way? What suggestions can you make for transitions between paragraphs that would make connections clearer and easier to follow?

10. The Sentences. Choose three sentences you consider the most interesting or best written — stylistically effective, entertaining, or otherwise memorable. Then choose three sentences you see as weak — confusing, awkward, or uninspiring. Advise your peer on how to revise those three weak sentences.

11. The Words. Circle the words that are particularly effective; underline those that are weak, vague, or unclear. Do any words need to be defined or replaced? Are there any potentially offensive words in the draft?

12. The Tone. What dominant impression does the draft create — serious, humorous, satiric, persuasive, argumentative, or objective? Is the tone appropriate to the topic and audience? Is it consistent? Mark specific places where the writer's voice comes through most clearly. Ask the writer if this is the intended tone — and if he finds your comments surprising.

13. <u>The Conclusion</u>. Does the draft conclude in a memorable way? Does it end abruptly? trail off? restate the introduction? How else might this draft end? If you like the conclusion, give two reasons why.

14. <u>Final Thoughts</u>. What are the main strengths of this draft? weaknesses? What surprised you — and why? What do you want to know more about? What is the writer's single most important comment or point?

Responses to workshop questions like those in Example 3.4 are more useful when they are written down and clipped to the original draft than if they are just discussed. When the questions are used as a worksheet to elicit written answers, students may initially take twenty-five or thirty minutes to work through them while reviewing an essay. But as the term progresses, they will work more quickly.

Online and Electronic Peer Response

The questions listed in Example 3.4 can also serve as a guide for students responding to drafts electronically. If you're teaching in a computer-supported classroom, you might ask students to respond to each others' drafts online in class. If you've already worked in class on effective peer-response strategies (whether you teach in a computer-supported classroom or not), you might ask students to email their drafts to each other or post their drafts to a course Web site and respond outside of class. Asking students to respond to each other's essays outside of class can save class time — but be sure to reserve some time for students to talk face-to-face in peer-response groups, so they can ask questions and make sure they understand the comments others have made on their work.

If you require electronic peer response, be sure students have the hardware and software necessary to complete the task. If you're teaching in a wired or wireless classroom, you likely will already have chosen the program you wish to use (see the section on computerized learning technologies in Chapter 1), but if students do not have access to a common program designed for peer response (such as Bedford/St. Martin's *Comment*), you will have to weigh the benefits and pitfalls of other methods of electronic peer response. Most students have access to email and can insert comments in [brackets], ALL CAPS, or **bold** directly in a classmate's text. Often, however, formatting is lost in inserting a text into the body of an email message, and, therefore, it can be difficult to read. If your students use a common word-processing program, such as Microsoft Word, they can utilize the Track Changes feature (in the Tools pull-down menu), which allows them to make changes, insert comments, and highlight parts of the text. This feature also allows writers to accept and reject changes, deleting comments after they have addressed the issues raised. Not all students, though, have access to the same word-processing program. Whatever method you choose, be sure to provide a handout that explains how students should use the technology.

Evaluating Peer-Response Groups

After one or two sessions during which students work in their writing groups on their own, try asking for a brief, written evaluation of the group's effectiveness:

1. What does your writing group do well?
2. What has helped you as a writer? What has helped you as a reader?
3. Suggest one thing your group could do differently to improve its effectiveness. Complete this statement: "Next time let's try _____."
4. What are you contributing to the group?
5. What would you like to do better?

Have students discuss their evaluations at a subsequent group meeting and implement some of their own suggestions. Later have them evaluate the groups again:

1. What has your group accomplished so far?
2. What has your group been most helpful with? What has it been least helpful with? Explain.
3. What has each group member contributed?
4. How can you help make your group more effective?

In this way — and especially when you use these questions as the basis of whole-class analysis and discussion — you can keep loose tabs on each group's work and reinforce the idea that students are responsible for the success of their groups. In addition, the groups will learn from the successes and trials of other groups as well as from the contributions of individual group members.

Understanding Cultural and Multilingual Differences in Peer-Response Groups

Asking students to evaluate their peer-response groups periodically will help you and them recognize differences in how and what group members contribute. Students — influenced by personality, gender, cultural differences, and a range of other kinds of differences — will adopt various roles, creating complex group dynamics. One student might be authoritarian, directly telling others how to change their work; another might ask questions, probing for more information; another might try to mediate suggestions, playing a collaborative role; while another might be silent or resistant or simply unsure of what to contribute. Students' educational backgrounds, expectations, and preferences for the kinds of responses they find useful will further complicate the dynamics.

Students need to understand that communication is influenced by cultural context and that working in groups requires flexibility and openness to others and their ideas. In their article "Variation in EFL-ESL Peer Response," Adina Levine, Brenda Oded, Ulla Connor, and Iveta Asons assert that "students may use culturally diverse rules for how much and what kind of criticism should be expressed" (2). Drawing on earlier studies of ESL peer response, they also observe, more specifically, "While both Chinese and Spanish-speaking students preferred critical comments to help them improve their drafts, and both preferred teacher feedback to student feedback, they differed on the amount and kind of talk that was needed to identify problems" (2). Given such variation, it's imprudent to make sweeping generalizations about how students' cultural backgrounds affect peer response, but Levine's study, which examines "the nature of peer response in the foreign language and second language writing of student populations in two different learning settings: Israel and the U.S." (8), and other similar studies provide a starting point for addressing and working with such differences.

Ilona Leki, in "Meaning and Development of Academic Literacy in a Second Language" (included in Part III of this book), takes a broader view of cultural differences, not simply as they relate to peer response but, rather, to the larger realm of academic literacy. At the end of her article, she writes, "Given how complex literacy issues in second, third, or fourth languages can become, perhaps the only reasonable stance to take, at least initially, is one of modest flexibility and willingness to learn from others, one in which 'You do a lot of observing and then you think about it'" (341). Such observation can take place when students evaluate their own peer-response groups, pointing to their own strengths and to areas they wish to improve.

STUDENT CONFERENCES

Another way to mediate cultural differences and respond directly to the needs of individuals is through student conferences. The student-teacher conference has a number of functions, but the primary ones have to do with getting to know your students better as writers, intervening more directly in their composing processes, and letting them know you care about how they are doing. The student conference gives you the opportunity to explain writing strategies, discuss the strengths and weaknesses of a student's work, plan and examine future work, and in general establish the kind of relationship that will foster strong teacher-student interaction. Most important, though, the conference allows the student to talk about his or her writing, ideas, and plans.

Unfortunately, in spite of all these desirable goals and possibilities, you usually can't rely solely on your office hours for fostering contact with your students, especially if you teach at an institution where many students are balancing responsibilities of work, school, family, and home. Probably the best way to ensure personal contact and effect useful help with revisions, then, is by instituting a system of conferences held in the office, in the classroom, or electronically. Mandatory conferences need to be specified as such from the beginning of the course, preferably on the syllabus. You will need to check with your WPA to learn whether it is acceptable to use occasional class time for individual conferences. For instance, you may be permitted to assign writing groups a task that they will accomplish outside of class and use class time to meet individually with class members whose schedules do not permit meeting at other times. The number of conferences you schedule with your students is up to you. Some teachers specify only one or two conferences per term; others ask their students to meet with them weekly or biweekly.

Conferences work best when they have one of the following purposes:

- Discussion of a plan or draft for a new assignment.
- Discussion of the content or structural revisions of a draft in progress.
- Discussion of the progress of any long-term ongoing project (a research essay, for instance).
- Discussion of a process, particularly changes in a student's writing process, and the sharing of anecdotes about writing (since you, the teacher, are a writer, too, with your own blocks, ruts, successes).
- Discussion of activities meant to deal with specific and identified patterns of formal problems: syntactic errors, verb endings, and the like.

Usually the conversation focuses on a draft the student has submitted. Each conference should draw on past work and past discussions in order to support and stimulate the student's future work. Student-teacher conferences, then, are always conversations about writing — and about moving forward. Through one-on-one discussion of students' work (previous, in hand, or planned), you get to know your students, demonstrate your interest in their work, and provide a responsive audience and individualized instruction. The students, meanwhile, get to talk about their intentions and their work to an interested and expert mentor. Getting students to take an active part in conferences, however, is not always easy. Many of them are more than willing to let the teacher dominate any discussion, particularly during a one-on-one conference. Others may be intimidated by the very idea of meeting alone with the teacher or of having the teacher's complete attention. To students used to blending into the crowd of the classroom, the potential for miscommunication or misjudgment may seem high. But as soon as they realize that the direction of the conference belongs to them, rather than to you, they will be more comfortable meeting and talking about their work.

Therefore, in addition to the very real advantage of helping students "own" their learning and writing, conferences provide a safe space to discuss ongoing problems or issues of concern. For instance, if a student has been absent or tardy often, you can show your concern: "I've noticed you've missed three classes already this term. Is there some problem or issue I should know about?" Or if a student is especially quiet in class, you can ask how you can help provide a space for her to speak: "I've noticed that you're very quiet in class. I'm sure you have a lot to say. Would it be helpful if I called on you?" Problems in the classroom often stem from issues outside class, and you can guide students to the appropriate resources for help, such as the counseling center or disability services office. Conferences also provide a good time to learn about how your classroom practices are working. You might ask, "How's your writing group going?" or "What kinds of classroom activities have been most or least helpful to you in your writing?" Students' answers to such questions will help you modify classroom practices before the end-of-the-term evaluations come back and it's too late to make changes.

Using a regular conference system means your teaching will be more interactive than presentational, and your students' learning will be more collaborative and active. If students view writing as a complex, long-term, interactive process of prewriting, drafting, receiving feedback, and revising, they will seek responses from you and from their peers. Regularly scheduled conferences are simply an extension of this process: Writers talk themselves through their drafts, over the rough spots, and into new territories, while you, as the reader-teacher, provide a knowledgeable, supportive audience. Students (all writers, for that matter) are encouraged when they know somebody cares enough to read, respond to, and talk about what they write.

However you decide to structure conferences for your course, let your students know your reasons for doing so, and establish a schedule as early in the term as possible so students will know what kind of feedback to expect and when. They should understand that yours is not the only word and that feedback from their peers — individually, in writing groups, in whole-class workshops — and from writing center tutors are useful as well. Using all of these methods of feedback will give students a variety of responses to their work, emphasizing a broader audience for that work (and keeping you from carrying the total weight of being the only respondent).

Scripting the Conference

In a conference, it is a good idea to assume the writer knows the work better than you do. The student wrote the essay and knows the kind of effort that went into it, what was hard and what was easy. The writer may also have thought about purpose, audience, and possibilities for revision. Your questions and responses will help the student see the draft in a fresh or less subjective way. In conferences, then, you use your experience as a reader to teach students how to read their own work.

Successful conferences are usually based on a script. Whether you stick to or diverge from that script depends on the conference, but having a script means you have a plan. When you open a conference with such scripted questions as "How can I help you?" and "What is your purpose in this piece of writing?" you set the direction for the conference yet allow the student to steer. Other open-ended, scripted questions that can help students get going include the following:

- What are the stronger sections? the weaker? Why?
- Who is your audience?
- What are you pleased with? What are you not so happy with?
- What did you learn in writing this?
- Is this finished? If not, what would you like to change?

- What surprised you in this essay?
- What did you discover while writing this?
- What is the key line or passage? Why is it so important?

If you can teach the student to use the conference as a chance to communicate with a supportive, informed reader, you will both relax a little and become two writers, or perhaps a writer and a writing coach, working together to push a draft forward and, ultimately, to improve the student's overall writing and reading skills. Often it is helpful to let the student know exactly what you understand from the reading. Tell the student what you think she is getting at in the essay so that she can compare your reading and understanding with what she hoped readers would understand. If you missed the point, the student will see the need for appropriate revision.

Student investment in a conference also ensures student "ownership" of the essay under discussion. It is all too easy for teachers to appropriate students' work by being too much the director, by revising for students instead of helping them choose the course of the revision. The issue here is one of responsibility, and responsibility depends entirely on the nature of the discussion and the spirit in which advice is given and received. For example, a student who questions the introduction to his essay does so because he suspects there is a better place to begin. And with his question, he opens the door for you to point to one or more spots that might work as a better beginning. You might give a mini-lesson on audience, tension, tone, even argumentation — depending on the nature of the assignment — as you discuss introductions and what they can do. It is always left to the students to evaluate your advice, to weigh what they have learned in the conference and to consider their own instincts before deciding what to do in the next draft. A discussion initiated by the student about possible leads differs considerably from one initiated by the teacher saying that the introduction should be replaced by the third paragraph. In the latter case, the student's responsibility (and initiative) for the assignment is lost. When an essay improves as the result of a revision, the student should "own" the improvement.

A successful conference should end with at least one concrete assignment, one that shows you and the student agree on your expectations for the next stage of work. In addition, both you and the student should come away with a clear sense of what has been accomplished. You should know what expectations have been raised, what task comes next, and why.

Student-teacher conferences about drafts may be demanding, but they are a much more efficient way to help students understand content and questions of organization than just marking up their essays. For these conferences to be useful, they must be dialogic; meetings in which students can ask you questions, explain themselves, react to suggestions. In these ways the bond between writer and reader becomes real and personal. The more conferences you hold with your students, the better they will come to understand the concept of an audience and the responsibilities of a writer.

EVERYBODY'S ISSUES

Absenteeism and Tardiness

In writing courses, the most common classroom-management problem has nothing to do with classroom order or activities—it is absenteeism. The temptation to skip classes can be great for FY students, who may for the first time in their lives be in a situation in which no one is forcing them to go to school. In dealing with absenteeism, teachers must first consider that this is college and they have no way to compel attendance.

Even before the term begins, you should be familiar with your school's policy on class attendance and should work with it as best you can. In general, unless your department has a specific written policy, teachers may be forbidden or discouraged from using grades to compel attendance in writing courses. Some schools will not allow you to fail a student who never comes to class but writes the assigned essays. Still, you have options. You can, of course, make class participation and writing-group work a part of the final grade so that the grades of those students who do not attend class will suffer. In addition, brief in-class writing assignments and group projects will encourage steady attendance.

Often the best way to deal with absenteeism is to plan the course so as to discourage it. Try this: Give information about graded assignments on one class day, hold editing workshops on another class day, have graded essays due on yet another class day. In other words, fill up the week with requests for specific actions, and provide meaningful progress toward a goal. If a student misses a class, the goal becomes harder to attain and the tasks at hand become more difficult. If a student skips a writing-group session and then receives a poor grade on an essay because the support for his thesis is vague, and if he realizes his writing group would have pointed out this shortcoming, he will quickly become aware of the concrete advantages of attending class.

Whatever your policy on absenteeism may be, you should spell it out clearly in the syllabus so that when problems do occur you can point to the written policy. If a student misses two or more classes in a row, you may wish to call or send an email, showing your concern. Students often have valid reasons for missing classes (illness or family emergency), but if the problem persists, it is best to know about the situation early enough to advise students of their options (including withdrawing from the course). You will also need to decide whether you want to—or if your institution requires you to—distinguish between excused and unexcused absences.

You may also encounter students who consistently show up for class five, ten, even fifteen minutes late. Here again, your school may have a policy, but usually this matter is best settled privately. Speak to the student after class or in conference, and find out whether there is a valid reason for the lateness. Surprisingly often, students do have good excuses—a long walk across campus between classes, an inconsiderate teacher running late in a previous class, personal responsibilities of different sorts—but just as often the lateness is a result of late rising, poor planning, or careless habits.

If the student's reasons for lateness do not seem valid, state politely but seriously that students who are late will be marked as absent. If you take attendance at the start of each class, students will quickly realize that latecomers are marked as absent. Treating students as responsible adults and showing an interest in them can have a good effect: Tardy students often begin appearing in class on time.

Late Essays

Late essays — written assignments handed in (often slipped surreptitiously under your office door or into your office mailbox) after their due date — can be another problem, but only if you allow them to be. State in your syllabus that you will not accept late essays: "No late assignments. Period." Or, if your composition program allows it, make the consequences for late assignments clear in the syllabus: "Grades will be reduced by one-half of a letter grade for each day an assignment is late." When the inevitable requests for extensions appear or when the late essays show up, you can adjust the policy as seems fit and fair. It is often better to announce an unyielding policy initially and then adjust it than to announce a liberal policy, see it abused, and then try to establish a harder line. If you do receive a late essay that has not been explained in advance, one common way of dealing with it is to note the time and date it reached you, write "late essay" on it, and lower the grade. You can also give it credit without reading it, which will keep the student from being penalized for not turning in the essay but will not add to the student's grade average. You can, of course, choose instead not to accept it.

Plagiarism, Intellectual Property, and Academic Integrity

All of us go to books, teachers, friends, experts, movies, and Web sites for information and ideas that we then use in our decision making, thinking, and writing. If we have strong opinions about the superiority of foreign-made over U.S.-made cars, for example, chances are we came to those opinions through conversations and reading. Yet we often neglect to mention the sources for our opinions and focus instead on the ideas themselves. We're so used to taking the credit for our opinions that we rarely name our sources; doing so seems unnecessary. Sometimes we want to take all the credit for what we think are our own unique thoughts; at other times, we don't really consider where our thoughts or opinions came from. In some cultures, it's considered impolite or even disrespectful to note your sources; indeed, our concept of plagiarism doesn't exist in some cultures, and it has changed over time even in our own.

Writing students in North America, however, don't enjoy the luxury of eliding their sources. When students present the work or thinking of others as their own, it's called plagiarism, whether their intention was to compensate for academic-performance anxiety, steal someone else's ideas and get away with it, or take full credit in all innocence for what became their ultimate opinion.

Plagiarism can range from downloading an entire essay from the Web and submitting it for a grade to lifting the opening paragraph from a recent *Time* article. It can be as obvious as a beautifully written passage from Terry Tempest Williams amid a jumble of otherwise impenetrable prose, or it can be as subtle as an artfully worked-in argument from a sociology text. Most important, it can be deliberate or accidental; students can plagiarize with anything from full knowledge of the consequences to none at all. The range of attitudes can be based on experience, knowledge, or cultural background. However, whatever the reasons for or degree of plagiarism, it spells a problem that you'll want to approach quickly and efficiently.

Defining the Terms. Given the current academic climate's insistence on a responsible use of sources, it's important that you and your students have a clear understanding of academic integrity, plagiarism, and intellectual property (one's ideas and work). Plagiarism — the use of someone else's words, ideas, or, images without giving credit to the source — can result in serious consequences. At some colleges, students who plagiarize fail the course automatically; at others, they are expelled. In academic circles, plagiarism is a serious offense: professors who plagiarized, even inadvertently, have had their degrees revoked or their books withdrawn from publication. Outside academic life, eminent political, business, and scientific leaders have been stripped of candidacies, positions, and awards because of plagiarism. Therefore, you'll want your students to be able to acknowledge directly and credit specifically the intellectual property of others. They must be able to give credit where credit is due.

Example 3.5 shows Penn State's guide to plagiarism, which is provided to incoming students so they won't *un*knowingly commit plagiarism.

However, students and teachers are often confused by what exactly constitutes plagiarism — in other words, exactly when and where *is* credit due? It's important that you teach students which types of sources to acknowledge. Information that is well known or that you gather yourself does not need to be cited. But what exactly can be considered "well known"? In chapter 16 of *The St. Martin's Handbook*, Sixth Edition, Lunsford offers the following list of materials that do not require acknowledgment:

> *Your own words, observations, surveys, and so on*
> *Common knowledge*
> *Facts available in many sources*
> *Drawings or other visuals you create on your own* (283)

Lunsford also offers the following list of materials that must be cited and included in a bibliography or a Works Cited list:

> *Quotations*
> *Paraphrases or summaries of a source*
> *Ideas you glean from a source*
> *Facts that aren't widely known*
> *Graphs, tables, and other statistical information from a source*

Photographs, video, or sound taken from sources
Organization or structure taken from a source
Help or advice from an instructor or another student (283)

Example 3.5   **PENN STATE'S GUIDE TO UNDERSTANDING PLAGIARISM**

The Source

> The U.S. has only lost approximately 30 percent of its original forest area,
> most of this in the nineteenth century. The loss has not been higher mainly
> because population pressure has never been as great there as in Europe.
> The doubling of U.S. farmland from 1880 to 1920 happened almost without
> affecting the total forest area as most was converted from grasslands.
>
>   –Bjorn Lomborg, *The Skeptical Environmentalist*

Word-for-Word Plagiarism

In the following example, the writer tacks on a new opening part of the first
sentence in the hope that the reader won't notice that the rest of the paragraph
is simply copied from the source. The plagiarized words are italicized.

> Despite the outcry from environmentalist groups like Earth First! and the
> Sierra Club, it is important to note that *the U.S. has only lost approximately
> 30 percent of its original forest area, most of this in the nineteenth century.
> The loss has not been higher mainly because population pressure has never
> been as great there as in Europe. The doubling of U.S. farmland from 1880
> to 1920 happened almost without affecting the total forest area as most
> was converted from grasslands.*

Quotation marks around all the copied text, followed by a parenthetical citation,
would avoid plagiarism in this case. But even if that were done, a reader might
wonder why so much was quoted from Lomborg in the first place. Beyond that, a
reader might wonder why you chose to use a quote here instead of paraphrase this
passage, which as a whole is not very quotable, especially with the odd reference
to Europe. Using exact quotes should be reserved for situations where the original
author has stated the idea in a better way than any paraphrase you might come
up with. In the above case, the information could be summed up and simply

paraphrased, with a proper citation, because the idea, even in your words, belongs to someone else. Furthermore, a paper consisting largely of quoted passages and little original writing would be relatively worthless.

Plagiarizing by Paraphrase

In the following case, the exact ideas in the source are followed very closely — too closely — simply by substituting your own words and sentences for those of the original.

Original	Paraphrase
The United States has only lost approximately 30 percent of its original forest area, most of this in the nineteenth century.	Only 30 percent of the original forest area in the United States has been lost.
The loss has not been higher mainly because population pressure has never been as great there as in Europe.	Europe has fared slightly worse due to greater population pressure.
The doubling of U.S. farmland from 1880 to 1920 happened almost without affecting the total forest area as most was converted from grasslands.	Even though U.S. farmland doubled from 1880 to 1920, little forest area was affected since the farms appeared on grasslands.

The ideas in the right column appear to be original. Obviously, they are just Lomborg's ideas presented in different words without any acknowledgment. Plagiarism can be avoided easily here by introducing the paraphrased section with an attribution to Lomborg and then following up with a parenthetical citation. Such an introduction is underlined here:

> Bjorn Lomborg points out that despite environmentalists' outcries.... (page number).

Properly used, paraphrase is a valuable rhetorical technique. You should use it to simplify or summarize so that others' ideas or information, properly attributed in the introduction and documented in a parenthetical citation, may be woven into the pattern of your own ideas. You should not use paraphrase simply to avoid quotation; you should use it to express another's important ideas in your own words when those ideas are not expressed in a way that is useful to quote directly.

Mosaic Plagiarism

This is a more sophisticated kind of plagiarism wherein phrases and terms are lifted from the source and sprinkled in among your own prose. Words and phrases lifted verbatim or with only slight changes are italicized:

> Environmentalist groups have long bemoaned the loss of U.S. forests, particularly in this age of population growth and urbanization. Yet, *the U.S. has only lost approximately 30 percent of its original forest area, and most of this in the nineteenth century.* There are a few main reasons for this. First, *population pressure has never been as great* in this country *as in Europe.* Second, the explosion of *U.S. farmland, when it doubled from 1880 to 1920, happened almost without affecting the total forest area as most was converted from grasslands.*

Mosaic plagiarism may be caused by sloppy note-taking, but it always looks thoroughly dishonest and intentional and will be judged as such. In the above example, just adding an introduction and a parenthetical citation will not solve the plagiarism problem since no quotation marks are used where required. But adding them would raise the question of why those short phrases and basic statements of fact and opinion are worth quoting word for word. The best solution is to paraphrase everything: rewrite the plagiarized parts in your own words, introduce the passage properly, and add a parenthetical citation.

Summary

Using quotation marks around someone else's words avoids the charge of plagiarism, but when overdone, makes for a patchwork paper with little flow to it. When most of what you want to say comes from a single source, either quote directly or paraphrase. In both cases, introduce your borrowed words or ideas by attributing them to the author and then follow them with a parenthetical citation.

The secret of using sources productively is to make them work for you to support and amplify your ideas. If you find, as you work at paraphrasing, quoting, and citing, that you are only pasting sources together with a few of your own words and ideas thrown in — that too much of your paper comes from your sources and not enough from your own mind — then go back and start over. Try rewriting the paper without looking at your sources, just using your own ideas, after you have completed a draft entirely of your own, add the specific words and ideas from your sources to support what you want to say.

If you have any doubts about the way you are using sources, talk to your instructor as soon as you can.

Source: http://english.la.psu.edu/facultystaff/plagiarism.htm

---

Specific Department Plagiarism Policy. Some departments have official plagiarism policies that you must explain to the class early on in the term, adhere to, and enforce. It's important to include a copy of the plagiarism statement with your syllabus, so students can refer to it at any time. The English Department at Penn State, for example, has a detailed plagiarism policy that is summarized in the following statement: "The Department of English insists on strict standards of academic honesty in all courses. Therefore, plagiarism, the act of passing off someone else's words or ideas as your own, will be penalized severely."

Teaching toward the Prevention of Plagiarism. Of course, the best policy for dealing with plagiarism is to avoid inviting it in the first place. Successful teachers avoid writing assignments that lend themselves to easy answers found in readily available sources, those that populate various online paper mills and for-hire essay-writing sites, and those that have been around the department (or in the fraternity file) for years. Another way to prevent plagiarism is to suggest essay topics that must be personalized in some way. And if you make certain that all students' essays have gone through several revisions and that all early drafts are turned in with the typed final versions, you can be pretty sure your students have written their own essays. When assigning research projects, you might ask your students to keep and submit research portfolios, which include notes on their sources as well as multiple drafts of their papers. These portfolios can provide a forum for the teacher to intervene early and prevent any plagiarism-related issues. Good assignment planning and classroom management can make plagiarism difficult — sometimes more difficult, in fact, than writing the essay.

When you've taught your students how to acknowledge the work of others responsibly, explained your university's plagiarism policy, and designed writing assignments and policies that discourage plagiarism, you've done just about all you can. Even teachers who take the time to explain the many good reasons for citing sources receive plagiarized essays. You can stress that by crediting their sources, students not only demonstrate the extra research they've conducted; they also place their own intellectual endeavor in the context of the conversation that has come before. By crediting their sources, students thank those whose work they've built on. In short, crediting sources provides a means of establishing the student's ethos as a writer. Failure to credit sources corrupts the textual conversation, misleads readers, and destroys the credibility of the writer and the work. By raising these issues, you'll provide a forum for discussing the ethical and cultural dimensions of citing, paraphrasing, and quoting sources; concepts of intellectual property; and academic integrity.

Internet Plagiarism.   Even the best teachers sometimes have to deal with intentional plagiarism, and given the ease of downloading papers from the Internet, it's no surprise. There are more than 250 different term paper sites on the Web, each one allowing college essays to be downloaded, tweaked to provide some seeming evidence of originality, and passed off as the student's own. Some sites, such as <*http://www.termpapersites.com*>, list several member sites, advertising free essays or ones that can be custom ordered. Taken together, term-paper sites represent a genuine threat to the integrity of teaching writing in the United States. The Kimbel Library of Coastal Carolina University offers an online list of active Internet paper mills, compiled in conjunction with a teaching effectiveness seminar; the list is updated every six months. (For more information, see the Web site listed at the end of this chapter.)

Confronting Plagiarism.   One of the most uncomfortable issues teachers face is suspecting a student of plagiarizing, but there isn't an experienced teacher among us who hasn't had to deal with the issue. Before the widespread use of computers, teachers went to the library to try to locate the original source — the "smoking gun" — before they could confront, let alone punish, a student suspected of plagiarism. Today, many schools use Web plagiarism trackers and plagiarism-detection software (such as <www.turnitin.com>, <www.plagiarism.com> and <www.canexus.com>) as a means of identifying plagiarized or purchased research papers as well as the plagiarized source. Many teachers, however, have raised concerns about the unauthorized archiving of students' work and the climate of suspicion plagiarism trackers create. Your judgment as a teacher will likely be better than any plagiarism tracker; after all, if you didn't think it was plagiarized in the first place, why would you submit it to the Web site for identification as a plagiarized essay? If you suspect that a student has downloaded an essay from the Internet, you can simply type a phrase from that essay into a search engine such as Google, which checks the results against most paper mills.

   If you do find indisputable evidence of plagiarism, you need to determine how to proceed. Consider whether the student intended dishonesty or whether the uncited material is a result of ignorance, carelessness, or turpitude. Most teachers would rather not set the wheels of institutional punishment going unless they are sure the student intended dishonesty. Instead, they will try to deal with the student's failure in the context of the class, by asking the student to rewrite the essay or by giving that one essay a failing grade. Pressing plagiarism cases publicly is time-consuming and unpleasant, and only where the intent to deceive is clear and the case is obvious and provable is it common for a teacher to invoke the full majesty of the academic code against a plagiarist.

As in other areas, however, you need to know your institution's policy on reporting plagiarism. (For scholarly discussions of plagiarism, see Curzan and Damour, pp. 118–22; Haswell and Lu; Kroll; and Lunsford, Chapter 18 of *The St. Martin's Handbook,* Sixth Edition. See also the Web site <www.bedford stmartins.com/plagiarism>, which offers a discussion of plagiarism and a series of interactive exercises and tutorials that help students learn about responsible use of sources; also included are helpful research tools for teachers and students, such as <www.bedfordresearcher.com> and <www.bedford stmartins.com/modeldocs>.)

WORKS CITED

Anson, Chris, et al. *Scenarios for Teaching Writing.* Urbana: NCTE, 1993.

Brookfield, Stephen D., and Stephen Preskill. *Discussion as a Way of Teaching: Tools and Techniques for Democratic Classrooms.* San Francisco: Jossey-Bass, 1999.

Curzan, Anne, and Lisa Damour. *First Day to Final Grade: A Graduate Student's Guide to Teaching.* Ann Arbor: U of Michigan P, 2000.

Elbow, Peter, and Pat Belanoff. *Sharing and Responding.* New York: Random, 1989.

Haswell, Richard H., and Min-Zhan Lu. *CompTales.* New York: Longman, 2000. 52, 53, 61, 81, 90, 96, 97.

Kroll, Barry. "How College Freshmen View Plagiarism." *Written Communication* 5 (Apr. 1988): 203–27.

Levine, Adina, Brenda Oded, Ulla Connor, Iveta Asons. "Variation in EFL-ESL Peer Response." *TESL-EJ* 6.3 (Dec. 2002): 1–18.

Lunsford, Andrea. *The St. Martin's Handbook.* 6th ed. Boston: Bedford/St. Martin's, 2008.

Polanyi, Michael. *Personal Knowledge: Towards a Post-Critical Philosophy.* New York: Harper, 1964.

Weaver, Richard. *Language Is Sermonic.* Ed. Richard L. Johannesen, Rennard Strickland, and Ralph T. Eubanks. Baton Rouge: Louisiana State UP, 1970.

Wysocki, Anne Frances, Johndan Johnson-Eilola, Cynthia L. Selfe, and Geoffrey Sirc. *Writing New Media: Theory and Applications for Expanding the Teaching of Composition.* Logan: Utah State UP, 2004.

Useful Web Sites

Bedford Researcher
<www.bedfordresearcher.com>

Bedford/St. Martin's Model Documents Gallery
<www.bedfordstmartins.com/modeldocs>

Bedford/St. Martin's Plagiarism Workshop
<www.bedfordstmartins.com/plagiarism>

Eve 2.4 Essays Verification Engine

Kimbel Library: Internet Paper Mills
<http://www.coastal.edu/library/presentations/mills2.html>

Plagiarism.com
<www.plagiarism.com>

St. Martin's Handbook, **Sixth Edition Site**
<www.bedfordstmartins.com/smhandbook>

Turnitin.com

CHAPTER

4

Successful Writing Assignments

Here's my dilemma when attempting to design successful writing assignments. I want to be specific enough so that students understand the assignment itself and the kinds of concepts or rhetorical tools that they should use when writing their essays. But I also want to make sure that I'm not too specific and directive so that they can still be creative while they are choosing their topics, composing their essays, and revising their drafts.

–Jess Enoch

ASSIGNMENTS

Initiating student writing and designing and evaluating writing assignments are at the heart of a composition teacher's job. The life of a writing teacher has often been described as a perpetual search for effective topics, writing prompts, and assignments: No matter how polished their courses seem, all good writing teachers remain on the lookout for more fruitful ways to help students develop their writing abilities.

There's no best way to run a writing program, let alone design a writing course, but there are basic issues to take into consideration as you think about your course and assignments. Even if your composition program has provided you with textbooks and a syllabus, you'll still need to take two basic issues into consideration as you plan your course: What genres will you ask your students to write? Will your students have a free choice of topics? Some FY writing teachers (and programs) specify every feature of every writing assignment, from topic and genre to deadline and format, while others encourage students to make their own choices. There are advantages to both course designs as well as to many of the designs that fall somewhere in between. Some students thrive in a tightly designed writing course, finding security in established boundaries even though others might feel that they're simply doing what the teacher wants, writing artificial essays about uninteresting subjects. In a course offering more freedom and options, some students blossom. They experiment with different forms and genres and feel emotionally invested in their writing, more so than if they had to respond to a teacher's specifications; nevertheless, other students in that same class might feel as though they've been set adrift. The benefits for teachers also vary: some teachers feel more comfortable evaluating essays that are all alike in terms of format, length, and genre, whereas others are invigorated by a stack of student essays on a variety of topics, some in innovative forms.

In *Genre and Writing*, Wendy Bishop and Hans Ostrom encourage teachers "to be aware of the power of discourses and genres that we have claimed for ourselves," arguing that "we need to return this power to our students, encouraging alternate understandings of genre as form *and* as social practice" (1). That is, the assignments teachers give (as well as the kinds of scholarly work they do) can help create, break, or reinforce conventions. Bishop and Ostrom, as well as other composition scholars, want teachers to consider the potential effects of the choices they make in giving assignments. The assignments you give will help shape the way your students view writing and its purposes — and they will also shape you.

For a first-time teacher, following a preset syllabus and series of writing assignments designed by experienced, successful teachers can be a good idea. Whether these carefully developed and sequenced assignments come from your composition program or from a good textbook doesn't matter, as long as they are assignments that you can use with confidence. Depending on whether the textbook is a rhetoric, rhetorically arranged reader, thematic reader, or handbook, you'll find a wide variety of assignments that reflect different philosophies of teaching, learning, and writing. Just a glance at the textbooks shelved in your composition office will reveal a range of writing assignments: basic rhetorical methods of development; arguments; personal essays; Web site construction; literacy studies, including narratives and autobiographies; institutional and political critiques; traditional rhetorical exercises, including imitation; and research projects, including collaborative research and ethnographies. Some assignments, for instance, encourage writing to learn; others present writing as a way to communicate something the writer has already learned.

The assignments in textbooks have been developed by experienced teachers; Often, they've been tested by a number of teachers across the nation who have helped refine and improve them. Therefore, if the pedagogical theories supported by the textbook you're using are close to your own, chances are the book's assignments will work well for you, too. As you create assignments for your classes, carefully consider what you want students to learn and what kinds of writing you want to read — and then choose, refine, or design writing assignments that will help you achieve these goals. If you're using a textbook as a starting place, remember that you can adjust the topics and specifications to suit your purposes and your class. (See the sample assignments at the end of this chapter.) The following discussion offers guidelines and examples on the assumption that you will provide specifications for your own writing assignments.

Assignment Sequences

Sequenced writing assignments have been used in composition classes for decades. Most teachers are familiar with sequences based on the work of nineteenth-century Scottish logician Alexander Bain. The Bain sequence divides writing into four "modes of discourse": narration, description, exposition, and argumentation (118–21). The first two modes, which are the most concrete, can serve as the bases for initial course assignments; they allow students to draw on their own experiences and observations for subject matter, seldom forcing any higher-level generalizations or deductions. The second two modes, which are the most abstract, are reserved for later assignments, when students will presumably be better able to manipulate nonpersonal ideas and concepts in an expository or a persuasive fashion.

The supposition of this sequence of assignments is that students gain confidence in their writing by first using the more concrete and personal modes of narration and description and are then better able to use the abstract modes. Unfortunately, skill with narration and description does not automatically carry over to exposition and argumentation; students who are confident and even entertaining when narrating experiences and describing concrete objects sometimes flounder when asked to generalize, organize, or argue for abstract concepts. Likewise, skill with exposition and argumentation does not necessarily indicate a student's expertise in narration and description. All good writing takes practice, and Bain's modes of discourse, when taught not as mere forms of arrangement but as methods of development to be combined and built upon, can be useful.

Increasingly, however, teachers have chosen sequences of assignments that are not based so much on rhetorical methods of development (or what many have called "modes of discourse") as on the ways in which deliberate sequencing can help students see themselves as writers — and readers. As David Bartholomae and Anthony Petrosky tell us, good assignments "bring forward the image of the reader and writer represented in our students' textual performances ... so that they can reimagine themselves as readers and writers" (*Facts* 8). The authors remind us that for most of our students, every response to an assignment is an act of the student writer "inventing the university," evolving a way of imagining and fitting into the academic community. Experienced students and teachers tend to take the discourse of academia for granted; it is the water in which we swim. But for new college students, this community can often seem threatening or mysterious — the ocean during a storm. It is important that our assignments provide them with a life jacket, a way of using their personal experience and ability to keep them afloat as they gain new information, knowledge, and ability.

Bartholomae and Petrosky's *Facts, Artifacts, and Counterfacts* describes a writing course based on a sequence of assignments that brings together a series of readings and a carefully designed progression of twenty-four responsive and encapsulating writing tasks. Many of the readings focus on personal experience and autobiography, and the assignments ask students gradually to consider and reconsider the writers' methods of autobiography and then to write about the readings and about themselves. It is a sophisticated and widely admired teaching method built around the idea of gradually accumulating genuine authority as a writer by becoming a careful, critical reader.

Bartholomae and Petrosky's *Ways of Reading*, another useful text for a course based on sequenced writing assignments, provides eighteen writing sequences on topics ranging from "The Aims of Education" to "Writing with Style." The linked readings and assignments encourage close and critical reading and help students consider such theoretical concepts as Pratt's "contact zones," Foucault's "panopticon," and Freire's "banking concept" of education; these readings and assignments also help students interrogate and gain experience writing in a variety of forms. If you're interested in learning more about this text you can check out the course companion Web site at bedfordstmartins.com/waysofreading, which includes a link to more information on this text as well as a link to information on Bartholomae and Petrosky's *Ways of Reading Words and Images,* a text with eight main readings and a sequence of five writing assignments that consider textual and visual literacy.

Whether you're using an already established sequence of assignments or creating your own, it is important that each assignment is connected to the others and that your students expand their repertoire. In creating the sequence, you must first consider the skills you wish students to develop and how they can best learn those skills through a series of related tasks. If you want students, for example, to recognize effective uses of research to support an argument, you could:

1. Assign readings that incorporate outside sources effectively.
2. For homework or an in-class writing, ask students to write a one-paragraph *summary* of the argument of one of those readings.
3. Ask students to write a two-page *analysis* of how the writer incorporates the sources to support or complicate the argument.
4. Ask students to write a two-page *assessment* of how effective the sources are in supporting the argument.

After students work through the process of analyzing and assessing another author's argument and use of sources, you can build on this competency by teaching students how to create their own arguments and how to incorporate outside sources into their work. The next step would be to provide sources for students, perhaps giving them a packet of readings on a topic on which you want them to write. In doing so, you can focus your attention on teaching students to create their own arguments and to support those arguments without giving them the added responsibility of finding their own sources (that will come later).

5. Ask students to write an introductory paragraph that includes a clear thesis.
6. Ask them to locate ten to twelve quotations from the packet of readings that support or help complicate their argument.
7. Ask them to write a two-page assessment of which quotations will be most useful and to reflect on how they will incorporate those sources into their paper.

Students will then be ready to begin drafting. Once they have completed their drafts, they can work in peer-response groups to summarize their classmates' arguments, analyze how the outside sources are incorporated, and assess the efficacy of the argument and support. Such an arrangement of assignments creates a logical progression in which the assignments inform each other.

Later in the term, you can ask students to locate their own sources, adding lessons in electronic and library research. In any sequence of assignments, try to connect each assignment both to skills that have been practiced previously and to skills that will follow.

In general, the organization of contemporary textbooks will help you follow a logical sequence. In *Making Sense,* for example, Cheryl Glenn provides assignments organized according to the rhetorical methods of description, narration, exemplification, classification and division, comparison and contrast, process analysis, cause-and-consequence analysis, definition, and argument. (For a sequence of formal assignments based on *Making Sense,* see pp. 107–12). Although the book devotes a chapter to each of these methods, the assignments help students see how various separate rhetorical strategies overlap and interact in complex ways. At the end of each reading, Glenn includes a prompt on combining rhetorical methods, asking students to analyze how professional writers combine them; the writing assignments also encourage such observations and practice. In the following example from *Making Sense,* the prompt helps students consider how William Zinsser combines methods in his essay "College Pressures":

> How does Zinsser use *narration, description,* and *cause-and-consequence analysis* to support his argument? Mark the passages that use each of these methods of development. How does each passage contribute to the overall argument? (300)

To extend this prompt, you could ask students to identify the different rhetorical methods they have used in one of their own arguments. As you encourage students to expand their repertoire, be sure to provide examples of how others use the skills and methods you're trying to teach. Such examples help students better understand the purpose of your assignment sequence and how they can build upon the knowledge they have and extend the skills they have begun to practice.

Assignments Based in Literature

Some first-year writing courses are primarily based on the reading of literature; in this case, you will probably use an anthology containing "apparatus" — that is, questions and assignments following each selection that are created by the editors of the textbook. But, as many teachers have recognized for half a century, teaching a writing course using literature is very different from teaching a literature course. In their 1958 article, John Hart, Robert Slack, and Neal Woodruff Jr. list three conditions that must be met in order to use literary assignments in the writing class: (1) the teacher must resist the temptation to *teach* literature (that is, the *technae* of literary form, biography, and literary judgment); (2) the literary works chosen for use must be the kind students can understand themselves without a great deal of help from the teacher or class discussion; and (3) every writing assignment must be planned so that students examine a significant feature of the work being read and work on a particular kind of compositional problem (237–39).

In the 1970s and 1980s, many composition teachers moved away from using literature in the composition classroom because, as Michael Gamer observes, "it was associated with approaches to teaching that were counterproductive to what we wanted to have happen in a writing classroom" (281). But as Gamer also observes, "Individual texts and disciplines do not determine pedagogy nearly so much as do the choices of particular teachers in particular classrooms" (281). He argues that "the multidisciplinary nature of imaginative texts can help students to make connections between the bewildering array of courses across many disciplines that they have to take while in college" (285). In this section, we offer some productive ways of incorporating literature into the composition classroom while still keeping the focus on students' writing. (For more on the conversation about literature in the composition classroom, see Lindemann, "No Place"; Tate, "A Place"; and the March 1995 Symposium on Literature in the Composition Classroom published in *College English,* which includes articles by Gamer, Lindemann, Peterson, Steinberg, and Tate, cited at the end of this chapter.)

So what is the appropriate way to use literature in the composition classroom? While there are many possible answers to this question — and the assignments in various textbooks offer provisional answers — it is, at the very least, important to remember that most of our FY students are not (and are not going to be) English majors and that the level of literary experience we may assume from our own educational experiences may not be theirs. The important criterion here is that FY students find meaning in what they read before anything else useful can be done, and this can only be accomplished by choosing texts carefully and spending extensive class time discussing them (Glenn, "Reading-Writing Connection" 103). As Edward P. J. Corbett says, the test for literary assignments is this simple question: "Can my students, with their present equipment, fulfill this assignment, . . . develop this topic or thesis, without a lot of specialized knowledge about the techniques of creative literature, simply with the data that . . . can [be] glean[ed] from a careful reading of the text at hand and from [their] experience of living in the world?" (200). This is not to suggest that you can't help students learn new concepts and theories to apply to their reading, but you will need to limit your teaching of new material so that students can focus on applying what they're learning to their writing.

In the course design section of *Scenarios for Teaching Writing: Contexts for Discussion and Reflective Practice,* Chris Anson et al. relate Dan Howells's process of developing a literature-based writing course, one that would *enact* "ideas about textuality and the generation of readers' responses" — not just *present* those ideas (142). While *Scenarios for Teaching Writing* does not offer, in this case, models for assignments on teaching literature-based composition, it does suggest that the groupings of readings will certainly shape the kinds of questions students ask and, likewise, the kinds of assignments teachers can and will give. If you're using a literature anthology, before creating your assignments you need to think carefully about (1) how much material you can cover in order to use literature to teach writing (you'll most likely be reading fewer pieces than you would in a literature class), (2) whether you'll focus on one or several genres, (3) what genres you'll ask students to write about (that is, will they write analyses of poems and write poems?), and (4) how you will structure the readings to emphasize the development of good writing.

Writing literary assignments is both a science and an art. Make sure that when writing out assignments you choose key terms with care. The words you use in an assignment will reveal its important elements. For that reason, you'll want to teach your students to read through the wording of their literary assignments with as much care as they read their writing assignments for other classes. You'll also want to provide them with specific information about whether they should use secondary sources — and if so, how many sources and in what ways (including, for example, the amount of direct citation and quotation) — and how to provide evidence for each claim.

In the rhetorically arranged reader *Subjects/Strategies,* Paul Eschholz and Alfred Rosa offer several assignments based on works of fiction for use in a literature-based writing course. For example, in the following assignment, students are asked to read Julia Alvarez's piece of short fiction, "Snow," examine Alvarez's use of fictional narrative to produce an argument, and point out the other rhetorical strategies used:

> In commenting on how she chose to write "Snow," Alvarez said, "Rather than becoming polemical or railing against nuclear weapons, I thought I might best 'prove' the destructiveness of nuclear weapons if I showed how a simple, poignant, and 'natural' moment becomes in this nuclear age a moment of possible holocaust for a child." How did Alvarez turn a straightforward narrative of an event into a powerful argument? Besides narration, what other rhetorical strategies does she use? (533)

Assignments like this one merge the concerns of literature and writing classrooms in a way that is workable for FY students.

If you will be assigning an essay analyzing a literary work, a sequence of shorter assignments can allow students to prepare for it. Literary analysis is not, as some students seem to think, an unnatural genre distinct from all other writing, and it should build on the expository skills from earlier assignments. A composition course that teaches literary analysis may be structured around the same sources of information that feed nonfiction writing: memory, close reading, and critical research. Students first look within themselves for material and then cast a progressively wider net. Their work culminates in the literary essay, which may incorporate all of these sources of information. A series of assignments — narrative or descriptive essays, then profiles based on interviews (perhaps with one another), and then a critical essay that brings together and discusses several readings — will move students naturally toward an analytical essay. In this sequence, the research essay encourages students to look at the text in the widest sense, often examining topics that have been written about by many people and listening to what diverse voices have to say about it.

This approach may demand that students — and their instructors — alter the way they have viewed literary analysis: it is more than going to the library and reading books and articles or doing sophisticated Web searches. The work that goes into any research essay should stimulate a student's understanding of the wide range of opinions surrounding their research topic as well as the ever-developing writing and planning skills necessary to enrich their developing understanding and opinion about the topic.

Web Assignments

Increasingly, writing teachers comfortable with technology are moving beyond traditional writing assignments and asking their students to work on Web projects. Writing for the Web, of course, is different from writing traditional academic essays. Paragraphs tend to be much shorter, and the visual aspect is nearly as important as the words. If you and your students already have some experience creating Web sites and if you're discussing visual literacy in your class, you may wish to have your students create Web sites. You can work on one Web site as an entire class, have students work in small groups or pairs, or have students create their own individual sites. Whatever formation you choose, the sites should somehow be related to the class. For example, students could create a hypertextual version of an essay they've already written, or they could create a site introducing others to the work and focus of the class. You should make your expectations clear — explaining how students' work will be assessed and evaluated — because the skills and competencies they'll need for Web projects differ somewhat from those associated with more traditional writing assignments.

Here are some general guidelines for assigning Web design projects:

1. Familiarize yourself with the Web-authoring programs to which your students have access. Microsoft Office comes equipped with Front-Page. If you are teaching in a computer-equipped classroom, your school may have purchased other Web-authoring programs such as Macromedia's Dreamweaver. Since most students (and many teachers) will not have knowledge of HTML, a Web-authoring program can make the process easier.

2. Check into whether students will have access to school Web space or if they'll need to go through a commercial server. Many commercial servers provide "free" Web space, but such space does come with a price: pop-up advertisements over which neither the author of the Web site nor the viewer has much control.

3. Look at and evaluate several existing Web sites together as a class before asking students to create their own sites. Discussing what is or is not effective on other sites will help your students get ideas for their own sites. For examples of what not to do, take your students to "Vincent Flanders' Web Pages That Suck" (listed at the end of this chapter). Through viewing and discussing both positive and negative

examples, students will gain a better understanding of content and design issues, including the significance of organizational structure, design consistency, color, images, and navigational ease.

4. Discuss with students the purpose of and audience for the Web sites they'll be creating. Such concerns will help determine the text, images, and design for their sites. If you foreground such issues, students will better know what to include and what to leave out.

5. Provide step-by-step handouts for your students and addresses of helpful Web sites. In order to write step-by-step instructions for your students, you will likely have to create a Web site of your own and track the process you went through. Alternately (or in addition), you can provide students with Web sites that provide clear guidelines, such as *PC World's* article, "Instant Web Sites" (listed at the end of this chapter). This article provides directions as well as links to templates for billboard sites, galleries, and interactive blogs. Also make a list of sites from which students can get free images and graphics, starting with Cool Archive <coolarchive.com> to point students to additional resources. In your list of resources, discuss copyright and intellectual property issues, reminding students both to ask permission for using images and to cite their sources.

6. Give students a series of deadlines for completing different parts of the project. Just as you would have drafts, peer response, and conferences for traditional papers, you can do the same for Web projects.

7. If possible, schedule some office hours in a computer lab or in a space where you and your students have access to a computer, so you can view and work on the Web project in conference sessions. Once students complete their Web sites, provide some time and space for them to showcase their work. If you're not already teaching in a computer-supported classroom, you may wish to schedule a class period in a lab, use a digital projector and laptop in a traditional classroom, or have students email their Web site addresses to the class or post them on a class discussion page or Web site.

Oral Assignments

If you ask students to do presentations or to create texts that are meant to be spoken (a radio essay, for example), you will need to teach the different components of texts meant to be read silently and those meant to be delivered orally. Sentence structures that appear simple — even choppy — on the page are often quite effective when spoken. Repeated phrases that seem redundant on the page become clear — even powerful — when read aloud. Furthermore, the bulleted lists, white space, and bracketed cues that would be odd in formal essays translate well into oral texts.

As you create your assignment, there are several elements of the rhetorical situation you will need to consider:

- What is the purpose of the assignment? (To inform, persuade, entertain?)
- What will the content or topic be? How will this assignment build on earlier assignments? (Will students rewrite an essay they have already written to make it suitable for oral delivery? Will they present on a topic they have already researched but not yet written about?)
- Who is the audience? (Should students see you, their classmates, or someone else as the primary audience?)
- When students present what they have written, what format should they use? (Should they read from the text, speak from notes, or memorize the text?)
- How much time will they have to speak/read? (Do students need to reserve time for questions and comments — or time to pass out handouts?)

In addition to these considerations, students will also need to know whether handouts are expected or optional, and they will need to know how the presentations will be evaluated. Will you evaluate students primarily on the written product (whether the piece is written in such a way that it could be delivered effectively), their oral delivery (clarity of voice, eye contact, gestures), or some mix of both?

Because you may be combining two assignments (an assignment for writing or revising a text for oral delivery, as well as an assignment to make an oral presentation), your written assignment to students might be longer than usual. Example 4.1 provides such an assignment. (For further discussion of oral delivery and its relationship to writing, see Chapter 10.)

Example 4.1   **SAMPLE ASSIGNMENT: REVISING A TEXT AND DELIVERING IT ORALLY**

Having, as a class, attended two creative nonfiction readings and discussed both how the writers created memorable prose and how their delivery enhanced the effective elements already in the text, you will turn to one of your own creative nonfiction essays, revise it for oral delivery, and do a reading of a selection from your piece for the class. The purpose of this assignment is twofold: first, you will gain experience revising a text written originally for silent reading, turning it into a text for oral delivery; second, you will gain practice presenting your work in front of an audience. Your classmates and I will be your audience, so you should choose a selection that illustrates effective elements of the genre: consideration of tone, attention to detail, character development, and so on.

Although you will be reading your text, you should practice enough that you can look up often, making eye contact with your audience. You will read for ten minutes and reserve an additional two minutes for questions from your classmates. Be prepared in the question/answer time to discuss the ways in which you revised your initial essay. When you hand in the revised text, also staple a copy of your original essay to the back.

Assignments That Call for the Use of Visual Components

Any assignment — print text, digital, or oral — can make use of visuals, such as photographs, graphics, drawings, even videos. Visuals can be both a primary vehicle of and an aid to communication. That is, a carefully organized montage of pictures can communicate without words, but for the purpose of this text, we assume that you will be asking students to use visuals to support and further an argument or effect they have already worked to develop in writing.

Like other assignments, those that call for the use of visuals should be sequenced carefully, providing students an opportunity (1) to reflect on their own visual literacy — what they already know and can bring to the assignment — both in writing and in class discussions; (2) to analyze and evaluate various uses of images in texts; and (3) to use visuals effectively in their own texts, incorporating them appropriately and documenting sources properly. (For additional discussion of visual literacy and specific assignments, see Chapter 10. See also, Selfe's "Toward New Media Texts: Taking Up the Challenges of Visual Literacy" included in Part III.)

One popular assignment in composition classes is a literacy narrative, asking students to reflect on their own memories of reading and writing or to tell a story about their own acquisition of new literacy. Visuals can work especially well in a literacy narrative assignment. In "Toward New Media Texts," (pp. 479–504) Cynthia Selfe provides an assignment for a visual essay, one that, in a section for teachers, details goals, time required, a sequence of assignments, and a useful vocabulary (including definitions for "visual impact," "visual coherence," "visual salience," and "visual organization"). For students, her assignment provides objectives, tasks, suggested format, information on documenting images from online sources, and information on creating and documenting images for poster board essays (499–500). Additionally, she provides guides for composer/designer reflection as well as reader/reviewer reflection (501–02). Although Selfe provides a more detailed assignment in her article, Example 4.2 offers a shortened version of Selfe's assignment.

Example 4.2   **VISUAL ESSAY ASSIGNMENT**

"Compose a visual essay that represents and reflects on

1. the range of different literacy practices, values, and understandings you have developed over your lifetime (from birth to now)
2. how you have developed these literacies (where, how, who helped)
3. your feelings about these literacies" (488).

Your essay "should demonstrate a high degree of visual impact" and "overall coherence," and it "should identify 2–4 major points as particularly important (using strategies to make these points prominent and stand out from other elements: size, color, contrast, placement, etc.)" (488).

Defining Good Assignments

What a Good Assignment Is Not.   Before we turn to defining good assignments, we want to spend a little time talking about what a good assignment is *not* — and the reasons why it is not. A good assignment is not one that can be answered with a simple true/false or yes/no answer: "Do the SAT exams have too much power over students' lives?" Such assignments do not offer a writer enough purpose or give enough direction, and students are often at a loss for a place to go after they have formulated their simple answers. A good assignment is not one that leads to unfocused or too-short answers. For example, "How do you feel about the ozone layer?" does not give students enough direction.

A good assignment is also not one that assumes too much student knowledge. "What are the good and bad points of U.S. foreign policy?" or "Is America decaying as the Roman Empire did?" would be far too broad, and even a minimal answer would require students to do a considerable amount of reading and research. Nor is a good assignment one that poses too many questions in its attempt to elicit a specific response:

> In the reality television show *Survivor,* what do producers wish to suggest about society? What do the competitions, the injunction to "Outwit, Outplay, Outlast," and the fact that there can only be one "survivor" at the end suggest about human relationships — and their relationship to nature? What image does the show provide of different cultures? of group dynamics? of moral leadership? What ethical message does the show give its viewers?

This sort of assignment means to help students by supplying them with many possibilities, but it can provoke panic as inexperienced writers scramble to deal with each question separately.

Finally, a good assignment is not one that asks students for too personal an answer: "Has there ever been a time in your life when you felt you just couldn't go on?" or "What was the most exciting thing that ever happened to you?"

Though you might sometimes get compelling writing in response to such visceral topics, some students will be put off and not wish to answer them, while others will revel in the chance to advertise their angst or detail their road trip to Daytona Beach — or worse. Either way, you are likely to get some bad writing, replete with evasions, clichés, or an experience so troublesome that you cannot think of any way to respond to it.

What Is a Good Assignment?   If good assignments are not any of these things, then what are they? In *Teaching Expository Writing*, William Irmscher lists a number of useful criteria (69–71). Foremost, a good assignment has to have a purpose. If you ask students to write a meaningless exercise, that is what you will get. (If, on the other hand, the assignment is meant as exercise or practice, then simply be honest with yourself as well as your students about your pedagogical purpose.) An assignment such as "Describe your dorm room in specific detail" has no purpose but to make students write; the response to such an assignment is meaningless as communication (except, of course, if you simply want them to get practice in noticing and writing about details). If the assignment is extended, though, to "Describe your dorm room, and explain how various details in it reflect your personality and habits," it becomes a rhetorical problem. The answer to the assignment now has a purpose, a reason for saying what it says.

Irmscher tells us that a good assignment is also meaningful within students' experience. *Meaningful* here does not necessarily mean "completely personal," but if students can tap some of their experiences, then they might have a starting place for accessing the world of opinion or fact. Though you can perhaps talk coherently about the recession during the Reagan era or the English-Only movement of the 1990s, many seventeen- and eighteen-year-olds might consider these subjects to be topics for historical research. The subjects that students can be expected to write about well without doing research are those that fall within their own range of experience — the economy as it relates to their own neighborhood or circle of family and friends, or the English-only issue as it relates to their high school experiences. In *Assigning, Responding, Evaluating*, Edward M. White offers several sample assignments, including one that asks students to draw from their own experiences even as they consider the choices they make in writing for different audiences: "Think of the last really good cultural, social, or sports event you attended, and describe it in three different ways: first to your best friend, then to your parents, and then to a group of high school students attending an open house at your college. Finally, describe the variations in content, organization, and wording that writing for different audiences led you to make" (11).

A good assignment, says Irmscher, also asks for writing about specific and immediate situations rather than abstract and theoretical ones. "Discuss the problem of sexism" will not elicit the strong, specific writing that an assignment tied to concrete reality will: "Discuss how you first became aware of sexism and how it has affected the way you deal with men and women." When you pose a hypothetical situation in an assignment, make certain it is one students can conceptualize. "If you had been Abraham Lincoln in 1861..." is the sort of assignment that will only invite wearying and uninformed fantasy, whereas "Write a letter to the board of trustees explaining why it should reconsider its decision to raise tuition by $300 per year" is a hypothetical situation (or perhaps it is not) that students can approach in an informed and realistic manner. A good assignment should suggest a single major question to which the thesis statement of the essay is the answer. "Is smoking tobacco harmful, and should the tobacco laws be changed?" asks for several different, though related, theses. It is better to stay with a single question whose ramifications can then be explored: "Discuss why tobacco should or should not be legal, supporting your argument with details from your own experience or the experiences of people you know."

The written assignment itself should be neither too long nor too short. It should generally be no longer than two or three paragraphs. Too long and too complex an assignment will frustrate and confuse students. Too short an assignment, on the other hand, will fail to give sufficient guidance.

A good assignment, then, must be many things. Ideally, it should help students practice specific stylistic and organizational skills. (If you want your students to format their essays in a particular way, specify the format that you want to read. See "Creating a Syllabus" in Chapter 1.) A good assignment should furnish enough data (from format and page length to rhetorical method and topic limits) to give students an idea of where to start, and it should evoke a response that is the product of discovering more about the interanimation of that data. A good assignment should encourage students to do their best writing and should give the teacher her best chance to help them do just that.

A final word on assignments: do not be reluctant to change or jettison assignments that do not work out. As we mentioned earlier, every writing teacher is always on the lookout for new and better topics, not because the old ones are necessarily bad but because good teachers constantly search for better ways of teaching. You may also find that you get tired of reading students' responses, even good responses, to an old assignment. When you find boredom setting in, it is time to change assignments, as much for your students' sake as for your own.

Creating Assignments and Explaining Them to Students

After you decide on the length, number, and sequence of assignments, you can get down to the business of creating each one. You will want to write down all assignments beforehand and pass out copies of them to your students, rather than writing them on the board or reading them aloud. Providing written assignments allows you to be as specific as you wish to be — to put into words exactly what you want your students to do and learn — and helps prevent misunderstandings by the students.

When you hand out an assignment, take some time to go over the wording and explain how to read writing prompts in general. Students need to know, for all their classes, that words such as *analyze, describe,* and *explain* tell them the strategy, even the rhetorical method of development, to use and often determine the form of their response. Example 4.3, from *Making Sense* by Cheryl Glenn, provides an activity that will help students consider their own understanding of important words in assignments:

Example 4.3 **MAKING SENSE OF COLLEGE-LEVEL WRITING ASSIGNMENTS**

In preparation for making sense of your college-level writing assignments, take a minute to write out what each of the following terms means to you:

inform	describe	entertain	analyze	define
persuade	prove	compare	argue	explore
convince	evaluate	propose	formulate	classify
observe	report	explain		

Working with one or two classmates, compare your answers. Discuss your group's response with the rest of the class. You may be surprised by the range of definitions you and your classmates give these important academic terms. (Glenn 17–18)

Discussing strategy words with students (and providing them the actual definitions for these words) is a good way to begin your larger discussion of the criteria that will be used to evaluate their drafts and essays. In a sense, criteria for the evaluation of essays are the theoretical heart of any course in rhetoric or writing, but you need to boil them all down to specifics for each new assignment. For each type of assignment, a slightly different kind of invention works best and a slightly different group of forms or genres is appropriate, as are different levels of descriptive detail or narration and different methods of logical development. In a new assignment to a class, you need to describe thoroughly what you want to see, from specific thesis statements to levels of support, formal structure, use of personal pronouns, use of dialogue, various conventions, and so forth. Some of these criteria will be spelled out in the wording of the assignment, but some you should present and discuss in class. As you continue teaching, it is a good idea to ask students whose essays are particularly effective whether you can make photocopies of their work for use in subsequent semesters. Such models of successful responses to assignments can help students immensely by letting them see concretely what your necessarily abstract criteria can produce.

REVISION

As the sample syllabi in Chapter 1 suggest, the revision of students' drafts before the essays are submitted for a grade is an important element of college writing courses. Including a revision option is, of course, up to you (unless your department has a policy requiring or forbidding one), but most successful writing teachers are committed supporters of the revision option. Their experience has shown them that the reasons for allowing revision seem to outweigh by far any inconveniences. In many writing classes, in fact, revision isn't just an option: it's structured into the course schedule with first, second, and final drafts due on particular days. Sometimes the teacher reads all the drafts; at other times the teacher reads the first and final drafts, asking students to work on other drafts in their peer-response groups. If your writing course uses portfolios, your students may be writing new essays even as they revise their earlier pieces throughout the term. (For more on the use of portfolios, see Chapter 5, "Evaluating Student Essays"; for more on revision see Flower et al.; Sommers; and Yagelski, cited at the end of this chapter.)

Using the revision option in a composition course can transform the relationship between the teacher and the student: Instead of serving as the judge and jury, the teacher joins the student in improving that student's writing. The teacher is released from the burden of putting a grade on every piece of writing at the same time that the student is released from the pressure of always writing toward a grade. In other words, the revision option provides a less-judgmental relationship between teacher and student. Furthermore, it invites students into the editing process, a process that is difficult to understand if all their written work is graded and then filed away without their having any chance to reexamine or change it. Research into the composing process has revealed that far too many students sit down at the keyboard and write out their essay, submitting it with little or no editing or revision. Far too many students still see writing as a one-shot, make-it-or-break-it event. Because the very idea of revision (let alone large-scale revision) is alien to these students, providing a revision option allows them to approach the task of editing as an authentic "re-seeing" of their writing. All of our students deserve to learn that self-evaluation and self-correction are elements crucial to successful writing.

A revision option can work in several different ways, but all of them involve the same general idea: someone responds to and/or evaluates a student's essay and then returns it to the writer, who then has the option of revising it. Sometimes it's the teacher who collects, reads, and responds to all the essays; at other times it's a member of the writing group who considers the draft. The mechanics of turning in and responding to essays differ from system to system (some teachers grade drafts, others simply provide comments to aid in revision), but all have in common a focus on rewriting.

Revisions are usually the focus of conferences and peer-response group or workshop sessions, but you needn't use either of these systems. Another system using a revision routine might work as follows: students must turn in essay 1 on the day it is due. They will either mark the essay DRAFT, which indicates that the writer wants the essay evaluated but not graded, or they will leave it unmarked, which indicates that the essay is to be evaluated and graded. You evaluate all the essays but grade only those considered final efforts. On the drafts your task is to provide guidance in revising, not merely in editing. You are looking not for a neater or more "correct" copy of an essay but for a re-envisioned essay. Thus your terminal or closing comments will contain far more specific suggestions and criticisms than will those on a graded essay. The terminal comments on a pre-liminary draft must serve as blueprints or suggestions for revision, whereas those on a final essay must, by the nature of the grading process, be more concerned with justifying the grade and giving closure to the assignment.

The next week, you return the students' essays and give those students who had turned in drafts a week to ten days in which to revise their drafts, which must then be turned in for a final grade. If a draft is very good, as occasionally one is, the student may return it unchanged; most students, however, rewrite their essays. When the final versions are handed in, ask that the original draft be clipped to the revision so that the changes will be evident. Also ask that any comments from workshop members be attached as well. On this second sweep through essay 1, you will read the essay, write comments in the margins, note any remaining formal errors (usually with a checkmark), write a short com-ment on the success of the revision and the general quality of the essay, and return it to the writer for the last time.

In the week before the final drafts of essay 1 are due, rough drafts of the next assignment, essay 2, will have come in and perhaps a few early revisions of essay 1 will have arrived as well. By the time you get all the final versions of essay 1, you will be seeing the rough drafts of essay 3. During any given week, therefore, you may be evaluating or grading as many as three assignments. It is not as confusing as it sounds. Here is a diagram:

Week 2

Monday   *Friday*
Drafts of essay 1 due

Week 3

Monday   *Friday*
Drafts of essay 1 returned   Drafts of essay 2 due
Some final drafts of essay 1 turned
in this week

Week 4

Monday   *Friday*
Final drafts of essay 1 due   Drafts of essay 3 due
Drafts of essay 2 returned
Some final drafts of essay 2 turned
in this week

Week 5

Monday   *Friday*
Final drafts of essay 1 returned
Final drafts of essay 2 due
Drafts of essay 3 returned
Some final drafts of essay 3 turned
in this week

Other permutations of the revision system work better for some teachers. For example, you may permit students to submit multiple versions of an essay, especially if the class is working in peer-response groups. Other teachers may allow only one or two revisions during the term. (For an example of a revision-essay assignment, see p. 108 of this chapter.) Still others allow students to submit their revisions during a "revision week" at the end of the term. This option allows students more time in which to revise, but it also results in a great influx of essays — in various states of revision — to be read and graded during that final, hectic week. Teachers who grade all essays as they come in and then regrade those that students choose to revise give students a clear idea of how they are doing in terms of grades. In such a system, however, the grading process is burdensome for the teacher because the terminal comment on a graded essay is expected to justify the letter grade rather than provide suggestions for revision.

The most common objection to the revision option is that it creates more work for the teacher. And in some ways, it does. In a class of twenty-four students that demands six graded essays from each student, the teacher must read and evaluate 144 essays. If revision is allowed, the number of essays to be evaluated naturally increases — whether it's the writing group or the teacher who does the evaluation. But there is not as much extra work for the teacher as there might seem to be at first. The revision option places more of the added responsibility on the student. Reading for evaluation takes less time than the combined effort of reading for evaluation, assigning a grade, and justifying the grade; and the final reading and grading of the revision take less time than reading for evaluation and justifying the grade. Once you get the system down, you should be able to read for evaluation and write a terminal comment in roughly ten minutes. Grading the revised version takes only about seven minutes because you already know the writer's purpose. In neither reading should you give small, formal errors the amount of attention that you would give such errors in a single reading. In the first reading, in fact, you mark no errors at all, although you may mention serious error patterns in your terminal comment. In the second reading, errors get only a checkmark. The act of revision generally means that the final essay will have fewer formal problems.

This paean to the revision option should not obscure the problems the revision option can present. The most obvious one is the students' temptation to use the teacher only as an editor. If you mark all the formal errors on each rough draft, you will lead your students to believe that their revision need be no more than a simple reprinting of the essay with the formal errors corrected.

If you want to mark errors in drafts, do so with a simple checkmark over the error, which the writer must then identify and correct. Encourage students to rely on one another as editors and proofreaders before submitting drafts; if you can develop peer-response groups, your pedagogical life can be better. Don't hesitate to say, "This draft isn't ready for me."

The second problem that revision presents is psychological: Students tend to believe that an essay that has been revised in a formal process will automatically receive a higher grade than one the teacher sees only once — the A-for-effort misconception. If a draft merits a D and the revision raises the grade to a C, the student often has a hard time understanding why, with all the changes he made, the essay is not worth an A or a B. Students may see any essay without serious formal errors as worthy of an A or a B, not realizing that its content is vacuous or its organization incoherent. (See Chapter 5, "Evaluating Student Essays," for a sample rubric for grading.) Such issues make for useful classroom discussion and exploration. After an assignment has been graded, the class can analyze the criteria for evaluation and grading. Some students, used to grade inflation, simply cannot get used to receiving Cs and even lower grades, especially if the work is formally perfect or they received high grades in high school. One way around this expectation is to assign an essay no grade at all until after at least one revision has been submitted or until you can declare the essay "acceptable" (usually the equivalent of a passing grade or a C).

As you evaluate the merits of a revision option, keep in mind that revision of written work is immensely useful to students. No longer is an essay a one-shot deal, submitted in fear or resignation because it must soar or crash on its maiden voyage. The opportunity for revision can foster commitment to the assignment and real intellectual growth. By allowing students to reflect on and improve their writing, a teacher allows them to see writing for what it is: a process of re-seeing a subject, a process that isn't completed until the writer is ready to say, "I can do no more."

SAMPLE ASSIGNMENTS

1. Literacy Narrative (3–4 double-spaced pages, with a title)

   Due: September 16 (10%)

In this class, we will examine your literacy in broad ways, not just in terms of your ability to read and write. This assignment will help you imagine your literacy in terms of how you react to and interpret language in particular ways, and how you produce and use language to achieve certain kinds of goals.

Please write a short narration (3–4 typed pages, double-spaced) recounting a significant literacy event or development in your life. In the broadest sense, this assignment asks you to reflect in some way on the roles that reading, writing, and community have played in your life — to consider, in other words, how you became the literate person you are now and are still in the process of becoming.

By re-creating or retelling a sequence of occurrences that relates to your literacy development, you will be using narration for a specific purpose: to argue a point, create a mood, or provide an example. Whatever your purpose, you need to determine exactly what point you want to make; it should be a general point that you'll bring to life with specific, relevant, and representative examples. You also want to keep a specific audience of readers in mind as you write. Therefore, the key to writing a successful narrative is to *choose:* you need to choose the most important details, characters, and dialogue to make certain that the setting, point of view, and organizational pattern work to your advantage.

2. Process Analysis Essay (3–4 double-spaced pages, with a title)

Due: October 4 (10%)

Like narration, process analysis is chronological — that is, organized according to time — but narration is concerned with a one-time event, whereas process analysis focuses on an event that might be replicable or duplicated. Your 3–4-page process analysis essay should fulfill one of two purposes: supply detailed directions for replication of the process (directional process analysis), or supply information about how a process works or is done (informational process analysis).

Your process analysis should (1) focus on a specific process; (2) fulfill a clear purpose that you clarify in your thesis statement; (3) consider the needs and interests of a specific audience; and (4) be organized step by step, explaining why each step is important. Like the writing you did for your literacy narrative, the process analysis essay also needs clear, pertinent details and examples in each step as well as transitions to help your reader move from one step to the next. Also, your thesis statement should explain what your audience will gain or learn by following your process analysis.

3. Definition Essay (3–4 double-spaced pages, with a title)

Due: October 25 (10%)

The purpose of your definition essay is to inform or argue by (1) classifying the term in a broader category and then (2) differentiating that term from other terms in the same category, stating its distinguishing characteristics. Your one-sentence definition should serve as the basis of your thesis statement. As you focus on your subject for defining, you have to decide if yours will be an extended definition or a historical, negative, or stipulative definition — as well as whether yours will be objective or subjective. Unless otherwise specified, your audience will be first-year writing students in our program. However, if your definition is contingent on another, more specific audience, then specify it. You can develop your definition only by considering who your audience members are, what they already know about your topic, what they need to know, and how they feel about it. So when choosing a topic for definition, think carefully about a specific group of people who would be interested in or benefit from your definition — and then direct your definition to that group.

You should develop your essay, then, by clarifying, redefining, explaining, or arguing for a new or different definition of the term, one for which you've provided detailed support and examples. Your definition, then, should aim to expand your audience's thinking about the term, the nature of the problem, or the current situation *as* a problem. (This essay might serve as a prelude to your final writing assignment, a recommendation for a specific solution to a problem.)

Whatever your topic, audience, and purpose, your essay must include definitions of important terms in the controversy, some history and background information, a thorough explanation of all the different points of view on the issue, and *two outside sources*. Remember that to do a credible job of informing your audience to consider new points of view, you need to supplement and verify your information beyond your personal knowledge and experience (hence, the two required outside sources).

How might you deliver your essay? It could be a letter, a talk that includes the points of view of the audience, or an article for a magazine or newspaper that presents the issue to its readers. Or, you might imagine it as a lengthy memo to a person or group, such as a legislator or a particular group that needs to be informed before it takes a stand on the issue. In any case, it must have exigence — that is, the situation must call for a rhetorical response (in this case, your definition). Whatever form of delivery you choose, avoid writing a descriptive, encyclopedia-like article for general readers.

4. Revision Essay (3–4 double-spaced pages, with a title)

Due: November 6 (15%)

The revision essay asks you to revise — or "re-see" — an assignment you've already submitted. To get started on the revision process, follow the guidelines in "How to Respond in Helpful Ways to a Peer's Draft" [p. 71] and respond to one of your submitted essays, either the definition or the process analysis. Then, using your peer's response, your teacher's response, and your own response, significantly rethink your essay.

In order for a revised essay to receive an improved grade, "cosmetic" revision will not be enough. In other words, don't re-see the merely superficial features of your graded essay and don't stop at fixing up a few things here and there, changing a few words, correcting typos, or attending to sentence-level errors. Concentrate instead on a *significant revision:*

- Refine and focus your thesis statement.
- Expand and develop your supporting assertions using new evidence, examples, and illustrations.
- Include and respond to counterarguments.
- Develop more fully your introduction and conclusion.
- Significantly modify or change your thesis — and thus your argument (you could even argue the opposite of the original), which means that you'll use different lines of reasoning and respond to different counterarguments.
- Write to a different audience (which will require changes in the overall argument as well).
- Rearrange your argument.
- Improve your style and tone, appropriately.

Note: You must turn in the original essay with the revision. And it goes without saying that your revision should take into account the comments (from your teacher and peers) on the original.

5. Causal Analysis Essay (3–4 double-spaced pages, with a title)

Due: November 22 (15%)

Like a process analysis, causal analysis links actions or events along a timeline, but it differs from process analysis in that it tells us why something happens, is happening, or will probably happen. Therefore, a causal analysis can serve one or more of four main purposes: to entertain, inform, speculate, and argue. Whether we're enrolling in a fitness program, appearing in traffic court, diagnosing a child's illness, or assessing an investment, we're analyzing causes, often for a specific audience. Because purpose and audience are nearly inseparable, it's often impossible to decide which to think about first. But if you consider your general subject, then you can begin to determine the exigence for your writing and your purpose. Your audience will be those readers best served by your purpose, so you'll need to consider the values they hold and the information they need.

Your thesis statement should introduce your subject to that audience, suggest the reason you're analyzing it, and state the ideas about the causes or consequences you want your readers to accept. Unless you're absolutely certain, using qualifiers such as *probably* and *most likely* will enhance your credibility with readers. You also need to think critically about different causes or consequences (primary, contributory, immediate, remote, and so on) as well as about whether you want to explain the causes or consequences in chronological or emphatic order, using transitional words or phrases to help your readers follow your line of thinking.

What conclusions can you draw from your analysis? what inferences? what implications? If you answer these three questions, your conclusion will offer you an opportunity to push your own thinking as well as that of your audience—and you'll write a meaningful conclusion, one that goes beyond a weary restatement of your introduction.

6. Recommendation Essay (3–4 double-spaced pages, with a title)

Due: December 13 (20%)

Look around you—at your living quarters, your campus, your town, and the world at large. What specific issue concerns you as a student, male or female? as a citizen? as an environmentalist, an artist, and so on? Why does that problem exist? How might it be solved? What are the negative consequences? Could a specific policy, issue, situation, or problem be changed? (Your recommendation essay might grow out of the topic you examine in your causal analysis essay.)

A recommendation essay points to a specific problem, a set of circumstances that creates a problem, or a set of consequences that flows from that problem. It then proposes and argues for a process, policy, or procedure for solving the problem, using logical reasoning to try to get an audience to accept the recommendation. Whether you're arguing that a certain action should (or should not) be taken or that a situation or policy should be changed, you need to do the following:

1. Identify the problem and the negative effects it has on a specific community.
2. Identify the exigence for writing.
3. Imagine an audience who is also (or should be) invested in this issue — and establish common ground with that audience, using rhetorical appeals.
4. Determine your claim, which will become the basis of your thesis statement.
5. Determine your purpose.
6. Create a solution, and identify the negative and positive consequences of the solution.
7. Order your recommendation either chronologically or emphatically, using transition words.
8. Consider the implications of your recommendation in your conclusion, in terms of its possibility and purposefulness.

WORKS CITED

Anson, Chris M., et al. *Scenarios for Teaching Writing: Contexts for Discussion and Reflective Practice.* Urbana: NCTE, 1993.

Bain, Alexander. *English Composition and Rhetoric.* London: Longmans, 1877.

Bartholomae, David, and Anthony R. Petrosky. *Facts, Artifacts, and Counterfacts.* Portsmouth: Boynton/Cook, 1986.

——. *Ways of Reading.* 7th ed. Boston: Bedford/St. Martin's, 2005.

Bishop, Wendy, and Hans Ostrom, eds. *Genre and Writing: Issues, Arguments, Alternatives.* Portsmouth: Boynton/Cook, 1997.

Corbett, Edward P. J. "A Composition Course Based upon Literature." *Teaching High-School Composition.* Ed. Gary Tate and Edward P. J. Corbett. New York: Oxford UP, 1970. 195–204.

Eschholz, Paul, and Alfred Rosa. *Subjects/Strategies.* 10th ed. Boston: Bedford/St. Martin's, 2005.

Flower, Linda S., et al. "Detection, Diagnosis, and the Strategies of Revision." *CCC* 37 (Feb. 1986): 16–55.

Gamer, Michael. "Fictionalizing the Disciplines: Literature and the Boundaries of Knowledge." *CE* 57 (Mar. 1995): 281–86.

Glenn, Cheryl. *Making Sense: A Real-World Rhetorical Reader*. Boston: Bedford/ St. Martin's, 2005.

———. "The Reading-Writing Connection: What's Process Got to Do with It?" *When Writing Teachers Teach Literature*. Ed. Toby Fulwiler and Art Young. Portsmouth: Boynton/Cook, 1995. 99–118.

Hart, John A., Robert C. Slack, and Neal Woodruff Jr. "Literature in the Composition Course." *CCC* 11 (1958): 236–41.

Irmscher, William F. *Teaching Expository Writing*. New York: Holt, 1979.

Lindemann, Erika. "Freshman Composition: No Place for Literature." *CE* 55 (Mar. 1993): 311–16.

———. "Three Views of English 101." *CE* 57 (Mar. 1995): 287–302.

Lunsford, Andrea. *The St. Martin's Handbook*. 6th ed. Boston: Bedford/St. Martin's, 2008.

Peterson, Jane. "Through the Looking-Glass: A Response." *CE* 57 (Mar. 1995): 310–18.

Sommers, Nancy. "Revision Strategies of Student Writers and Experienced Adult Writers." *CCC* 31 (Dec. 1980): 378–88.

Steinberg, Erwin R. "Imaginative Literature in Composition Classrooms?" *CE* 57 (Mar. 1995): 266–80.

Tate, Gary. "Notes on the Dying of a Conversation." *CE* 57 (Mar. 1995): 303–9.

———. "A Place for Literature in Freshman Composition." *CE* 55 (Mar. 1993): 317–21.

White, Edward M. *Assigning, Responding, Evaluating: A Writing Teacher's Guide*. 3rd ed. Boston: Bedford/St. Martin's, 1999.

Wysocki, Anne Frances, Johndan Johnson-Eilola, Cynthia L. Selfe, Geoffrey Sirc. *Writing New Media: Theory and Applications for Expanding the Teaching of Composition*. Logan: Utah State UP, 2004.

Yagelski, Robert P. "The Role of Classroom Context in the Revision Strategies of Student Writers." *Research in the Teaching of English* 29 (May 1995): 216–38.

Useful Web Sites

Cool Archive
<coolarchive.com>

Instant Web Sites
<pcworld.about.com/magazine/2201p123id113447.htm>.

Vincent Flanders' Web Pages That Suck

5

Evaluating Student Essays

I didn't think grading papers would be a big deal, but when I saw the stack on my desk, I suddenly got intimidated. Reading through the first one, I had no idea how to assign it a grade. But I took a deep breath, reviewed the grading standards, and reread the essay. It was still tough, but I no longer felt hopeless. And I'm guessing that as I do more of it, I'll get even more confident.

–Keith Gibson

In a sense, it is unfortunate that we have to grade student essays at all; far too often a grade halts further work on and thought about a piece of writing. If we could limit our responses to advice for revision and evaluation of progress, we could create a supportive, rather than a competitive or judgmental, atmosphere in our classrooms. However, most colleges and universities require us to grade student essays, so we need to concentrate on specific ways to make our evaluations useful and meaningful. If approached cautiously and thoughtfully, evaluating and marking our students' work can serve as an encouraging record of student progress — but only if we supply students with useful information.

Unless your department favors a holistic grading system, you will be using the more common method of grading: professional evaluation. In preparing to grade and evaluate your first stack of essays, you must consider some questions. First, are you expected to enforce departmental grading standards? If your department or writing program has such standards, you must be prepared to grade accordingly, for in all probability the standards were instituted in a serious attempt to reduce grade inflation and standardize grades within the composition program. (For more information on grading, see Anson; Curzan and Damour; Davis; and Zak and Weaver, cited at the end of this chapter.) Regardless of whether you have to follow departmental guidelines, the question of enforcing standards usually comes down to practical questions you will have to answer for yourself: Will you assume that every essay can be, or must be, revised to meet a higher standard? Will you assume that every essay starts out as a potential A and, with each flaw, discredits itself, gradually becoming a B, a C, and so on? Or will you assume that each essay begins as a C — an average or competent essay — and then rises above or falls below that middle ground? To a great degree, the answers to these questions will depend on the ethos of the program in which you're teaching, your teaching experience, and your own

[margin annotations: "Opt. or district grading systems", "Questions"]

experience as a student receiving grades. (For more information on writing assessments, see White, Lutz, and Kamusikiri, cited at the end of this chapter.)

Teachers who begin the work of evaluation with the assumption that all essays should be A's tend to see only what is wrong with the essays that don't meet that standard. Those teachers who start from the position that most FY essays are average—or C's—are perhaps grudging with their A's. Whichever position you start from, you will have to reach some decision about one other question: Will improvement—presumably the goal of your writing course—be taken into consideration during final grading? What about students who start out writing C-level essays and work up to B-level work—should they be given a B even if their grade average is only a C-plus? This question can be answered in the following two ways, assuming you want to make improvement a consideration. *[margin notes: Begin w/ A's. Begin w/ C's. Improvement.]*

One method of treating improvement is to set up your schedule of written assignments so that later assignments are worth a larger percentage of the grade for the course, thus weighting the final grade in favor of improvement late in the course (the syllabi at the end of Chapter 1 do this). The second method is to use the concept of "degree of difficulty," assigning more cognitively demanding topics as the course progresses, with the most difficult writing assignment earning the highest grade percentage. Thus an essay creditable in the second week would seem simplistic in the eighth week. The first method often works better for newer teachers since the second method, establishing degrees of assignment difficulty, is learned only with experience. *[margin note: Improvement]*

Finally, you'll want to think carefully about how to address your students. The written comments you make on a student's essay will often be the basis of your relationship with that student. It is important that you consider this relationship as you comment and grade and that your responses to students' writing be part of a respectful conversation. We expect students to respect our knowledge of the subject and our good intentions toward them; in return, we must respect their attempts to fulfill our expectations and to move forward in their learning. Pamela Gay, in "Dialogizing Response in the Writing Classroom: Students Answer Back," encourages teachers to provide opportunities for students to respond to comments on their texts. Peter Elbow offers similar advice, encouraging teachers to take five minutes after handing back essays to have students write a note to the teacher in response (359). Such interaction will help you see more clearly how students are interpreting (and sometimes misinterpreting) the comments you make. Since you're likely to encounter a wide range of abilities and motivations as you evaluate your students' essays, you'll need to consider each student's work separately because comparisons are inherently invidious. Allowing students to respond in writing to your comments on their work is one way of reminding yourself that each student is an individual—and that each will respond differently to the kinds of comments you make. *[margin notes: Addressing Students. Students respond to comments. Don't compare.]*

Your students may constitute a diverse group in terms of age, background, ability, culture, and ethnicity. To all of them, however, you represent—though you may not always feel comfortable with it—the academic community; many will see you as a sort of gatekeeper of discourse and opportunity. Although some of them may hesitate to join in the conversation of what they see as your community, you should assume and respect their desire to be a part of it, and you should take responsibility for helping them become a part of it. Remember that, as you write your comments and suggestions, some of your students' backgrounds may be far different from yours and that of the academic community. You will want, therefore, to represent academic conventions to them with a sympathetic, as well as a judicious, eye.

Be sympathetic

STANDARDS AND EVALUATION

Formal Standards

As all experienced writing teachers know, formal errors in standardized English are by far the easiest to mark, recognize, and correct. You mark a spelling error here, a sentence fragment there. There is a natural feeling after having marked formal errors that you have done a solid, creditable job of reading a student's essay, when you may not have responded to content issues at all.

That false sense of having completed a job makes formal evaluation seductive. Because of it, teachers are often tempted to base most of their grade on the formal qualities of the essay and not enough on the content. One can easily see why: Formal evaluation is concrete and quantitative; it demands few complex judgment calls and ignores content evaluation. When teachers fill a student essay with red marks, they may think they've done a thorough reading of it — so why do more? Justifying a D on the basis of three fragments and nine misspelled words is easier than dealing with the complex, sometimes arbitrary world of content: thesis statements, patterns of development, assertions, and support. A piece of writing consists of far more than its grammar and punctuation, however. If we stress nothing but formal grading, we quickly become pedants, obsessed with correctness to the detriment of meaning. We do have a responsibility to evaluate formal errors, for as Mina Shaughnessy says, they are "unintentional and unprofitable intrusions upon the consciousness of the reader" that "demand energy without giving any return" (12). We must mark them, but we should not give them more than their due.

Tempting to let this dominate.

In 2006, to update the research done in 1988 by Connors and Lunsford (see "Frequency of Formal Errors in Current College Writing" in Part III of this book), Andrea A. Lunsford and Karen J. Lunsford surveyed nearly nine hundred student essays and identified the twenty errors most often made by students, who now almost uniformly compose on computers. Here, in order of occurrence, is the new list of the twenty most common error patterns (Lunsford, p. 1):

20 common errors.

1. Wrong word
2. Missing comma after an introductory element
3. Incomplete or missing documentation
4. Vague pronoun reference
5. Spelling (including homonyms)

6. Mechanical error with a quotation
7. Unnecessary comma
8. Unnecessary or missing capitalization
9. Missing word
10. Faulty sentence structure
11. Missing comma with a nonrestrictive element
12. Unnecessary shift in verb tense
13. Missing comma in a compound sentence
14. Unnecessary or missing apostrophe (including *its/it's*)
15. Fused (run-on) sentence
16. Comma splice
17. Lack of pronoun-antecedent agreement
18. Poorly integrated quotation
19. Unnecessary or missing hyphen
20. Sentence fragment

You will need to determine, of course, how much emphasis you want to give to each kind of formal error. Within any group of serious errors, many teachers distinguish between *sentence-level* or *syntactic errors* (sentence fragments, fused sentences, comma splices) and *word-level errors* (spelling, verb forms, agreement). Syntactic errors are considered much more serious than word-level errors because these more global errors often present the reader with a situation in which it is impossible to know what the writer meant. When teachers quantitatively count errors, they nearly always count syntactic errors and word-level errors separately.

Another issue to consider when responding to formal elements in student writing is the extent to which deviations from standardized English may be the result of differences in dialects, languages, and cultures. There are many sources that provide guidance for considering and respecting a variety of language uses; such sources can help you gain a better understanding of important differences among students and their language practices. (See the essays by Ball, Cai, and Valdés and Sanders, in Cooper and Odell's *Evaluating Writing;* and Elbow's chapter "Inviting the Mother Tongue: Beyond 'Mistakes,' 'Bad English,' and 'Wrong Language'" in *Everyone Can Write,* cited at the end of this chapter.)

Once again, looking at an essay in terms of its formal and mechanical problems is an important part of your task but only a small part of it. Read your students' writing with an eye to discerning their error patterns. By seeing patterns rather than individual mistakes, students can work on breaking those patterns one at a time, concentrating on a series of single goals in a way that does not overwhelm them. *Patterns of error.*

Standards of Content

Unlike formal correctness, in which conventions are generally agreed upon (a comma splice is, after all, a comma splice), content is a much more abstract business. And despite the fact that content is every bit as important as form, writing teachers are less confident about their ability to judge ideas and organization and therefore may be tempted to give these aspects of composition less than their due when grading.

In response to content, teachers must make serious judgments that inform the evaluation or the final grade of an essay. Usually grades for content are assigned on the basis of the success of the essay in four specific areas, which Paul Diederich calls *ideas, organization, wording,* and *flavor* (55–57).

Connors and Lunsford's "Teachers' Rhetorical Comments on Student Papers" shows that more teachers comment on *ideas* than on any other single area. More than 56 percent of the essays they examined contained teachers' comments on ideas and their support (208). In general, comments on ideas are based on the following questions:

1. How well does the essay respond to the assignment?
2. How novel, original, or well presented is the thesis of the essay?
3. Are the arguments or main points of the essay well supported by explanatory or exemplary material?
4. Is the thesis carried to its logical conclusion?

Connors and Lunsford's study reveals that, after comments on supporting evidence and examples, teachers are most likely to comment on an essay's *organization.* Comments on organization are based on questions such as the following:

1. Does the essay have a coherent plan?
2. Is the plan followed out completely and logically?
3. Is the plan balanced, and does it serve the purpose of the essay?
4. Are the paragraphs within the essay well developed?

Issues of *wording* can impinge on the formal standards of a work; but with respect to content, comments on wording are more concerned with word choice than with grammatical correctness. Addressed are such questions as the following:

1. Does the essay use words precisely?
2. Does the essay use words in any delightful or original fashion?

Finally, there is the level of *flavor,* the term Diederich uses for what others might call *style.* More than 33 percent of the essays analyzed by Connors and Lunsford contained comments on issues of flavor or style in response to the following questions:

1. Is the writing pleasing to the reader?
2. Does the writer come across as someone the reader might like and trust?
3. Does the writer sound intelligent and knowledgeable?
4. Are the sentence structures effective?

Although these guidelines can help you grade content, it is ultimately you who must decide whether an essay says something significant, has a strong central idea, adheres to standards of logic in development, and supports its contentions with facts. All teachers know the uncomfortable sense of final responsibility that goes with the territory of teaching, so don't hesitate to share your problems, solutions, and evaluation questions with your colleagues.

Evaluating Formal Standards and Standards of Content When Responding to ESL Student Writing

In many ways, responding to and evaluating ESL student writing isn't any different from providing feedback to students for whom English is their first language. That is, you should always first make positive comments, acknowledging what a student has done well — complimenting good ideas, logical organization, or effective details and examples.

Once you have found elements that work well, you can consider those content elements that still need work. For example, you can comment on the clarity of one idea and ask the student to bring that same clarity to another, showing the student how to build upon successes.

Although content should be your primary focus, when responding to ESL student writing, sentence-level issues often seem more pressing because it can be difficult to get to the ideas when idioms, sentence structure, verb forms and tenses, prepositions, articles, and punctuation press against the conventions of standardized English. If the number of formal errors seems overwhelming, look for patterns of error instead of marking each one. You will likely find that you can categorize the areas on which the student still needs to work. For example, you might find six instances of confusing word order, twelve sentences in which the subject and verb do not agree, eighteen missing or misused articles, and eleven places where the student has used the wrong form of a word. Instead of ranking these errors numerically, however, your next step is to consider which errors most interfere with understanding. Some errors — such as using the wrong part of speech or an incorrect preposition — will often confuse readers, preventing them from understanding the writer's point; other errors, though, such as a missing article, will simply irritate or amuse readers without preventing communication. You will want to give more attention to the errors that interfere with the writer's message.

You can then make a list of the most serious errors and sit down with the student after class or during a scheduled conference to go over the areas that require the most attention in revision (or if you're dealing with a final draft, you can provide a list of goals for the student to work toward for the next assignment). When you talk with the student about the errors, point first to the places where the student does something well. If there are six places where the student has used a preposition correctly, draw attention to those areas and then ask the student which preposition would work in the places where you recognize preposition errors. A handbook provides another helpful resource for ESL students, who often know the rules of grammar and punctuation even better than native speakers. If the handbook you are using includes a verb tense chart or a section on parts of speech, you can talk through those sections in reference to the student's paper. At other times, though, no rule exists for what you want the student to know, and you simply have to act as an informant, perhaps explaining an idiom or acknowledging an exception to a rule the student has put into practice.

Marking patterns of error rather than every mistake (regardless of its level of seriousness) will give both you and the student perspective on the writing. Instead of seeing an essay with forty-seven errors, you and the student can see a well-organized essay that includes appropriate details and examples — and also needs work in three or four specific areas. As you evaluate and grade the essay, that perspective will be important, and as the student considers the assignments to come, she will have specific areas on which to focus.

GENERAL ROUTINES FOR EVALUATION

I don't copyedit.

Multiple Readings

If you are not using the multidraft evaluation process discussed in Chapter 4 (pp. 104–07), you might consider another efficient procedure for handling essays, one suggested many years ago by Richard Larson (152–55). First, read over the essay quickly, making no marks but trying to get a sense of the organization and the general nature of the work. Try to decide during this initial reading what you like about the essay and what elements need work. Next, reread the essay more slowly, marking it for errors and writing marginal comments. You may read it paragraph by paragraph this time, thinking less about overall organization. Finally, reread the essay quickly, this time taking into consideration its overall purpose, its good and bad features, the number of formal errors, and your marginal notes and comments. After this reading, write your terminal comment and grade the essay.

Next, make a note of the essay in your student file. Compare its successes and failures with those of the student's past essays, and note any improvement or decline. You might at this point add to your terminal comment a sentence or two concerning the essay's success compared with previous efforts. Finally, you can put the essay in your out basket and take up another one. This general routine seems time-consuming at first, but with experience, you should be able to evaluate a two-or three-page essay in about ten minutes.

Elbow "liking"

Evaluation Sheet.

There are other evaluation procedures, of course. Some teachers use evaluation sheets detailing areas of content, organization, and style. The teacher fills out a sheet for each essay and clips it to the essay instead of making comments directly on the student's work. The evaluation sheets can be formatted so that each student submits the same sheet for all assignments, providing an easy way for both student and teacher to track progress, particularly with regard to trouble spots. Some teachers have experimented successfully with making audio recordings of their comments and returning each student's essay along with a cassette or CD containing the comments (this method, however,

Audio

assumes that students have access to technology that will enable them to listen to the comments.) Both checklists and recordings are useful but require more setup than does the Larson procedure, and in most ways, they are simply permutations of it.

Electronic.

Other teachers respond electronically, using the track changes feature of Microsoft Word or providing a secure Web site (such as the ones offered by Bedford/St. Martin's *Comment*) to which students can upload their papers. Whether you have students email their papers to you or upload them to Blackboard, *Comment,* or some other secure site, you will need to teach students the technology they are expected to use. If you have students send their papers by email, be sure your virus protection software is up-to-date.

The final task, of course, is to return students' essays. You should return student work as quickly as possible — no doubt you can remember the anxiety of waiting for your own teachers to get essays back to you. If you are commenting electronically, you can return papers quickly by email or have students log on to the site you're using. Although responding electronically can allow you to return papers as quickly as you're able to read and respond to them, it also invites quick responses — sometimes reactions from students. Be prepared for email responses and questions or ask students to wait a day or two before responding. Likewise, if you're returning papers in class, some students may rush to your desk, asking to speak with you immediately about their grades. You may want to ask them to look carefully at their essays and your comments and to set up a meeting during your office hours if they have questions and concerns. Time and reflection helps diffuse immediate emotional reactions to a grade and allows a student to prepare for a more productive meeting with you.

MARGINAL COMMENTS *I don't do this.*

A good number of the marks you make on students' essays will be marginal comments about specific words, sentences, and paragraphs. Making marginal comments allows you to be specific in your praise or questioning — you can call attention to strengths or weaknesses where they occur. Marginal comments may deal with substantive matters, arrangement, tone, support, and style. (For detailed discussions of both marginal and terminal comments, see Cooper and Odell; Elbow; S. Smith; and Straub and Lunsford, cited at the end of this chapter.)

In writing marginal comments, you want to balance advice and criticism with praise. Try to avoid the temptation to comment only on form or to point out only errors. You can use conventional editing symbols (if you explain to students what they mean), but do not let them be your only marginal effort. Nor should you use a mere question mark if you do not understand a section; *No abbreviations!* instead, spell out your question. If reasoning is faulty, do not merely write "logic" or "coh?"; let the student know what is wrong, and try to provide some direction for revision. Teacher shorthand can be very confusing to students, leaving them perplexed, as the following humorous example illustrates. In his poem "Amphibians Have Feelings Too," Gerald Locklin recounts the story of a teacher who "kept scrawling / FRAG in the margin" of a student's papers until

> The last day of the semesters rolled around
> and after everyone else had left
> this student came up to the desk and said,
> 'Mr. Odin, there's just one thing I'd like to ask you.'
> 'Sure. What is it?'
> 'Why have you been writing FROG on my paper all semester?' (107)

FROG!

To limit such confusions, it is more useful to write comments as if you are having a conversation with the text. Elbow reminds teachers to make "comments on students' writing sound like they come from a human reader rather than from an impersonal machine or a magisterial, all-knowing God source" (359). For example, according to Elbow, instead of writing "awk" in the margin, you might write, "I stumbled here" (359), thereby helping your students see that their writing has an effect on real readers.

Converse with the text

What other sorts of marginal comments are effective? Remember that praise is always welcome. If students write something impressive or make stylistic choices that seem effective or appealing, do not hesitate to tell them. A simple "Good!" or "Yes!" next to the sentence can mean a great deal to a struggling writer, as you may recall from your own papers annotated with red ink. In addition, a simple question such as "Evidence?" or "Does this follow?" or "Proof of this?" or "How did you make this move?" or "Seems obvious. Is it true?" can lead students to question their assertions more effectively than will a page of rhetorical injunctions.

Mary Beaven mentions three sorts of marginal comments that she has found particularly helpful:

1. Asking for more information on a point that the student has made.
2. Mirroring, reflecting, or rephrasing the student's ideas, perceptions, or feelings in a nonjudgmental way.
3. Sharing personal information about times when you, the teacher, have felt or thought similarly. (139)

All of these sorts of comments are text-specific; they thus make students feel as if the teacher is genuinely interested in what they have written. Note also that the kinds of marginal comments *you* use will likely be the kinds of marginal comments students themselves use in their peer-response groups, so try to model the use of helpful comments.

Marginal comments are nearly always short — single sentences or phrases. As Nancy Sommers points out, marginal comments tend to "freeze" students in the current draft, whereas terminal comments often invite a new draft (151). It is best, therefore, to limit your marginal comments when evaluating first drafts. If you write a response to every feature of an essay (from punctuation and usage to logic and style), you will put in a tremendous amount of work, and your students are likely to be put off. For many good reasons, students tend to believe that the more a teacher comments on their work (even when the commentary is in the form of praise), the worse the work is. So consider three or four marginal comments per page an upper limit, at least for substantive comments. Anne Curzan and Lisa Damour remind teachers that

KEY

the key to writing good comments on students' work is striking the balance between too little and too much. Bear in mind how frustrated you have been over the years when you have put time into an assignment only to get it back with a check mark [sic] on the first page. As importantly, remember that students can absorb only so much constructive criticism in one shot. Focus your comments on one or two major problems and perhaps one minor one (e.g., a grammatical problem)[,] and accept the fact that you cannot cover all the bases in your response to one assignment. (142)

Purely formal marginal or interlinear comments on errors are another area entirely. You must decide for yourself on a system for noting such errors, and you must explain that system to students. (See the section on "Formal Standards" earlier in this chapter.) Much will depend on your philosophy.

Two teachers are likely to see the same page of student writing in two completely different ways: One might mark a fragment, a comma splice, and three misspellings, whereas the other might mark those errors plus four misuses of the comma, three awkward phrasings, a misplaced modifier, and five questionable word choices. A great deal depends on the stage of the composing process the student is concentrating on. ESL and BW teachers, for instance, tend to concentrate on global errors that obstruct meaning before pointing out errors that violate conventions of standardized English. (For more on the variation among teacher responses, see Anson, pp. 35–42; and Straub and Lunsford, cited at the end of this chapter.)

ME

Members of the minimalist school of marking errors leave minor faults alone unless they are the only errors in an essay. In "Minimal Marking," Richard Haswell explains this method: "All surface mistakes in a student's paper are left totally unmarked within the text. These are unquestionable errors in spelling, punctuation, capitalization, and grammar.... Each of these mistakes is indicated only with a check in the margin by the line in which it occurs" (601). Haswell's method may seem radical, but the sight of an essay whose margins are completely filled with criticism can make any writer despair.

Certainly after the term has run for a few weeks and students have become aware of their individual error patterns, you may find that simply placing a checkmark over an error is effective. This system asks students to discover for themselves the cause of and solution for their errors and saves you from having to continue as editor. Because checkmarks are also considerably faster to apply, you can devote more time to an attentive rhetorical reading of the essay and thus to providing substantive comments.

TERMINAL COMMENTS

Terminal, or general, comments are probably the most important message you give students about their essays, even more important than the grades you assign. (We are calling all general comments *terminal* comments because Connors and Lunsford's research indicates that 84 percent of all teachers place their longer comments at the end of a student paper rather than at the beginning.) Students turn first to their grades and then to your comments, which they interpret as a justification of the grade. Therefore, terminal comments must do a great deal in a short space: they must document the strengths and weaknesses of an essay, let the student know whether she responded well to your assignment, help create a psychological environment in which the student is willing to revise or write again, encourage and discourage specific writing behaviors, and set specific goals that you think the student can meet.

The type of terminal comment you make will depend on your purpose — on whether, for example, you are justifying an irrevocable grade or making suggestions for revision. The task of justifying a grade often forces a teacher to focus the terminal comment in a closed way on the successes and problems of the essay. It is a kind of autopsy report on a moribund essay, one that will not see further development. Advice on revision, however, can focus on the future and build on an analysis of error patterns and the student's ongoing writing experience. Both sorts of terminal comments share certain components, though, and more than anything else the difference between them is a matter of the percentages of these components that each contains.

Extensive research by Connors and Lunsford indicates that the most common kind of terminal comment that composition teachers make on a student essay — 42 percent of all terminal comments — opens with praise for some aspect of the essay and then makes suggestions for other areas of the essay that need work (207). In addition, terminal comments most commonly begin with larger-scale issues — content, organization, general effectiveness — and then discuss the smaller-scale issues of form and mechanics; thus, teachers often move from global to local concerns. More than 75 percent of terminal comments deal with the large-scale rhetorical issues in student essays (207). The average length of terminal comments, according to the sample studied, is about thirty-one words, but the most effective comments are somewhat longer (211).

After analyzing the most effective comments, Connors and Lunsford derived several characteristics of a good terminal comment. First, every terminal comment should focus on general qualities, presenting the teacher's impression of the essay as a whole. Second, a good terminal comment devotes a large part of its content to an evaluation of the essay's thesis and how well the thesis is supported, answering the question, "How well does the thesis respond to the assignment?" If a thesis is thought of as a promise of what the essay will include, the terminal comment should evaluate how well the essay keeps this promise. The evaluation must take in content, organization, and style, concentrating all of this information in a short space.

In addition, Connors and Lunsford write that the teacher should maintain a serious yet interested tone — not risking humor at the writer's expense unless the essay has earned an A. The teacher's comment should include praise for the effective elements of the essay as well as mention of the elements that need work. It should point out improvements made since previous efforts and encourage revision. Except perhaps to mention one or two of the most important error patterns, the teacher need not spend time pointing out formal errors or summarizing material covered in the marginal comments. In general, a terminal comment need not ever contain more than 150 words and seldom more than 100.

Meeting these goals is not as difficult as you might think. After an entire afternoon of grading, you will have gained a sense of your class as a continuum of writing abilities. Even when fatigue sets in and your critical apparatus gets creaky, you will see how each essay compares with the ones that came before and with those of the rest of the class this time. But if you are still uncertain about your ability to write good comments or want to look at examples of comments that good teachers make, your colleagues are a natural resource. Inquire about teachers in the department who are highly respected, and ask them whether they would be willing to check your annotations and show you theirs. Colleagues constantly help one another with revisions of their own scholarly writing, so it is natural to seek help in the same way when you want to improve your writing of terminal comments. Also consider the most worthwhile and helpful comments you have received on your own essays.

Researchers in the field of composition studies agree that teachers would do well to avoid two extremes: harsh or disrespectful comments that usurp student control over the text, and minimal or generic comments that seem disengaged from the text and offer little real response or help. As Elbow observes, "Most students benefit when they feel that writing is a transaction with human beings rather than an 'exercise in getting something right or wrong'" (359). Somewhere between the two extremes of taking over a student's writing and being disengaged from it is where we try to be: reading carefully and offering genuine commentary from the continuum of generic knowledge that we do, after all, possess. Both aggressive willingness to take over and direct students' work and coy withdrawal from sharing our valuable evaluative opinions serve students badly. As Richard Straub puts it, "The best responding styles will create us on the page in ways that fit in with our classroom purposes, allow us to take advantage of our strengths as teachers, and enable us to interact as productively as we can with our students. Ultimately, they will allow us to make comments that are ways of teaching" (248). Your terminal comments should show students that you have read their work carefully, that you care about helping them improve their writing, and that you know enough about the subject to be able to help them effectively. As in all features of teaching, your terminal comments will be useful to students only if they demonstrate humanity and competence.

THE GRADE

The comments you make in the margins and at the end of an essay are the truly important responses that the student gets from you about his writing, but the grade remains the first thing the student looks for. Although professional grading can be difficult, it can be made easier for you and for all new teachers if you can organize or attend a departmental grading seminar. Such a seminar will bring together new and experienced teachers to discuss and practice grading. This group need not meet more than once or twice and need not be large, but in one afternoon, the experienced teachers can share many of their techniques and standards with the new teachers — and everyone can learn from one another.

The grading seminar works best when the participants bring copies of several unmarked essays, enough so that every teacher present receives a copy. Each teacher should mark and grade her copy of the essay separately and contribute to the discussion following the marking session. Out of this discussion of the problems and strengths of each essay will come a stronger sense of context and unity for both new and experienced teachers.

Though they can be difficult to organize, such seminars are extremely useful in giving new teachers a sense of how to grade essays. They also introduce teachers to the philosophy and practice of holistic grading, which involves a group evaluation by trained "raters."

If you have to proceed alone, however, make certain that your grading system corresponds to that used by your school, lest you find out at the end of the term that you must adapt your system to some other one. Before you grade your first essay, find out whether your school uses a four-point system or a five-point system and whether you can give plus/minus grades. If your department, your program, or even those with whom you share an office have devised standards of grading that you agree to follow, you can avoid many anxieties about grading.

As you grade, be on the alert for the B fallacy: the temptation to overuse the B. This grade does, after all, seem like a nice compromise: an essay is not A quality, but a C is so…average. To many teachers, new and experienced alike, a C seems like a condemnation. Why not a B? If you think you are assigning too many B's and are vaguely dissatisfied with and confused by this practice, try to get back on track by asking yourself what elements in the essay deserve that grade. What, in short, makes this essay better than average? Is it word choice? organization? expression of ideas? If you can honestly point to a specific area in which the essay is better than most others you've seen, it may deserve the B. If you can find no specific area in which the essay excels, you can be fairly certain it is indeed average.

METHODS AND CRITERIA FOR GRADING

Course-Based Grading Criteria

Many teachers using the professional evaluation method have found that a system of course-based (or individual class-based) grading criteria works to involve their students in the evaluation process. Course-based evaluation does not put all grading responsibility into students' hands, of course, but by involving all the members of your class in important decisions — about what they want to learn and have you evaluate — you make grading seem less arbitrary and individual.

To work with your students to develop course-based evaluation, you should plan one or two sessions on grading criteria early in the term. Let students know that these sessions are important and that the weightings and criteria that result from them will be in use for the rest of the course. Begin the sessions by asking each student to list on paper the writing skills and issues that seem most important for the class to cover and emphasize. Then assemble students into groups of three, and ask them to compare lists and be prepared to present the group's choices of important issues to the class. After the groups have met for ten minutes or so, ask each group to elect a person to place its list on the board. This will produce seven or eight such lists ranging from "understand assignments" and "use the Web for research" to "correct comma use" and "document sources properly." There will be a tremendous amount of overlap, of course, so you will need to point out and erase repetitive categories. You will still be left with as many as thirty possible issues or criteria. Number them on the board.

Next, ask each student to vote for a weighting on the criteria that are listed — from five points for most heavily weighted criteria to one point for least important criteria. From this initial tally, which you can write on the board, the larger number of issues can be whittled down to a smaller number, usually from five to ten. At this point the class needs to discuss the weighting of these criteria: which are to be more important and which less, the standards to be used in judging, and the ways in which you will apply these standards. Usually the outcome of these discussions will be a sheet of criteria that you draw up on the basis of the class determination. Everyone in the class receives a copy of these criteria, and you use the weighted criterion issues in both your evaluations and final grading. Here is an example of an evaluation-criteria sheet produced by one of our FY classes:

Evaluation Criteria — English 101, Section 22

1. Final essays will have a clear central idea that is supported by examples.
2. Paragraphs and sentences will have good transitions linking them so as to allow smooth reading.
3. Introductions will catch the reader's attention in some interesting way.
4. Sentences will have different lengths and types.
5. All sentences will have proper grammatical construction.
6. Research materials will be properly quoted and cited.
7. Essays will be neat and readable.
8. Essays will show several different types of writing, including narration, explanation, comparison/contrast, and analysis.

Although the criteria your class comes up with may not align exactly with either the criteria you might apply or with the weighting you would give, you will find that students usually have a remarkably accurate idea of what sorts of standards might be usefully applied to their writing. Moreover, the discussion of what is central and what is less important to their writing makes them participants in the process rather than mere pawns of other powers. Most students appreciate the opportunity to be involved in the process, though some might prefer that the teacher establish the grading criteria.

Rubrics

One way of establishing grading criteria is to create your own rubric, one that makes your expectations explicit and allows students to set goals for themselves. Because people often disagree about what constitutes good writing, it's important to clarify your expectations — for yourself and for your students. When used as guidelines, rubrics can be helpful in communicating with students and in ensuring that your evaluation process is as fair and consistent as possible. The disadvantages of some rubrics, however, are that they can become too systematic and replace individual comments, especially when you assign numerical values to the constitutive parts of each essay and use the rubric only in the context of grading. Rubrics that assign numerical values to each part of an essay (clear and graceful transitions = 7 points, functional transitions = 5 points) cause students to think more about what they "got points 'off' for" rather than how they can become better writers overall.

Rubrics can take many shapes and be used in a variety of ways. Sometimes, they take the form of a checklist, detailing what you expect from a particular assignment. Other times, teachers structure them according to grades: what an A essay looks like, what a B essay looks like, and so on. Another structure for rubrics is a prioritized list: You put the most important components of the essay higher on the list (thesis, support, organization, and so on), creating a kind of hierarchy of concerns on which to focus. The shape of the rubric you use (if you use one) will likely depend on your purpose: Will you use it as a way of defining your expectations for the kind of writing students will do? as a way of structuring your course? as peer-response guidelines? as a self-checklist for students before essays are due? as a guide for responding to students' essays? as a scoring device?

Example 5.1, from the Penn State University composition department, shows a rubric that establishes criteria for evaluation and describes how such criteria translate into particular grades. Examples of other rubrics are available from the University Writing Program at Virginia Polytechnic Institute Web site, listed at the end of this chapter. The Web site also offers paragraph descriptions of what a teacher might expect from essays earning particular grades and a writing assessment checklist, including a list of criteria in the form of questions ("Do the introduction and conclusion focus clearly on the main point?" for example), boxes to check (excellent, fair, poor), a space for comments, and an area to record strengths of the work and suggestions for change.

While the paragraph descriptions work well in helping teachers discuss expectations for a successful essay and as a reminder of grading criteria for completed essays, the writing assessment checklist works well when attached to a draft or as a point of discussion in conferences, providing guidance for revision. In any case, rubrics — though helpful in making expectations explicit — should not replace marginal and terminal comments on students' essays. If you do use a rubric, remember to emphasize to students that the process of writing and response is complex. Strong writing is more than its constituent parts, and there are aspects of both the writing and reading process for which rubrics cannot account. Likewise, responding well to a student's writing requires more than placing checkmarks and circles on a rubric.

Example 5.1   PENN STATE UNIVERSITY'S ENGLISH 15 GRADING STANDARDS

These grading standards establish four major criteria for evaluation at each grade level: purpose, reasoning and content, organization, and expression. Obviously, every essay will not fit neatly into one grade category; some essays may, for instance, have some characteristics of B and some of C. The final grade the essay receives depends on the weight the instructor gives each criterion and whether the essay was received on time.

The A Essay

1. The A essay fulfills the assignment — and does so in a fresh and mature manner, using purposeful language that leads to knowledge making. The essay effectively meets the needs of the rhetorical situation in terms of establishing the writer's stance, attention to audience, purpose for writing, and sensitivity to context. Furthermore, the writer demonstrates expertise in employing the artistic appeals of ethos, logos, and pathos appropriately.

2. The topic itself is clearly defined, focused, and supported. The essay has a clear thesis that is supported with specific (and appropriate) evidence, examples, and details. Any outside sources of information are used carefully and cited appropriately. The valid reasoning within the essay demonstrates good judgment and an awareness of the topic's complexities.

3. The organization — chronological, spatial, or emphatic — is appropriate for the purpose and subject of the essay. The introduction establishes a context, purpose, and audience for writing and contains a focused

thesis statement. The following paragraphs are controlled by (explicit or implicit) topic sentences; they are well developed; and they progress logically from what precedes them. (If appropriate, headings and subheadings are used.) The conclusion moves beyond a mere restatement of the introduction, offering implications for or the significance of the topic.

4. The prose is clear, readable, and sometimes memorable. It contains few surface errors, none of which seriously undermines the overall effectiveness of the paper for educated readers. It demonstrates fluency in stylistic flourishes (subordination, variation of sentence and paragraph lengths, interesting vocabulary).

The B Essay

1. The assignment has been followed and fulfilled. The essay establishes the writer's stance and demonstrates a clear sense of audience, purpose, and context.

2. The topic is fairly well defined, focused, and supported. The thesis statement is adequate (but could be sharpened), especially for the quality of supporting evidence the writer has used. The reasoning and support are thorough and more than adequate. The writer demonstrates a thoughtful awareness of complexity and other points of view.

3. The B essay has an effective introduction and conclusion. The order of information is logical, and the reader can follow it because of well-chosen transitions and (explicit or implicit) topic sentences. Paragraph divisions are logical, and the paragraphs use enough specific detail to satisfy the reader.

4. The prose expression is clear and readable. Sentence structure is appropriate for educated readers, including the appropriate use of subordination, emphasis, varied sentences, and modifiers. Few sentence-level errors (comma splices, fragments, or fused sentences) appear. Vocabulary is precise and appropriate; punctuation, usage, and spelling conform to the conventions of standardized English discussed in class.

The C Essay

1. The assignment has been followed, and the essay demonstrates a measure of response to the rhetorical situation, insofar as the essay demonstrates some sense of audience and purpose.
2. The topic is defined only generally; the thesis statement is also general. The supporting evidence, gathered honestly and used responsibly, is, nevertheless, often obvious and easily accessible. The writer demonstrates little awareness of the topic's complexity or other points of view; therefore, the C essay usually exhibits minor imperfections or inconsistencies in development, organization, and reasoning.
3. The organization is fairly clear. The reader could outline the presentation, despite the occasional lack of topic sentences. Paragraphs have adequate development and are divided appropriately. Transitions may be mechanical, but they foster coherence.
4. The expression is competent. Sentence structure is relatively simple, relying on simple and compound sentences. The essay is generally free of sentence-level errors; word choice is correct though limited. The essay contains errors in spelling, usage, and punctuation that reveal a lack of familiarity with the conventions of standardized English discussed in class.

The D Essay

1. The D essay attempts to follow the assignment, but demonstrates little awareness of the rhetorical situation in terms of the writer's stance, audience, purpose, and context. For example, the essay might over- or underestimate (or ignore) the audience's prior knowledge, assumptions, or beliefs. The writer may have little sense of purpose.
2. The essay may not have any thesis statement, or, at best, a flawed one. Obvious evidence may be missing, and irrelevant evidence may be present. Whatever the status of the evidence, it is inadequately interpreted and rests on an insufficient understanding of the rhetorical situation. Or it may rely too heavily on evidence from published sources without adding original analysis.

3. Organization is simply deficient: Introductions or conclusions are not clearly marked or functional; paragraphs are neither coherently developed nor arranged; topic sentences are consistently missing, murky, or inappropriate; transitions are missing or flawed.

4. The D essay may have numerous and consistent errors in spelling, usage, and punctuation that reveal unfamiliarity with the conventions of standardized English discussed in class (or a lack of careful proofreading).

The F Essay

1. The F essay is inappropriate in terms of the purpose of the assignment and the rhetorical situation. If the essay relates vaguely to the assignment, it has no clear purpose or direction.

2. The essay falls seriously short of the minimum length requirements; therefore, it is insufficiently developed and does not go beyond the obvious.

3. The F essay is plagued by more than one of the organizational deficiencies of a D essay.

4. Numerous and consistent errors of spelling, usage, and punctuation hinder communication.

5. It may be plagiarized: Either it is someone else's essay, or this essay has used sources improperly and/or without documentation.

Contract Grading

Contract grading is a related but different system, and it may be best left in the hands of experienced FY writing teachers. It involves working out a specific individual contract with each student about how much work he or she will do, what kinds of work will be done, and what standards will be applied. Students' grades are based on the degree to which their work meets the criteria of the contract, and they can each contract for different grades. One student might contract, for instance, for an A if he completed seven 5-page essays of at least two drafts per essay, twenty journal entries of at least a page each, and class-work contributions each day. A B-range grade would be for less achievement, and so on. Some students choose to contract for B's or even for C's.

In an appendix to *Everyone Can Write*, Peter Elbow includes examples of contracts that he uses in writing courses. He begins with a letter to his FY students, one that explains the contract-grading system, offers sample contracts for a B and an A, and then spells out his goals as a teacher in the "Final Thoughts" section. Example 5.2 shows his contract for a B. You'll want to consult Elbow's text for the full versions of his sample contracts. While the details of your contract might differ from the specifics of Elbow's, reflecting your own values and expectations, his contract provides a starting place — an example of what teachers might expect in terms of student behavior in class and in terms of their approach to assignments.

Finally, although contract grading can be a useful technique, in order for teachers to use it successfully, some experience with standard grading techniques is necessary. While for now, at least, it would probably be wise to wait before using contract grading, when and if you are ready to do so, be sure to talk with other teachers who have used this method successfully and ask for examples of their contracts. (For more information on contract grading, see Elbow; see also John A. Smith's "Contracting English Composition," which describes a system of contract grading in an introductory college composition course; both are cited at the end of this chapter.)

Example 5.2   **PETER ELBOW'S EXAMPLE OF A CONTRACT FOR A GRADE OF B**

You are guaranteed a B for the final grade if you meet the following conditions:

1. Don't miss more than one week's worth of classes.

2. Don't be habitually late. (If you are late or miss a class, you are responsible for finding out any assignments that were made.)

3. Don't have more than one late major assignment and one late smaller assignment.

4. Keep up your journal assignments.

5. Work cooperatively in groups. Be willing to share some of your writing, listen supportively to the writing of others and, when they want it, give full and thoughtful responses.

6. Major assignments need to meet the following conditions:

   - Include a process letter, all previous notes and drafts. And all feedback you have received.

   - *Revisions.* When the assignment is to revise, make it more than just a correcting or fixing. Your revision needs to reshape or extend or complicate or substantially clarify your ideas — or relate your ideas to new things. Revisions don't have to be better but they must be different — not just touched up but changed in some genuine way.

- *Mechanics, copy-editing.* When the assignment is for a *final draft,* it must be well copy-edited — that is, free from virtually all mistakes in spelling and grammar. It's fine to get help in copy-editing. I don't ask for careful copy-editing on early and midprocess drafts, but it's crucial for final drafts.

- *Effort.* Your papers need to show solid effort. This doesn't mean that you have to suffer; it's fine to have fun and even fool around with assignments. It just means that I need to see solid work.

- *Perplexity.* For every paper, you need to find some genuine question or perplexity. That is, don't just tell four obvious reasons why dishonesty is bad or why democracy is good. Root your paper in a felt *question* about honesty or democracy — a problem or an itch that itches *you.* (By the way, this is a crucial skill to learn for success in college: how to *find* a question that interests you — even in a boring assignment.)

- *Thinking.* Having found a perplexity, then use your paper to do some *figuring out.* Make some intellectual gears turn. Thus your paper needs to *move* or *go somewhere* — needs to have a line of thinking.

- Please don't panic because of these last three conditions. I recognize that if you emphasize effort, perplexity, and thinking, you will have a harder time making your papers intellectually tidy and structurally well organized. It's okay if your essays have some loose ends, some signs of struggle — especially in early drafts. But this lack of unity or neatness needs to be a sign of *effort,* not lack of effort.

Your final grade will fall rapidly below a B if you don't meet these conditions. (417–18)

Portfolio Grading

The last twenty years have seen a great deal of interest in moving from the evaluation of individual student essays to a larger consideration of the student's overall writing ability. In practical terms, this means considering a portfolio of the student's writing. The term *portfolio* comes from Latin words meaning "to carry" and "sheets, or leaves, of paper," and until recently the word was usually associated with the large, flat cases in which artists carry samples of their work. Writing teachers have begun to use the term in a similar way, to indicate a folder, case, or notebook in which the whole range of writing a student does during a term is stored. (Yancey and Weiser's edited collection, *Situating Portfolios: Four Perspectives,* cited at the end of this chapter, is a particularly helpful guide to theories and models of portfolio assessment; see also Belanoff and Dickson; Black et al.; Calfree and Perfumo; Murphy; and Yancey.)

Much of the conversation surrounding portfolio evaluation has to do with using the process in whole writing programs, either to determine a student's placement in the program or to determine exit standards from basic writing courses. (For information on portfolio assessment in whole programs, see Belanoff and Elbow; Hamp-Lyons and Condon; and Roemer, Schultz, and Durst, cited at the end of this chapter.) Your program may indeed use some version of portfolio assessment, in which case you will be trained in the appropriate methods. In this section, however, we discuss how individual teachers can use portfolios to work with students and evaluate their work.

Why should you consider using portfolios? Many teachers use them because they had been dissatisfied with the system of evaluating individual essays. Grading essays separately provides snapshots of what students are doing on particular topics in a given week, but the aggregate may not be a coherent picture of the students' progress or abilities. Assigning a grade each week moves the course along in a linear way, but the teacher often has difficulty envisioning progress because he remembers each assignment largely in the form of a letter in a grade book. Teachers are left with thin data to go on when summing up their students' abilities at the end of the term.

Portfolios, on the other hand, provide a physical record of where students begin, how they progress during the term, and where their writing abilities seem to be heading as the course ends. Rather than showing a series of letter-grade snapshots, a portfolio demonstrates the kind of progress a student has made, the ways in which the student used successive drafts to work through the writing process, the student's strengths and weaknesses in choosing topics and working on different types of assignments, and the themes in the student's work. The portfolio serves students and teachers as a continual source of material for conversation, documenting where things have been and where they are going in their editorial relationship. For teachers, portfolios encourage what Bonnie Sunstein and Joseph Potts call "reflexive theorizing" about their teaching and expectations in a writing course (9).

And, finally, the portfolio gives students exactly what it has always given artists: a place to store, and from which to show, their best work. Some teachers require students to keep in their portfolio everything they write for the class, including in-class writings, journals, notes, prewriting, draft and final essays, and other exercises and assignments. Others, though, allow students more freedom in selecting and ordering their material, asking students to choose their strongest pieces and to order them in a way that best represents their growth and strength as a writer. Whether you ask your students to keep everything or to pick and choose, portfolios usually contain examples of several different kinds of writing, and they often contain different drafts of each assignment.

Usually, students are asked to write either a cover letter describing each assignment in the portfolio or an opening reflective essay in which they introduce the work they've chosen to include. In their descriptions or reflective introduction, they discuss the rhetorical techniques and moves they made in each essay, the strengths and weaknesses, and how each piece relates to the readings in the course. They also have the opportunity to consider the progress they've made and what specific elements they want to continue working on in their writing.

Reflective cover letters benefit both students and teachers. Through this process of putting the portfolio together and reflecting on their writing, students often come to better understand how various components of the course fit together. Students also have the opportunity to explain their revision choices and contextualize their work, providing teachers more information with which to determine a final grade. If students effectively use their cover letters to explain their rationale for revision and if they can clearly articulate both their strengths and weaknesses, teachers can more efficiently see the progress students have made.

Example 5.3 provides a portfolio assignment that gives students guidance on assembling the portfolio.

Example 5.3   PORTFOLIO ASSIGNMENT

The final portfolio, as you know, will count for a large percentage of your grade in our class. As a result, you will probably want to work on your portfolio from now to the end of term. Here are some issues you should consider:

What to Include

You must include the final, revised draft of your research-based argument (along with earlier drafts) and at least four other assignments, also with drafts; but you may also decide to include all of the work you have done for our course as part of your portfolio. That means that you might wish to submit some thoughtful and well-written listserv postings, substantive responses you have made to a group member's work, or your study notes as well as drafts and final revisions of all your assignments.

How to Prepare the Cover Letter

A very important part of this assignment concerns the cover letter you write to us. The job of the cover letter, which is crucial to your success, is to

- introduce your portfolio;
- describe the contents of your portfolio, using specific details and explaining the rationale for your choices;
- comment on specific, concrete strengths and weaknesses in your writing, particularly noting areas of improvement you can identify from first draft to revision;
- evaluate the overall effectiveness of the portfolio and suggest the grade you believe it has earned;
- reflect on what you have learned about writing, and about improving writing, during this term's work; and
- discuss your future plans for developing your writing abilities.

It probably goes without saying by now that we will be looking carefully at the kind of claims, warrants, reasons, backing, and qualifiers you use; at how well you deploy ethical, emotional, and logical proofs; and at the stylistic qualities of your prose. Polish, polish, polish!

How to Format the Portfolio

The choice here is yours, but be sure to save time for thinking carefully about format: how do you intend to display your work? Will you present a Webfolio? What kind of cover or binder will you prepare? What will you put in your table of contents? Do you want to add an "acknowledgments" page? How will you use color, graphics, and so on? In short, think about the concrete object here — and how you want it to represent you.

What We'll Be Responding To

When we sit down to read, study, and evaluate your portfolios — a process we really look forward to and enjoy — we will be looking very carefully at several key elements:

- Imaginative presentation of the portfolio. Here we want to see how you decide to put the portfolio together, literally how it looks as a material or electronic object, what its parts are, how it is presented as a "final" product.
- Quality and effectiveness of the cover letter. Here we want to see your mind at work, detailing your choices, explaining them, making a compelling

rationale for those choices — and then analyzing the pieces in the portfolio, showing in what ways your writing has changed, progressed, and so forth. Finally, we will be looking for evidence here that you have read and understood the textbooks in the course, that you know some things about the rhetorical canons of invention, arrangement, style, and so on that you can put to good use in your analysis.

- Quality of the revisions you have done on pieces in your portfolio. Of special importance, of course, will be the final revision of your research-based argument. In this final draft, we will be looking for

  1. a clearly articulated claim supported by strong evidence and good reasons;
  2. effective appeals to audience;
  3. a clear structure, with logical connections among parts;
  4. sophisticated interweaving of sources throughout your essay;
  5. use of vivid and memorable language;
  6. effective sentence variety;
  7. effective use of visuals, images, and so on;
  8. a powerful opening and closing; and
  9. flawless editing.

Handout created by Andrea Lunsford

There are several ways in which you can use portfolios in your course, and you should check with your WPA for advice on which ones are appropriate for your program. The least elaborate writing portfolio is a simple folder for storing assignments. As each assignment is graded and completed, the student adds it to the portfolio, along with notes, drafts, and workshop comments. The teacher continues to keep a grade book — but at the end of the term calls for each student's portfolio. The portfolio, then, is evidence the teacher can examine for information about the student's development during the semester, perhaps using it to determine part of the final grade.

Even such a simple use of portfolios has advantages, especially if the course involves student-teacher conferences. The portfolio is brought to every conference and provides the basis for a discussion of the student's progress. Such longitudinal conferences are greatly enhanced by the inclusion of a table of contents that shows exactly what the folder contains. Notes, drafts, and final versions are marked with number-letter designations, keyed to the table of contents, and placed in the portfolio in sequential order. See Example 5.4 for the opening of a typical table of contents.

Example 5.4   **SAMPLE PORTFOLIO TABLE OF CONTENTS**

This folder contains important material. If found, please return to

Owner   _____

Address _____

Phone   _____

Email   _____

Assignment 1

Topic:

    1a. First draft; length and date:

    1b. Workshop evaluations; names of readers and date(s):

    1c. Conference(s); notes and date(s):

    1d. Final draft; length and date:

Final grade:

Student's comment on grade and teacher's evaluation:

A more comprehensive portfolio plays a central role in determining the final grade, though it does not completely leave the evaluation of essays until the end of the course. In this system, students keep a portfolio like the one described previously, but instead of assigning each essay a final grade within a few weeks of its submission, the teacher reads work submitted during the semester for acceptability. Acceptability, which may correspond to a grade of C or lower, merely indicates that a draft is finished enough to be left for a time while the student goes on to new work. The drafts and notes go into the portfolio, and the student drafts the next essay. The table of contents for this sort of portfolio uses slightly different notations (see Example 5.5). At the end of the semester, the teacher asks students to choose a specified number of accepted drafts for final revision and grading. These are placed in a separate portfolio, which is due at the end of the term; each essay within it is graded separately.

Example 5.5   **PORTFOLIO TABLE OF CONTENTS**

Assignment 1

Topic:

     1a. First draft; length and date:

     1b. Workshop evaluations; names of readers and dates:

     1c. Conference(s); notes and date(s):

     1d. Second draft; length and date:

     1e. Third draft; length and date (if needed):

Date of Acceptability:

Student's comment on accepted draft:

Revision intention:

In addition to acting as a physical storage system, the portfolio acts as a mental "cold storage" system. As all writers know, revising work too soon after drafting it is not easy; writers have a hard time getting emotional distance from something just created. So by storing "acceptable" essays in a portfolio, students are assured of having basically workable drafts and the time and distance that make final revisions fruitful.

The final system using portfolios is probably the most rarely used, at least by individual teachers. In it, the portfolio itself, rather than individual essays, is the focus of the course. In this system, no essay is ever graded individually. Students continue to work on assignments or topics until they wish to move on to the next one, and they may be asked to write evaluations of their essays or reflections on how their work is developing.

The teacher may or may not use this system in conjunction with some version of the acceptability system. At the end of the semester, the teacher looks through the entire portfolio, usually in conference with the student, and grades it as a whole, taking into consideration effort, progress, the work of peers, and the quality of each piece of writing. This is a significant departure from the standard methods involved in student evaluation, and you should make certain your program allows it before you institute this most thorough of portfolio systems.

Most teachers who use portfolios assign a large percentage of the final grade to the portfolio, often as much as 50–70 percent. You may wish to assign grades to some assignments early in the term so that students are aware of your grading style and criteria. Some students believe that if they revise multiple times, they are guaranteed an A on their portfolio at the end of the term. Even if you're not assigning grades on individual essays or assignments, be prepared to let students know how they're doing in the course at any point during the term. One of the advantages of using portfolios is that you don't have to grade every assignment. You can comment on students' work, expecting that they will revise before the end of the term. If a student's work, however, is particularly weak — and especially if a student is in danger of failing the course — you need to let that student know his or her standing in the class and how it might be improved. Some teachers institute a policy of telling students if their work is below average. Even some of your strong writers, though, are likely to feel anxious if they're not receiving grades regularly. To calm grade anxiety, tell students that even though you're not formally grading each assignment, you are willing to talk with them during conferences or office hours about where they stand in the course. You may wish to assign tentative grades at specific times in the term or give students a written midterm evaluation that includes a tentative grade.

THE END OF THE TERM

Final Grades

That final grade next to a student's name represents your ultimate judgment on that student, usually the only judgment carried away from your class. It is both a difficult task and a relief, a closure, to mark down that letter. You have, of course, since before the first day been preparing a system that would allow you to judge each student's performance. In front of you are the following factors:

1. Grades for each written essay
2. Weight of each assignment (by percentage)
3. Test grades, if any
4. Amount of class participation
5. Faithfulness of homework and journal, if required
6. Amount of perceived improvement in writing ability

Of these six factors, the first three are easily amenable to a mathematical solution, and many teachers have devised ways to quantify the last three as well. To arrive at a mathematical "raw score" for a student is a bit time-consuming but not difficult. If each essay and test is weighted alike, you need only convert the letter grade to its numerical equivalent, add the numbers, divide by the number of assignments, and then convert the result back to a letter grade. Consider the example of student X, whose grades are B−, C, B+, D, C+, C+, B−, and C−. The following example assumes a four-point system:

Conversion Chart

A	4.0	B+	3.3	C+	2.3	D+	1.3
A−	3.7	B	3.0	C	2.0	D	1.0
		B−	2.7	C−	1.7	F	0.0

The student's grades thus convert to:

$$2.7 + 2.0 + 3.3 + 1.0 + 2.3 + 2.3 + 2.7 + 1.7 = 18.0$$

The next step is to divide the sum by the number of assignments:

$$18 \div 8 = 2.25$$

The result can be converted back into a grade or left in the form of a grade-point average. If you convert to a grade, you must establish your own cutoff points. In this case, a 2.25 GPA is closer to a C+ than to a C. The grade becomes more difficult to decide when the GPA is 2.5 or 2.85. In such cases, you must apply other criteria in deciding whether to lower the grade or raise it.

If your assignments are not all weighted the same, working out the raw score is a more complex process. Let's assume, for instance, that you are considering nine grades, which are weighted as follows (percentages refer to the percentage of the raw score):

Assignment 1	5%
Assignment 2	10
Assignment 3	15
Assignment 4	5
Assignment 5	10
Assignment 6	10
Assignment 7	15
Assignment 8	10
Assignment 9	20
Total	100%

The following table can help you figure the weighting of each assignment:

	5%	10%	15%	20%	25%	30%	40%
A	5.00	10.00	15.00	20.00	25.00	30.00	40.00
A−	4.75	9.50	14.25	19.00	23.75	28.50	38.00
B+	4.50	9.00	13.50	18.00	22.50	27.00	36.00
B	4.25	8.50	12.75	17.00	21.25	25.50	34.00
B−	4.10	8.20	12.30	16.40	20.50	24.60	32.80
C+	3.90	7.80	11.70	15.60	19.50	23.40	31.20
C	3.75	7.50	11.25	15.00	18.75	22.50	30.00
C−	3.60	7.20	10.80	14.40	18.00	21.60	28.80
D+	3.40	6.80	10.20	13.60	17.00	20.40	27.20
D	3.25	6.50	9.75	13.00	16.25	19.50	26.00
D−	3.10	6.20	9.30	12.40	15.50	18.60	24.80
F	2.50	5.00	7.50	10.00	12.50	15.00	20.00

Using the table is not difficult. Simply find the value of each grade indicated at the left according to the percentage value indicated at the top of each column, and add up the values for all assignments. The score for assignments that are all A's would be 100; that are all F's, 50. If you wish to convert the final numerical score to a grade, you can use this chart:

A = 96–100	C = 75–77
A– = 92–95	C– = 72–74
B+ = 88–91	D+ = 68–71
B = 85–87	D = 65–67
B– = 82–84	D– = 62–64
C+ = 78–81	F = 50–61

To give an example of this system in action, let us evaluate student Y's nine grades. They are, respectively, C+, D+, B–, A–, C–, C–, B, C+, and C–. Given the weighting of the grades previously mentioned, student Y's grades would be as follows:

Assignment 1 (5%) C+ = 3.90	Assignment 6 (10%) C– = 7.20
Assignment 2 (10%) D+ = 6.80	Assignment 7 (15%) B = 12.75
Assignment 3 (15%) B– = 12.30	Assignment 8 (10%) C+ = 7.80
Assignment 4 (5%) A– = 4.75	Assignment 9 (20%) C– = <u>14.40</u>
Assignment 5 (10%) C– = 7.20	**Total Score:** 77.10

The score of 77.1 equals either a C or a C+ on the grade scale. Once again, you will have to establish your own cutoff points. To simplify, you might move scores of half a point and greater to the next higher number and scores of less than half a point to the next lower number. Thus a rating of 77.1 would mean a raw score of C.

A spreadsheet can also help you calculate grades. To create a grading spreadsheet, start by entering the column headings in the columns of row one. You will need columns for the student name, two columns for each assignment (one for the raw score and one for the weighted score), and a column for the final grade.

	A	B	C	D	E	F	G	H	I
1	Last Name	First Name	Assign. 1	5%	Assign. 2	10%	Assign. 3	85%	Final Grade

Next enter formulas to calculate each weighted score, a formula that will multiply the raw score by the decimal equivalent of the percentage. For example, in cell D2 enter the formula = C2*.05. This formula will multiply the raw score you enter into column C by the weight of the assignment, 5% or .05.

	A	B	C	D	E	F	G	H	I
1	Last Name	First Name	Assign. 1 Raw Score	5%	Assign. 2 Raw Score	10%	Assign. 3 Raw Score	85%	Final Grade
2	Inu	Art		= C2*.05		= E2*.1		= G2*.85	

In the final grade column, enter a formula that adds all of the weighted scores. For this example, enter = D2 + F2 + H2. To check the accuracy of your formulas, enter test data for which you know the answer. For example, if you are planning on using a 4-point scale, enter a 4.0 in each raw score. If the final grade comes up to 4.0, you'll know that you have entered the formulas correctly.

Things get more complicated for those wishing to record raw scores as a letter grade rather than a numeric value. For those interested, the VLOOKUP function in Microsoft Excel is the best way to convert letter grades to a numeric value. Consult the Excel Help function or the Internet for help in using the VLOOKUP function.

Mathematical systems can aid us in figuring a final grade, but they are not all that goes into it. The raw score based on the graded assignments will certainly be the most important element in determining a final grade, but if we haven't already made allowances for them, we must add in our judgments of many subtle qualities that fall under the heading "class participation." Did the student attend classes and conferences faithfully? How serious was the student about making revisions? How hard did the student try? How willing was the student to help others in workshops and peer response? How much time did the student give to journal entries? These and other considerations must eventually go into the process of turning the raw mathematical score into a final grade. And ultimately, as with grades on individual papers, this decision is one that you, the teacher, must make alone.

The question of failing a student is painful, especially if you know the student has been trying hard to pass — it is less difficult to write down the F for a student who has given up coming to class or who has not written many assignments. But that desperate, struggling one is hard to fail.

No one wants to fail such students. If a student is in danger of failing, you may want to recommend dropping the course, seeking outside help, and picking it up again at a later time. Most students in this position will drop a class if they see there is no hope, but sometimes no amount of advice helps; the student cannot or does not drop out, and you are left with no alternative but writing down that damning F.

STUDENT EVALUATIONS OF COURSE AND TEACHER

Teachers have to make final judgments about their students in the form of grades, but students' judgments about the teacher and the course, important as they are, are often optional. Not all departments demand that teachers ask their students to fill out teacher or course-evaluation forms. Even if yours does not, however, you will learn a great deal about your course and your teaching by developing an evaluation form or using a departmental or school form and asking students to complete it. Evaluation forms should be filled out anonymously, either as homework or during one of the last days of classes. You may want to seal them — unread — in an envelope and ask one of your students to keep them until after you have turned in your grades.

If you don't have a departmental form to work from, you may want to use or adapt the following questions:

An Evaluation Form.   (Be sure to space questions to leave room for students' responses.)

1. How would you improve the content of the course?
2. What was the most useful assignment in the course? Explain.
3. What was the least useful assignment? Explain.
4. In what particular way was/were the textbook(s) helpful? for which assignment? What are the weaknesses of the textbook(s)? Do you recommend that it/they be used again?
5. What responses to and comments on your written work seemed helpful and encouraging or useless or discouraging? What specific advice do you have for the instructor?
6. How has the revision policy affected the way you do your writing? Do you have any suggestions that might improve this policy?
7. Do you believe the course requirements are fair? Why, or why not?
8. Did the peer-response sessions help you improve your work? How might the group structure be improved?
9. Did you know what the instructor's objectives for the course were? If so, did the instructor accomplish these objectives?
10. How might the instructor make in-class presentations more effective?
11. How did the grading policy compare to those in other courses in terms of clarity and fairness?
12. How helpful were the conferences? Would more or fewer be better?
13. What general comments do you have?

After you have turned in your grades, you can take some time to read these evaluations. We have found that they are more easily understood and applied if you let a few days or even several weeks go by before reading them. As you do, note in writing any elements that surprised you and any changes you plan to make on the basis of the evaluations. Sometimes you will be transported by your evaluations; sometimes you will be chagrined. But they are always important input for your teaching life, and they are worth your attention.

AFTERWORD

Your evaluations have been read and digested; your grade sheets have been marked, signed, and turned in. Nothing remains but the stack of students' theme folders (or portfolios) and your faithful grade book, filled with red and black hieroglyphics where previously only blank squares existed. Your first writing course is a memory; you are now a seasoned veteran, a resource for the nervous new teachers of next year. You will be able to help them by telling them what helped you and to welcome them to the conversation that is always going on among teachers of writing.

WORKS CITED

Anson, Chris, ed. *Writing and Response*. Urbana: NCTE, 1989.

Beaven, Mary H. "Individualized Goal Setting, Self-Evaluation, and Peer Evaluation." In Cooper and Odell, 135–56.

Belanoff, Pat, and Peter Elbow. "Using Portfolios to Increase Collaboration and Community in a Writing Program." *Journal of Writing Program Administration* 9 (1986): 27–39.

Belanoff, Pat, and Marcia Dickson. *Portfolios: Process and Product*. Portsmouth: Boynton/ Cook, 1991.

Black, Laurel, et al., eds. *New Directions in Portfolio Assessment: Reflective Practice, Critical Theory, and Large-Scale Scoring*. Portsmouth: Boynton/Cook, 1994.

Calfree, Robert, and Pam Perfumo, eds. *Writing Portfolios in the Classroom: Policy and Practice, Promise and Peril*. Hillsdale: Lawrence Erlbaum, 1996.

Connors, Robert J., and Andrea A. Lunsford. "Frequency of Formal Errors in Current College Writing, or Ma and Pa Kettle Do Research." *CCC* 39 (Dec. 1988): 395–409.

———. "Teachers' Rhetorical Comments on Student Papers." *CCC* 44 (1993): 200–23.

Cooper, Charles R., and Lee Odell, eds. *Evaluating Writing: Describing, Measuring, Judging*. Urbana: NCTE, 1977. See, especially, the essays by Ball (225–48), Cai (279–97), Cooper (3–32), and Valdés and Sanders (249–78).

Curzan, Anne, and Lisa Damour. *First Day to Final Grade*. Ann Arbor: U of Michigan P, 2000.

Davis, B. G. *Tools for Teaching*. San Francisco: Jossey-Bass, 1993.

Diederich, Paul B. *Measuring Growth in English*. Urbana: NCTE, 1974.

Elbow, Peter. *Everyone Can Write: Essays toward a Hopeful Theory of Writing and Teaching Writing*. New York: Oxford UP, 2000.

Gay, Pamela. "Dialogizing Response in the Writing Classroom: Students Answer Back." *Journal of Basic Writing* 17.1 (1998): 3–17.

Hamp-Lyons, Liz, and William Condon. "Questioning Assumptions about Portfolio-Based Assessment." *CCC* 44 (1993): 176–90.

Haswell, Richard. "Minimal Marking." *CE* 45 (1983): 600–4.

Larson, Richard. "Training New Teachers of Composition in the Writing of Comments on Themes." *CCC* 17 (1966): 152–55.

Locklin, Gerald. "Amphibians Have Feelings Too." *In Praise of Pedagogy*. Wendy Bishop and David Starkey, eds. Portland: Calendar Island P, 2000.

Lunsford, Andrea A. *The St. Martin's Handbook*, 6th ed. Boston: Bedford/St. Martin's, 2008.

Murphy, Sandra. "Assessing Portfolios." *Evaluating Writing: The Role of Teachers' Knowledge about Text, Learning, and Culture*. Urbana: NCTE, 1999. 114–35.

Roemer, Marjorie, Lucille M. Schultz, and Russel K. Durst. "Portfolios and the Process of Change." *CCC* 42 (1991): 455–69.

Shaughnessy, Mina P. *Errors and Expectations: A Guide for the Teacher of Basic Writing*. New York: Oxford UP, 1977.

Smith, John A. "Contracting English Composition: It Only Sounds Like an Illness." *Teaching English in the Two-Year College* 26.4 (May 1999): 427–30.

Smith, Summer. "The Genre of the End Comment: Conventions in Teacher Responses to Student Writing." *CCC* 48.2 (May 1997): 249–68.

Sommers, Nancy. "Responding to Student Writing." *CCC* 33 (1982): 148–56.

Straub, Richard. "The Concept of Control in Teacher Response: Defining the Varieties of 'Directive' and 'Facilitative' Commentary." *CCC* 47 (1996): 223–51.

Straub, Richard, and Ronald F. Lunsford. *Twelve Readers Reading: Responding to College Student Writing.* Cresskill: Hampton, 1995.

Sunstein, Bonnie S., and Joseph P. Potts. "Teachers' Portfolios: A Cultural Site for Literacy." *Council Chronicle* 3 (1993): 9.

White, Edward M., William D. Lutz, and Sandra Kamusikiri. *Assessment of Writing: Politics, Policies, Practices.* New York: MLA, 1995.

Yancey, Kathleen Blake. *Portfolios in the Writing Classroom.* Urbana: NCTE, 1992.

Yancey, Kathleen Blake, and Irwin Weiser, eds. *Situating Portfolios: Four Perspectives.* Logan: Utah State UP, 1997.

Zak, Frances, and Christopher C. Weaver, eds. *The Theory and Practice of Grading Writing.* Albany: State U of New York P, 1998.

PART

II

Rhetorical Practices

6

Teaching Invention

> *For students who experience difficulty figuring out what to say, flexible invention strategies can help them generate the kinds of ideas that turn into interesting, imaginative, committed essays that others will want to read. Instructors committed to creating a classroom space for students to establish unique voices may view teaching invention as too mechanical of a topic. Nevertheless, introducing and creating opportunities for students to use invention strategies can afford them useful, transferable tools for generating ideas not only in the first-year composition classroom but also as they engage new subjects and new materials in semesters to come.*
>
> –SCOTT WIBLE

Invention, the central, indispensable canon of rhetoric, traditionally means a systematic search for arguments. In composition classes, it has taken on a much broader meaning: a writer's search for all the kinds of material that can shape and determine what can be presented and even known. When writing arguments and analyses, invention strategies help students discover the *thesis,* or the central informing idea of a piece of writing, and all the *supporting material* that illustrates, exemplifies, or proves the validity of the thesis. For personal and lyric essays, narratives, and descriptive writing, invention techniques help writers draw from their memory and observations for the kinds of details that will add depth to their essays (for more on the connection between memory and invention, see Chapter 9; see also Ede, Glenn, and Lunsford, cited at the end of this chapter). No matter what forms and genres you ask your students to write, without content there can be no effective communication, and invention is the process that supplies writers and speakers with content.

Invention is particularly important in college writing courses because it helps students *generate* and *select from* material they will write about (Lauer, *Invention* 3). This process is often difficult, especially for students who have had little practice with it. When faced with a writing assignment, many students are troubled not by the lack of a subject or topic (often one is supplied), but by a seeming lack of anything important or coherent to write about it. Invention comes into play here, providing processes by which students can analyze the assigned or chosen subject in order to discover things to write. Most serious and experienced writers incorporate into their habits some system of invention that they use to plan and carry out their writing. For many this is a subconscious process, and to them, theories of and suggestions for teaching invention as a conscious activity may seem artificial.

Such discomfort with artificial systems is not new. The history of rhetoric is characterized by a continuing disagreement about the usefulness of systems and *topics*. (See Harrington; and Elbow's discussion of "The Neglect and Rediscovery of Invention" in *Everyone,* pp. 141–42, cited at the end of this chapter.) On the one hand are the idealists, rhetorical theorists who believe there can be no meaningful communication unless the speaker or writer is broadly educated; trained in philosophy, morals, ethics, and politics; and possessed of natural intellectual ability. For a person of this order, systems and *topics* might be secondarily useful, for subject matter flows primarily from individual meditations and wisdom, rather than from any artificial system of discovery. On the other hand are the realists, whose greatest spokesperson is Aristotle. The realists are aware that not everyone who needs to communicate possesses the broad educational background necessary to produce subject matter from personal resources; many people need an external system to consult in order to probe their subjects and discover subject matter and arguments. (For more on the rhetorical canon of invention, see Corbett and Connors; Kinneavy; Lauer, "Heuristics and Composition," *Invention in Contemporary Rhetoric,* and "Toward a Methodology"; Young; and Young and Liu, cited at the end of this chapter.)

The systems of invention discussed in this chapter will provide the assistance. Most FY students have had little opportunity to practice serious, extended, coherent writing, and (a no-longer-surprising) few of them have read even two books in the past year. Clearly, many of our students are in need of training in invention; without some introduction to the techniques of discovering subject matter and arguments, they might flounder all term in a morass of vague assertions and unsupported, ill-thought-out essays. They need a system that will buoy them until they can swim by themselves.

BRINGING THE RHETORICAL CANON OF INVENTION INTO THE WRITING CLASSROOM

In their introduction to *Landmark Essays: Rhetorical Invention in Writing,* Richard E. Young and Yameng Liu discuss the study of invention as both theoretically sophisticated and rooted in pedagogical practices. The essays in their collection span forty years and explore various issues related to the process of composing, such as "the nature of invention as an art, the role of rhetorical invention in the creation of knowledge, [and] the possibility for teaching invention" (xiii). Each of these issues is important not only to theoretical debates but also to classroom practices. This chapter sketches some of the debates about invention that have taken place in composition studies over the past forty-five years, but just as importantly it provides exercises and strategies that you can use to teach invention in your own classroom.

Since the early 1960s, the revival of rhetorical theory has reacquainted teachers with the primary elements of the rhetorical tradition — ethos/writer; pathos/audience; logos/text — and with the way these elements of the rhetorical triangle have played out in the canon of rhetoric. Close attention to the writer has resulted in much important work that essentially attempts to answer this twofold question: Where do a writer's ideas come from, and how are they formulated in writing? Such a question demands a new focus on invention, the first canon of rhetoric, and has led in two provocative and profitable directions.

The first direction, represented in the work of Richard Young and Janice Lauer (among others), aims toward deriving heuristic procedures or systematic strategies that will aid students in discovering and generating ideas about which they might write. Such strategies may be as simple as asking students about a subject: *who? what? when? where? why?* and *how?* — the traditional journalistic formula. Or they can be as complex as the matrix presented in Young, Becker, and Pike's *Rhetoric: Discovery and Change*. Essentially, this heuristic asks the student to look at any subject from different perspectives. A student writing about a campus demonstration, for example, might look at it as a "happening" frozen in time and space, as the result of a complex set of causes, as a cause of certain effects, or as one tiny part of a larger economic pattern. Looking at a subject in different ways loosens up the mind and jogs the writer out of a one-dimensional, or tunnel-vision, view of a subject.

We see the interest in procedural heuristics as related theoretically to the work of researchers interested in cognition. Coauthors Linda Flower and John Hayes are best known for their studies of writers' talk-aloud protocols, tape-recorded documents that catch a writer's thoughts about writing while the writing is actually in progress. In "Interpretive Acts," Flower and Hayes discuss a schema of discourse construction comprising social context, discourse conventions, language purposes and goals, and the activated knowledge of both the reader and the writer. The writer and the reader balance these elements to create and re-create a text.

The second direction of invention is characterized most notably by the work of Ken Macrorie and, more pervasively, Peter Elbow. Interested in how writers establish "voice" in writing and realize individual selves in discourse, Elbow's work with students presents dramatic evidence of such activity. In a series of influential books (*Writing without Teachers, Writing with Power, Embracing Contraries,* and *Everyone Can Write*), Elbow focuses on how writers come to know themselves and then share those selves with others. In "What Is Voice in Writing?" he deals with a question related to invention that has perplexed theorists and teachers of rhetoric for thousands of years — "Is ethos real virtue or the appearance of virtue?" — and links this question to the modern debate about the relationship between voice and identity (*Everyone Can Write* 188, 192). Elbow recognizes that voice and its relation to self and text are controversial issues, yet in the midst of controversy he works to make theories of voice and invention practical for teachers of writing.

The researchers and teachers surveyed in this chapter differ from one another in many ways, but they are alike in that their work is aimed primarily at that point of the rhetorical triangle that focuses on the writer's powers of invention. They want to know what makes writers tick and how teachers can help writers tick most effectively.

In this chapter, the term *invention* deals generally with strategies for helping students access materials that will guide and strengthen their writing, no matter what forms and genres they're working with. More specifically, the chapter also deals with invention as it relates to the development and expansion of three different but closely related elements: the *thesis statement,* a declarative sentence that serves as the backbone of an essay; the *subject matter,* which fills out, expands, and amplifies the thesis; and the *argument,* a specialized form of subject matter consisting of persuasive demonstrations of points that the writer wants to prove. Some of the techniques discussed here will work best for one or two of these elements, whereas others work for all three. You will easily see the characteristics of each technique, and you can choose those you wish to adapt according to what you want your students to learn. Before reviewing the invention techniques, however, you should be aware of a few facts about invention as a whole.

HEURISTIC SYSTEMS OF INVENTION

Nearly all the systems of invention covered in this chapter can be called *heuristic,* or questioning, systems. (The Greek word *heurisis* means "finding" and is related to Archimedes' cry of *"Eureka!* I have found it!") In her foundational study of invention, contemporary rhetorical theorist Janice Lauer defines heuristic procedure as

> a conscious and non-rigorous search model which explores a creative problem for seminal elements of a solution. The exploratory function of the procedure includes generative and evaluative powers: the model generously proposes solutions but also efficiently evaluates these solutions so that a decision can be made. Heuristic procedures must be distinguished from trial-and-error methods which are non-systematic and, hence, inefficient, and from rule-governed procedures which are rigorous and exhaustive processes involving a finite number of steps which infallibly produce the right solution. (*Invention* 4)

Although the systems described here differ widely in their approaches, with few exceptions they fit Lauer's definition. (For more recent work on invention, see Atwill and Lauer, cited at the end of this chapter.)

Writing in 1970 in "Heuristics and Composition," Lauer asserted that the then-emerging discipline of composition needed to appropriate theories from other fields if it was to establish a respectable theoretical foundation. She suggested that composition researchers and teachers should consult the extensive bibliography of psychological research on heuristics, which comprises most of her eight-page article. The works she cited included pioneering studies as well as more contemporary research, such as Herbert Simon, Cliff Shaw, and Allen Newell's cognitive investigations that greatly influenced Flower and Hayes's composition research.

Lauer's suggestion sparked a lively exchange with Ann Berthoff, in which the two debated the benefits, drawbacks, and philosophical and political bases of heuristics. In Berthoff's 1971 response, aptly entitled "The Problem of Problem Solving," she condemned heuristics as an indoctrination of mechanical procedures serving a bureaucratic and technological society, and she critiqued the researcher's failure to consider adequately the relationship between language and the world. In her "Response," Lauer argued that problem-solving strategies were not a dictatorial procedure to find "the right solution, the correct answer," using "a finite number of steps governed by explicit rules" (209). She defined heuristics as open-ended, "systematic, yet flexible guides to effective guessing" that seek reasonable answers (209). Lauer's work was foundational in composition studies, and those who responded provided important information for teachers who needed to decide for themselves not just whether to use heuristics but *how* to use them in flexible ways. In her 1979 "Toward a Methodology of Heuristic Procedures," Lauer proposes that the best invention techniques need to be (1) applicable to a wide variety of writing situations so that they will transcend a particular topic and can be internalized by the student; (2) flexible in their direction, allowing a thinker to return to a previous step or skip to an inviting one as the evolving idea suggests; and (3) highly generative, by involving the writer in various operations — such as visualizing, classifying, defining, rearranging, and dividing — that are known to stimulate insights.

In "Piaget, Problem-Solving, and Freshman Composition," Lee Odell asserts the need for, and the limitation of, teaching problem-solving strategies — because writing is "an aspect of a person's general intellectual development and cannot be fostered apart from that development," but "there can be no quick and painless way to develop a well-stocked mind, a disciplined intelligence, and a discriminating taste in language and fluency in its use" (36, 42). Heuristics can help fill the gap between the ideal writer's knowledge of all and everything and that writer's practical inability to use all of those resources. Building on this early work, Odell's recent scholarship on assessment looks at the extent to which a written "text reflects a mind at work, a writer wondering about things, trying to imagine what *might* be" ("Assessing Thinking" 7). Odell's understanding of writing — even of finished texts — is clearly linked to invention; he defines writing as "an act of discovery, an act of constructing meaning" and looks to students' texts for evidence of questioning minds (7).

Using Heuristic Strategies in the Classroom

In judging the heuristic procedures discussed in this chapter, you can run each one through Lauer's questions for testing heuristics (see Example 6.1). The three necessary characteristics of effective heuristic procedures, according to Lauer, are *transcendency, flexible order,* and *generative capacity.*

Example 6.1   **LAUER'S TEST FOR HEURISTIC MODELS**

1. Can writers transfer this model's questions or operations from one subject to another?
2. Does this model offer writers a direction of movement which is flexible and sensitive to the rhetorical situation?
3. Does this model engage writers in diverse kinds of heuristic procedures? ("Toward a Methodology" 269)

Each system described in this chapter is discrete. You can choose one and ignore the others, or you can use several concurrently or at different times. Because invention is a central skill in composition, you will want to introduce at least one system early in the course; otherwise, you may not have a coherent framework on which to hang the other elements of the writing process. Your students can practice some of these methods (for example, prewriting, freewriting, and brainstorming) with you in class. They can use the other methods at home, after you introduce them in classroom exercises. Ideally, your students will gradually assimilate these systems of invention into their subconscious, recalling them when needed.

The goal, then, is to make these artificial systems of discovery so much a part of the way students think about problems that the systems become second nature. Truly efficient writing is almost always done intuitively and then, at the revision stage, checked against models for completeness and correctness. You should not expect the process of subconscious assimilation to complete itself within ten or fifteen weeks. However, when a system of invention is conscientiously taught and practiced for that period of time, it will become a useful tool for students and, eventually, may become part of their thought processes.

CLASSICAL TOPICAL INVENTION

The tradition of classical rhetoric, as it developed from Aristotle and Cicero and then was codified by Quintilian, is the only complete system that we will deal with in this book; it remains one of the most definitive methodologies ever evolved by the Western mind. The rhetoric of the Renaissance was largely informed by it. Even the epistemological rhetoric of the eighteenth century is far less coherent as a system than is classical rhetoric in its finished form. In contrast to classical rhetoric, contemporary rhetoric is in its infancy, with many workable techniques but no fixed structure. Many books have been devoted to analyzing and explaining the structure and usefulness of the classical rhetorical tradition, but for our purposes, only a few techniques drawn from classical theory are useful.

The classical technique that we will concentrate on as an aid to invention is that of the *topics,* or seats of argument. The *topics* can be used to conceptualize and formulate the single-sentence declarative thesis that usually constitutes the backbone of an FY essay as well as to invent subject matter and arguments. Remember, though, that all classical techniques were originally devoted to the creation of persuasive discourse and that classical invention works most naturally in an argumentative mode; it should not be expected to work as well for nonexpository prose.

Aristotle is responsible for our first introduction to the *topics* or "seats of argument," but his doctrine was continued and amplified by the other classical rhetoricians. The *topics* were conceived of as actual mental "places" (the term itself comes from geography) to which the rhetorician could go to find arguments.

The system of *topics* described here is a modern arrangement of classical topical invention adapted from the work of Edward P. J. Corbett and Robert Connors; Richard P. Hughes and P. Albert Duhamel; and other teachers at the University of Chicago (including Bilsky et al.). These *topics* are not so much places to go for ready-made arguments as they are ways of probing one's subject in order to find the means to develop that subject. The four common *topics* that are most useful to students are *definition, analogy, consequence,* and *testimony.*

1. **Definition.**   The *topic* of definition involves the creation of a thesis by taking a fact or an idea and expanding on it by precisely identifying its nature. The subject can be referred to its class, or genus, and the argument made that whatever is true of the genus is true of the species: "A single-payer national health plan is a socialist policy — and should therefore be classed with other socialist policies." A far less powerful and less sophisticated form of definition is "the argument from the word" — the use of dictionary or etymological meanings to define things or ideas.

2. **Analogy.**   The *topic* of analogy is concerned with discovering resemblances or differences between two or more things, proceeding from known to unknown. It should always be kept in mind that no analogy is perfect and that all analogies deal in probabilities. Nonetheless, analogy is a useful tool for investigating comparisons and contrasts: "The first week of college is like the first week of boot camp." Another type of analogical reasoning is the argument from contraries, or negative analogy: "The marijuana laws are unlike Prohibition." Although analogy is often thought of only as a figure of speech, it is an important tool of demonstration as well.

3. **Consequence.**   The *topic* of consequence investigates phenomena in a cause-to-effect or effect-to-cause pattern. The best use of consequence is in the prediction of probabilities from patterns that have previously occurred: "Coal-burning power plants, automobiles, and other human-made sources of carbon dioxide pollution have led to global

warming, which—if not curbed—can have serious negative effects on the environment." The *topic* of consequence is prone to two fallacies. The first is the fallacy of *post hoc, ergo propter hoc,* "after this, therefore because of this." Just because one element precedes another element does not mean that the former is the cause of the latter. An extreme example of this fallacy is, "The Louisiana Purchase led to global warming." The second fallacy, *a priori,* claims but does not demonstrate a cause-effect relationship between two phenomena. To support the first cause-effect relationship claimed above, the writer would need to cite scientific studies that link these sources of carbon dioxide pollution to global warming and to provide evidence that global warming can have negative effects on the environment.

4. ***Testimony.*** The *topic* of testimony relies on appeals to an authority, some external source of argumentation. For example, the authority could be an expert opinion, statistics, or the law. This *topic* is not as useful today as it once was: our controversial age has produced so many authorities whose views are in conflict with one another that all too often they cancel one another out, and celebrities often give paid— and therefore untrustworthy—testimony in the form of advertising. Still, testimony can be a good starting place for an argument, especially when students have a familiarity with, and an understanding of, the source of the testimony.

Using Classical Topical Invention in the Classroom

When using classical topical invention in your classes, you'll need first to teach the use of the *topics* in general and then familiarize students with their use in generating theses, subject matter, and arguments. Classical invention takes just a short time to teach because it is elegantly simple. Students are often impressed when they learn the background of the technique—at last, a high-level classical skill!—and use it with enthusiasm once they have learned to apply the different terms.

Ultimately, a thesis or an argument must say something about the real world. Teaching the *topics* requires using examples, and good examples are to be had by applying each *topic* to a definite subject and coming up with several thesis statements. You may want to pass out examples for students to have in front of them as they begin to create their own theses. You won't find that drawing theses from the *topic* is difficult for you. In the following discussion of cloning, run through the topical-thesis mechanism.

Definition. Definition always answers the question "What is/was it?" in a variety of contexts. The subject can be defined in its immediate context, in a larger context, in different settings, in space, in time, or in a moral continuum. Here are some examples:

- Cloning is a form of asexual reproduction.
- Cloning humans is immoral.
- Cloning cells may one day make it possible to grow healthy organs.

Analogy.   Analogy always asks the question "What is it like or unlike?" and the subject of the analogy usually answers the question by explaining a lesser-known element in the context of a better-known element.

- A clone is like an identical twin.
- Cloning is, according to Josef Ratzinger (Pope Benedict XVI), "Nazi madness."
- Cloning opens Pandora's box.

Consequence.   Consequence always answers the question "What caused/causes/will cause it?" or "What did it cause/is it causing/will it cause?" It is not a *topic* to be taken lightly because, even in a thesis statement, it demands that the writer trace the chains of consequence to the end. Consequence can be either explanatory or predictive.

- If therapeutic cloning is made illegal, it will hinder scientific progress in finding new treatments for diseases.
- Cloning farm animals will help farmers produce higher-quality meat.
- The uproar over questionable cloning practices may cause U.S. lawmakers to ban human stem-cell research.

Testimony.   Testimony always answers the question "What does an authority say about it?" Authorities can range from experts and statistics to eyewitnesses and accepted wisdom.

- The National Right to Life organization opposes embryonic stem-cell research.
- The U.S. Food and Drug Administration questions the safety of food derived from cloned animals.
- Thomas Okarma, President and CEO of Geron Corporation, opposes human reproductive cloning but supports beneficial applications of therapeutic cloning technology.

These are just a few of the theses available for each topic. Using the *topics* to create theses demands some immediate knowledge of the subject, but students will derive theses and argumentative lines that are very specific. You can also see that some *topics* will be more fruitful than others. The *topics* of definition, analogy, and consequence are the most useful for creating theses, whereas testimony is most naturally suited to the buttressing of already created theses.

The *topics* are not magic formulas that can make something out of nothing, but they are useful in organizing masses of information. Students need not have more than a layperson's knowledge of cloning to come up with many of the preceding thesis statements, but after having created these theses, they will know more clearly what they do know. They will also have a much better idea of where they need to go to look up information they do not have at hand. As you work through the *topics* in class, spend enough time on each of the first three (testimony is more specialized) to allow your students to digest the examples you provide and to see the process by which you arrive at the statements under each topic. You may want to pass out a photocopied sheet with the examples of the *topics* in action on a particular subject. After you explain the examples and show how they derive from the *topics*, assign a few subjects and ask students to use the topical system to come up with at least three theses for each topic (perhaps nine theses in all). After this assignment has been written, either in class or as homework, ask students to volunteer to read their theses aloud in class. The next step is to ask students to come up with ideas for an essay on a topic relevant to another class they are currently enrolled in and to apply classical topical invention to that subject. At this point, students should be comfortable enough with the system — perhaps even openly pleased with it — to be able to reel off theses for other subjects without much trouble.

Once students have successfully used the *topics* to produce theses, they will readily see how they can use them to generate supporting subject matter. After they have chosen their thesis from among the myriad possibilities that the topical system offers, they are left with many other statements that are at least indicators of other informational lodes. Very often after choosing a thesis, students can structure their essays around other thesis statements that they need to change only slightly to make them subordinate to the main purpose of their essays.

If you have the time in class, ask your students to put together a rough topic outline of a projected essay by arranging as many of the theses they have generated as possible in an order that could be used to structure an essay (remind them that often they may have to change the direction of the theses slightly to subordinate them to the main thesis). Here is an example of such a rough outline using some of the theses generated about cloning:

> *Main thesis:* If therapeutic cloning is made illegal, it will hinder scientific progress in finding new treatments for diseases.
> *Subordinate thesis 1:* Scientists believe stem-cell research may lead to vaccines and breakthrough medicines to treat diseases.
>> *Minor thesis:* They believe cloned functional cells can replace damaged cells in the body.
>> *Minor thesis:* Patients with heart disease could benefit from new heart muscle cells.
>
> *Subordinate thesis 2:* The uproar over questionable cloning practices — such as cloning humans — may cause U.S. lawmakers to ban human stem-cell research.
>> *Minor thesis:* Reproductive cloning is not safe.
>> *Minor thesis:* There are ethical and moral objections to reproductive cloning.
>
> *Subordinate thesis 3:* It is important to consider reproductive cloning and therapeutic uses of cloning technology as separate issues.

Although this list is more structured than those that many students will come up with, it exemplifies how such a topic list can be constructed.

The preceding description shows a deductive use of the *topics*, in which the thesis statement is decided on and then subject matter is arranged according to the perceived needs of the thesis. The *topics* can, of course, also be used inductively, to explore the subject and gather a mass of potential material, with the student creating a thesis only after the subject material has been grouped or categorized. With this inductive use of the *topics*, it is necessary for students to leave the whole area of thesis creation until after they have used the topical system to gather subject matter. You may well find that students often cannot wait to begin to arrange the material under a thesis and so greet the stage of thesis creation with enthusiasm.

Classical invention, in its simplified form, can be satisfying to teach. You use a tradition of education that is as old as any in Western culture. And since it is easy enough for students to memorize, they can carry it with them for use in other classes. It is neither the simplest nor the most complex heuristic system, but it has a charm and a comprehensiveness that make it one of the most attractive.

JOURNAL WRITING

Over the last twenty-five years, journal writing has become an intrinsic part of many English classes. Journals serve as a repository of material and concepts that can lead to more formal essays; journal writing does not impose systematic techniques of invention and thus can have a salutary effect on students' feelings about writing (Gannett). Journal writing can take many forms. Some forms are more structured than others, while all forms are used for different pedagogical purposes:

- *Writing logs:* The writing log helps students reflect on their writing processes, providing a place for them to keep track of their thoughts about writing and particular assignments — both while they are working on the assignment and after they've completed it. Reading a writing log that they have kept over a period of time can help students identify their own strengths and weaknesses as writers. The writing log can also be used as a place to record ideas for future writing assignments.
- *Reading journals:* The reading journal helps students make sense of and reflect on their reading assignments; in it, students can wrestle with ideas, note correspondences with and differences between the reading and their own experience, and prepare for class discussions. One effective format for the reading journal is the double-entry notebook, in which students write facts or quotations from their reading on one side of the page and personal responses or observations on the other side. The reading journal works well in the literature-based composition class — or in any class requiring a substantial amount of reading.

- *Commonplace books:* Used by many writers, the commonplace book is a journal where students record not only experiences, ideas, observations, and images, but also quotations from their reading. The commonplace book, when used well and often, becomes a rich source for informal essays, often containing powerful details as well as the voices of others. It is especially helpful to writers of creative nonfiction.

- *Research journals:* A research journal helps students keep track of their research process and the development of their ideas on a particular topic; like the reading journal and commonplace book, it can also include quotations and the student's thoughts or responses to the ideas of others. When combined with a research project, the research journal helps ensure students are thinking regularly about their project, provides a record of their development of ideas, allows students to respond informally to their reading, and may encourage more personal investment in the research process.

- *"Everyday" journals:* Many students already keep personal "everyday journals" or their more public, online counterparts: blogs. Some teachers assign journals simply because they want students to write every day. Teachers might provide general prompts if students get stuck (such as, "What book or movie has affected your thinking?" or "What person do you most admire? Explain."), but the topics for everyday journal writing are generally chosen by students themselves. In addition to encouraging students to write daily, these journals often become repositories of ideas for formal essays.

Using Journals in the Classroom

For students to get the most from journal writing, it is necessary to introduce them to the art of keeping a journal. First, acquaint your students with the definition of *journal* — a record of reactions, not actions. A journal is not a diary, nor is it a record of events. If you fail to be specific about this, students may end up writing diary entries — "Got up at 7:30, went to Commons for breakfast, saw Diane." Students need to be shown, and then convinced, that a journal is a record of a mind and its thoughts, rather than a record of a body and its movements. (For an essay on journal writing written for students, see Anson and Beach, cited at the end of this chapter.) One good way of demonstrating this difference is by showing students excerpts from the journals of established writers — such as Plath, Thoreau, Pepys, Woolf, and Hawthorne — or from student writing submitted in previous classes. Compared to keeping a journal, keeping a diary will soon seem to most of your students like a lame activity.

Along with familiarizing students with good examples of journal writing, you may want to provide particular prompts that will help get them started. Example 6.2 offers journal prompts that could be used for either writing logs or everyday journals. Provide just enough prompts so that students will occasionally have to grope for a sense of their own will to write something; too many questions and suggestions can be a crutch. Encourage students to move beyond each prompt to more self-directed writing.

One potential problem with journal writing for FY students is their tendency to rely on ready-made opinions, premanufactured wisdom, and clichés. Because some students have not yet begun to question their parents' or their friends' norms, they sometimes repeat the most appalling prejudices as if they had invented them. A ready-made challenge to such secondhand thought is the requirement that students be as concrete in their entries as possible. Discourage generalizing and opining unless the opinion can be tied to some actual experience in the student's life. (This is, after all, good argumentation — no assertions should be made without concrete support.) Macrorie suggests that students write journal entries on the same topic over a period of time, from "different and developing viewpoints" (*Telling Writing* 137). Such writing gives students the distance they need to reflect on, deepen, and enrich their perceptions and thus make their stories more moving and effective. But most important, Macrorie tells us, journals are the best starting place and the best storehouse for ideas: "A journal is a place for confusion and certainty, for the half-formed and the completed" (*Telling Writing* 141).

Example 6.2 JOURNAL PROMPTS

Journal Statements

You will submit ten *single-spaced* journal statements of one page each throughout the term: no more than one each Wednesday (you get to pick the Wednesdays). The purpose of the journal statements is twofold: (1) to help you think strategically about your writing assignments; and (2) to help you both examine yourself as a writer and imagine yourself as a writer who sets goals and develops specific, effective steps to achieve them.

The subject of each of your journal statements should be different. The following options — some on writing in general, others specifically about this course — should help get you started on the weekly journal assignment.

Journal 1: What are two of your strengths as a writer? What are two of your writing weaknesses? Specifically, how would you like to improve as a writer? What could you do or learn to make such improvements?

Journal 2: What expectations do you have for the course? What is your feeling toward first-year college writing? What has been your experience in a writing classroom? What did you like or dislike?

Journal 3: Informational process analyses should provide a specific audience with information it needs to replicate a process. Use this journal entry to describe possible topics for your process analysis essay, considering the following questions: What sorts of directions or instructions could students on campus, incoming students, or people in your community benefit from? Why?

Journal 4: Look at two editorials from this week's campus newspaper. What are the writers' goals? What kinds of appeals do the writers make? Explain the (in)appropriateness of each writer's use of rhetorical appeals.

Journal 5: Spend several minutes freewriting about particular difficulties that you have encountered thus far when drafting your process analysis. Specifically, what strategies have you used to work through these problems? What special concerns about your first draft would you like your peer reviewer to address during this week's draft workshop?

Journal 6: How do you define literacy? How can you measure it? How might your definition differ from that of your classmates?

Journal 7: Write for several minutes about the pressures you feel as a college student.

Journal 8: How do you respond to any writing assignment? In other words, is your reaction always the same, or does it vary, depending on the course, the teacher, or the level of instructional detail or freedom?

Journal 9: What specific revision strategies that we have discussed could you use to revise your process analysis assignment? Why will these strategies help you to create a more effective essay?

Journal 10: Do you ever get frustrated while driving or shopping? Why? What kinds of incidents, events, or situations can lead to your frustration?

Journal 11: Think for a minute about a special problem or talent you have. Maybe you're shy, behind in your classwork, overly committed, out of shape, or out of money; maybe you're highly motivated, popular, or particularly witty. Make a list of both the causes and consequences of your problem or gift. Which list provides you with more information about your problem or talent?

Journal 12: Write about the specific parts of the composing process that are most difficult for you. What particularly pressing concerns do you have when drafting your essays? What presents you with the most trouble? Why?

Journal 13: What are your feelings about the role of technology in education?

Journal 14: Reflect on your writing progress during the course of this semester. Consider the following questions as you write: How did you envision your writing at the beginning of the semester? How do you "see" your writing now? What improvements or discoveries have you made? What setbacks or successes have you experienced?

Elbow also recommends having students keep a journal, what he calls a "freewriting diary." He warns that it is "not a complete account of your day; just a brief mind sample from each day" (*Writing without Teachers* 9). Like Macrorie, Elbow sees the "freewriting diary" as the mother lode of ideas for essays. Elbow writes that "freewriting helps you to think of topics to write about. Just keep writing," he tells his readers; "follow threads where they lead and you will get the ideas, experiences, feelings, or people that are just asking to be written about" (*Writing with Power* 15).

You, too, should join your students in the journal-keeping practice, recording your own classroom experiences and your responses to your students' journals and essays. Nancy Comley, when she was director of FY writing at Queens College, City University of New York, encouraged her teaching assistants to keep their own journals. Comley writes that

> through the journal one comes to know oneself better as a teacher, and in the discipline of keeping a journal the teacher can experience what students experience when they are told to write and do not really feel like it. As part of the journal, I suggest that each teacher keep a folder of the progress (or lack of it) of two of his or her students, noting the students' interaction with the class and the teacher as well as evaluating their written work. Such data can form the basis for a seminar paper presenting these case histories, augmenting journal observations with student conferences and with research done into special problems or strengths the students had as writers. (55–56)

Encouraging teachers to keep a journal is in keeping with Comley's sage pedagogical advice: Never give an assignment you have not tried yourself.

Evaluating Journals

The issue of whether to evaluate journals is simple to answer: don't. Instead, read the entries to ensure that the student has made a sincere effort and assign a grade based on the number of pages a student turns in; four a week for ten weeks might earn an A; three a week, a B; and so on. Students are expected to write for themselves, yet they know that the instructor will see everything in the journal. While some teachers put no marks on journals except for a date after the last entry, others initiate a written conversation with the students, and still others write on separate sheets of paper that they insert into the journals. At times, you may find an entry directed to you — an invitation to reply.

Journals, then, shouldn't be judged by the standards you might bring to a student essay. The fact that students' journals do have an audience, however — namely, the teacher — means that they "do not speak privately," as Ken Macrorie puts it in *Telling Writing* (130). Macrorie insists that journals

> can be read with profit by other persons than the writer. They may be personal or even intimate, but if the writer wants an entry to be seen by others, it will be such that they can understand, enjoy, be moved by [it]. (131)

Helping students distinguish between what is personal and what is private is an important task for teachers who assign and read student journals. Emphasizing that you won't be grading the journals but that you will be reading them should help students work toward balancing the different demands of writing for themselves versus writing for others.

BRAINSTORMING

Using Brainstorming in the Classroom

Brainstorming is the invention method used by most professional and academic writers. The technique of brainstorming is simple: the writer decides on a subject, sits down in a quiet place with pen and paper or computer, and writes down everything that comes to mind about the subject. Alex Osborne codified the main rules of brainstorming in the late 1950s:

1. Don't criticize or evaluate any ideas during the session. Simply write down every idea that emerges. Save the criticism and evaluation until later.
2. Use your imagination for "free wheeling." The wilder the idea the better, because it might lead to some valuable insights later.
3. Strive for quantity. The more ideas, the better chance for a winner to emerge.
4. Combine and improve ideas as you proceed. (84)

The writer, in other words, free-associates, writing down as many ideas as possible. After doing so, the writer either tries to structure the information in some way — by recopying it in a different order or by numbering the items, crossing some out, adding to others — or finds the list suggestive enough as it stands and begins to work.

Brainstorming is extremely simple — and effective. The most widely used inventive technique, brainstorming moves in naturally to fill the void if no structured method is ever taught. Research suggests that if an inventive system is not internalized by around age twenty, brainstorming is adopted, probably because it represents the natural way the mind grapples with the storage and retrieval of information. Most professional and academic writers were never taught systematic invention and therefore turned to brainstorming.

Sometimes, young, self-conscious writers who have little specialized educational experience are initially stymied by brainstorming, for their stores of knowledge and general intellectual resources aren't as developed as those of experienced writers. Hence, they go dry when confronted with the task of listing ideas about an abstract topic. You may want to walk such writers through the brainstorming system by doing a sample exercise on the board or in small groups before you turn them loose with their own ideas. Brainstorming works well as a collaborative exercise, allowing students to feed off each other's ideas and draw from and extend each other's knowledge.

CLUSTERING

In *Writing the Natural Way,* Gabriele Lusser Rico describes clustering. Based on theories of the brain's hemispheric specialization, Rico's creative search process taps the right hemisphere of the brain, the hemisphere sensitive "to wholeness, image, and the unforced rhythms of language" (12). Usually, Rico tells us, beginning writers rely solely on the left hemisphere, the hemisphere of reason, linearity, and logic. By clustering, they can learn to tap the other hemisphere as well and produce writings that demonstrate

> a coherence, unity, and sense of wholeness; a recurrence of words and phrases, ideas, or images that [reflect] a pattern sensitivity; an awareness of the nuances of language rhythms; a significant and natural use of images and metaphors; and a powerful "creative tension." Another by-product of clustering seem[s] to be a significant drop in errors of punctuation, awkward phrasing, even spelling. (11)

Using Clustering in the Classroom

Clustering is an easy-to-use invention activity because there is no right or wrong way to cluster. Rico guarantees that the words will come and that writing eventually takes over. Students' clusters — and your own — are likely to be messy, drawing on both memory and association and displaying a mix of images, experiences and ideas. Here are Rico's simple directions for clustering, using the word *afraid* as an example:

1. Write the word *afraid* in the upper third of the page, leaving the lower two-thirds of the page for writing, and circle it. We'll start with this word because even the most hesitant of us will discover many associations triggered by it.
2. Now get comfortable with the process of clustering by letting your playful, creative...mind make connections. Keep the childlike attitude of newness and wonder and spill whatever associations come to you onto paper. What comes to mind when you think of the word? Avoid judging or choosing. Simply let go and write. Let the words or phrases radiate outward from the nucleus word, and draw a circle around each of them. Connect those associations that seem related with lines. Add arrows to indicate direction, if you wish, but don't think too long or analyze. There is an "unthinking" quality to this process that suspends time.

3. Continue jotting down associations and ideas triggered by the word *afraid* for a minute or two, immersing yourself in the process. Since there is no *one* way to let the cluster spill onto the page, let yourself be guided by the patterning... [abilities of your] mind, connecting each association as you see fit without worrying about it. Let clustering happen naturally. It will, if you don't inhibit it with objections from your censoring...mind. If you reach a plateau where nothing spills out, "doodle" a bit by putting arrows on your existing cluster.

4. You will know when to stop clustering through a sudden, strong urge to write, usually after one or two minutes, when you feel a shift that says "Aha! I think I know what I want to say." If it doesn't happen suddenly, this awareness of a direction will creep up on you more gradually, as though someone were slowly unveiling a sculpture....Just know you will experience a mental shift characterized by the certain, satisfying feeling that you have something to write about.

5. You're ready to write. Scan [your] clustered perceptions and insights....Something therein will suggest your first sentence to you, and you're off. Students rarely, if ever, report difficulty writing that first sentence; on the contrary, they report it as being effortless. Should you feel stuck, however, write about anything from the cluster to get you started. The next thing and the next thing after that will come because your [right hemisphere] has already perceived a pattern of meaning. Trust it. (36–37)

Like brainstorming, clustering works best when it's done very quickly, when students don't have time to edit or overthink their responses. Remind them that it's good if their clusters are messy, if they go off on tangents. When a cluster works well, students are surprised by how much material they were able to develop and the connections that their minds naturally made — even without conscious thought. When you model clustering for your students, allow a volunteer to suggest the starting place, the center word that you will work from. Don't try to explain the process as you're clustering; wait until after you're done and then take them through the process of your own clustering, explaining the associations you made and where you might go from there if you were to write about something that came up in your cluster. Students can practice clustering in pairs, too, choosing the same center word and then comparing their clusters. Such an activity allows students both to recognize their own individual ideas and associations and to see how much knowledge is communally constructed.

FREEWRITING

Unlike the heuristic-type invention techniques discussed in this chapter, freewriting is not a device through which experience can be consciously processed, nor do freewriting exercises (in their pure form) provide theses, arguments, or subject matter. Rather, freewriting — like clustering — is a ritual that can elicit possible subjects to which the conscious mind may not have easy access. What freewriting does best is loosen the inhibitions of the inexperienced writer. Thus, while freewriting differs strikingly from some of the other techniques discussed in this chapter, it follows well from both brainstorming and clustering. Once students have scanned their brainstorming lists or cluster diagrams and have an idea for a topic or first line, they are ready to freewrite — to begin putting the ideas suggested by their lists or cluster into prose, even as they hold out the possibility of discovering even more new material.

Freewriting, of course, does not need to follow another invention activity such as brainstorming or clustering. Freewriting itself can be a good starting place for invention. A number of writers over the past sixty years have developed freewriting exercises as methods of getting potential writers used to the idea of writing. Perhaps the first mention of freewriting-type exercises is in Dorothea Brande's 1934 book *Becoming a Writer,* in which the author suggests freewriting as a way for young would-be novelists to get in touch with their subconscious selves. Brande advocates writing "when the unconscious is in the ascendent":

> The best way to do this is to rise half an hour, or a full hour, earlier than you customarily rise. Just as soon as you can — and without talking, without reading — begin to write. Write anything that comes to your head. Write any sort of early morning revery, rapidly and uncritically. The excellence or ultimate worth of what you write is of no importance yet. Forget that you have any critical faculty at all. (50–51)

Brande's technique, the ancestor of freewriting, was largely ignored by teachers of expository writing until the 1950s, when Ken Macrorie, who had read *Becoming a Writer,* began to use an updated version of it in his composition classes. He modified Brande's directions for use in general composition and told his students to "go home and write anything that comes to your mind. Don't stop. Write for ten minutes or till you've filled a full page." This exercise produced writing that was often incoherent but that was also often striking in its transcendence of the dullness and clichéd thought teachers too often come to expect in English papers (*Uptaught* 20). Macrorie popularized the freewriting technique with his books *Uptaught* and *Telling Writing,* but it was Peter Elbow who developed and refined freewriting, making it a well-known tool. In his *Writing without Teachers* (which every writing teacher should read for the author's opinions on how to teach and learn writing), Elbow presents the most carefully wrought freewriting plan published thus far.

Using Freewriting in the Classroom

Freewriting is a kind of structured brainstorming, a method of exploring a topic by writing about it — or whatever else it brings to mind — for a certain number of minutes without stopping. It consists of a series of exercises, conducted either in class or at home, during which students start with a blank piece of paper, think about their topic, and then simply let their minds wander while they write. For as long as their time limit, they write down everything that occurs to them (in complete sentences as much as possible). They must not stop for anything. If they can't think of what to write next, they can write

"I can't think of what to write next" over and over until something else occurs to them. When their time is up, they can look at what they've written. They may find much that is unusable, irrelevant, or nonsensical. But they may also find important insights and ideas that they didn't know they had; freewriting has a way of jogging loose such ideas. As soon as a word or an idea appears on paper, it often triggers others.

The point of freewriting is to concentrate on writing, taking no time to worry about what others might think of it. When writers struggle to keep words — any words — flowing, they overload their "academic superego," which is usually concerned with content, criticism, spelling, grammar, and any of the other formal or content-based issues of correctness that so easily turn into writing blocks. In other words, they are writing — for five, ten, or fifteen minutes. Here are Elbow's directions for freewriting:

> Don't stop for anything. Go quickly without rushing. Never stop to look back, to cross something out, to wonder how to spell something, to wonder what word or thought to use, to think about what you are doing. If you can't think of a word or a spelling, just use a squiggle or else write, "I can't think of it." Just put down something. The easiest thing is just to put down whatever is in your mind. If you get stuck, it's fine to write, "I can't think what to say" as many times as you want, or repeat the last word you wrote over and over again, or anything else. The only requirement is that you never stop. (*Writing without Teachers* 3)

The requirement that the student never stop writing is matched by an equally powerful mandate to the teacher: never grade or evaluate freewriting exercises in any way. You can collect and read them — they are often fascinating illustrations of the working of the mind — but they must not be judged. To judge or grade freewriting would obviate the purpose of the exercise; this writing is free, not to be held accountable in the same way as other, more structured kinds of writing. Be sure to tell students that you will not be grading their freewriting. The value of freewriting lies in its capacity to release students from the often self-imposed halter of societal expectations. If you grade or judge such creations, you will convey the message that this writing is not free.

Most teachers who use pure freewriting use it at the opening of each class, every day for at least four or five weeks of the term. A session or two of freewriting, though interesting, is insufficient. For long-term gains, students must freewrite frequently and regularly. Only then will the act of writing stop being the unnatural exercise that some students see it as and start being a part of a writer's habit. Regular freewriting in class has two particularly worthwhile effects, says William Irmscher: "It creates the expectation that writing classes are places where people come to write, and it makes writing habitual" (*Teaching Expository Writing* 82–83). Students can also freewrite outside of class. You can assign freewriting as homework, grading it only according to whether or not it is done.

As students become more used to being pushed by a time constraint, their freewriting will become more coherent — the superego adapts and learns to work under pressure, although not with the deadly efficiency it once had. As this occurs, you can begin to intersperse directed writing assignments with the freewriting assignments. Or you may consider phasing out the pure freewriting exercises altogether.

Combined with brainstorming and clustering, freewriting can be used as an aid to writing longer pieces. But you won't want to try this combination of techniques until students are comfortable with each one individually. Combining techniques is most fruitful when students use them at home, since they require an extended period of time. Example 6.3 provides an exercise that helps students combine the brainstorming, clustering, and freewriting invention techniques.

The Benefits of Freewriting

Pure freewriting does not provide the neatness of the heuristic systems nor even the coherent processes of some other invention techniques, but as long as you explain its purpose and make certain that students don't see it as busywork, freewriting can accomplish two important goals.

First, it can familiarize beginning writers with the physical act of writing. Mina Shaughnessy suggests that it is hard for some teachers to understand exactly how little experience many FY students have had in writing (14–15). Their handwriting may be immature, and their command of sentence structure may suffer because they cannot match their writing process with their thought process. Freewriting forces them to produce, without the conscious editorial mechanism making the writing process harder than it is. A full five or six weeks of directed freewriting can make a difference.

Second, freewriting demystifies the writing process. After simply pouring out their thoughts in a freewriting exercise, students can no longer view the ability to write as a divine gift that has been denied them. They soon come to realize the difference between writing and editing, a difference crucial to their willingness and their ability to write. Freewriting primes the pump for more structured writing by demonstrating that a writer normally cannot, and need not, produce a perfectly finished essay on the first try, that the process has many steps, and that the most seemingly unpromising gibberish can yield valuable material.

Example 6.3   **COMBINING INVENTION TECHNIQUES**

Give students a subject to write about, and then suggest the following pattern:

1. Brainstorm for ten minutes.
2. Choose one item from your brainstorming list.
3. Cluster that word or idea for five minutes.
4. Set a timer or an alarm clock for twenty minutes, and freewrite for the entire time. Don't stop, and use only the brainstormed list and cluster as a basis for ideas.

Although students may grow tired while writing and may discard much of what they write, this piece of writing (or maybe the next one) will be the first draft of an essay that they can edit and you can grade. This technique works best when you assign the topics a week or so before the essays are due. Successful topics range from "the meaning of the funny papers" to "feminism" — topics even teenage students have lived with for many years.

WORKS CITED

Anson, Chris M., and Richard Beach. "Journeys in Journaling." *The Subject Is Writing.* 2nd ed. Ed. Wendy Bishop. Portsmouth: Boynton/Cook, 1999. 20–29.

Atwill, Janet, and Janice M. Lauer, eds. *Perspectives on Rhetorical Invention.* Knoxville: U of Tennessee P, 2003.

Berthoff, Ann. "The Problem of Problem Solving." *CCC* 22 (1971): 237–42.

Bilsky, Manuel, et al. "Looking for an Argument." *CE* 14 (1953): 210–16.

Brande, Dorothea. *Becoming a Writer.* 1934. New York: Harcourt, 1970.

Comley, Nancy R. "The Teaching Seminar: Writing Isn't Just Rhetoric." *Training the New Teacher of College Composition.* Ed. Charles W. Bridges. Urbana: NCTE, 1986. 47–58.

Corbett, Edward P. J., and Robert J. Connors. *Classical Rhetoric for the Modern Student.* 4th ed. New York: Oxford UP, 1998.

Ede, Lisa, Cheryl Glenn, and Andrea Lunsford. "Border Crossings: Intersections of Rhetoric and Feminism." *Rhetorica* 4 (Autumn 1995): 401–41.

Elbow, Peter. *Embracing Contraries.* New York: Oxford UP, 1986.

———. *Everyone Can Write.* New York: Oxford UP, 2000.

———. *Writing without Teachers.* New York: Oxford UP, 1973.

———. *Writing with Power.* New York: Oxford UP, 1981.

Flower, Linda. "Interpretive Acts: Cognition and the Construction of Discourse." *Poetics* 16 (1987): 109–30.

Flower, Linda, and John Hayes. "Uncovering Cognitive Processes in Writing: An Introduction to Protocol Analysis." *Research on Writing.* Ed. Peter Mosenthal, Sean Walmsley, and Lynn Tamor. London: Longman, 1982, 207–20.

Gannett, Cinthia. *Gender and the Journal.* Albany: State U of New York, 1990.

Harrington, Elbert W. *Rhetoric and the Scientific Method of Inquiry: A Study of Invention.* Boulder: U of Colorado P, 1948.

Hughes, Richard P., and P. Albert Duhamel. *Rhetoric: Principles and Usage.* Englewood Cliffs: Prentice, 1967.

Irmscher, William F. *Teaching Expository Writing.* New York: Holt, 1979.

Kinneavy, James. *A Theory of Discourse.* 1971. New York: Norton, 1980.

Lauer, Janice. "Heuristics and Composition." *CCC* 21 (1970): 396–404.

———. *Invention in Contemporary Rhetoric: Heuristic Procedures.* Diss. U of Michigan, 1970.

———. "Response to Anne E. Berthoff, 'The Problem of Problem Solving.'" *CCC* 23 (1972): 208–10.

———. "Toward a Methodology of Heuristic Procedures." *CCC* 30 (1979): 268–69.

Lauer, Janice, Janet Emig, and Andrea A. Lunsford. *Four Worlds of Writing.* 4th ed. New York: HarperCollins, 1995.

Macrorie, Ken. *Telling Writing.* Rochelle Park: Hayden, 1970.

____. *Uptaught.* Rochelle Park: Hayden, 1970.

Odell, Lee. "Assessing Thinking: Glimpsing a Mind at Work." *Evaluating Writing.* Ed. Charles R. Cooper and Lee Odell. Urbana: NCTE, 1999.

____. "Piaget, Problem-Solving, and Freshman Composition." *CCC* 24 (1973): 36–42.

Osborne, Alex F. *Applied Imagination.* New York: Scribner, 1957.

Rico, Gabriele Lusser. *Writing the Natural Way.* Los Angeles: Tarcher, 1983.

Shaughnessy, Mina. *Errors and Expectations: A Guide for the Teacher of Basic Writing.* New York: Oxford UP, 1977.

Young, Richard E. "Invention: A Topographical Survey." *Teaching Composition: Ten Bibliographic Essays.* Ed. Gary Tate. Fort Worth: Texas Christian UP, 1976, 1–44.

Young, Richard E., Alton L. Becker, and Kenneth L. Pike. *Rhetoric: Discovery and Change.* New York: Harcourt, 1970.

Young, Richard E., and Yameng Liu, eds. *Landmark Essays: Rhetorical Invention in Writing.* Davis: Hermagoras, 1994.

7

Teaching Arrangement and Form

Every time I review my marginal comments on student essays, I cringe. Among such stock phrases as "awkward construction" and "no need for a semicolon here — use a period," there is always one comment that stands out for both its banality and its lack of sense. This time, it's "choppy transition — aim at a more natural flow." Natural flow? Who am I kidding? Arrangement is the most contrived act of all.

—Steve Schneider

One of the continuing criticisms of classical rhetoric is its seemingly arbitrary canonical divisions: Is there any essential reason for assuming that the process of generating discourse should be divided into the restrictive classifications of invention, arrangement, style, memory, and delivery? And if these divisions are arbitrary, having no real connection to the composing process, why use them in a book like this?

Controversial though they may be, the divisions of rhetoric are useful conventions. Were we to try to describe the composing process as the seamless interaction of form and content that it apparently is, our discussion would have to be considerably deeper and more theoretical than space allows here. Separating invention and arrangement is a convenient tool for discussing certain features of process composing, even though the two operations are deeply interrelated and, except in certain invention techniques such as freewriting and brainstorming, rarely carried out separately by practiced writers. Experienced writers know that invention, arrangement, and style are inextricably intertwined, that no approach to one can ever ignore the others.

Because of this intimate relationship between form and content, Richard Larson writes that "form in complete essays has not been the subject of much theoretical investigation" (45). Invention, with its many open-ended systems, has received much more recent attention, reflecting a move away from formal requirements in general and a move toward self-ordered expression. Still, no one can claim that expectations about the characteristics of the different genres do not exist, and thus the demands of arrangement remain an integral part of rhetoric.

The arrangement of material in an essay grows out of a complex blend of the author's purpose and knowledge of the subject, as well as the formal expectations of the audience. In the course of ten or fifteen weeks, though, few teachers can present, and even fewer students can grasp, all of the intricacies in the marriage of form and content and all of the techniques used by experienced writers. Students can, however, begin to appreciate these intricacies in the material that is familiar to them. For example, you might ask students to examine the patterns of arrangement in articles and essays written by academics in other fields of study and to deduce the writers' conventional formats wherever possible. You can also introduce students to both the conventional and creative forms of arrangement covered here, which include simple and short formats that can be adapted to nearly any subject matter, longer and more complex ones used specifically in argumentation, and options for arranging creative essays. You can demonstrate and assign one, two, or all of these patterns of arrangement. You and your students should remember, however, that these patterns are not absolutes; they must be seen as convenient devices, not as rigid structures.

RHETORICAL FORM

Specific internal arrangement of elements creates rhetorical form, which may also be called genre, mode, or organization. Some teachers argue that preconceived arrangement (or formal structure) is artificial, that all organization should grow naturally out of the writer's purpose. Others see readily identifiable organization and form as the first step toward successful communication. Each teacher must gradually develop a conception of form and learn to strike a balance between form and content. This chapter can only suggest the various available alternatives that have long been used in the teaching of rhetoric.

Forms and arrangements can sometimes be assigned and used artificially; therefore, when we discuss form with our students, we must remind them (and ourselves) of the relationships between structure and content: that purpose, the needs of the audience, and the subject should dictate arrangement — not vice versa. We cannot, then, merely offer our students one or two prefabricated, all-purpose arrangements. Instead, we must regularly ask students to recognize the interconnections between form and content and between genre and intention, and we must work to assist them in the subtle task of creating forms that fit their ideas and emphases.

Whatever methods of arrangement or form you choose to teach, you want your students to realize that the conventions can be adapted and changed according to the needs of a particular subject and a particular audience. Methods of arrangement can provide a rough framework on which to build an essay, but they should neither limit the development of an essay nor demand sections that are clearly unnecessary.

The prescriptive forms discussed in this chapter, then, should be thought of and taught as stepping-stones only, not as ends in themselves. You will want to teach your students to transcend them as well as to use them. Kenneth Burke conveys an immensely important message in telling us that "form is an arousing and fulfillment of desires, ... correct in so far as it gratifies the needs ... it creates" (124). Form must grow from the human desires for both the familiar and the novel. If the prescriptive forms we give our students can help them realize this primary purpose, then we can offer the forms with the certainty that they will provide scaffolding only until the students can dismantle them and build on their own.

CLASSICALLY DESCENDED ARRANGEMENTS

The first theorists to propose generic forms for rhetoric were the Greeks, whose ideas were then rendered more formally and more technically by Roman rhetoricians. The first arrangement we have record of is from Aristotle, who may have been responding to the complicated, "improved" methods of arrangement detailed by his sophistic competition when he wrote, "A speech has two parts. You must state your case, and you must prove it....The current division is absurd" (*Rhetoric* 1414b). With the exception of the three-part essay, which has been generalized and modernized, all classical arrangements descend from Aristotle, and all are essentially argumentative in nature — like classical rhetoric itself. These arrangements, organized formally rather than according to content, rarely suit narrative or descriptive writing and can confuse students who try to use them for nonargumentative purposes. In *Classical Rhetoric for the Modern Student,* Edward P. J. Corbett and Robert Connors point out that instead of being topically organized, classical arrangements are "determined by the *functions* of the various parts of a discourse" (259).

The elements discussed as parts of each method of arrangement have no necessary correlation with paragraphs. Some students are tempted to think of a six-part essay as a six-paragraph essay, but except for some minor and very prescriptive forms, such as the five-paragraph theme, each element in a discourse scheme consists of a minimum of a single paragraph. Therefore, a four-part essay might consist of a single paragraph for the introduction, three paragraphs for the statement of fact, four paragraphs for the argument, and a single paragraph for the conclusion. Since each element can theoretically consist of an unlimited number of paragraphs, you should beware of letting your students fall into the habit of perceiving each element as a single paragraph.

The Three-Part Arrangement

"A whole," says Aristotle, "is that which has a beginning, a middle, and an end" (*Poetics* 24). Aristotle's observation — original, true, and now obvious — is the starting place for the most widely accepted method of rhetorical arrangement, the three-part arrangement. Like the dramatic works Aristotle was describing, a complete discourse, such as a successful essay, has three parts: an introduction, a body of some length, and a conclusion. From the simplest single-paragraph exercise to a forty-page research essay, every writing assignment is expected to contain these three parts.

The simplicity of this arrangement has positive and negative aspects. On the one hand, it is easy to teach and demonstrate, it is not overly structured, and it is the one truly universal pattern of arrangement, workable for exposition and argumentation alike. On the other hand, it provides little actual guidance in structuring an essay, especially if the assignment calls for a response longer than five hundred words. With such longer essays, students often find that although they are able to shape their introductions and conclusions, the bodies of their essays are amorphous. Nothing in the three-part essay provides interior structure to guide beginning writers in constructing the body of their essays, nearly always the longest part. The three-part arrangement, then, is most suitable for assignments of under five hundred words. Each of the three parts can be taught separately.

The Introduction. "The Introduction," writes Aristotle, "is the beginning of a speech,... paving the way... for what is to follow.... The writer should... begin with what best takes his fancy, and then strike up his theme and lead into it" (*Rhetoric* 1414b). In the three-part essay, the introduction has two main tasks. First, it must catch and hold the reader's attention with an opening "hook" — an introductory section that does not announce the thesis of the essay but instead begins to relate the as-yet-unannounced thesis in some brief, attention-catching way. The introduction can open with an anecdote, an aphorism, an argumentative observation, or a quotation. Donald Hall calls such an opening strategy a "quiet zinger,... something exciting or intriguing and at the same time relevant to the material that follows" (38).

Second, the introduction must quickly focus the attention of the reader on the thesis. This central informing principle of the essay is determined by the writer's purpose, subject, and audience. It is usually found in the form of a single-sentence declarative statement near the end of the introduction. The thesis statement represents the essay-length equivalent of the topic sentence of a paragraph; it is general enough to announce what the essay plans to do yet specific enough to suggest what the essay will not do. Sheridan Baker makes the controversial suggestion that the thesis statement is always the most specific sentence in the opening paragraph and should always come at the end of that paragraph. Although this is an easy-to-teach truism that may help students structure their introductions, critics have disputed how accurately it reflects the practice of experienced and published writers.

The Body of the Essay. According to Aristotle, the body of the essay is a middle. In truth, little more can be said of the middle in terms of the theory of the three-part essay, but in practice, writers can choose from many organizational plans. Some teachers trail off into generalities when they discuss the body of the essay, talking about "shaping purpose," "order of development," and "correct use of transitions" — necessary considerations but of little help to students adrift between their first and last paragraphs.

The body of the three-part essay can take many shapes: Writers can develop their essays according to the physical aspects, chronology, or logic or association of the subject matter; or by illustrating points, defining terms, dividing and classifying, comparing and contrasting, analyzing causes and effects, or considering problems and solutions. Whatever organizational plan writers choose, they want to be sure that the main points of the body relate not

---

Box 7.1 **PRINCIPLES OF ORGANIZATION**

Space — *where* bits of information occur within a setting
Time — *when* bits of information occur, usually chronologically
Logic — *how* bits of information are related logically
Association — *how* bits of information are related in terms of images, motifs, personal memories, and so on (Lunsford 64–68)

---

only to the thesis but to one another. Box 7.1 shows the four general principles of organization offered by Lunsford in *The St. Martin's Handbook*.

The Conclusion.   Like the introduction, the conclusion presents special challenges, for it should indicate that a full discussion has taken place. Often the conclusion begins with a restatement of the thesis and ends with more general statements that grow out of it, reversing the common general-to-specific pattern of the introduction. This restatement is usually somewhat more complex than the original thesis statement, since now the writer assumes that readers can marshal all of the facts of the situation as they have been presented in the body of the essay. A typical, if obvious, example of the opening of a conclusion might be "Thus, as we have seen," followed by the reworded thesis.

In addition to reiterating the consequence and import of the thesis, however, the conclusion should include a graceful or memorable rhetorical note. Writers can draw on a number of techniques to conclude effectively and give their text a sense of ending: a provocative question, a quotation, a vivid image, a call for action, or a warning. Baker writes that a successful conclusion satisfies the reader because it "conveys a sense of assurance and repose, of business completed" (22). William Zinsser, however, insists that

> the perfect ending should take the reader slightly by surprise and yet seem exactly right to him. He didn't expect the [piece] to end so soon, or so abruptly, or to say what it said. But he knows it when he sees it. (78–79)

Zinsser goes on to tell writers of nonfiction that when they are ready to stop, they should stop: "If you have presented all the facts and made the point that you want to make, look for the nearest exit" (79). Often, however, the best conclusions are those that answer the "so what?" of the thesis statement and overall argument.

Using the Three-Part Arrangement in the Classroom

Although it is applicable to many modes of discourse, the classical three-part arrangement simply does not provide enough internal structure to help students put together the middle sections of their essays. The three-part form is

useful mainly as an introduction to the conventions of introductions and conclusions. The easiest way to consider the body of an essay is to teach patterns
of other, more fully developed arrangements.

After introducing the basic three-part structure, you can discuss the importance of introductions and conclusions. Try to choose examples that put
special emphasis on the structures of these parts, and ask students to respond
to your examples. You might assign a series of short, in-class essays on topics
your students have chosen. So that students concentrate on recognizable introductions and conclusions, you might allow them to dispense with the writing
of the body of each essay and to submit instead a rough outline or list of
components.

An Exercise for Small Groups

This exercise is especially useful when students work in writing groups: After
each short essay assignment is written in class, ask students to work with their
group to evaluate the introductions and conclusions. They might answer specific questions, such as those listed in Example 7.1. You might put the most
effective introductions and conclusions on the blackboard so that the entire
class can see them. After students have conferred and improved one another's
work and after the introductions and conclusions have been hammered
into a final form, allow those students who have become intrigued by the
ideas they've been working with to complete the essay for a grade. Several days
of this kind of practice can give students competence in beginning and ending
their essays.

Example 7.1   QUESTIONS FOR SMALL GROUPS

- What does the opening of this essay accomplish?
- How does it "hook" the reader?
- How can you help the writer improve the opening?
- Does the essay end in a memorable way? Or does it seem to trail off into
  vagueness or end abruptly?
- If you like the conclusion, what about it do you like?
- Can you help the writer improve the conclusion?

The Four-Part Arrangement

After blasting the hair-splitting pedagogues of his day and declaring that an
oration has only two parts, Aristotle relented and admitted that as speakers
actually practice rhetoric, a discourse generally has four parts: the *proem* or

introduction, the *statement of fact,* the *confirmation* or *argument,* and the *epilogue* or *conclusion* (*Rhetoric* 200). Specifically an argumentative form, this four-part arrangement does not adapt well to narrative or description.

The Introduction.   Called the *proem* (from the Greek word *proemium,* meaning "before the song") by Aristotle and the *exordium* (from the Latin weaving term for "beginning a web") by the author of the Roman handbook *Rhetorica ad herenium,* the introduction to the four-part essay has two functions, one major and one minor. The major task is to inform the audience of the purpose or object of the essay; the minor task is to create a rapport, or relationship of trust, with the audience. The introduction to the four-part essay, then, performs functions similar to that of the introduction to the three-part essay. It draws readers into the discourse with the promise of interesting information and informs them of the main purpose while rendering them well-disposed toward the writer and the subject.

"The most essential function and distinctive property of the introduction," writes Aristotle, "[is] to show what the aim of the speech is" (*Rhetoric* 202). Corbett and Connors tell us that the introduction serves two important audience-centered functions: it orients the audience within the subject, and even more importantly, it seeks to convince readers that what is being introduced is worthy of their attention (260). In a fashion similar to the "quiet zinger" that opens the three-part essay, the four-part essay can catch readers' attention by using different devices. Richard Whately describes five different types of introductions that can arouse the reader's interest (see Box 7.2). The usefulness of these types of introductions is not limited to the four-part essay, though they do complement

---

Box 7.2   **WHATELY'S TYPES OF INTRODUCTIONS**

Inquisitive introductions show that the subject in question is "important, curious, or otherwise interesting."

Paradoxical introductions dwell on characteristics of the subject that seem improbable but are nonetheless real. This form of introduction searches for strange and curious perspectives on the subject.

Corrective introductions show that the subject has been "neglected, misunderstood, or misrepresented by others." As Whately says, this immediately removes the danger that the subject will be thought trite or hackneyed.

Preparatory introductions explain peculiarities in the way the subject will be handled, warn against misconceptions about the subject, or apologize for some deficiency in the presentation.

Narrative introductions lead to the subject by narrating a story or anecdote. (189–92)

argumentative subject matter. The various introductions can accomplish the major task of acquainting the audience with the subject as well as the minor task of rendering the reader attentive to and well-disposed toward the writer.

In rendering an audience benevolent, writers must be aware of certain elements concerning the rhetorical situation in which they find themselves. In *Classical Rhetoric for the Modern Student*, Corbett offers five questions that writers must ask themselves regarding their rhetorical situation before they can be certain of the conditions for their discourse:

1. What do I have to say?
2. To or before whom is it being said?
3. Under what circumstances?
4. What are the predispositions of the audience?
5. How much time or space do I have? (290)

The introduction is the best place to establish "bridges" between writer and reader by pointing to shared beliefs and attitudes — that is, by creating what Burke calls identification of the writer with the audience and the audience with the writer.

The Statement of Fact.   The Romans called the statement of fact the *narratio,* and it is sometimes today referred to as the *narration* or *background.* But Corbett's term *statement of fact* works well, especially since we now use *narration* to signify dramatized activities. This section of a discourse also presents more than just background. The statement of fact is a nonargumentative, expository presentation of the objective facts concerning the situation or problem — the subject — under discussion.

The statement of fact may contain circumstances, details, summaries, even narrative in the modern sense. It sets forth the background of the problem and very often explains the central point as well. Perhaps the best general advice remains Quintilian's, who in the first century A.D., recommended that the statement of fact be *lucid, brief,* and *plausible.* Writers can order a statement of fact in a number of different ways: in chronological order, from general situation to specific details, from specific to general, or according to topics. The tone of the statement of fact should be neutral, calm, and matter-of-fact, free of overt stylistic mannerisms and obvious bias. Writers are best served by understatement, for readers will readily trust a writer they deem to be striving for fairness.

The Confirmation.   Also called the *argument,* the confirmation is central to the four-part essay and is often the longest section. Corbett tells us that the confirmation is easily used in expository as well as argumentative prose; Historically, it has been used mainly in argumentation. Simply put, the confirmation is used to prove the writer's case. With the audience rendered attentive by the introduction and informed by the statement of fact, the writer is ready to show the reasons why her position concerning the facts should be accepted and believed. Most of the argumentative material discovered in the invention process is used in this section.

Aristotle theorizes that argumentative discourse deals with two different sorts of questions: deliberative (or political) oratory is always concerned with the future, and forensic (or judicial) oratory is always concerned with the past. If the question is about events in the past, the confirmation will try to prove the following:

1. Whether an act was committed
2. Whether an act committed did harm
3. Whether the harm of the act is less or more than alleged
4. Whether a harmful act was justified

If the question is about a course for the future, the confirmation will try to prove that

1. A certain thing can or cannot be done. If it can be done, then the confirmation tries to prove that
2. It is just or unjust
3. It will do harm or good
4. It has not the importance the opposition attaches to it

After deciding on a question and a position, the writer can move into the argument, choosing from definitions, demonstrations of cause or effect, analogies, authoritative testimony, maxims, personal experiences — evidence of all sorts — in order to prove a point.

The writer can build an argument in different ways, but classical rhetoricians offer a rough plan. If there are, for instance, three specific lines of argument available to the writer — one strong, one moderately convincing, and one weak — they should be grouped thus: the moderate argument first, the weak argument second, and the strong argument last. This arrangement begins and ends the confirmation on notes of relative strength and prevents the writer's position from appearing initially weak or finally anticlimactic.

The Conclusion.   Called the *epilogue* by the Greeks and the *peroration* by the Romans (from *per-oratio*, a "finishing off of the oration"), the conclusion, according to Aristotle's *Rhetoric*, has four possible tasks:

1. It renders the audience once again well-disposed toward the writer and ill-disposed toward the writer's opponent.
2. It magnifies the writer's points and minimizes those of the opposition.
3. It puts the audience in the proper mood.
4. It refreshes the memory of the audience by summarizing the main points of the argument.

Most conclusions do recapitulate the main points, or at least the central thesis, of the discourse. The other three possible tasks are less concrete. Although the conclusion tends to be the most obviously emotional of all the sections, the use of *pathos* (emotional appeal) in written assignments is a dangerous technique for beginners, in whose hands it can all too easily degenerate into *bathos* (laughable emotional appeal). The best conclusions restate or expand their main points and then sign off gracefully with a stylistic flourish that signals the end of the discourse.

Using the Four-Part Arrangement in the Classroom

Although the four-part arrangement gives more direction to an essay than does the three-part arrangement, it is not as adaptable to different sorts of discourse. The four-part pattern generally demands subject-directed, nonpersonal writing that can support an argumentative thesis. For an essay with such an arrangement, students usually need several days in which to conceptualize and investigate their subjects. They will also need to apply techniques of invention or do research on their subjects before writing their first drafts. Some teachers prefer to provide the subjects on which their students are to write four-part essays, at least in the beginning, because this arrangement works best when applied to rigidly defined questions.

You may want to assign subjects that need little or no research and that support several different argumentative theses. You can decide whether to begin with a question involving actions in the past (a forensic question) or one involving future policy (a deliberative question). Here are some possible forensic and deliberative topics:

Forensic Topics

- The conduct of FEMA after Hurricane Katrina in 2005
- Law schools' objections to military recruiters on campus
- Gangsta rap's role in the increase in urban violence

Deliberative Topics

- Should the federal government institute a national identification-card system?
- Is mandatory recycling good for the state?
- Should all undergraduates be required to have proficiency in a foreign language?

Obviously, deliberative topics change as the issues of the day change. Current campus controversies make excellent topics.

While students can certainly master the forms in a week, that amount of time does not allow for a topic to be thoroughly researched. You may want to overlook the generalizations and the abstract, vague arguments your students make while they learn to apply the four parts of the arrangement. You can also give them some peer-response group work that reinforces what they are learning about arrangement.

After your students complete their first drafts of the four-part essay assignment, ask them to join their peer-response groups and read one another's drafts. Have them evaluate each other's drafts by asking the questions listed in

Example 7.2. Many teachers like to drift among the peer-response groups as they work and remind students that any form must be adapted to its content. To help students adapt form to content, you may want to talk with students individually while the groups are meeting.

Example 7.2   PEER-RESPONSE QUESTIONS FOR THE FIRST DRAFT OF A FOUR-PART ESSAY

Introduction

- Do the first four sentences attract my interest?
- Is the subject clearly defined in the introduction?
- Is the introduction too long?
- Does the introduction seem to be aimed at a specific audience? What is that audience?
- Do I want to know more, to keep reading? Why or why not?

Statement of Fact

- Does this section clearly explain the nature of the problem or situation?
- Is there anything not told that I need to know?
- Does the problem or situation continue to interest me?

Confirmation

- Is the argumentation convincing?
- Does the order of presentation seem reasonable?
- Has any obvious argument been left out?
- Has the opposing position been competently refuted?

Conclusion

- Has the case been summarized well?
- Do I feel well-disposed toward the writer? Why or why not?
- Does the ending seem graceful?

After the groups complete their discussions and evaluations of the draft essays, ask the students to submit typed copies of their essays. You may want to distribute copies of the essays (without the student writers' names) and review with the class the strengths and weaknesses of each argument. Often students will volunteer drafts of their essays for class review if they know they can remain anonymous.

The more that students know about the formal qualities of the four-part form and what is successful in argument, the easier it will be for them to write their next essays.

Two More-Detailed Arrangements

The Five-Part Arrangement.   The classical oration form used by Cicero and Quintilian was a four-part form, but the Latin rhetoricians went on to divide the third part, the confirmation, into *confirmatio* and *reprehensio*. Cicero said that "the aim of confirmation is to prove our own case and that of refutation (*reprehensio*) is to refute the case of our opponents" (337). Thus, the classical oration is composed of five parts:

1. *Exordium*, or introduction
2. *Narratio*, or statement of facts
3. *Confirmatio*, or proof of the case
4. *Reprehensio*, or refutation of opposing arguments
5. *Peroratio*, or conclusion

Setting off the refutation in its own section is not a meaningful change from the four-part arrangement, since the confirmation of the four-part essay can also be refutative. Still, a separate section of refutation makes the task of dealing with opposing arguments mandatory; hence, it can provide more structure for an essay. Although the refutation does not always present the writer's own positive arguments, it usually does — that is, unless the opposing arguments are so powerful or so well accepted that the audience would not listen to an opposing confirmation without first being prepared by the refutation.

Corbett tells us that refutation is based on *appeals to reason, emotional appeals, ethical or personal appeals* of the writer, or *wit*. Refutation can usually be accomplished in one of two ways: (1) the writer denies the truth of one of the premises on which the opposing argument is built; or (2) the writer objects to the inferences drawn by the opposition from premises that cannot be broken down.

The Six-Part Arrangement.   Most detailed of all the classically descended arrangements is the six-part arrangement, recommended by Hugh Blair in his influential book, *Lectures on Rhetoric and Belles-Lettres,* published in 1783. Blair's arrangement was largely influenced by the classical theorists, but Blair was also a practitioner of pulpit oratory. Hence, his arrangement shows both classical and sermonic elements. His discourse model is composed of six elements:

1. exordium, or introduction
2. statement and division of the subject
3. narration, or explication

4. reasoning, or arguments
5. pathetic or emotional part
6. conclusion (341)

In this breakdown, the introduction captures the attention of the audience, renders the reader benevolent, and so on. Like some of the classical theorists, Blair distinguishes two sorts of introductions: the *principium,* a direct opening addressed to well-disposed audiences, and the *insinuatio,* a subtler method that prepares a hostile audience for arguments counter to their opinions.

The *insinuatio* generally opens by first admitting the most powerful points made by the opposition, by showing how the writer holds the same views asthe audience on general philosophical questions, or by dealing with ingrained audience prejudices. The *principium* can proceed with the knowledge that the audience is sympathetic, going directly to the task of rendering readers attentive.

In Blair's arrangement, as in the three-part arrangement, the thesis is clearly stated at the end of the introduction, but here the thesis is immediately followed by the "division," or announcement of the plan of the essay, which is Blair's first large departure from the four-part essay. Both the statement and the division should be short and succinct. According to Blair, the division should avoid "unnecessary multiplication of heads" (Golden and Corbett 114). In other words, it should contain as simple an outline as possible, presented in a natural, nonmechanistic fashion.

The next two sections, "narration" and "reasoning," correspond to the statement of fact and the confirmation in the four-part essay. However, Blair's model then proposes that a new division of arrangement, termed the pathetic part, follow the argumentation section. The word *pathetic* in this case refers to the pathetic or emotional appeal of classical rhetoric. Thus, after presenting an argument, the writer would appeal to the audience's feelings; in addition, the writer would begin to draw the discourse to a close.

Blair recommends using a formula remarkably similar to T. S. Eliot's "objective correlative" for arousing the emotions of the audience: The writer must connect the audience's emotions with a specific instance, object, or person. A writer arguing against nuclear power, for instance, might close his arguments with specific examples of nuclear harm — factory workers made sterile by isotope poisoning or workers killed in grisly fashion at Chernobyl, for example. A writer arguing for nuclear generation of electricity might paint a picture of poor people freezing to death because the cost of heating without nuclear power is too great for them to bear.

In the pathetic part, the writer should conclude the arguments with a powerful emotional appeal, one that will bring together the arguments and lead readers to act on their feelings. The pathetic appeal at the end of the arguments can be very effective.

The pathetic part should also be short, Blair says, and must not rely on any stylistic or oratorical flourishes; therefore, the language should be bold, ardent, and simple. And finally, Blair warns, writers should not attempt to create a pathetic effect if they themselves are not moved, for the result of such attempts will not only be ineffective and artificial but hypocritical as well.

Following the pathetic part of this six-part form is the conclusion, which is similar to the conclusion presented in the less-detailed arrangements discussed earlier in the chapter.

Using the More-Detailed Arrangements in the Classroom

For the advanced or honors student, the more detailed forms are profitable. Based on the four-part essay, these forms are best taught as mere extensions of it. Teachers who provide advanced students with a more complex arrangement often find that the students are unwilling to go back to the less-detailed structure and its larger burden of decision. Often teachers present both of the more-detailed forms, spending time on the four-part structure and then progressing to the classical oration and Blair's arrangement. Each successive structure subsumes those that precede it.

Because your students will probably need more time to think through and develop their argumentative essays than they will need for any other type of discourse, your choice for this assignment is of paramount importance. Even when they understand the argumentative arrangement, students cannot assemble their essays overnight. The forensic and deliberative topics mentioned earlier can be profitably applied to these arrangements. But by the time you have reached the stage of teaching these forms, it is often close to the end of the term, and students will be able to choose their own topics. Having been led through the four-part form, they know which topics can be well argued and which will present problems. Sometimes, however, the class will need to work together, coming up with and developing topics for stumped classmates.

Both the five- and the six-part forms provide specific sorts of practice, the five-part form in refutation and the six-part form in emotional appeals of a certain sort. Before they begin to write, students using the five-part form should be able to list at least two arguments their opposition would be likely to use; otherwise, their refutations could be too general or indistinguishable from their confirmations. Students using the six-part form must keep in mind the difference between pathos and bathos and avoid embarrassing attempts to sway the emotions. The six-part form is best used by honors or upper-level students whose emotional perceptions are likely to be informed by the rational judgment necessary for effective pathetic or emotional appeal.

To familiarize your students with the soon-to-be-assigned form, you may want to hand out a model of the form. You will want to exemplify as well as introduce each element in a new argument. Some teachers elicit an argumentative subject from the class and then, with the class, outline the course of that argument on the board. Students often have strong ideas of how one specific form of arrangement best suits a particular argument. Working together in this way is the best practice you can give your students.

During each stage of teaching these prescriptive arrangements, you want to illustrate the flexibility of the demands made by these forms. The more complex the pattern of arrangement, the greater the chance that one or more sections will be extraneous or actually harmful to the discourse. Students must learn to use common sense in deciding whether or to what degree the method of arrangement fits their needs and the needs of their audience.

OTHER PATTERNS OF ARRANGEMENT

Arrangements for Rhetorical Methods

In the 1970s, rhetorical theorist Frank J. D'Angelo isolated what he considered to be the ten most common patterns of arrangement: narration, process analysis, cause-effect, description, definition, analysis, classification, exemplification, comparison, and analogy. He then presented each in the form of a model or fixed outline that students could use as a plan for essays of their own. Other rhetoricians, too, have listed and dealt with some of these patterns of arrangement — indeed, insofar as they recapitulate the classical topics, they can be said to go back to Aristotle. Many textbooks, in fact, are organized according to "patterns of exposition," "modes," or "rhetorical methods." In her rhetorically arranged textbook, *Making Sense,* Cheryl Glenn explores in depth the "nine rhetorical methods everyone uses to make sense of the world" and argues that we use these methods as powerful tools for understanding and creating the kinds of texts and images we encounter every day (v). Instead of prescribing fixed outlines for arrangement, Glenn offers guidance for organizing texts that make use of such rhetorical methods as description, narration, exemplification, classification and division, comparison and contrast, process analysis, cause-and-consequence analysis, definition, and argument. What follows is a condensed version of the principles of arrangement that Glenn details, including guidance for helping writers achieve their purposes, even as they anticipate their readers' needs. These patterns of arrangement can be used both for paragraphs and whole essays.

Arrangement for Description.   Three methods for arranging descriptive essays include a "spatial organizational pattern, with the details arranged according to their location," a chronological pattern, and an emphatic pattern, in which details are arranged in order of importance (Glenn 58–59). Because sensory details are central to description, point of view — what Glenn defines as "the assumed eye and mind of the writer" — is important to both spatial and chronological order. Glenn also suggests that students keep their audiences in mind as they write descriptions, considering "an order that reflects the audience's physical or mental point of view" rather than their own, moving from most familiar (to the reader) to least familiar, from most remote (from the reader) to closest, from least persuasive (to the reader) to most persuasive (60). You can also remind students that photographs and other kinds of images can help suggest an organizational format, guiding the writer and visually ground-ing the reader.

Arrangement for Narrative.   Glenn notes that most narratives follow a chronolog-ical order, often building to a climax and then making or reaffirming a point or lesson (144). Yet she also discusses variations to strict chronological order in writing narratives, such as using flashbacks, "a glimpse of the past that illumi-nates the present," or flashforwards, "a technique that takes readers to future events" (145). She also reaffirms the importance of guiding readers through the use of transitional words and phrases — such as *first, then,* and *next* — and appropriate verb tense (148).

Arrangement for Exemplification.   In exemplification, each paragraph must be related to the thesis or generalization, and examples must be organized in a purposeful order (emphatically or chronologically, for example), an order that makes the connections both between each example and in relation to the thesis clear (Glenn 217).

Arrangement for Classification and Division.   When classifying and dividing, the pur-pose and thesis statement determine arrangement. The organization might be chronological, emphatic ("starting with the least important category or part and ending with the most important — which could be the largest, the most complex, the most entertaining, or the most persuasive"), or logical (Glenn 286). In any case, students should use details to provide balance, topic sen-tences and transitional words to provide clarity, and a strong conclusion to explain the importance of the classification and division (286).

Arrangement for Comparison and Contrast.   Writers doing comparisons and con-trasts usually organize their texts in one of two ways: either by making "a point-by-point case" for each subject individually or by comparing and contrasting each corresponding point of each subject (one point rather than one subject at a time) (Glenn 364).

Arrangement for Process Analysis.   As Glenn observes, "a process analysis is pre-sented as a chronological sequence of actions or steps," usually in a fixed order, in which the steps and the results are consistent (438). Generally, the writer includes every step in the process, unless readers already know — or don't need to know — particular steps. As in other rhetorical methods, necessary details and transitions are significant in a process analysis.

Arrangement for Cause and Consequence.   One possibility for opening a cause and consequence essay is to begin "with a description of the event or situation" to be analyzed and then to introduce the thesis, which should explain whether the writer will focus on causes, consequences, or both (Glenn 498). After the intro-duction, there are various options for arrangement: narrating the causes and effects in chronological or reverse chronological order — or, alternately, ordering "the causes emphatically, from least to most important" (498). Depending on the material students are working with, either of these arrangements can be effective, so long as the order remains consistent and the conclusion is strong, perhaps revealing the larger or long-term implications.

Arrangement for Definition.   While there is no fixed organization for writing definitions, as in any other essay the arrangement must be tied to the writer's purpose — in this case either informing or persuading. The writer must first establish a "definition for the term or concept and then support [that] definition by using examples, descriptions, comparisons and contrast, narratives, or another method of development" (Glenn 585). Finally, the writer must conclude in a way that will help readers decide what to do with the information the writer has offered.

Arrangement for Argument.   Much of the information presented so far in this chapter has been geared toward writing effective arguments. Whether using a three-part arrangement or a more-detailed format, students should make a clear and supportable claim; balance appeals to reason, character, and emotion; and avoid logical fallacies. What Glenn adds to these traditional expectations is the potential power of images to enhance logical, ethical, and pathetic appeals. The placement of such images — and how they are introduced and explained — can provide strong support for a well-developed argument.

As you teach arrangements for the rhetorical methods, note that many of the arrangement strategies overlap, and that although neither the methods for developing nor the ways of organizing texts are discrete, they still remain useful.

Arrangements for Creative Nonfiction Essays

If you're asking students to write personal or lyric essays, there are many patterns of arrangement available to them. Narration, description, and comparison-contrast are all common rhetorical methods of developing creative nonfiction, and their patterns of arrangement provide useful starting places. But just as writers of creative nonfiction can rarely depend on one method of development, neither can they depend on one discrete pattern of arrangement to fulfill their writing purposes. One method or pattern is simply too restrictive for the more amorphous essay form. Thus, many of the very best creative nonfiction essays draw from several patterns.

Though many students will have experience writing traditional narratives in which the narration follows a chronological arrangement, they often need to learn additional techniques in order to imagine new ways of structuring their material to achieve a particular effect. Lyric essays, for example — although they may contain narrative sections — almost always move away from a strict chronological arrangement. An arrangement common to both lyric and narrative essays is association. As Lunsford notes in *The St. Martin's Handbook*, "associational organization is most often used in personal narrative, where writers can use a chain of associations to render an experience vividly for readers" (68). Personal narrative, too, comes in many forms — each with various options for arrangement.

In "Collage, Montage, Mosaic, Vignette, Episode, Segment," Robert L. Root Jr. introduces teachers to some of the terminology related to various forms of personal essays and options for arrangement in creative nonfiction. He acknowledges that the terminology is not fixed: What Root refers to as the "segmented essay" (a piece written in loosely connected sections, rather than chronological narrative) is what Peter Elbow calls a "collage essay." Root points to additional terms and adjectives suggested by contemporary authors: Rebecca Blevins Faery uses the adjectives "fragmented" and "polyphonic" to describe a similar form, and Carl Klaus suggests the term "disjunctive" (362). Still another option is "mosaics," Mark Rudman's term for patterned essays (363). Mosaics — like Elbow's collage — suggest a visual metaphor, which might help students imagine a form that creates a larger picture or effect by using many smaller parts or sections. (For examples and further discussion of these types of essays, see DePeter, cited at the end of this chapter; Elbow's "Your Cheatin' Art: A Collage" in *Everyone*; and Fontaine and Quaas, cited at the end of this chapter.)

Using Arrangements for Creative Nonfiction Essays in the Classroom

One advantage to teaching segmented essays is that choosing an arrangement that differs from a traditional linear form can help students think about — and even understand — their experiences in a new way. Just as a collage or mosaic is organized according to patterns of color and shape to create an overall effect, so too can an essay be organized by the emotional color or shape of a series of related experiences. The essay can also be shaped around an idea or abstraction (fear or comfort, for instance), an object or image related to an idea (such as Susan Griffin's "Red Shoes"), or a memory and reflection on one's telling of the story (Patricia Hampl's "Memory and Imagination" provides a fitting example).

Such essays provide interesting opportunities for revision as well. If you can move students away from an attachment to linear narrative (the too familiar "This is how it happened, so I can't change it"), they will begin to see and talk about the important effects of arrangement. Students can literally cut up (disassemble) their essays and move the various sections around to create different movements.

A danger of such forms is that, if they're not done well or if the audience for such essays has expectations for a more traditionally arranged piece, they can lose readers. The connections between sections are often intuitive and associational, and providing clues for readers can sometimes be difficult for less experienced writers. There are, however, certain patterns of arrangement with which many readers will be familiar. In a slightly different format, Root offers the strategies for arrangement listed in Box 7.3.

An additional means of helping students imagine alternate ways of arranging essays is to lead a discussion on the organization of their favorite movies or television shows. Although these show are now in syndication, many students will be familiar with *Seinfeld* and *Friends*, for example, sitcoms that often have

---

Box 7.3   **ARRANGEMENT STRATEGIES FOR CREATIVE
                NONFICTION ESSAYS**

Juxtaposition — arranging one item alongside another item so that they comment back and forth on one another

Parallelism — alternating or intertwining one continuous strand with another (present/past tense)

Patterning — choosing an extraliterary design and arranging literary segments accordingly (Root uses Nancy Willard's "The Friendship Tarot," in which Willard uses tarot cards as an organizational guide, as an example)

Accumulation — arranging a series of segments or scenes or episodes so that they add or enrich or alter meaning with each addition

Journaling — writing in episodes or reconstructing the journal experience in drafts (Root 367)

---

two or three seemingly independent stories in each episode but then tie the stories together (often through irony and humor) in a final scene. Students will also be able to recall movies that use flashbacks or ones that show the same scene or situation from several different perspectives. For instance, in *Dead Man Walking,* viewers watch Susan Sarandon's character (Sister Helen Prejean) try to make sense of a crime through a series of flashbacks, and each flashback is revised as she learns more of what really happened. (A similar arrangement is used in *Memento,* and students will be able to provide many other examples.) Though you and your students may not have seen all the same films or television shows, through discussion you can come up with specific patterns of arrangement that are repeatedly used in popular culture. And students can use similar patterns of arrangement in their own essays.

An Exercise for Linking Invention and Arrangement

The following exercise will help students recognize important connections between invention and arrangement strategies. Since the arrangement of creative nonfiction prose is often — though not always — associational, clustering is an effective invention technique (see Chapter 6 for more on clustering). Ask students to create a cluster from a word that might call up physical, metaphorical, experiential, and visual associations. The word *cold,* for instance, might work well. Depending on their experiences and associations, clusters might include any of the following: *snow, ice, steel, sneeze, stare, chill, shiver, goosebumps, frost.* The cluster might also include places or people. Have students choose five of the words from their clusters that are most suggestive to them; they may choose one branch of the cluster or words from several different branches.

Next, ask students to use each of the five words as a different section heading, using white space to separate each segment, and to write a short vignette under each word. One vignette might be a memory, another might be a character sketch of an especially "cold" person, another might be a philosophical reflection on ice, and still another might be a description of goosebumps. The sense of coldness will provide overall coherence to the essay, and the associations students make through repeating imagery of coldness will enhance cohesion.

After writing this piece, students will have created a segmented essay. They can now try a word of their own choosing as the center word for their cluster and the organizational center of their essay. They can include as many sections as they desire in their next piece, and they can experiment with different patterns of arrangement in organizing their material.

TECHNIQUES OF EDITING AND PLANNING

Although arrangement in creative nonfiction essays tends to be somewhat organic, much of this chapter addresses methods of arrangement that are "transcendent"; that is, they prefigure the essays patterned on them. Some rhetoricians call these arrangements generative, on the theory that form can help generate content. Some of the prescriptive arrangements we have seen are fairly flexible, but many teachers distrust the idea of prescriptive or transcendent arrangements. Rather than using preexisting arrangements, such teachers subscribe to the organic model of composition, one in which invention, arrangement, and style are informed by writers' perceptions of their subject, purpose, and audience. Most mature writers do compose organically, but it can be argued that they do so because they have completely internalized prescriptive forms. In any case, many teachers continue to offer students section-by-section prescriptive arrangements; otherwise, they may feel they have little more to offer than vague maxims: "organize your points clearly," "strive for unity, order, and coherence," and "don't ramble or digress."

As a teacher, you *can* offer students sound advice without being prescriptive. Following are some techniques for editing and rearranging sections.

Using the Outline in the Classroom

Outlines can be used successfully as an editorial or revision technique, rather than as a tool for generating and arranging material initially. After all, writing is an epistemological tool, and composition researchers are proving that writing is a way of knowing. As the famous E. M. Forster quotation goes, "How can I know what I think until I see what I say?"

Many successful writers draw up an ordered list of topics before they write, but the list is more note-taking for possibilities than it is any kind of set plan. Many teachers, therefore, suggest that their students turn to ordering lists or brainstorming lists for the generative part of the composing process, and then use outlines in the editing stage of composition.

The two most useful sorts of outlines for composition are the *topic outline* and its more complex sibling, the *topic-sentence outline*. The topic outline, as its name suggests, is a listing of the sections of the proposed essay, its topics and their subtopics, with a key word or a short clause attached to each letter or number as a designation of content. For the topic-sentence outline, the writer creates a topic sentence for each paragraph in the proposed essay and orders these topic sentences as the topics and subtopics of the essay; thus the major and minor ideas of the essay can be ranked according to their importance or the writer's purpose.

As you may imagine, this second sort of outline is extremely difficult to create beforehand. Yet both these outlines can be turned around and written after the first draft of the essay has been completed. What were once devices for creating frustration can become easily usable and illuminating tools for editing. If your students have initial difficulties coming up with outlines for their own work, you can ask them to create an outline from a text written by someone else. A possible topic outline to use as an example could be extrapolated from William Zinsser's "College Pressures," which uses methods of classification and division and cause and effect. For the purpose of this example, we focus mainly on classification, though cause and effect will become evident in the expansion of the topic outline:

- Introduction — four kinds of pressures
- Classification 1: economic pressure
- Classification 2: parental pressure
- Classification 3: peer pressure
- Classification 4: self-induced pressure
- Conclusion — four kinds of pressures

From this simple topic outline, each idea can be expanded into a topic sentence:

- There are four types of pressures that university students face.
- Because of economic pressures, students pursue safe subjects and high grades rather than intellectual curiosity.
- Parental pressures often lead students to pursue careers that offer prestige and money rather than personal fulfillment.
- Competition with classmates raises the bar, and students feel compelled to do more.
- As a result of heightened competition, students put too much pressure on themselves.
- All these pressures put together often cause students a great deal of anxiety.

Though both the simple topic outline and the expanded sentence outline are based on a reading of Zinsser's essay, after working through the process, students will be ready to create outlines of their own essays. Example 7.3 will walk you through the steps.

Example 7.3 **HELPING STUDENTS CREATE AN OUTLINE OF A DRAFT ESSAY**

After your students complete their first drafts using one of the forms of arrangement (either one covered in this chapter or one proceeding intuitively), ask them to draw up an outline of the paragraphs in their drafts. Do not insist on sets and subsets at this point; merely suggest a numbered list, each number representing a paragraph. After each number, the student should write a short sentence summarizing the paragraph.

After each paragraph has been thus represented and charted, each student will have what is in essence a map of the argument of the essay. At this point, have students meet in peer-response groups to exchange lists and discuss them for ten minutes or so. Questions to be asked about each list include the following:

1. Are there any paragraphs or topics that don't seem to relate well to the development of the subject?
2. Is there anything that should be cut?
3. Might one or several paragraphs work better in another position in the essay?
4. Is there any important part of the essay that seems to be missing?

After writing and discussing their outlines, students will have a much clearer idea of what changes need to be made in the paragraph arrangement of a rough draft. Generally, adding a few paragraphs and cutting or rearranging a few others will be the result, yielding a much more conscientiously organized final draft. The practice that the students will get in paragraph-level transitions is an extra bonus.

The same sort of after-the-fact outlining can also be done using the simpler topic outline, but the sentence outline produces clearer realizations about what the writer is saying as the argument proceeds.

Using Winterowd's "Grammar of Coherence" Technique in the Classroom

In "The Grammar of Coherence," W. Ross Winterowd argues that beyond the sentence level — that is, at the level of paragraphs and essay-units (what Willis Pitkin calls "discourse blocs") — *transitions* control coherence (830). Form and coherence, says Winterowd, are synonymous at the paragraph and discourse-bloc level, and we perceive coherence as consistent relationships among transitions. Thus, recognizing and controlling these transitional relationships are important skills for students, and the editorial technique that can promote them is implicit in Winterowd's discussion.

Winterowd identifies (and names) seven transitional relationships among parts of an essay (see Box 7.4). The application of knowledge of these seven relationships can help students order the parts of their essays. Winterowd suggests that this list of transitional relationships can be used for many generative and analytic purposes, but here we examine it as a tool for maintaining coherence among the parts of an essay.

To use this list for maintaining coherence, first introduce your students to the transitional concepts, using illustrative handouts. Winterowd suggests that these concepts are much more easily illustrated than defined or explained, especially for beginning writers. A look through any readily available anthology of essays will usually provide good material for examples. Choose blocks of two or three paragraphs — the shorter the better. After talking for a few minutes about the transitional relationships in the examples, ask students to do a short imitation exercise as homework, copying the transitional form of several of the examples while substituting their own content. The next step is to go directly to the anthology and work orally on the transitional links between paragraphs. By this time, students should be able to manipulate the terms fairly confidently.

After the imitation exercise and class work have been completed, ask students to bring to class one of the essays they have already written and had evaluated. Then ask them to go over the essay, marking each paragraph as it relates to the previous one. Each paragraph will be marked *alternativity, causativity*, and so forth. After the imitation practice, this task is not as hard as it sounds; most students will see the transitional relationships fairly easily. There will, of course, be the occasional mystery paragraph, which students can discuss with a friend or with the entire class. This exercise provides students with an immediate method for analyzing their essays for coherence and for learning to strike or regroup selected paragraphs that have no observable relation to the surrounding paragraphs.

Box 7.4 **WINTEROWD'S SEVEN TRANSITIONAL RELATIONSHIPS**

Coordination: expressed by the terms *and, furthermore, too, in addition, also, again*

Obversativity: expressed by *but, yet, however, on the other hand*

Causativity: expressed by *for, because, as a result*

Conclusativity: expressed by *so, therefore, thus, for this reason*

Alternativity: expressed by *or*

Inclusativity: expressed by a colon

Sequentiality: expressed by *first...second...third, earlier...later, and so forth*

After having practiced this exercise on finished essays, your students should be ready to use the method on rough drafts of in-progress essays. Winterowd's system works well for checking arrangements already generated. You may want to ask your students to work in writing groups to check one another's essays for transitional relationships between paragraphs. Although essays with clear transitions between paragraphs and between blocks of discourse may have other problems, they will generally be coherent. Continually using this method in class will help students gain an intuitive grasp of transitions that will prove beneficial in the drafting process.

WORKS CITED

Aristotle. *Poetics*. Trans. S. H. Butcher. *Criticism: The Major Texts*. Ed. W. J. Bate. New York: Harcourt, 1970.

———. *Rhetoric*. Trans. Rhys Roberts. New York: Modern Library, 1954.

Baker, Sheridan. *The Practical Stylist*. 3rd ed. New York: Crowell, 1969.

Blair, Hugh. *Lectures on Rhetoric and Belles-Lettres*. 1783. Philadelphia: Zell, 1866.

Burke, Kenneth. *Counter-Statement*. Los Altos: Hermes, 1953.

Cicero. *De Partitione Oratoria*. Trans. H. Rackham. London: Heinemann, 1960.

Corbett, Edward P. J. *Classical Rhetoric for the Modern Student*. 3rd ed. New York: Oxford UP, 1990.

Corbett, Edward P. J., and Robert J. Connors. *Classical Rhetoric for the Modern Student*. 4th ed. New York: Oxford UP, 1999.

D'Angelo, Frank J. *A Conceptual Theory of Rhetoric*. Cambridge: Winthrop, 1975.

———. *Process and Thought in Composition*. Cambridge: Winthrop, 1977.

DePeter, Ronald A. "Fractured Narratives: Explorations in Style." *Elements of Alternate Style*. Ed. Wendy Bishop. Portsmouth: Boynton/Cook, 1997. 26–34.

Elbow, Peter. *Everyone Can Write*. New York: Oxford UP, 2000.

Faery, Rebecca Blevins. "Text and Context: The Essay and the Politics of Disjunctive Form." *What Do I Know? Reading, Writing, and Teaching the Essay*. Ed. Janis Forman. Portsmouth: Boynton/Cook, 1996. 55–68.

Fontaine, Sheryl I., and Francie Quaas. "Transforming Connections and Building Bridges: Assigning Reading, and Evaluating the Collage Essay." *Teaching Writing Creatively*. Ed. David Starkey. Portsmouth: Boynton/Cook, 1998. 111–25.

Glenn, Cheryl. *Making Sense*, 2nd edition. Boston: Bedford / St. Martin's, 2005.

Golden, James, and Edward P. J. Corbett. *The Rhetoric of Blair, Campbell, and Whately*. Carbondale: Southern Illinois UP, 1990.

Griffin, Susan. *The Eros of Everyday Life*. New York: Doubleday, 1995.

Hall, Donald. *Writing Well*. 2nd ed. Boston: Little, 1976.

Hampl, Patricia. "Memory and Imagination." *The Fourth Genre*. Ed. Robert L. Root Jr. and Michael Steinberg. Boston: Allyn, 1999. 297–305.

Klaus, Carl. "Excursions of the Mind: Toward a Poetics of Uncertainty in the Disjunctive Essay." *What Do I Know? Reading, Writing, and Teaching the Essay*. Ed. Janis Forman. Portsmouth: Boynton/Cook, 1996. 39–53.

Larson, Richard. "Structure and Form in Non-Fiction Prose." *Teaching Composition: Twelve Bibliographic Essays*. 2nd ed. Ed. Gary Tate. Fort Worth: Texas Christian UP, 1987. 45–72.

Lunsford, Andrea. *The St. Martin's Handbook*. 6th ed. Boston: Bedford / St. Martin's, 2008.

Pitkin, Willis. "Discourse Blocs." *CCC* 20 (1969): 138–48.

Root, Robert L., Jr. "Collage, Montage, Mosaic, Vignette, Episode, Segment." *The Fourth Genre*. Ed. Robert L. Root Jr. and Michael Steinberg. Boston: Allyn, 1999. 358–68.

Rudman, Mark. "Mosaic on Walking." The Best American Essays 1991. Ed. Joyce Carol Oates. Boston: Ticknor and Fields, 1991: 138–53.

Whately, Richard. *Elements of Rhetoric*. 6th ed. London: Fellowes, 1841.

Willard, Nancy. "The Friendship Tarot." *Between Friends*. Ed. Mickey Pearlman. Boston: Houghton, 1994. 195–203.

Winterowd, W. Ross. "The Grammar of Coherence." *CE* 31 (1970): 828–35.

Zinsser, William. "College Pressures. From *Blair and Ketchum's Country Journal*, Vol. 6, No. 4, April 1979.

——. *On Writing Well*. 3rd ed. New York: Harper, 1985.

8

Teaching Style

I ask my students, "Would you wear the same clothes to accompany your grandmother to your cousin's wedding as you would to accompany your friends to a rock concert? It depends on who has to look at you." I want my students to understand that style is not just ornamentation or some kind of special genius that comes from inside, but that it's real stuff. They can touch it. They can try on different ones.

−STEVE THOMAS

Once considered little more than the study of schemes, tropes, and rhetorical flourishes, style has become one of the most important canons of rhetoric — at least, Edward P. J. Corbett tells us, if success is measured by the sheer number of works published ("Approaches" 83). Besides Corbett, who has written a classic work on stylistic analysis, other scholars have taken the study of style into the realms of poetry, creative nonfiction, and other forms of literary writing. Style also lurks behind much contemporary deconstructive and reader-response literary criticism, and cultural critics have considered the socioeconomic ramifications of style and revision, deepening our understanding of the connections among style, substance, and meaning along historical as well as contemporary continua. Lisa Ede, Cheryl Glenn, and Andrea Lunsford, in an article that explores connections between feminism and rhetoric, define style as "the material embodiment of the relationships among self, text, and world" (423). One goal of teaching style in your writing classes is to help students explore these relationships through writing.

Style, in other words, is not just "style." All composition teachers can benefit from a background in stylistics, and one of the easiest ways to obtain such a background is to borrow the duality that W. Ross Winterowd creates in *Contemporary Rhetoric.* Winterowd divides the study of style into two areas: *theoretical stylistics,* concerned primarily with the nature and existence of style, the application of stylistic criteria to literary studies, and the linguistic attributes of different styles; and *pedagogic stylistics,* which deals with the problem of teaching students to recognize and develop styles in their own writing (252). This chapter deals almost completely with works on pedagogic stylistics, which are far fewer in number than works in the fascinating — but not always classroom-practical — field of theoretical stylistics.

STYLE: THEORY AND PEDAGOGIC PRACTICE

Milic's Three Theories of Style

Perhaps the central theoretical problem presented by the study of style is the question of whether style as an entity really exists. Is it, as Chatman and Levin claim, "the totality of impressions which a literary work produces," or is it merely "sundry and ornamental linguistic devices" tacked on to a given content-meaning (*Literary Style* 337–38)? There is no agreement at all on this question among the foremost theorists of style in our time, yet all writing teachers must answer this question for themselves before they can decide on a teaching method.

Three distinct views of the nature of style have emerged, says the eminent theorist Louis T. Milic, who identifies and describes these views in "Theories of Style and Their Implications for the Teaching of Composition" (126). Milic's first theory, given the daunting name *Crocean aesthetic monism,* is based on the critical theories of twentieth-century Italian philosopher Benedetto Croce. Milic writes that Crocean aesthetic monism, the most modern theory of style,

> is an organic view which denies the possibility of any separation between content and form. Any discussion of style in Croce's view is useless and irrelevant, for the work or art (the composition) is a unified whole, with no seam between meaning and style. ("Theories" 67)

In Crocean theory, then, the sentences *John gave me the book* and *The book was given to me by John* have different semantic meanings as well as different syntactic forms.

The second theory is what Milic calls *individualist* or *psychological monism* and is best summed up by the famous aphorism of the French naturalist Georges de Buffon, *"Le style c'est l'homme même,"* usually translated as "Style is the man." Psychological monism holds that a writer cannot help writing the way he does for that is the dynamic expression of his personality. This theory claims that no writer can truly imitate another's style, for no two life experiences are the same; it further holds that the main formative influences on writers are their education and their reading ("Typology of Styles" 442). Both the psychological and the Crocean theories are monisms in that they perceive style and content as a unity, inseparable from each other, either because different locutions say different things or because an individual's style is her habitual and consistent selection from the expressive resources available in language, which is not consciously amendable to any great degree.

The third theory of style, and the one most applicable to teaching, is what Milic calls the *theory of ornate form,* or *rhetorical dualism.* The assumption behind rhetorical dualism is that "ideas exist wordlessly and can be dressed in a variety of outfits depending on the need or the occasion" ("Theories" 67). As the critic Michael Riffaterre puts it, "Style is understood as an emphasis (expressive, affective, or aesthetic) added to the information conveyed by the linguistic structure, without alteration of meaning." In other words, "language expresses and style stresses" (Riffaterre 443).

Milic points out that the two monisms make the teaching of style a rather hopeless enterprise, since for the Croceans, there is no "style," form and content being one; and for the individualists, style is an expression of personality, and we cannot expect writers to change their personality. These monisms render all of the resources of rhetoric useless ("Theories" 69). In order to retain options, then, teachers must be dualists, at least to some degree. Although dualistic theory cannot be proved true empirically, it still seems to be the only approach we have to improving students' writing style. If we cannot tell a student that the struggle to find the best words to express an idea is a real struggle, then we cannot teach style at all.

A confessed individualist himself, Milic is aware that dualism must be adopted at least conditionally if we are to teach style. In an important essay, "Rhetorical Choice and Stylistic Option," he tries to resolve the division between his beliefs and the pedagogic options offered by dualism. He argues that most of what we call style is actually the production of a huge unconscious element that he terms the *language-generating mechanism.* This mechanism, processing subconscious choices and operating at a speed that the conscious mind cannot possibly match, creates most of what we call style. After these decisions have been made, an editing process takes over that can make any stylistic changes the author consciously desires.

Milic distinguishes between *stylistic options,* decisions made unconsciously while the language-generating mechanism is proceeding, and *rhetorical choices,* decisions made consciously while the mechanism is at rest. Rhetorical choices, in other words, are an evaluation of what has been intuitively created by the language-generating mechanism, an editorial element that can be practiced consciously and thus something we can teach our students. Of course, certain rhetorical choices can become habits of mind and thus stylistic options. The process of adding to the repertoire of the language-generating mechanism is what we hope to accomplish. Milic thus seems to integrate successfully his roles as theorist and teacher.

In this chapter, then, we focus on rhetorical choices because they are the only elements of style that can be handled consciously. In the realm of pedagogic stylistics, we must keep our discussion at a considerably lower level of abstraction than is characteristic of most of the works mentioned by Corbett in his bibliographic essay "Approaches to the Study of Style." The possibilities of our changing a student's style in ten or fifteen weeks are limited; Milic tells us that the process of learning to write takes a dozen years and must begin much earlier than age eighteen. Style is the hardest canon to teach, linked as it is to reading. Only avid and accomplished readers can generate and perceive style, recognizing it in a contextual continuum. The more models and styles a writer knows or is aware of, the more raw data there are to feed the language-generating mechanism and the more informed are the choices that can be made both intuitively and consciously.

A Pedagogic Focus on Rhetorical Choices

So, how do we teach style? In "Teaching Style: A Possible Anatomy," Winston Weathers mentions several obligatory tasks for those who aim to teach style at the college level. The first task is "making the teaching of style significant and relevant for our students" (144). Many beginning writers view the concept of style with suspicion, as if it were something that only effete snobs should be interested in. Thus, Weathers tells us, it is our task to justify the study of style on the grounds of better communication and as a proof of individuality. Style can be taught as a gesture of personal freedom or as a rebellion against rigid systems of conformist language, rather than as dainty humanism or mere aesthetic luxury.

Students convinced that style is indeed a gesture of personal freedom will invest maximum effort in stylistic concerns. Bill Roorbach, in *Writing Life Stories,* wants students to learn about style by "forgetting about style." He writes:

> In this exercise you are to throw a fit.... Break the bass drum of your punctuation with the pedal of your adjectives. Ram your stout verb sticks through your adverbial tom-toms. Nix prolixity. Fling symbols out the windows; listen to the crash. (140)

Of course, this exercise does anything but convince students to forget about style. Rather, it helps students to play with language and interrogate their own preconceived notions of what "style" means.

The second task Weathers mentions is that of revealing style as a measurable and viable subject matter. Style seems vague and mysterious to many beginning writers because they have mostly been exposed to the metaphysical approach to style, in which arbitrarily chosen adjectives are used to identify different styles — the "abrupt," the "tense," the "fast-moving," the "leisurely," and the popular "flowing" styles. As a result of hearing styles described in these nebulous terms, students cannot see how such an amorphous entity might be approached or changed. Therefore, they need to be exposed to the actual components, the nuts and bolts, of style — words, phrases, clauses, sentences, paragraphs — and to the methods of analyzing them before they can begin to use them to control their rhetorical options.

For example, in writing the preceding exercise, Roorbach does not forget about style at all, for the assignment itself is ripe for stylistic analysis. You might ask students first to identify Roorbach's tone (colloquial in most parts; angry or violent, perhaps) and then to consider how he achieves that tone through the rhetorical choices he makes: using short imperative and declarative sentences; starting sentences with monosyllabic, active (not to mention violent) verbs; incorporating metaphors; being attentive to sound (such as the onomatopoeia of "crash" and the near rhyme of "fling symbols out the windows"). Students will quickly see that "getting mad" on the page involves many stylistic choices. As teachers, we have important tools for explaining these stylistic features.

In "A Primer for Teaching Style," Richard Graves tells us that the following four explanatory methods are primary:

1. We can identify the technical name of a particular stylistic feature or concept.
2. We can give a definition or description of the feature.

3. We can provide a schematic description of the feature.
4. We can provide an example or illustration of the feature. (187)

The goals of these methods are recognition and then gradual mastery of the different features. Explanations such as this one can be used in both stylistic analyses and exercises in imitation, the central practical activities described in this chapter. In addition to demonstrating discrete skills, though, every essay a student writes must be informed by certain questions of style. Like the other canons of rhetoric, style must be approached philosophically as well as practically.

Choosing a Rhetorical Stance

The study of style needs to be prefaced by a careful discussion of both the purpose of each piece of writing a student does and the interrelationships among author, subject (work), universe, and audience. M. H. Abrams presents a useful diagram of these elements in *The Mirror and the Lamp* (8).

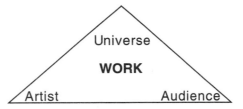

These four elements, based on the rhetorical theory of Aristotle, form a central construct in modern communication theory. Composition teachers use a version of this construct called the *communication triangle* to help students formulate their concepts of the whole rhetorical situation in which they find themselves.

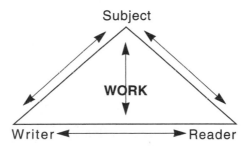

Each of these elements suggests a question that writers must face every time they sit down to write, and a significant factor in each question must necessarily be style. No one factor can predominate in a successful piece of writing, however, and Wayne Booth's famous essay, "The Rhetorical Stance," offers a well-expressed overview of this complexity. The "rhetorical stance" he discusses

depends on discovering and maintaining in any writing situation a proper balance among the three elements that are at work in any communicative effort:

the available arguments about the subject itself, the interests and peculiarities of the audience, and voice, the implied character of the speaker. (74)

A "corruption" of the rhetorical stance, according to Booth, overemphasizes any one of the three elements of the communication triangle of author-audience-subject. Students' compositions are prone to all three sorts of corruptions or imbalances.

One type of imbalance, the *pedant's stance*, occurs when the writer concentrates only on the subject while ignoring the author-audience relationship. This reliance on nothing but subject-based discourse makes the pedant's stance dry and uninteresting. It makes no concessions to a personal voice or to the reader's interest. It is the sort of depersonalized prose that students often think their teachers want to hear. Ken Macrorie's famous term for it is *Engfish,* and it is found in its purest form at a relatively high academic level — as "dissertation style."

Example: One may observe an attempt at the pedant's stance in this sentence; note how the formal tone distances the reader.

Another sort of imbalance is the *advertiser's stance,* which concentrates on impressing the audience and underplays the subject. This imbalance is not so frequent as the pedant's stance, mainly because only experienced writers will attempt it. Booth tells us that the "advertiser" overvalues pure effect. Student "advertisers" are likely to write directly to the teacher, attempting to charm by using candor, humor, or personal attention — often a novel experience for the teacher.

Example: Have you ever wondered what the advertiser's stance might look like in a sentence? Sure you have. We all have; haven't we?

Related to the advertiser's stance is the *entertainer's stance,* which "sacrifices substance to personality and charm" (78). An imbalance in favor of the speaker's ethical appeal, this stance is the rarest corruption of the rhetorical stance found in student's essays. Most students are unaware of the methods used by writers to generate ethical appeal; hence, their imbalances are likely to tilt in other directions. Many FY writers were taught in high school never to use *I* in their writing — the key word of the entertainer's stance.

Example: I want so much to show you what it means to write from an entertainer's stance, but I feel it's far more important to be true to my own voice, my own style.

Booth's questions of rhetorical balance are essential to an understanding of the methods available for the manipulation of stylistic choices. The question of the relationship between writer and subject is important, but more central to students' understanding of style will be the question of their relationships as writers to their audience — an audience that, in the final analysis, will usually be composed only of you, their teacher. Obviously, students will attempt to choose a style that will suit their identified readership, and the voice they choose for a letter to a close friend will be very different from the one they choose for an essay to be read by their English teacher. But the danger of artificiality in the voice chosen for the essay is all too real.

Considering the Audience for Student Essays

Teachers and scholars have explored the problem of the teacher as the final audience for student-written texts by trying to create other plausible audiences, with the most obvious sorts of such assignments being letters to the editor of a local newspaper, letters to the president of the United States or to the university or college president. Some assignments have been created that specify a complex writing situation, complete with subject and audience; one example is an assignment that asks students to define and give examples of "conventional diction" to a group of ninth-grade French students who know basic English but who need more information about how Americans really use it.

The problem with these plausible or created audiences (not including the ethical problems some teachers have with the artificial aspect of hypothetical audiences) stems from the fact that the students are always aware that behind the "editor" or the "French students" stands the teacher, who ultimately wields the power of the grade. This awareness makes the assignment even more complex. The student knows that in reality she is writing the way the teacher thinks the student should write to the editor or for ninth graders, not the way the student really would write to them. In other words, a student must try to write for another person's concept of a fictional audience. It is no wonder that students often freeze solidly into take-no-chances dullness in such assignments.

The alternative, to specify no audience at all, leaves the student in a simpler — but no less difficult — situation. Most FY students, accustomed to the rich contextual responses of oral communication, find it difficult to conceptualize the abstract, fictionalized "universal audience" that the Belgian rhetorician Chaim Perelman says is the ultimate audience for written discourse (402).

FY students also have trouble adjusting their styles, which may be sharp and skillful at the oral level, to what seem to them the difficult conventions of non-contextual written discourse. As a result, they tend to write pedantically, on the assumptions that stressing the subject is the safest thing to do and that as college students they need to sound "grown-up." They cannot create a fictional audience easily, so they tend to write into the void.

The problem of audience is not easily solved, since both overspecification and underspecification of audience can have unfortunate consequences. One compromise is to admit that the teacher is the audience and to attempt to work accordingly. However, if you choose to specify an audience other than yourself, you'll need to imaginatively place yourself in the position of that audience, considering the various factors that would influence how that audience would likely receive the writer's text. A related option, especially if you allow students to choose their own topics and forms, is to have students identify their own audience. Students can be asked to carefully weigh all the elements of the rhetorical situation (including, among other factors, style and audience) and to report on their attention to these elements by providing answers to the questions in Example 8.1 with their final drafts. Your task as teacher would thus be to evaluate the extent to which the piece of writing works, given the rhetorical situation the student has imagined.

Example 8.1   **REPORTING ON THE RHETORICAL SITUATION**

1. What is your subject?
2. What audience are you addressing?
3. What exigence are you responding to? (the "so what?" question)
4. What is your purpose?
5. What genre or form have you chosen to deliver your message?
6. What specific rhetorical strategies (including stylistic features) will help you achieve your purpose?

LEVELS OF STYLE

Intimately related to the question of audience is the concept of different levels of style. Cicero mentions the high, middle, and low styles of oratory and suggests that each has its place and purpose. In the early days of teaching composition, however, this sort of liberalism was supplanted by prescriptive judgments about the different levels of style. Style was either right or wrong, correct or incorrect, and in general only an attempt to write in a high, "literary" style was acceptable. Gradually, this dichotomy between good and bad gave way to the three hierarchical levels of style that many of us were raised on: formal or literary style; informal or colloquial style; and vulgar or illiterate style. Of the three, only formal style was considered proper for writing; the other two instead reflected the way people talk or the style of letters to friends. (The vulgar style was how *they* talked, not how *we* talk.) Toward the middle of the twentieth century, this hierarchy was liberalized, becoming a continuum from which any stylistic form could be chosen (Marckwardt viii).

Certain levels of stylistic formality *do* correspond better than others to the needs and perceptions of readers of particular genres. Contemporary writers of the personal essay, for example, tend to choose a style somewhere between colloquial and formal. And those writing articles or academic arguments tend to choose a more formal style. For this reason, we can — depending on the form and context — teach a particular level of style not as more correct but as more appropriate for specific rhetorical situations, knowing that the level of style will change depending on the writer's purpose, the reader's expectations, the demands of the form, and the context. See Example 8.2 for an exercise designed to help you discuss the nature and effects of different levels of style.

Example 8.2 **STYLE TRANSLATIONS**

1. To discuss and demonstrate different levels of style, ask students to bring in samples of various kinds of discourse: a business letter, an email from a friend, the transcript from an online chat, the most recent State of the Union Address, and excerpts from personal essays and theoretical articles.

2. Have students read and discuss their samples in small groups, seeking to name the level of style each writer uses.

3. Then ask students to translate one or two passages into a style different from the one in which it was originally written. If the piece was formal, for example, ask students to translate it into more colloquial language.

4. Have them read their translations to the class.

5. Discuss the challenges students faced with their translations, including how meaning changed (or didn't change) depending on the level of style.

In *Style: An Anti-Textbook,* Richard Lanham condemns the utilitarian prose and the "plain style" most commonly taught in FY writing classes, asserting that language as play should be the key concept in composition classes. "Style," says Lanham, "must be taught for and as what it is — a pleasure, a grace, a joy, a delight" (20). Given the limitations under which most writing teachers labor, you may not get that far. Students cannot learn to control style in three or four months, but if you provide them with good models and classroom exercises, they will become aware of style as a concrete, often controllable entity.

EXERCISES FOR DEVELOPING STYLE

Most FY students declare that they have no writing style — that mysterious "extra" quality that only professional writers possess. It's no wonder they feel this way: Even if they have been introduced to style, the introduction was probably to literary style, a vague quality described by their teacher as "vigorous" or "curt" or "smooth" that can be found only in the writing of Hawthorne or Baldwin or Woolf. Style, nebulous and qualitative, is not to be found in students' writing — so they think.

As Winston Weathers points out, though, "improvement in student style comes not by osmosis, but through exercises" ("Teaching Style" 146). Classroom practice helps reinforce the notion that no writer, not even a student writer, is a prisoner of unchangeable ways of writing. By introducing students to the exercises included here, you can begin to make style understandable to your students and demonstrate that they, too, can develop their own style. (For detailed information on conducting stylistic analyses of both student and professional writing, see Corbett and Connors, cited at the end of this chapter.)

IMITATION

Hans Ostrom, in " 'Carom Shots': Reconceptualizing Imitation and Its Uses in Creative Writing Courses," discusses the ideological and pedagogical reservations many teachers of writing and literature have about imitation. Some teachers want to empower students by helping them find "their own voices," rather than imitating others' writing; others want to venerate "great authors" and keep students from messing with supposed perfection. Many teachers value "originality" and find imitation exercises suspect. While we don't advocate asking students to imitate someone else's work to the point that they begin to write and sound exclusively like their favorite author, we do recognize the value of imitation for helping students expand their own stylistic repertoires.

Different imitation techniques, whether they consist of direct copying, composition based on models, or controlled mutation of sentence structures, all have one thing in common: they lead students to internalize the structures of the piece being imitated. With those structures internalized, a student is free to make the informed choices that are the wellspring of creativity. William Gruber puts it succinctly when he suggests that imitation does not affect creativity but assists in design:

> Standing behind imitation as a teaching method is the simple assumption that an inability to write is an inability to design — an inability to shape effectively the thought of a sentence, a paragraph, or an essay. (493–94)

Imitation exercises provide students with practice in that "ability to design" that is the basis of a mature prose style.

Using Imitation Exercises in the Classroom

Edward P. J. Corbett's central statement on imitation and a large number of exercises in copying and creative imitation are found in his *Classical Rhetoric for the Modern Student*. Corbett recommends several different sorts of exercises, the first and simplest of which involves "copying passages, word for word, from admired authors" (424). This task is not quite as simple as it may seem, though; Corbett offers the following rules to help students derive benefit from this exercise:

1. You must not spend more than fifteen or twenty minutes copying at any one time. If you extend this exercise much beyond twenty minutes at any one sitting, your attention will begin to wander, and you will find yourself merely copying words.

2. You must do this copying with a pencil or pen. [Keyboarding] is so fast and so mechanical that you can copy off whole passages without paying any attention to the features of an author's style. Copying by hand, you transcribe the passage at such a pace that you have time to observe the choice and disposition of words, the patterns of sentences, and the length and variety of sentences.

3. You must not spend too much time with any one author. If you concentrate on a single author's style, you may find yourself falling into the "servile imitation" that rhetoricians warned of. The aim of this exercise is not to acquire someone else's style but to lay the groundwork for developing your own style by getting the "feel" of a variety of styles.

4. You must read the entire passage before starting to copy it so that you can capture the thought and the manner of the passage as a whole. When you are copying, it is advisable to read each sentence through before transcribing it. After you have finished copying the passage, you should read your transcription so that you once again get a sense of the passage as a whole.

5. You must copy the passage slowly and accurately. If you are going to dash through this exercise, you might as well not do it at all. A mechanical way of insuring accuracy...is to make your handwriting as legible as you can. (*Classical Rhetoric* 425)

Corbett provides a number of specimens for imitation in *Classical Rhetoric,* prose styles ranging from the King James Bible to Mary Wollstonecraft's *Vindication of the Rights of Women* to Alice Walker's *The Color Purple.*

For students who have spent some time copying passages, Corbett recommends a second kind of imitation exercise, *pattern practice.* In this, students choose or are given single sentences to use as patterns, after which they design sentences of their own. "The aim of this exercise," says Corbett, "is not to achieve a word-for-word correspondence with the model but rather to achieve an awareness of the variety of sentence structure of which the English language is capable" (*Classical Rhetoric* 443). The model sentences need not be followed slavishly, but Corbett suggests that the student observe at least the same kind, number, and order of phrases and clauses. Here are a few of Corbett's model sentences and examples of imitations:

MODEL SENTENCE: He went through the narrow alley of Temple Bar quickly, muttering to himself that they could all go to hell because he was going to have a good night of it. –James Joyce, "Counterparts"
IMITATION: They stood outside on the wet pavement of the terrace, pretending that they had not heard us when we called to them from the library.

MODEL SENTENCE: To regain the stage in its own character, not as a mere emulation of prose, poetry must find its own poetic way to the mastery the stage demands — the mastery of action. –Archibald MacLeish, "The Poet as Playwright"
IMITATION: To discover our own natures, not the personalities imposed on us by others, we must honestly assess the values we cherish — in short, our "philosophy of life. " (*Classical Rhetoric* 444–45)

The kind of imitation that Ostrom advocates is less structured than Corbett's exercises. Ostrom emphasizes that the imitation assignments he gives students are "different from an 'apprentice's' modeling of a 'master's' work" (167). His method of imitation is "more of a carom shot, one text playing off another" (167). He illustrates it by explaining his combined use of imitation and micronarration in a fiction writing course: After students read Gertrude Stein, for example, they write micro-stories (short fictions of one or two pages) that "jazz around with language in some way, not necessarily Stein's way" (167). He discusses how this exercise encourages students to see texts as invitations "to manipulate language in a similar way" (168). Combined with Corbett's methods for analyzing a text's stylistic features, Ostrom's method of imitation can help students first learn to articulate what is going on stylistically in another person's text and then to work on style in their own writing.

Such exercises in imitation can also help students begin to understand the context in which they create writing. Without knowledge of what has been done by others, there can be no profound originality. Speaking of his own instruction through the use of imitation, Winston Churchill said, "Thus I got into my bones the essential structure of the ordinary British sentence — which is a noble thing." If you can help your students get the structure of ordinary sentences "into their bones," the time and effort you devote to imitation exercises will be worthwhile.

There are many ways to introduce imitation exercises into a FY class, and you can decide how you wish to approach them based on the amount of time you have available. Some kinds of imitation can be done as homework, but others require the sort of encouragement that you can provide only in a classroom. One important point applies to all sorts of imitation, however: If you choose to use this technique, be prepared to work with it throughout the entire term to gain benefits from it. Donna Gorrell's *Copy/Write*, Winston Weathers's *An Alternate Style*, David Starkey's collection *Teaching Writing Creatively*, and Wendy Bishop's collection *Elements of an Alternate Style* provide additional ideas and exercises.

You may encounter some resistance in teaching imitation. Some students are initially suspicious of the method, seeing it as a block to their originality. They may balk at the rigidity of some of the exercises. Higher-level students sometimes see it as beneath their capacities (and obviously, for some students, it will be). Other students, however, delight in what imitation has to offer: a chance to write differently, to break tired habits of writing they may have fallen into. While some students will struggle, others will flourish. To help those who struggle with imitation, ask for volunteers to read both original passages and their imitations aloud in class.

In teaching imitation, you will have to keep reminding your students of the two criteria for success: (1) the more removed the new content is from that of the original, the better the imitation will be; and (2) the structure of an imitation should coincide perfectly with the given rhetorical model. Asking students to revise something they've already written will almost always guarantee that the content differs between the imitation and the piece being imitated. In Example 8.3 students are asked to produce distinctive imitations.

Example 8.3   **AN EXERCISE IN IMITATION, REVISION, AND REFLECTION**

- Choose a passage (two paragraphs or so) from a favorite prose writer's work.
- Copy the passage by hand, paying particular attention to sentence patterns.
- Now choose a passage from an essay you have written.
- Rewrite your own passage using the exact same sentence structures (and order) used by your favorite author in the passage you copied.
- Then write a paragraph reflecting on the choices and changes you made in revising your work in terms of another writer's sentence patterns. What did you add? What did you cut? Did this exercise make you think about your own style in a different way?

LANGUAGE VARIETY

In her often anthologized essay "Mother Tongue," Chinese American writer Amy Tan writes, "Language is the tool of my trade. And I use them all — all the Englishes I grew up with" (147). Later in the essay, she lists some of the Englishes she uses in her novel *The Joy Luck Club:*

> . . . the English I spoke to my mother, which for lack of a better term might be described as "simple"; the English she used with me, which for lack of a better term might be described as "broken"; my translation of her Chinese, which could certainly be described as "watered down"; and what I imagined to be her translation of her Chinese if she could speak in perfect English, her internal language, and for that I sought to preserve the essence, but neither an English nor a Chinese structure. (152)

Even if English is, for most of your students, their first language, they most likely speak — and possibly write — several varieties of English. Because students may not, at first, understand what you mean by "varieties of language," it's helpful to provide examples.

In *The St. Martin's Handbook,* Andrea Lunsford encourages her readers to recognize the characteristics of particular *geographic regions,* of particular *occupations or professions,* [and] of particular *social, cultural, or ethnic groups* (519). Although there are other varieties of English — and you can ask your students to think of additional categories — these three groupings provide a fitting starting place for examples:

- In her essay "On a Hill Far Away," Annie Dillard writes of talking with a young boy in rural Virginia: " 'Do you know how to catch a fish when you haven't got a rod, or a line, or a hook?'. He was smiling, warming up for a little dialect, being a kid in a book. He must read a lot. 'First, you get you a *stick. . . .*' He explained what sort of stick. 'Then you pull you a thread of honey-suckle...and if you need a *hook. . . .*'" (82).

- In "Testimony," a speech that the naturalist and writer Terry Tempest Williams delivered before a congressional subcommittee, students will recognize several occupational languages at work. In the following passage, Williams draws from medical and scientific vocabularies: "I can tell you that my mother, who had ovarian cancer, didn't know she had any more options after a radical hysterectomy, Cytoxan, cisplatin, Adriamycin treatments, and six weeks of radiation therapy had failed to offer her a cure. Pacific yew, *Taxus brevifolia*, taxol were not words in her vocabulary, or in her doctor's vocabulary for that matter" (126).

- Garrett Hongo, in "Kubota," writes about his Hawaiian-born Japanese grandfather and the stories "Kubota" (his grandfather) would tell, including a moral: " 'study *ha-ahd*,' he'd say with pidgin emphasis. 'Learn read good. Learn speak da kine *good* English.' The message is the familiar one taught to [m]any children of immigrants: succeed through education" (69).

In each of these examples, the writers intentionally shift among different varieties of English in order to achieve a particular effect. Utilizing such shifts is one way of affecting style. (It's also important to remember that the issues surrounding language variety are not limited to style; they affect many other aspects of teaching and learning. For more on language variety and diversity, see Chapter 11, "Invitation to Further Study." See also Ball; Ball and Lardner; Delpit and Dowdy; Gilyard; Jordan; and Smitherman, *The Need for Story* and *The Skin That We Speak,* cited at the end of this chapter.)

Such shifts can sometimes be difficult for less experienced writers, and so your students will likely look to you for guidance. As Lunsford explains, "The key to shifting among varieties of English and among languages is appropriateness: when will such a shift reach your audience and help you make a particular point?" (519). In the writing your students will do in your class, much will depend on the forms and genres you ask them to write. For example, if you ask them to write personal essays or other forms of creative nonfiction, it may be appropriate to shift varieties of language through dialogue, for doing so can reveal character. Shifts are also appropriate when students write the kinds of alternate-styled texts we discuss later in this chapter: double-voiced texts, for example, require shifts — often from an academic to a more personal voice. However, if you assign traditional argumentative essays, students will need to know specifically what — if any — place shifting among varieties of English should have in their writing for your class.

In the "Hint Sheet" section of *The Subject Is Writing,* Wendy Bishop offers fifteen prompts to help students consider language communities. We've included several of these questions in Example 8.4 (for the full list, you'll want to consult Bishop's book). You can use these questions as prompts for in-class writing, as journal prompts, or — with some tinkering — even as prompts for fully developed essays.

Example 8.4 **BISHOP'S PROMPTS FOR WRITING ABOUT LANGUAGE COMMUNITIES**

1. What languages do you speak? When do you speak them and to whom?
2. Under what circumstances does your dialect (register, vocabulary) change? Tell a story about this.
3. Do you have a peer group that uses a certain language? Give examples.
4. Do you or someone you know work in a profession with its own language? For instance, what is the language of school? What is the language of therapy? What is advertising language?
5. Have you lost a language? Where, how, why? (*Subject* 209–10)

Teaching an Awareness of Language Variety

Throughout "Mother Tongue," Amy Tan recalls times when she became aware of the particular variety of English she used at any given time. For instance, when her mother attended a talk Tan was giving to an academic audience, Tan became aware of the way "a speech filled with carefully wrought grammatical phrases" suddenly seemed burdened "with nominalized forms, past perfect tenses, conditional phrases, all the forms of standard English [she] had learned in school and through books, the forms of English [she] did not use at home" with her mother (147). Often, we become aware of the many languages we use only when others do not understand what we are trying to say. Example 8.5 lists some questions you can ask students to help them consider the variety of "Englishes" they use. Helping students gain an awareness of their own varieties of language in daily speech can help them use — or not use — such language patterns in their writing.

Example 8.5 **THE "ENGLISHES" YOU SPEAK AND WRITE**

- What words or phrases common in your own vocabulary have others questioned, laughed at, commented on, or not understood? (Examples might range from the regionally influenced "might could have" or "the plants need watered" to terms such as "my bad" or "true that," phrases that have meaning among friends but that may leave parents perplexed.)

- How would you classify these terms and phrases? Which ones are regionally influenced? family influenced? culturally influenced? learned from your peers?
- Which varieties of English do you use in your writing for school? Are there any you'd like to use in your writing that you don't use already? Are there any you use in writing that you'd rather not use?

In "Inviting the Mother Tongue: Beyond 'Mistakes,' 'Bad English,' and 'Wrong Language,' " (*Everyone Can Write*) Peter Elbow describes in personal terms the conflict many writing teachers feel: "On the one hand, I feel an obligation to invite all my students to use their own language and not make them conform to the language and culture of mainstream English" (323). "On the other hand," Elbow continues, "I feel an obligation to give all my students access to the written language of power and prestige" (323). Elbow goes on to observe — as has Geneva Smitherman and other scholars — that the choice does not entail an "either/or" decision. Smitherman argues that the "mother tongue language or dialect...can establish the firm foundation upon which to build and expand the learner's linguistic repertoire" ("National Public Policy" 172). The rhetorical and linguistic habits of various cultures and geographic regions are not only effective forms of communication but can also be stylistically powerful. We need only to look at the work of such writers as Gloria Anzaldúa, Alice Walker, Amy Tan, bell hooks, Zora Neale Hurston, Henry Louis Gates Jr., Geneva Smitherman, and Barbara Mellix, who have a command of both standard English and various dialects (additional "Englishes"), to understand the power of using more than one kind of English in writing. Many of these writers have published essays and books that reflect on the choices they make about language use in writing; these texts can help your students reflect on similar issues as well. (See, for example, Barbara Mellix's "From Outside, In," cited at the end of this chapter.)

You may be thinking, *Okay: I recognize the value of teaching standard English and of encouraging my students to use their home languages in writing, but how do I do both in a one-semester course?* Elbow suggests inviting "students to leave their exercises and low-stakes writing in the home dialect," and on major essays to "invite copy-editing into *two* final drafts: one into correct SWE [standard written English] and one into the best form of the student's home dialect" (342). Another solution is to teach a variety of forms: personal essays that lend themselves to a variety of diverse language uses as well as to the rhetorical/stylistic features of more traditional academic arguments. Alternate-styled texts — such as collage essays and double-voiced texts — allow for additional possibilities, giving students a recognizable form for intentionally shifting between voices or dialects in writing. In any case, the key is to emphasize intention, purpose, context, and audience. That is, whenever students switch among language varieties in their essays, they should have a reason for doing so and an awareness of how such switches might affect their audience.

Language Varieties and Varying Syntax

Related to an awareness of English language varieties is the important stylistic practice of varying syntax. While not all writing teachers want their students to draw from all the varieties of language they have at their disposal (some teachers focus more on teaching a particular kind of academic discourse), nearly all writing teachers look for syntactic variety. You can tell students repeatedly to vary sentence structure, but unless they have models, unless they understand the real effects of rhythm in both speech and writing, they are not likely to understand what you mean — or how they can use certain language patterns to good effect *and* how to change patterns that are not effective.

Language practices that are influenced by factors such as geographic region, ethnicity, or culture can also affect writing at the sentence level, producing a kind of rhythm — for good or ill. Just as rhythm is recognizable in patterns of speech, so it is in patterns of writing at the level of syntax. Bill Roorbach, in *Writing Life Stories,* helps students become more aware of language variety by asking them to be attentive to the rhythm of their writing:

> A sense of rhythm is a cultural sense, a sense of tradition. Do your sentences pick up the cadences of childhood rhymes? Of marching bands? Of biblical phrasing? Of television scripts? Of the squad room? Of a preacher's repetition?...Variety, as in all things, is key. (150)

In other words, rhythm in writing (which is influenced by the structure and length of sentences, word choice, repetition, and punctuation) is in many ways linked to culture and tradition — from what we've internalized from reading, from listening, and from simply living. Example 8.6 shows an exercise that Roorbach uses to help his students practice being attentive to rhythm in their reading and writing and work toward variety in their writing. (For additional exercises on structural variety and rhythm in written discourse, see Chapter 10 in Joe Glaser's *Understanding Style,* cited at the end of this chapter.)

Example 8.6   ROORBACH'S "TAP YOUR FEET" EXERCISE

Pull out the work of a favorite writer, and read it listening and feeling for rhythm and rhythms. Tap your feet as you read out loud. Look for repeated words or phrases that set up a beat. Listen for sentences that rise, for sentences that fall. Where does the prose stop? What kinds of words create pauses?...How do paragraph lengths fit into the music of the work? Is there a visual rhythm? Can you sing any lines?

Then pull out another author, and do it again. What accounts for the changes you hear in rhythm?

Finally, pull out your own draft, and read the same way. Are you satisfied? Can you get more music in there? More of a beat? More aural surprises? More variety?

I'll make your charge more concrete: Do you start most sentences with the subject? Do you always subordinate in the same way? Do you avoid alliteration, repetition? Does every paragraph end on a rising note, or falling? Does every sentence have about the same number of beats, every paragraph the same number of sentences?

Shake it up, baby! (152–53)

ALTERNATE STYLES: GRAMMAR B

Winston Weathers's *An Alternate Style: Options in Composition* is perhaps the most accessible text for students interested in expanding their repertoire of stylistic options. Weathers writes that

> one of our major tasks as teachers of composition is to identify compositional options and teach students the mastery of the options and the liberating use of them. We must identify options in all areas of vocabulary, usage, sentence forms, dictional levels, paragraph types, ways of organizing material into whole compositions: options in all that we mean by style. Without options, there can be no rhetoric, for there can be no adjustment to the diversity of communication occasions that confront us in our various lives. (5)

Thus, it ultimately rests with teachers to introduce students to their stylistic options. Once students stop viewing their styles as predestined and unchangeable and begin to perceive style as quantitative and plastic, they can begin to seek what Richard Lanham calls "grace" and "delight" in their writing as they learn how to control their rhetorical choices and stylistic options.

Weathers defines Grammar B as "a mature and alternate (*not* experimental) style used by competent writers and offering students of writing a well-tested set of options that, added to the traditional grammar of style, will give them a much greater opportunity to put into effective language all the things they have to say" (*Alternate Style* 8). Some elements of alternate style (see Weathers for others) include crots, or sections of sentences that work together but may be only loosely connected to the sentences that follow; labyrinthine sentences, which are long, winding sentences that may use embedded phrases, lists, multiple forms of punctuation, and explanations within explanations; sentence fragments; double voices that suggest two sides of a story or different attitudes toward the same subject; and lists. Weathers cites examples of how these stylistic features have been used by literary writers; if you're using a reader, you can point out examples from it to students.

Using Alternate Styles in the Classroom

Though still available in many university libraries and some used bookstores, Weathers's *An Alternate Style: Options in Composition* is out of print. However, a more recent book based on Weathers's work can help you introduce a range of styles to your composition class: *Elements of Alternate Style: Essays on Writing and Revision,* edited by Wendy Bishop, includes both essays and exercises meant to introduce students to elements of alternate style and to give them an opportunity to apply what they learn in writing new compositions and revising pieces they've already written. The essays are short, directed to student writers, and full of exercises and examples. In "'You Want Us to Do WHAT?' How to Get the Most Out of Unexpected Writing Assignments," for example, Ruth Mirtz includes an assignment sheet that explains Weathers's terms and offers guidelines for revising an essay previously written using Grammar A (traditional grammar) by using the techniques of Grammar B:

> Don't change topics/it's too late now.
>
> If you conceive of a Grammar B-like device that fits what you want to say (that is, breaks one rule of Grammar A to good effect), do it.
>
> Don't change font styles every other word or add obscure symbols and call it Grammar B. It won't B.
>
> Have fun. Play. Take a Chance. If it Fails because you tried something that didn't work, it didn't Fail. If it fails because you didn't try, it failed.
>
> Do as the handout describes, not as it does. This handout uses too many Grammar B techniques because it's trying to illustrate possibilities rather than make sense.
>
> The POINT of this assignment, which I place at the end of the handout instead of [at] the Grammar A position at the beginning of the handout, is to understand better what Grammar A is all about by using Grammar B, to explore what Grammar A (and Grammar B, perhaps) fails to express, to be politically aware (instead of politically correct) of who gets to make rules like Grammar A and who doesn't, who gets to use Grammar B and why, what the rules of Grammar A accomplish in terms of communication, expression, meaning-making, to explore further the concept of revision by writing a radically different version of a paper and comparing the effect, and to imagine more possibilities and power in language than Grammar A (or our assumptions and ignorances about Grammar A) allow us. (107)

By carrying out such an assignment and then comparing their earlier drafts to their revisions, students potentially come to understand better how style can change not only how people read and respond to their work but also how they themselves think about and understand an experience or topic.

Alternate styles can be used for a variety of pedagogical purposes — to help students recognize stylistic options, to produce radical revisions, even to teach Grammar A. In asking students to attempt alternate styles, it is important to reiterate that one reason traditional rules of grammar exist is that they are effective in helping guide readers. Writers who use alternate styles also must keep their readers in mind. There are times when the teaching and practice of Grammar A and Grammar B can be mutually reinforcing.

Example 8.7 provides an assignment for a labyrinthine sentence. By giving students such an assignment, you provide an example of what is expected and can spend time in class analyzing the grammatical features that work well in labyrinthine sentences: lists, embedded clauses and phrases, resumptive modifiers, parentheticals, and so on. The assignment also provides an opportunity to discuss rules of punctuation, such as when it is appropriate to use semicolons or dashes. Thus, through analyzing and practicing this element of alternate style, students learn more about sentence variety and grammatical complexity — all while writing one long sentence.

Example 8.7   **LABYRINTHINE SENTENCE ASSIGNMENT**

Though I fully understand the great challenge — even the difficulty — of such a task, for your labyrinthine sentence assignment (of at least two hundred words), you need to construct a very long, circuitous sentence: one that leads and directs your readers, taking them through the labyrinthine with both grace and ease (and maybe even a pleasant surprise), never becoming overly repetitious or wordy (avoiding filler words or the overuse of adjectives and adverbs); one that is grammatically correct, showing careful attention to each word, clause, and phrase and how these elements (along with the various parts of speech) work together to create meaning; one that is correctly punctuated, using the full range of options available to you — including dashes, colons, commas, parentheses, semicolons, and some end punctuation; one that is coherent, demonstrating control and a command of language, syntactic structure, and subject matter; one that shows an attention to vocabulary, using words that are precise and appropriate in diction, sound, and sense; and one that is as interesting as it is complex; for in order to complete this assignment effectively and successfully, you will need to be patient, flexible, and creative — sensitive to almost every aspect of writing as you demonstrate the considerable effort involved in the craft of language.

In case you're wondering, the preceding sentence contains 210 words. It can be done.

Evaluating Alternate Styles

You may be wondering how to respond to, evaluate, even grade alternate styles. The labyrinthine sentence assignment in Example 8.7 can be evaluated according to standard English and the elements referred to in the assignment itself. For many other alternate style assignments, however, there are few established criteria against which to measure student responses. You might intuitively know what works and what doesn't, but how do you translate your gut-level responses into language that will help students further refine their writing? If the evaluation of traditional assignments seems subjective to students, the evaluation of alternate style assignments must seem even more so. And how do you evaluate an assignment when you've asked students to take risks?

Wendy Bishop, in the appendix to *Elements of Alternate Style,* gives guidance on how to respond to, evaluate, and grade alternate-style texts. She provides two sets of questions — questions students can ask about their own pieces and questions teachers and classmates can ask in response to their reading. The questions students can ask themselves include the following:

- Can I describe why this writing requires this style/format?
- Are there places in the writing that I covered up, patched, [or] ignored problems I was having [with] understanding my own writing goals or aims?
- If I recast this as a traditionally styled writing, what would I lose and what would I gain?
- In my final draft, am I paying attention to the reader? Have I done everything I can to "teach" the reader how to read my piece while still maintaining the integrity of my writing goals and ideas? (175)

Notice how these questions encourage students to balance the attention they give to each element of the communication triangle (subject, writer, reader, and work) discussed earlier in this chapter.

Bishop also provides guidance for teachers and classmates responding to alternate-style texts, including the following prompts:

- Here's how I read your text. Here's where I had trouble reading your text and why.
- Can you tell us what effects you were hoping for, where you achieved them and where you think you may have fallen short?
- What do you wish you had done (what would you still like to do) to push this text even f[u]rther? Why haven't you? How can you? (175-76)

These questions ask writers to consider reader response, to interrogate their own intentions and the extent to which they were able to carry out their purposes, and to keep working.

For grading alternate-style texts, Bishop suggests using process cover sheets (which are similar to the portfolio cover letters discussed in Chapter 5). Bishop provides a series of questions, directs writers to choose six out of eight of them to answer, and asks them to compose a letter that includes those answers. She also offers the following grading options:

1. Grade the letter as a traditional persuasive essay for the insights discussed and explored, and don't grade the project beyond done/not done.
2. Grade both the letter and the project as part of an entire class portfolio. This may mean allowing for more experimentation (even individually productive "failure") by evaluating this "slot" in the portfolio as done/not done (in good faith).
3. Grade the text on the basis of traditional criteria — a mixture of assignment

goals and [the] teacher's estimate of the degree to which those goals were met, using the process cover sheet to add depth to this subjective evaluation.

4. Grade using a combination of these options. (177)

Whether you use instruction and practice in writing alternate styles as in-class exercises, as fully developed essays, as revision techniques, or to encourage students to consider the effects of stylistic differences in what they read and write, such instruction can be quite valuable in helping students expand their stylistic range.

WORKS CITED

Abrams, M. H. *The Mirror and the Lamp*. New York: Oxford UP, 1953.

Ball, Arnetha F. "Cultural Preference and the Expository Writing of African-American Adolescents." *Written Communication* 9.4 (1992): 501–32.

Ball, Arnetha, and Ted Lardner. "Dispositions Toward Language: Teacher Constructs and the Ann Arbor Black English Case." *CCC* 48 (1997): 469–85.

Bishop, Wendy, ed. *Elements of Alternate Style: Essays on Writing and Revision*. Portsmouth: Boynton/Cook, 1997.

———. *The Subject Is Writing*. 2nd ed. Portsmouth: Boynton/Cook, 1999.

Booth, Wayne. "The Rhetorical Stance." *Contemporary Rhetoric: Conceptual Background with Readings*. Ed. W. Ross Winterowd. New York: Harcourt, 1975. 71–79.

Chatman, Seymour, and Samuel R. Levin, eds. *Literary Style: A Symposium*. London: Oxford UP, 1971.

———. *Essays on the Language of Literature*. Boston: Houghton, 1967.

Corbett, Edward P. J. "Approaches to the Study of Style." *Teaching Composition: Twelve Bibliographic Essays*. 2nd ed. Ed. Gary Tate. Fort Worth: Texas Christian UP, 1987. 83–130.

———. *Rhetorical Analyses of Literary Works*. New York: Oxford UP, 1969.

Corbett, Edward P. J., and Robert Connors. *Classical Rhetoric for the Modern Student*. 4th ed. New York: Oxford UP, 1999.

Delpit, Lisa, and Joanne Kilgour Dowdy, eds. *The Skin That We Speak*. New York: Norton, 2002.

Dillard, Annie. *Teaching a Stone to Talk*. New York: Harper, 1982.

Ede, Lisa, Cheryl Glenn, and Andrea Lunsford. "Border Crossings: Intersections of Rhetoric and Feminism." *Rhetorica* XIII.4 (Autumn 1995): 410–41.

Elbow, Peter. *Everyone Can Write*. New York: Oxford UP, 2000.

Gilyard, Keith. *Voices of the Self*. Detroit: Wayne State UP, 1991.

Glaser, Joe. *Understanding Style: Practical Ways to Improve Your Writing*. New York: Oxford UP, 1999.

Gorrell, Donna. *Copy/Write: Basic Writing through Controlled Composition*. Boston: Little, 1982.

Graves, Richard. "A Primer for Teaching Style." *CCC* 25 (1974): 186–90.

Gruber, William. " 'Servile Copying' and the Teaching of English." *CE* 39 (1977): 491–97.

Hongo, Garrett. "Kubota." *The Best American Essays: College Edition*. Ed. Robert Atwan. Boston: Houghton, 1998. 64–76.

Irmscher, William F. *Teaching Expository Writing*. New York: Holt, 1979.

Joos, Martin. *The Five Clocks*. New York: Harcourt, 1961.

Jordan, June. "Nobody Mean More to Me Than You: And the Future Life of Willie Jordan." *City Kids, City Teachers: Reports from the Front Row.* Ed. William Ayers and Patricia Ford. New York: New, 1996. 176–93.

Kiefer, Kathleen, and Charles R. Smith. "Improving Students' Revising and Editing: The Writer's Workbench." *The Computer in Composition Instruction: A Writer's Tool.* Ed. William Wresch. Urbana: NCTE, 1984. 65–82.

Lanham, Richard. *Style: An Anti-Textbook.* New Haven: Yale UP, 1974.

Lunsford, Andrea A. *The St. Martin's Handbook.* 6th ed. Boston: Bedford / St. Martin's, 2008.

Macrorie, Ken. *Uptaught.* Rochelle Park: Hayden, 1970.

Marckwardt, Albert H. Introduction. *The Five Clocks.* Martin Joos. New York: Harcourt, 1961. i–x.

Mellix, Barbara. "From Outside, In." *The Fourth Genre.* Ed. Robert L. Root Jr. and Michael Steinberg. Boston: Allyn, 113–20.

Milic, Louis T. "Against the Typology of Styles." *Literary Style: A Symposium.* Ed. Seymour Chatman and Samuel R. Levin. London: Oxford UP, 1971. 442–50.

____. "Rhetorical Choice and Stylistic Option: The Conscious and Unconscious Poles." *Literary Style: A Symposium.* Ed. Seymour Chatman and Samuel R. Levin. London: Oxford UP, 1971. 77–88.

____. "Theories of Style and Their Implications for Teaching Composition." CCC 16 (1965): 66–69, 126.

Miller, Edmund. *Exercises in Style.* Normal: Illinois State UP, 1980.

Mirtz, Ruth. " 'You Want Us to Do WHAT?': How to Get the Most Out of Unexpected Writing Assignments." *Elements of Alternate Style: Essays on Writing and Revision.* Ed. Wendy Bishop. Portsmouth: Boynton/Cook, 1997. 105–15.

Ostrom, Hans. " 'Carom Shots': Reconceptualizing Imitation and Its Uses in Creative Writing Courses." *Teaching Writing Creatively.* Ed. David Starkey. Portsmouth: Boynton/Cook, 1998. 164–71.

Perelman, Chaim. "The New Rhetoric: A Theory of Practical Reasoning." *The Rhetoric of Western Thought.* Ed. James L. Golden et al. Dubuque: Kendall-Hunt, 1983. 402–23.

Riffaterre, Michael. "Criteria for Style Analysis." *Literary Style: A Symposium.* Ed. Seymour Chatman and Samuel R. Levin. London: Oxford UP, 1971. 442–50.

Roorbach, Bill. *Writing Life Stories.* Cincinnati: Story, 1998.

Smitherman, Geneva. " 'The Blacker the Berry, the Sweeter the Juice': African American Student Writers." *The Need for Story: Cultural Diversity in the Classroom and Community.* Urbana: NCTE, 1994. 80–101.

____. "Toward a National Public Policy on Language." *The Skin That We Speak.* Ed. Lisa Delpit and Joanne Kilgour Dowdy. New York: New, 2002. 163–78.

Starkey, David, ed. *Teaching Writing Creatively.* Portsmouth: Boynton/Cook, 1998.

Tan, Amy. "Mother Tongue." *The Best American Essays: College Edition.* Ed. Robert Atwan. Boston: Houghton, 1998. 146–53.

Tate, Gary, ed. *Teaching Composition: Twelve Bibliographic Essays.* 2nd ed. Fort Worth: Texas Christian UP, 1987.

Weathers, Winston. *An Alternate Style: Options in Composition.* Rochelle Park: Hayden, 1980.

____. "Teaching Style: A Possible Anatomy." CCC 21 (1970): 114–49.

Weaver, Richard. *Ideas Have Consequences.* Chicago: U of Chicago P, 1948.

Williams, Terry Tempest. *An Unspoken Hunger.* New York: Pantheon, 1994.

Winterowd, W. Ross, ed. *Contemporary Rhetoric: Conceptual Background with Readings.* New York: Harcourt, 1975.

9

Teaching Memory

In the writing courses I teach, I often begin personal writing assignments with invitations for students to explore their memories. I ask students to respond in writing to questions like, "At what time in your life were you the most content? Discouraged?" I also ask students to recall memories of significant people — appearance, mannerisms, significant experiences, dialogue. I have found that by encouraging student-writers to pay attention to the importance of memory in their drafting processes, I am also helping them become more detailed and analytical in all of their writing projects.

— AMY HODGES HAMILTON

"Memory has been forgotten," asserts Kathleen Welch in a critique of writing textbooks that give no attention to the final two canons of rhetoric: memory and delivery (153). Much of this "forgetfulness" can be attributed to the common belief that rhetorical memory is concerned simply with memorizing speeches. Edward P. J. Corbett, who does not include a section on memory in his influential text *Classical Rhetoric for the Modern Student,* explains, "The reason for the neglect of this aspect of rhetoric is probably that not much can be said, in a theoretical way, about the process of memorizing; and after rhetoric came to be concerned mainly with written discourse, there was no further need to deal with memorizing" (22). Although there may be little need to deal with memorizing in a book on teaching writing, we — like other scholars of rhetoric — are finding ways to remember memory and the role it can play in teaching writing.

Winifred Bryan Horner, in her introduction to *Rhetorical Memory and Delivery,* calls for further attention to memory and delivery, for — as she argues — all of the canons "are necessary for a full understanding of a communication act, whether it be written, spoken, electronic, or some combination of any or all of these" (ix). Responding to the calls of Welch, Horner, and other scholars of rhetoric and composition, we devote this chapter to exploring the ways a fresh understanding of memory can invigorate the teaching of writing, and we give equal attention to delivery in Chapter 10.

Instead of seeing "memory" as linked exclusively to the memorization of speeches, we prefer Sharon Crowley's claim, in "Modern Rhetoric and Memory," that memory "is a heuristic, a way of stimulating selection, reworking, and amplification of *all* that writers know" (44). This expanded definition provides many useful entries into the study of memory and its uses for the teaching of writing.

MEMORY IN THE COMPOSITION CLASSROOM

Drawing on Patrick Mahony's 1969 study "McLuhan in the Light of Classical Rhetoric," John Frederick Reynolds argues for "four interrelated approaches to memory in modern composition studies: memory as mnemonics, memory as memorableness, memory as data bases, and memory as psychology" (7). Developing these ideas further, Reynolds suggests that composition teachers can help students develop "sight mnemonics" or "visual sensibility" in relation to texts, allowing students better to retrieve or remember what they have read (8). Further, students can practice the rhetorical art of memory by making their own writing memorable to readers by writing about significant situations, including details, and using powerful language—all elements of contemporary memoir or creative nonfiction.

In figuring memory as databases, Reynolds points to Horner's important distinction between individual memory and cultural memory (which is stored in books, on computers, in databases, in recordings, even in public memorials) (11). Finally, in seeing memory as psychology, Reynolds quotes Mahony's idea of " 'a oneness of memory, electronic technology, and the human unconscious' " (quoted in Reynolds 6). Welch, too, sees a connection between memory and psychology, arguing in *Electric Rhetoric* that the "idea of memory as shards of consciousness, or mentalité, and the connection of memory to psychology (cognitive and depth, to name two kinds) continues to be an important area in the historicizing and production of discourses" (153). A consideration of both individual memory and cultural memory can be particularly useful in teaching this rhetorical canon.

The study of memory has important implications for the many kinds of writing students do in composition courses, particularly personal writing and research-based writing. These categories ("personal" and "research-based"), of course, are not mutually exclusive. Strong personal writing requires research, and research essays should be informed and driven by students' concerns and marked by a personal voice. Both kinds of writing demand attention to memory in similar ways:

1. Through invention exercises: Both classical rhetoricians and contemporary scholars link the rhetorical canons of invention and memory, for without invention, it is impossible to draw upon and use stored knowledge—whether it is stored in a person's mind or externally in books or databases.
2. Through research: Individual memories and arguments often need to be supplemented, confirmed, challenged, or extended by research.
3. Memory as communal: Both those who write from their own memories and those who use other texts as sources must recognize the communal nature of memory.
4. Through experiences, images, and ideas worth communicating—and communicating well: writers often remember particular images and

experiences for a reason, but they may need to work to make the idea behind those images and experiences not only communicable but also memorable to readers.

Although, for ease of arrangement, we have separated the discussion of memory as it relates to personal and research writing, we encourage you and your students to see the important ways these categories overlap and inform each other.

REMEMBERING AND MAKING WRITING MEMORABLE: TEACHING MEMOIR AND PERSONAL WRITING

Nonfiction writer and novelist Bill Roorbach opens his chapter "Memory" in *Writing Life Stories* with an epigraph from E.L. Doctorow: "'When you use memories as a source, they're no different from any other source — the composition still has to be made" (qtd. in Roorbach 18). This reminder — that memories are sources like any others — is important for students who are sometimes tempted to believe that writing from experience or about memories involves a simple transcription of what "really happened."

Writers, like psychologists, understand that memory is complicated, limited, and faulty. As Roorbach states, "What's remembered, recorded, is never the event, no matter how precise the measurement" (19). Roorbach claims, further, that readers come "to memoir understanding that memory is faulty, that the writer is going to challenge the limits of memory" (21). Challenging the limits of memory, students should be reminded, is not the same thing as making things up completely, as the critical response to James Frey's supposed memoir *A Million Little Pieces* illustrates. But the difference between "what really happened" and "what I remember, why I remember it, and *how I interpret it* in the context of my essay" is worth discussing in class. (One useful source for beginning such a discussion is Patricia Hampl's essay "Memory and Imagination" from *I Could Tell You Stories,* cited at the end of this chapter. In this essay, Hampl reflects on the complexity of truth and imagination, telling a story that contains literal inaccuracies and then reflecting on why she told the story as she did.)

Whether you're asking students to write memoir, a personal essay, or some other autobiographical piece that requires attention to memory (such as a literacy narrative), the key elements of such essays are the same. Richard Bullock, who includes guidance for writing both literacy narratives and memoirs in *The Norton Field Guide to Writing,* identifies such features as a well-told story, vivid detail, and clear significance (29–30, 149–50). Such features come from memory as evoked through invention as well as through research that uses external aids to memory; such qualities, too, make writing memorable for readers.

Invention

As Crowley reminds us, memory "is associative, global; it privileges disquisition, repetition, digression, allusion, allegory" (43). Invention strategies such as brainstorming, clustering, and freewriting demonstrate and emphasize the associative power of memory (see Chapter 6 for detailed discussions of these invention techniques). Clustering, in particular, provides students a visual representation of the connections their minds naturally make between images and memories they may not have consciously related. Like a word-association game, one image or experience reminds them of another and then another, expanding connections from the center word or idea.

Invention exercises provide a perfect starting place for accessing memories. Example 9.1 provides a series of invention exercises for students beginning to write literacy narratives.

Example 9.1   **REMEMBERING CHILDHOOD LITERACY**

1. For five minutes, brainstorm a list of books you remember from childhood (they might be books your family owned, ones you borrowed from the library, ones you read in school, or books someone else read to you).

2. For three minutes, brainstorm a list of people who read to you or to whom you read (parents, grandparents, siblings, teachers, neighbors, and so on).

3. Pick an element from one of these lists (a book title or the name of a person) and use it as a central word for a cluster. Cluster for five minutes.

4. Look at your cluster. Are there any associations or experiences you wrote down that interest or surprise you? Freewrite for thirty minutes on the element that interests or surprises you the most.

Note: Although this example uses books and reading as its focus, you can modify it to focus on writing.

After doing the invention exercises, students will likely be surprised by how much they remember about their childhood literacy. Equally interesting is how much their invention exercises will overlap with their classmates' work.

Memory as Communal

Crowley suggests in "Modern Rhetoric and Memory" that citizens are shaped by their knowledge of culture and history, which is "stored in memory" (36). Books, of course, are cultural artifacts, and for students who grew up in similar cultures, family and educational rituals of reading will likely have similarities (reading before bed, story time in school, reading aloud one at a time in class, and so on). As an extension of the invention exercises, you can ask students to write on the board the name of one of the books they read (or that was read to them) as children. As students write the names of books on the board, you'll likely hear exclamations of "Oh, yeah! I remember that one!"

As students discuss what they have in common (how many read *Winnie the Pooh,* the *Chronicles of Narnia,* or Dr. Seuss), they can become resources for each other, supplying details others might have forgotten. They can also recognize the ways particulars are, if not universal, at least culturally and historically formed — that writing about their memories communicates to others on some level because readers can identify with those memories.

Research

Although we discuss the complexities of research more thoroughly later in this chapter (in the sections on writing research essays), personal writing can also be informed through research. External memory aids — such as memory books or scrapbooks, boxes of childhood memorabilia (some parents organize a box for each child, but unorganized collections are just as likely to be found in closets, drawers, attics, or basements), photo albums, and journals or diaries (or old report cards for those writing literacy narratives) — prove to be indispensable resources for including detail in personal writing. (For more on research as it relates to personal writing, see Goldthwaite's "This, Too, Is Research" included in Bishop and Zemliansky, cited at the end of this chapter.)

Experience, Image, Idea

Crowley writes, "People who know nothing outside their own experience cannot compose discourse that anyone else cares about" (43). That is not to say that writing from experience produces vacant or worthless writing, but that writers must consider the ideas that arise from and are suggested by their experiences or the images that stick in memory. Experience provides a source of knowledge, but as Doctorow reminds us, the composition must still be made. Students must relate experiences in engaging ways (through scene, dialogue, concrete detail, attention to language and form) and consider the "so what?" question important to any form of writing. In memoir and other forms of personal writing, the "so what?" question does not need to be answered explicitly through a thesis statement at the beginning or a moral tacked on at the end, but the writer should have a sense of purpose, and that purpose should suggest an idea — something readers can take from the piece.

Well-rendered experiences, those written with attention to image and detail, can make the idea of a piece memorable to readers. Eighteenth-century rhetorician George Campbell writes in *The Philosophy of Rhetoric* that "vivid ideas are not only more powerful than languid ideas in commanding and preserving attention, they are not only more efficacious in producing conviction, but they are also more easily retained" (925). One reason that people have told stories throughout generations and in every culture is that story helps make ideas memorable; teaching students the intricacies of powerful narrative and lyrical writing can help make their writing memorable too. Example 9.2 provides an exercise to help students test how memorable their writing is to readers.

Example 9.2   **WHAT READERS REMEMBER — AND WHY**

1. If you're using a collection of essays in your composition class, read one short, particularly well-written essay from that collection aloud to the class.

2. After you read the essay, ask students to tell you what they remember about the piece — what words or phrases stood out (often they'll point to strong verbs or metaphors and similes), what characters they remember (often it will be a well-developed major character or even a quirky minor character), and what idea they took from the piece.

3. As a class, determine why those features or textual elements were memorable.

4. Do the same exercise with a student essay.

Students can also do this exercise in peer-response groups, reading their essays aloud and asking their peers to tell them what was memorable, but it's worth doing the exercise at least once as an entire class because sometimes what's memorable is what students need to revise away from: awkward phrasing, the use of a word that, although interesting, is not precise (sometimes, when you ask students to use memorable words, they'll consult a thesaurus and use words that sound good but don't necessarily fit in terms of meaning), a character who is stereotyped, and so on. The question of *why* some element stands out in memory remains important.

MEMORY AS DATABASE: TEACHING RESEARCH ASSIGNMENTS

Even though a large percentage of college writing programs specifically require research assignments, most teachers and students continue to be stymied by them. Why? Because we all seem to forget that we're already researchers. Every one of us does research every day: whether we're looking in the telephone book to find a doctor, reading music reviews in *Rolling Stone* to decide which CD to buy, or checking out a political candidate's Web site, we're researching.

We conduct research in order to make informed decisions, come to an opinion, learn how to do something, make sense of the world or the people around us.

If your program requires a research assignment, then you'll want to begin talking early in the term about the amount of research students conduct on a regular basis. You'll also want to find time to ask them about the reasons they research, their methods and sources, and the amount of time successful research can take. We think you'll be surprised at how lively your class can become when your students begin tapping their own expertise. Furthermore, these early talks can help guide your students toward a topic or critical question that interests them, even if the general topic itself is teacher-generated.

The research assignment is often weighted more than other writing assignments for several reasons. First, it's usually a longer assignment, an extended essay of *at least* fifteen hundred words (or six typed pages). Second, besides asking students to demonstrate the usual essay-writing skills, the research assignment demands that they demonstrate their mastery of library and Internet research skills and of careful, thorough documentation. This assignment offers students the chance to read widely and deeply on a particular subject, to use outside sources and voices to prove or support their argument, and to think critically about an issue to the point that they arrive at an informed, well-supported opinion. It's much more (and much more interesting) than merely stringing together quotations; the research assignment gives students an opportunity to weave together and balance their own voice and opinions with those of their outside sources. In other words, this assignment provides students a forum for entering an intellectual conversation. Finally, because the overall assignment is usually composed of a series of smaller assignments (from an initial list of ten sources and an annotated bibliography to a tentative thesis statement and a first-draft opening paragraph), it can take from several weeks to an entire term to fulfill.

Even though the assignment may hover over them for a month or more, when students have some kind of personal connection with their topic, the research, analysis, synthesis, and interpretation can be intellectually invigorating for them. Following their progress can be just as interesting for their teacher. Thus, the research assignment can be the most important and most interesting assignment in the writing course, building powerfully on everything that came before it (particularly if it's not presented as a separate writing entity or genre).

The research assignment provides the teacher with the chance to take on a form that students may think inviolable and to demonstrate that the shape of every piece of writing is determined by the writer's purpose. This assignment can also show students that finding information from outside sources (home, library, Internet, other people, observation) is not a specialized activity but something all writers do to find out what they want or need to know — something they themselves do every day. The research assignment even promises students as great a chance for personal discovery and creativity as any piece of personal writing they've done during the term. In addition, it provides an opportunity to introduce students to the quickly changing world of academic research, which will undergird all the other work they do in college.

There are many useful texts and handbooks that can help guide you and your students through the research process. One especially helpful source is Wendy Bishop and Pavel Zemliansky's *The Subject Is Research,* which includes essays on many aspects of writing research essays (such as "Finding the Voices of Others without Losing Your Own," "The Internet Can Be a Wonderful Place, But...," and "Interviewing"), prompts for "sharing ideas" at the end of each section, and "Hint Sheets," which are practical assignments and guides for both teachers and students. The essays and sample assignments are very accessible, written with FY writing students in mind, and help demystify the research process.

INTERNET RESEARCH IN THE WRITING CLASS

The world of research has changed dramatically during the last fifteen years, and teachers who ask students to do research and to write up research essays must take these newer technologies into account. Gone are the days when a teacher could simply explain the search capabilities of the library's computer system and the serials section in the campus library and then leave students to work away within those safe limits. The capabilities of the Internet have opened up vast new resources, but these resources must be used with awareness of their strengths and limitations.

More than two decades ago, the rapidly developing world of computers began to allow searches of large data banks for specific keywords. For some time, this kind of computer data searching was so complex and specialized that trained reference specialists had to do it, and many libraries subscribed to for-pay data services that allowed such searches. But the rapid advance of storage and network technologies increasingly allowed huge amounts of data to be stored in very small media such as CD-ROMs or accessed over the Internet via file transfers, gopher searches, and eventually over the World Wide Web. As of this writing, the Web has expanded its capabilities and its availability to the point where almost every college student has access to it. If students do not have computers with Web access in their dorm rooms or at home (even on their mobile phones or other hand-held devices), they nearly all can access the Web at the college library or at a computer lab on campus. The Web and the Internet have thus become standard elements of research, tools with which every writing teacher needs to be familiar.

The World Wide Web

The best-known and most widely used Internet resource is, of course, the World Wide Web. The Web presents to students tremendous opportunities, but as a research tool it is a double-edged sword. The ease with which keyword searches can be done on the Web, and the plethora of material that many such searches turn up, can give students the illusion that they need do little more than find and print out a few Web sites to have completed all their necessary research. Although any student research must now include the Web, no genuinely thorough information search can stop with it. One of our tasks as teachers of research and research writing must be to show students what the Web can do — and what it cannot do.

Increasingly, the Web is becoming an excellent source for serious research, providing information on manuscript and archival collections, electronic indexes and abstracts, online journals, and even searchable electronic copies of entire books. Using electronic books and searching the school library from one's home or dorm room can save valuable time, but students need guidance on how to use the Internet effectively to conduct research.

Although there are several textbooks and many Web sites completely devoted to Web research, the most important resources for your students are those immediately available in the reference section of the college library. The Web does not replace resources available through carefully constructed library information sources. When discussing electronic Web searches, the best advice about specific local offerings and sources will come from your reference librarians, who are specially trained to introduce students to the electronic resources available. One absolutely dependable element of the world of electronic searching is that it changes faster than any book can follow, and new tools and possibilities arise almost daily. You can probably keep up with many of these changes yourself — enough to give your students a general overview of possibilities — but for current local searches and services, no resource beats the reference department. Introduce students to it as soon as you can.

The most important reason for sending students to the library as soon as possible is the extraordinary difference between the electronic resources of the library and those of the World Wide Web. Library resources, including contemporary-linked bibliographic services and online databases, are controlled, monitored for quality and validity, and defined and moderated by experts. In contrast, the Web is a free-fire zone of information. It is an amazing phenomenon, flashing thousands of possibilities and myriad colors, pictures, and data bits at its enraptured beholders, but teachers cannot lose sight of the Web's essential nature. It is, among other things:

1. a bulletin board used to display personal prejudices and enthusiasms
2. a commercial billboard deeply tied into a variety of economic and advertising purposes, some of them subtly hidden
3. an uncontrolled arena of data, with no moderation and no checks on bias, completeness of presentation, or factuality
4. a free aesthetic space, in which the quality of any presentation has more to do with the intensity of the presenter than with the truth of the presentation

All of these elements of the Web's nature mean that it is wonderful for exploring some questions and issues and almost useless for exploring others. The Web tosses so much data at a user that sifting through it is often as much work as finding the information in a more ordered source.

The essential point that students must understand about the Web is that it cannot be the *only* place they go for information on a research topic. For very general background or "ground-level" information, student researchers used to turn to encyclopedias (and, of course, some went no farther). Now they have a tendency to turn to Yahoo!, Google, or AltaVista for easy keyword searches, chugging around the Web looking for easy access to background information or lucky hits into specialized Web sites. These base-level search engines are the equivalent of encyclopedia entries. But once students need to move beyond that base level, Web research starts to get much less certain.

The nature of the research topic can determine whether the Web will provide gold or lead. In general, the Web is a great source for information about popular culture, though much of that information may be outdated, biased, or commercially based. It is much less dependable for detailed information on less popular or more abstract subjects. You may be able to easily find an entire detailed history and discography of the Grateful Dead and find almost nothing about Pope John XXII, or the Synod of Dort, or phlogiston. Or, even worse, the Web may pop up a few brief facts about these issues but allow no deeper access or more helpful links. The problem is that a researcher already must know a good deal about the question or issue before she can determine whether Web research is providing a treasure trove or a heap of chaff. There certainly are many sites that seem to offer specialized materials, but judging and sifting through those materials is often only possible if you already have a solid grasp of the subject — which many students do not.

A Web Exercise

Students will listen with patience to any caveats you provide them about Web research, but many students will still see the Web as the most immediately accessible, and therefore more useful, source of information. Sometimes, certainly, it can be, but an exercise illustrating the Web's strengths and limitations is a good idea. Try this one. Divide the class into groups of three students, and assign each group one of the following research topics. (As you see, there are three general sorts of topics here: the "old chestnut" argument topics, topics drawn from popular culture, and more specific (and thus genuine) topics drawn from across the disciplines.)

A

1. capital punishment
2. abortion
3. euthanasia
4. animal rights

B

1. Howard Stern
2. Lindsay Lohan
3. Celine Dion
4. Angelina Jolie and Brad Pitt

C

1. Albigensianism and the Catholic Church
2. the Heisenberg Uncertainty Principle and philosophy
3. Andrea Dworkin and feminist legal theory
4. the Viagra black market in Canada

Assign each group one topic to research on the Web, using general browsers and search engines to find as many sites as possible about the topic in one evening. Each group is to print out the homepage of each important site they find and answer the following questions about each important site:

1. Who is responsible for the Web site? What do you know about them?
2. What is the Web site's general attitude toward the subject?
3. What is the level of originality of the material?
4. How authoritative or trustworthy does the material seem? Why?
5. How completely does the site deal with the subject at hand?
6. What sorts of links does the site contain? How do these links add to the authority of the site? How complete and recent are they?
7. How is the site biased?
8. When was the site last updated?

After a day or two, ask each group to present a ten-minute summary of its findings to the class, including handouts of some of the homepages the group found to illustrate points. Following each of these reports, you can stimulate discussion about the strengths and limitations of Web research on each topic. As you would suspect, the "old chestnuts" will provide plenty of grist for students, but will present corresponding problems of selection and quality control as well as a need for constant checking for site biases. Although the popular culture topics will also generate numerous hits, many of them will be shallow, repetitious, academically useless, or overtly commercial. Finally, the specific disciplinary questions will require careful searches but may not generate much Web data. Two days spent in class discussion on these research problems and issues will well repay the time.

For detailed information on Web-site evaluation, see "Evaluating Web Pages: Techniques to Apply & Questions to Ask" on the UC Berkeley Web site, listed at the end of this chapter. This site provides questions to ask, helpful information on determining the reliability of a source, and links to other useful sources.

RESEARCH WRITING IN THE CLASSROOM

To begin, a short introductory lecture or classroom discussion should help students understand what a college research essay is *not*. For one thing, it is not a research report or an extended summary of what is known about a topic. It also is not a recycled encyclopedia entry. Like any other type of essay students have written for your class, the research essay must have a purpose, and part of the challenge of writing a research essay is discovering that purpose. To discover the purpose, students must look beyond their own experiences, find out what they want to know, and explore their interests openly. Their reactions to this process are as important to the research essay as they were to the personal essays they may have written at the beginning of the course.

Not enforcing all the protocols of the traditional FY composition-course research paper may not be an option in your program; but if you can, modify the assignment, turning it into a research essay. Though it is important that students learn to document sources and build all their essays around a controlling idea or thesis, they should be given some freedom in choosing the form in which to express what they discover. They may want to use first-person pronouns and include personal experiences and observations. In the future, whenever students are asked to write a formal research essay, they will be expected to follow the specific conventions of the discipline in which they are working. They will conduct research in the discipline and write scholarly essays for those best equipped to guide them: the faculty members in their discipline. The best that the teacher of an FY writing course can do is give students a feel for the excitement of research, impress upon them the ethics of honest reporting, and stress the importance of following discipline-specific guidelines.

What must drive the research assignment, then, is not a desire to "get it right" formally but the student's curiosity and desire to explore. This motivation is best served by an open, or at least democratically structured, choice of topics. As early as the first few weeks of the semester, challenge students to think about how their own experiences raise questions that research can help answer. Some of the best research topics (and essay topics, too) grow out of the writer's experiences. For example, one of our students survived an abusive relationship with her boyfriend and wondered why she had stayed with him as long as she did. She wrote an essay that focused on the paradox in which many victims of abuse feel dependent on their abusers. Another student visited graveyards on Cape Cod, searching for the headstone of an ancestor. He noticed certain recurring designs on the older headstones and wondered about their significance. And when a class got into a discussion of "political correctness" on campus, some students wanted to explore and debate the subject; there was a topic for a whole group of students.

Sometimes, too, research topics grow out of essay topics that were discarded because they seemed to demand more background than could be handled in a short work. Other topics may stem from class discussion, newspaper articles or editorials, lectures by visiting speakers, late-night conversations, and even a reference work's subject index, as when a student looks up a general area of interest (for example, advertising) and then focuses on narrower subject headings (advertising — effects on children).

Example 9.3 provides a brainstorming exercise that can help get your students thinking about what makes them curious — and, therefore, what they wish to research further.

Example 9.3 **SEARCHING THE STOREHOUSE OF IDEAS: AN INVENTION EXERCISE**

1. Brainstorm for five minutes to generate a list of things about which you know something but would like to know more. Make the list as long as you can. Whenever possible, be specific, and don't censor yourself.

2. Brainstorm for another five minutes, making a list of things about which you don't know much but would like to learn more. Write down whatever comes to mind.

3. Look at both lists, and circle the one item that piques your curiosity more than any other item does.

4. Now take another five minutes, and build a list of questions about the item you chose. If that topic goes nowhere — that is, if you can't come up with a strong list of questions about the topic that you'd like to learn the answers to — try another topic from your brainstormed list.

Students who have the freedom to act on their own curiosity can't dismiss an unsuccessful essay with the excuse that the assigned topic was boring. More important, such freedom fosters conditions that can make research genuinely rewarding — for example, late-night moments browsing the Web or in the library when students stumble on a source that suddenly opens a door to their topic. In doing research, students can experience, often for the first time, the same joy of discovery they may have experienced when they wrote personal essays. The key is that they are in command of the journey.

If your program demands that all students in a class choose from just a few topics, however, you might devote a class period to brainstorming and sharpening one or more topics that the class will tackle. Ask each student to bring in two research topics they would be interested in writing about. Then assign the students to workshop groups, having the members of each group discuss their various suggestions for ten minutes and come up with a group-sponsored list of four or five subjects. As the groups report back on their subjects, write the topics down in a numbered list on the board. This should give you twelve to twenty possible subjects. Students may then vote on how much they like the subjects, using a numerical system — from four points for "really want to write on this one" to one point for "have no interest at all in this." Using a process of elimination, you can reduce your twenty topics to two or three within a relatively short time, and your students may then feel that they have a stake in the selection of their topic.

The rewards of allowing students to choose their topics can be great: When allowed to find out for themselves whether a topic is fruitful or fruitless, most students overcome their alienation from research and come to approach all research essays with more confidence. They also come to see that what they think does indeed matter, and that through research, they can become authorities capable of interpreting and analyzing information.

A Model Five-Week Assignment

Although there are many variations on the research essay, typically it is an eight- to ten-page documented piece, researched and written in just over a month. By providing a structure within the course that supports students' activities, you can facilitate the tasks of conducting research and writing an essay based on it.

Although all teachers agree that procrastination is the enemy of good research writing, many students have never researched and written an essay more than twenty-four hours before it was due. The following five week model incorporates short weekly assignments that allow you to supervise students' progression toward the completion of interesting research essays.

Week 1: Invention.   At the beginning of the term, encourage students to begin collecting possible topics for research. Ask, for example, "What have you seen or experienced or read that raises questions that research might help answer?" They might want to know about the major areas of study that lead to the best chances of employment and to the most lucrative job offers, the effects of step-families on student achievement, or whether the United States should embrace nuclear power as a solution to energy problems. Several weeks before you begin the assignment, remind students to consider their tentative topics, including those that promise the possibility of interviews. The key is to stress the extent to which the success of their projects depends on their curiosity about the topics; in fact, you may want to provide them with an opportunity to discuss their potential topics in their writing groups.

Despite your emphasis on curiosity, many students will continue to hold some stale assumptions about research and research essays being only form and facts. Therefore, begin the week by bringing these assumptions into the open. Ask students to complete the following freewriting exercise:

1. Write *research and research essays* at the top of a page in your notebook, and spend five minutes freewriting about any initial thoughts, preconceived notions, or prejudices that come to mind when you focus on these words.

2. Skip a few lines, and freewrite for another five minutes, this time focusing on people, anecdotes, situations, and specific experiences that come to mind when you think of these words.
3. Now spend five minutes making a list of sayings, clichés, rules, principles, and ideas about research and research essays that you've heard, including those you believe to be untrue.

This exercise can serve as the means for launching a class discussion about how the research assignment may differ from other writing assignments students have done in the past. In writing a research essay, the point is not simply to collect and document information on a topic but to do something with the information. Usually a controlling question will inform and guide the research and writing.

Students must also be helped to discover that research, in the hands of a good writer, is lively as well as informative. You may want to provide the class with copies of a strong research-based essay or article that challenges the assumption that facts "kill" writing. Popular magazines that value good writing — *New Yorker, Harper's, New Republic, Rolling Stone,* and *Sports Illustrated* — are a good source. Or look to the work of some of the best essayists who also happen to be first-rate researchers: Sandra Steingraber, Barry Lopez, Joan Didion, Lewis Thomas, Terry Tempest Williams, and John McPhee. A successful student research essay, either from your files or a real student's work in a textbook such as Lunsford's *The St. Martin's Handbook,* will work as well. Any research-based essay, student or professional, that features lively writing and an engaging treatment will challenge the prejudice that writing based on research is boring.

Suggest that students read the essay looking for literary devices that hold their interest, and follow up with a discussion about what a research-based essay shares with any other essay type: a distinct voice and point of view, concrete information, a discrete focus, and perhaps even the telling of a story. Most important, though, help students see that the writer of the research essay has the same motivation as the writer of the personal essay: the desire to make sense of something. Both writers share their discoveries with their readers.

This first week you'll need to confront one final problem: library-phobia. Even students who feel as though they mastered their hometown or local libraries may find the campus library intimidating. Some students will wish to retreat to the false security of Web-only searches in the privacy of their dorms. To help them learn about the range of resources available, a library tour is the best option. Most university libraries offer orientation programs, ranging from tours to in-class presentations, but we have found it useful to accompany our classes to the library by devoting a large part of one class to a library tour. When students are ready to begin their research, they're ready to learn about the appropriate sources, and they are often more comfortable asking their teacher specific questions than they are asking a reference librarian, whom they do not know.

For many students, this tour may be the first introduction to the world of the college library, with its computerized searches, serial files, bound volumes of journals, reference room or section, and staff of librarians. You will want, at the least, to explain the basics of the research procedure: how to search a subject index, how to use indexes and bibliographies to expand a search, how to take useful notes, and how to keep track of sources. Suggest that when students are ready to begin their research, those who have chosen similar topics work together and share their findings, so that no student is left without help or a place from which to begin. Suggest, too, that those who find particularly useful sources note their names and location in the library and share the information with the class.

Most colleges offer access to electronic databases that can be indispensable to researchers. Students will need help accessing the electronic journals indexes or helpful research databases such as LexisNexis. They will also need an introduction to the kinds of databases most useful for the research they wish to carry out. You might wish to create a handout with essential information, including the Web site students should use to access the databases provided by the college, the ones you think will be most helpful to students, and the appropriate username and password if they wish to access such databases off campus.

Tours can be supplemented with library exercises that encourage hands-on experience with key college reference sources. One approach is a kind of scavenger hunt: before leaving the library, hand out slips of paper with specific questions ("How and when did Virginia Woolf die?") or ask students to write down one question related to their research. Students can then exchange questions and spend at least twenty-five minutes searching for the answers to one another's questions. When the library session is over and everyone returns to class, students may announce the answers they discovered and discuss any issues that came up during their brief research experience.

A more comprehensive exercise may be assigned as homework. For example, devise a worksheet that requires students to consult increasingly specialized reference materials, from magazine, newspaper, and government-document indexes to general academic indexes and indexes to discipline-specific journals. Have students jot down answers to specific questions about each reference work they consult. This exercise can be especially effective if it is designed to get students started on their own topics.

When you meet with students in conferences, urge them to talk about the research topics they are considering. Always challenge their curiosity: "Why are you interested in that?" Ask that students come to class the following week ready to discuss their tentative topics.

Week 2: Focusing Topics. When your students come to class with their tentative topics, be prepared for generality. Many students will begin with the big picture: "My topic is advertising," or "I want to write about whales." These general topics are not necessarily a bad place to begin. They give researchers plenty of room in which to roam until they discover what they are really interested in.

But a lack of focus plagues college research essays (and most other essays), and the sooner students narrow the topic, the better. Among other things, a narrower focus makes the research process more efficient; instead of being compelled to glance at forty articles on the depletion of rain forests, a student can choose the five articles that deal with its impact on native peoples. A narrow focus also means that the writer is more likely to reveal less obvious aspects of the subject. At this point, your job is to help students narrow their focus to the point where they are making a specific comment or asking a specific question about their chosen topic.

All writing answers questions. That's especially true of the research essay. Students simply need to decide which question they are most interested in exploring. Try this focusing exercise at the beginning of the second week:

1. Ask students to bring a tentative topic idea and a felt-tipped marker to class. Give every student a large piece of newsprint (or other kind of paper), and have students tape it to a convenient place on the wall.

2. Have students write their topic idea in a few words at the top of the paper (for example, "child abuse," "steroid use," and so forth).

3. Have them take a few minutes to state why they chose the topic. (Did they read something about it? discuss it in class? Is it based on personal experience?)

4. Ask each student to spend about five minutes listing what he or she knows about the topic. Some students may know very little, whereas others may know some striking statistics, something about the extent of the problem, the names of important persons involved, pertinent schools of thought, common misconceptions, or facts they have observed on their own.

5. Ask students to spend fifteen or twenty minutes building a list of questions about their topic that they would like to learn the answers to.

6. As students are finishing up, encourage them to move around the room and look at the gallery of topics. Now they can help one another. Ask them to stop at each sheet of paper and do two things: add a question they would like answered about the stated topic, and check the one question (it could be their own) they find most interesting.

This exercise rarely fails to impress students with the range of interesting topics their peers have chosen, and the list of questions helps them see the many angles on their chosen topic. The one question that will provide the focus for each student's essay may even be somewhere on that sheet of paper. By taking the exercise a few steps further, you can challenge each student to find that question:

7. Ask students to look over their lists of questions and circle the one they find most interesting. Urge them to choose a specific "focusing" question rather than a general one. They should write this question at the top of a fresh sheet of paper.

8. Ask that they build a new list of questions in response to the following question: "What do I need to find out in order to answer my focusing question?" For example, if the student's focusing question is "Why do many college students abuse alcohol?" that student would then need to research the consumption patterns among college students: "Do they differ from those in the general population?" "Do drinking patterns vary by gender?" "How frequently do college students seek treatment?" "How often does abuse end in tragedy?" "Have efforts by colleges to curtail abuse succeeded anywhere?" "Why, or why not?" Many of these questions may also have appeared on the first sheet of paper. Urge students to cull the first list as they build their new list.

If the exercise is successful, students will leave the class with a clear sense of the direction they want their research to take. In conferences, help the undecided students settle on a tentative focus (or two). They can change their minds later, but for now they need a discrete trail to follow.

A follow-up class discussion of the library exercise would also be useful. Ask students where they ran into problems and what references proved to be gold mines. Spend some time discussing how to evaluate sources. Most students will be unfamiliar with college-level indexes. Their favorite sources for high-school research essays were probably online encyclopedias and general Web search engines. They should be pushed to dig more deeply and to turn to more authoritative sources. Encourage them to work toward the bottom of an inverted pyramid of sources (see Figure 9.1), where they are most likely to find more surprising, more specific, and more reliable information. Explain what

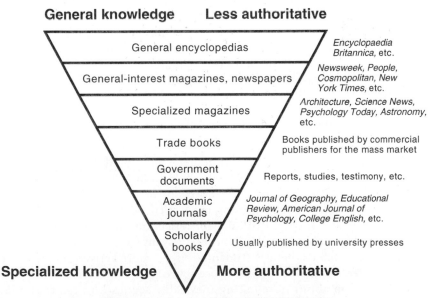

Figure 9.1 Inverted Pyramid of Sources

makes an article in the *Journal of Alcohol Studies* more authoritative than one in *Good Housekeeping* (even if it isn't better written).

Week 3: Research.   Begin the week with a discussion of note-taking. This skill has unfortunately suffered from the wide availability of photocopiers and the copy-and-paste command on computers. The student reasons, "Why do any writing from a source when I can make a copy and bring it home or simply copy from a Web page and paste into a word-processing program?" The answer is simple: By taking the time to write about sources as they research, students are in effect starting to write their essays. Note-taking is thus a kind of prewriting. In addition, taking good notes helps the student researcher internalize and personalize the information, lessening the chances of unintentionally plagiarizing by copying and pasting and then losing track of the original source.

Students struggle with their research material to gain control of it. When students are swamped with information, their voices may get lost in the chorus of experts. But by paraphrasing, summarizing, and analyzing sources, students begin to establish authority over their own essays.

Despite their experience, many students aren't sure what distinguishes a paraphrase from a summary or even what constitutes plagiarism. Some students have never used notes to synthesize or analyze source material — let alone to support their opinions. In class, hand out a page containing passages from a Web site or print source. Then show two paraphrases of a passage, one of which is plagiarized. Use these two examples as a basis for discussing the improper use of a source. Then ask each student to paraphrase a different passage from the source and to work in pairs to check each other's work for plagiarism. Their questions can be the basis for further discussion. (For additional information on plagiarism, see Penn State's Guide to Understanding Plagiarism in Chapter 3.)

Ask students to summarize in their own words the central ideas in a larger source. Then talk about what seems worth quoting from the sample passage and what constitutes a strong quotation. Finally, introduce another type of note-taking — analysis or commentary, in which the writer reflects on what the source says and how it relates to the purpose of the research essay. This kind of writing is probably most important of all because it encourages students to make active use of the information, shaving it and shaping it.

Though many students are familiar with using note cards in the research process — and note cards do have advantages — you can also suggest the double-entry journal technique made popular by Ann Berthoff. According to this method, students divide each page of a notebook into two vertical columns (or write only on every other page), using the left column for quotations, paraphrases, or facts and the right column for reflections on these notes, such as freewriting on their notes (41–47). The chief advantage of this approach is the right column, which challenges students to read more actively, analyze their sources, and determine why — or if — those sources are important.

The discussion about note-taking inevitably segues into another about documentation conventions. At this point, you can review the basics of the

Modern Language Association (MLA) and American Psychological Association (APA) formats for documenting sources. Students inevitably worry about the formal aspects of citing their sources, especially Internet sources, so point them to the appropriate sources for the documentation format you expect them to use.

In conferences, keep pressing students to narrow the focus of their subjects even if they are not sure they can find enough information. Encourage them to deepen their library searches by checking more specialized indexes and to broaden the scope of their hunt by considering nonlibrary sources — interviews, informal surveys, campus lectures, films, and so forth. Though some students may have started their research with a clear thesis in mind, most others will not yet be sure what they want to write about. Challenge these students to consider some tentative ideas, articulate a trial thesis, or pose a controlling question.

Week 4: Beginning Drafts.   Some students will feel ready to attempt a draft at this point; others will be immersed in collecting information; and still others may decide to abandon their topic altogether. Here is where you can help move the process along. Because research, like writing, is a recursive process, you'll want to use assignments and discussion during week 4 to prod your students to complete a first draft.

Try beginning the week with the following in-class exercise on voice. Students often think research essays are supposed to sound, as one student wrote, as though they were "generated by individuals who can facilitate and implement effective word usage at a level that far surpasses themselves" — in other words, as if they weren't written by human beings. With the following exercise, you can inspire a critical discussion of the reasons — good and bad — that scholarly writing often adopts an impersonal, detached voice, as well as why these reasons may not apply to less formal research essays. At the very least, students should understand that the voice for their essays should be appropriate to their purpose, subject, audience, and, most important, who they are.

1. Assume that you're a fashion-conscious person with imported leather shoes and exquisitely tasteful designer clothes. Today, as you were getting out of a taxicab, another taxi whizzed by you, splashing you with a wave of muddy water. Spend ten minutes composing a letter to a friend, describing the incident.
2. Now assume that you're the driver of the first taxicab. Spend ten minutes composing a story to tell your friends over lunch, describing the same incident.

After listening to several examples of each version read aloud in class, students may recognize that they can write effectively in more than one voice. You might point out the voices they have used — in their college admission essays, in letters to their parents, and especially in their research essays. Reinforce the point that no single voice is appropriate to research writing; as with any piece of writing, the writer of a research essay assumes a voice that best serves the writer's purpose. Urge students not to abandon the "real" voices they discovered in their personal essays but to adapt that voice to the new rhetorical situation, for then their ideas will be more memorable to readers.

You might follow up this discussion with an assignment that asks students to write three distinctly different one- or two-paragraph leads for their essays, paying special attention to voice. Consider providing examples of published or student work, with different kinds of introductions — for example, introductions that use a scene, a quotation, a description, an anecdote, a profile, a question, a case study, or a comparison. Ask your students to share their three introductions with the class, and ask the readers to mark the lead that most encourages them to read on and to explain why it does. Beginnings have an enormous influence over the direction of a piece of writing; working on three different ways to start an essay may point students in a useful direction. This exercise also reintroduces the idea of writing for an audience: each lead may well be aimed at a different audience.

As students begin their drafts, they should try to nail down the controlling idea around which they will build the essay. Doing so is not easy. Swamped with expert information, much of it contradictory, they may be unsure of what they think — let alone what they want to argue. Careful note-taking should have helped them overcome the feeling that they are in over their heads. Just as important, however, is for them to tune out the voices of their sources and take some time to listen to their own voice. Assign the following freewriting exercise to help students reflect on the purpose of their essays and perhaps come up with a thesis statement:

An Exercise for Formulating a Thesis

1. Quickly read over your notes, and review your most important sources. Your head may be swimming with information. Now clear off your desk. Begin freewriting a narrative of how your thinking about your topic has developed since you began working on your research essay. What did you think when you started? What did you discover? What did you think then? What do you think now? Write fast for ten minutes.

2. Skip a few lines, and freewrite for another ten minutes, focusing on specific stories, anecdotes, people, case studies, and observations that stand out in your mind when you reflect on what you've learned. Describe them in as much detail as you can.

3. Spend another ten minutes writing a dialogue between yourself and someone you imagine you are talking to about your topic (your instructor, roommate, or friend, for example). Begin by trying to answer the question you think that person would be most likely to ask about your topic, and go on from there.

4. Finally, spend five minutes composing a one- or two-sentence answer to this question about your topic: "So what?"

When this exercise works, several things happen. First, when students have drowned out the chorus of experts and can write in their own voice, they establish their authority over the material. Second, through freewriting they produce writing that they can use in their drafts. The dialogue in step 3 can help them determine how to structure the essay, whereas the final question challenges them to state their point succinctly.

In conferences this week, discuss the two preceding exercises. Also be prepared for lots of questions about documentation, the library, and essay format.

Week 5: Completing the Draft.   The drafts are due at the end of this week. With the five-week approach, any revisions are made subsequently. But students have probably never revised a research essay, and they put an enormous effort into producing a strong first draft. No matter how curious they are about the topic, they are looking forward to being done with it.

You may want to provide exercises and class discussion this week that will assist students with their writing. You might showcase some research essays from previous terms that demonstrate inventive approaches. You can also introduce the conventional ways of structuring an essay: by posing a question and proposing an answer; by describing cause and effect or effect and cause; by narrating events chronologically; by posing a problem and proposing a solution; by comparing and contrasting; by treating the known and then the unknown; by discussing the simple and then the complex, the specific and then the general, or the general and then the specific. And you might show how successful essays often effectively mix two or more of these conventions.

You'll undoubtedly also need to discuss in some detail the format of the essay, especially that of the works-cited section. In addition, address how visual devices make an essay more readable: block quotations, bulleted lists, subheadings or subtitles, and diagrams. Briefly discuss methods of weaving quotations into the text, and reiterate the importance of attribution.

Also remind students of the devices writers use to make a work memorable. It might be helpful to list some of these methods on the board:

People on the page. Ultimately, what makes a subject interesting is its effect on people. Demonstrate this effect by pointing to profiles, case studies, or quotations from interviews. People love stories: They bring a point to life, and they arouse a reader's curiosity about what will happen next. Research essays can make use of anecdotes or can even tell the story of what the writer learned, serving as a kind of narrative of thought.

Strong openings and conclusions. Students should recognize strong openings and conclusions and how they improve a paper.

Tone. Discuss what the tone of a work reveals about the writer's relationship to the subject.

Active voice. Remind students to avoid passive-voice constructions, a bane of research writing. Find examples, and discuss the reasons the passive voice is so often lifeless.

Detail. The meat of strong writing is specific, concrete information. In a research essay, details aren't just sensory; they can be statistics, unusual facts, strong quotations — any sort of memorable, convincing point.

Surprise. Readers like to be surprised. Ask students to consider what they can tell their audience that might be surprising. Ask what surprised them from their research and whether they can use a surprise to hook their readers early on in the essay.

At the end of the week, when your students print out their essays and bring them to class, they will feel as if they are finished. Having labored over their essays for five weeks, they are likely to find the prospect of revision difficult to face. Because they may have difficulty seeing the possibilities for further development, you may want to end the week with an exercise in essay resuscitation. Ask students to bring to class another copy of their draft, scissors, and tape.

An Exercise in Revision

1. Cut out each paragraph from your essay, and shuffle the pieces.
2. Go through the paragraphs, and look for the core paragraph, the one that most clearly reveals the purpose of your essay. It may be the paragraph that contains the thesis. Set it aside.
3. Go through the remaining stack of paragraphs, and make two piles: paragraphs that are relevant to the core in some way, and those that seem to have little to do with it. You may find that part of a paragraph seems unimportant and the rest is useful. Cut away what is unimportant, and set it aside.
4. Working with the pile of relevant paragraphs and your core paragraph, rebuild your essay. Try new beginnings, new conclusions, and new middles. Don't worry about transitions; you can add those later. Look especially for gaps, places where you should add information. Splice in your ideas for new material. Tape the pieces of paper together when you have an order that seems promising, even if it is the same one you started with.

In conferences or in class, discuss what the cut-and-paste exercise suggests about where to go next. This exercise is most useful in helping students conduct a "purpose test" on their drafts, encouraging them to ask, "Is every piece of information contributing to a convincing thesis?" They should not consider it a setback that their work ended up in pieces, but as a chance to take another, fresher look.

Additional Assignments

The five-week schedule described in the preceding section helps students produce eight- to ten-page research essays that rely heavily on library work. It can be adapted for the production of shorter or even longer essays. An alternative to the five-week schedule is the three-part research assignment (see

Example 9.4), which students work on for much of the term. This assignment is course-related, allowing students to delve more deeply into some aspect of the course that interests them. If you included a list of suggested readings with your syllabus, students will have a head start on the research process and a model of the kinds of texts they will find most helpful. Though less detailed than the five-week assignment, the three-part assignment encourages in-depth research and scholarly inquiry and allows students to consider their own personal investment in their research topic.

Other approaches are based on the notion that the writer's curiosity should drive the process. The collaborative research project, in which students work in small groups on subjects of shared interest, each finding his or her own angle, is an example of one such approach. In some cases, students even collaborate on writing the essay and then present their findings to the class. In this case, you will have another important way to help students consider the rhetorical canon of memory: providing guidelines for presenting a text orally.

Of the "universal treasure-house" of memory, Cicero writes, "It is clear that unless this faculty is applied as a guard over the ideas and words that we have devised and thought out for our speech, all the qualities of the orator, however brilliant, will go to waste" (61). If you ask students to do presentations on their research, they can benefit both from structuring their ideas in a way that is memorable for them as speakers (so that they are not tempted to simply read the text and forgo making necessary eye contact) and memorable for listeners. In doing so, they will have to return to their research, culling the most memorable ideas and putting them in an order that will make sense to listeners.

Example 9.4   **THREE-PART RESEARCH ASSIGNMENT**

Part 1: Essay on Course-Related Issues

In this 3- to 4-page, double-spaced essay, you will begin exploring your final research paper by working on a course-related issue early on. You may want to write about a particular topic we've discussed (such as the relationship between visual and word-based rhetoric) or about the rhetorical methods you'd like to explore further (such as whether narrative or description can also be a form of argument). Whatever you choose to write about, you'll want to demonstrate that you've been keeping up with the reading, in-class writing, and discussion. Do your best to convince your reader that this topic is important to you, either personally or academically.

You need a title, an introductory paragraph, a compelling thesis statement (or controlling idea), well-developed paragraphs that illustrate or explore your topic, and a tentative list of bibliographic materials/sources. Your research must investigate some facet of writing or reading or a rhetorical concept.

Part 2: Overview of Research-Based Assignment

Please map out an overview of your ongoing research-based assignment. (Although length is negotiable, five to six double-spaced pages should be enough.) The purpose of this assignment is to lead you into the thick of your topic and force you to get organized and focused! By this time in the term, though, you're probably already feeling somewhat knowledgeable — if not also opinionated — about your topic. Broken into full sections, each with a heading, this overview should include the following items:

1. The significance of your topic (why you're writing about it, why it's a worthy topic for investigation for this course)
2. Your conception and definition of your topic (how you're thinking about your topic and defining your terms)
3. The relation of this topic to your intellectual, academic, literate, cultural, or emotional development (and, if you're collaborating with a writing partner, an explanation of how the two of you are working together)
4. The way you are entering the ongoing intellectual (and perhaps emotional) conversations surrounding this topic (who the leading researchers on this topic are, their opinions, the main currents of thought, how you are joining into the conversation)
5. Your research method (how you are conducting your research — at the library, on the Web, through interviews, ethnographic studies, personal experience)
6. Your plan of work (the timeline for the work you have left to do)
7. Your updated bibliography

This assignment will help you become more fluent in your topic and will strongly inform your final research project. You will not, however, be able to paste large passages of this assignment into your final project. If you're not already working collaboratively, you'll need to work on this assignment in your writing group.

Part 3: Putting Together the Term-Long, Research-Based Project
Your paper will be long enough to merit headings. Here are some provisional
headings for you to consider:

Title.

Introduction. (You may want to keep this heading as is.) Here's where you
provide an overview and, perhaps, a very brief look at what some of your
sources say about your topic. Eventually you come to the critical question
that fuels your research.

Background of the Problem or Critical Question. (You may want to keep this
heading — or change it to something that works better for your essay.) In
this section you provide the history or background of your problem or
critical question. It's also a place for you to show off your reading and
knowledge.

Response to the Problem or Critical Question. (Again, experiment with this
heading.) I mean "response" loosely: here you move from the background of
the problem or question to your so-called response or solution, which will
feature your thesis statement. The background and response parts of your
essay might end up as one section rather than two.

Body of the Text. (This section will be the longest part of your research essay.
You will need to think of appropriate headings and subheadings for this
section.) You want to introduce the sections/features of your argument, the
basic assertions that support your thesis statement. For each major assertion/
development, you may want a separate subheading. Many of the readings in
our textbook use subheadings, so you have examples of how this is done.

Conclusion. After doing so much research, some writers have difficulty
coming up with their own conclusion. One successful way to work on your
conclusion is to think about it in three subsections (which rarely merit separate subheadings): (1) the clear-cut or obvious conclusions you can draw
from your research; (2) the inferences you can make (though not obvious,
given your knowledge of the subject, you feel confident making them); and
(3) the implications of your research for others; that is, where someone else
might pick up where you've left off.

(continued)

Works Cited. This list begins a new page at the end of the essay and should follow MLA style. See Chapter 18 in *The St. Martin's Handbook,* Sixth Edition, for detailed information on documenting sources.

WORKS CITED

Berthoff, Ann E. *The Making of Meaning.* Portsmouth: Boynton/Cook, 1981.

Bishop, Wendy, and Pavel Zemliansky, eds. *The Subject Is Research.* Portsmouth: Boynton/Cook, 2001.

Bullock, Richard. *The Norton Field Guide to Writing.* New York: Norton, 2006.

Campbell, George. "From *The Philosophy of Rhetoric.*" *The Rhetorical Tradition,* 2nd edition. Eds. Patricia Bizzell and Bruce Herzberg. Boston: Bedford 2001. 902–46.

Cicero. *On The Ideal Orator.* Trans. James M. May and Jakob Wisse. New York: Oxford UP, 2001.

Corbett, Edward P.J. and Robert Connors. *Classical Rhetoric for the Modern Student,* 4th edition. New York: Oxford UP, 1999.

Crowley, Sharon. "Modern Rhetoric and Memory." *Rhetorical Memory and Delivery: Classical Concepts for Contemporary Compositions and Communication.* Ed. John Frederick Reynolds. Hillsdale: Erlbaum, 1993.

Frey, James. *A Million Little Pieces.* New York: Doubleday, 2003.

Hampl, Patricia. *I Could Tell You Stories: Sojourns in the Land of Memory.* New York: Norton, 1999.

Horner, Winifred Bryan. "Introduction." *Rhetorical Memory and Delivery: Classical Concepts for Contemporary Compositions and Communication.* Ed. John Frederick Reynolds. Hillsdale: Erlbaum, 1993.

Lunsford, Andrea A. *The St. Martin's Handbook,* 6th edition. New York: Bedford/St. Martin's, 2008.

Reynolds, John Frederick, ed. *Rhetorical Memory and Delivery: Classical Concepts for Contemporary Compositions and Communication.* Hillsdale: Erlbaum, 1993.

Roorbach, Bill. *Writing Life Stories.* Cincinnati: Story, 1998.

Welch, Kathleen. *Electric Rhetoric: Classical Rhetoric, Oralism, and New Literacy.* Cambridge: MIT P, 1999.

Useful Web Site

UC Berkeley Teaching Libraries: Evaluating Web Pages
http://www.lib.berkeley.edu/TeachingLib/Guides/Internet/Evaluate.html

10

Teaching Delivery

[T]oday's composition for me is explicitly materially laden, informed and invented by way of print of various kinds (markers, pens, and pencils); by way of word processors and printers and plotter printers; by way of other software (e.g., Excel, Adobe Photoshop); by way of digital cameras; by way of Web searches; by way of sticky notes and white boards and Smart Boards and tackboards and classroom walls and hallways.

— Kathleen Blake Yancey, *Delivering College Composition*

DELIVERING WRITING

According to Cicero, delivery "must be regulated by the movement of the body, by gesture, by facial expression, voice, and movement" (61). Because of this association with oratory, delivery — like the rhetorical canon of memory — has long been neglected in rhetoric texts devoted to writing. However, in the past fifteen years, prompted in large part by fast-paced changes in technology, scholars of rhetoric and composition have also been recognizing the significance of delivery in textual performance (especially since computers allow for the use of sounds, images, colors, icons, and interactivity — blurring the boundary between performance and text) and other kinds of multimedia performances in which writing plays a significant role, such as speeches written to be read, or presentations supported by visual accompaniments that include both text and images.

Of course, the technological conditions in which one writes and teaches have always had an effect on writing and pedagogy. Quintilian, in his *Institutes of Oratory,* dealt not only with the kinds of oral delivery Cicero wrote about, but also written delivery as it was influenced by the technology of his time. Quintilian observes that "we can write best on *waxen tablets,* from which there is the greatest facility for erasing" and encourages students to "take care to leave some pages blank, on which we may have free scope for making any additions; since want of room sometimes causes a reluctance to correct, or, at least, what was written first makes a confused mixture with what is inserted" (Book X, chapter III, 290). He further expresses his preference for waxen tablets over parchment paper because "the frequent movement of the hand backwards and forwards, while dipping the pen in ink, causes delay, and interrupts the current of thought" (Book X, chapter III, 290). Such relationships among theory, practice, and the technologies of writing call for continued intensive study in our rapidly changing time.

DELIVERING PEDAGOGY

As Yancey reminds us, the term *delivery* can be used not only to refer to oratory and writing, but also to pedagogy. Yancey and other scholars have been investigating the varied ways instruction in college composition courses is "delivered" to differing populations and in various contexts. Yancey, in *Delivering College Composition*, pinpoints some important questions and issues related to delivering composition pedagogy when she asks, "What is composing? How should it be delivered?" She encourages teachers and researchers to think carefully "about what college composing is, how it is best learned, and what that might mean for a curricular space that is affected and shaped by—indeed in dialogue with—a corresponding physical space" (12). Consideration of these questions and issues will inform both the arrangement and content of this chapter on delivery: What is the nature of composition? What literacies do composing and the teaching of composition demand, utilize, invite? In what ways do material conditions, including physical space, affect the work that composition teachers and students do?

BLURRED BOUNDARIES: THE CHANGING NATURE OF WRITING, READING, AUDIENCE, AND CONTEXT

In the twenty-first century, how do teachers and scholars of writing define our subject? It is almost a cliché today to say that the traditional rhetorical triangle of writer, reader, and text has exploded out at every angle. Post-structuralist critiques have made discussion of a monolithic student writer problematic; while work on double consciousness (following W. E. B. DuBois) and multiple voices (Anzaldúa, hooks, Royster) has undermined the concept of a writer's singular "voice" while highlighting the ways in which writing is collaborative (Lunsford and Ede, "Collaborative Learning" and "Let Them Write"; and Ede and Lunsford, *Singular Texts*).

And what of the concept of reader or audience? In his well-known article "The Writer's Audience Is Always a Fiction," Walter Ong writes:

> A history of literature could be written in terms of the ways in which audiences have successfully been fictionalized from the time when writing broke away from oral performance, for, just as each genre grows out of what went before it, so each new role that readers are made to assume is related to previous roles. (12)

Readers, we know, both play and resist roles called for by written texts rather than passively receiving the messages writers construct. Readers actively shape (and are shaped by) the reading process by re-reading, writing in margins, writing notes or other texts of their own in response, reading aloud, discussing ideas, interpreting, misinterpreting, remembering, forgetting, dismissing, accepting, synthesizing, making connections, articulating objects, and playing a host of other roles in addition (see Eberly; Ede and Lunsford; Park; Royster; and Selzer).

The notion of what constitutes a text has also expanded almost out of bounds; first of all, post-structuralists continue to argue that all the world is a text; and, second, what constitutes a text continues to shift with the emergence of new media and technologies.

New media and technology also blur the boundaries separating the traditional language arts: reading, writing, speaking, and listening. When we watch television, for example, we are reading as well as listening, and we may be talking back or even composing our own countertexts. When the president addresses the nation, he appears to be engaged in an oral presentation, when in fact, he is reading a written text. When a student sits at a computer studying a Web site rich with audio, images, and video, what are all the literate acts in which she is engaged?

These blurred boundaries offer opportunities to create richly mediated texts that are exciting for teachers and students alike, but these opportunities also bring challenges, such as the pressing need for new and expanded definitions of writing and reading as well as writers and readers.

Teaching Blurred Boundaries: Establishing Goals — and Delivering on Them

As Marvin Diogenes and Andrea A. Lunsford observe in "Toward Delivering New Definitions of Writing," "For the present generation of college-aged students, reared and schooled in a culture of cable TV, computers, poetry slams, zines, the Internet, and the World Wide Web, writing is no longer a stable, black-and-white affair: writing is Technicolor, oral, and thoroughly integrated with visual and audio displays" (142). With an understanding not only of their student population at Stanford but also the exigencies of twenty-first-century communication, Diogenes, Lunsford, and their colleagues in Stanford University's Program in Writing and Rhetoric have been working to "deliver an enlarged, enhanced definition of writing," one that includes attention to the teaching of "oral, visual, and multimedia rhetoric" (146).

In their article, they list the goals for a course that would work toward expanding the definition of writing. Such goals include, but are not limited to, the following:

- To identify, evaluate, and synthesize materials across a range of media and to explore how to present these materials effectively in support of the student's own arguments.
- To analyze the rhetoric of oral, visual, and multimedia documents with attention to how purpose, audience, and context help shape decisions about format, structure, and persuasive appeals.
- To learn to design appropriate and effective oral and multimedia texts.
- To reflect systematically on oral, visual, and multimedia rhetoric and writing. (Diogenes and Lunsford 147)

Their pedagogical strategy for achieving these goals was to design a sequence of assignments that led to a multimedia research-based argument. (For more on creating sequenced writing assignments, see Chapter 4.) The assignments included tasks such as "substantive writing, research, collaboration, and delivery of the argument in one or more media" as well as attention to the process of completing a large project — from proposal to research to drafting and revising to presenting findings publicly (148). Diogenes and Lunsford go on to describe the final assignment, "a reflective essay that essentially analyzed [students'] work in the course, noting how various media shaped their writing, how their rhetorical choices were affected by various media, and how they used a new medium effectively in the presentation of research" (148). Although in their article Diogenes and Lunsford do not describe the assignments in as much depth as they would to students actually carrying them out, their description does show how the sequence repeats certain activities such as research, rhetorical analysis, and presentation — providing students multiple opportunities to analyze and practice various forms of delivery.

Using Diogenes and Lunsford's goals and description as a guide, it is possible to design a sequence of your own. Example 10.1 provides a sample sequence (See Chapter 9 for detailed information on and step-by-step guidelines for teaching research-based assignments).

Example 10.1   **AN ASSIGNMENT SEQUENCE FOR CREATING AND ANALYZING MULTIMEDIA RHETORIC**

Project proposal: Write a 2-page proposal for your research-based argument that explains your topic, focus, and the potential significance of your argument. (5%)

Annotated bibliography: Provide an annotated bibliography that includes the six most important sources for your research-based argument. In addition to traditional print-based texts, your sources can also include visual, oral, or multimedia texts. (5%)

Comparative analysis: Choose three sources (from your list of six) that offer significant perspectives on the topic you have chosen for your research-based argument. Write a 5-page comparative analysis of these three sources. Your analysis should indicate the strengths and weaknesses of each piece and also consider the rhetorical appeals each piece uses. (10%)

Research-based argument: Write an 8-page argumentative essay in which you draw on and integrate the sources you have used in your previous two assignments. (30%)

Rhetorical analysis 1: In a 3-page essay, analyze the rhetorical strategies you used to make your research-based argument persuasive to an academic audience (your instructor and classmates). How did your purpose, audience, and context shape the choices you made? (10%)

Persuasive piece: Identify an audience outside of the university that might be interested in your research, and choose a form that would best convey your argument to that audience. You might write a magazine article, prepare a pamphlet, create a commercial, or even write a song. Your goal is to present your topic and research to a more general audience, an audience that would be interested in your topic but might not have a scholarly background in your research area. (20%)

Rhetorical analysis 2: In a 3-page essay, analyze the rhetorical strategies you used to make your argument persuasive to your chosen audience. How did your purpose, audience, and context shape the choices you made? (10%)

Multimedia presentation: I have reserved the last two weeks of class for presentations. Prepare a 12-minute presentation in which you discuss your research experience and present your findings to the class. Be prepared to discuss your research-based argument and to present your persuasive piece, indicating its intended audience. (10%)

Other Options for Exploring Blurred Boundaries in the Classroom

There are many textbooks that provide readings, assignments, and guidance for analyzing and creating multimedia texts. Bedford/St. Martin's, for example, offers texts such as *Writing in a Visual Age, ReMix,* and *Seeing & Writing.* Christine Alfano and Alyssa O'Brien's *Envision: Persuasive Writing for a Visual World* links particularly well with the goals Diogenes and Lunsford describe in their article. (Alfano and O'Brien are both lecturers in Stanford University's Program in Writing and Rhetoric.) *Envision* introduces students to visual rhetoric and provides guidance for composing research arguments and multimedia presentations. The Web site for this text, <wps.ablongman.com/long_alfano_envision_1>, provides additional resources for students and instructors, including exercises, assignments, sample student writing, and other resources. (See Chapter 1 for O'Brien's syllabus, which uses *Envision* as its primary text and provides a sequence of writing assignments.)

Even if you do not use a textbook that is explicitly devoted to the creation and analysis of multimedia texts, it is possible to see blurred boundaries everywhere: from the increasing use of visuals in student papers to the frequent inclusion of CD-ROMs or DVDs in pockets of textbooks. Most composition textbooks have interactive Web sites with materials for both teachers and students. Furthermore, we are all bombarded with advertisements and emails that work in multimedia ways to command attention and persuade to action. Through analyzing, creating, presenting, and evaluating such multifaceted texts, students will learn not only to better understand the blurred boundaries of composition but also to develop and practice the multiple literacy skills required to perform such tasks in rhetorically sophisticated and responsible ways. Example 4.2 provides an exercise in analysis. (Chapter 4, Successful Writing Assignments, provides practical advice for and additional assignments dealing with Web, oral, and visual texts.)

Example 10.2   **ANALYZING BLURRED BOUNDARIES — AN IN-CLASS EXERCISE**

1. Using a computer connected to the World Wide Web as well as a digital projector, go to MySpace.com, Xanga.com, or Facebook.com (for Facebook, you must register to search users, but it is a useful source since it is geared toward college students) and project a chosen user profile. (Given the sometimes explicit nature of such profiles, it's wise to choose one — preferably featuring various forms of writing, images, and sound — before you're standing in front of the class.)

2. Ask students to list the many genres and forms of writing used in the profile. (Many profiles have lists, poetry, song lyrics, blogs, email, public bulletins, instant message logs, manifestos, reviews, narratives, comments from "friends," and a variety of other forms.)

3. Ask students to list the potential audience(s), both intended and unintended, for the profile (close friends, acquaintances, strangers, stalkers, family members, law enforcement, employers, and so on).

4. As a class, analyze the use of images and sounds in constructing the user's identity. What do viewers (think they) know about the individual by the pictures, icons, and other images used? What might chosen sound and/or video clips say about the individual?

5. Analyze the "friends" linked to the person: How many friends does this person have? Why do they have so many or so few? What do these friends look like? What does the user's choice of friends say about him or her?

(A more in-depth approach would lead to analyzing each friend's profile too, which can be very time-consuming. You could choose a few friends to analyze as a class or suggest that students do that kind of analysis outside of class.)

6. Ask students to consider the extent to which delivery is controlled by the layout of the program. What information is the user required to provide? What choices are left to the user in terms of layout, design, and information provided? Students who have profiles on such sites will be able to fill in information unavailable to those visiting such sites for the first time. (Although there is some flexibility in how individuals represent themselves, certain features in programs are mandatory. MySpace profiles of individuals, for example, require the posting of "status" — for which the user is given only five options from which to choose: swinger, single, in a relationship, married, divorced — and "zodiac sign.")

7. After analyzing such elements, work as a class to consider the multiple ways — through various genres, images, sounds, and design — individuals compose and "deliver" selves (and are composed by audiences and influences beyond their control) in such interactive electronic spaces.

Often, students are savvier at using technology than they are at analyzing their use of technology (and the opposite is often true for teachers). In carrying out such an exercise collaboratively, students will quickly recognize the complicated rhetorical choices individuals make — sometimes consciously, other times unconsciously — and may also gain a better understanding of the potential effects of such choices.

MULTIPLE LITERACIES

Closely related to the changing nature of writing and other rhetorical concerns is the issue of how first-year composition incorporates, interrogates, and expands students' multiple literacies. In addition to studying multiple literacies in school settings (Yagelski), teacher-researchers increasingly seek to learn more about student literacies at home (Heath); in communities and other non-school settings (Ball; Flower; Mahiri; Moss, *Literacy* and *Community Text*); and at work (Bazerman; Lovitt and Goswami; Odell and Goswami; Selzer). One important way to incorporate attention to delivery in the writing classroom is to examine how out-of-school literate behaviors interact with those demanded in school, exploring the full range of literacies students possess and then linking those literacies to the goals of both the teacher and students.

One Approach to Considering Multiple Literacies: Defining Computer Literacies

In *Multiliteracies for a Digital Age,* Stuart A. Selber encourages readers to reimagine computer literacy, to focus — as Neil Postman has also urged — "on the consequences and contexts of technology rather than merely on the technology itself" (1). Selber details three vital forms of literacy that students need to acquire in relation to computers: functional literacy, critical literacy, and rhetorical literacy. Tables 10.1, 10.2, and 10.3 display both visually and textually the parameters Selber sets for such literacies.

TABLE 10.1 Selber's Parameters of a Functional Approach to Computer Literacy

Parameters	Qualities of a Functionally Literate Student
Educational Goals	A functionally literate student uses computers effectively in achieving educational goals.
Social Conventions	A functionally literate student understands the social conventions that help determine computer use.
Specialized Discourses	A functionally literate student makes use of the specialized discourses associated with computers.
Management Activities	A functionally literate student effectively manages his or her online world.
Technological Impasses	A functionally literate student resolves technological impasses confidently and strategically.

Source: Selber 45.

TABLE 10.2 Selber's Parameters of a Critical Approach to Computer Literacy

Parameters	Qualities of a Critically Literate Student
Design Cultures	A critically literate student scrutinizes the dominant perspectives that shape computer design cultures and their artifacts.
Use Contexts	A critically literate student sees use contexts as an inseparable aspect of computers that helps to contextualize and constitute them.
Institutional Forces	A critically literate student understands the institutional forces that shape computer use.
Popular Representations	A critically literate student scrutinizes representations of computers in the public imagination.

Source: Selber 96.

TABLE 10.3 Selber's Parameters of a Rhetorical Approach to Computer Literacy

Parameters	Qualities of a Rhetorically Literate Student
Persuasion	A rhetorically literate student understands that persuasion permeates interface design contexts in both implicit and explicit ways and that it always involves larger structures and forces (e.g., use contexts, ideology).
Deliberation	A rhetorically literate student understands that interface design problems are ill-defined problems whose solutions are representational arguments that have been arrived at through various deliberative activities.
Reflection	A rhetorically literate student articulates his or her interface design knowledge at a conscious level and subjects [...] actions and practices to critical assessment.
Social Action	A rhetorically literate student sees interface design as a form of social versus technical action.

Source: Selber 147.

Using Selber's Approach in the Classroom

Selber's approach to computer literacy demonstrates the ways that a seemingly "singular" literacy can be broken up into constituent parts and understood in its complexity. That is, any literacy requires multiple literacies. With this understanding of complexity, Selber's ideas can be used in a number of ways in the composition classroom.

1. Using an overhead, a digital projector, or handouts, provide students with Selber's tables. Ask students what literacies they need in order to understand the information in the tables. Are there concepts they don't understand? Are there words they need to have defined? Is important information or context missing? Where would they go to find the information they need in order to understand Selber's ideas? (Be sure to provide students the bibliographic information for Selber's book!)

2. If students feel literate enough to understand Selber's tables, ask them to use the tables as a checklist, checking off the computer literacies they already have (and making notes on the extent to which they have those literacies, since specific literacies are often better measured on a continuum rather than understood as something a person has or doesn't have). What literacies do they wish to gain or strengthen? How might they go about doing so?

3. Ask students to think about another literacy — something other than computer literacy — with which they feel comfortable. They might choose waiting tables, fixing cars, dancing, carpentry, mastering a particular computer game, or any other skill or competency. Once students have chosen a literacy, ask them to make their own tables, demonstrating the multifaceted nature of their own chosen literacy. Do the terms "functional," "critical," and "rhetorical" also apply to the literacy they've chosen? If not, what different terms would they use? What supporting terms help clarify their understanding of a chosen literacy? (This project can also be carried out in groups.)

By carrying out one or all of these exercises, students can begin to understand the complexity and multiplicity of any given literacy and will be better prepared to consider the various ways literacies overlap and inform each other.

You can then move from a discussion of the literacies students use outside of school to a discussion of the terms *functional, critical,* and *rhetorical* as they apply to writing, reading, speaking, and listening — the very literacies first-year writing seeks to improve. What does it mean to be functionally, critically, and rhetorically literate in these areas?

Expanding Consideration of Multiple Literacies in the Classroom

One way to explore the questions asked above is to have students brainstorm lists (a separate page for each list) of all the kinds of reading, writing, speaking, and listening they do — and in what contexts they perform these acts. After students have composed (either in groups or individually) their seemingly discrete lists, ask them to consider the places of overlap: for example, in writing a paper for school, do they also read, speak, and listen? When they listen to a lecture, do they also take down notes, read the words on the chalkboard or projection screen, and read the instructor's and their classmates' body language? Almost every activity — inside or outside of school — requires some level of visual, aural, and gestural literacy. Students must also be aware, however, of the difference between a literacy of delivery (writing texts and speaking) and a literacy of reception (reading, listening, observing). That is, knowing how to read body language is not the same as having the skill to use body language effectively in an oral presentation. Although learning to read body language is important to learning to use it, it is possible to be functionally literate in one skill and not the other. Examining this difference will help reinforce the multiple skills and knowledge sets required for functional, critical, and rhetorical literacies.

This general discussion of multiple literacies can then be applied to a more specific classroom activity, the analysis of an assignment, as described in Example 10.3.

Example 10.3   **MULTIPLE LITERACIES FOR SPECIFIC ASSIGNMENTS**

1. Choose one of the assignments in your syllabus — preferably the one students will be working on next — and ask students to list the literacies required in order to fulfill the assignment. Will they need to do research? (Will such research require skill in using an online database, a search engine, field research, or skill in incorporating and citing sources?) Will students be analyzing a text or a situation? (Will they need knowledge of a specific terminology or theory in order to do so?) What form or genre have students been asked to write in? (What are the conventions they need to know how to use?)

2. After they've considered the multiple literacies required to fulfill the assignment, ask them to list the ones with which they feel most comfortable and least comfortable. When you read their lists or discuss them in class, you will have a better sense of how you can help students carry out the assignment most effectively, helping them build the skills needed to do what you've asked.

3. Finally, discuss with students the tools and media they have the option of using in their delivery of the final "product." If you're asking them to hand in word-processed papers using a specific format, typeface, and citation style, explain why. If you're requiring the use of visuals, discuss the complexities of attribution and fair use. If students have considerable leeway in the form of delivery they choose, discuss what parameters they should work within. Different mediums require knowledge of different conventions, conventions that must be taught.

The need for skill in and knowledge of multiple and overlapping literacies is inescapable, but by analyzing the skills and competencies you want students to develop, you can help make the process of learning less overwhelming, less mysterious, and more exciting as students recognize the options they have. (For another assignment on considering multiple literacies, see the Visual Essay Assignment in Chapter 4; also, see Chapter 8 for information and exercises related to language variety.)

DELIVERING PEDAGOGY: EXTRA-TEXTUAL SPACES

We conclude this chapter by expanding the notion of delivery to include, as Yancey and her colleagues have done in *Delivering College Composition*, consideration of material conditions that affect the teaching and learning of composition. She and the colleagues who wrote essays for her edited collection use the lens of *delivery* to "look at college composition in diverse institutions and regions of the country," studying specific "classrooms, sites, and programs" from research universities, comprehensive universities, and liberal arts colleges to high schools and cyberclassrooms" (ix). One facet of that exploration is a closer look at how material conditions, including physical space, affect the work composition teachers and students do. In Chapter 11, we encourage more study of these important issues.

One Approach to Delivery in Extra-Textual Spaces

In his essay "Design, Delivery, and Narcolepsy," Todd Taylor considers "the body language of instructors and students operating in the architectural space of a four-walled, institutional classroom" (128). Taylor's concern is why students often fall asleep in class — and what teachers can learn from such behavior. He considers teachers' and administrators' lack of attention to the "lives of students: what they think about, their priorities, what they want, who they are, how their minds and bodies operate" (138) and argues that attention to such elements might lead to profitable changes in matters ranging from classroom design to what time the school day begins to the genres taught and to what is discussed in class.

Using Taylor's Approach in the Classroom

Taylor encourages attention to the actual design of classroom spaces, what he calls "the ergonomics of delivery," and how such ergonomics "both reflect and reshape pedagogical design" (130). One example of how space can affect pedagogy is the difficulty of encouraging small group work in a room in which chairs are bolted to the floor. Your students will be able to find many more examples as they work through the questions and activities suggested in Example 10.4.

Example 10.4   **ANALYZING DELIVERY IN CLASSROOM SPACES**

1. Ask students to list the methods of instruction and aids to learning used in your composition classroom (e.g., lecture, whole-class discussions, small group work, peer response, reading aloud, reading silently, writing

on the chalkboard, writing on paper, writing with the use of computers, etc.). Which of these activities are students actively involved in? Which ones are carried out primarily by the teacher? Which ones aid most in their learning of the subject matter?

2. Next, ask students to write about the physical space of the classroom: its size; the presence or absence of climate control (a usable thermostat); the presence or absence of windows (and whether they open); the proximity of the classroom to other classrooms, hallways, buildings, offices, streets; the number of chairs/desks, their arrangement (rows, circle, half-circle), their size, and whether there are any for left-handers; the presence and arrangement of other equipment in the room (chalkboard, overhead projector, TV/DVD/VHS, digital projector, computers, clock, etc.); the location of doors; the kind and quality of lighting; the extent to which the room is accessible to those with disabilities (learning disabilities, mobility impairment, blindness, deafness).

3. Finally, ask students to reread their responses to questions one and two and make a claim concerning the extent to which the physical space of the classroom shapes, interrupts, and/or aids their learning.

In doing this classroom exercise, you might meet student resistance ("It's your job, not mine, to set up the classroom in a way conducive to learning") or excuses for poor performance ("I can't perform well on in-class writings because of bad lighting and hallway noise"), but even what at first come across as excuses can provide useful information for teachers. Although you cannot unbolt the desks from the floor or eliminate all hallway noise, you can request a different classroom for the next term or make other changes. For example, if you use overheads and you learn students have difficulty reading them, you can enlarge the print, create handouts, or post the material to your class Web site.

The benefit of this exercise for students is that it can expand their understanding of delivery and help them recognize the ways that not only individuals but also objects and physical spaces influence communication. This exercise can also be used as a precursor for an assignment in which students analyze the other places in which they write — dorm rooms, libraries, coffee shops — perhaps prompting students to modify their own surroundings or to seek out other places more conducive to writing. In engaging such thoughts and discussions, students will have a better sense of the multiple ways the study of writing — in its numerous forms — is "delivered" and how they can deliver their own texts to others in effective ways.

WORKS CITED

Alfano, Christine, and Alyssa O'Brien. *Envision: Persuasive Writing in a Visual World.* New York: Longman Publishers, 2005.

Anzaldúa, Gloria. *Borderlands/La Frontera.* San Francisco: Lute, 1987.

Ball, Arnetha. "Cultural Preference and the Expository Writing of African American Adolescents." *Written Communication* 9 (1992): 501–32.

Bazerman, Charles. *Shaping Written Knowledge: The Genre and Activity of the Experimental Article in Science.* Madison: U of Wisconsin P, 1988.

Cicero. *On The Ideal Orator.* Trans. James M. May and Jakob Wisse. New York: Oxford UP, 2001.

Diogenes, Marvin and Andrea A. Lunsford. "Toward Delivering New Definitions of Writing." *Delivering College Composition: The Fifth Canon.* Ed. Kathleen Blake Yancey. Portsmouth: Boynton/Cook, 2006. (141–54)

DuBois, W. E. B.. *The Souls of Black Folk: Essays and Sketches.* 1903. New York: Modern Library, 2003.

Eberly, Rosa A. "From *Writers, Audiences, and Communities* to *Publics:* Writing Classrooms as Protopublic Spaces." *Rhetoric Review* 18.1 (1999): 165–78.

Ede, Lisa, and Andrea A. Lunsford. *Singular Texts/Plural Authors: Perspectives on Collaborative Writing.* Carbondale: Southern Illinois UP, 1990.

Flower, Linda. *Learning to Rival.* Mahwah: Erlbaum, 2000.

Heath, Shirley Brice. *Ways with Words: Language, Life, and Work in Communities and Classrooms.* Cambridge: Cambridge UP, 1983.

hooks, bell. *Talking Back: Thinking Feminist, Thinking Black.* Boston: South End, 1989.

Latterell, Catherine G. *ReMix (Reading and Composing Culture).* New York: Bedford/St. Martin's, 2006.

Lovitt, Carl, and Dixie Goswami. *Exploring the Rhetoric of International Professional Communication: An Agenda for Teachers and Researchers.* Amityville: Baywood, 1999.

Lunsford, Andrea, and Lisa Ede. "Collaborative Learning: Lessons from the World of Work." *Writing Program Administration* 9 (1986): 17–27.

———. "Let Them Write-Together." *English Quarterly* 18 (1985): 119–27.

Lyon, Scott. "Rhetorical Sovereignty: What Do American Indians Want from Writing?" *CCC* 51.3 (Feb. 2000): 447–68.

Mahiri, Jabari, ed. *What They Don't Learn in School.* New York: Lang, 2002.

McQuade, Donald, and Christine McQuade. *Seeing & Writing 3.* New York: Bedford/St. Martin's, 2006.

Moss, Beverly. *Literacy across Communities.* Cresskill: Hampton, 1994.

———. *A Community Text Arises.* Cresskill: Hampton, 2002.

Odell, Lee, and Dixie Goswami. *Writing in Non-Academic Settings.* New York: Guilford, 1985.

———. "The Writer's Audience Is Always a Fiction." *PMLA* 90 (January 1975): 9–21.

Odell, Lee, and Susan Katz. *Writing in a Visual Age.* New York: Bedford/St. Martin's, 2005.

Park, Douglas. "Analyzing Audiences." *CCC* 37.4 (1986): 478–88.

Quintilian. *Institutes of Oratory.* Trans. John Shelby Watson. London: George Bell and Sons, 1891.

Royster, Jacqueline Jones. "When the First Voice You Hear Is Not Your Own." *CCC* 47.1 (1996): 29–40.

Selber, Stuart A. *Multiliteracies for a Digital Age.* Carbondale: Southern Illinois UP, 2004.

Selzer, Jack. "The Composing Processes of an Engineer." *CCC* 34.2 (1983): 178–87.

Taylor, Todd. "Design, Delivery, and Narcolepsy." *Delivering College Composition: The Fifth Canon.* Ed. Kathleen Blake Yancey. Portsmouth: Boynton/Cook, 2006. 127–40.

Yagelski, Robert. *Literacy Matters.* New York: Teachers College P, 2000.

Yancey, Kathleen Blake, ed. *Delivering College Composition: The Fifth Canon.* Portsmouth: Boynton/Cook, 2006.

11

Invitation to Further Study

When I began to look in the composition studies literature for answers to my questions about teaching, I found that researchers were borrowing from fields as rich as English studies and cognitive psychology, but they were still coming to relatively few answers, themselves. What could have been a frustrating discovery about the nature of composition studies, though, was a revelation to me: Students — and student writing — are so complex that they elude easy categorization in any well-written article. I was, finally, reunited with the real reason I wanted to teach: to be challenged by my students. When I understood that, I understood I was in the thick of composition studies.

—Jay Jordan

If theory is tested when we put it into practice, the reverse holds true as well: All our classroom practices need to be reexamined continually in the light of contemporary scholarly discussions. Beginning teachers are often interested in finding out why certain theories translate well into practice, whereas others that seem to have equal potential fail miserably. Even after a year in the classroom, during which they have experienced successes, teachers often cannot explain those successes in terms of their theoretical base. Fortunately for those interested in the theory and practice of composition, arenas in which to explore the complex relationship between theory and practice are easily found.

WAYS INTO THE SCHOLARLY AND PEDAGOGICAL CONVERSATION

Professional organizations — such as the Conference on College Composition and Communication (CCCC), the Modern Language Association (MLA), the Rhetoric Society of America (RSA), the International Society for the History of Rhetoric (ISHR), the National Council of Teachers of English (NCTE), Teachers of English to Speakers of Other Languages (TESOL), Writing Program Administrators (WPA), The National Writing Centers Association (NWCA), the Conference on Computers and Composition, Language and Learning across the Curriculum (LALAC), and state and local organizations — offer a way to learn about the current concerns in this field as well as a wide arena for scholarly activity on writing and rhetoric. Many teachers and scholars of writing feel that attending one of these organizations' national or state meetings every year provides the excitement of learning and sharing that sustains them through their next year of hard work.

The NCTE is the most broad-based of these organizations, for its membership comprises teachers of language arts, literature, and writing from pre-kindergarten through college. For college-level writing teachers, perhaps the most stimulating and useful professional meeting is the CCCC, held annually in March. Over a four-day period, the CCCC offers hundreds of sessions that attempt a balance among pedagogy, theory, and research in writing and rhetoric. Like most other organizations, it also offers graduate students special membership and conference rates.

Some professional organizations publish their own journals. *College Composition and Communication* (*CCC*), *College English* (*CE*), *English Journal* (*EJ*), *Teaching English in the Two-Year College* (*TETYC*), and *Research in the Teaching of English* (*RTE*) are all published by the NCTE, and subscriptions to some of these journals are automatic on joining the organization. Numerous journals are published by other organizations or institutions (including university and commercial presses): *Journal of Business and Technical Writing; Contemporary Issues in Technology and Teacher Education Journal; Language and Learning across the Disciplines; TESOL Journal; Writing Program Administration* (*WPA*); *Rhetoric Society Quarterly* (*RSQ*); *Rhetorica; Composition Studies; Reader; Dialogue; JAC: A Journal of Advanced Composition; Pre/Text; Computers and Composition; Journal of Basic Writing; Journal of Teaching Writing; Writing Center Journal; Written Communication; Kairos: A Journal for Teachers of Writing in Webbed Environments;* and *Writing on the Edge.*

Many of the journals mentioned thus far are available online at the sponsoring organizations' Web sites, where visitors can check out the latest information on calls for papers, upcoming publications, conferences, and other events (see the list of Useful Web Sites at the end of this chapter). In addition, beginning teachers of writing may want to join one or more listservs in rhetoric and composition (see the list with subscription information at the end of the chapter). If you've never subscribed to a listserv before, the easiest way to start is to browse the listservs sponsored by the NCTE at <http://www.ncte.org/member/community/listservs/119605.htm>, where you can learn more about each listserv and easily sign up for one or more.

The last twenty-five years have seen a veritable explosion of new publications in the field of composition and rhetoric. When the field emerged as its own discipline in the late 1960s, only three journals existed; today that number has expanded tenfold. Perhaps best of all for beginning teachers, almost all these journals welcome new voices in the profession, offering opportunities for publication that did not exist thirty years ago.

Just as journals have proliferated in the field, so have book series. The major publisher of works in rhetoric and composition since the 1960s, Southern Illinois University Press, led the way with the *Landmarks in Rhetoric* series, to which it has added other series, most notably *Studies in Rhetoric and Feminisms,* edited by Shirley Logan and Cheryl Glenn, and *Rhetorical Philosophy and Theory,* edited by David Blakesley. In cooperation with the NCTE, Southern Illinois University Press also sponsors a monograph series, *Studies in Writing and Rhetoric,* intended to highlight the best current research in the field. Other publishers that sponsor important series in rhetoric and composition include the University of Pittsburgh Press, Southern Methodist University Press, University of Wisconsin Press, Utah State University Press, Boynton/Cook, Ablex, University of Michigan Press, Hampton Press, and State University of New York Press.

COMPOSITION/RHETORIC AND ITS CONCERNS

The proliferation of journals, book series, conferences, and graduate programs devoted to composition/rhetoric suggests that this field represents an umbrella under which many areas of study cluster together. Like other fields (English studies, for example, encompasses both British and American literature across all historical periods as well as critical theory, narrative theory, and often folklore, creative writing, and applied linguistics), composition/rhetoric is a large endeavor, bringing together researchers and teachers interested in subjects as diverse as the history and theory of rhetoric; feminist writing pedagogies; the history, theory, and pedagogy of composition; composition and technology; literacy studies; disability studies; and specific areas of writing or groups of writers, such as writing across the curriculum, writing in the disciplines, basic writing, advanced composition, and multilingual writers. This array of subjects calls for a range of methodologies as well. Thus scholars of composition/rhetoric draw on historiography, rhetorical analysis, discourse analysis, feminist analysis, ethnography (and other forms of qualitative research), and social science methodology (such as quantitative analysis of survey data).

CENTRAL CONCERNS

Across this range of subfields and methods lie several central concerns, three of which seem particularly important to the work of writing teachers.

The Content of First-Year Writing

The first pressing concern is the question of what should be the content of first-year writing. This general question prompts more specific inquiries, such as:

- What theories should shape the teaching of composition: process theory, rhetorical theory, cultural studies, feminist theory? (Tate, Rupiper, Schick). Should first-year writing classes focus on the writing process (Tobin and Newkirk), or are post-process theories of writing of greater pedagogical importance? (Kent).
- What forms and genres should we teach students to write? personal narratives and other forms of creative nonfiction? research papers and other forms of academic argument? Web sites and other electronic texts? letters to the editor and other forms that prompt civic engagement?
- How should readings be used in the writing classroom? Should teachers and students give equal attention to reading and writing? Should texts be

used as models to develop better writing, as content for the discussion of ideas and politics, as sources for the development of critical reading strategies?

The ways in which composition scholars, textbook authors, writing program administrators, and individual teachers answer these questions shapes the field of composition studies, writing programs, and particular classrooms.

Across the nation, composition programs are flourishing in wildly divergent directions. Is there any foundation common to all of these programs? Should there be?

Evaluation and Response

The second concern, which runs across all levels of education, is that of evaluation and response. Whom are we testing, in the name of what standards, and for whose purposes? While we as a nation seem completely devoted to assessing and testing, the reasons for doing so are far from clear. Even more troubling is the fact that current theories of testing (like most of the tests themselves) rest on a questionable epistemology, one that views knowledge as quantitative, externalized, and statistically verifiable. Although such a view has been under attack since the early twentieth century in almost every field, it still underlies most testing efforts today.

Perhaps most pressing for the classroom teacher of composition is the question of how best to measure the success of students' writing. Gone are the days when a C+ at the top of a student's paper would speak for itself. Indeed, the highly publicized grade inflation now evident at most colleges and universities suggests that C+ is not the grade it used to be. Adding to the complexity of this issue is the current debate over the role that standard academic English has played in restricting access to higher education. The struggle for language rights — represented by the uproar over Ebonics and the place of vernacular discourses in school writing — is but one aspect of this important debate. Given the range of voices, styles, genres, discourses, and language varieties available to student writers, how should teachers of writing respond to and evaluate student texts?

Most writing teachers today recommend making a clear distinction between what some call "formative" and "normative" response and evaluation. *Formative responses* are defined as those that are most effective when students are in the process of forming their thoughts in drafts. At this point, teacher response may provide an overall evaluation of where the draft stands and how much work (and what kind of work) the student writer still needs to do. Even more important than such general information, however, are probing questions, encouragement, ideas for sources, and general "talking back" to the student text. We like to think of the teacher's role in providing formative responses to drafts as that of the ideal coach, rather than that of an arbiter who eventually carries out the final judgment on the text (that is, the final, or *normative*, response).

But even the best formative or coaching response is limited to the teacher's perspective, which is why so many writing teachers engage all students in a class in responding to and evaluating one another's work. Effective peer response is difficult to engage students in, and it requires several weeks of practice — with the teacher responding to the quality and helpfulness of each student's response. But research and experience show that once students see how much they can gain from attending to the responses of their peers, the drafts improve exponentially. (For more information on peer response, see Chapter 3.) Another strategy for engaging students in assessing their own work is the use of a final portfolio in your writing class. If you decide to use a portfolio, you may give tentative or preliminary grades on the "final" drafts of assignments as they come in, but students may present a "final final" draft of some or all of their assignments in the portfolio, accompanied by a letter in which they reflect on their own development as writers and analyze the results of their final presentations. (For more on portfolios and evaluation, see Chapter 5. For additional discussions of response and evaluation, see Anson; Cooper and Odell; Goldstein; Smitherman, "Blacker the Berry" and *Talkin and Testifyin;* Sommers; Yancey; and Yancey and Weiser, cited at the end of this chapter.)

Diversity in the Writing Classroom

The third major concern of writing teachers and researchers relates directly to difficulties of evaluation and response. Once composition scholars began to question the ways in which focusing on the writing process led inevitably to essentializing students, the full impact of diversity in writing classes became unavoidable. Even a supposedly homogeneous group of students will reveal wide diversity, and most of our classrooms are far from homogeneous. Growing recognition of the role material and personal contexts — gender, sexual orientation, race, ethnicity, socioeconomic class, age, ability, religion, culture, and linguistic background — play in student writing has led to a generation of exciting scholarship. Among the studies we find most compelling are Geneva Smitherman's *Talkin and Testifyin;* Lisa Delpit and Joann Dowdy's *The Skin That We Speak;* Ralph Cintron's *Angels' Town;* Beverly Moss's *Literacy across Communities;* Morris Young's "Standard English and Student Bodies"; Xiao-Ming Li's *"Good Writing" in Cross-Cultural Context;* Min-Zhan Lu's *Shanghai Quartet;* Scott Richard Lyons's "Rhetorical Sovereignty: What Do American Indians Want from Writing?"; Jacqueline Jones Royster and Jean Williams's "History in the Spaces Left"; Elaine Richardson's " 'To Protect and Serve': African American Female Literacies," Sarah Sloane's "Invisible Diversity"; Brenda Brueggemann's *Lend Me Your Ear* and her coauthored article "Becoming Visible: Lessons in Disability"; Gwendolyn Pough's "Empowering Rhetoric: Black Students Writing Black Panthers"; and Jaime Mejia's "Arts of the U.S.-Mexico Contact Zone." These works have added in deeply significant ways to our knowledge about student writers and student writing.

It should not be surprising that one of the many lessons we learn from these scholarly works is a grammatical one, for structures of hierarchy and power are inscribed in our language as well as in the ways we talk about gender, race, class, and clan and in the ways we read, write, think, and respond. Unless we learn this lesson, we may listen to our very diverse students in class and read this important scholarship to little or no avail. The time has never been more ripe for all teachers to gain insights from studying important works such as those listed here as a central part of their pedagogy.

ANOTHER INVITATION TO FURTHER RESEARCH

These three areas of concern represent only a few of the issues facing writing teachers today. In spite of more than four decades of intense scholarship and research, we have only begun to fill in the outlines of theories of language and learning that will shape the discourse of education in the twenty-first century. Unlike some other areas of English studies, which have been intensively examined for centuries, composition and rhetoric offer many areas in which the surface has hardly been scratched.

In short, exciting scholarly and pedagogical work awaits if you find yourself drawn to it. We hope that this book helps you settle into teaching writing with enthusiasm and confidence. We also hope it raises many questions you may want to pursue as teacher, scholar, and writer.

WORKS CITED

Anson, Chris. *Writing and Response: Theory, Practice, and Research.* Urbana: NCTE, 1989.

Brueggemann, Brenda Jo. *Lend Me Your Ear: Rhetorical Constructions of Deafness.* Washington: Gallaudet UP, 1999.

Brueggemann, Brenda Jo, et al. "Becoming Visible: Lessons in Disability." *CCC* 52 (Feb. 2001): 368–98.

Cooper, Charles, and Lee Odell. *Evaluating Writing: Describing, Measuring, Judging.* Urbana: NCTE, 1997.

Cintron, Ralph. *Angels' Town: Chero Ways, Gang Life, and Rhetorics of the Everyday.* Boston: Beacon, 1997.

Delpit, Lisa, and Joann Dowdy. *The Skin That We Speak: Thoughts on Language and Culture in the Classroom.* New York: Norton, 2002.

Goldstein, Lynn. "For Kyla: What Does the Research Say about Responding to ESL Writers?" *On Second Language Writing.* Ed. Tony Silva and Paul Kei Matsuda. Mahwah: Erlbaum, 2001. 73–89.

Kent, Thomas, ed. *Post-Process Theory: Beyond the Writing-Process Paradigm.* Carbondale: Southern Illinois UP, 1999.

Li, Xiao-Ming. *"Good Writing" in Cross-Cultural Context.* Albany: State U of New York P, 1996.

Lu, Min-Zhan. *Shanghai Quartet :The Crossings of Four Women of China.* Pittsburgh: Duquesne UP, 2001.

Lyons, Scott Richard. "Rhetorical Sovereignty: What Do American Indians Want from Writing?" *CCC* 51.3 (Feb. 2000): 447–68.

Mejia, Jaime. "Arts of the U.S.-Mexico Contact Zone." *Crossing Borderlands*. Ed. Andrea A. Lunsford and Lahoucine Ouzgane. Pittsburgh: U of Pittsburgh P, forthcoming.

Moss, Beverly. *Literacies across Communities*. Cresskill: Hampton, 1994.

Pough, Gwendolyn. "Empowering Rhetoric: Black Students Writing Black Panthers." *CCC* 53.3 (Feb. 2002): 466–86.

Richardson, Elaine. " 'To Protect and Serve': African American Female Literacies." *CCC* 53.4 (June 2002): 675–704.

Royster, Jacqueline Jones, and Jean Williams. "History in the Spaces Left: African American Presence and Narratives of Composition Studies." *CCC* 50.4 (1999): 563–84.

Sloane, Sarah. "Invisible Diversity: Gay and Lesbian Students Writing Our Way Into the Academy." *Writing Ourselves into the Story*. Ed. Sheryl I. Fontaine and Susan Hunter. Carbondale: Southern Illinois UP, 1993. 29–39.

Smitherman, Geneva. "The Blacker the Berry, the Sweeter the Juice: African American Student Writers." *The Need for Story: Cultural Diversity in Classroom and Community*. Ed. A. H. Dyson and C. Genishi. Urbana: NCTE. 80–101.

———. *Talkin and Testifyin*. Detroit: Wayne State UP, 1977.

Sommers, Nancy. "Responding to Student Writing." *CCC* 32 (May 1982): 148–56.

Tate, Gary, Amy Rupiper, and Kurt Schick, eds. *A Guide to Composition Pedagogies*. New York: Oxford UP, 2001.

Tobin, Lad, and Thomas Newkirk. *Taking Stock: The Writing Process Movement in the '90s*. Portsmouth: Boynton / Cook, 1994.

Yancey, Kathleen Blake. *Portfolios in the Writing Classroom*. Urbana: NCTE, 1992.

Yancey, Kathleen Blake, and Irwin Weiser, eds. *Situating Portfolios: Four Perspectives*. Logan: Utah State UP, 1997.

Young, Morris. "Standard English and Student Bodies: Institutionalizing Race and Literacy in Hawaii." *CE* 64.4 (Mar. 2002): 405–31.

Useful Web Sites

Online Rhetoric and Composition Journals

College Composition and Communication (CCC)
http://www.ncte.org/pubs/journals/ccc

College English (CE)
http://www.ncte.org/pubs/journals/ce

Composition Studies
http://www.compositionstudies.tcu.edu/

Computers and Composition
http://www.bgsu.edu/cconline/

JAC: A Journal of Advanced Composition
http://jac.gsu.edu

Journal of Teaching Writing
http://www.iupui.edu/~jtw

Kairos: A Journal for Teachers of Writing in Webbed Environments
http://english.ttu.edu/kairos

Pre/Text
http://www.pre-text.com

Radical Teacher
http://www.radicalteacher.org/

Rhetoric Review
http://www.rhetoricreview.com

Rhetoric Society Quarterly (RSQ)
http://rhetoricsociety.org/

Teaching English in the Two-Year College (TETYC)
http://www.ncte.org/pubs/journals/tetyc

Writing on the Edge
http://wwwenglish.ucdavis.edu/compos/woe

The Writing Instructor
http://www.writinginstructor.com

Writing Program Administration (WPA)
http://www.cas.ilstu.edu/English/Hesse/journal.htm

SUGGESTED READINGS FOR TEACHERS OF WRITING

Twenty-five years ago, a graduate student or new teacher interested in entering the field of composition/rhetoric could attempt to read all the major contributions to the field, including the canonical texts in the history of rhetoric. Today, thanks to the inspired work of many scholars noted in this chapter and especially to the work of people of color and women, who have opened up the canon and led the way in expanding the concept of literacy, no such attempt at "coverage" is possible. And we think that's a good thing: Knowledge production should be as free and varied as possible.

We conclude this invitation to further study, then, with a list of commonly used reference works and brief lists of books and articles in eight areas of study. Reading these selected works will give you something more important than coverage: an entry into the conversations that currently animate the field.

Bibliographies and Other Reference Works

Braddock, Richard, Richard Lloyd-Jones, and Lowell Schoer. *Research in Written Composition*. Urbana: NCTE, 1963.
Cooper, Charles R., and Lee Odell, eds. *Research on Composing: Points of Departure*. Urbana: NCTE, 1978.
Enos, Theresa, ed. *The Encyclopedia of Rhetoric and Composition*. New York: Garland, 1996.
Hawisher, Gail E., and Cynthia L. Selfe. CCCC *Bibliography of Composition and Rhetoric, 1993*. Carbondale: Southern Illinois UP, 1995.
Hillocks, George C. *Research on Written Composition: New Directions for Teaching*. Urbana: NCTE, 1986.

Lindemann, Erika. *Longman Bibliography of Composition and Rhetoric, 1986.* New York: Longman, 1988.

―――. *CCCC Bibliography of Composition and Rhetoric, 1990.* Carbondale: Southern Illinois UP, 1993.

Moran, Michael G., and Martin J. Jacobi. *Research in Basic Writing: Bibliographic Sourcebook.* New York: Greenwood, 1990.

Moran, Michael G., and Debra Journet. *Research in Technical Communication: A Bibliographic Sourcebook.* Westport: Greenwood, 1985.

Moran, Michael G., and Ronald F. Lunsford. *Research in Composition and Rhetoric: A Bibliographic Sourcebook.* Westport: Greenwood, 1984.

Reynolds, Nedra, Bruce Herzberg, and Patricia Bizzell. *The Bedford Bibliography for Teachers of Writing.* 6th ed. Boston: Bedford / St. Martin's, 2003.

Stygall, Gail, and Kathy Murphy. *CCCC Bibliography of Composition and Rhetoric, 1995.* Carbondale: Southern Illinois UP, 1999.

Tate, Gary, ed. *Teaching Composition: Twelve Bibliographical Essays.* Fort Worth: Texas Christian UP, 1987.

Rhetorical History, Theory, and Practice

Beale, Walter. *A Pragmatic Theory of Rhetoric.* Carbondale: Southern Illinois UP, 1987.

Bizzell, Patricia, and Bruce Herzberg, eds. *The Rhetorical Tradition.* 2nd ed. Boston: Bedford / St. Martin's, 2001.

Burke, Kenneth. *Language as Symbolic Action.* Berkeley: U of California P, 1966.

Feminist Historiography in Rhetoric. Ed. Patricia Bizzell. Spec. issue of *Rhetoric Society Quarterly* 32.1 (Winter 2002): 7–124.

Glenn, Cheryl. *Rhetoric Retold: Regendering the Tradition from Antiquity to the Renaissance.* Carbondale: Southern Illinois UP, 1997.

―――. *Unspoken: A Rhetoric of Silence.* Carbondale: Southern Illinois UP, 2004.

Johnson, Nan. *Gender and Rhetorical Space in American Life, 1866–1910.* Carbondale: Southern Illinois UP, 2002.

Kates, Susan. *Activist Rhetorics and American Higher Education, 1885–1937.* Carbondale: Southern Illinois UP, 2001.

Logan, Shirley Wilson. *We Are Coming: The Persuasive Discourse of Nineteenth Century Black Women.* Carbondale: Southern Illinois UP, 1999.

Lunsford, Andrea A., ed. *Reclaiming Rhetorica.* Pittsburgh: U of Pittsburgh P, 1995.

Neel, Jasper. *Aristotle's Voice: Rhetoric, Theory, and Writing in America.* Carbondale: Southern Illinois UP, 1994.

―――. *Plato, Derrida, and Writing.* Carbondale: Southern Illinois UP, 1988.

Poulakos, John, and Takis Poulakos. *Classical Rhetorical Theory.* Boston: Houghton, 1999.

Ritchie, Joy, and Kate Ronald. *Available Means: An Anthology of Women's Rhetoric.* Pittsburgh: U of Pittsburgh P, 2001.

Swearingen, C. Jan. *Rhetoric and Irony: Western Literacy and Western Lies.* New York: Oxford UP, 1991.

Villanueva, Victor. *Bootstraps: From an American Academic of Color.* Urbana: NCTE, 1993.

Vitanza, Victor J. *Negation, Subjectivity, and the History of Rhetoric.* Albany: State U of New York P, 1997.

Welch, Kathleen. *The Contemporary Reception of Classical Rhetoric.* Hillsdale: Erlbaum, 1990.

―――. *Electric Rhetoric.* Cambridge: MIT P, 1999.

Composition History and Theory

Adams, Katherine. *A Group of their Own: College Writing Courses and American Women Writers, 1880–1940*. Albany: State U of New York P, 2001.

Berlin, James. *Rhetoric and Reality: Writing Instruction in American Colleges, 1900–1985*. Carbondale: Southern Illinois UP, 1987.

——. "Rhetoric and Ideology in the Writing Class." *CE* 50.5 (Sept. 1988): 477–94.

Brereton, John. *The Origins of Composition Studies in American Colleges, 1875–1925: A Documentary History*. Pittsburgh: U of Pittsburgh P, 1995.

Brueggemann, Brenda. *Lend Me Your Ear: Rhetorical Constructions of Deafness*. Washington: Gallaudet UP, 1999.

Connors, Robert. *Composition/Rhetoric: Backgrounds, Theory, and Pedagogy*. Pittsburgh: U of Pittsburgh P, 1997.

Crowley, Sharon. *Composition in the University: Historical and Polemical Essays*. Pittsburgh: U of Pittsburgh P, 1998.

Faigley, Lester. *Fragments of Rationality: Postmodernity and the Subject of Composition*. Pittsburgh: U of Pittsburgh P, 1992.

Flower, Linda. *The Construction of Negotiated Meaning: A Social Cognitive Theory of Writing*. Carbondale: Southern Illinois UP, 1994.

Gere, Anne Ruggles. *Intimate Practices: Literacy and Cultural Work in U.S. Women's Clubs, 1880–1920*. Urbana: U of Illinois P, 1997.

Harris, Joseph. *A Teaching Subject: Composition Since 1966*. Upper Saddle River: Prentice, 1997.

Miller, Richard E. *As If Learning Mattered: Reforming Higher Education*. Ithaca: Cornell UP, 1998.

Miller, Susan. *Textual Carnivals: The Politics of Composition*. Carbondale: Southern Illinois UP, 1991.

Miller, Tom. *The Formation of College English*. Pittsburgh: U of Pittsburgh P, 1997.

Olson, Gary A. *Rhetoric and Composition as Intellectual Work*. Carbondale: Southern Illinois UP, 2002.

Composition Practice and Pedagogy

Bishop, Wendy. *Something Old, Something New: College Writing Teachers and Classroom Change*. Carbondale: Southern Illinois UP, 1990.

——. *Teaching Lives: Essays and Stories*. Logan: Utah State UP, 1997.

Bloom, Lynn Z. *Composition Studies as a Creative Art: Teaching, Writing, Scholarship, Administration*. Logan: Utah State UP, 1998.

Brodkey, Linda. *Writing Permitted in Designated Areas Only*. Minneapolis: U of Minnesota P, 1996.

Elbow, Peter. *Everyone Can Write*. New York: Oxford UP, 2000.

Halasek, Kay. *A Pedagogy of Possibilities*. Carbondale: Southern Illinois UP, 1999.

Harris, Joseph. *A Teaching Subject: Composition Since 1966*. Upper Saddle River: Prentice, 1997.

Hunter, Susan, and Ray Wallace. *The Place of Grammar in Writing Instruction*. Portsmouth: Boynton/Cook, 1995.

North, Stephen. *The Making of Knowledge in Composition*. Portsmouth: Boynton/Cook, 1987.

Rose, Mike. *Possible Lives*. Boston: Houghton, 1995.

Sullivan, Patricia, and Donna Qualley, eds. *Pedagogy in the Age of Politics.* Urbana: NCTE, 1994.

Wiley, Mark, Barbara Gleason, and Louise Phelps. *Composition in Four Keys.* Mountain View: Mayfield, 1996.

Literacy Studies

Brandt, Deborah. *Literacy as Involvement: The Acts of Writers, Readers, and Texts.* Carbondale: Southern Illinois UP, 1990.

Cushman, Ellen, et al. *Literacy: A Critical Sourcebook.* Boston: Bedford / St. Martin's, 2001.

Flower, Linda. *Learning to Rival.* Mahwah: Erlbaum, 2000.

Gilyard, Keith. *Voices of the Self.* Detroit: Wayne State UP, 1991.

Heath, Shirley Brice. *Ways with Words.* New York: Cambridge UP, 1983.

Hobbs, Catherine, ed. *Nineteenth Century Women Learn to Write.* Charlottesville: U of Virginia P, 1995.

Mahiri, Jabari, ed. *What They Don't Learn in School.* New York: Lang, 2002.

Moss, Beverly. *Literacy across Communities.* Cresskill: Hampton, 1994.

Royster, Jacqueline Jones. *Traces of a Stream.* Pittsburgh: U of Pittsburgh P, 2000.

Selfe, Cynthia, and Susan Hilligoss. *Literacy and Computers: The Complications of Teaching and Learning with Technology.* New York: MLA, 1994.

Street, Brian. *Cross-Cultural Approaches to Literacy.* New York: Cambridge UP, 1993.

Stuckey, J. Elspeth. *The Violence of Literacy.* Portsmouth: Boynton/Cook, 1991.

Trimbur, John. *Popular Literacy: Studies in Cultural Practices and Politics.* Pittsburgh: U of Pittsburgh P, 2001.

Tuman, Myron. *A Preface to Literacy: An Inquiry into Pedagogy, Practice, and Progress.* Tuscaloosa: U of Alabama P, 1987.

Yagelski, Robert. *Literacy Matters.* New York: Teachers College P, 2000.

Axes of Difference

Ball, Arnetha, and Ted Lardner. "Dispositions toward Language: Teacher Constructs of Knowledge and the Ann Arbor Black English Case." *CCC* 48.4 (Dec. 1997): 469–85.

Belcher, Diane, and Ulla Connor, eds. *Reflections on Multiliterate Lives.* Clevedon: Multilingual Matters, 2001.

Cook, William W. "Writing in the Spaces Left." *CCC* 44.1 (1993): 9–25.

Delpit, Lisa. *Other People's Children.* New York: New, 1995.

Delpit, Lisa, and Joanne Dowdy, eds. *The Skin That We Speak: Thoughts on Language and Culture in the Classroom.* New York: Norton, 2002.

Flynn, Elizabeth. *Feminism beyond Modernism.* Carbondale: Southern Illinois UP, 2002.

Foster, David, and David Russell. *Writing and Learning in Cross-National Perspectives.* Urbana: NCTE, 2002.

Fox, Helen. *Listening to the World: Cultural Issues in Academic Writing.* Urbana: NCTE, 1994.

Gilyard, Keith, ed. *Race, Rhetoric, and Composition.* Portsmouth: Boynton/Cook, 1999.

hooks, bell. *Teaching to Transgress: Education and the Practice of Freedom.* New York: Routledge, 1994.

Jarratt, Susan, and Lynn Worsham. *Feminism and Composition Studies: In Other Words.* New York: MLA, 1994.

Li, Xiao-Ming. *"Good Writing" in Cross-Cultural Context.* Albany: State U of New York P, 1996.

Lyons, Scott Richard. "Rhetorical Sovereignty: What Do American Indians Want from Writing?" *CCC* 51.3 (Feb. 2000): 447–68.

Malinowitz, Harriet. *Textual Orientations: Lesbian and Gay Students and the Making of Discourse Communities.* Portsmouth: Boynton/Cook, 1994.

Moss, Beverly. *A Community Text Arises.* Cresskill: Hampton, 2002.

Royster, Jacqueline Jones, and Jean Williams. "History in the Spaces Left: African American Presence and Narratives of Composition Studies." *CCC* 50.4 (June 1999): 563–84.

Severeino, Carol, Juan Guerra, and Johnella Butler, eds. *Writing in Multicultural Settings.* New York: MLA, 1997.

Silva, Tony, and Paul Kei Matsuda, eds. *On Second Language Writing.* Mahwah: Erlbaum, 2001.

Smitherman, Geneva. *Talkin and Testifyin.* Detroit: Wayne State UP, 1997.

———. *Talkin that Talk.* New York: Routledge, 2000.

Walters, Keith, and Beverly Moss. "Axes of Difference in the Writing Classroom: Rethinking Diversity." *Theory and Practice in the Teaching of Writing.* Ed. Lee Odell. Carbondale: Southern Illinois UP, 1993. 132–85.

Computers, Technology, and New Media

Blair, Kristine, and Pamela Takayoshi, eds. *Feminist Cyberscapes: Mapping Gendered Academic Spaces.* Norwood: Ablex, 1999.

DeWitt, Scott Lloyd. *Writing Inventions: Identities, Technologies, Pedagogies.* Albany: State U of New York P, 2001.

Duffelmeyer, Barbara B. "Critical Computer Literacy: Computers in First-Year Composition as Topic and Environment." *Computers and Composition* 17.3 (Dec. 2000): 289–307.

Grabill, Jeff. "Utopic Visions, the Technopoor, and Public Access: Writing Technologies in a Community Literacy Program." *Computers and Composition* 15.3 (1998): 297–315.

Grusin, Richard, and Jay David Bolter. *Remediation: Understanding the New Media.* Cambridge: MIT P, 1999.

Gurak, Laura. *Cyberliteracy.* New Haven: Yale UP, 2001.

Hawisher, Gail, et al. *Computers and the Teaching of Writing in American Higher Education, 1979–1994: A History.* Norwood: Ablex, 1996.

Hawisher, Gail, and Cynthia Selfe, eds. *Passions, Pedagogies, and Twenty-first Century Technology.* Logan: Utah State UP, 1999.

———. *Literate Lives in the Information Age: Stories from the United States.* Mahwah: Erlbaum, 2004.

Johnson-Eilola, Johndan. *Nostalgic Angels: Rearticulating Hypertext Writing.* Norwood: Ablex, 1997.

Johnson-Eilola, Johndan, and Stuart A. Selber. "Policing Ourselves: Defining the Boundaries of Appropriate Discussion in Online Forums." *Computers and Composition* 13 (1996): 269–91.

Manovich, Lev. *The Language of New Media.* Cambridge: MIT P, 2002.

Palmquist, Mike, Katie Kiefer, James Hartvigensen, and Barbara Goodlew. *Transitions: Teaching in Computer Supported and Traditional Classrooms.* Greenwich: Ablex, 1998.

Porter, James. *Rhetorical Ethics and Internetworked Writing.* Greenwich, CT: Ablex, 1998.

Regan, Alison E., and John D. Zuern. "Community Service Learning and Computermediated Advanced Composition." *Computers and Composition* 17.2 (2000): 177–96.

Reiss, Donna, Dickie Selfe, and Art Young, eds. *Electronic Communication across the Curriculum.* Urbana: NCTE, 1998.

Selber, Stuart A. *Multiliteracies for a Digital Age.* Carbondale: Southern Illinois UP, 2004.

Selfe, Cynthia. *Technology and Literacy in the Twenty-first Century: The Importance of Paying Attention.* Carbondale: Southern Illinois UP, 1999.

Selfe, Richard. *Sustainable Computer Environments: Cultures of Support in English Studies and Language Arts.* Cresskill: Hampton P, 2004.

Wysocki, Anne Frances, Johndan Johnson-Eilola, and Cynthia L. Selfe. *Writing New Media: Theory and Applications for Expanding the Teaching of Composition.* Logan: Utah State UP, 2004.

FY Writing Programs: Models and Administrative Practices

Anson, Chris, et al. *Scenarios for Teaching Writing.* Urbana: NCTE, 1993.

Bartholomae, David, and Anthony Petrosky. *Facts, Artifacts, Counterfacts.* Montclair: Boynton/Cook. 1986.

Berlin, James. *Rhetorics, Poetics, Cultures: Refiguring English Studies.* Urbana: NCTE, 1996.

Brereton, John, ed. *Traditions of Inquiry.* New York: Oxford UP, 1985.

Carden, Patricia. "Designing a Course." *Teaching Prose: A Guide for Writing Instructors.* Ed. Fredric V. Bogel and Katherine K. Gottschalk. New York: Norton, 1988. 20–45.

Coles, William. *The Plural I—and After.* Portsmouth: Boynton/Cook, 1988.

Donovan, Timothy, and Benjamin McClelland, eds. *Eight Approaches to Teaching Composition.* Urbana: NCTE, 1980.

Elbow, Peter, and Pat Belanoff. *A Community of Writers: A Workshop Course in Writing.* Boston: McGraw, 2002.

Fahnestock, Jeanne, and Marie Secor. "Teaching Argument: A Theory of Types." *CCC* 34 (Feb. 1983): 20–30.

Foster, David. *A Primer for Writing Teachers: Theories, Theorists, Issues, Problems.* 2nd ed. Portsmouth: Boynton/Cook, 1993.

Hartzog, Carol P. *Composition and the Academy: A Study of Writing Program Administration.* New York: MLA, 1996.

Janangelo, Joseph, and Kristine Hansen. *Resituating Writing: Constructing and Administering Writing Programs.* Portsmouth: Boynton/Cook, 1995.

Julier, Laura. "Community-Service Pedagogy." *A Guide to Composition Pedagogies.* Ed. Gary Tate, Amy Rupiper, and Kurt Schick. New York: Oxford UP, 2001. 132–48.

Kiniry, Malcolm, and Ellen Strenski. "Sequencing Expository Writing: A Recursive Approach." *CCC* 36 (May 1985): 191–202.

Pytlik, Betty P., and Sarah Liggett, eds. *Preparing College Teachers of Writing : Histories, Theories, Programs, Practices.* New York: Oxford UP, 2001.

Shor, Ira, and Caroline Pari. *Critical Literacy in Action.* Portsmouth: Boynton/Cook, 1999.

Tate, Gary, Amy Rupiper, and Kurt Schick. *A Guide to Composition Pedagogies.* New York: Oxford UP, 2001.

Tinberg, Howard B. *Border Talk: Writing and Knowledge in the Two-Year College.* Urbana: NCTE, 1997.

Walvoord, Barbara. *Helping Students Write Well: A Guide for Teachers in All Disciplines.* 2nd ed. New York: MLA, 1986.

Pedagogic Issues for College Teachers

Fishman, Stephen M., and Lucille McCarthy. *John Dewey and the Challenge of Classroom Practice.* New York: Teachers College P, 1998.

hooks, bell. *Teaching to Transgress: Education and the Practice of Freedom.* New York: Routledge, 1994.

Light, Richard. *Making the Most of College.* Cambridge: Harvard UP, 2001.

Macedo, Donaldo. *Literacies of Power.* Boulder: Westview, 1994.

Roen, Duane, Veronica Pantoja, Lauren Yena, Susan K. Miller, and Eric Waggoner, eds. *Strategies for Teaching First-Year Composition.* Urbana: NCTE, 2002.

Salvatori, Mariolina. *Pedagogy: A Disturbing History, 1819–1929.* Pittsburgh: U of Pittsburgh P, 1996.

Sternglass, Marilyn. *Time to Know Them: A Longitudinal Study of Writing and Learning at the College Level.* Mahwah: Erlbaum, 1997.

Stock, Patricia Lambert, and Eileen Schell. *Moving a Mountain.* Urbana: NCTE, 2001.

III

An Anthology of Essays

INTRODUCTION

We hope that the first two parts of this book have helped you organize, plan, and make choices about the writing course you teach. Our central purpose has been to focus on the practical concerns of real writing teachers in real class-rooms, and we've tried to keep that purpose in sight. But we also realize that the concerns of teachers are often theoretical as well as practical.

Part III includes readings from composition studies that address theoretical concerns. Like the first two parts, this one is included to help you be the most effective and the most informed teacher you can be. In addition, we hope that this collection of essays (some of the best we know) will serve to reinforce our invitation to you to join the field of composition studies. We'd like you to become a reader of, as well as a contributor to, the ongoing conversation in the field. Teaching writing is the ground for almost everything else that goes on in composition studies, but in the last forty years, the field has become an established scholarly discipline as well — one that we hope will interest you.

The essays reprinted here consider composition theory and practice, particularly in terms of the social conditions that inform literacy practices and policies. These discussions serve as the basis for much of what we do in the classroom — the theories we choose to build on, the traditions and wisdom we challenge, and the speculations we deem most promising. These discussions also reflect current social and literate practices outside of the classroom. Parts I and II suggest that every teaching practice is theoretical as well as social. Part III demonstrates just how social exigencies shape the intimate relation-ship between theory and practice. Rhetorical theory, in its relation to pedagogy, is neither arcane nor archaic knowledge, nor is it merely desirable knowledge for a writing teacher to possess. Rhetorical theory is the very stuff that makes a writing teacher effective. A great deal of this theoretical background may be intuitive — learned through practice, simple listening, commonsense awareness of life and social interactions. But sometimes rhetorical theory becomes more useful when it is foregrounded and contextualized, pedagogically and socially. For this reason, we have chosen the essays that follow. To provide context, we have included original publication information in a footnote near the start of each essay.

Our theories — the ideas we evolve to explain what has happened and to predict on that basis what will happen — arise inside and outside our class-rooms and are shared in hallway conversations, meetings, workshops, and jour-nal articles. From there, they are carried back into the world of action — for those of us in composition studies, back to our classrooms through our teach-ing and the textbooks we write and use. The best textbook is simply the best teaching on a much larger scale — a repository of successful ideas and tech-niques available to other teachers and their students.

Our own research and the research available to us help keep us current in the ongoing discussion about writing and the teaching of writing. But this conversation is not a recent one: it has been going on in different forms for over twenty-five hundred years, and it will continue long after we are gone. The late Kenneth Burke, in one of his most famous passages, likens such ongoing conversation to a parlor that we all may visit for a while:

> Imagine you enter a parlor. You come late. When you arrive, others have long pre-ceded you, and they are engaged in a heated discussion, a discussion too heated for them to pause and tell you exactly what it is about. In fact, the discussion had already begun long before any of them got there, so that no one present is quali-fied to retrace for you all the steps that had gone before. You listen for a while, until you decide that you have caught the tenor of the argument; then you put in your oar. Someone answers; you answer him; another comes to your defense; another aligns himself against you, to either the embarrassment or gratification of your opponent, depending upon the quality of your ally's assistance. However, the discussion is interminable. The hour grows late, you must depart. And you do depart, with the discussion still vigorously in progress. (110–11)

Of course, even some good teachers have never entered this conversation. But from our own experiences, we can testify to the excitement, usefulness, and inspiration that can come from joining a national community of people who are all working on the same questions and issues. Besides addressing the basic issues surrounding students' writing and teaching students to write, our conversation also addresses issues of working with students whose strongest language or dialect is not standard English.

Therefore, the essays included here speak not only to the established concerns of basic writers, process writing, teachers' responses, and grammar, but also to the possibilities of exploring a range of literate practices as they play out in language variation, the reading and writing relationship, and identity. In considering these issues, we have chosen those articles that have been the most helpful to us, especially when we were looking to understand our own teaching. And that, for us, is the bottom line: the scholarship and theory collected here returns to our teaching and to our students' learning. Counter to popular thinking, we teachers do not live in an ivory tower. Every day, most of us are called back to the people and places that are truly important to us, our students and our writing classes.

WORK CITED

Burke, Kenneth. *The Philosophy of Literary Form*. Berkeley: U of California P, 1941.

Janet Emig

Writing as a Mode of Learning

Writing represents a unique mode of learning—not merely valuable, not merely special, but unique. That will be my contention in this paper. The thesis is straightforward. Writing serves learning uniquely because writing as process-and-product possesses a cluster of attributes that correspond uniquely to certain powerful learning strategies.

Although the notion is clearly debatable, it is scarcely a private belief. Some of the most distinguished contemporary psychologists have at least implied such a role for writing as heuristic. Lev Vygotsky, A. R. Luria, and Jerome Bruner, for example, have all pointed out that higher cognitive functions, such as analysis and synthesis, seem to develop most fully only with the support system of verbal language—particularly, it seems, of written language.[1] Some of their arguments and evidence will be incorporated here.

Here I have a prior purpose: to describe as tellingly as possible *how* writing uniquely corresponds to certain powerful learning strategies. Making such a case for the uniqueness of writing should logically and theoretically involve establishing many contrasts, distinctions between (1) writing and all other verbal language processes—listening, reading, and especially talking; (2) writing and all other forms of composing, such as composing a painting, a symphony, a dance, a film, a building; and (3) composing in words and composing in the two other major graphic symbol systems of mathematical equations and scientific formulae. For the purpose of this paper, the task is simpler, since most students are not permitted by most curricula to discover the values of composing, say, in dance, or even in film; and most students are not sophisticated enough to create, to originate formulations, using the highly abstruse symbol system of equations and formulae. Verbal language represents the most *available* medium for composing; in fact, the significance of sheer availability in its selection as a mode for learning can probably not be overstressed. But the uniqueness of writing among the verbal languaging processes does need to be established and supported if only because so many curricula and courses in English still consist almost exclusively of reading and listening.

---

[1] Lev S. Vygotsky, *Thought and Language,* trans. Eugenia Hanfmann and Gertrude Vakar (Cambridge: The M. I. T. Press, 1962); A. R. Luria and F. Ia. Yudovich, *Speech and the Development of Mental Processes in the Child,* ed. Joan Simon (Baltimore: Penguin, 1971); Jerome S. Bruner, *The Relevance of Education* (New York: W. W. Norton and Co., 1971).

This article is reprinted from *College Composition and Communication* 28 (May 1977): 122–28.

WRITING AS A UNIQUE LANGUAGING PROCESS

Traditionally, the four languaging processes of listening, talking, reading, and writing are paired in either of two ways. The more informative seems to be the division many linguists make between first-order and second-order processes, with talking and listening characterized as first-order processes; reading and writing, as second-order. First-order processes are acquired without formal or systematic instruction; the second-order processes of reading and writing tend to be learned initially only with the aid of formal and systematic instruction.

The less useful distinction is that between listening and reading as receptive functions and talking and writing as productive functions. Critics of these terms like Louise Rosenblatt rightfully point out that the connotation of passivity too often accompanies the notion of receptivity when reading, like listening, is a vital, construing act.

An additional distinction, so simple it may have been previously overlooked, resides in two criteria: the matters of origination and of graphic recording. Writing is originating and creating a unique verbal construct that is graphically recorded. Reading is creating or re-creating *but not* originating a verbal construct that is graphically recorded. Listening is creating or re-creating but not originating a verbal construct that is *not* graphically recorded. Talking is creating *and* originating a verbal construct that is *not* graphically recorded (except for the circuitous routing of a transcribed tape). Note that a distinction is being made between creating and originating, separable processes.

For talking, the nearest languaging process, additional distinctions should probably be made. (What follows is not a denigration of talk as a valuable mode of learning.) A silent classroom or one filled only with the teacher's voice is anathema to learning. For evidence of the cognitive value of talk, one can look to some of the persuasive monographs coming from the London Schools Council project on writing: *From Information to Understanding* by Nancy Martin or *From Talking to Writing* by Peter Medway.[2] We also know that for some of us, talking is a valuable, even necessary, form of pre-writing. In his curriculum, James Moffett makes the value of such talk quite explicit.

But to say that talking is a valuable form of pre-writing is not to say that writing is talk recorded, an inaccuracy appearing in far too many composition texts. Rather, a number of contemporary trans-disciplinary sources suggest that talking and writing may emanate from different organic sources and represent quite different, possibly distinct, language functions. In *Thought and Language,* Vygotsky notes that "written speech is a separate linguistic function, differing from oral speech in both structure and mode of functioning."[3] The

---

[2] Nancy Martin, *From Information to Understanding* (London: Schools Council Project Writing across the Curriculum, 11–13, 1973); Peter Medway, *From Talking to Writing* (London: Schools Council Project Writing across the Curriculum, 11–13, 1973).

[3] Vygotsky, p. 98.

socio-linguist Dell Hymes, in a valuable issue of *Daedalus,* "Language as a Human Problem," makes a comparable point: "That speech and writing are not simply interchangeable, and have developed historically in ways at least partly autonomous, is obvious."[4] At the first session of the Buffalo Conference on Researching Composition (4–5 October 1975), the first point of unanimity among the participant-speakers with interests in developmental psychology, media, dreams and aphasia was that talking and writing were markedly different functions.[5] Some of us who work rather steadily with writing research agree. We also believe that there are hazards, conceptually and pedagogically, in creating too complete an analogy between talking and writing, in blurring the very real differences between the two.

What are these differences?

1. Writing is learned behavior; talking is natural, even irrepressible, behavior.
2. Writing then is an artificial process; talking is not.
3. Writing is a technological device–not the wheel, but early enough to qualify as primary technology; talking is organic, natural, earlier.
4. Most writing is slower than most talking.
5. Writing is stark, barren, even naked as a medium; talking is rich, luxuriant, inherently redundant.
6. Talk leans on the environment; writing must provide its own context.
7. With writing, the audience is usually absent; with talking, the listener is usually present.
8. Writing usually results in a visible graphic product; talking usually does not.
9. Perhaps because there is a product involved, writing tends to be a more responsible and committed act than talking.
10. It can be said that throughout history, an aura, an ambience, a mystique has usually encircled the written word; the spoken word has for the most part proved ephemeral and [been] treated mundanely....
11. Because writing is often our representation of the world made visible, embodying both process and product, writing is more readily a form and source of learning than talking.

UNIQUE CORRESPONDENCES BETWEEN LEARNING AND WRITING

What then are some *unique* correspondences between learning and writing? To begin with some definitions: Learning can be defined in many ways, according to one's predilections and training, with all statements about learning

---

[4] Dell Hymes, "On the Origins and Foundations of Inequality among Speakers," *Daedalus,* 102 (Summer, 1973), 69.

[5] Participant-speakers were Loren Barrett, University of Michigan; Gerald O'Grady, SUNY/Buffalo; Hollis Frampton, SUNY/Buffalo; and Janet Emig, Rutgers.

of course hypothetical. Definitions range from the chemophysiological ("Learning is changed patterns of protein synthesis in relevant portions of the cortex")[6] to transactive views drawn from both philosophy and psychology (John Dewey, Jean Piaget) that learning is the re-organization or confirmation of a cognitive scheme in light of an experience.[7] What the speculations seem to share is consensus about certain features and strategies that characterize successful learning. These include the importance of the classic attributes of reinforcement and feedback. In most hypotheses, successful learning is also connective and selective. Additionally, it makes use of propositions, hypotheses, and other elegant summarizers. Finally, it is active, engaged, personal — more specifically, self-rhythmed — in nature.

Jerome Bruner, like Jean Piaget, through a comparable set of categories, posits three major ways in which we represent and deal with actuality: (1) enactive — we learn "by doing"; (2) iconic — we learn "by depiction in an image"; and (3) representational or symbolic — we learn "by restatement in words."[8] To overstate the matter, in enactive learning, the hand predominates; in iconic, the eye; and in symbolic, the brain.

What is striking about writing as a process is that, by its very nature, all three ways of dealing with actuality are simultaneously or almost simultaneously deployed. That is, the symbolic transformation of experience through the specific symbol system of verbal language is shaped into an icon, the graphic product by the enactive hand. If the most efficacious learning occurs when learning is reinforced, then writing through its inherent reinforcing cycle involving hand, eye, and brain marks a uniquely powerful multirepresentational mode for learning.

Writing is also integrative in perhaps the most basic possible sense: the organic, the functional. Writing involves the fullest possible functioning of the brain, which entails the active participation in the process of both the left and right hemispheres. Writing is markedly bispheral, although in some popular accounts, writing is inaccurately presented as a chiefly left-hemisphere activity, perhaps because the linear written product is somehow regarded as analogue for the process that created it; and the left hemisphere seems to process material linearly.

The right hemisphere, however, seems to make at least three, perhaps four, major contributions to the writing process — probably, to the creative process genetically. First, several researchers, such as Geschwind and Snyder of Harvard and Zaidal of Cal Tech, through markedly different experiments, have very

---

[6] George Steiner, *After Babel: Aspects of Language and Translation* (New York: Oxford University Press, 1975), p. 287.

[7] John Dewey, *Experience and Education* (New York: Macmillan, 1938); Jean Piaget, *Biology and Knowledge: An Essay on the Relations between Organic Regulations and Cognitive Processes* (Chicago: University of Chicago Press, 1971).

[8] Bruner, pp. 7–8.

tentatively suggested that the right hemisphere is the sphere, even the *seat,* of emotions.[9] Second — or perhaps as an illustration of the first — Howard Gardner, in his important study of the brain-damaged, notes that our sense of emotional appropriateness in discourse may reside in the right sphere:

> Emotional appropriateness, in sum — being related not only to *what* is said, but to how it is said and to what is *not* said, as well — is crucially dependent on right hemisphere intactness.[10]

Third, the right hemisphere seems to be the source of intuition, of sudden gestalts, of flashes of images, of abstractions occurring as visual or spatial wholes, as the initiating metaphors in the creative process. A familiar example: William Faulkner noted in his *Paris Review* interview that *The Sound and the Fury* began as the image of a little girl's muddy drawers as she sat in a tree watching her grandmother's funeral.[11]

Also, a unique form of feedback, as well as reinforcement, exists with writing, because information from the *process* is immediately and visibly available as that portion of the *product* already written. The importance for learning of a product in a familiar and available medium for immediate, literal (that is, visual) re-scanning and review cannot perhaps be overstated. In his remarkable study of purportedly blind sculptors, Géza Révész found that without sight, persons cannot move beyond a literal transcription of elements into any manner of symbolic transformation — by definition, the central requirement for reformulation and re-interpretation, i.e., revision, that most aptly named process.[12]

As noted in the second paragraph, Vygotsky and Luria, like Bruner, have written importantly about the connections between learning and writing. In his essay "The Psychobiology of Psychology," Bruner lists as one of six axioms regarding learning: "We are connective."[13] Another correspondence then between learning and writing: in *Thought and Language,* Vygotsky notes that writing makes a unique demand in that the writer must engage in "deliberate semantics" — in Vygotsky's elegant phrase, "deliberate structuring of the web of meaning."[14] Such structuring is required because, for Vygotsky, writing centrally represents an expansion of inner speech, that mode whereby we talk to ourselves, which is "maximally compact" and "almost entirely predicative"; written

[9] Boyce Rensberger, "Language Ability Found in Right Side of Brain," *New York Times,* 1 August 1975, p. 14.

[10] Howard Gardner, *The Shattered Mind: The Person after Brain Damage* (New York: Alfred A. Knopf, 1975), p. 372.

[11] William Faulkner, *Writers at Work: The Paris Review Interviews,* ed. Malcolm Cowley (New York: The Viking Press, 1959), p. 130.

[12] Géza Révész, *Psychology and Art of the Blind,* trans. H. A. Wolff (London: Longmans-Green, 1950).

[13] Bruner, p. 126.

[14] Vygotsky, p. 100.

speech is a mode which is "maximally detailed" and which requires explicitly supplied subjects and topics. The medium then of written verbal language requires the establishment of systematic connections and relationships. Clear writing by definition is that writing which signals without ambiguity the nature of conceptual relationships, whether they be coordinate, subordinate, superordinate, causal, or something other.

Successful learning is also engaged, committed, personal learning. Indeed, impersonal learning may be an anomalous concept, like the very notion of objectivism itself. As Michael Polanyi states simply at the beginning of *Personal Knowledge:* "the ideal of strict objectivism is absurd." (How many courses and curricula in English, science, and all else does that one sentence reduce to rubble?) Indeed, the theme of *Personal Knowledge* is that

> into every act of knowing there enters a passionate contribution of the person knowing what is being known, . . . this coefficient is no mere imperfection but a vital component of his knowledge.[15]

In *Zen and the Art of Motorcycle Maintenance,* Robert Pirsig states a comparable theme:

> The Quality which creates the world emerges as *a relationship* between man and his experience. He is a *participant* in the creation of all things.[16]

Finally, the psychologist George Kelly has as the central notion in his subtle and compelling theory of personal constructs man as a scientist steadily and actively engaged in making and re-making his hypotheses about the nature of the universe.[17]

We are acquiring as well some empirical confirmation about the importance of engagement in, as well as self-selection of, a subject for the student learning to write and writing to learn. The recent Sanders and Littlefield study, reported in *Research in the Teaching of English,* is persuasive evidence on this point, as well as being a model for a certain type of research.[18]

As Luria implies in the quotation [below], writing is self-rhythmed. One writes best as one learns best, at one's own pace. Or to connect the two processes, writing can sponsor learning because it can match its pace. Support for the importance of self-pacing to learning can be found in Benjamin Bloom's important study "Time and Learning."[19] Evidence for the significance of self-pacing to writing can be found in the reason Jean-Paul Sartre gave last summer for not

---

[15] Michael Polanyi, *Personal Knowledge: Toward a Post-Critical Philosophy* (Chicago: University of Chicago Press, 1958), p. viii.

[16] Robert Pirsig, *Zen and the Art of Motorcycle Maintenance* (New York: William Morrow and Co., Inc., 1974), p. 212.

[17] George Kelly, *A Theory of Personality: The Psychology of Personal Constructs* (New York: W. W. Norton and Co., 1963).

[18] Sara E. Sanders and John H. Littlefield, "Perhaps Test Essays Can Reflect Significant Improvement in Freshman Composition: Report on a Successful Attempt," *RTE,* 9 (Fall, 1975), 145–153.

[19] Benjamin Bloom, "Time and Learning," *American Psychologist,* 29 (September, 1974), 682–688.

using the tape-recorder when he announced that blindness in his second eye
had forced him to give up writing:

> I think there is an enormous difference between speaking and writing. One
> rereads what one rewrites. But one can read slowly or quickly: in other words, you
> do not know how long you will have to take deliberating over a sentence....If I
> listen to a tape recorder, the listening speed is determined by the speed at which
> the tape turns and not by my own needs. Therefore I will always be either lagging
> behind or running ahead of the machine.[20]

Writing is connective as a process in a more subtle and perhaps more significant way, as Luria points out in what may be the most powerful paragraph of
rationale ever supplied for writing as a heuristic:

> Written speech is bound up with the inhibition of immediate synpractical con-
> nections. It assumes a much slower, repeated mediating process of analysis and
> synthesis, which makes it possible not only to develop the required thought, but
> even to revert to its earlier stages, thus transforming the sequential chain of con-
> nections in a simultaneous, self-reviewing structure. Written speech thus repre-
> sents a new and powerful instrument of thought.[21]

But first to explicate: writing inhibits "immediate synpractical connections."
Luria defines *synpraxis* as "concrete-active" situations in which language does
not exist independently but as a "fragment" of an ongoing action "outside of
which it is incomprehensible."[22] In *Language and Learning,* James Britton defines
it succinctly as "speech-cum-action."[23] Writing, unlike talking, restrains dependence upon the actual situation. Writing as a mode is inherently more self-
reliant than speaking. Moreover, as Bruner states in explicating Vygotsky,
"Writing virtually forces a remoteness of reference on the language user."[24]

Luria notes what has already been noted above: that writing, typically, is a
"much slower" process than talking. But then he points out the relation of this
slower pace to learning: this slower pace allows for — indeed encourages — the
shuttling among past, present, and future. Writing, in other words, connects
the three major tenses of our experience to make meaning. And the two major
modes by which these three aspects are united are the processes of analysis and
synthesis: analysis, the breaking of entities into their constituent parts; and synthesis, combining or fusing these, often into fresh arrangements or amalgams.

Finally, writing is epigenetic, with the complex evolutionary development of
thought steadily and graphically visible and available throughout as a record
of the journey, from jottings and notes to full discursive formulations.

[20] Jean-Paul Sartre, "Sartre at Seventy: An Interview," with Michael Contat, *New York Review of
Books,* 7 August 1975.

[21] Luria, p. 118.

[22] Luria, p. 50.

[23] James Britton, *Language and Learning* (Baltimore: Penguin, 1971), pp. 10–11.

[24] Bruner, p. 47.

For a summary of the correspondence stressed here between certain learning strategies and certain attributes of writing, see Figure 1.

This essay represents a first effort to make a certain kind of case for writing—specifically, to show its unique value for learning. It is at once over-elaborate and under-specific. Too much of the formulation is in the off-putting jargon of the learning theorist, when my own predilection would have been to emulate George Kelly and to avoid terms like *reinforcement* and *feedback* since their use implies that I live inside a certain paradigm about learning I don't truly inhabit. Yet I hope that the essay will start a crucial line of inquiry; for unless the losses to learners of not writing are compellingly described and substantiated by experimental and speculative research, writing itself as a central academic process may not long endure.

Selected Characteristics of Successful Learning Strategies	Selected Attributes of Writing, Process and Product
(1) Profits from multi-representational and integrative reinforcement	(1) Represents process [as] uniquely multi-representational and integrative
(2) Seeks self-provided feedback:	(2) Represents powerful instance of self-provided feedback:
(a) immediate	(a) provides product uniquely available for immediate feedback (review and re-evaluation)
(b) long-term	(b) provides record of evolution of thought since writing is epigenetic as process-and-product
(3) Is connective:	(3) Provides connections:
(a) makes generative conceptual groupings, synthetic and analytic	(a) establishes explicit and systematic conceptual groupings through lexical, syntactic, and rhetorical devices
(b) proceeds from propositions, hypotheses, and other elegant summarizers	(b) represents most available means (verbal language) for economic recording of abstract formulations
(4) Is active, engaged, personal—notably, self-rhythmed	(4) Is active, engaged, personal—notably, self-rhythmed

Figure 1.   Unique cluster of correspondences between certain learning strategies and certain attributes of writing

Robert J. Connors and Andrea A. Lunsford

Frequency of Formal Errors in Current College Writing, or Ma and Pa Kettle Do Research

PROEM: IN WHICH THE CHARACTERS ARE INTRODUCED

The labyrinthine project of which this research is a part represents an ongoing activity for us, something we engage in because we like to work together, have a long friendship, and share many interests. As we worked on this error research together, however, we started somewhere along the line to feel less and less like the white-coated Researchers of our dreams and more and more like characters we called Ma and Pa Kettle — good-hearted bumblers striving to understand a world whose complexity was more than a little daunting. Being fans of classical rhetoric, *prosopopoeia, letteraturizzazione,* and the like, as well as enthusiasts for intertextuality, *plaisir de texte, differance,* etc., we offer this account of our travails — with apologies to Marjorie Main and Percy Kilbride.

EXORDIUM: THE KETTLES SMELL A PROBLEM

Marking and judging formal and mechanical errors in student papers is one area in which composition studies seems to have a multiple-personality disorder. On the one hand, our mellow, student-centered, process-based selves tend to condemn marking formal errors at all. Doing it represents the Bad Old Days. Ms. Fidditch and Mr. Flutesnoot with sharpened red pencils, spilling innocent blood across the page. Useless detail work. Inhumane, perfectionist standards, making our students feel stupid, wrong, trivial, misunderstood. Joseph Williams has pointed out how arbitrary and context-bound our judgments of formal error are. And certainly our noting of errors on student papers gives no one any great joy; as Peter Elbow says, English is most often associated *either* with grammar or with high literature — "two things designed to make folks feel most out of it."

Nevertheless, very few of us can deny that an outright comma splice, "its/it's" error, or misspelled common word distracts us. So our more traditional pedagogical selves feel a touch guilty when we ignore student error patterns altogether, even in the sacrosanct drafting stage of composing. Not even the

---

This article is reprinted from *College Composition and Communication* 39 (December, 1988): 395–409.

most liberal of process-oriented teachers completely ignores the problem of mechanical and formal errors. As Mina Shaughnessy put it, errors are "unintentional and unprofitable intrusions upon the consciousness of the reader.... They demand energy without giving back any return in meaning" (12). Errors are not merely mechanical, therefore, but rhetorical as well. The world judges a writer by her mastery of conventions, and we all know it. Students, parents, university colleagues, and administrators expect us to deal somehow with those unmet rhetorical expectations, and like it or not, pointing out errors seems to most of us part of what we do.

Of course, every teacher has his or her ideas of what errors are common and important, but testing those intuitive ideas is something else again. We became interested in error-frequency research as a result of our historical studies, when we realized that no major nationwide analysis of actual college essays had been conducted, to our knowledge, since the late 1930s. As part of the background for a text we were writing and because the research seemed fascinating, we determined to collect a large number of college student essays from the 1980s, analyze them, and determine what the major patterns of formal and mechanical error in current student writing might be.

NARRATIO: MA AND PA VISIT THE LIBRARY

Coming to this research as historians rather than as trained experimenters has given us a humility based on several different sources. Since we are not formally trained in research design, we have constantly relied on help from more expert friends and colleagues. Creating a sense of our limitations even more keenly, however, have been our historical studies. No one looking into the history of research on composition errors in this country can emerge very confident about definitions, terms, and preconceptions. In almost no other pedagogical area we have studied do the investigators and writers seem so time-bound, so shackled by their ideas of what errors *are*, so blinkered by the definitions and demarcations that are part of their historical scene. And, ineluctably, we must see ourselves and our study as history-bound as well. Thus we write not as the torchbearers of some new truth, but as two more in the long line of people applying their contemporary perspectives to a numbering and ordering system and hoping for something of use from it.

The tradition of research into error patterns is as old as composition teaching, of course, but before the growth of the social-science model in education it was carried on informally. Teachers had "the list" of serious and common errors in their heads, and their lists were probably substantially similar (although "serious" and "common" were not necessarily overlapping categories).[1] Beginning around 1910, however, teachers and educational researchers began trying to taxonomize errors and chart their frequency. The great heyday of error-frequency seems to have occurred between 1915 and 1935. During those two decades, no fewer than thirty studies of error frequency were conducted.[2] Unfortunately, most of these studies were flawed in some way: too small a data sample, too regional a data sample, different definitions of errors, faulty methodologies (Harap 440). Most early error research is hard to understand today because the researchers used terms widely understood at the time but now incomprehensible or at best strange. Some of the studies were very seriously conducted, however, and deserve further discussion later in this paper.

After the middle 1930s, error-frequency research waned as the progressive-education movement gained strength and the "experience curriculum" in English replaced older correctness-based methods. Our historical research indicates that the last large-scale research into student patterns of formal error was conducted in 1938–39 by John C. Hodges, author of the *Harbrace College Handbook*. Hodges collected 20,000 student papers that had been marked by sixteen different teachers, mainly from the University of Tennessee at Knoxville. He analyzed these papers and created a taxonomy of errors, using his findings to inform the thirty-four-part organization of his *Harbrace Handbook,* a text which quickly became and remains today the most popular college handbook of writing.

However Hodges may have constructed his study, his results fifty years later seem problematic at best. Small-scale studies of changes in student writing over the past thirty years have shown that formal error patterns have shifted radically ever since the 1950s. The kinds and quantities of formal errors revealed in Mina Shaughnessy's work with basic writers in the 1970s were new and shocking to many teachers of writing. We sensed that the time had come for a study that would attempt to answer two questions: (1) what are the most common patterns of student writing errors being made in the 1980s in the United States? and (2) which of these patterns are marked most consistently by American teachers?

CONFIRMATIO 1: THE KETTLES GET CRACKING

The first task we faced was gathering data. We needed teacher-marked papers from American college freshmen and sophomores in a representative range of different kinds of schools and a representative range of geographic areas. We did not want to try to gather the isolated sample of timed examination-style writing that is often studied, although such a sample would probably have been easier to obtain than the actual marked papers we sought. We wanted "themes in the raw," the actual commerce of writing courses all across America. We wanted papers that had been personally marked or graded, filled with every uncontrolled and uncontrollable sign of both student and teacher personalities.

Gathering these papers presented a number of obstacles. In terms of ideal methodology, the data-gathering would be untouched by self-selection among teachers, and we could randomly choose our sources. After worrying about this problem, we finally could conceive of no way to gather upwards of 20,000 papers (the number of papers Hodges had looked at) without appealing to teachers who had marked them. We could think of no way to go directly to students, and, though some departments stockpile student themes, we did not wish to weight our study toward any one school or department. We had to ask composition teachers for help.

And help us they did. In response to a direct mail appeal to more than 1,500 teachers who had used or expressed interest in handbooks, we had received by September 1985 more than 21,500 papers from 300 teachers all across America.[3]

To say that the variety in the papers we were sent was striking is a serious understatement. They ranged in length from a partial page to over twenty pages. About 30% were typed, the rest handwritten. Some were annotated marginally until they looked like the Book of Kells, while others merely sported a few scrawled words and a grade. Some were pathologically neat, and others looked dashed off on the jog between classes. Some were formally perfect, while others approximated Mina Shaughnessy's more extreme examples of basic writing. Altogether, the 21,500+ papers, each one carefully stamped by paper number and batch number, filled approximately thirty feet of hastily-installed shelving. It was an imposing mass.

We had originally been enthusiastic (and naive) enough to believe that with help we might somehow look over and analyze 20,000 papers. Wrong. Examining an average paper even for mechanical lapses, we soon realized, took at the very least ten busy minutes; to examine all of them would require over 3,000 Ma-and-Pa-hours. We simply could not do it. But we could analyze a carefully stratified sample of 3,000 randomly chosen papers. Such an analysis would give us data that were very reliable. Relieved that we would not have to try to look at 20,000 papers, we went to work on the stratification.[4] After stratifying our batches of papers by region, size of school, and type of school, we used the table of random numbers and the numbers that had been stamped on each paper as it came in to pull 3,000 papers from our tonnage of papers. Thus we had our randomized, stratified sample, ready for analysis.

CONFUTATIO: MA AND PA SUCK EGGS

But — analyzed using what? From very early on in the research, we realized that trying to introduce strict "scientific" definitions into an area so essentially values-driven as formal error marking would be a foolhardy mistake. We accepted Williams' contention that it is "necessary to shift our attention from error treated strictly as an isolated item on a page, to error perceived as a flawed verbal transaction between a writer and a reader" (153). Williams' thoughtful article on "The Phenomenology of Error" had, in fact, persuaded us that some sort of reader-response treatment of errors would be far more useful than an attempt to standardize error patterns in a pseudo-scientific fashion based on Hodges' or any other handbook.

We were made even more distrustful of any absolutist claims by our further examination of previous error-frequency research. Looking into the history of

this kind of research showed us clearly how teachers' ideas about error definition and classification have always been absolute products of their times and
cultures. What seem to us the most common and permanent of terms and definitions are likely to be newer and far more transient than we know. Errors like
"stringy sentences" and "use of *would* for simple past tense forms" seemed
obvious and serious to teachers in 1925 or 1917 but obscure to us today.[5]

While phenomena and adaptable definitions do continue from decade to
decade, we knew that any system we might adopt, however defensible or
linguistically sound it might seem to us, would someday represent one more
historical curiosity. "Comma splice?" some researcher in the future will mur-
mur, "What a strange term for Connors and Lunsford to use. Where could it
have come from?"[6] Teachers have always marked different phenomena as
errors, called them different things, given them different weights. Error-pattern
study is essentially the examination of an ever-shifting pattern of skills judged
by an ever-shifting pattern of prejudices. We wanted to try looking at this situation as it existed in the 1980s, but clearly the instrument we needed could not
be algorithmic and would not be historically stable.

We settled, finally, on several general understandings. First, examining what
teachers had marked on these papers was as important as trying to ascertain
what was "really there" in terms of formal error patterns. Second, we could
only analyze for a limited number of error patterns — perhaps twenty in all.
And finally, we had no taxonomy of errors we felt we could trust. We would
have to generate our own, then, using our own culture- and time-bound definitions and perceptions as best we could.

CONFIRMATIO II: MA AND PA HIT THE ROAD

Producing that taxonomy meant looking closely at the papers. Using the random number tables again, we pulled 300 papers from the remaining piles. Each
of us took 150, and we set out inductively to note every formal error pattern we
could discover in the two piles of papers. During this incredibly boring part of
the study, we tried to ignore any elements of paper content or organization
except as they were necessary to identify errors. Every error marked by teachers
was included in our listing, of course, but we found many that had not been
marked at all, and some that were not even easily definable. What follows is the
list of errors and the numbers of errors we discovered in that first careful
scrutiny of 300 papers:

Error or Error Pattern	No. in 300 Papers
Spelling	450
No comma after introductory element	138
Comma splice	124
Wrong word	102
Lack of possessive apostrophe	99

Vague pronoun reference	90
No comma in compound sentence	87
Pronoun agreement	83
Sentence fragment	82
No comma in non-restrictive phrase	75
Subject-verb agreement	59
Unnecessary comma with restrictive phrase	50
Unnecessary words/style rewrite	49
Wrong tense	46
Dangling or misplaced modifier	42
Run-on sentence	39
Wrong or missing preposition	38
Lack of comma in series	35
"Its"/"it's" error	34
Tense shift	31
Pronoun shift/point of view shift	31
Wrong/missing inflected endings	31
Comma with quotation marks error	28
Missing words	27
Capitalization	24
"Which/that" for "who/whom"	21
Unidiomatic word use	17
Comma between subject and verb	14
Unnecessary apostrophe after "s"	11
Unnecessary comma in complex sentence	11
Hyphenation errors	9
Comma before direct object	6
Unidiomatic sentence pattern	6
Title underlining	6
Garbled sentence	4
Adjectival for adverbial form "-ly"	4

In addition, the following errors appeared fewer than 4 times in 300 papers:

Wrong pronoun
Wrong use of dashes
Confusion of "a"/"an"
Missing articles ("the")
Missing question mark
Wrong verb form
Lack of transition
Missing/incorrect quotation marks
Incorrect comma use with parentheses
Use of comma instead of "that"
Missing comma before "etc."
Incorrect semicolon use

Repetition of words
Unclear gerund modifier
Double negative
Missing apostrophe in contraction
Colon misuse
Lack of parallelism

As expected, many old favorites appear on these lists. To our surprise, however, some errors we were used to thinking of as very common and serious proved to be at least not so common as we had thought. Others, which were not thought of as serious (or even, in some cases, as actual errors), seemed very common.

Our next step was to calibrate our readings, making certain we were both counting apples as apples, and to determine the cutoff point in this list, the errors we would actually count in the 3,000 papers. Since spelling errors predominated by a factor of 300% (which in itself was a surprising margin), we chose not to deal further with spelling in this analysis, but to develop a separate line of research on spelling. Below spelling, we decided to go arbitrarily with the top twenty error patterns, cutting off below "wrong inflected ending." These were the twenty error patterns we would train our analysts to tote up.

Now we had a sample and we had an instrument, however rough. Next we needed to gather a group of representative teachers who could do the actual analysis. Fifty teaching assistants, instructors, and professors from the Ohio State University English Department volunteered to help us with the analysis. The usual question of inter-rater reliability did not seem pressing to us, because what we were looking for seemed so essentially charged with social conditioning and personal predilection. Since we did not think that we could always "scientifically" determine what was real error and what was style or usage variation, our best idea was to rationalize the arbitrariness inherent in the project by spreading out the analytical decisions.

On a Friday afternoon in January 1986 we worked with the fifty raters, going over the definitions and examples we had come up with for the "top twenty," as we were by then calling them. It was a grueling Friday and Saturday. We trained raters to recognize error patterns all Friday afternoon in the dusty, stuffy old English Library at OSU — the air of which Thurber must have breathed, and probably the very same air, considering how hard the windows were to open. On returning to our hotel that night, we found it occupied by the Ohio chapter of the Pentecostal Youth, who had been given permission to run around the hotel giggling and shouting until 3:30 a.m. In despair, we turned our TV volumes all the way up on the white-noise stations that had gone off the air. They sounded like the Reichenbach Falls and almost drowned out the hoo-raw in the hallway. After 3:30 it did indeed quiet down some, and we fell into troublous sleep. The next day the Pentecostal Youth had vanished, and Ma & Pa had research to do.

AMPLIFICATIO: MA AND PA HUNKER DOWN

The following day, rating began at 9:00 a.m. and, with a short lunch break, we had completed the last paper by 5:00 p.m. We paused occasionally to calibrate our ratings, to redefine some term, or to share some irresistible piece of student prose. (Top prize went to the notorious "One Night," one student's response to an assignment asking for "analysis." This essay's abstract announced it as "an analysis of the realm of different feelings experienced in one night by a man and wife in love.") The rating sheets and papers were reordered and bundled up, and we all went out for dinner.[7]

The results of this exercise became real for us when we totaled up the numbers on all of the raters' sheets. Here was the information we had been seeking, what all our efforts had been directed toward. It was exciting to finally see in black and white what we had been wondering about. What we found appears in Table 1 [p. 298].

PERORATIO: THE KETTLES SAY, "AW, SHUCKS"

The results of this research by no means represent a final word on any question involving formal errors or teacher marking patterns. We can, however, draw several intriguing, if tentative, generalizations.

First, teachers' ideas about what constitutes a serious, markable error vary widely. As most of us may have expected, some teachers pounce on every "very unique" as a pet peeve, some rail at "Every student...their...." The most prevalent "error," failure to place a comma after an introductory word or phrase, was a *bête noire* for some teachers but was ignored by many more. Papers marked by the same teacher might at different times evince different patterns of formal marking. Teachers' reasons for marking specific errors and patterns of error in their students' papers are complex, and in many cases they are no doubt guided by the perceived needs of the student writing the paper and by the stage of the composing process the paper has achieved.

Second, teachers do not seem to mark as many errors as we often think they do. On average, college English teachers mark only 43% of the most serious errors in the papers they evaluate. In contrast to the popular picture of English teachers mad to mark up every error, our results show that even the most-often marked errors are only marked two-thirds of the time. The less-marked patterns (and remember, these are the Top Twenty error patterns overall) are marked only once for every four times they appear. The number of errors found compared to the number of errors marked suggests a fascinating possibility for future research: detailed observation of teacher marking, accompanied by talk-aloud protocols. Such research seems to us a natural follow-up to the findings presented here.[8]

Third, the reasons teachers mark any given error seem to result from a complex formula that takes into account at least two factors: how serious or

TABLE 1

Error or Error Pattern	No. Found in 3,000 Papers	% of Total Errors	No. Found Marked by Teacher	% Marked by Teacher	Rank by No. of Errors Marked by Teacher
1. No comma after introductory element	3,299	11.5%	995	30%	2
2. Vague pronoun reference	2,809	9.8%	892	32%	4
3. No comma in compound sentence	2,446	8.6%	719	29%	7
4. Wrong word	2,217	7.8%	1,114	50%	1
5. No comma in non-restrictive element	1,864	6.5%	580	31%	10
6. Wrong/missing inflected endings	1,679	5.9%	857	51%	5
7. Wrong or missing preposition	1,580	5.5%	679	43%	8
8. Comma splice	1,565	5.5%	850	54%	6
9. Possessive apostrophe error	1,458	5.1%	906	62%	3
10. Tense shift	1,453	5.1%	484	33%	12
11. Unnecessary shift in person	1,347	4.7%	410	30%	14
12. Sentence fragment	1,217	4.2%	671	55%	9
13. Wrong tense or verb form	952	3.3%	465	49%	13
14. Subject-verb agreement	909	3.2%	534	58%	11
15. Lack of comma in series	781	2.7%	184	24%	19
16. Pronoun agreement error	752	2.6%	365	48%	15
17. Unnecessary comma with restrictive element	693	2.4%	239	34%	17
18. Run-on or fused sentence	681	2.4%	308	45%	16
19. Dangling or misplaced modifier	577	2.0%	167	29%	20
20. Its/it's error	292	1.0%	188	64%	18

annoying the error is perceived to be at a given time for both teacher and student, and how difficult it is to mark or explain. As Table 1 shows, the errors marked by the original teachers on our papers produce a different (although not completely dissimilar) ranking of errors than the formal count we asked our raters to do. Some of the lesser-marked errors we studied are clearly felt to be more stylistic than substantive. Certain of the comma errors seem simply not to bother teachers very much. Others, like wrong words or missing inflections, are much more frequently marked, and might be said to have a high "response quotient" for teachers. In addition, we sensed that in many cases errors went unmarked not because the teacher failed to see them, but because they were not germane to the lessons at hand. A teacher working very hard to help a student master subject-verb agreement with third-person singular nouns, for instance, might well ignore most other errors in a given paper.

Teachers' perceptions of the seriousness of a given error pattern seem, however, to be only part of the reason for marking an error. The sheer difficulty of explanation presented by some error patterns is another factor. Jotting "WW" in the margin to tip a student off to a diction problem is one thing; explaining a subtle shift in point of view in that same marginal space is quite another. Sentence fragments, comma splices, and wrong tenses, to name three classic "serious" errors, are all marked less often than possessive apostrophes. This is, we think, not due to teachers' perception that apostrophe errors are worse than sentence-boundary or tense problems, but to their quickness and ease of indication. The its/it's error and the possessive apostrophe, the two highest-marked patterns, are also two of the easiest errors to mark. This is, of course, not laziness; many composition teachers are so chronically overworked that we should not wonder that the errors most marked are those most quickly indicated.

Fourth, error patterns in student writing are shifting in certain ways, at least partially as a result of changing media trends within the culture. Conclusions must be especially tentative here, because the time-bound nature of studies of error makes comparisons difficult and definitions of errors counted in earlier research are hard to correlate. Our research turned up several earlier lists of serious errors in freshman composition, however, whose order is rather different from the order we discovered.

Roy Ivan Johnson, writing in 1917, reported on 198 papers written by 66 freshmen, and his list of the top-ten error patterns in his study is as follows (wherever possible, we have translated his terms into ours):

1. Spelling
2. Capitalization
3. Punctuation (mostly comma errors)
4. Careless omission or repetition
5. Apostrophe errors
6. Pronoun agreement
7. Verb tense errors and agreement
8. Ungrammatical sentence structure (fragments and run-ons)

9. Mistakes in the use of adjectives and adverbs
10. Mistakes in the use of prepositions and conjunctions

In 1930, Paul Witty and Roberta Green analyzed 170 papers written in a timed situation by freshmen. Here is their top-ten list, translated into our terms where possible:

1. Faulty connectives
2. Vague pronoun reference
3. Use of "would" for simple past tense forms
4. Confusion of forms from similarity of sound or meaning
5. Misplaced modifiers
6. Pronoun agreement
7. Fragments
8. Unclassif.ed errors
9. Dangling modifier
10. Wrong tense

As we mentioned earlier, the largest-scale analysis of errors was done by John C. Hodges in the late 1930s. Unfortunately, we know very little about Hodges' research. He never published any results in contemporary journals, and thus it is difficult to know his methods or even very much about his findings, because we can see them only as they are reflected in the *Harbrace Handbook,* which today still uses the exact arrangement that Hodges gave it in its first edition in 1941. In the "To the Instructor" preface of his first edition, Hodges says that his 20,000 themes "have been tabulated according to the corrections marked by sixteen instructors," which suggests that his raters looked only for teacher-marked errors (Hodges iii). In a footnote on the same page, Hodges gives the only published version of his top-ten list.

1. Comma
2. Spelling
3. Exactness
4. Agreement
5. Superfluous commas
6. Reference of pronouns
7. Apostrophe
8. Omission of words
9. Wordiness
10. Good use

That is all we know of Hodges' findings, but it does not seem unreasonable to assume that he reports them in order of frequency.

In terms of how patterns of error have changed, our findings are, of course, extremely tentative. Assuming that Hodges' *Harbrace* list constitutes some version of the error patterns he found in 1939, however, we note some distinct changes. In general, our list shows a proliferation of error patterns that seem to suggest declining familiarity with the visual look of a written page. Most strikingly, spelling errors have gone from second on the list to first by a factor of three. Spelling is the most obvious example of this lack of visual memory of printed pages seen, but the growth of other error patterns supports it as well.[9]

Some of the error patterns that seem to suggest this visual-memory problem were not found or listed in earlier studies but have come to light in ours. The many wrong word errors, the missing inflected endings, the wrong prepositions, even the "its"/"it's" errors — all suggest that students today may be less familiar with the visible aspects of written forms. These findings confirm the contrastive analysis between 2,000 papers from the 1950s and 2,000 papers from the 1970s that was carried out by Gary Sloan in 1979. Sloan determined that many elements of formal writing convention broke down severely between the fifties and seventies, including spelling, homophones, sentence structure elements, inflected endings, and others (157–59). Sloan notes that the effects of an oral — and we would stress, an *electronic* — culture on literacy skills are subversive. Students who do not read the "texts" of our culture will continue to come to school without the tacit visual knowledge of written conventions that "text-wise" writers carry with them effortlessly. Such changes in literate behavior have and will continue to affect us in multiple ways, including the ways we perceive, categorize, and judge "errors."

Finally, we feel we can report some good news. One very telling fact emerging from our research is our realization that college students are *not* making more formal errors in writing than they used to. The numbers of errors made by students in earlier studies and the numbers we found in the 1980s agree remarkably. Our findings chart out as follows:[10]

Study	Year	Average Paper Length	Errors per Paper	Errors per 100 words
Johnson	1917	162 words	3.42	2.11
Witty & Green	1930	231 words	5.18	2.24
Ma & Pa	1986	422 words	9.52	2.26

The consistency of these numbers seems to us extraordinary. It suggests that although the length of the average paper demanded in freshman composition has been steadily rising, the formal skills of students have not declined precipitously.

In the light of the "Johnny Can't Write" furor of the 1970s and the sometimes hysterical claims of educational decline oft heard today, these results are striking — and heartening. They suggest that in some ways we *are* doing a better job than we might have known. The number of errors has not gone down, but neither has it risen in the past five decades. In spite of open admissions, in spite of radical shifts in the demographics of college students, in spite of the huge escalation in the population percentage as well as in the sheer numbers of people attending American colleges, freshmen are still committing approximately the same number of formal errors per 100 words they were before World War I. In this case, not losing means that we are winning.

EPILOGOS

Our foray into the highways of research and the byways of the Pentecostal Youth are over for a time, and we are back on the farm. From our vantage point here on the porch, we can see that this labor has raised more questions than it has answered. Where, for instance, *do* our specific notions of error come from? Can we identify more precisely the relationship among error patterns in written student discourse and other forms of discourse, especially the mass media? Could we identify regional or other variations in error patterns? How might certain error patterns correlate with other patterns — say age, gender, habits of reading, etc.? How might they correlate with measures of writing apprehension, or the "ethos," the ideology of a specific curriculum? Most provocatively, could we derive a contemporary theory of error which would account for the written behaviors of all our students as well as the marking behavior of teachers? These are a few of the problems we'd like to fret over if and when we decide to take to the research road again.

NOTES

[1] As an example of shifting perceptions of student error patterns, it is worth noting that Charles T. Copeland and Henry M. Rideout, writing in 1901, identified the most serious and common grammatical error in Harvard freshman papers as a confusion of the rules for use of "shall" and "will" to express futurity (71n).

[2] For a list of most of these studies, see Harap 444–46.

[3] We wish here to express our gratitude to the College Division of St. Martin's Press, which graciously offered respondents a choice from the St. Martin's trade book list in exchange for thirty or more teacher-marked student papers or Xeroxes of student papers. We are especially grateful to Nancy Perry, Marilyn Moller, and Susan Manning, without whose help this research could never have been accomplished. From assistance with mailings to the considerable tasks of paper stacking, stamping, sorting, and filing, they made the task possible. Their support, both institutional and personal, is deeply appreciated.

The demographics of the papers we were sent were interesting, as we found when examining them for our stratified sample. After pulling all the papers that were illegible, or were not undergraduate papers, were too short to be useful, or were clearly papers from ESL courses, we were left with 19,615 papers. We divided up the U.S. into seven fairly standard geographical regions: (1) Northeast, (2) Southeast, (3) Midwest, (4) Mid-South, (5) Plains States, (6) Southwest (including Hawaii), (7) Northwest (including Alaska). Here are the raw numbers of how the papers were distributed as they came in to us:

Region	1	2	3	4	5	6	7	Total
Total number of papers	3,652	3,478	3,099	4,974	1,229	2,292	891	19,615
Total number of teachers	61	51	54	55	18	47	14	300
Total number of 4-year schools	47	35	40	39	14	24	7	206
Total number of 2-year schools	14	16	14	16	4	23	7	94

Total number of state schools	44	49	48	48	18	44	13	264
Total number of private schools	17	2	6	7	0	3	1	36
Number of schools with total enrollment under 1,000	2	2	0	1	1	1	1	8
Enrollment 1–3,000	9	13	7	11	3	5	4	52
Enrollment 3,000–5,000	13	5	5	14	2	7	2	48
Enrollment 5,000–10,000	19	9	16	10	6	7	4	71
Enrollment 10,000–20,000	14	9	13	13	1	15	2	67
Enrollment over 20,000	4	13	13	6	5	12	1	54

[4] We wanted to find out whether the sample of papers we had received mirrored the demographic realities of American higher education. If it did not, we would have to adjust it to represent the student and teacher populations that were really out there.

When we looked at *The Digest of Education Statistics,* we found that some of our numbers approximated educational statistics closely enough not to need adjustment. The breakdown between 4-year colleges and 2-year colleges, for instance, is 71%/29% in the statistical tables and 69%/31% in our sample. The state schools/private schools ratio is statistically 79%/21%, while our sample ratio was 88%/12%, but the over-representation of state schools did not seem serious enough to worry about for our purposes. In terms of enrollment, we found middle-sized schools slightly over-represented and very small and very large schools slightly under-represented, but in no case was the deviation more than 7% either way:

	% of students nationally	*% in sample*
Number of schools with total enrollment under 1,000	4	2
Enrollment 1,000–3,000	11	17
Enrollment 3,000–5,000	13	16
Enrollment 5,000–10,000	21	24
Enrollment 10,000–20,000	25	22
Enrollment over 20,000	25	18

We found the most serious discrepancies in the regional stratification, with some regions over- and others under-represented.

Region	*1*	*2*	*3*	*4*	*5*	*6*	*7*
% of students nationally	23	12	23	15	4	19	4
% of students in sample	19	18	15	25	6	12	5

On the basis of the regional discrepancy we found, we decided to stratify the sample papers regionally but not in any other way.

For help with the methodological problems we faced, and for advice on establishing a random stratified sample of 3,000 papers, many thanks to Charles Cooper. When the going gets tough, the tough go ask Charles for advice.

[5] These two examples of old-time error patterns are cited in Pressey and in Johnson.

[6] The term "comma fault" was by far the most popular term to describe this error pattern until the ubiquitous *Harbrace* seeded the clouds with its terms in 1941, advancing "comma splice," previously a term of tertiary choice, into a primary position by 1960.

[7] In addition to the error-rating sheets, on which the raters kept track of errors found and errors marked, we asked them to write down on a separate list every misspelled word in every paper they saw. This spelling research is only partially tabulated and will be presented in another study.

[8] We were also intrigued to find that of the 3,000 papers examined, only 276 had been marked using the letter-number system of any handbook. Handbooks may be widely used, but fewer than 10% of our papers relied on their systems. The rest had been marked using the common symbols and interlinear notes.

[9] With our spelling research partially tabulated at this point, we are struck by the prevalence of homophone errors in the list of the most commonly misspelled words. The growth of *too/to* and *their/there/they're* error patterns strongly suggests the sort of problem with visual familiarity suggested by our list of non-spelling errors.

[10] These comparisons are not absolutely exact, of course. Johnson counted spelling errors, while Witty and Green and we did not. The numbers in the chart for Johnson's research were derived by subtracting all spelling errors from his final error total.

WORKS CITED

Copeland, Charles T., and Henry M. Rideout. *Freshman English and Theme-Correcting at Harvard College.* Boston: Silver, Burdett, 1901.

Elbow, Peter. Unpublished document. English Coalition Conference. July 1987.

Harap, Henry. "The Most Common Grammatical Errors." *English Journal* 19 (June 1930): 440–46.

Hodges, John C. *Harbrace Handbook of English.* New York: Harcourt, Brace, 1941.

Johnson, Roy Ivan. "The Persistency of Error in English Composition." *School Review* 25 (Oct. 1917): 555–80.

Pressey, S. L. "A Statistical Study of Children's Errors in Sentence-Structures." *English Journal* 14 (Sept. 1925): 528–35.

Shaughnessy, Mina P. *Errors and Expectations.* New York: Oxford UP, 1977.

Sloan, Gary. "The Subversive Effects of an Oral Culture on Student Writing." *College Composition and Communication* 30 (May 1979): 156–60.

Snyder, Thomas D. *Digest of Education Statistics 1987.* Washington: Center for Education Statistics, 1987.

Williams, Joseph. "The Phenomenology of Error." *College Composition and Communication* 32 (May 1981): 152–68.

Witty, Paul A., and Roberta La Brant Green. "Composition Errors of College Students." *English Journal* 19 (May 1930): 388–93.

Patrick Hartwell

Grammar, Grammars, and the Teaching of Grammar

For me the grammar issue was settled at least twenty years ago with the conclusion offered by Richard Braddock, Richard Lloyd-Jones, and Lowell Schoer in 1963.

> In view of the widespread agreement of research studies based upon many types of students and teachers, the conclusion can be stated in strong and unqualified terms: the teaching of formal grammar has a negligible or, because it usually displaces some instruction and practice in composition, even a harmful effect on improvement in writing.[1]

Indeed, I would agree with Janet Emig that the grammar issue is a prime example of "magical thinking": the assumption that students will learn only what we teach and only because we teach.[2]

But the grammar issue, as we will see, is a complicated one. And, perhaps surprisingly, it remains controversial with the regular appearance of papers defending the teaching of formal grammar or attacking it.[3] Thus Janice

---

[1] *Research in Written Composition* (Urbana, Ill.: National Council of Teachers of English, 1963), pp. 37–38.

[2] "Non-magical Thinking: Presenting Writing Developmentally in Schools," in *Writing Process, Development and Communication,* Vol. II of *Writing: The Nature, Development and Teaching of Written Communication,* ed. Charles H. Frederiksen and Joseph F. Dominic (Hillsdale, N.J.: Lawrence Erlbaum, 1980), pp. 21–30.

[3] For arguments in favor of formal grammar teaching, see Patrick F. Basset, "Grammar—Can We Afford Not to Teach It?" *NASSP Bulletin,* 64, No. 10 (1980), 55–63; Mary Epes et al., "The COMP-LAB Project: Assessing the Effectiveness of a Laboratory-Centered Basic Writing Course on the College Level" (Jamaica, N.Y.: York College, CUNY, 1979) ERIC 194 908; June B. Evans, "The Analogous Ounce: The Analgesic for Relief," *English Journal,* 70, No. 2 (1981), 38–39; Sydney Greenbaum, "What Is Grammar and Why Teach It?" (a paper presented at the meeting of the National Council of Teachers of English, Boston, Nov. 1982) ERIC 222 917; Marjorie Smelstor, *A Guide to the Role of Grammar in Teaching Writing* (Madison: University of Wisconsin School of Education, 1978) ERIC 176 323; and A. M. Tibbetts, *Working Papers: A Teacher's Observations on Composition* (Glenview, Ill.: Scott, Foresman, 1982).

For attacks on formal grammar teaching, see Harvey A. Daniels, *Famous Last Words: The American Language Crisis Reconsidered* (Carbondale: Southern Illinois University Press, 1983); Suzette Haden Elgin, *Never Mind the Trees: What the English Teacher Really Needs to Know about Linguistics* (Berkeley: University of California College of Education, Bay Area Writing Project Occasional Paper No. 2, 1980) ERIC 198 536; Mike Rose, "Remedial Writing Courses: A Critique and a Proposal." *College English,* 45 (1983), 109–128; and Ron Shook, "Response to Martha Kolln," *College Composition and Communication,* 34 (1983), 491–495.

This article is reprinted from *College English* 47 (February 1985): 105–27.

Neuleib, writing on "The Relation of Formal Grammar to Composition" in *College Composition and Communication* (23 [1977], 247–250), is tempted "to sputter on paper" at reading the quotation above (p. 248), and Martha Kolln, writing in the same journal three years later ("Closing the Books on Alchemy," *CCC,* 32 [1981], 139–151), labels people like me "alchemists" for our perverse beliefs. Neuleib reviews five experimental studies, most of them concluding that formal grammar instruction has no effect on the quality of students' writing nor on their ability to avoid error. Yet she renders in effect a Scots verdict of "Not proven" and calls for more research on the issue. Similarly, Kolln reviews six experimental studies that arrive at similar conclusions, only one of them overlapping with the studies cited by Neuleib. She calls for more careful definition of the word *grammar*—her definition being "the internalized system that native speakers of a language share" (p. 140)—and she concludes with a stirring call to place grammar instruction at the center of the composition curriculum: "our goal should be to help students understand the system they know unconsciously as native speakers, to teach them the necessary categories and labels that will enable them to think about and talk about their language" (p. 150). Certainly our textbooks and our pedagogies—though they vary widely in what they see as "necessary categories and labels"—continue to emphasize mastery of formal grammar, and popular discussions of a presumed literacy crisis are almost unanimous in their call for a renewed emphasis on the teaching of formal grammar, seen as basic for success in writing.[4]

AN INSTRUCTIVE EXAMPLE

It is worth noting at the outset that both sides in this dispute—the grammarians and the anti-grammarians—articulate the issue in the same positivistic terms: what does experimental research tell us about the value of teaching formal grammar? But seventy-five years of experimental research has for all practical purposes told us nothing. The two sides are unable to agree on how to interpret such research. Studies are interpreted in terms of one's prior assumptions about the value of teaching grammar: their results seem not to change those assumptions. Thus the basis of the discussion, a basis shared by Kolln and Neuleib and by Braddock and his colleagues—"what does educational research tell us?"—seems designed to perpetuate, not to resolve, the issue. A single example will be instructive. In 1976 and then at greater length in 1979, W. B. Elley, I. H. Barham, H. Lamb, and M. Wyllie reported on a three-

---

[4] See, for example, Clifton Fadiman and James Howard, *Empty Pages: A Search for Writing Competence in School and Society* (Belmont, Cal.: Fearon Pitman, 1979); Edwin Newman, *A Civil Tongue* (Indianapolis, Ind.: Bobbs-Merrill, 1976); and *Strictly Speaking* (New York: Warner Books, 1974); John Simon, *Paradigms Lost* (New York: Clarkson N. Potter, 1980); A. M. Tibbets and Charlene Tibbets, *What's Happening to American English?* (New York: Scribner's, 1978); and "Why Johnny Can't Write," *Newsweek,* 8 Dec. 1975, pp. 58–63.

year experiment in New Zealand, comparing the relative effectiveness at the high school level of instruction in transformational grammar, instruction in traditional grammar, and no grammar instruction.[5] They concluded that the formal study of grammar, whether transformational or traditional, improved neither writing quality nor control over surface correctness.

> After two years, no differences were detected in writing performance or language competence; after three years small differences appeared in some minor conventions favoring the TG [transformational grammar] group, but these were more than offset by the *less* positive attitudes they showed towards their English studies. (p. 18)

Anthony Petrosky, in a review of research ("Grammar Instruction: What We Know," *English Journal,* 66, No. 9 [1977], 86–88), agreed with this conclusion, finding the study to be carefully designed, "representative of the best kind of educational research" (p. 86), its validity "unquestionable" (p. 88). Yet Janice Neuleib in her essay found the same conclusions to be "startling" and questioned whether the findings could be generalized beyond the target population, New Zealand high school students. Martha Kolln, when her attention is drawn to the study ("Reply to Ron Shook," *CCC,* 32 [1981], 139–151), thinks the whole experiment "suspicious." And John Mellon has been willing to use the study to defend the teaching of grammar; the study of Elley and his colleagues, he has argued, shows that teaching grammar does no harm.[6]

It would seem unlikely, therefore, that further experimental research, in and of itself, will resolve the grammar issue. Any experimental design can be nit-picked, any experimental population can be criticized, and any experimental conclusion can be questioned or, more often, ignored. In fact, it may well be that the grammar question is not open to resolution by experimental research, that, as Noam Chomsky has argued in *Reflections on Language* (New York: Pantheon, 1975), criticizing the trivialization of human learning by behavioral psychologists, the issue is simply misdefined.

> There will be "good experiments" only in domains that lie outside the organism's cognitive capacity. For example, there will be no "good experiments" in the study of human learning.
>
> This discipline...will, of necessity, avoid those domains in which an organism is specially designed to acquire rich cognitive structures that enter into its life in an intimate fashion. The discipline will be of virtually no intellectual interest, it seems to me, since it is restricting itself in principle to those questions that are guaranteed to tell us little about the nature of organisms. (p. 36)

---

[5] "The Role of Grammar in a Secondary School English Curriculum." *Research in the Teaching of English,* 10 (1976), 5–21; *The Role of Grammar in a Secondary School Curriculum* (Wellington: New Zealand Council of Teachers of English, 1979).

[6] "A Taxonomy of Compositional Competencies," in *Perspectives on Literacy,* ed. Richard Beach and P. David Pearson (Minneapolis: University of Minnesota College of Education, 1979), pp. 247–272.

ASKING THE RIGHT QUESTIONS

As a result, though I will look briefly at the tradition of experimental research, my primary goal in this essay is to articulate the grammar issue in different and, I would hope, more productive terms. Specifically, I want to ask four questions:

1. Why is the grammar issue so important? Why has it been the dominant focus of composition research for the last seventy-five years?
2. What definitions of the word grammar are needed to articulate the grammar issue intelligibly?
3. What do findings in cognate disciplines suggest about the value of formal grammar instruction?
4. What is our theory of language, and what does it predict about the value of formal grammar instruction? (This question — "What does our theory of language predict?" — seems a much more powerful question than "what does educational research tell us?")

In exploring these questions I will attempt to be fully explicit about issues, terms, and assumptions. I hope that both proponents and opponents of formal grammar instruction would agree that these are useful as shared points of reference: care in definition, full examination of the evidence, reference to relevant work in cognate disciplines, and explicit analysis of the theoretical bases of the issue.

But even with that gesture of harmony it will be difficult to articulate the issue in a balanced way, one that will be acceptable to both sides. After all, we are dealing with a professional dispute in which one side accuses the other of "magical thinking," and in turn that side responds by charging the other as "alchemists." Thus we might suspect that the grammar issue is itself embedded in larger models of the transmission of literacy, part of quite different assumptions about the teaching of composition.

Those of us who dismiss the teaching of formal grammar have a model of composition instruction that makes the grammar issue "uninteresting" in a scientific sense. Our model predicts a rich and complex interaction of learner and environment in mastering literacy, an interaction that has little to do with sequences of skills instruction as such. Those who defend the teaching of grammar tend to have a model of composition instruction that is rigidly skills-centered and rigidly sequential: the formal teaching of grammar, as the first step in that sequence, is the cornerstone or linchpin. Grammar teaching is thus supremely interesting, naturally a dominant focus for educational research. The controversy over the value of grammar instruction, then, is inseparable from two other issues: the issues of sequence in the teaching of composition and of the role of the composition teacher. Consider, for example, the force of these two issues in Janice Neuleib's conclusion: after calling for yet more experimental research on the value of teaching grammar, she ends with an absolute (and unsupported) claim about sequences and teacher roles in composition.

> We do know, however, that some things must be taught at different levels. Insistence on adherence to usage norms by composition teachers does improve usage. Students can learn to organize their papers if teachers do not accept papers that are disorganized. Perhaps composition teachers can teach those two abilities before they begin the more difficult tasks of developing syntactic sophistication and a winning style. ("The Relation of Formal Grammar to Composition," p. 250)

(One might want to ask, in passing, whether "usage norms" exist in the monolithic fashion the phrase suggests and whether refusing to accept disorganized papers is our best available pedagogy for teaching arrangement.)[7]

But I want to focus on the notion of sequence that makes the grammar issue so important: first grammar, then usage, then some absolute model of organization, all controlled by the teacher at the center of the learning process, with other matters, those of rhetorical weight — "syntactic sophistication and a winning style" — pushed off to the future. It is not surprising that we call each other names: those of us who question the value of teaching grammar are in fact shaking the whole elaborate edifice of traditional composition instruction.

THE FIVE MEANINGS OF "GRAMMAR"

Given its centrality to a well-established way of teaching composition, I need to go about the business of defining grammar rather carefully, particularly in view of Kolln's criticism of the lack of care in earlier discussions. Therefore I will build upon a seminal discussion of the word *grammar* offered a generation ago, in 1954, by W. Nelson Francis, often excerpted as "The Three Meanings of Grammar."[8] It is worth reprinting at length, if only to re-establish it as a reference point for future discussions.

> The first thing we mean by "grammar" is "the set of formal patterns in which the words of a language are arranged in order to convey larger meanings." It is not necessary that we be able to discuss these patterns self-consciously in order to be able to use them. In fact, all speakers of a language above the age of five or six know how to use its complex forms of organization with considerable skill; in this sense of the word — call it "Grammar 1" — they are thoroughly familiar with its grammar.
>
> The second meaning of "grammar" — call it "Grammar 2" — is "the branch of linguistic science which is concerned with the description, analysis, and formulization of formal language patterns." Just as gravity was in full operation before Newton's apple fell, so grammar in the first sense was in full operation before anyone formulated the first rule that began the history of grammar as a study.

[7] On usage norms, see Edward Finegan, *Attitudes toward English Usage: The History of a War of Words* (New York: Teachers College Press, 1980), and Jim Quinn, *American Tongue in Cheek: A Populist Guide to Language* (New York: Pantheon, 1980); on arrangement, see Patrick Hartwell, "Teaching Arrangement: A Pedagogy," *CE,* 40 (1979), 548–554.

[8] "Revolution in Grammar," *Quarterly Journal of Speech,* 40 (1954), 299–312.

The third sense in which people use the word "grammar" is "linguistic etiquette." This we may call "Grammar 3." The word in this sense is often coupled with a derogatory adjective: we say that the expression "he ain't here" is "bad grammar." ...

As has already been suggested, much confusion arises from mixing these meanings. One hears a good deal of criticism of teachers of English couched in such terms as "they don't teach grammar any more." Criticism of this sort is based on the wholly unproven assumption that teaching Grammar 2 will improve the student's proficiency in Grammar 1 or improve his manners in Grammar 3. Actually, the form of Grammar 2 which is usually taught is a very inaccurate and misleading analysis of the facts of Grammar 1; and it therefore is of highly questionable value in improving a person's ability to handle the structural patterns of his language. (pp. 300–301)

Francis' Grammar 3 is, of course, not grammar at all, but usage. One would like to assume that Joseph Williams' recent [1981] discussion of usage ("The Phenomenology of Error," *CCC*, 32 [1981], 152–168), along with his references, has placed those shibboleths in a proper perspective. But I doubt it, and I suspect that popular discussions of the grammar issue will be as flawed by the intrusion of usage issues as past discussions have been. At any rate I will make only passing reference to Grammar 3 — usage — naively assuming that this issue has been discussed elsewhere and that my readers are familiar with those discussions.

We need also to make further discriminations about Francis' Grammar 2, given that the purpose of his 1954 article was to substitute for one form of Grammar 2, that "inaccurate and misleading" form "which is usually taught," another form, that of American structuralist grammar. Here we can make use of a still earlier discussion, one going back to the days when *PMLA* was willing to publish articles on rhetoric and linguistics, to a 1927 article by Charles Carpenter Fries, "The Rules of the Common School Grammars" (42 [1927], 221–237). Fries there distinguished between the scientific tradition of language study (to which we will now delimit Francis' Grammar 2, scientific grammar) and the separate tradition of "the common school grammars," developed unscientifically, largely based on two inadequate principles — appeals to "logical principles," like "two negatives make a positive," and analogy to Latin grammar; thus, Charlton Laird's characterization, "the grammar of Latin, ingeniously warped to suggest English" (*Language in America* [New York: World, 1970], p. 294). There is, of course, a direct link between the "common school grammars" that Fries criticized in 1927 and the grammar-based texts of today, and thus it seems wise, as Karl W. Dykema suggests ("Where Our Grammar Came From," *CE*, 22 [1961], 455–465), to separate Grammar 2, "scientific grammar," from Grammar 4, "school grammar," the latter meaning, quite literally, "the grammars used in the schools."

Further, since Martha Kolln points to the adaptation of Christensen's sentence rhetoric in a recent sentence-combining text as an example of the proper emphasis on "grammar" ("Closing the Books on Alchemy," p. 140), it is worth separating out, as still another meaning of *grammar*, Grammar 5, "stylistic grammar," defined as "grammatical terms used in the interest of teaching prose style." And, since stylistic grammars abound, with widely variant terms and emphases, we might appropriately speak parenthetically of specific forms of Grammar 5 — Grammar 5 (Lanham): Grammar 5 (Strunk and White); Grammar 5 (Williams, *Style*); even Grammar 5 (Christensen, as adapted by Daiker, Kerek, and Morenberg).[9]

THE GRAMMAR IN OUR HEADS

With these definitions in mind, let us return to Francis' Grammar 1, admirably defined by Kolln as "the internalized system of rules that speakers of a language share" ("Closing the Books on Alchemy," p. 140), or, to put it more simply, the grammar in our heads. Three features of Grammar 1 need to be stressed: first, its special status as an "internalized system of rules," as tacit and unconscious knowledge; second, the abstract, even counterintuitive, nature of these rules, insofar as we are able to approximate them indirectly as Grammar 2 statements; and third, the way in which the form of one's Grammar 1 seems profoundly affected by the acquisition of literacy. This sort of review is designed to firm up our theory of language, so that we can ask what it predicts about the value of teaching formal grammar.

A simple thought experiment will isolate the special status of Grammar 1 knowledge. I have asked members of a number of different groups — from sixth graders to college freshmen to high-school teachers — to give me the rule for ordering adjectives of nationality, age, and number in English. The response is always the same: "We don't know the rule." Yet when I ask these groups to perform an active language task, they show productive control over the rule they have denied knowing. I ask them to arrange the following words in a natural order:

| French | the | young | girls | four |

I have never seen a native speaker of English who did not immediately produce the natural order, "the four young French girls." The rule is that in English the order of adjectives is first, number, second, age, and third, nationality. Native speakers can create analogous phrases using the rule — "the seventy-three aged Scandinavian lechers"; and the drive for meaning is so great that they will create contexts to make sense out of violations of the rule, as in foregrounding for emphasis: "I want to talk to the French four young girls." (I immediately envision a large room, perhaps a banquet hall, filled with tables at which are seated groups of four young girls, each group of a different nationality.) So Grammar 1 is eminently usable knowledge — the way we make our life through language —

[9] Richard A. Lanham, *Revising Prose* (New York: Scribner's, 1979); William Strunk and E. B. White, *The Elements of Style*, 3rd ed. (New York: Macmillan, 1979); Joseph Williams, *Style: Ten Lessons in Clarity and Grace* (Glenview, Ill.: Scott, Foresman, 1981); Christensen, "A Generative Rhetoric of the Sentence," *CCC*, 14 (1963), 155–161; Donald A. Daiker, Andrew Kerek, and Max Morenberg, *The Writer's Options: Combining to Composing*, 2nd ed. (New York: Harper & Row, 1982).

but it is not accessible knowledge; in a profound sense, we do not know that we have it. Thus neurolinguist Z. N. Pylyshyn speaks of Grammar 1 as "autonomous," separate from common-sense reasoning, and as "cognitively impenetrable," not available for direct examination.[10] In philosophy and linguistics, the distinction is made between formal, conscious, "knowing about" knowledge (like Grammar 2 knowledge) and tacit, unconscious, "knowing how" knowledge (like Grammar 1 knowledge). The importance of this distinction for the teaching of composition—it provides a powerful theoretical justification for mistrusting the ability of Grammar 2 (or Grammar 4) knowledge to affect Grammar 1 performance—was pointed out in this journal by Martin Steinmann, Jr. in 1966 ("Rhetorical Research," *CE,* 27 [1966], 278–285).

Further, the more we learn about Grammar 1—and most linguists would agree that we know surprisingly little about it—the more abstract and implicit it seems. This abstractness can be illustrated with an experiment, devised by Lise Menn and reported by Morris Halle, about our rule for forming plurals in speech. It is obvious that we do indeed have a "rule" for forming plurals, for we do not memorize the plural of each noun separately. You will demonstrate productive control over that rule by forming the spoken plurals of the nonsense words below:

thole   flitch   plast

Halle offers two ways of formalizing a Grammar 2 equivalent of this Grammar 1 ability. One form of the rule is the following, stated in terms of speech sounds:

  a. If the noun ends in s z š ž č ǰ/, add /Iz/;
  b. otherwise, if the noun ends in /p t k f Ø/, add /s/;
  c. otherwise, add /z/.[11]

This rule comes close to what we literate adults consider to be an adequate rule for plurals in writing, like the rules, for example, taken from a recent "common school grammar," Eric Gould's *Reading into Writing: A Rhetoric, Reader, and Handbook* (Boston: Houghton Mifflin, 1983):

> *Plurals* can be tricky. If you are unsure of a plural, then check it in the dictionary.
>
> The general rules are
> Add *s* to the singular: *girls, tables*

---

[10] "A Psychological Approach," in *Psychobiology of Language,* ed. M. Studdert-Kennedy (Cambridge, Mass.: MIT Press, 1983), pp. 16–19. See also Noam Chomsky, "Language and Unconscious Knowledge," in *Psychoanalysis and Language: Psychiatry and the Humanities,* Vol. III, ed. Joseph H. Smith (New Haven, Conn.: Yale University Press, 1978), pp. 3–44.

[11] Morris Halle, "Knowledge Unlearned and Untaught: What Speakers Know about the Sounds of Their Language," in *Linguistic Theory and Psychological Reality,* ed. Halle, Joan Bresnan, and George A. Miller (Cambridge, Mass.: MIT Press, 1978), pp. 135–140.

Add *es* to nouns ending in *ch, sh, x* or *s: churches, boxes, wishes*

Add *es* to nouns ending in *y* and preceded by a vowel once you have changed *y* to *i: monies, companies.* (p. 666)

(But note the persistent inadequacy of such Grammar 4 rules: here, as I read it, the rule is inadequate to explain the plurals of *ray* and *tray,* even to explain the collective noun *monies,* not a plural at all, formed from the mass noun *money* and offered as an example.) A second form of the rule would make use of much more abstract entities, sound features:

    a. If the noun ends with a sound that is [coronal, strident], add /ɨz/;

    b. otherwise, if the noun ends with a sound that is [non-voiced], add /s/;

    c. otherwise, add /z/.

(The notion of "sound features" is itself rather abstract, perhaps new to readers not trained in linguistics. But such readers should be able to recognize that the spoken plurals of *lip* and *duck,* the sound [s], differ from the spoken plurals of *sea* and *gnu,* the sound [z], only in that the sounds of the latter are "voiced" — one's vocal cords vibrate — while the sounds of the former are "non-voiced.")

To test the psychologically operative rule, the Grammar 1 rule, native speakers of English were asked to form the plural of the last name of the composer Johann Sebastian *Bach,* a sound [x], unique in American (though not in Scottish) English. If speakers follow the first rule above, using word endings, they would reject a) and b), then apply c), producing the plural as /baxz/, with word-final /z/. (If writers were to follow the rule of the common school grammar, they would produce the written plural *Baches,* apparently, given the form of the rule, on analogy with *churches.*) If speakers follow the second rule, they would have to analyze the sound [x] as [non-labial, non-coronal, dorsal, non-voiced, and non-strident], producing the plural as /baxs/, with word-final /s/. Native speakers of American English overwhelmingly produce the plural as /baxs/. They use knowledge that Halle characterizes as "unlearned and untaught" (p. 140).

Now such a conclusion is counterintuitive — certainly it departs maximally from Grammar 4 rules for forming plurals. It seems that native speakers of English behave as if they have productive control, as Grammar 1 knowledge, of abstract sound features (± coronal, ± strident, and so on) which are available as conscious, Grammar 2 knowledge only to trained linguists — and, indeed, formally available only within the last hundred years or so. ("Behave as if," in that last sentence, is a necessary hedge, to underscore the difficulty of "knowing about" Grammar 1.)

Moreover, as the example of plural rules suggests, the form of the Grammar 1 in the heads of literate adults seems profoundly affected by the acquisition of literacy. Obviously, literate adults have access to different morphological codes: the abstract print *-s* underlying the predictable /s/ and /z/ plurals, the abstract print *-ed* underlying the spoken past tense markers /t/, as in "walked," /əd/, as in "surrounded," /d/, as in "scored," and the symbol /Ø/ for no surface realization, as in the relaxed standard pronunciation of "I walked to the store." Literate adults also have access to distinctions preserved only in the code of print (for example, the distinction between "a good sailer" and "a good sailor" that Mark Aranoff points out in "An English Spelling Convention," *Linguistic Inquiry,* 9 [1978], 299–303). More significantly, Irene Moscowitz speculates that the ability of third graders to form abstract nouns on analogy with pairs like *divine::divinity* and *serene::serenity,* where the spoken vowel changes but the spelling preserves meaning, is a factor of knowing how to read. Carol Chomsky finds a three-stage developmental sequence in the grammatical performance of seven-year-olds, related to measures of kind and variety of reading; and Rita S. Brause finds a nine-stage development sequence in the ability to understand semantic ambiguity, extending from fourth graders to graduate students.[12] John Mills and Gordon Hemsley find that level of education, and presumably level of literacy, influence judgments of grammaticality, concluding that literacy changes the deep structure of one's internal grammar; Jean Whyte finds that oral language functions develop differently in readers and non-readers; José Morais, Jésus Alegria, and Paul Bertelson find that illiterate adults are unable to add or delete sounds at the beginning of nonsense words, suggesting that awareness of speech as a series of phones is provided by learning to read an alphabetic code. Two experiments — one conducted by Charles A. Ferguson, the other by Mary E. Hamilton and David Barton — find that adults' ability to recognize segmentation in speech is related to degree of literacy, not to amount of schooling or general ability.[13]

It is worth noting that none of these investigators would suggest that the developmental sequences they have uncovered be isolated and taught as discrete skills. They are natural concomitants of literacy, and they seem best characterized not as isolated rules but as developing schemata, broad strategies for approaching written language.

GRAMMAR 2

We can, of course, attempt to approximate the rules or schemata of Grammar 1 by writing fully explicit descriptions that model the competence of a native speaker. Such rules, like the rules for pluralizing nouns or ordering adjectives

---

[12] Moscowitz, "On the Status of Vowel Shift in English," in *Cognitive Development and the Acquisition of Language,* ed. T. E. Moore (New York: Academic Press, 1973), pp. 223–260; Chomsky, "Stages in Language Development and Reading Exposure," *Harvard Educational Review,* 42 (1972), 1–33; and Brause, "Developmental Aspects of the Ability to Understand Semantic Ambiguity, with Implications for Teachers," *RTE,* 11 (1977), 39–48.

[13] Mills and Hemsley, "The Effect of Levels of Education on Judgments of Grammatical Acceptability," *Language and Speech,* 19 (1976), 324–342; Whyte, "Levels of Language Competence and Reading Ability: An Exploratory Investigation," *Journal of Research in Reading,* 5 (1982), 123–132; Morais et al., "Does Awareness of Speech is a Series of Phones Arise Spontaneously?" *Cognition,* 7 (1979), 323–331; Ferguson, *Cognitive Effects of Literacy: Linguistic Awareness in Adult Non-readers* (Washington, D.C.: National Institute of Education Final Report, 1981) ERIC 222 857; Hamilton and Barton, "A Word Is a Word: Metalinguistic Skills in Adults of Varying Literacy Levels" (Stanford, Cal.: Stanford University Department of Linguistics, 1980) ERIC 222 859.

discussed above, are the goal of the science of linguistics, that is, Grammar 2. There are a number of scientific grammars — an older structuralist model and several versions within a generative-transformational paradigm, not to mention isolated schools like tagmemic grammar, Montague grammar, and the like. In fact, we cannot think of Grammar 2 as a stable entity, for its form changes with each new issue of each linguistics journal, as new "rules of grammar" are proposed and debated. Thus Grammar 2, though of great theoretical interest to the composition teacher, is of little practical use in the classroom, as Constance Weaver has pointed out (*Grammar for Teachers* [Urbana, Ill.: NCTE, 1979], pp. 3–6). Indeed Grammar 2 is a scientific model of Grammar 1, not a description of it, so that questions of psychological reality, while important, are less important than other, more theoretical factors, such as the elegance of formulation or the global power of rules. We might, for example, wish to replace the rule for ordering adjectives of age, number, and nationality cited above with a more general rule — what linguists call a "fuzzy" rule — that adjectives in English are ordered by their abstract quality of "nouniness": adjectives that are very much like nouns, like *French* or *Scandinavian,* come physically closer to nouns than do adjectives that are less "nouny," like *four* or *aged.* But our motivation for accepting the broader rule would be its global power, not its psychological reality.[14]

I try to consider a hostile reader, one committed to the teaching of grammar, and I try to think of ways to hammer in the central point of this distinction, that the rules of Grammar 2 are simply unconnected to productive control over Grammar 1. I can argue from authority: Noam Chomsky has touched on this point whenever he has concerned himself with the implications of linguistics for language teaching, and years ago transformationalist Mark Lester stated unequivocally, "there simply appears to be no correlation between a writer's study of language and his ability to write."[15] I can cite analogies offered by others: Francis Christensen's analogy in an essay originally published in 1962 that formal grammar study would be "to invite a centipede to attend to the sequence of his legs in motion,"[16] or James Britton's analogy, offered informally after a conference presentation, that grammar study would be like forcing starving people to master the use of a knife and fork before

[14] On the question of the psychological reality of Grammar 2 descriptions, see Maria Black and Shulamith Chiat, "Psycholinguistics without 'Psychological Reality,'" *Linguistics,* 19 (1981), 37–61; Joan Bresnan, ed., *The Mental Representation of Grammatical Relations* (Cambridge, Mass.: MIT Press, 1982); and Michael H. Long, "Inside the 'Black Box': Methodological Issues in Classroom Research on Language Learning," *Language Learning,* 30 (1980), 1–42.

[15] Chomsky, "The Current Scene in Linguistics," *CE,* 27 (1966), 587–595; and "Linguistic Theory," in *Language Teaching: Broader Contexts,* ed. Robert C. Meade, Jr. (New York: Modern Language Association, 1966), pp. 43–49; Mark Lester, "The Value of Transformational Grammar in Teaching Composition," *CCC,* 16 (1967), 228.

[16] Christensen, "Between Two Worlds," in *Notes toward a New Rhetoric: Nine Essays for Teachers,* rev. ed., ed. Bonniejean Christensen (New York: Harper & Row, 1978), pp. 1–22.

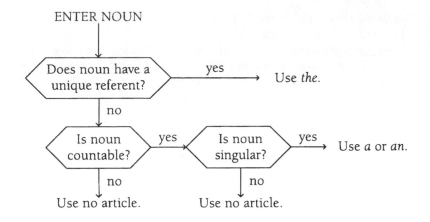

allowing them to eat. I can offer analogies of my own, contemplating the wisdom of asking a pool player to master the physics of momentum before taking up a cue or of making a prospective driver get a degree in automotive engineering before engaging the clutch. I consider a hypothetical argument, that if Grammar 2 knowledge affected Grammar 1 performance, then linguists would be our best writers. (I can certify that they are, on the whole, not.) Such a position, after all, is only in accord with other domains of science: the formula for catching a fly ball in baseball ("Playing It by Ear," *Scientific American,* 248, No. 4 [1983], 76) is of such complexity that it is beyond my understanding — and, I would suspect, that of many workaday centerfielders. But perhaps I can best hammer in this claim — that Grammar 2 knowledge has no effect on Grammar 1 performance — by offering a demonstration.

The diagram above is an attempt by Thomas N. Huckin and Leslie A. Olsen (*English for Science and Technology* [New York: McGraw-Hill, 1983]) to offer, for students of English as a second language, a fully explicit formulation of what is, for native speakers, a trivial rule of the language — the choice of definite article, indefinite article, or no definite article. There are obvious limits to such a formulation, for article choice in English is less a matter of rule than of idiom ("I went to college" versus "I went to a university" versus British "I went to university"), real-world knowledge (using indefinite "I went into a house" instantiates definite "I looked at the ceiling," and indefinite "I visited a university" instantiates definite "I talked with the professors"), and stylistic choice (the last sentence above might alternatively end with "the choice of the definite article, the indefinite article, or no article"). Huckin and Olsen invite nonnative speakers to use the rule consciously to justify article choice in technical prose, such as the passage below from P. F. Brandwein (*Matter: An Earth Science* [New York: Harcourt Brace Jovanovich, 1975]). I invite you to spend a couple of minutes doing the same thing, with the understanding that this exercise is a test case: you are using a very explicit rule to justify a fairly straightforward issue of grammatical choice.

> Imagine a cannon on top of _____ highest mountain on earth. It is firing _____ cannonballs horizontally. _____ first cannonball fired follows its path. As _____ cannonball moves, _____ gravity pulls it down, and it soon hits _____ ground. Now _____ velocity with which each succeeding cannonball is fired is increased. Thus, _____ cannonball goes farther each time. Cannonball 2 goes farther than _____ cannonball 1 although each is being pulled by _____ gravity toward the earth all _____ time. _____ last cannonball is fired with such tremendous velocity that it goes completely around _____ earth. It returns to _____ mountaintop and continues around the earth again and again. _____ cannonball's inertia causes it to continue in motion indefinitely in _____ orbit around earth. In such a situation, we could consider _____ cannonball to be _____ artificial satellite, just like _____ weather satellites launched by _____ U. S. Weather Service. (p. 209)

Most native speakers of English who have attempted this exercise report a great deal of frustration, a curious sense of working against, rather than with, the rule. The rule, however valuable it may be for non-native speakers, is, for the most part, simply unusable for native speakers of the language.

COGNATE AREAS OF RESEARCH

We can corroborate this demonstration by turning to research in two cognate areas, studies of the induction of rules of artificial languages and studies of the role of formal rules in second language acquisition. Psychologists have studied the ability of subjects to learn artificial languages, usually constructed of nonsense syllables or letter strings. Such languages can be described by phrase structure rules:

$$S \Rightarrow VX$$
$$X \Rightarrow MX$$

More clearly, they can be presented as flow diagrams, as below:

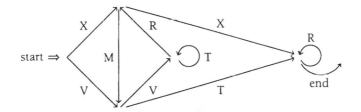

This diagram produces "sentences" like the following:

VVTRXRR.	XMVTTRX.	XXRR.
XMVRMT.	VVTTRMT.	XMTRRR.

The following "sentences" would be "ungrammatical" in this language:

    *VMXTT.   *RTXVVT.   *TRVXXVVM.

Arthur S. Reber, in a classic 1967 experiment, demonstrated that mere exposure to grammatical sentences produced tacit learning: subjects who copied several grammatical sentences performed far above chance in judging the grammaticality of other letter strings. Further experiments have shown that providing subjects with formal rules — giving them the flow diagram above, for example — remarkably degrades performance: subjects given the "rules of the language" do much less well in acquiring the rules than do subjects not given the rules. Indeed, even telling subjects that they are to induce the rules of an artificial language degrades performance. Such laboratory experiments are admittedly contrived, but they confirm predictions that our theory of language would make about the value of formal rules in language learning.[17]

The thrust of recent research in second language learning similarly works to constrain the value of formal grammar rules. The most explicit statement of the value of formal rules is that of Stephen D. Krashen's monitor model.[18] Krashen divides second language mastery into *acquisition* — tacit, informal mastery, akin to first language acquisition — and *formal learning* — conscious application of Grammar 2 rules, which he calls "monitoring" output. In another essay Krashen uses his model to predict a highly individual use of the monitor and a highly constrained role for formal rules:

> Some adults (and very few children) are able to use conscious rules to increase the grammatical accuracy of their output, and even for these people, very strict conditions need to be met before the conscious grammar can be applied.[19]

In *Principles and Practice in Second Language Acquisition* (New York: Pergamon, 1982) Krashen outlines these conditions by means of a series of concentric circles, beginning with a large circle denoting the rules of English and a smaller circle denoting the subset of those rules described by formal linguists (adding that most linguists would protest that the size of this circle is much too large).

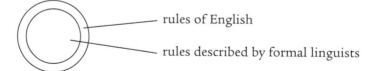

                            rules of English

                            rules described by formal linguists

---

[17] Reber, "Implicit Learning of Artificial Grammars," *Journal of Verbal Learning and Verbal Behavior,* 6 (1967), 855–863; "Implicit Learning of Synthetic Languages: The Role of Instructional Set," *Journal of Experimental Psychology: Human Learning and Memory,* 2 (1976), 889–894; and Reber, Saul M. Kassin, Selma Lewis, and Gary Cantor, "On the Relationship between Implicit and Explicit Modes in the Learning of a Complex Rule Structure," *Journal of Experimental Psychology: Human Learning and Memory,* 6 (1980), 492–502.

[18] "Individual Variation in the Use of the Monitor," in *Principles of Second Language Learning,* ed. W. Richie (New York: Academic Press, 1978), pp. 175–185.

[19] "Applications of Psycholinguistic Research to the Classroom," in *Practical Applications of Research in Foreign Language Teaching,* ed. D. J. James (Lincolnwood, Ill.: National Textbook, 1983), p. 61.

Krashen then adds smaller circles, as shown below — a subset of the rules described by formal linguists that would be known to applied linguists, a subset of those rules that would be available to the best teachers, and then a subset of those rules that teachers might choose to present to second language learners:

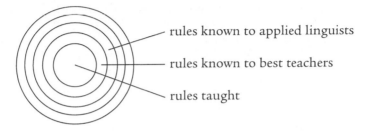

— rules known to applied linguists

— rules known to best teachers

— rules taught

Of course, as Krashen notes, not all the rules taught will be learned, and not all those learned will be available, as what he calls "mental baggage" (p. 94), for conscious use.

An experiment by Ellen Bialystock, asking English speakers learning French to judge the grammaticality of taped sentences, complicates this issue, for reaction time data suggest that learners first make an intuitive judgment of grammaticality, using implicit or Grammar 1 knowledge, and only then search for formal explanations, using explicit or Grammar 2 knowledge.[20] This distinction would suggest that Grammar 2 knowledge is of use to second language learners only after the principle has already been mastered as tacit Grammar 1 knowledge. In the terms of Krashen's model, learning never becomes acquisition (*Principles*, p. 86).

An ingenious experiment by Herbert W. Seliger complicates the issue yet further ("On the Nature and Function of Language Rules in Language Learning," *TESOL Quarterly,* 13 [1979], 359–369). Seliger asked native and non-native speakers of English to orally identify pictures of objects (e.g., "an apple," "a pear," "a book," "an umbrella"), noting whether they used the correct form of the indefinite articles *a* and *an*. He then asked each speaker to state the rule for choosing between *a* and *an*. He found no correlation between the ability to state the rule and the ability to apply it correctly, either with native or non-native speakers. Indeed, three of four adult non-native speakers in his sample produced a correct form of the rule, but they did not apply it in speaking. A strong conclusion from this experiment would be that formal rules of grammar seem to have no value whatsoever. Seliger, however, suggests a more paradoxical interpretation. Rules are of no use, he agrees, but some people think they are, and for these people, assuming that they have internalized the rules, even inadequate rules are of heuristic value, for they allow them to access the internal rules they actually use.

---

[20] "Some Evidence for the Integrity and Interaction of Two Knowledge Sources," in *New Dimensions in Second Language Acquisition Research,* ed. Roger W. Andersen (Rowley, Mass.: Newbury House, 1981), pp. 62–74.

THE INCANTATIONS OF THE "COMMON SCHOOL GRAMMARS"

Such a paradox may explain the fascination we have as teachers with "rules of grammar" of the Grammar 4 variety, the "rules" of the "common school grammars." Again and again such rules are inadequate to the facts of written language; you will recall that we have known this since [Fries's] 1927 study. R. Scott Baldwin and James M. Coady, studying how readers respond to punctuation signals ("Psycholinguistic Approaches to a Theory of Punctuation," *Journal of Reading Behavior,* 10 [1978], 363–383), conclude that conventional rules of punctuation are "a complete sham" (p. 375). My own favorite is the Grammar 4 rule for showing possession, always expressed in terms of adding -*'s* or -*s'* to nouns, while our internal grammar, if you think about it, adds possession to noun phrases, albeit under severe stylistic constraints: "the horses of the Queen of England" are "the Queen of England's horses" and "the feathers of the duck over there" are "the duck over there's feathers." Suzette Haden Elgin refers to the "rules" of Grammar 4 as "incantations" (*Never Mind the Trees,* p. 9: see footnote 3).

It may simply be that as hyperliterate adults we are conscious of "using rules" when we are in fact doing something else, something far more complex, accessing tacit heuristics honed by print literacy itself. We can clarify this notion by reaching for an acronym coined by technical writers to explain the readability of complex prose — COIK: "clear only if known." The rules of Grammar 4 — no, we can at this point be more honest — the incantations of Grammar 4 are COIK. If you know how to signal possession in the code of print, then the advice to add -*'s* to nouns makes perfect sense, just as the collective noun *monies* is a fine example of changing -*y* to -*i* and adding -*es* to form the plural. But if you have not grasped, tacitly, the abstract representation of possession in print, such incantations can only be opaque.

Worse yet, the advice given in "the common school grammars" is unconnected with anything remotely resembling literate adult behavior. Consider, as an example, the rule for not writing a sentence fragment as the rule is described in the best-selling college grammar text, John C. Hodges and Mary S. Whitten's *Harbrace College Handbook,* 9th ed. (New York: Harcourt Brace Jovanovich, 1982). In order to get to the advice, "as a rule, do not write a sentence fragment" (p. 25), the student must master the following learning tasks:

Recognizing verbs.
Recognizing subjects and verbs.
Recognizing all parts of speech. (*Harbrace* lists eight.)
Recognizing phrases and subordinate clauses. (*Harbrace* lists six types of phrases, and it offers incomplete lists of eight relative pronouns and eighteen subordinating conjunctions.)
Recognizing main clauses and types of sentences.

These learning tasks completed, the student is given the rule above, offered a page of exceptions, and then given the following advice (or is it an incantation?):

> Before handing in a composition,...proofread each word group written as a sentence. Test each one for completeness. First, be sure that it has at least one subject and one predicate. Next, be sure that the word group is not a dependent clause beginning with a subordinating conjunction or a relative clause. (p. 27)

The school grammar approach defines a sentence fragment as a conceptual error — as not having conscious knowledge of the school grammar definition of *sentence*. It demands heavy emphasis on rote memory, and it asks students to behave in ways patently removed from the behaviors of mature writers. (I have never in my life tested a sentence for completeness, and I am a better writer — and probably a better person — as a consequence.) It may be, of course, that some developing writers, at some points in their development, may benefit from such advice — or, more to the point, may think that they benefit — but, as Thomas Friedman points out in "Teaching Error, Nurturing Confusion" (*CE*, 45 [1983], 390–399), our theory of language tells us that such advice is, at the best, COIK. As the Maine joke has it, about a tourist asking directions from a farmer, "you can't get there from here."

REDEFINING ERROR

In the specific case of sentence fragments, Mina P. Shaughnessy (*Errors and Expectations* [New York: Oxford University Press, 1977]) argues that such errors are not conceptual failures at all, but performance errors — mistakes in punctuation. Muriel Harris's error counts support this view ("Mending the Fragmented Free Modifier," *CCC*, 32 [1981], 175–182). Case studies show example after example of errors that occur *because of* instruction — one thinks, for example, of David Bartholomae's student explaining that he added an *-s* to *children* "because it's a plural" ("The Study of Error," *CCC*, 31 [1980], 262). Surveys, such as that by Muriel Harris ("Contradictory Perceptions of the Rules of Writing," *CCC*, 30 [1979], 218–220), and our own observations suggest that students consistently misunderstand such Grammar 4 explanations (COIK, you will recall). For example, from Patrick Hartwell and Robert H. Bentley and from Mike Rose, we have two separate anecdotal accounts of students, cited for punctuating a *because*-clause as a sentence, who have decided to avoid using *because*. More generally, Collette A. Daiute's analysis of errors made by college students shows that errors tend to appear at clause boundaries, suggesting short-term memory load and not conceptual deficiency as a cause of error.[21]

Thus, if you think seriously about error and its relationship to the worship of formal grammar study, we need to attempt some massive dislocation of our

---

[21] Hartwell and Bentley, *Some Suggestions for Using Open to Language* (New York: Oxford University Press, 1982), p. 73; Rose, *Writer's Block: The Cognitive Dimension* (Carbondale: Southern Illinois University Press, 1983), p. 99; Daiute, "Psycholinguistic Foundations of the Writing Process," *RTE*, 15 (1981), 5–22.

traditional thinking, to shuck off our hyperliterate perception of the value of formal rules, and to regain the confidence in the tacit power of unconscious knowledge that our theory of language gives us. Most students, reading their writing aloud, will correct in essence all errors of spelling, grammar, and, by intonation, punctuation, but usually without noticing that what they read departs from what they wrote.[22] And Richard H. Haswell ("Minimal Marking," *CE,* 45 [1983], 600–604) notes that his students correct 61.1% of their errors when they are identified with a simple mark in the margin rather than by error type. Such findings suggest that we need to redefine error, to see it not as a cognitive or linguistic problem, a problem of not knowing a "rule of grammar" (whatever that may mean), but rather, following the insight of Robert J. Bracewell ("Writing as a Cognitive Activity," *Visible Language,* 14 [1980], 400–422), as a problem of metacognition and metalinguistic awareness, a matter of accessing knowledges that, to be of any use, learners must have already internalized by means of exposure to the code. (Usage issues — Grammar 3 — probably represent a different order of problem. Both Joseph Emonds and Jeffrey Jochnowitz establish that the usage issues we worry most about are linguistically unnatural, departures from the grammar in our heads.)[23]

The notion of metalinguistic awareness seems crucial. The sentence below, created by Douglas R. Hofstadter ("Metamagical Themas," *Scientific American,* 235, No. 1 [1981], 22–32), is offered to clarify that notion; you are invited to examine it for a moment or two before continuing.

Their is four errors in this sentance. Can you find them?

Three errors announce themselves plainly enough, the misspellings of *there* and *sentence* and the use of *is* instead of *are*. (And, just to illustrate the perils of hyperliteracy, let it be noted that, through three years of drafts, I referred to the choice of *is* and *are* as a matter of "subject-verb agreement.") The fourth error resists detection, until one assesses the truth value of the sentence itself — the fourth error is that there are not four errors, only three. Such a sentence (Hofstadter calls it a "self-referencing sentence") asks you to look at it in two ways, simultaneously as statement and as linguistic artifact — in other words, to exercise metalinguistic awareness.

A broad range of cross-cultural studies suggests that metalinguistic awareness is a defining feature of print literacy. Thus Sylvia Scribner and Michael

---

[22] See Bartholomae, "The Study of Error"; Patrick Hartwell, "The Writing Center and the Paradoxes of Written-Down Speech," in *Writing Centers: Theory and Administration,* ed. Gary Olson (Urbana, Ill.: NCTE, 1984), pp. 48–61; and Sondra Perl, "A Look at Basic Writers in the Process of Composing," in *Basic Writing: A Collection of Essays for Teachers, Researchers, and Administrators* (Urbana, Ill.: NCTE, 1980), pp. 13–32.

[23] Emonds, *Adjacency in Grammar: The Theory of Language-Particular Rules* (New York: Academic Press, 1983); and Jochnowitz, "Everybody Likes Pizza, Doesn't He or She?" *American Speech,* 57 (1982), 198–203.

Cole, working with the triliterate Vai of Liberia (variously literate in English, through schooling; in Arabic, for religious purposes; and in an indigenous Vai script, used for personal affairs), find that metalinguistic awareness, broadly conceived, is the only cognitive skill underlying each of the three literacies. The one statistically significant skill shared by literate Vai was the recognition of word boundaries. Moreover, literate Vai tended to answer "yes" when asked (in Vai), "Can you call the sun the moon and the moon the sun?" while illiterate Vai tended to have grave doubts about such metalinguistic play. And in the United States Henry and Lila R. Gleitman report quite different responses by clerical workers and PhD candidates asked to interpret nonsense compounds like "house-bird glass": clerical workers focused on meaning and plausibility (for example, "a house-bird made of glass"), while PhD candidates focused on syntax (for example, "a very small drinking cup for canaries" or "a glass that protects house-birds").[24] More general research findings suggest a clear relationship between measures of metalinguistic awareness and measures of literacy level.[25] William Labov, speculating on literacy acquisition in inner-city ghettoes, contrasts "stimulus-bound" and "language-bound" individuals, suggesting that the latter seem to master literacy more easily.[26] The analysis here suggests that the causal relationship works the other way, that it is the mastery of written language that increases one's awareness of language as language.

This analysis has two implications. First, it makes the question of socially nonstandard dialects, always implicit in discussions of teaching formal gram-

---

[24] Scribner and Cole, *Psychology of Literacy* (Cambridge, Mass.: Harvard University Press, 1981); Gleitman and Gleitman, "Language Use and Language Judgment," in *Individual Differences in Language Ability and Language Behavior,* ed. Charles J. Fillmore, Daniel Kemper, and William S. Y. Wang (New York: Academic Press, 1979), pp. 103–126.

[25] There are several recent reviews of this developing body of research in psychology and child development: Irene Athey, "Language Development Factors Related to Reading Development," *Journal of Educational Research,* 76 (1983), 197–203; James Flood and Paula Menyuk, "Metalinguistic Development and Reading/Writing Achievement," *Claremont Reading Conference Yearbook,* 46 (1982), 122–132; and the following four essays: David T. Hakes, "The Development of Metalinguistic Abilities: What Develops?," pp. 162–210; Stan A. Kuczaj II and Brooke Harbaugh, "What Children Think about the Speaking Capabilities of Other Persons and Things," pp. 211–227; Karen Saywitz and Louise Cherry Wilkinson, "Age-Related Differences in Metalinguistic Awareness," pp. 229–250; and Harriet Salatas Waters and Virginia S. Tinsley, "The Development of Verbal Self-Regulation: Relationships between Language, Cognition, and Behavior," pp. 251–277; all in *Language, Thought, and Culture,* Vol. II of *Language Development,* ed. Stan Kuczaj, Jr. (Hillsdale, N.J.: Lawrence Erlbaum, 1982). See also Joanne R. Nurss, "Research in Review: Linguistic Awareness and Learning to Read," *Young Children,* 35, No. 3 (1980), 57–66.

[26] "Competing Value Systems in Inner City Schools," in *Children In and Out of School: Ethnography and Education,* ed. Perry Gilmore and Allan A. Glatthorn (Washington, D.C.: Center for Applied Linguistics, 1982), pp. 148–171; and "Locating the Frontier between Social and Psychological Factors in Linguistic Structure," in *Individual Differences in Language Ability and Language Behavior,* ed. Fillmore, Kemper, and Wang, pp. 327–340.

mar, into a non-issue.[27] Native speakers of English, regardless of dialect, show tacit mastery of the conventions of Standard English, and that mastery seems to transfer into abstract orthographic knowledge through interaction with print.[28] Developing writers show the same patterning of errors, regardless of dialect.[29] Studies of reading and of writing suggest that surface features of spoken dialect are simply irrelevant to mastering print literacy.[30] Print is a complex cultural code — or better yet, a system of codes — and my bet is that, regardless of instruction, one masters those codes from the top down, from pragmatic questions of voice, tone, audience, register, and rhetorical strategy, not from the bottom up, from grammar to usage to fixed forms of organization.

Second, this analysis forces us to posit multiple literacies, used for multiple purposes, rather than a single static literacy, engraved in "rules of grammar." These multiple literacies are evident in cross-cultural studies.[31] They are equally evident when we inquire into the uses of literacy in American communities.[32]

---

[27] See, for example, Thomas Farrell, "IQ and Standard English," *CCC,* 34 (1983), 470–484; and the responses by Karen L. Greenberg and Patrick Hartwell, *CCC,* [35, Dec. 1984].

[28] Jane W. Torrey, "Teaching Standard English to Speakers of Other Dialects," in *Applications of Linguistics: Selected Papers of the Second International Conference of Applied Linguistics,* ed. G. E. Perren and J. L. M. Trim (Cambridge University Press, 1971), pp. 423–428; James W. Beers and Edmund H. Henderson, "A Study of the Developing Orthographic Concepts among First Graders," *RTE,* 11 (1977), 133–148.

[29] See the error counts of Samuel A. Kirschner and G. Howard Poteet, "Non-Standard English Usage in the Writing of Black, White, and Hispanic Remedial English Students in an Urban Community College," *RTE, 7* (1973), 351–355; and Marilyn Sternglass, "Close Similarities in Dialect Features of Black and White College Students in Remedial Composition Classes," *TESOL Quarterly,* 8 (1974), 271–283.

[30] For reading, see the massive study by Kenneth S. Goodman and Yetta M. Goodman, *Reading of American Children Whose Language Is a Stable Rural Dialect of English or a Language Other Than English* (Washington, D.C.: National Institute of Education Final Report, 1978) ERIC 175 754; and the overview by Rudine Sims, "Dialect and Reading: Toward Redefining the Issues," in *Reader Meets Author/Bridging the Gap: A Psycholinguistic Approach,* ed. Judith A. Langer and M. Tricia Smith-Burke (Newark, Del.: International Reading Association, 1982), pp. 222–232. For writing, see Patrick Hartwell, "Dialect Interference in Writing: A Critical View," *RTE,* 14 (1980), 101–118; and the anthology edited by Barry M. Kroll and Roberta J. Vann, *Exploring Speaking Writing Relationships: Connections and Contrasts* (Urbana, Ill.: NCTE, 1981).

[31] See, for example, Eric A. Havelock, *The Literary Revolution in Greece and Its Cultural Consequences* (Princeton, N.J.: Princeton University Press, 1982); Lesley Milroy on literacy in Dublin, *Language and Social Networks* (Oxford: Basil Blackwell, 1980); Ron Scollon and Suzanne B. K. Scollon on literacy in central Alaska, *Interethnic Communication: An Athabascan Case* (Austin, Tex.: Southwest Educational Development Laboratory Working Papers in Sociolinguistics, No. 59, 1979) ERIC 175 276; and Scribner and Cole on literacy in Liberia, *Psychology of Literacy* (see footnote 24).

[32] See, for example, the anthology edited by Deborah Tannen, *Spoken and Written Language: Exploring Orality and Literacy* (Norwood, N.J.: Ablex, 1982); and Shirley Brice Heath's continuing work: "Protean Shapes in Literacy Events: Ever-Shifting Oral and Literate Traditions," in *Spoken and Written Language,* pp. 91–117; *Ways with Words: Language, Life and Work in Communities and Classrooms* (New York: Cambridge University Press, 1983); and "What No Bedtime Story Means," *Language in Society,* 11 (1982), 49–76.

Further, given that students, at all levels, show widely variant interactions with print literacy, there would seem to be little to do with grammar — with Grammar 2 or with Grammar 4 — that we could isolate as a basis for formal instruction.[33]

GRAMMAR 5: STYLISTIC GRAMMAR

Similarly, when we turn to Grammar 5, "grammatical terms used in the interest of teaching prose style," so central to Martha Kolln's argument for teaching formal grammar, we find that the grammar issue is simply beside the point. There are two fully-articulated positions about "stylistic grammar," which I will label "romantic" and "classic," following Richard Lloyd-Jones and Richard E. Young.[34] The romantic position is that stylistic grammars, though perhaps useful for teachers, have little place in the teaching of composition, for students must struggle with and through language toward meaning. This position rests on a theory of language ultimately philosophical rather than linguistic (witness, for example, the contempt for linguists in Ann Berthoff's *The Making of Meaning: Metaphors, Models, and Maxims for Writing Teachers* [Montclair, N.J.: Boynton/Cook, 1981]); it is articulated as a theory of style by Donald A. Murray and, on somewhat different grounds (that stylistic grammars encourage overuse of the monitor), by Ian Pringle. The classic position, on the other hand, is that we can find ways to offer developing writers helpful suggestions about prose style, suggestions such as Francis Christensen's emphasis on the cumulative sentence, developed by observing the practice of skilled writers, and Joseph Williams' advice about predication, developed by psycholinguistic studies of comprehension.[35] James A. Berlin's . . . survey of composition theory

---

[33] For studies at the elementary level, see Dell H. Hymes et al., eds., *Ethnographic Monitoring of Children's Acquisition of Reading/Language Arts Skills In and Out of the Classroom* (Washington, D.C.: National Institute of Education Final Report, 1981) ERIC 208 096. For studies at the secondary level, see James L. Collins and Michael M. Williamson, "Spoken Language and Semantic Abbreviation in Writing," *RTE,* 15 (1981), 23–36. And for studies at the college level, see Patrick Hartwell and Gene LoPresti, "Sentence Combining as Kid-Watching," in *Sentence Combining: Toward a Rhetorical Perspective,* ed. Donald A. Daiker, Andrew Kerek, and Max Morenberg (Carbondale: Southern Illinois University Press, [1985, pp. 107–126]).

[34] Lloyd-Jones, "Romantic Revels—I Am Not You," *CCC,* 23 (1972), 251–271; and Young, "Concepts of Art and the Teaching of Writing," in *The Rhetorical Tradition and Modern Writing,* ed. James J. Murphy (New York: Modern Language Association, 1982), pp. 130–141.

[35] For the romantic position, see Ann E. Berthoff, "Tolstoy, Vygotsky, and the Making of Meaning," *CCC,* 29 (1978), 249–255; Kenneth Dowst, "The Epistemic Approach," in *Eight Approaches to Teaching Composition,* ed. Timothy Donovan and Ben G. McClellan (Urbana, Ill.: NCTE, 1980), pp. 65–85; Peter Elbow, "The Challenge for Sentence Combining"; and Donald Murray, "Following Language toward Meaning," both in *Sentence Combining: Toward a Rhetorical Perspective* (see footnote 33); and Ian Pringle, "Why Teach Style? A Review-Essay," *CCC,* 34 (1983), 91–98.

For the classic position, see Christensen's "A Generative Rhetoric of the Sentence"; and Joseph Williams' "Defining Complexity," *CE,* 41 (1979), 595–609; and his *Style: Ten Lessons in Clarity and Grace* (see footnote 9).

(*CE,* 45 [1982], 765–777) probably understates the gulf between these two positions and the radically different conceptions of language that underlie them, but it does establish that they share an overriding assumption in common: that one learns to control the language of print by manipulating language in meaningful contexts, not by learning about language in isolation, as by the study of formal grammar. Thus even classic theorists, who choose to present a vocabulary of style to students, do so only as a vehicle for encouraging productive control of communicative structures.

We might put the matter in the following terms. Writers need to develop skills at two levels. One, broadly rhetorical, involves communication in meaningful contexts (the strategies, registers, and procedures of discourse across a range of modes, audiences, contexts, and purposes). The other, broadly metalinguistic rather than linguistic, involves active manipulation of language with conscious attention to surface form. This second level may be developed tacitly, as a natural adjunct to developing rhetorical competencies — I take this to be the position of romantic theorists. It may be developed formally, by manipulating language for stylistic effect, and such manipulation may involve, for pedagogical continuity, a vocabulary of style. But it is primarily developed by any kind of language activity that enhances the awareness of language as language.[36] David T. Hakes, summarizing the research on metalinguistic awareness, notes how far we are from understanding this process:

> the optimal conditions for becoming metalinguistically competent involve growing up in a literate environment with adult models who are themselves metalinguistically competent and who foster the growth of that competence in a variety of ways, as yet little understood. ("The Development of Metalinguistic Abilities," p. 205; see footnote 25)

Such a model places language, at all levels, at the center of the curriculum, but not as "necessary categories and labels" (Kolln, "Closing the Books on Alchemy," p. 150), but as literal stuff, verbal clay, to be molded and probed, shaped and reshaped, and, above all, enjoyed.

THE TRADITION OF EXPERIMENTAL RESEARCH

Thus, when we turn back to experimental research on the value of formal grammar instruction, we do so with firm predictions given us by our theory of language. Our theory would predict that formal grammar instruction, whether instruction in scientific grammar or instruction in "the common school gram-

---

[36] Courtney B. Cazden and David K. Dickinson, "Language and Education: Standardization versus Cultural Pluralism," in *Language in the USA,* ed. Charles A. Ferguson and Shirley Brice Heath (New York: Cambridge University Press, 1981), pp. 446–468; and Carol Chomsky, "Developing Facility with Language Structure," in *Discovering Language with Children,* ed. Gay Su Pinnell (Urbana, Ill.: NCTE, 1980), pp. 56–59.

mar," would have little to do with control over surface correctness nor with quality of writing. It would predict that any form of active involvement with language would be preferable to instruction in rules or definitions (or incantations). In essence, this is what the research tells us. In 1893, the Committee of Ten (*Report of the Committee of Ten on Secondary School Studies* [Washington, D.C.: U.S. Government Printing Office, 1893]) put grammar at the center of the English curriculum, and its report established the rigidly sequential mode of instruction common for the last century. But the committee explicitly noted that grammar instruction did not aid correctness, arguing instead that it improved the ability to think logically (an argument developed from the role of the "grammarian" in the classical rhetorical tradition, essentially a teacher of literature—see, for example, the etymology of *grammar* in the *Oxford English Dictionary*).

But Franklin S. Hoyt, in a 1906 experiment, found no relationship between the study of grammar and the ability to think logically; his research led him to conclude what I am constrained to argue more than seventy-five years later, that there is no "relationship between a knowledge of technical grammar and the ability to use English and to interpret language" ("The Place of Grammar in the Elementary Curriculum," *Teachers College Record, 7* [1906], 483–484). Later studies, through the 1920s, focused on the relationship of knowledge of grammar and ability to recognize error; experiments reported by James Boraas in 1917 and by William Asker in 1923 are typical of those that reported no correlation. In the 1930s, with the development of the functional grammar movement, it was common to compare the study of formal grammar with one form or another of active manipulation of language; experiments by I. O. Ash in 1935 and Ellen Frogner in 1939 are typical of studies showing the superiority of active involvement with language.[37] In a 1959 article, "Grammar in Language Teaching" (*Elementary English, 36* [1959], 412–421), John J. DeBoer noted the consistency of these findings.

> The impressive fact is . . . that in all these studies, carried out in places and at times far removed from each other, often by highly experienced and disinterested investigators, the results have been consistently negative so far as the value of grammar in the improvement of language expression is concerned. (p. 417)

In 1960 Ingrid M. Strom, reviewing more than fifty experimental studies, came to a similarly strong and unqualified conclusion:

> direct methods of instruction, focusing on writing activities and the structuring of ideas, are more efficient in teaching sentence structure, usage, punctuation,

---

[37] Boraas, "Formal English Grammar and the Practical Mastery of English." Diss. University of Illinois, 1917; Asker, "Does Knowledge of Grammar Function?" *School and Society,* 17 (27 January 1923), 109–111; Ash, "An Experimental Evaluation of the Stylistic Approach in Teaching Composition in the Junior High School," *Journal of Experimental Education,* 4 (1935), 54–62; and Frogner, "A Study of the Relative Efficacy of a Grammatical and a Thought Approach to the Improvement of Sentence Structure in Grades Nine and Eleven," *School Review,* 47 (1939), 663–675.

and other related factors than are such methods as nomenclature drill, diagramming, and rote memorization of grammatical rules.[38]

In 1963 two research reviews appeared, one by Braddock, Lloyd-Jones, and Schoer, cited at the beginning of this paper, and one by Henry C. Meckel, whose conclusions, though more guarded, are in essential agreement.[39] In 1969 J. Stephen Sherwin devoted one-fourth of his *Four Problems in Teaching English: A Critique of Research* (Scranton, Penn.: International Textbook, 1969) to the grammar issue, concluding that "instruction in formal grammar is an ineffective way to help students achieve proficiency in writing" (p. 135). Some early experiments in sentence combining, such as those by Donald R. Bateman and Frank J. Zidonis and by John C. Mellon, showed improvement in measures of syntactic complexity with instruction in transformational grammar keyed to sentence-combining practice. But a later study by Frank O'Hare achieved the same gains with no grammar instruction, suggesting to Sandra L. Stotsky and to Richard Van de Veghe that active manipulation of language, not the grammar unit, explained the earlier results.[40] More recent summaries of research — by Elizabeth I. Haynes, Hilary Taylor Holbrook, and Marcia Farr Whiteman — support similar conclusions. Indirect evidence for this position is provided by surveys reported by Betty Bamberg in 1978 and 1981, showing that time spent in grammar instruction in high school is the least important factor, of eight factors examined, in separating regular from remedial writers at the college level.[41]

More generally, Patrick Scott and Bruce Castner, in "Reference Sources for Composition Research: A Practical Survey" (*CE*, 45 [1983], 756–768), note that much current research is not informed by an awareness of the past. Put simply, we are constrained to reinvent the wheel. My concern here has been with a far more serious problem: that too often the wheel we reinvent is square.

---

[38] "Research on Grammar and Usage and Its Implications for Teaching Writing," *Bulletin of the School of Education,* Indiana University, 36 (1960), pp. 13–14.

[39] Meckel, "Research on Teaching Composition and Literature," in *Handbook of Research on Teaching,* ed. N. L. Gage (Chicago: Rand McNally, 1963), pp. 966–1006.

[40] Bateman and Zidonis, *The Effect of a Study of Transformational Grammar on the Writing of Ninth and Tenth Graders* (Urbana, Ill.: NCTE, 1966); Mellon, *Transformational Sentence Combining: A Method for Enhancing the Development of Fluency in English Composition* (Urbana, Ill.: NCTE, 1969); O'Hare, *Sentence-Combining: Improving Student Writing without Formal Grammar Instruction* (Urbana, Ill.: NCTE, 1971); Stotsky, "Sentence-Combining as a Curricular Activity: Its Effect on Written Language Development," *RTE,* 9 (1975), 30–72; and Van de Veghe, "Research in Written Composition: Fifteen Years of Investigation," ERIC 157 095.

[41] Haynes, "Using Research in Preparing to Teach Writing," *English Journal,* 69, No. 1 (1978), 82–88; Holbrook, "ERIC/RCS Report: Whither (Wither) Grammar," *Language Arts,* 60 (1983), 259–263; Whiteman, "What We Can Learn from Writing Research," *Theory into Practice,* 19 (1980), 150–156; Bamberg, "Composition in the Secondary English Curriculum: Some Current Trends and Directions for the Eighties," *RTE,* 15 (1981), 257–266; and "Composition Instruction Does Make a Difference: A Comparison of the High School Preparation of College Freshmen in Regular and Remedial English Classes," *RTE,* 12 (1978), 47–59.

It is, after all, a question of power. Janet Emig, developing a consensus from composition research, and Aaron S. Carton and Lawrence V. Castiglione, developing the implications of language theory for education, come to the same conclusion: that the thrust of current research and theory is to take power from the teacher and to give that power to the learner.[42] At no point in the English curriculum is the question of power more blatantly posed than in the issue of formal grammar instruction. It is time that we, as teachers, formulate theories of language and literacy and let those theories guide our teaching, and it is time that we, as researchers, move on to more interesting areas of inquiry.

[42] Emig, "Inquiry Paradigms and Writing," *CCC,* 33 (1982), 64–75; Carton and Castiglione, "Educational Linguistics: Defining the Domain," in *Psycholinguistic Research: Implications and Applications,* ed. Doris Aaronson and Robert W. Rieber (Hillsdale, N.J.: Lawrence Erlbaum, 1979), pp. 497–520.

Ilona Leki

Meaning and Development of Academic Literacy in a Second Language

As English continues to expand into a global language (Kachru, 1992; Penny-cook, 1994), English learners worldwide experience pressure to develop literacy in English, often a high level of academic literacy. Yet, book titles such as *The Violence of Literacy* (Stuckey, 1991) and references to literacy as genocidal (Purcell-Gates, 1998) point to a growing recognition that literacy is neither innocent nor unproblematic. The potential negative consequences of enforced literacy described by these writers hold ethical implications for those of us involved in English literacy development and require us to examine the issues raised by second- (or third- or fourth-) language literacy and to become more fully aware of the complexity of the enterprise. This complexity entails differing conceptions of the meaning and role of literacy across cultures. It is my hope that such a cross-cultural approach to thinking about literacy will help to engender sympathy and respect for learners of English as an additional language by promoting a better understanding of the task they face in acquiring English academic literacy.

Even from the perspective only of native language literacy (Street, 1995), it is clear that literacy, certainly including academic literacy, is not a single, uniform, unitary skill and that literacy can be properly understood only from the perspective of a social context and not as the possession or personal cognitive ability of a single individual. If literacy is neither a unitary skill nor a personal possession independent of context, then what it means to be academically literate necessarily varies from one culture to the next. Being academically literate in Chinese, for example, means, among other things, having knowledge of thousands of characters and enough familiarity with the works of writers of antiquity to be able to quote them without hesitation in certain contexts. This concept of academic literacy is not the same for English. Attempting to move across cultures and languages into new literacies, academic or otherwise, complicates literacy acquisition qualitatively.

This chapter examines four of the complicating issues raised by the development of academic literacy in English as a second language (ESL): correctness, range, identity, and discourse community values.

This article is reprinted from Brian Huot, Charles Bazerman, and Beth Stroble (Eds.), *Multiple Literacies for the 21st century*. Cresswood: Hampton Press. (2004) 115–128.

CORRECTNESS

When I first started teaching, the grammar and vocabulary idiosyncrasies of second language (L2) writers were actually called "illiteracies." In other words, if L2 English learners made grammar and vocabulary errors, no matter how competent they were in their own languages, they were, for some, illiterate. These days most trained teachers of L2 academic literacy think of the language variances of L2 writers either as interlanguage forms (Selinker, 1972; i.e., intermediary grammars that are systematic and rule-governed but exhibit features unlike target language features) or as a type of *contact variety* of English, a term that comes from studies of pidgins and creoles and refers to mediating language forms that develop when people who do not speak each other's languages attempt to communicate.

Whatever such forms are called, questions of correctness do arise, if only in terms of whether or not the contact language forms are comprehensible to the members of an academically literate community. These issues of correctness arise not just in terms of producing text but also in interpreting text. How "correct" does a reading have to be to qualify as an instantiation of academic literacy in an L2? Peirce and Stein (1995) recount a striking case of conflicting instantiations of English academic literacy. A group of Black South African high school students whose first language (L1) was not English were asked to participate in piloting a text to be used in an English language proficiency test for university admissions. The text was based on a newspaper story about a group of 80 monkeys, four of whom were shot in the effort to stop their wild rampage against a home in Durban, where they attacked a boy, two policemen, and the house itself. (The monkeys had apparently become enraged at the entrapment of a mother monkey and her baby.) As one of the White L1 English authors explained, she and her colleagues took the text to be "a simple factual report" about this incident with monkeys in Durban. The Black high school students doing the pilot test, however, regarded the text as racist, one of them interpreting the passage as being "about Black people, who are the 'monkeys' 'on the rampage' in White people's homes" (p. 56). Another said "It's about who owns the land — the monkeys think the land belongs to them but the Whites think they own the land" (p. 56). Although the text was withdrawn as a test item, these students, who hoped eventually to be admitted to the university, were obviously not participants in the same interpretive community as the White test makers. Had the piloting not occurred, the students' "misinterpretation" may well have been read as a simple lack of L2 English academic literacy.

But the issue of correct interpretation can arise at the most basic level. For example, in responding to one student's text written under some time constraints in a composition class, I wrote something like "It's too bad you didn't have more time to finish." He was mortified because as he understood it, I was telling him his paper was bad, "too bad." When issues of correctness and comprehensibility arise, the question becomes, how correct does something have to be to be comprehensible? How distant and unlikely can an interpretive frame be and still qualify as a literate reading in L2? How closely does the reading and writing of an L2 English learner have to match that of other members of an L1 English literate culture, including in terms of grammatical accuracy, and what are the consequences when the mismatch leads to misunderstanding?

RANGE

Range of literate abilities is also a very important issue for L2 English students. Normally, we would probably associate academic literacy with the ability to use and produce texts in a fairly wide range of general academic contexts. This is the meaning of academic literacy that undergirds the undergraduate general education curriculum. But with L2 learners once again we may need a different perspective. For example, one of the participants (Yang) in a research project of mine majored in nursing. Although she was trained as a physician and practiced medicine in the People's Republic of China, when she came to the United States, she was in her middle 30s and had not really studied English beyond high school. She had a great deal of difficulty making herself understood orally and produced contact variety writing. In fact, the first report she wrote for a nursing class was simply returned to her as unacceptable because of the problems her professor noted in language. Yang's general extemporaneous written work never really got much better in the three years of her nursing program, but she eventually graduated with a solid B average because all of her exams in the nursing program were multiple choice; whenever she had to write a paper she always made use of the writing center and of her husband's and her young adolescent daughter's better command of grammar and vocabulary to screen the paper before she turned it in; and much of the writing required of her at the university was in the form of nursing care plans that are written in symbols and abbreviations as incomprehensible to most English users as a foreign language. In sum, the range of her academic literacy was quite narrow although I believe no one would challenge its depth within her field of expertise. Nevertheless, her L2 academic literacy, one that is so narrow and so dependent, again pushes at the margins of what it means to have L2 academic literacy.

IDENTITY ISSUES

Issues of identity arise to some degree in any language learning situation, but the poignancy of the issues are seen most clearly through the example of Fan Shen (1989), whose frequently quoted article appeared in *College Composition and Communication*. As Shen explained, he was a Chinese graduate student studying American literature and having trouble with his writing. His professor told him to stop worrying about being so academic in his writing and to just be himself. That advice made Shen realize that he could not in fact be himself in English because when he was himself, he was Chinese, and when his real Chinese self wrote something, it was not what his American professors were looking for. In order to write what they expected of him, he had to create and pretend to be a different self, an English-speaking self, one that did not mind arrogantly writing in the first person, one who put himself forward as having himself thought up these ideas he wrote and defended, rather than his Chinese self who did not write in the first person and whose native rhetoric required him to look to the authority of other writers and credit them with the ideas he wrote about. He had to pretend to be self-confident and assertive instead of circumspect, tentative, and suggestive as he really was. He managed, but only by becoming someone else, by creating an alter ego, a bold self-centered English-speaking person. Asking that someone create an alter ego is quite a lot to ask in the name of English academic literacy development. Why was it not possible for Shen to remain a Chinese person in his English writing?

Shen was a graduate student and possibly a visa student. That is, enough of his emotional and intellectual development had already taken place in Chinese so that he was able to resist the English assault against his Chinese self productively. The tension between identity and the development of L2 academic literacy presents an even more problematic and painful set of issues for younger students, particularly those who come to the United States as permanent residents. First, Cognitive Academic Language Proficiency (CALP), a concept proposed by Cummins (1979), develops somewhat independently from what Cummins called Basic Interpersonal Communicative Skills (BICS). In other words, although permanent resident students may be quite capable of handling their real-world communicative needs, including everyday reading and writing needs, that proficiency is of a different nature from the kinds of proficiency needed to succeed in academically oriented tasks. CALP takes a relatively long time to develop, long enough so that permanent resident students entering English medium high schools may in fact get to graduation before having developed academic proficiency in English (Collier, 1987). Bosher (1998) further suggests that this situation is exacerbated for refugee students, whose education may be interrupted by stays in refugee camps en route to permanent residences; to complicate matters, these students may not be academically literate in their first language (Fu, 1995; for a less academic perspective on these issues, see also Fadiman, 1997).

When permanent resident students enter college, we sometimes witness the sad and frustrating result of the educational system's response to these students, who communicate well in the everyday world but whose academic literacy is less well developed. In moving and eye-opening research on L2 students' experiences in the transition between high school and college, Harklau (2000) explored the situation of a small group of permanent resident students whose identities were in effect constructed for them by their teachers and classmates in high school, identities that they embraced. The four whom Harklau studied were considered top students in their high schools because they always did their homework as required, they tried hard academically and seemed to think education was important and teachers were to be respected, and they behaved well in class, so unlike native U.S. students with their disregard for schooling, as their teachers said.

These L2 students' teachers in high school praised them to the domestic students as models, pointing out how they obviously valued education despite their language "handicaps." With their first semester in college, however, their identities were reconstructed, not as model students, but first and foremost as ESL students, as students who had to be separated out from the other graduates of U.S. high schools because their proficiency in English (presumably in writing) was judged to be insufficient to allow them to take mainstream freshman writing classes. This reinterpretation of their identities was an embarrassment and a humiliation for these students, who had up to this point been taking all their high school classes with the U.S. students; they dressed like them, liked the same entertainments, lived like U.S. teenagers, and had been praised for their efforts in high school despite their language problems. They had become fully invested in their English-speaking identities. Now, after all this time succeeding in English, they were redefined, in the name of academic literacy, as failures in English, not primarily as model students but as ESL students.

ACADEMIC DISCOURSE COMMUNITY VALUES

At least in part, the development of academic literacy entails sharing the values of an academic discourse community, including subscribing to its expressed or tacit assumptions about what it means to be academically literate, that is, what it means to be one of the members of the literacy club, as Smith (1988) said. The academic discourse community in this U.S. culture currently values, among other things, critical thinking, developing "voice," and avoiding plagiarism. It might be useful to examine these values by first looking at different conceptions of what academic literacy means and how it is acquired in different cultures in order to make the point that beliefs about and attitudes toward literacy themselves form a part of literacy and that the acquisition of academic literacy in an L2 can be impeded by clashing culture-bound, often implicitly held values. The point of such an examination is to problematize these values as local and historical rather than universal and eternal. This critique then is intended to underscore the status of L1 English academic values as contingent and so to work against the colonizing of other literacies and concomitant devaluation of the literacy knowledge and practices of L2 English learners.

Although the research exists (see, e.g., Street, 1993), we in the United States have not focused much on research on cross-cultural academic literacy besides the large volume of work on contrastive rhetoric, which is fairly limited in scope, dealing mainly with patterns of text structure, not with values, beliefs, attitudes toward, or development of academic literacy (see also, Carson, 1992). One possible insight from contrastive rhetoric that moves beyond organizational issues appears in the often cited, although perhaps somewhat controversial, work by Hinds (1987) on Reader- and Writer-Responsible text. From his analyses of texts in Japanese and English, Hinds concluded that in some cultures, such as the United States, the burden of communication falls on the writer. That is, it is the writer's responsibility to make the meaning of a text as transparent as possible for the reader by explicitly explaining what the main point of the text is, how the text is divided, how various parts of the text are related to each other. On the other hand, other cultures prefer Reader-Responsible writing. In this case, it is the reader's responsibility to read between the lines, to intuit the meaning the writer only hints at, to see through disparate parts of the text to their underlying unity. If in fact such cultural preferences exist, it is easy to see why a highly literate reader and writer from a Reader-Responsible academic culture would have some difficulty seeing the value of and thus being willing to take on the habits and preferences of someone from a Writer-Responsible culture, and vice versa. In other words, if Hinds' studies hold up, U.S. reader/writers might find Japanese writing diffuse, suggestive, but unclear; Japanese reader/writers might find U.S. writing lockstep, simplistic, overly specified.

In addition to studying texts across cultures in an attempt to understand the nature of academic literacy, we might look cross-culturally at literacy training. In describing literacy training and practices in Korea, Lee and Scarcella (1992) noted that in grammar school Korean children are encouraged to keep daily journals that are collected once a week though not graded or corrected, that children are regularly asked to write to commemorate special occasions, and that many urban Korean families with children subscribe to special daily newspapers for children that report world, national, and local news, among other things. As adults, Koreans particularly appreciate poetry and short fiction. In fact, Lee and Scarcella reported that Koreans are, amazingly, accustomed to constructing poems on the spot. They refer to an article in the *Los Angeles Times* from 1988 that described a radio talk show host in Korea going out onto the street and randomly asking people to construct poems to express their opinions on the then current government corruption scandal.

However, although the Korean "person on the street" reported on in the article seems able and willing to create poetry, essay writing is not taught in schools and so not practiced much, with the general public apparently feeling, according to these authors, that only experts in a subject area are qualified to write essays on that topic. They also report the comments of a Korean university student who claims that the really good Korean writers spend a great deal of time planning what they will write, gathering their thoughts, and so once an essay is written, writers are unlikely to be inclined to spend time revising it. By contrast, the U.S. literate community seems to hold strong beliefs about the value of revising. Ability and willingness to revise practically define U.S. notions of expertise in writing.

Moving to China for a glimpse of other ways with words, we learn from Kohn (1992) something about reading instruction in the PRC. In Chinese reading classes, children are taught to read slowly and be sure they know each word before moving on; to reread difficult sentences until the meaning is clear; to look up definitions of all unknown words in a dictionary. As Kohn points out, this list of dos and don'ts is almost exactly the opposite of what current reading instruction theory recommends in this country, particularly in the instruction of L2 reading, where learners are encouraged to read fast to get the gist; use background knowledge to guess meaning; focus on main ideas, not details; and guess the meanings of unknown words instead of looking them up right away.

Clearly, attitudes and beliefs about academic literacy and literacy acquisition differ across cultures. With these differences as a backdrop, we might now turn to some of the values and beliefs that undergird academic literacy practices in this culture. One of the currently most pervasive and highly prized stances before text in this culture is that required for critical thinking. Critical thinking appears to mean approaching text with a combination of skepticism and analysis. It also appears to be taken for granted that critical thinking represents a universal good, and it is sometimes argued that for students from countries that value rote memorization in education (with all the negative connotations this term indexes), critical thinking is a skill or attitude that is especially important to teach to L2 students, suggesting that they in particular, because of their educational backgrounds, lack the ability to take such an approach. It is also only recently that writing researchers are finally beginning to examine critical thinking with a bit of critical distance.

Atkinson (1997) links the notion of critical thinking with the glorification of individualism, standing alone against the crowd or against the received wisdom of a particular text. He points out that not all countries have this obsession with the power and importance of the individual above the group that undergirds current notions of critical thinking, and so we should be clear that this notion of critical thinking is culture bound, preferred by some academically literate communities as a way of approaching text at this particular time. It is neither a universal value nor an expression of the universal good. Atkinson's analysis is important for those of us who deal with students who come from cultures where the proper approach to a text is not a critical approach, from cultures that encourage a less individualistic stance before text. His discussion reminds us of the arrogance of believing that, because at this moment in time we feel that a critical approach works well for us, we must require it of every student that comes our way, not as an option but as the only appropriate form of intellectual engagement.

But perhaps more important to remember is that, although the U.S. academic discourse community currently finds the critical thinking approach to text useful and other cultures may find this approach to text less interesting, useful, or appropriate for whatever reason, not adopting a critical thinking stance before a text in an educational context cannot be equated with an inability to think critically. It would in fact be ludicrous to make such an assumption. After all, what culture, what part of the world does not at one time or another witness the political unrest and/or protest that can be one of the consequences of thinking critically, analytically, skeptically? Certainly, L2 English students can and do think critically, without our help, and very often their critical thinking is directed at the United States, at what we do here in general and at what we do in our classes in particular. Those who despair that these students are not critical enough need to have more conversations with them. But approaching a text, especially certain kinds of texts, with a primary view to finding fault with it may simply not be an appropriate stance to take before a text, at least not certain texts and perhaps not in an initial encounter. What might those certain texts be? They might easily be religious texts, but they might well also be academic texts in academic settings, especially on subjects the students do not know much about, and most especially on subjects related to a culture that is not their own (see, e.g., Johns, 1991).

Like critical thinking, another value associated in this culture with academic literacy and taught in writing classes, although mentioned only rarely in disciplinary courses across the curriculum, is the development of an authorial voice. An apparent goal of writing classes in this culture is the development of a sense of individual difference: to set oneself apart from the others, to be unlike other writers, to let individual voices stand out and be heard. Such a stance is open to the criticism, in a post-structuralist context, that it emphasizes to students the discredited notion of the unified, autonomous subjectivity, posits the notion as natural and universal rather than constructed and determined, and thus casts as unnatural anyone for whom such an emphasis on individualism is not automatic.

In addition to reemphasizing our heavy bias toward individualism, the notion of voice appears to be associated, at least to some degree, with a willingness to self-disclose and herein lies another potential problem for L2 writing development. On one hand, not all cultures encourage young people to self-disclose in classrooms, to talk about their personal experiences and opinions; that simply is not what school is for. And on the other hand, in other educational systems, that kind of self-disclosure may in fact be considered very appropriate but exclusively for schoolchildren, not for adults at a university, who would be expected to be able to exercise self-control and to find ways to self-disclose among their family and friends, not in a classroom.

In other words, while English writing teachers value voice in student writing, it too must be considered contingent, valued in a particular time and place, but not an essential component of academic literacy and so perhaps not worth hammering on too much in L2 reading/writing classes. (For further discussion of voice in L2 writing, see the special issue on voice in the *Journal of Second Language Writing*, Belcher & Hirvela, 2001.)

And finally, plagiarism. Although critical thinking and voice are relative newcomers to the list of qualities that writers are currently being encouraged to exhibit, the nearly absolute requirement to avoid plagiarism has been around much longer. But not forever. Strictures against plagiarism are neither universal nor ahistorical; they appear to have begun in the English-speaking world during the Renaissance and for specific historical reasons. Pennycook (1996) traces the history of plagiarism in the West and helps us to put into perspective this currently greatest of literacy sins. The reason it is important to see plagiarism as a notion limited to a particular time and place is to blunt the hysteria with which accusations of plagiarism are surrounded. Blunting this hysteria is especially important when dealing with L2 students for at least three reasons. First, in many cultures citing someone else's work without saying who the source is marks the writer as particularly steeped in literate culture. It is a sign of respect toward the reader as well, indicating the writer's belief that the reader is too literate to require a source reference.

The second reason not to exaggerate the importance of plagiarism is related to culturally dependent notions of what it is to learn. For example, in an incident at my school, a group of Malaysian students came to see me in despair that their history teacher was giving them Fs on a recent exam because he was accusing them of plagiarism. As they adamantly maintained, they had not plagiarized. They had simply done what good students do; they had memorized portions of the textbook. During the exam they wrote exactly the correct answer, taken from the textbook word for word, from memory, not copied from the book, which is what they understood we meant here by plagiarism. They had learned the material by heart, which to them meant, really learned it. Clearly, their view of learning clashed with the view the professor had. He had faith in the idea that only if you can more or less say something in your own words can you claim to have learned it. I leave open the question of how well "your own words" are able to accurately retain the meaning of what you might be trying to learn. In any case, this teacher did not want these students to use the textbook author's words.

But the third reason to view plagiarism with a bit more distance is that in a sense L2 students are always using others' words. How can they not? Because of a limited linguistic repertoire in their L2, they may simply have no other way available to them to restate what they just read. They may not be able to tell if an attempted paraphrase in fact paraphrases an original text. Or having limited options themselves, they may find the original captures for them the one best way to say something. As one student said, "If you have a ... text in perfect English, that's exactly ... what you should say and this is the best way. Then [because you don't want to plagiarize] you have to find another way. This is funny. ... So you have to change it and then it gets worse. Kind of sad" (Leki & Carson, 1997, p. 59). This is not to say that L2 English learners do not need to be aware of the great store this culture puts in "using your own words," only that plagiarism elicits emotional reactions from teachers and perhaps others that are entirely out of proportion to the event, and L2 literacy teachers need to be aware of our own deep enculturation on the topic.

To set the beliefs and practices of these different discourse communities in contrast, then, we find some cultures where reading instruction recommends careful focus on detail to understand text and others where the focus is on global approaches to help understand a text; some where poetry is part of everyday life but expressing personal opinion in essays is left to experts in the subject area and others where essay writing, developing individual voice, and expressing personal opinion constitute the quintessence of knowing how to write; some that value implicitness above overexplaining, others that consider implicitness to be vague, maybe even deceitful, and value straightforward, clearly explicit approaches instead.

But how much do these differences matter? Could we not just recognize that there are differences and move on? To try to answer these questions, it might be useful to look at the experience of one more L2 learner, highly literate in her L1, English, and very motivated to develop L2 literacy. Bell (1995) describes her attempt to learn Chinese and explains how implicit clashing assumptions about literacy on her part and on the part of her Chinese tutor led to frustration and feelings of failure. Bell began studying written Chinese at the same time as she began oral Chinese. She felt she progressed well in oral Chinese but began to feel increasingly miserable about what she perceived as her lack of progress in written Chinese. Her Chinese writing tutor would introduce one character at a time, showing how the strokes are made and in what order and Bell would then be asked to practice, practice, practice that same character.

But Cindy, her tutor, was never satisfied; her feedback was consistently that the characters lacked balance and that Bell needed to concentrate more, feedback that became increasingly irritating and incomprehensible to Bell as the months went on and she was still practicing the same characters over and over. She finally came to realize that what was getting in her way were certain basic assumptions she had about learning, deeply held convictions that had made of her all her life an efficient and accomplished learner in her own culture. She examines two particularly striking clashes of assumptions. First, Bell assumed that the characters she was learning could more or less be split into their forms and their content, that her goal was to be able to recognize and generally reproduce a character, and that she could clean up the niceties of reproducing the forms perfectly later. That is, as long as the characters were recognizable for what they were, superficial issues like neatness and attractiveness could be worried about later. But for Cindy, the Chinese tutor, appearance was essential; form was inextricably linked to content; presentation, not just ideas, was crucial. There was no first sloppy draft and then going back to clean it up; in Cindy's view, for Bell to develop the mental discipline to succeed (i.e., to become literate), each character needed to be perfect each time.

The second area in which Bell's and Cindy's assumptions conflicted had to do with learning style. Bell had become a successful academic through her engaged, questioning, active learning style. When she tried to use the same style with Cindy in learning to write Chinese, Cindy told her that "the way to learn is to receive.... You do a lot of observing and then you think about it" (p. 698). Cindy is clearly not talking about passive rote learning; you do a lot of observing and then you think about it, she says. But it is possible that the attitude toward learning that Cindy expresses here may be interpreted in U.S. culture as passive, unquestioning, unengaged, and the people, say Chinese, who use this style and believe in this way of learning (and for good reason because they have probably become academically successful using it), these people may well be viewed in U.S. culture as not thinking critically, not developing personal voice, maybe likely to plagiarize by wanting to copy text word for word. As we see in Bell's example, it is difficult to understand cross-cultural literacies without first examining the assumptions of our own L1 literacy and then being willing to challenge or suspend the values tied to it.

The question of academic discourse communities finally presents itself to L2 literacy teachers in two forms. First, if beliefs and attitudes about L1 literacy and about the acquisition of L1 literacy inform approaches and attitudes toward L2 literacy acquisition, L2 literacy teachers need to do more to understand the kinds of literacy expectations and attitudes students bring with them from their families and their home cultures and to build on those expectations. Remaining ignorant of other cultures' approaches to literacy may cause us to misunderstand our students' actions and motivations and to misinterpret the causes of obstacles they may be experiencing in acquiring L2 literacy.

Second, L2 reading/writing teachers need to think long and hard about our own academic discourse community. What is it? Specifically, what community do we belong to? As we introduce L2 students to academic literacy, whose discourse community are we representing to them? In the course of doing research on professors' expectations about writing across disciplines, I learned that in our College of Agriculture, before turning in papers to their professors, students are asked to run a computer check of the length of each of the sentences in their reports. The computers there are programmed to flag any sentences longer than 21 words. I was stunned to learn this. In my L2 writing classes I encouraged students to try to combine short sentences into longer ones, telling them, as I believe, that in English we tend to value embedding at the sentence level; complex sentences lend an air of maturity to writing. Apparently, however, this belief is not shared in the discourse community of the College of Agriculture. There, longer sentences are discouraged as more likely to be confusing than short sentences. Whose discourse community was I representing in what I was teaching my students, my L2 English students who are in college to study engineering, business, agriculture, computer science, math, biology? Clearly, I was representing the English department's discourse community to my students as the very holder of the meaning of what it is to be literate — the English department, the academic discourse community that is the most likely to assign essays to write rather than reports, the one that values personal disclosure to develop a writer's voice, the one that encourages, even requires, students to express personal opinions on topics they may know very little about, the one literacy community that my L2 English students are the very least likely to want to join. I would argue that it is important to keep reminding ourselves that different communities value different aspects of reading and writing, and English department literacy values are not universal and do not define literacy in general. This knowledge, however, puts L2 reading/writing teachers in the odd and conflicted situation of trying to introduce L2 English students to literacy communities we ourselves do not belong to and of belonging to a community they have no reason to be introduced to.

In view of the place of English in the world today and the role it sometimes plays in both empowering and dramatically constraining the lives and futures of people from different L1 backgrounds, I feel an interrogation of the characteristics of L1 English literacy and its place among the other literacies in the world is a task that L1 English literates are morally and ethically obliged to undertake. Given how complex literacy issues in second, third, or fourth languages can become, perhaps the only reasonable stance to take, at least initially, is one of modest flexibility and willingness to learn from others, one in which "You do a lot of observing and then you think about it."

REFERENCES

Atkinson, D. (1997). A Critical Approach to Critical Thinking in TESOL. *TESOL Quarterly, 31*, 71–94.

Belcher, D., & Hirvela, A. (Eds.). (2001). *Journal of Second Language Writing, 10* [Special issue on Voice in L2 Writing].

Bell, J. (1995). The Relationship between L1 and L2 Literacy: Some Complicating Factors. *TESOL Quarterly, 29*, 687–704.

Bosher, S. (1998). The Composing Process of Three Southeast Asian Writers at the Post-secondary Level. *Journal of Second Language Writing, 7*, 205–241.

Carson, J. (1992). Becoming Biliterate: First Language Influences. *Journal of Second Language Writing, 1*, 37–60.

Collier, V. (1987). Age and Acquisition of Second Language for Academic Purposes. *TESOL Quarterly, 21*, 617–641.

Cummins, J. (1979). Linguistic Interdependence and the Educational Development of Bilingual Children. *Review of Education Research, 49*, 222–251.

Fadiman, A. (1997). *The Spirit Catches You and You Fall Down.* New York: Farrar, Straus & Giroux.

Fu, D. (1995). *My Trouble Is My English.* Portsmouth, NH: Boynton/Cook.

Harklau, L. (2000). From "Good Kids" to the "Worst": Representation of English Language Learners across Educational Settings. *TESOL Quarterly, 34*, 35–67.

Hinds, J. (1987). Reader vs. Writer Responsibility: A New Typology. In U. Connor & R. Kaplan (Eds.), *Writing across Languages: Analysis of L2 Text* (pp. 141–152). Reading, MS: Addison-Wesley.

Johns, A.M. (1991). Interpreting an English Competency Examination: The Frustrations of an ESL Science Student. *Written Communication, 8*, 379–401.

Kachru, B. (1992). *The Other Tongue: English across Cultures.* Urbana: University of Illinois Press.

Kohn, J. (1992). Literacy Strategies for Chinese University Learners. In F. Dubin & N. Kuhlman (Eds.), *Cross-Culture Literacy: Global Perspectives on Reading and Writing* (pp. 113–125). Englewood Cliffs, NJ: Prentice-Hall.

Lee, C., & Scarcella, R. (1992). Building upon Korean Writing Practices: Genres, Values, and Beliefs. In F. Dubin & N. Kuhlman (Eds.), *Cross-culture literacy: Global Perspectives on Reading and Writing* (pp. 143–161). Englewood Cliffs, NJ: Prentice-Hall.

Leki, I., & Carson, J. (1997). "Completely Different Worlds": EAP and the Writing Experiences of ESL Students in University Courses. *TESOL Quarterly, 31*, 39–69.

Peirce, B., & Stein, P. (1995). Why the "Monkeys Passage" Bombed: Tests, Genres, and Teaching. *Harvard Educational Review, 65*, 50–65.

Pennycook, A. (1994). *The Cultural Politics of English as an International Language*. New York: Longman.

Pennycook, A. (1996). Borrowing Others' Words: Text, Ownership, Memory, and Plagiarism. *TESOL Quarterly, 30,* 201–230.

Purcell-Gates, V. (1998, October). *Literacy at Home and Beyond*. Paper presented at Watson Conference on Rhetoric and Composition, Louisville, KY.

Selinker, L. (1972). Interlanguage. *International Review of Applied Linguistics, 10,* 209–231.

Shen, F. (1989). The Classroom and the Wider Culture: Identity as a Key to Learning English Composition. *College Composition and Communication, 40,* 459–466.

Smith, F. (1988). *Joining the Literacy Club*. Princeton, NJ: Princeton University Press.

Street, B. (Ed.). (1993). *Cross-cultural Approaches to Literacy*. New York: Cambridge.

Street, B. (1995). *Social Literacies: Critical Approaches to Literacy in Development, Ethnography and Education*. New York: Longman.

Stuckey, J. (1991). *The Violence of Literacy*. Portsmouth, NH: Boynton/Cook.

Wendy Bishop

Helping Peer Writing Groups Succeed

Imagine you are entering a freshman level composition classroom. It is the tenth week of a fifteen–week semester. The teacher sits to one side of the room, conferencing with a single student about the student's paper which rests on a table between them. The rest of the twenty-student class has been divided into peer writing groups of four to five students. The class is noisy, for each group is busy discussing a paper and students talk freely, offering revision suggestions. The writer and a group historian note these suggestions, and a group monitor moves the discussion on, seeing to it that the group reviews at least some of each member's writing before the one hour class is over.

After the teacher conferences with several students, she then moves for a time from group to group, offering additional suggestions and encouragement, and checking on work accomplished. A few minutes before the class ends, the groups briefly summarize their work and each discussion is transcribed into written notes by the group historian. Finally, the teacher checks to make sure that the class as a whole is clear about future class sessions and/or assignments.

I have just described an idealized but obtainable writing classroom, one in which students join together in collaborative work and develop their writing abilities in a non-threatening environment. The teacher is guide and assistant to the work at hand. This holistic approach to writing and the teaching of writing makes many new demands on both students and teachers who need to change their attitudes and expectations to participate in such a classroom. Because of these sometimes unexpected demands, teachers trying to introduce peer writing groups into their curriculum often feel let down by a method that has been presented in glowing terms yet can prove problematic in practice. Has group work been overrated? Have teachers been deceived? Or, have teachers become confused by the apparent simplicity of a rather complex teaching method?

I would like to explore these questions by reviewing research that discusses the use of peer writing groups, by profiling successful and unsuccessful peer writing groups and, finally, by offering a plan for preparing and training students for the method. Such a plan must also include guidelines for evaluating the effectiveness of peer writing groups in the composition classroom.

This article is Chapter 2 of Wendy Bishop, *Teaching Lives: Essays and Stories*. Logan, Utah State University Press. (1997) 14–24.

343

RESEARCH ON PEER WRITING GROUPS

The value of using peer writing groups as a teaching method, if not over-rated has sometimes been oversimplified. A brief review of current research and practice shows this. In general, collaborative peer writing groups do benefit the student. The claims for the efficacy of the method are many and various. Mary Beaven, discussing peer evaluation, claims that the collaborative method allows students to develop audience awareness, to check their perceptions of reality, to strengthen their interpersonal skills, and to take risks; the entire process results in improvement in writing and students' ability to revise. Thom Hawkins agrees that students strengthen their interpersonal skills and risk-taking or creative abilities.

Kenneth Bruffee found that peer tutors and tutees at work in a collaborative environment deal with higher order concerns such as paper focus and development. Tutees feel comfortable enough with peers to bring up these concerns which go beyond the usage level, and the writing abilities of tutors also improves as a direct result of the collaborative writing act. Researchers like Francine Danis, who found that 75% of the students in her study correctly identified both major and minor writing problems, and Anne Gere, who felt that student responses (grades five to twelve) did deal with meaning, would seem to support Bruffee's contention that students in peer groups do more than simply act as proofreaders of each other's work. Other research by Anne Gere and Robert Abbott reaffirmed the power of peer writing groups to stay focused on discussions about writing. Their research also shows that group discussions where teachers are present are significantly different from those in which teachers are absent.

Drawbacks to the method must be noted. First, collaborative learning can be time consuming (see Beaven and Abercrombie), for those writing about this method agree that some training of group members is necessary. Mary Beaven also notes that some instructors are unable to allow students the freedom required (student- rather than teacher-centered, discussion rather than lecture dominated classrooms) and therefore end up doing double work, designing *and controlling,* directing *and correcting* the groups. This problem seems to be one of teacher awareness and training rather than an inherent flaw in the method.

A final criticism develops from close research observation of groups and from student evaluations. Francine Danis found that students are not always sure of their group role, aren't able to stand back from their own writing, don't know what they want to know, and have a reluctance to offer critical comments. Elizabeth Flynn felt students lacked critical ability and attributed this to students' tendencies to supply missing information in a paper in order to make sense out of what they were reading. Again, these are problems that can be somewhat alleviated by student and teacher preparation for the method. The fact that students do need to develop a critical vocabulary from which to discuss their works is supported in Kenneth Bruffee's articles concerning the importance of language communities. Clearly, there is a need to introduce writing students to the vocabulary and terminology of the composition community.[1]

PROFILES OF PEER WRITING GROUPS

Now let us enter another freshman composition classroom. Again, it is the tenth week of a fifteen-week semester. Again, the teacher is conferencing with one student and four or five peer writing groups are in session. We will observe three of the groups.

In Group A, students form a tightly knit circle. Members are discussing organizational changes that would benefit a group member's paper. The writer of the paper listens and makes notes as does the group secretary. Soon, the group monitor reminds the group that other papers remain to be discussed. The transition to the next paper is made smoothly. If the teacher were to come over to the group, she could slip into a nearby seat and participate; talk would continue, although it would be altered somewhat by the group's awareness of her presence.

If you asked members of Group A how the group method was working, members would most likely be enthusiastic, pointing out changes they have made in papers as a result of the discussion, showing how every member of the group helps by offering suggestions, explaining that they appreciate the teacher's comments but also enjoy developing their writing skills together. Group A is a successful, fully-developed peer writing group.

Here is an evaluation from a member of such a group:

> This is the first time I've had an English class where groups were formed. I found that I had an easier time talking in the groups then in class discussion. So I must say that it has value in letting me get my ideas across to other people in class, with much less apprehension.

Group B looks a lot like Group A. Most of the members are concentrating on a single paper. However, comments on this paper are tentative. The group gets stalled on a grammar point that no one is really interested in discussing nor competent to decide. When this happens, the writer of the paper starts to explain what she meant to do in the paper and other group members look bored. They've heard her talk like this before. Still, the members are polite and wait until the writer stops talking before moving on to another point: they find several misspellings in the paper. When the class ends, this group has only discussed two of four papers as the monitor forgot to move them on. The historian suggests that the group forego the end of session summary and no one cares. When the teacher moves toward the group, discussion wanes and dies awkwardly. When asked how the group is doing, members can't articulate their group's progress, but insist that everything is okay. Talk picks up slowly as the teacher moves away.

Group B is finding the group method only mildly successful, for members are never really sure if they are talking about writing "in the right way." They don't feel that other members give them truly honest evaluation of their work and don't trust the evaluations they do receive. They are confused when they get teacher-graded papers returned that have low grades. They wonder why group members didn't catch more of the problems the teacher marked. They feel comfortable with each other but are sometimes lazy and unsure of their own abilities to discuss or change their writing. They accept working in groups but are constantly waiting for something to happen. Group B is an under-developed peer writing group.

Here is an evaluation from a member of such a group:

> I do like the idea of the groups. But could you please float around & insert "starter" statements for some groups if need be? Sometimes our group doesn't go very far under the analysis that we write in our journals.

Group C looks different than either Group A or Group B and looks differ-ent every time members try to start working together. Members of this group often don't come to class or come late and try to leave early. Some members are easily distracted; they look through their own bags or papers or watch other groups covertly. When this group does have more than one or two members, a single student may dominate the talk. No one has volunteered or been elected for the positions of historian and monitor. Often the group drifts, finishing work too quickly or not moving along at all. When the teacher comes to join this group, a single member enters into a private dialogue with her. Other group members may try to avoid contact with the teacher, both in and out of class.

Group C is sure the group method is useless. No one in the group knows what is going on and the class is boring. The dominant member is resentful, feeling he is doing too much work, and the other members feel they are in the grip of yet another un-elected teacher–dictator. Group members feel unsure of their own writing and do not see how they can teach each other. They have strong suspicions that the teacher is holding back something or is too lazy to really teach them. Group C is not simply underdeveloped; it is really not a peer writing group at all.

Here is an evaluation from a member of such a group:

> Individuals a little lax in group to have assignments read (including myself). We don't know what to write about, probably because we don't know what you want and don't know how to find it in the stories.
>   What are we looking for?

The observer of this writing class and the teacher might agree: when peer groups are fully developed (Group A), the method is exciting and rewarding for students and teacher alike, but when peer group interactions are under-developed (Group B) or break down (Group C), the method is discouraging and group work all too often feels like a matter of luck.

Obviously, these profiles are only useful in that they give a teacher a way to begin to sort out group interaction patterns. Each teacher will vary in the way she labels her groups. For instance, I evaluate group success on a continuum between fully developed and under-developed groups as distinct from non-cohering groups. Diana George in her article "Writing with Peer Groups in Composition" distinguishes between task-oriented, leaderless, and dysfunctional. In both cases, in-class observations have taken place and serious consideration has been given to groups in order for a teacher to improve future group work. By profiling her own writing groups, a teacher can learn how writing peer groups can become useless and sometimes lifeless. If even one of several important problems is present in a group, such a problem can quickly move the group from success to failure. Therefore, teachers need to be aware of the attributes of successful groups and learn what can be done to move groups from failure to success and doing so will enable composition teachers to feel more comfortable using peer writing groups.

The following list shows ways groups can fail or succeed and notes the names of researchers or writers who touch on these concerns when discussing peer writing groups. I have developed my profiles of group weaknesses and strengths after reading these writers and observing composition and literature classes which I conducted by group method at the University of Alaska, Fairbanks campus, from fall 1985 to spring 1987.

Ways Peer Writing Groups Fail

1. Too much or too little leadership (Hawkins; Elbow 1977; George).
2. Poor attendance or participation or preparation of some students leading to resentment between members (Hawkins; Flynn 1982).
3. Unclear group goals; group doesn't value work or works too quickly (Johnson and Johnson; Hawkins; George).
4. Group doesn't feel confident of group members' expertise or members are afraid to offer criticism (Lagana; Danis; Flynn).
5. Group doesn't understand new role of instructor (Ziv).
6. Group never develops adequate vocabulary for discussing writing (Danis; Bruffee).
7. Group fails to record suggestions or to make changes based on members' suggestions (George).

Ways Peer Writing Groups Succeed

1. Group successfully involves all members (Johnson and Johnson; Hawkins; Elbow).
2. Group works to clarify goals and assignments (Johnson and Johnson; Elbow 1977; Danis).
3. Group develops a common vocabulary for discussing writing (Beaven; Bruffee; Danis).
4. Group learns to identify major writing problems such as organization, tone, and focus, as well as minor writing problems such as spelling errors, and so on (Bruffee; Danis; Gere; Gere and Abbot).
5. Group learns to value group work and to see instructor as a resource which the group can call on freely (Rogers; Danis; Flynn).

Most writers are in agreement, students and teachers need preparation and training for successful peer group work. Those teachers who divide students into groups merely to provide momentary relief from the lecture classroom will develop failures similar to those listed above.

PREPARING FOR PEER WRITING GROUPS

Although the peer writing groups profiled in this paper show students critiquing each other's drafts, groups can serve a broader variety of purposes. Students can work together to discuss readings, to complete exercises, to explore writing invention strategies, and to help members with forming very early drafts. Additionally, the peer group method can be adapted to classes at the primary and secondary level, to advanced or creative writing classes, and to diverse academic disciplines.

Teachers who want to use peer writing groups in their classroom should plan ahead. They need to realize that the group method rests on a theory of collaborative learning and they will be more successful if they read widely in this area. While reading, a teacher should ask several questions:

1. Do I understand the theory behind peer writing groups?
2. Do I have a clear use for this method in my classroom?
3. What are my goals for students when using this method?

Additionally, because group work is based on a theory of learning that students may be unfamiliar with or resistant to, the well prepared teacher will acquaint students with concepts of collaborative learning through prepared handouts, class discussion, and continual monitoring of group work. After gaining a deeper understanding through reading, teachers need to visualize the place of peer writing groups in their entire curriculum. Students need to develop a group identity and participate in a new writing community. To function well, group members must be present, which requires a class attendance policy. A teacher might decide to use groups for a certain percentage of class time. I have found using groups 50 to 75% of my available class periods most effective. This percentage allows my students to develop a group identity yet regroup into a class on a regular basis in order to maintain a class identity also.

Classroom communities are formed by the school registrar, academic departments, and the enrolling student. How should peer group communities be formed? To start, teachers may divide a class into sets of four to five students or students may start working collaboratively in pairs and then pairs may be joined. Although many criteria could be presented for forming such groups, nothing in the peer group literature supports any one in particular. First week diagnostic writings may be used to organize groups with a balance of strong and weak writers. Students may rate themselves on matters such as ability to lead, to help, to take risks, and so on, and groups may be balanced with a member strong in each area. In addition, I try to balance groups by gender and by age.

Once groups are formed, there is no certain number of sessions needed to develop a strong sense of group community. Some groups develop rapport immediately and some take much longer. Groups can develop a radical (sometimes disruptive) streak and also a conservative (and equally disruptive) bent. Groups work best when they are balanced, focused, and comfortable. Depending on my course goals, I try to let groups work together for at least four sessions, and I rarely leave a group together for an entire semester.

The more groups are used, the more adept a teacher becomes in divining group personalities. Sometimes a teacher needs to intervene and change group membership (placing an overly dominant member in another, more challenging group, and so on), but often it is wiser to let the group itself solve group problems. Ideally, groups that stay together over a long period develop a strong group identity and sense of shared community. Equally, groups that change membership, partially or wholly, are often revitalized and ready to undertake new course challenges with greater enthusiasm.

Because groups develop as real writing communities, choosing a group name can help members identify with their new community. Ordering and clarifying group members' roles such as monitor and historian and general member also assures that group work will be carried on in an orderly manner. Groups are formed to work together, so group projects should be clearly articulated in handout form or as directions on the chalkboard, and group work should be real work, contributing to each member's writing development.

Time should be allowed for groups to share their work, conclusions, and progress with the whole class in order to support the class as a larger community and to keep groups from becoming too isolated. Reporting on what the group accomplished each session, in the form of historian's notes in a group folder, provides useful artifacts for group self-evaluation and teacher evaluation of the group session. To review, when forming groups for the first time, I ask the members to give themselves a name and to chose a monitor (timekeeper) and historian (secretary). Each group is given a folder for saving work and recording discussions.

TRAINING PEER WRITING GROUPS

To work well together, peer writing groups need training in two areas in particular: group roles and writing response. It is not enough to ask the groups to elect a monitor and a historian, but those individuals should have clear directions as to their roles. If a monitor does not act as the group caretaker, making sure each member gets time to respond to writing and time to have writing discussed and making sure the group performs the group tasks in time to share with the whole class, then the group will risk failure. If the historian does not record group discussions, there will be little continuity from session to session and no product to show the group and the teacher where the group has been and what it has done. When groups are first formed, handouts to elected members, as well as a handout detailing the responsibilities of a member in general — attendance, support, sharing, and so on — can speed the training in this area.

Even more important, group members will be teaching each other to talk about writing. This talk can be initiated by the teacher, reinforced by the class text, and nurtured by whole class discussion, but it will be brought to fruition in the group itself as members learn to improve their writing. In this effort, the teacher functions as the conduit linking the class to the academic community. She may begin by teaching the class necessary terminology (concerning writing process and writing analysis) and by training writers and readers to work together through role playing, reviewing sample essays, and so on. In their initial critique sessions, groups can work to answer set questions or can learn to develop their own critical concerns for papers. If composition terms such as prewriting, drafting, revising, focus, organization, and tone are introduced in class discussion, show up on group handouts, are reinforced in peer writing group discussions, and recorded in group minutes, such terms will soon become part of the peer group's working vocabulary.

MONITORING PEER WRITING GROUPS

During group work, the teacher is extremely busy, although not necessarily appearing so, for she is the group and class facilitator, deciding when to intervene in groups and when to reconvene the groups into a class to share results, review strategies, or speed up information dissemination. Sometimes the best thing a teacher can do is to listen and watch her groups quietly and unobtrusively; sometimes she must participate in groups to insure that each group is working efficiently, but there is no single right way to help groups succeed.

A teacher needs to experiment, but she should do so carefully. She should keep records of her groups (a personal journal is a good place to start), for she learns from each one of them. She can monitor groups by sight (regularly noting what is happening in each by direct observation); by sound (listening to tape recordings of groups at a later date); by direct contact (visits to and participation in groups); and by reviewing group or individual artifacts (learning logs, group weekly reports, group self-evaluations [,] questionnaires). It is important to remember that the teacher should be actively involved with the groups on a class by class basis.

EVALUATING PEER WRITING GROUPS

A teacher can evaluate the effectiveness of her peer writing groups, although few methods for doing so are quantifiable. Good evaluation results from good planning and from sensitive and careful review throughout and at the end of each course.

Teachers can determine if students are attaining [...] goals she set for group work. Group folders when examined tell a story of good attendance, completed work, and enlarged understanding. Self-evaluation on the part of students and teacher can chronicle success with the method and pinpoint areas for future work and improvement. And, most important, gains in individual student writing can be assessed.

In brief, a teacher can use any of the monitoring documents (group folders, tapes of group work, group self-evaluations, and so on) as well as her own journal of group work to develop a fairly clear profile of how successful each group was.

Measurements of student growth in collaborative learning techniques and writing in general can be accomplished with pre and post testing in the following areas:

1. pre and post written descriptions of what students feel can be accomplished in writing groups,
2. pre and post written descriptions of students' writing process,
3. pre and post writing apprehension tests,
4. pre and post essay samples.

Teachers would hope to find that post written descriptions of the group method show a greater understanding of and enjoyment of the method. Post descriptions of students' writing process should show a greater awareness of the writing process in general and as it relates to an individual student. Post writing apprehension tests should show a decline in writing apprehension. And post essay samples should show an improvement in writing when holistically evaluated (Bishop "Qualitative").

A teacher who hopes to use peer writing groups in her classroom should prepare for success. She needs to understand her writing groups will not always be completely effective but can be made more effective if she is willing to train herself and her students. In a sense, a teacher using peer writing groups must become a researcher in her own classroom. She plans for her class, trains group members, monitors and evaluates them, and, the next semester, begins the process again, refining and developing her talents as a group facilitator based on her own observations. This teacher will be willing to experiment, to redefine group failures as steps in a larger process that leads to success, and to have realistic expectations for this holistic teaching method. Before long, those expectations will be met and, hopefully, surpassed.

NOTE

[1] This review of research into writing peer groups was completed in 1986, and significant amounts of work have been done on this subject since that time. I'd send readers to *Small Groups in Writing Workshops: Invitations to a Writer's Life* (Robert Brooke, Ruth Mirtz, and Rick Evans) for recent scholarship and bibliographic references.

Nancy Sommers

Responding to Student Writing

More than any other enterprise in the teaching of writing, responding to and commenting on student writing consumes the largest proportion of our time. Most teachers estimate that it takes them at least 20 to 40 minutes to comment on an individual student paper, and those 20 to 40 minutes times 20 students per class, times 8 papers, more or less, during the course of a semester add up to an enormous amount of time. With so much time and energy directed to a single activity, it is important for us to understand the nature of the enterprise. For it seems, paradoxically enough, that although commenting on student writing is the most widely used method for responding to student writing, it is the least understood. We do not know in any definitive way what constitutes thoughtful commentary or what effect, if any, our comments have on helping our students become more effective writers.

Theoretically, at least, we know that we comment on our students' writing for the same reasons professional editors comment on the work of professional writers or for the same reasons we ask our colleagues to read and respond to our own writing. As writers we need and want thoughtful commentary to show us when we have communicated our ideas and when not, raising questions from a reader's point of view that may not have occurred to us as writers. We want to know if our writing has communicated our intended meaning and, if not, what questions or discrepancies our reader sees that we, as writers, are blind to.

In commenting on our students' writing, however, we have an additional pedagogical purpose. As teachers, we know that most students find it difficult to imagine a reader's response in advance, and to use such responses as a guide in composing. Thus, we comment on student writing to dramatize the presence of a reader, to help our students to become that questioning reader themselves, because, ultimately, we believe that becoming such a reader will help them to evaluate what they have written and develop control over their writing.[1]

Even more specifically, however, we comment on student writing because we believe that it is necessary for us to offer assistance to student writers when they are in the process of composing a text, rather than after the text has been completed. Comments create the motive for doing something different in the next draft; thoughtful comments create the motive for revising. Without comments from their teachers or from their peers, student writers will revise in a consistently narrow and predictable way. Without comments from readers, students assume that their writing has communicated their meaning and perceive no need for revising the substance of their text.[2]

This article is reprinted from *College Composition and Communication* 33 (May 1982): 148–56.

Yet as much as we as informed professionals believe in the soundness of this approach to responding to student writing, we also realize that we don't know how our theory squares with teachers' actual practice—do teachers comment and students revise as the theory predicts they should? For the past year my colleagues Lil Brannon, Cyril Knoblauch, and I have been researching this problem, attempting to discover not only what messages teachers give their students through their comments, but also what determines which of these comments the students choose to use or to ignore when revising. Our research has been entirely focused on comments teachers write to motivate revisions. We have studied the commenting styles of thirty-five teachers at New York University and the University of Oklahoma, studying the comments these teachers wrote on first and second drafts, and interviewing a representative number of these teachers and their students. All teachers also commented on the same set of three student essays. As an additional reference point one of the student essays was typed into the computer that had been programmed with the "Writer's Workbench," a package of twenty-three programs developed by Bell Laboratories to help computers and writers work together to improve a text rapidly. Within a few minutes, the computer delivered editorial comments on the student's text, identifying all spelling and punctuation errors, isolating problems with wordy or misused phrases, and suggesting alternatives, offering stylistic analysis of sentence types, sentence beginnings, and sentence lengths, and finally, giving our freshman essay a Kincaid readability score of eighth-grade which, as the computer program informed us, "is a low score for this type of document." The sharp contrast between the teachers' comments and those of the computer highlighted how arbitrary and idiosyncratic most of our teachers' comments are. Besides, the calm, reasonable language of the computer provided quite a contrast to the hostility and mean-spiritedness of most of the teachers' comments.

The first finding from our research on styles of commenting is that *teachers' comments can take students' attention away from their own purposes in writing a particular text and focus that attention on the teachers' purpose in commenting.* The teacher appropriates the text from the student by confusing the student's purpose in writing the text with her own purpose in commenting. Students make the changes the teacher wants rather than those that the student perceives are necessary, since the teachers' concerns imposed on the text create the reasons for the subsequent changes. We have all heard our perplexed students say to us when confused by our comments: "I don't understand how you want me to change this" or "Tell me what you want me to do." In the beginning of the process there was the writer, her words, and her desire to communicate her ideas. But after the comments of the teacher are imposed on the first or second draft, the student's attention dramatically shifts from "This is what I want to say" to "This is what *you* the teacher are asking me to do."

This appropriation of the text by the teacher happens particularly when teachers identify errors in usage, diction, and style in a first draft and ask students to correct these errors when they revise; such comments give the student an impression of the importance of these errors that is all out of proportion to how they should view these errors at this point in the process. The comments create the concern that these "accidents of discourse" need to be attended to before the meaning of the text is attended to.

It would not be so bad if students were only commanded to correct errors, but, more often than not, students are given contradictory messages; they are commanded to edit a sentence to avoid an error or to condense a sentence to achieve greater brevity of style, and then told in the margins that the particular paragraph needs to be more specific or to be developed more. An example of this problem can be seen in the following student paragraph:

> *wordy – be precise*   *which Sunday?*   *comma needed*
> Every year [on one Sunday in the middle of January]
>   *word choice*
> tens of millions of people cancel all events, plans
> or work to watch the Super Bowl. This audience in-
>   *wordy*
> cludes [little boys and girls, old people, and house-
>   *Be specific – what reasons?*
> wives and men.] Many reasons have been given to ex-
>   *and why*
> plain why the Super Bowl has become so popular that
>   *what spots?*
> commercial spots/cost up to $100,000.00. One explana-
> *awkward*
> tion is that people like to take sides and root for a
>   *another what?*   *spelling*
> team. Another is that some people like the pagentry
>   *too*
> and excitement of the event. These reasons alone,
>   *colloquial*
> however, do not explain a happening as big as the
> Super Bowl.
>
> *(left margin, vertical)* You need to do more research.
>
> *(right margin, vertical)* This paragraph needs to be expanded in order to be more interesting to the reader.

In commenting on this draft, the teacher has shown the student how to edit the sentences, but then commands the student to expand the paragraph in order to make it more interesting to a reader. The interlinear comments and the marginal comments represent two separate tasks for this student; the inter-linear comments encourage the student to see the text as a fixed piece, frozen in time, that just needs some editing. The marginal comments, however, sug-gest that the meaning of the text is not fixed, but rather that the student still needs to develop the meaning by doing some more research. Students are commanded to edit and develop at the same time; the remarkable contradic-tion of developing a paragraph after editing the sentences in it represents the confusion we encountered in our teachers' commenting styles. These different signals given to students, to edit and develop, to condense and elaborate, represent also the failure of teachers' comments to direct genuine revision of a text as a whole.

Moreover, the comments are worded in such a way that it is difficult for students to know what is the most important problem in the text and what problems are of lesser importance. No scale of concerns is offered to a student with the result that a comment about spelling or a comment about an awkward sentence is given weight equal to a comment about organization or logic. The comment that seemed to represent this problem best was one teacher's command to his student: "Check your commas and semicolons and think more about what you are thinking about." The language of the comments makes it difficult for a student to sort out and decide what is most important and what is least important.

When the teacher appropriates the text for the student in this way, students are encouraged to see their writing as a series of parts — words, sentences, paragraphs — and not as a whole discourse. The comments encourage the students to believe that their first drafts are finished drafts, not invention drafts, and that all they need to do is patch and polish their writing. That is, teachers' comments do not provide their students with an inherent reason for revising the structure and meaning of their texts, since the comments suggest to students that the meaning of their text is already there, finished, produced, and all that is necessary is a better word or phrase. The processes of revising, editing, and proofreading are collapsed and reduced to a single trivial activity, and the students' misunderstanding of the revision process as a rewording activity is reinforced by their teachers' comments.

It is possible, and it quite often happens, that students follow every comment and fix their texts appropriately as requested, but their texts are not improved substantially, or, even worse, their revised drafts are inferior to their previous drafts. Since the teachers' comments take the students' attention away from their own original purposes, students concentrate more, as I have noted, on what the teachers commanded them to do than on what they are trying to say. Sometimes students do not understand the purpose behind their teachers' comments and take these comments very literally. At other times students understand the comments, but the teacher has misread the text and the comments, unfortunately, are not applicable. For instance, we repeatedly saw comments in which teachers commanded students to reduce and condense what was written, when in fact what the text really needed at this stage was to be expanded in conception and scope.

The process of revising always involves a risk. But, too often revision becomes a balancing act for students in which they make the changes that are requested but do not take the risk of changing anything that was not commented on, even if the students sense that other changes are needed. A more effective text does not often evolve from such changes alone, yet the student does not want to take the chance of reducing a finished, albeit inadequate, paragraph to chaos — to fragments — in order to rebuild it, if such changes have not been requested by the teacher.

The second finding from our study is that *most teachers' comments are not text-specific and could be interchanged, rubber-stamped, from text to text.* The comments are not anchored in the particulars of the students' texts, but rather are a series of vague directives that are not text-specific. Students are commanded to "think more about [their] audience, avoid colloquial language, avoid the passive, avoid prepositions at the end of sentences or conjunctions at the beginning of sentences, be clear, be specific, be precise, but above all, think more about what [they] are thinking about." The comments on the following student paragraph illustrate this problem:

Begin by telling your reader what you are going to write about

In the sixties it was drugs, in the seventies it was

avoid "one of the"

rock and roll. Now in the eighties, one of the most

controversial subjects is nuclear power. The United

elaborate

States is in great need of its own source of power.

Because of environmentalists, coal is not an accept-

able source of energy. [Solar and wind power have not

be specific

yet received the technology necessary to use them.] It

avoid "it seems"

seems that nuclear power is the only feasible means

right now for obtaining self-sufficient power. How-

ever, too large a percentage of the population are

against nuclear power claiming it is unsafe. With as

be precise

many problems as the United States is having concern-

ing energy, it seems a shame that the public is so

quick to "can" a very feasible means of power. Nuclear

energy should not be given up on, but rather, more

nuclear plants should be built.

think more about your reader

Thesis sentence needed.

One could easily remove all the comments from this paragraph and rubber-stamp them on another student text, and they would make as much or as little sense on the second text as they do here.

We have observed an overwhelming similarity in the generalities and abstract commands given to students. There seems to be among teachers an accepted, albeit unwritten canon for commenting on student texts. This uniform code of commands, requests, and pleadings demonstrates that the teacher holds a license for vagueness while the student is commanded to be specific. The students we interviewed admitted to having a great difficulty with these vague directives. The students stated that when a teacher writes in the margins or as an end comment, "choose precise language," or "think more about your audience," revising becomes a guessing game. In effect, the teacher is saying to the student, "Somewhere in this paper is imprecise language or lack of awareness of an audience and you must find it." The problem presented by these vague commands is compounded for the students when they are not offered any strategies for carrying out these commands. Students are told that they have done something wrong and that there is something in their text that needs to be fixed before the text is acceptable. But to tell students that they have done something wrong is not to tell them what to do about it. In order to offer a useful revision strategy to a student, the teacher must anchor that strategy in the specifics of the student's text. For instance, to tell our student, the author of the above paragraph, "to be specific," or "to elaborate," does not show our student what questions the reader has about the meaning of the text, or what breaks in the logic exist, that could be resolved if the writer supplied information; nor is the student shown how to achieve the desired specificity.

Instead of offering strategies, the teachers offer what is interpreted by students as rules for composing; the comments suggest to students that writing is just a matter of following rules. Indeed, the teachers seem to impose a series of abstract rules about written products even when some of them are not appropriate for the specific text the student is creating.[5] For instance, the student author of our sample paragraph presented above is commanded to follow the conventional rules for writing a five-paragraph essay — to begin the introductory paragraph by telling his reader what he is going to say and to end the paragraph with a thesis sentence. Somehow these abstract rules about what five-paragraph products should look like do not seem applicable to the problems this student must confront when revising, nor are the rules specific strategies he could use when revising. There are many inchoate ideas ready to be exploited in this paragraph, but the rules do not help the student to take stock of his (or her) ideas and use the opportunity he has, during revision, to develop those ideas.

The problem here is a confusion of process and product; what one has to say about the process is different from what one has to say about the product. Teachers who use this method of commenting are formulating their comments as if these drafts were finished drafts and were not going to be revised. Their commenting vocabularies have not been adapted to revision and they comment on first drafts as if they were justifying a grade or as if the first draft were the final draft.

Our summary finding, therefore, from this research on styles of commenting is that the news from the classroom is not good. For the most part, teachers do not respond to student writing with the kind of thoughtful commentary which will help students to engage with the issues they are writing about or which will help them think about their purposes and goals in writing a specific text. In defense of our teachers, however, they told us that responding to student writing was rarely stressed in their teacher-training or in writing workshops; they had been trained in various prewriting techniques, in constructing assignments, and in evaluating papers for grades, but rarely in the process of reading a student text for meaning or in offering commentary to motivate revision. The problem is that most of us as teachers of writing have been trained to read and interpret literary texts for meaning, but, unfortunately, we have not been trained to act upon the same set of assumptions in reading student texts as we follow in reading literary texts.[4] Thus, we read student texts with biases about what the writer should have said or about what he or she should have written, and our biases determine how we will comprehend the text. We read with our preconceptions and preoccupations, expecting to find errors, and the result is that we find errors and misread our students' texts.[5] We find what we look for; instead of reading and responding to the meaning of a text, we correct our students' writing. We need to reverse this approach. Instead of finding errors or showing students how to patch up parts of their texts, we need to sabotage our students' conviction that the drafts they have written are complete and coherent. Our comments need to offer student revision tasks of a different order of complexity and sophistication from the ones that they themselves identify, by forcing students back into the chaos, back to the point where they are shaping and restructuring their meaning.[6]

For if the content of a text is lacking in substance and meaning, if the order of the parts must be rearranged significantly in the next draft, if paragraphs must be restructured for logic and clarity, then many sentences are likely to be changed or deleted anyway. There seems to be no point in having students correct usage errors or condense sentences that are likely to disappear before the next draft is completed. In fact, to identify such problems in a text at this early first draft stage, when such problems are likely to abound, can give a student a disproportionate sense of their importance at this stage in the writing process.[7] In responding to our students' writing, we should be guided by the recognition that it is not spelling or usage problems that we as writers first worry about when drafting and revising our texts.

We need to develop an appropriate level of response for commenting on a first draft, and to differentiate that from the level suitable to a second or third draft. Our comments need to be suited to the draft we are reading. In a first or second draft, we need to respond as any reader would, registering questions, reflecting befuddlement, and noting places where we are puzzled about the meaning of the text. Comments should point to breaks in logic, disruptions in meaning, or missing information. Our goal in commenting on early drafts should be to engage students with the issues they are considering and help them clarify their purposes and reasons in writing their specific text.

For instance, the major rhetorical problem of the essay written by the student who wrote the [second] paragraph (the paragraph on nuclear power) [p. 356]...was that the student had two principal arguments running through his text, each of which brought the other into question. On the one hand, he argued that we must use nuclear power, unpleasant as it is, because we have nothing else to use; though nuclear energy is a problematic source of energy, it is the best of a bad lot. On the other hand, he also argued that nuclear energy is really quite safe and therefore should be our primary resource. Comments on this student's first draft need to point out this break in logic and show the student that if we accept his first argument, then his second argument sounds fishy. But if we accept his second argument, his first argument sounds contradictory. The teacher's comments need to engage this student writer with this basic rhetorical and conceptual problem in his first draft rather than impose a series of abstract commands and rules upon his text.

Written comments need to be viewed not as an end in themselves—a way for teachers to satisfy themselves that they have done their jobs—but rather as a means for helping students to become more effective writers. As a means for helping students, they have limitations; they are, in fact, disembodied remarks – one absent writer responding to another absent writer. The key to successful commenting is to have what is said in the comments and what is done in the classroom mutually reinforce and enrich each other. Commenting on papers assists the writing course in achieving its purpose; classroom activities and the comments we write to our students need to be connected. Written comments need to be an extension of the teacher's voice—an extension of the teacher as reader. Exercises in such activities as revising a whole text or individual paragraphs together in class, noting how the sense of the whole dictates the smaller changes, looking at options, evaluating actual choices, and then discussing the effect of these changes on revised drafts—such exercises need to be designed to take students through the cycles of revising and to help them overcome their anxiety about revising: that anxiety we all feel at reducing what looks like a finished draft into fragments and chaos.

The challenge we face as teachers is to develop comments which will provide an inherent reason for students to revise; it is a sense of revision as discovery, as a repeated process of beginning again, as starting out new, that our students have not learned. We need to show our students how to seek, in the possibility of revision, the dissonances of discovery—to show them through our comments why new choices would positively change their texts, and thus to show them the potential for development implicit in their own writing.

NOTES

[1]C. H. Knoblauch and Lil Brannon, "Teacher Commentary on Student Writing: The State of the Art," *Freshman English News,* 10 (Fall 1981), 1–3.

[2]For an extended discussion of revision strategies of student writers see Nancy Sommers, "Revision Strategies of Student Writers and Experienced Adult Writers," *College Composition and Communication,* 31 (December 1980), 378–388.

[3]Nancy Sommers and Ronald Schleifer, "Means and Ends: Some Assumptions of Student Writers," *Composition and Teaching,* 2 (December 1980), 69–76.

[4]Janet Emig and Robert P. Parker, Jr., "Responding to Student Writing: Building a Theory of the Evaluating Process," unpublished paper, Rutgers University.

[5]For an extended discussion of this problem see Joseph Williams, "The Phenomenology of Error," *College Composition and Communication,* 32 (May 1981), 152–168.

[6]Ann Berthoff. *The Making of Meaning* (Montclair, N.J.: Boynton/Cook Publishers, 1981).

[7]W. U. McDonald, "The Revising Process and the Marking of Student Papers," *College Composition and Communication,* 24 (May 1978), 167–170.

Lynn Z. Bloom

Why I (Used to) Hate to Give Grades

When I was but a sprig on the family tree, growing up in the New Hampshire college town where my father, Professor Zimmerman, taught chemistry and chemical engineering, an emblematic cartoon by William Steig appeared in *The New Yorker*. It depicted a downcast youth glancing surreptitiously at a report card held with distaste by a man in a suit looming bulbously from his armchair. The caption, "B-plus isn't good enough for a Zimmerman!" — yes, that really was the name in the cartoon — so succinctly expressed the family ethos that my parents made dozens of copies. The cartoon became their Christmas card that year. When my siblings and I were in college, "the B-plus joke" as we had come to call it, would arrive, anonymously, at midterm and final exam times. As the grandchildren arrived they, too, were blessed with copies of their own. "The B-plus joke" has become the subject of long distance phone calls, impromptu seminars at family reunions, and considerable sardonic mirth.

That a B-plus was in fact *never* good enough for a Zimmerman, however, is my lifelong legacy. Its message will be inscribed on my grave.

Over the years I've filled up a depressing stack of grade books. Their limp, academic-green covers conceal a myriad of cryptic symbols, which in turn embed stories of work and goofing-off, hope and despair, brilliance and just-going-along-for-the-ride. Although I have always — well, usually — looked forward to reading papers, and can even tolerate reading exams, the calculus of giving grades had become, over time, preferable only to doing the income tax. Until last year.

It's easy to understand why giving grades was so grim, as I explain in the first half of this essay. This half focuses on the nature and problems presented by *grading* — the letters, numbers, percents and other forms of tallies — the characters that appear in grade books, on transcripts, and in other forms of score keeping, individually and in the aggregate. When I say *grading* I mean exactly that. I am not confusing *grading* with other ways of responding to student writing — such as extensive comments, oral or written (on screen or hard copy), preferably on early or intermediate drafts.

But when the semester's approaching end made it necessary once again to assign grades it dawned on me, for reasons that will be made clear in this paper's second half, to put not only the burden of proof but the burden of articulating that proof on the students. Who could have a more vested interest in the outcome of grading than the very recipients themselves? The process by which this worked transformed a tension-filled monologue (myself muttering to myself) to a constructive dialogue between students and teacher — a dramatic

This article is reprinted from *College Composition and Communication* 48.3 (Oct. 1997): 261–71.

"B-plus is not good enough for a Zimmerman!"

Drawing by W. Steig © 1958 The New Yorker Magazine, Inc.

alteration for the better. With adaptations to course level and type of class, this method has a potentially wide application.

WHY GRADES ARE MISLEADING

Grades exist for an institution's administrative convenience. Letters, numbers, and percents can be tallied, averaged, fiddled with, and fudged to satisfy a variety of institutional purposes. Under the guise of fake precision schools, like other advertisers, can announce, "Our students are better [or worse] than _____." Fill in the blanks: *they were last year.* But what about the year before? *yours.* All of yours? in comparison with all of ours, or only selected populations — say, all pre-meds — under certain circumstances — preparing for the MCAT? *students in other school systems.* Which students? Which systems?

    Grades fit record-keeping formats. Grades fill slots on forms. If transcripts didn't exist, registrars would invent them or their equivalent. They'd have to — to accommodate not a rage for precision but an institutional need for shorthand, a way to code, store, and transmit information in a compact way. Grades are an efficient means of reducing complicated information to a simple code that can be interpreted with alleged unambiguity by whoever sees the symbols and knows the context — and many others who know nothing whatever about the context. Does the meaning of the A, or the B+, or the C− in practice our grading scales sink no lower except for no-shows — reside in the mind of the grader?

the reader of the transcript? the student who thinks, irrespective of the actual grade, that it should have been better? Why ask — the meaning is crystal clear.

Grades look precise. They aren't. As we who have tried for years to convey the nuances of a host of meanings know only too well, the process of grading attempts to put a precise label on an imprecise assessment of a host of disparate components (such as subject, substance, organization, development, style, accuracy and finesse in using sources, grammar and mechanics, ethos — and perhaps format and punctuality). To amalgamate such disparities under a single symbol is comparable to trying to make strawberry jam — pure, elegant, tangy — by combining the strawberries not only with apples and oranges, but bananas, grapes, blueberries.... Truth in labeling requires that we call a fruit salad a fruit salad, and list the components in order of importance. What if other ingredients (broccoli, carrots — dare I say bologna?) enter the mixture, and further distort the categories?

Grades look objective. They aren't. Each and every grade reflects the cultural biases, values, standards, norms, prejudices, and taboos of the time and culture (with its complex host of subcultures) in which it's given. No teacher, no student (nor anyone else) can escape the tastes of their time — even rebels work against the current grain, in defiance of the echoes of other voices, other rooms. Although many, perhaps most, of these social constructs are present in all our reading and writing, they are seldom acknowledged, rarely articulated. But they inescapably inform our individual teaching of writing — the assignments we give, the range — however broad or narrow — of what we expect the students to write, and how we respond to it, in commenting and in grading.

Does a given paper deserve a good grade because the revision literally incorporates every single suggestion the teacher made on the first draft? because the student — as we hear time after time after time — worked so hard on it? because the student is just learning English/returning to school after long absence /plays football/works a forty-hour week/comes from a disadvantaged background/is laboring under insurmountable obstacles? because the student is — and why not? — such a nice person?

Will a given paper be downgraded because it's late? sloppy? plagiarized? the sixtieth paper we've read on the subject in three weeks? because the author takes a stand that we find reprehensible, offensive, immoral, even criminal? Grading dresses up the art of marking papers in scientists' clothes. But the better the writers, the more they inspire in us as readers and consequently, as commentators on the work, the passion that makes humanists of us all. As graders we can be fair, but as human beings we can never be objective.

Grades label not only papers but their writers. We say we're only responding to the text, not to the character of the writer behind it, but our students know better. They know from experience what it is to be labeled "An *A* Student." "A *B* Student." "A *C* student." Or worse. When I gave freshman Dewayne (name changed to protect the innocent) a generous B on doggerel verse he had written to honor his — yes — dog, he took umbrage, "*Hero* deserves more than a B. He's the best dog in Bean Blossom Township." Exactly. If the students are in graduate school, "A B+ isn't good enough for a Zimmerman" is their mantra. "Love me love my paper," they cry, and try as we may to look only at the words on the page, we cannot ignore the writer behind as well as in the text, or the stereotypes that cling to the A, the B, or the C student, clad in the velcro grade to which a host of connotations, positive and pernicious, cling.

WHY GRADES ARE BIG TROUBLE

Grades are big trouble because they undermine good teaching. Current composition theorists agree, in principle anyway, on the importance of dialogic discussions in which all students have a right to speak up and speak out, writing workshops, and revisions that incorporate the writer's resultant insights. But grades automatically signal who is more equal than all the rest put together. The teacher, who has the power and authority to award the grade, therefore has the power to impose her views on the directions the discussions and the resulting papers should go. But what if the teacher misses the point? What if the teacher's rage for order overrides the student's need to say something important to him, prompted by an assigned reading but tangential to the teacher's conception of the writing assignment?

"Just tell me what you want," our students ask — "and I'll give it to you in order to get a good grade" is the unspoken half of that sentence. "Abandon personal investment all ye who enter here" might be their motto. For when students engage in that transaction they give up both passion and concern. In consequence, they relinquish ownership of their writing and with it commitment to their subject, engagement with its ideas and point of view, and a willingness to rewrite beyond the minimum. If the students tailor their writing to contours of the teacher's views, how can they engage in the critical thinking and tough-minded independent learning we claim to encourage? No wonder such papers are boring; the teacher has already predetermined what they will say.

Grades are big trouble because they inhibit, even block, student discussion and response to the course material. In transactions between teacher and students such as those described above, only the bold, the hyperconfident, or the naive have the courage to speak for themselves instead of becoming their teachers' ventriloquists.

With most writing assignments we give, we expect the resulting papers to fall within a predictable range, however wide or narrow the latitude. Yet we've all had the experience of the paper that's out of bounds — in which the writer marches to a different beat, down a different avenue, even out of the universe established in the classroom. Once we've ruled out plagiarism — the knee-jerk reaction to aberrant papers — how do we respond to a paper when the student has ignored our careful cues? How do we respond to the fairly common paper that begins to discuss, say, the assigned literary text at hand but that incorporates (some would say *wanders to*) an examination of an issue in the writer's life inspired by something analogous in the text? Do we automatically treat the paper's altered direction as a problem in organization, and see the writing as bent out of shape? Or do we acknowledge such shifts in perspective and structure as ways the student has chosen to make the subject her own? What if the assigned literary analysis begins in the detached stance and vocabulary of a literary critic, but alters to a passionate, personal voice that reflects the change in focus?

These are not questions that can be answered in the abstract, but only with specific references to the paper at hand. If we expect our students to function as engaged, critical readers and writers, then we should encourage and accommodate writing that is full of, in Annie Dillard's words, "unwrapped gifts" for the teacher and "free surprises" for the authors, writing that they care about. We can provide appropriate encouragement, direction, and critical queries — preferably on early and intermediate drafts — much more effectively in commentary than in grades. If students and teachers alike write early and write often, there should be no major problems of organization, development, tone in the final version of the paper — by which time a grade (if given) should be almost irrelevant.

Grades are big trouble because they look fixed and permanent. It's a tossup as to which is worse, a false appearance of permanence, or an actually unchangeable grade. One scenario occurs when the teacher, attempting to be kind as well as to encourage revision, allows the student to rewrite and rewrite, and rewrite the paper in anticipation of a better grade. This procedure not only promises to inundate the teacher with revised old papers on top of the unrevised new ones that continue in response to new assignments, it also signals that grades are negotiable, temporary markers on the road that leads ultimately to A's, if both teacher and student have sufficient stamina to stay the course. And why not? — if the teacher has provided numerous corrections at each stage, at some point she'll be grading her own writing rather than the student's, anyway.

If, on the other hand, the grade given initially can't be changed, why should the student bother to revise the paper? If grades were out of the picture, the real reasons for revising — such as clarity, emphasis, argument, style — would become manifest, and the implication that writers revise essentially to improve their grades would become irrelevant. When Hemingway said he rewrote the last page of *A Farewell to Arms* thirty-nine times, he was "just getting the words right."

Grades are big trouble because they're dishonest. Oh, not necessarily in my course, and naturally not in yours, but that nationwide grade inflation is rampant is not news. For practical purposes undergraduate grading scales in most schools have in the past two decades been reduced from five points to three—A to C, with Fs reserved for no-shows, and graduate grades reduced from three points to two (A to B).

A SERENDIPITOUS SOLUTION

At the beginning of the fall semester this paper, originally titled "Why I Hate to Give Grades," stopped at this point. It dangled over the abyss of the inevitable, inexorable need of my institution — like most others — to assign grades to the work of every student in nearly every course (with the exception of the occasional pass/fail undergraduate course, and continuing credit for graduate students working on dissertations). I didn't know how to end it.

So I took "Why I Hate to Give Grades" to the first meeting of my advanced Writing Workshop in Creative Nonfiction — fifteen juniors and seniors selected by portfolio admission. We all wore shorts (it was hot), but I was the only one professing nonchalance under a big-brimmed red straw hat instead of the *chapeau du jour*, a baseball cap on backward. For although I wanted to set the example of how the workshop would operate in reading and commenting on papers ("What works well in this paper? What could be done to make it better?"), I didn't want these still-strangers to see my uncertain face as I read my work-in-progress.

My reading of that paper proved critical, in ways both intentional and inadvertent. I meant to signal that all of us, myself included, were colleagues in a writing community governed by clearheadedness, candor, and courtesy. I meant to affirm that good ideas were the heart of this course, and that revision was its soul. I wanted the students to acknowledge that nearly everything anyone wrote — or rewrote — could be made still better.

My reading also, of course, illustrated that it was appropriate to discuss unfinished work — a good way to raise questions and solve problems. In retrospect, I can see that the appearance of an unfinished work at the outset of the course may have also signaled that it was all right not to finish anything. Because I myself am often working on several papers concurrently, shifting from one to the other as the insight, or the research data emerges, it seemed reasonable to allow my students the same latitude. However, at some point the work must end; either deadlines descend or the writer has done all she can with a paper and has to let it go. Next time, in the interests of smoothing the roughness that exists even after several drafts, I'll require that at least two major papers be brought to closure; the writer can always open them up later on.

Moreover, by explaining "Why I Hate to Give Grades," I conveyed another message whose power I didn't realize until well into the semester — that grades were incidental, that the emphasis was on the writings themselves. "I really do hate to give grades," I told the class when I returned their warmup papers, "Why I Write," retitled by one writer, "Why I Wrong." "I want you to focus on making your writing better, and not to get hung up on a letter grade. I tell you what," I said, "let me know when you've finished a paper to your satisfaction, and then I'll give you its grade. However," I was compelled to add, "throughout the semester I'll be keeping a running record of your grades, on the originals as well as the revisions. As a fail-safe mechanism, I'll tell you if your grade on any given version is dipping below C level." The grungy green gradebook came to mind — but never to class.

During the semester the students had to write seven papers (some later papers could expand their predecessors), and turn in revisions on alternate weeks. All original versions, and many revisions, were discussed in class, either in small groups or by the class as a whole. I also wrote extensive commentary, usually on the initial version; the author and I each got a copy of the printout. After the second paper I virtually stopped marking the numerous errors of spelling and mechanics and the absence of titles on the papers; by then even the most cavalier students in this freewheeling group (one student's warmup was "Why I Rant") understood that house rules insisted on the absence of the former and the presence of the latter.

Preoccupation with the texts, and the rhythm of paper-and-revision, paper-and-revision obscured the fact that after ten weeks into the semester not one student had ever asked me for a grade on any paper, in class or in conference. The class response groups, like their writing, had taken on an extracurricular life of their own in which a number of the students analyzed each others' work and spurred each other on. That I didn't know about these meetings until the semester's end attests to an ideal shift of focus. For in becoming each others' audience, the students' reciprocal critiques validated their work and bypassed grading.

Amanda's group typifies the entire class, except for the two who disappeared by mid-semester, though one burly lad surfaced briefly, first with pink-eye, later with pink hair. Amanda explained, in her semester's-end commentary: "While I used to keep my writing strictly to myself, working with class peers has loosened me up a bit. Mike and Jeff have been very encouraging throughout the course of my work, exactly what I need to feel comfortable." In order to avoid feeling constrained, even "shut down by strict guidelines," Amanda decided to "find inspiration" in writing for her friends. "And it made a difference," she said, "Jeff's 'Vision Quest' paper encouraged me to write about my Mt. Washington experience.... He told me he stayed up all night writing his paper in its entirety. To be honest, I was jealous. And for the next week I tried to do the same thing." She continues, "I attacked my paper with such hopeful energy that I wrote more in the next few weeks" than in the rest of the semester. "I proudly showed my versions to Jeff, acting out the conversations, explaining and unfolding all of the conflicts and interactions in such a way that I explored the subject many times more deeply than I originally had thought. He has been so encouraging, and inspiring in his own writing, that my account of Washington has taken on a deeply personal significance. I see it now as a metaphor for my life experience since last summer."

"Well," I finally said as the semester's end lurked two weeks away. "I have to give you a semester grade, and no one has asked for a grade yet. Does this mean that your works are still in progress?" They nodded. "O.K. Then when you bring in your completed portfolio for our final conference, include a letter to me in which you identify the grade you think you deserve for the semester, and your rationale for this grade, based on your four best papers. What would the odds be that you could write four more of this quality? This letter will contain a critical analysis of your own work and you'll write it as you would any other critical paper, considering such features as" — I distributed the criteria — "significance of topic; organization; nature and solidity of evidence; language, style, tone; creation of authorial persona and ethos; spelling, mechanics, syntax. Moreover," I added, "explain what problems you had as a writer at the beginning of the semester, and what progress you've made in solving them. Also, include an estimate of your contributions to the writers' workshop." They nodded again. "Do you want me to bring my written assessment of your work to conference too?" I thought of the Evergreen State model. Groans and grimaces. "O.K. It's your show."

The students' self-assessment, while claiming preemptive authority, would also require them to shoulder the burden of proof. I did not realize until we discussed their analyses in conference how much of the burden that removed from me. In all instances but one I agreed exactly with the students' analyses of their performances as writers and critics. There was a single exception. Suzy, the best writer in the class, grossly undervalued work that the rest of us considered superb — taut, complex, original, and precise. For instance, her paper on anorexia begins, "I see them everywhere I go: the skinny girls with the gaunt faces and matchstick legs, an ass way too flat and underfed, and eyes that are hard with purpose. They carry their bodies forward, holding their hips out before their smile." In conference, I told Suzy how good her work was and, flipping through her portfolio, I showed her why.

Because the other students and I agreed on the substance of their self-evaluations — content, form, style, growth over time — conferences were the easiest I had experienced in three decades of teaching, and the most expeditious. The material was all there, in the portfolios and in the interpretations. Had I disagreed with their analyses, as I did with Suzy's, I'd have said so and explained why. That we were able to agree so consistently reaffirms the tenor of the feedback that the students had been receiving throughout the semester, in every class and on every paper.

We did not, however, always concur on grades. On the whole, my grades were about a half-step lower than the students', because of differences in emphasis. But because our points of agreement were so numerous, it was also easy to tell the students in person why (in most cases) they'd be getting some form of B instead of the A they desired, but didn't necessarily expect. Thus when Cory wrote, "I want an A and I'll understand a B+," it was easy for me to counter with a B and to explain why Jeff, a student risen from the ashes of his dropout self, his literary aspirations not only rekindled but inspiring Amanda's work, affirmed, "I'm very happy to tell you that I aced this class and confirmed that I am a good writer, good enough to even continue onto graduate school and maybe one day to earn my keep through my writing. I deserve an A+ for this course." "Not quite," I said, "Your writing is tougher and much better; it still needs work" — again the portfolio showed why — "but keep at it."

In conference I could readily acknowledge the students' eagerness for a grade that accommodated their perceived growth, including their newfound willingness to take risks in writing about subjects that came to mean a great deal to them ("true heartfelt renditions of a young girl's feelings and emotions"), to experiment with structure and style, and to revise and revise and revise again. In the same conference, when we perused their portfolios together, the students could acknowledge that even though they'd come a long way their writing still had miles to go before they could match the authority and grace of texts like Suzy's. The sole student who suggested an A based on punctiliousness, punctuation, and perfect attendance conceded that depth and development were overriding virtues. In a point of tact but also of truth, we all agreed that with the students' momentum and morale on their current high, if the course could have lasted for another semester, or even eight more weeks.... As I filled out the grade sheets in a half-hour instead of my usual day of agonized indecisiveness, I realized that the semester-long communication culminated in grades that were perceived as just and (except for the under-confident Suzy) surprised no one.

BUT WOULD THIS WORK WIDELY?

At my back I can hear the skeptics scoff. OK, so you could avoid giving grades in that class because they were advanced students in a merit-based elective; the students were highly motivated, working in a community of writers who received continuous feedback on their work, in and out of class. But I'm teaching a subject-matter course _____ [fill in the blank]; if I had to spend as much time on writing as you did we'd never get anything else done. And what about freshmen — or grad students — who require continuous grades to reassure them that they're not flunking out? What about large lecture courses where to comment so extensively on papers would cause instant teacher meltdown? (I personally will have more answers after I've experimented with this scheme in other, very different types of courses.)

But teachers working with Writing-across-the-Curriculum programs have already devised solutions that address most of these matters, and more — ways to assign lots of writing and to manage the paper load through a combination of peer feedback, selective teacher commentary, TA support in large lecture courses, and shifting more responsibility onto the students themselves. If each and every writing assignment incorporates not only the key language of its subject, but of its disciplinary-based form, structure, and style, students will understand what the teacher wants and will have the language both to write in and to discuss their work. Whether or not students have received grades throughout the semester, on papers and on tests — where it would probably be much more confusing to eschew grades than to assign them — there's no reason they can't be asked to submit a semester's end progress report. Again, this could be discipline-specific, and (if desired) it could be designed to accompany a portfolio of the semester's work. At minimum, it would comprise a critique of the student's work, and rationale for the semester grade as the basis for discussion with the professor (in small classes) or teaching assistants (in larger classes). The instructor could specify in advance that the conference is to be a colloquy, not a last-ditch attempt to lobby for a better grade. If needed, the conference could be abbreviated, or conducted through e-mail commentary on the student's self-critique, though, like Socrates, I think there is considerable virtue in person-to-person dialogue.

Yes, this solution places a great deal of trust in the students. The instructor trusts that they'll understand what the course is about, what they're supposed to have learned and done in it, and what level of proficiency they've attained relative to where they began, their peers, and college standards. This means that teachers have to be clear about course aims and assignments, consistent in responding (or in training assistants to respond) to student work, and to student self-assessments. Fortunately, we are truly blessed to teach in an educational system where the teachers are strong, the papers are good looking, and all the students are above average. So it shouldn't be hard.

Jacqueline Jones Royster

When the First Voice
You Hear Is Not Your Own

This essay emerged from my desire to examine closely moments of personal challenge that seem to have import for cross-boundary discourse. These types of moments have constituted an ongoing source of curiosity for me in terms of my own need to understand human difference as a complex reality, a reality that I have found most intriguing within the context of the academic world. From a collectivity of such moments over the years, I have concluded that the most salient point to acknowledge is that "subject" position really is everything.

Using subject position as a terministic screen in cross-boundary discourse permits analysis to operate kaleidoscopically, thereby permitting interpretation to be richly informed by the converging of dialectical perspectives. Subjectivity as a defining value pays attention dynamically to context, ways of knowing, language abilities, and experience, and by doing so it has a consequent potential to deepen, broaden, and enrich our interpretive views in dynamic ways as well. Analytical lenses include the process, results, and impact of negotiating identity, establishing authority, developing strategies for action, carrying forth intent with a particular type of agency, and being compelled by external factors and internal sensibilities to adjust belief and action (or not). In a fundamental way, this enterprise supports the sense of rhetoric, composition, and literacy studies as a field of study that embraces the imperative to understand truths and consequences of language use more fully. This enterprise supports also the imperative to reconsider the beliefs and values which inevitably permit our attitudes and actions in discourse communities (including colleges, universities, and classrooms) to be systematic, even systemic.

Adopting subjectivity as a defining value, therefore, is instructive. However, the multidimensionality of the instruction also reveals the need for a shift in paradigms, a need that I find especially evident with regard to the notion of "voice," as a central manifestation of subjectivity. My task in this essay, therefore, is threefold. First, I present three scenes which serve as my personal testimony as "subject." These scenes are singular in terms of their being my own stories, but I believe that they are also plural, constituting experiential data that I share with many. My sense of things is that individual stories placed one against another against another build credibility and offer, as in this case, a litany of evidence from which a call for transformation in theory and practice might rightfully begin. My intent is to suggest that my stories in the company of others demand thoughtful response.

This article is reprinted from *College Composition and Communication* 47.1 (Feb. 1996): 29–40.

Second, I draw from these scenes a specific direction for transformation, suggesting dimensions of the nature of voicing that remain problematic. My intent is to demonstrate that our critical approaches to voice, again as a central manifestation of subjectivity, are currently skewed toward voice as a spoken or written phenomenon. This intent merges the second task with the third in that I proceed to suggest that theories and practices should be transformed. The call for action in cross-boundary exchange is to refine theory and practice so that they include voicing as a phenomenon that is constructed and expressed visually and orally, *and* as a phenomenon that has import also in being a *thing* heard, perceived, and reconstructed.

SCENE ONE

I have been compelled on too many occasions to count to sit as a well-mannered Other, silently, in a state of tolerance that requires me to be as expressionless as I can manage, while colleagues who occupy a place of entitlement different from my own talk about the history and achievements of people from my ethnic group, or even about their perceptions of our struggles. I have been compelled to listen as they have comfortably claimed the authority to engage in the construction of knowledge and meaning about me and mine, without paying even a passing nod to the fact that sometimes a substantive version of that knowledge might already exist, or to how it might have already been constructed, or to the meanings that might have already been assigned that might make me quite impatient with gaps in their understanding of my community, or to the fact that I, or somebody within my ethnic group, might have an opinion about what they are doing. I have been compelled to listen to speakers, well-meaning though they may think they are, who signal to me rather clearly that subject position is everything. I have come to recognize, however, that when the subject matter is me and the voice is not mine, my sense of order and rightness is disrupted. In metaphoric fashion, these "authorities" let me know, once again, that Columbus has discovered America and claims it now, claims it still for a European crown.

Such scenes bring me to the very edge of a principle that I value deeply as a teacher and a scholar, the principle of the right to inquiry and discovery. When the discovering hits so close to home, however, my response is visceral, not just intellectual, and I am made to look over a precipice. I have found it extremely difficult to allow the voices and experiences of people that I care about deeply to be taken and handled so carelessly and without accountability by strangers.

At the extreme, the African American community, as my personal example, has seen and continues to see its contributions and achievements called into question in grossly negative ways, as in the case of *The Bell Curve*. Such interpretations of who we are as a people open to general interrogation, once again, the innate capacities of "the race" as a whole. As has been the case throughout our history in this country, we are put in jeopardy and on trial in a way that should not exist but does. We are compelled to respond to a rendering of our potential that demands, not that we account for attitudes, actions, and conditions, but that we defend ourselves as human beings. Such interpretations of human potential create a type of discourse that serves as a distraction, as noise that drains off energy and sabotages the work of identifying substantive problems within and across cultural boundaries and the work also of finding solutions that have import, not simply for "a race," but for human beings whose living conditions, values, and preferences vary.

All such close encounters, the extraordinarily insidious ones and the ordinary ones, are definable through the lens of subjectivity, particularly in terms of the power and authority to speak and to make meaning. An analysis of subject position reveals that these interpretations by those outside of the community are not random acts of unkindness. Instead, they embody ways of seeing, knowing, being, and acting that probably suggest as much about the speaker and the context as they do about the targeted subject matter. The advantage with this type of analysis, of course, is that we see the obvious need to contextualize the stranger's perspective among other interpretations and to recognize that an interpretive view is just that — interpretive. A second advantage is that we also see that in our nation's practices these types of interpretations, regardless of how superficial or libelous they may actually be within the context of a more comprehensive view, tend to have considerable consequence in the lives of the targeted group, people in this case whose own voices and perspectives remain still largely under considered and uncredited.

Essentially, though, having a mechanism to see the under considered helps us see the extent to which we add continually to the pile of evidence in this country of cross-cultural misconduct. These types of close encounters that disregard dialectical views are a type of free touching of the powerless by the power-full. This analytical perspective encourages us to acknowledge that marginalized communities are not in a good position to ward off the intrusion of those authorized in mainstream communities to engage in willful action. Historically, such actions have included everything from the displacement of native people from their homelands, to the use of unknowing human subjects in dangerous experiments, to the appropriation and misappropriation of cultural artifacts — art, literature, music, and so on. An insight using the lens of subjectivity, however, is a recognition of the ways in which these moments are indeed moments of violation, perhaps even ultimate violation.

This record of misconduct means that for people like me, on an instinctive level, all outsiders are rightly perceived as suspect. I suspect the genuineness of their interest, the altruism of their actions, and the probability that whatever is being said or done is not to the ultimate benefit and understanding of the people who are subject matter but not subjects. People in the neighborhood where I grew up would say, "Where is their home training?" Imbedded in the question is the idea that when you visit other people's "home places," especially when you have not been invited, you simply can not go tramping around the house like you own the place, no matter how smart you are, or how much imagination you can muster, or how much authority and entitlement outside that home you may be privileged to hold. And you certainly can not go around name calling, saying things like, "You people are intellectually inferior and have a limited capacity to achieve," without taking into account who the family is, what its living has been like, and what its history and achievement have been about.

The concept of "home training" underscores the reality that point of view matters and that we must be trained to respect points of view other than our own. It acknowledges that when we are away from home, we need to know that what we think we see in places that we do not really know very well may not actually be what is there at all. So often, it really is a matter of time, place, resources, and our ability to perceive. Coming to judgment too quickly, drawing on information too narrowly, and saying hurtful, discrediting, dehumanizing things without undisputed proof are not appropriate. Such behavior is not good manners. What comes to mind for me is another saying that I heard constantly when I was growing up, "Do unto others as you would have them do unto you." In this case, we would be implored to draw conclusions about others with care and, when we do draw conclusions, to use the same type of sense and sensibility that we would ideally like for others to use in drawing conclusions about us.

This scene convinces me that what we need in a pressing way in this country and in our very own field is to articulate codes of behavior that can sustain more concretely notions of honor, respect, and good manners across boundaries, with cultural boundaries embodying the need most vividly. Turning the light back onto myself, though, at the same time that my sense of violation may indeed be real, there is the compelling reality that many communities in our nation need to be taken seriously. We all deserve to be taken seriously, which means that critical inquiry and discovery are absolutely necessary. Those of us who love our own communities, we think, most deeply, most uncompromisingly, without reservation for what they are and also are not, must set aside our misgivings about strangers in the interest of the possibility of deeper understanding (and for the more idealistic among us, the possibility of global peace). Those of us who hold these communities close to our hearts, protect them, and embrace them; those who want to preserve the goodness of the minds and souls in them; those who want to preserve consciously, critically, and also lovingly the record of good work within them must take high risk and give over the exclusivity of our rights to know.

It seems to me that the agreement for inquiry and discovery needs to be deliberately reciprocal. All of us, strangers and community members, need to find ways to sustain productivity in what Pratt calls contact zones, areas of engagement that in all likelihood will remain contentious. We need to get over our tendencies to be too possessive and to resist locking ourselves into the tunnels of our own visions and direct experience. As community members, we must learn to have new faith in the advantage of sharing. As strangers, we must learn to treat the loved people and places of Others with care and to understand that, when we do not act respectfully and responsibly, we leave ourselves rightly open to wrath. The challenge is not to work with a fear of abuse or a fear of retalia-tion, however. The challenge is to teach, to engage in research, to write, and to speak with Others with the determination to operate not only with professional and personal integrity, but also with the specific knowledge that communities and their ancestors are watching. If we can set aside our rights to exclusivity in our own home cultures, if we can set aside the tendencies that we all have to think too narrowly, we actually leave open an important possibility. In our nation, we have little idea of the potential that a variety of subjectivities — oper-ating with honor, respect, and reasonable codes of conduct — can bring to crit-ical inquiry or critical problems. What might happen if we treated differences in subject position as critical pieces of the whole, vital to thorough under-standing, and central to both problem-finding and problem-solving? This soci-ety has not, as yet, really allowed that privilege in a substantial way.

SCENE TWO

As indicated in Scene One, I tend to be enraged at what Tillie Olsen has called the "trespass vision," a vision that comes from intellect and imagination (62), but typically not from lived experience, and sometimes not from the serious study of the subject matter. However, like W. E. B. Du Bois, I've chosen not to be distracted or consumed by my rage at voyeurs, tourists, and trespassers, but to look at what I can do. I see the critical importance of the role of negotiator, someone who can cross boundaries and serve as guide and translator for Others.

In 1903, Du Bois demonstrated this role in *The Souls of Black Folk*. In the "Forethought" of that book, he says: "Leaving, then, the world of the white man, I have stepped within the Veil, raising it that you may view faintly its deeper recesses — the meaning of its religion, the passion of its human sorrow, and the struggle of its greater souls" (1). He sets his rhetorical purpose to be to cross, or at least to straddle boundaries with the intent of shedding light, a light that has the potential of being useful to people on both sides of the veil. Like Du Bois, I've accepted the idea that what I call my "home place" is a cul-tural community that exists still quite significantly beyond the confines of a well-insulated community that we call the "mainstream," and that between this world and the one that I call home, systems of insulation impede the vision and narrow the ability to recognize human potential and to understand human history both microscopically and telescopically.

Like Du Bois, I've dedicated myself to raising this veil, to overriding these systems of insulation by raising another voice, my voice in the interest of clar-ity and accuracy. What I have found too often, however, is that, unlike those who have been entitled to talk about me and mine, when I talk about my own, I face what I call the power and function of deep disbelief, and what Du Bois described as, "the sense of always looking at one's self through the eyes of others, of measuring one's soul by the tape of a world that looks on in amused contempt and pity" (5).

An example comes to mind. When I talk about African-American women, especially those who were writing non-fiction prose in the nineteenth century, I can expect, even today after so much contemporary scholarship on such writers, to see people who are quite flabbergasted by anything that I share. Reflected on their faces and in their questions and comments, if anyone can manage to speak back to me, is a depth of surprise that is always discomforting. I sense that the surprise, or the silence, if there is little response, does not come from the simple ignorance of unfortunate souls who just happen not to know what I have spent years coming to know. What I suspect is that this type of surprise rather "naturally" emerges in a society that so obviously has the habit of expecting nothing of value, nothing of consequence, nothing of importance, nothing at all positive from its Others, so that anything is a surprise; everything is an exception; and nothing of substance can really be claimed as a result.

In identifying this phenomenon, Chandra Talpade Mohanty speaks powerfully about the ways in which this culture coopts, dissipates, and displaces voices. As demonstrated by my example, one method of absorption that has worked quite well has been essentially rhetorical. In discussing nineteenth century African American women's work, I bring tales of difference and adventure. I bring cultural proofs and instructive examples, all of which invariably must serve as rites of passage to credibility. I also bring the power of story telling. These tales of adventure in odd places are the transitions by which to historicize and theorize anew with these writers re-inscribed in a rightful place. Such a process respects long-standing practices in African-based cultures of theorizing in narrative form. As Barbara Christian says, we theorize "in the stories we create, in riddles and proverbs, in the play with language, since dynamic rather than fixed ideas seem more to our liking" (336).

The problem is that in order to construct new histories and theories such stories must be perceived not just as "simple stories" to delight and entertain, but as vital layers of a transformative process. A reference point is Langston Hughes and his Simple stories, stories that are a model example of how apparent simplicity has the capacity to unmask truths in ways that are remarkably accessible — through metaphor, analogy, parable, and symbol. However, the problem of articulating new paradigms through stories becomes intractable, if those who are empowered to define impact and consequence decide that the stories are simply stories and that the record of achievement is perceived, as Audre Lorde has said, as "the random droppings of birds" (Foreword xi).

If I take my cue from the life of Ida Wells, and I am bold enough and defiant enough to go beyond the presentation of my stories as juicy tidbits for the delectation of audiences, to actually shift or even subvert a paradigm, I'm much more likely to receive a wide-eyed stare and to have the value and validity of my conceptual position held at a distance, in doubt, and wonderfully absorbed in the silence of appreciation. Through the systems of deep disbelief I become a storyteller, a performer. With such absorptive ability in the systems of interpretation, I have greater difficulty being perceived as a person who theorizes without the mediating voices of those from the inner sanctum, or as a person who might name myself a philosopher, a theorist, a historian who creates paradigms that allow the experiences and the insights of people like me to belong.

What I am compelled to ask when veils seem more like walls is who has the privilege of speaking first? How do we negotiate the privilege of interpretation? When I have tried to fulfill my role as negotiator, I have often walked away knowing that I have spoken, but also knowing, as Anna Julia Cooper knew in 1892, that my voice, like her voice, is still a muted one. I speak, but I can not be heard. Worse, I am heard but I am not believed. Worse yet, I speak but I am not deemed believable. These moments of deep disbelief have helped me to understand much more clearly the wisdom of Audre Lorde when she said: "I have come to believe over and over again that what is most important to me must be spoken, made verbal and shared, even at the risk of having it bruised or misunderstood" (*Sister* 40). Lorde teaches me that, despite whatever frustration and vulnerability I might feel, despite my fear that no one is listening to me or is curious enough to try to understand my voice, it is still better to speak (*Black* 31). I set aside the distractions and permeating noise outside of myself, and I listen, as Howard Thurman recommended, to the sound of the genuine within. I go to a place inside myself and, as Opal Palmer Adisa explains, I listen and learn to "speak without clenching my teeth" (56).

SCENE THREE

There have been occasions when I have indeed been heard and positively received. Even at these times, however, I sometimes can not escape responses that make me most weary. One case in point occurred after a presentation in which I had glossed a scene in a novel that required cultural understanding. When the characters spoke in the scene, I rendered their voices, speaking and explaining, speaking and explaining, trying to translate the experience, to share the sounds of my historical place and to connect those sounds with systems of belief so that deeper understanding of the scene might emerge, and so that those outside of the immediacy of my home culture, the one represented in the novel, might see and understand more and be able to make more useful connections to their own worlds and experiences.

One, very well-intentioned response to what I did that day was, "How wonderful it was that you were willing to share with us your 'authentic' voice!" I said, "My 'authentic' voice?" She said, "Oh yes! I've never heard you talk like that, you know, so relaxed. I mean, you're usually great, but this was really great! You weren't so formal. You didn't have to speak in an appropriated academic language. You sounded 'natural.' It was nice to hear you be yourself." I said, "Oh, I see. Yes, I do have a range of voices, and I take quite a bit of pleasure actually in being able to use any of them at will." Not understanding the point that I was trying to make gently, she said, "But this time, it was really you. Thank you."

The conversation continued, but I stopped paying attention. What I didn't feel like saying in a more direct way, a response that my friend surely would have perceived as angry, was that all my voices are authentic, and like bell hooks, I find it "a necessary aspect of self-affirmation not to feel compelled to choose one voice over another, not to claim one as more authentic, but rather to construct social realities that celebrate, acknowledge, and affirm differences, variety" (12). Like hooks, I claim all my voices as my own very much authentic voices, even when it's difficult for others to imagine a person like me having the capacity to do that.

From moments of challenge like this one, I realize that we do not have a paradigm that really allows for what scholars in cultural and postcolonial studies (Anzuldua, Spivak, Mohanty, Bhaba) have called hybrid people — people who either have the capacity by right of history and development, or who might have created the capacity by right of history and development, to move with dexterity across cultural boundaries, to make themselves comfortable, and to make sense amid the chaos of difference.

As Cornel West points out, most African Americans, for example, dream in English, not in Yoruba, or Hausa, or Wolof. Hybrid people, as demonstrated by the history of Africans in the Western hemisphere, manage a fusion process that allows for survival, certainly. However, it also allows for the development of a peculiar expertise that extends one's range of abilities well beyond ordinary limits, and it supports the opportunity for the development of new and remarkable creative expression, like spirituals, jazz, blues, and what I suspect is happening also with the essay as genre in the hands of African American women. West notes that somebody gave Charlie Parker a saxophone, Miles Davis a trumpet, Hubert Laws a flute, and Les McCann a piano. I suggest that somebody also gave Maria Stewart, Gertrude Mossell, Frances Harper, Alice Walker, Audre Lorde, Toni Morrison, Patricia Williams, June Jordan, bell hooks, Angela Davis and a cadre of other African American women a pencil, a pen, a computer keyboard. In both instances, genius emerges from hybridity, from Africans who, over the course of time and circumstance, have come to dream in English, and I venture to say that all of their voices are authentic.

In sharing these three scenes, I emphasize that there is a pressing need to construct paradigms that permit us to engage in better practices in cross-boundary discourse, whether we are teaching, researching, writing, or talking with Others, whoever those Others happen to be. I would like to emphasize, again, that we look again at "voice" and situate it within a world of symbols, sound, and sense, recognizing that this world operates symphonically. Although the systems of voice production are indeed highly integrated and appear to have singularity in the ways that we come to sound, voicing actually sets in motion multiple systems [;] prominent among them are systems for speaking but present also are the systems for hearing. We speak within systems that we know significantly through our abilities to negotiate noise and to construct within that noise sense and sensibility.

Several questions come to mind. How can we teach, engage in research, write about, and talk across boundaries *with* others, instead of for, about, and around them? My experiences tell me that we need to do more than just talk and talk back. I believe that in this model we miss a critical moment. We need to talk, yes, and to talk back, yes, but when do we listen? How do we listen? How do we demonstrate that we honor and respect the person talking and what that person is saying, or what the person might say if we valued someone other than ourselves having a turn to speak? How do we translate listening into language and action, into the creation of an appropriate response? How do we really "talk back" rather than talk also? The goal is not, "You talk, I talk." The goal is better practices so that we can exchange perspectives, negotiate meaning, and create understanding with the intent of being in a good position to cooperate, when, like now, cooperation is absolutely necessary.

When I think about this goal, what stands out most is that these questions apply in so much of academic life right now. They certainly apply as we go into classrooms and insist that our students trust us and what we contend is in their best interest. In light of a record in classrooms that seriously questions the range of our abilities to recognize potential, or to appreciate students as non-generic human beings, or to appreciate that they bring with them, always, knowledge, we ask a lot when we ask them to trust. Too often, still, institutionalized equations for placement, positive matriculation, progress, and achievement name, categorize, rank, and file, while our true-to-life students fall between the cracks. I look again to Opal Palmer Adisa for an instructive example. She says:

> Presently, many academics advocate theories which, rather than illuminating the works under scrutiny, obfuscate and problematize these works so that students are rendered speechless. Consequently, the students constantly question what they know, and often, unfortunately, they conclude that they know nothing. (54)

Students may find what we do to be alienating and disheartening. Even when our intentions are quite honorable, silence can descend. Their experiences are not seen, and their voices are not heard. We can find ourselves participating, sometimes consciously, sometimes not, in what Patricia Williams calls "spirit murder" (55). I am reminded in a disconcerting way of a troubling scene from Alex Haley's *Roots*. We engage in practices that say quite insistently to a variety of students in a variety of ways, "Your name is Toby." Why wouldn't students wonder: Who can I trust here? Under what kinds of conditions? When? Why?

In addition to better practices in our classrooms, however, we can also question our ability to talk convincingly with deans, presidents, legislators, and the general public about what we do, how we do it, and why. We have not been conscientious about keeping lines of communication open, and we are now experiencing the consequences of talking primarily to ourselves as we watch funds being cut, programs being eliminated, and national agencies that are vital to our interests being bandied about as if they are post-it notes, randomly stuck on by some ill-informed spendthrift. We must learn to raise a politically active voice with a socially responsible mandate to make a rightful place for education in a country that seems always ready to place the needs of quality education on a sideboard instead of on the table. Seemingly, we have been forever content to let voices other than our own speak authoritatively about our areas of expertise and about us. It is time to speak for ourselves, in our own interests, in the interest of our work, and in the interest of our students.

Better practices are not limited, though, even to these concerns. Of more immediate concern to me this year, given my role as Chair of CCCC, is how to talk across boundaries within our own organization as teachers of English among other teachers of English and Language Arts from kindergarten through university with interests as varied as those implied by the sections, conferences, and committees of our parent organization, the National Council of Teachers of English (NCTE). Each of the groups within NCTE has its own set of needs, expectations, and concerns, multiplied across the amazing variety of institutional sites across which we work. In times of limited resources and a full slate of critical problems, we must find reasonable ways to negotiate so that we can all thrive reasonably well in the same place.

In our own case, for years, now, CCCC has recognized changes in our relationships with NCTE. Since the mid-1980s we have grown exponentially. The field of rhetoric and composition has blossomed and diversified. The climate for higher education has increasingly degenerated, and we have struggled in the midst of change to forge a more satisfying identity and a more positive and productive working relationship with others in NCTE who are facing crises of their own. After 50 years in NCTE, we have grown up, and we have to figure out a new way of being and doing in making sure that we can face our challenges well. We are now in the second year of a concerted effort to engage in a multi-leveled conversation that we hope will leave CCCC well-positioned to face a new century and ongoing challenges. Much, however, depends on the ways in which we talk and listen and talk again in crossing boundaries and creating, or not, the common ground of engagement.

As I look at the lay of this land, I endorse Henry David Thoreau's statement when he said, "Only that day dawns to which we are awake" (267). So my appeal is to urge us all to be awake, awake and listening, awake and operating deliberately on codes of better conduct in the interest of keeping our boundaries fluid, our discourse invigorated with multiple perspectives, and our policies and practices well-tuned toward a clearer respect for human potential and achievement from whatever their source and a clearer understanding that voicing at its best is not just well-spoken but also well-heard.

WORKS CITED

Adisa, Opal Palmer. "I Must Write What I Know So I'll Know That I've Known It All Along." *Sage: A Scholarly Journal on Black Women* 9.2 (1995): 54–57.

Anzaldua, Gloria. *Borderlands/La Frontera.* San Francisco: Aunt Lute. 1987.

Bhabha, Homi K. *The Location of Culture.* London: Routledge, 1994.

Christian, Barbara. "The Race for Theory." *Cultural Critique* 6 (1987): 335–45.

Cooper, Anna Julia. *A Voice from the South*. New York: Oxford UP, 1988.

Du Bois, W. E. B. *The Souls of Black Folk*. New York: Grammercy, 1994.

Haley, Alex. *Roots*. Garden City: Doubleday, 1976.

Hernstein, Richard J., and Charles Murray. *The Bell Curve: Intelligence and Class Structure in American Life*. New York: Free, 1994.

hooks, bell. *Talking Back: Thinking Feminist, Thinking Black*. Boston: South End, 1989.

Lorde, Audre, *The Black Unicorn*. New York: Norton, 1978.

____. Foreword. *Wild Women in the Whirlwind*. Ed. Joanne M. Braxton and Andree Nicola McLaughlin. New Brunswick: Rutgers UP. 1990. xi-xiii.

____. *Sister Outsider*. Freedom: The Crossing Press, 1984.

Mohanty, Chandra Talpade. "On Race and Voice: Challenges for Liberal Education in the 1990s." *Cultural Critique* 14 (Winter 1989-90): 179-208.

____. "Decolonizing Education: Feminisms and the Politics of Multiculturalism in the 'New' World Order." Ohio State University. Columbus, April 1994.

Olsen, Tillie, *Silences*. New York: Delta, 1978.

Pratt, Mary Louise. "Arts of the Contact Zone." *Profession 91* (1991): 33-40.

Spivak, Gayatri Chakravorty. *In Other Worlds: Essays in Cultural Politics*. New York: Routledge, 1988.

Thoreau, Henry David. *Walden*. New York: Vintage, 1991.

Thurman, Howard. "The Sound of the Genuine." Spelman College, Atlanta, April 1981.

West, Cornel. "Race Matters." Ohio State U, Columbus, OH, February 1995.

Williams, Patricia. *The Alchemy of Race and Rights*. Cambridge: Harvard UP, 1991.

David Bartholomae

Inventing the University

Education may well be, as of right, the instrument whereby every individual, in a society like our own, can gain access to any kind of discourse. But we well know that in its distribution, in what it permits and in what it prevents, it follows the well-trodden battle-lines of social conflict. Every educational system is a political means of maintaining or of modifying the appropriation of discourse with the knowledge and the powers it carries with it.

–FOUCAULT, "THE DISCOURSE ON LANGUAGE"

Every time a student sits down to write for us, he has to invent the university for the occasion — invent the university, that is, or a branch of it, like History or Anthropology or Economics or English. He has to learn to speak our language, to speak as we do, to try on the peculiar ways of knowing, selecting, evaluating, reporting, concluding, and arguing that define the discourse of our community. Or perhaps I should say the *various* discourses of our community, since it is in the nature of a liberal arts education that a student, after the first year or two, must learn to try on a variety of voices and interpretive schemes — to write, for example, as a literary critic one day and an experimental psychologist the next, to work within fields where the rules governing the presentation of examples or the development of an argument are both distinct and, even to a professional, mysterious.

The students have to appropriate (or be appropriated by) a specialized discourse, and they have to do this as though they were easily and comfortably one with their audience, as though they were members of the academy, or historians or anthropologists or economists; they have to invent the university by assembling and mimicking its language, finding some compromise between idiosyncrasy, a personal history, and the requirements of convention, the history of a discipline. They must learn to speak our language. Or they must dare to speak it, or to carry off the bluff, since speaking and writing will most certainly be required long before the skill is "learned." And this, understandably, causes problems.

Let me look quickly at an example. Here is an essay written by a college freshman, a basic writer:

> In the past time I thought that an incident was creative was when I had to make a clay model of the earth, but not of the classical or your everyday model of the earth which consists of the two cores, the mantle and the crust. I thought of these things in a dimension of which it would be unique, but easy to comprehend. Of course, your materials to work with were basic and limited at the same time, but

This article is reprinted from *When a Writer Can't Write: Studies in Writer's Block and Other Composing Process Problems.* Ed. Mike Rose. New York: Guilford, 1985. 273–85.

thought help to put this limit into a right attitude or frame of mind to work with the clay.

In the beginning of the clay model, I had to research and learn the different dimensions of the earth (in magnitude, quantity, state of matter, etc.). After this, I learned how to put this into the clay and come up with something different than any other person in my class at the time. In my opinion color coordination and shape was the key to my creativity of the clay model of the earth.

Creativity is the venture of the mind at work with the mechanics relay to the limbs from the cranium, which stores and triggers this action. It can be a burst of energy released at a precise time a thought is being transmitted. This can cause a frenzy of the human body, but it depends on the characteristics of the individual and how they can relay the message clearly enough through mechanics of the body to us as an observer. Then we must determine if it is creative or a learned process varied by the individual's thought process. Creativity is indeed a tool which has to exist, or our world will not succeed into the future and progress like it should.

I am continually impressed by the patience and good will of our students. This student was writing a placement essay during freshman orientation. (The problem set to him was "Describe a time when you did something you felt to be creative. Then, on the basis of the incident you have described, go on to draw some general conclusions about 'creativity.'") He knew that university faculty would be reading and evaluating his essay, and so he wrote for them.

In some ways it is a remarkable performance. He is trying on the discourse even though he doesn't have the knowledge that makes the discourse more than a routine, a set of conventional rituals and gestures. And he does this, I think, even though he *knows* he doesn't have the knowledge that makes the discourse more than a routine. He defines himself as a researcher, working systematically, and not as a kid in a high school class: "I thought of these things in a dimension of…"; "had to research and learn the different dimensions of the earth (in magnitude, quantity, state of matter, etc.)." He moves quickly into a specialized language (his approximation of our jargon) and draws both a general, textbook-like conclusion ("Creativity is the venture of the mind at work…") and a resounding peroration ("Creativity is indeed a tool which has to exist, or our world will not succeed into the future and progress like it should"). The writer has even, with that "indeed" and with the qualifications and the parenthetical expressions of the opening paragraphs, picked up the rhythm of our prose. And through it all he speaks with an impressive air of authority.

There is an elaborate but, I will argue, a necessary and enabling fiction at work here as the student dramatizes his experience in a "setting" — the setting required by the discourse — where he can speak to us as a companion, a fellow researcher. As I read the essay, there is only one moment when the fiction is broken, when we are addressed differently. The student says, "Of course, your materials to work with were basic and limited at the same time, but thought help to put this limit into a right attitude or frame of mind to work with the clay." At this point, I think, we become students and he the teacher, giving us a lesson (as in, "You take your pencil in your right hand and put your paper in front of you"). This is, however, one of the most characteristic slips of basic writers. It is very hard for them to take on the role—the voice, the person—of an authority whose authority is rooted in scholarship, analysis, or research. They slip, then, into the more immediately available and realizable voice of authority, the voice of a teacher giving a lesson or the voice of a parent lecturing at the dinner table. They offer advice or homilies rather than "academic" conclusions. There is a similar break in the final paragraph, where the conclusion that pushes for a definition ("Creativity is the venture of the mind at work with the mechanics relay to the limbs from the cranium...") is replaced by a conclusion which speaks in the voice of an Elder ("Creativity is indeed a tool which has to exist, or our world will not succeed into the future and progress like it should").

It is not uncommon, then, to find such breaks in the concluding sections of essays written by basic writers. Here is the concluding section of an essay written by a student about his work as a mechanic. He had been asked to generalize about "work" after reviewing an on-the-job experience or incident that "stuck in his mind" as somehow significant: "How could two repairmen miss a leak? Lack of pride? No incentive? Lazy? I don't know." At this point the writer is in a perfect position to speculate, to move from the problem to an analysis of the problem. Here is how the paragraph continues, however (and notice the change in pronoun reference):

> From this point on, I take my time, do it right, and don't let customers get under your skin. If they have a complaint, tell them to call your boss and he'll be more than glad to handle it. Most important, worry about yourself, and keep a clear eye on everyone, for there's always someone trying to take advantage of you, anytime and anyplace.

We get neither a technical discussion nor an "academic" discussion but a Lesson on Life.[1] This is the language he uses to address the general question "How could two repairmen miss a leak?" The other brand of conclusion, the more academic one, would have required him to speak of his experience in our terms; it would, that is, have required a special vocabulary, a special system of presentation, and an interpretive scheme (or a set of commonplaces) he could use to identify and talk about the mystery of human error. The writer certainly had access to the range of acceptable commonplaces for such an explanation: "lack of pride," "no incentive," "lazy." Each would dictate its own set of phrases, examples, and conclusions, and we, his teachers, would know how to write out each argument, just as we would know how to write out more specialized arguments of our own. A "commonplace," then, is a culturally or institutionally authorized concept or statement that carries with it its own necessary elaboration. We all use commonplaces to orient ourselves in the world; they provide a point of reference and a set of "prearticulated" explanations that are readily available to organize and interpret experience. The phrase "lack of pride" carries with it its own account for the repairman's error just as, at another point in time, a reference to "original sin" would provide an explanation, or just as, in a certain university classroom, a reference to "alienation" would enable a writer to continue and complete the discussion. While there is a way in which these terms are interchangeable, they are not all permissible. A student in a composition class would most likely be turned away from a discussion of original sin. Commonplaces are the "controlling ideas" of our composition textbooks, textbooks that not only insist upon a set form for expository writing but a set view of public life.[2]

When the student above says, "I don't know," he is not saying, then, that he has nothing to say. He is saying that he is not in a position to carry on this discussion. And so we are addressed as apprentices rather than as teachers or scholars. To speak to us as a person of status or privilege, the writer can either speak to us in our terms — in the privileged language of university discourse — or, in default (or in defiance), he can speak to us as though we were children, offering us the wisdom of experience.

I think it is possible to say that the language of the "Clay Model" paper has come through the writer and not from the writer. The writer has located himself (he has located the self that is represented by the *I* on the page) in a context that is, finally, beyond him, not his own and not available to his immediate procedures for inventing and arranging text. I would not, that is, call this essay an example of "writer-based" prose. I would not say that it is egocentric or that it represents the "interior monologue of a writer thinking and talking to himself" (Flower 63). It is, rather, the record of a writer who has lost himself in the discourse of his readers. There is a context beyond the reader that is not the world but a way of talking about the world, a way of talking that determines the use of examples, the possible conclusions, the acceptable commonplaces, and the key words of an essay on the construction of a clay model of the earth. This writer has entered the discourse without successfully approximating it.

Linda Flower has argued that the difficulty inexperienced writers have with writing can be understood as a difficulty in negotiating the transition between writer-based and reader-based prose. Expert writers, in other words, can better imagine how a reader will respond to a text and can transform or restructure what they have to say around a goal shared with a reader. Teaching students to revise for readers, then, will better prepare them to write initially with a reader in mind. The success of this pedagogy depends upon the degree to which a writer can imagine and conform to a reader's goals. The difficulty of this act of imagination, and the burden of such conformity, are so much at the heart of the problem that a teacher must pause and take stock before offering revision as a solution. Students like the student who wrote the "Clay Model" paper are not so much trapped in a private language as they are shut out from one of the privileged languages of public life, a language they are aware of but cannot control.

Our students, I've said, have to appropriate (or be appropriated by) a specialized discourse, and they have to do this as though they were easily or comfortably one with their audience. If you look at the situation this way, suddenly the problem of audience awareness becomes enormously complicated. One of the common assumptions of both composition research and composition teaching is that at some "stage" in the process of composing an essay a writer's ideas or his motives must be tailored to the needs and expectations of his audience. A writer has to "build bridges" between his point of view and his readers'. He has to anticipate and acknowledge his readers' assumptions and biases. He must begin with "common points of departure" before introducing new or controversial arguments. There is a version of the pastoral at work here. It is assumed that a person of low status (like a shepherd) can speak to a person of power (like a courtier), but only (at least so far as the language is concerned) if he is not a shepherd at all, but actually a member of the court out in the field in disguise.

Writers who can successfully manipulate an audience (or, to use a less pointed language, writers who can accommodate their motives to their readers' expectations) are writers who can both imagine and write from a position of privilege. They must, that is, see themselves within a privileged discourse, one that already includes and excludes groups of readers. They must be either equal to or more powerful than those they would address. The writing, then, must somehow transform the political and social relationships between basic writing students and their teachers.

If my students are going to write for me by knowing who I am — and if this means more than knowing my prejudices, psyching me out — it means knowing what I know; it means having the knowledge of a professor of English. They have, then, to know what I know and how I know what I know (the interpretive schemes that define the way I would work out the problems I set for them); they have to learn to write what I would write, or to offer up some approximation of that discourse. The problem of audience awareness, then, is a problem of power and finesse. It cannot be addressed, as it is in most classroom exercises, by giving students privilege and denying the situation of the classroom, by having students write to an outsider, someone excluded from their privileged circle: "Write about 'To His Coy Mistress,' not for your teacher, but for the students in your class"; "Describe Pittsburgh to someone who has never been there"; "Explain to a high school senior how best to prepare for college"; "Describe baseball to a Martian."

Exercises such as these allow students to imagine the needs and goals of a reader, and they bring those needs and goals forward as a dominant constraint in the construction of an essay. And they argue, implicitly, what is generally true about writing — that it is an act of aggression disguised as an act of charity. What they fail to address is the central problem of academic writing, where students must assume the right of speaking to someone who knows Pittsburgh or "To His Coy Mistress" better than they do, a reader for whom the general commonplaces and the readily available utterances about a subject are inadequate. It should be clear that when I say that I know Pittsburgh better than my basic writing students, I am talking about a way of knowing that is also a way of writing. There may be much that they know that I don't know, but in the setting of the university classroom, I have a way of talking about the town that is "better" (and for arbitrary reasons) than theirs.

I think that all writers, in order to write, must imagine for themselves the privilege of being "insiders" — that is, of being both inside an established and powerful discourse, and of being granted a special right to speak. And I think that right to speak is seldom conferred upon us — upon any of us, teachers or students — by virtue of the fact that we have invented or discovered an original idea. Leading students to believe that they are responsible for something new or original, unless they understand what those words mean with regard to writing, is a dangerous and counterproductive practice. We do have the right to expect students to be active and engaged, but that is more a matter of being continually and stylistically working against the inevitable presence of conventional language; it is not a matter of inventing a language that is new.

When students are writing for a teacher, writing becomes more problematic than it is for the students who are describing baseball to a Martian. The students, in effect, have to assume privilege without having any. And since students assume privilege by locating themselves within the discourse of a particular community — within a set of specifically acceptable gestures and commonplaces — learning, at least as it is defined in the liberal arts curriculum, becomes more a matter of imitation or parody than a matter of invention and discovery.

What our beginning students need to learn is to extend themselves into the commonplaces, set phrases, rituals, gestures, habits of mind, tricks of persuasion, obligatory conclusions, and necessary connections that determine the "what might be said" and constitute knowledge within the various branches of our academic community. The course of instruction that would make this possible would be based on a sequence of illustrated assignments and would allow for successive approximations of academic or "disciplinary" discourse. Students will not take on our peculiar ways of reading, writing, speaking, and thinking all at once. Nor will the command of a subject like sociology, at least as that command is represented by the successful completion of a multiple choice exam, enable students to write sociology. Our colleges and universities, by and large, have failed to involve basic writing students in scholarly projects, projects that would allow them to act as though they were colleagues in an academic enterprise. Much of the written work students do is test-taking, report or summary, work that places them outside the working discourse of the academic community, where they are expected to admire and report on what we do, rather than inside that discourse, where they can do its work and participate in a common enterprise.[3] This is a failure of teachers and curriculum designers who, even if they speak of writing as a mode of learning, all too often represent writing as a "tool" to be used by [an] educated mind.

Pat Bizzell is one of the most important scholars writing now on basic writers and on the special requirements of academic discourse.[4] In a recent [1982] essay, "Cognition, Convention, and Certainty: What We Need to Know about Writing," she argues that the problems of basic writers might be

> better understood in terms of their unfamiliarity with the academic discourse community, combined, perhaps, with such limited experience outside their native

discourse communities that they are unaware that there is such a thing as a discourse community with conventions to be mastered. What is underdeveloped is their knowledge both of the ways experience is constituted and interpreted in the academic discourse community and of the fact that all discourse communities constitute and interpret experience. (230)

One response to the problems of basic writers, then, would be to determine just what the community's conventions are, so that those conventions can be written out, "demystified," and taught in our classrooms. Teachers, as a result, could be more precise and helpful when they ask students to "think," "argue," "describe," or "define." Another response would be to examine the essays written by basic writers — their approximations of academic discourse — to determine more clearly where the problems lie. If we look at their writing, and if we look at it in the context of other student writing, we can better see the points of discord when students try to write their way into the university.

The purpose of the remainder of this paper will be to examine some of the most striking and characteristic problems as they are presented in the expository essays of basic writers. I will be concerned, then, with university discourse in its most generalized form — that is, as represented by introductory courses — and not with the special conventions required by advanced work in the various disciplines. And I will be concerned with the difficult, and often violent, accommodations that occur when students locate themselves in a discourse that is not "naturally" or immediately theirs.

I have reviewed five hundred essays written in response to the "creativity" question used during one of our placement exams. (The essay cited at the opening of this paper was one of that group.) Some of the essays were written by basic writers (or, more properly, those essays led readers to identify the writers as "basic writers"); some were written by students who "passed" (who were granted immediate access to the community of writers at the university). As I read these essays, I was looking to determine the stylistic resources that enabled writers to locate themselves within an "academic" discourse. My bias as a reader should be clear by now. I was not looking to see how the writer might represent the skills demanded by a neutral language (a language whose key features were paragraphs, topic sentences, transitions, and the like — features of a clear and orderly mind). I was looking to see what happened when a writer entered into a language to locate himself (a textual self) and his subject, and I was looking to see how once entered, that language made or unmade a writer.

Here is one essay. Its writer was classified as a basic writer. Since the essay is relatively free of sentence level errors, that decision must have been rooted in some perceived failure of the discourse itself.

> I am very interested in music, and I try to be creative in my interpretation of music. While in high school, I was a member of a jazz ensemble. The members of the ensemble were given chances to improvise and be creative in various songs. I feel that this was a great experience for me, as well as the other members. I was proud to know that I could use my imagination and feelings to create music other than what was written.

> Creativity to me, means being free to express yourself in a way that is unique to you, not having to conform to certain rules and guidelines. Music is only one of the many areas in which people are given opportunities to show their creativity. Sculpting, carving, building, art, and acting are just a few more areas where people can show their creativity.
>
> Through my music I conveyed feelings and thoughts which were important to me. Music was my means of showing creativity. In whatever form creativity takes, whether it be music, art, or science, it is an important aspect of our lives because it enables us to be individuals.

Notice, in this essay, the key gesture, one that appears in all but a few of the essays I read. The student defines as his own that which is a commonplace. "Creativity, to *me,* means being free to express yourself in a way that is unique to you, not having to conform to certain rules and guidelines." This act of appropriation constitutes his authority; it constitutes his authority as a writer and not just as a musician (that is, as someone with a story to tell). There were many essays in the set that told only a story, where the writer's established presence was as a musician or a skier or someone who painted designs on a van, but not as a person removed from that experience interpreting it, treating it as a metaphor for something else (creativity). Unless those stories were long, detailed, and very well told (unless the writer was doing more than saying, "I am a skier or a musician or a van-painter"), those writers were all given low ratings.

Notice also that the writer of the jazz paper locates himself and his experience in relation to the commonplace (creativity is unique expression; it is not having to conform to rules or guidelines) regardless of whether it is true or not. Anyone who improvises "knows" that improvisation follows rules and guidelines. It is the power of the commonplace (its truth as a recognizable, and, the writer believes, as a final statement) that justifies the example and completes the essay. The example, in other words, has value because it stands within the field of the commonplace. It is not the occasion for what one might call an "objective" analysis or a "close" reading. It could also be said that the essay stops with the articulation of the commonplace. The following sections speak only to the power of that statement. The reference to "sculpting, carving, building, art, and acting" attest to the universal of the commonplace (and it attests to the writer's nervousness with the status he has appropriated for himself — he is saying, "Now, I'm not the only one here who's done something unique"). The commonplace stands by itself. For this writer, it does not need to be elaborated. By virtue of having written it, he has completed the essay and established the contract by which we may be spoken to as equals: "In whatever form creativity takes, whether it be music, art, or science, it is an important aspect of *our lives* because it enables *us* to be individuals." (For me to break that contract, to argue that *my* life is not represented in that essay, is one way for me to begin as a teacher with that student in that essay.)

I said that the writer of the jazz paper offered up a commonplace regardless of whether it was "true" or not, and this, I said, was an example of the power of a commonplace to determine the meaning of an example. A commonplace determines a system of interpretation that can be used to "place" an example within a standard system of belief. You can see a similar process at work in this essay.

> During the football season, the team was supposed to wear the same type of cleats and the same type socks, I figured that I would change this a little by wearing my white shoes instead of black and to cover up the team socks with a pair of my own white ones. I thought that this looked better than what we were wearing, and I told a few of the other people on the team to change too. They agreed that it did look better and they changed there combination to go along with mine. After the game people came up to us and said that it looked very good the way we wore our socks, and they wanted to know why we changed from the rest of the team.
>
>   I feel that creativity comes from when a person lets his imagination come up with ideas and he is not afraid to express them. Once you create something to do it will be original and unique because it came about from your own imagination and if any one else tries to copy it, it won't be the same because you thought of it first from your own ideas.

This is not an elegant paper, but it seems seamless, tidy. If the paper on the clay model of the earth showed an ill-fit between the writer and his project, here the discourse seems natural, smooth. You could reproduce this paper and hand it out to a class, and it would take a lot of prompting before the students sense something fishy and one of the more aggressive ones might say, "Sure he came up with the idea of wearing white shoes and white socks. Him and Bill White-shoes Johnson. Come on. He copied the very thing he said was his own idea, 'original and unique.'"

The "I" of this text, the "I" who "figured," "thought," and "felt" is located in a conventional rhetoric of the self that turns imagination into origination (I made it), that argues an ethic of production (I made it and it is mine), and that argues a tight scheme of intention (I made it because I decided to make it). The rhetoric seems invisible because it is so common. This "I" (the maker) is also located in a version of history that dominates classroom accounts of history. It is an example of the "Great Man" theory, where history is rolling along—the English novel is dominated by a central, intrusive narrative presence; America is in the throes of a great depression; during football season the team was supposed to wear the same kind of cleats and socks—until a figure appears, one who can shape history—Henry James, FDR, the writer of the football paper—and everything is changed. In the argument of the football paper, "I figured," "I thought," "I told," "they agreed," and, as a consequence, "I feel that creativity *comes from* when a person lets his imagination come up with ideas and he is not afraid to express them." The story of appropriation becomes a narrative of courage and conquest. The writer was able to write that story when he was able to imagine himself in that discourse. Getting him out of it will be a difficult matter indeed.

There are ways, I think, that a writer can shape history in the very act of writing it. Some students are able to enter into a discourse, but, by stylistic maneuvers, to take possession of it at the same time. They don't originate a discourse, but they locate themselves within it aggressively, self-consciously.

Here is one particularly successful essay. Notice the specialized vocabulary, but also the way in which the text continually refers to its own language and to the language of others.

> Throughout my life, I have been interested and intrigued by music. My mother has often told me of the times, before I went to school, when I would "conduct" the orchestra on her records. I continued to listen to music and eventually started to play the guitar and the clarinet. Finally, at about the age of twelve, I started to sit down and to try to write songs. Even though my instrumental skills were far from my own high standards, I would spend much of my spare time during the day with a guitar around my neck, trying to produce a piece of music.
>
> Each of these sessions, as I remember them, had a rather set format. I would sit in my bedroom, strumming different combinations of the five or six chords I could play, until I heard a series which sounded particularly good to me. After this, I set the music to a suitable rhythm (usually dependent on the mood at the time), and ran through the tune until I could play it fairly easily. Only after this section was complete did I go on to writing lyrics, which generally followed along the lines of the current popular songs on the radio.
>
> At the time of the writing, I felt that my songs were, in themselves, an original creation of my own; that is, I, alone, made them. However, I now see that, in this sense of the word, I was not creative. The songs themselves seem to be an over-simplified form of the music I listened to at the time.
>
> In a more fitting sense, however, I *was* being creative. Since I did not purposely copy my favorite songs, I was, effectively, originating my songs from my own "process of creativity." To achieve my goal, I needed what a composer would call "inspiration" for my piece. In this case the inspiration was the current hit on the radio. Perhaps with my present point of view, I feel that I used too much "inspiration" in my songs, but, at that time, I did not.
>
> Creativity, therefore, is a process which, in my case, involved a certain series of "small creations" if you like. As well, it is something, the appreciation of which varies with one's point of view, that point of view being set by the person's experience, tastes, and his own personal view of creativity. The less experienced tend to allow for less originality, while the more experienced demand real originality to classify something a "creation." Either way, a term as abstract as this is perfectly correct, and open to interpretation.

This writer is consistent and dramatically conscious of herself forming something to say out of what has been said *and* out of what she has been saying in the act of writing this paper. "Creativity" begins, in this paper, as "original creation." What she thought was "creativity," however, she now calls "imitation," and, as she says, "in this sense of the word" she was not "creative." In another sense, however, she says that she *was* creative since she didn't purposefully copy the songs but used them as "inspiration."

The writing in this piece (that is, the work of the writer within the essay) goes on in spite of, or against, the language that keeps pressing to give another name to her experience as a song writer and to bring the discussion to closure. (Think of the quick closure of the football shoes paper in comparison.) Its style is difficult, highly qualified. It relies on quotation marks and parody to set off the language and attitudes that belong to the discourse (or the discourses) it would reject, that it would not take as its own proper location.[5]

In the papers I've examined in this essay, the writers have shown a varied awareness of the codes — or the competing codes — that operate within a discourse. To speak with authority student writers have not only to speak in another's voice but through another's "code"; and they not only have to do this, they have to speak in the voice and through the codes of those of us with power and wisdom; and they not only have to do this, they have to do it before they know what they are doing, before they have a project to participate in and before, at least in terms of our disciplines, they have anything to say. Our students may be able to enter into a conventional discourse and speak, not as themselves, but through the voice of the community. The university, however, is the place where "common" wisdom is only of negative value; it is something to work against. The movement toward a more specialized discourse begins (or perhaps, best begins) when a student can both define a position of privilege, a position that sets him against a "common" discourse, and when he can work self-consciously, critically, against not only the "common" code but his own.

The stages of development that I've suggested are not necessarily marked by corresponding levels in the type or frequency of error, at least not by the type or frequency of sentence level errors. I am arguing, then, that a basic writer is not necessarily a writer who makes a lot of mistakes. In fact, one of the problems with curricula designed to aid basic writers is that they too often begin with the assumption that the key distinguishing feature of a basic writer is the presence of sentence level error. Students are placed in courses because their placement essays show a high frequency of such errors and those courses are designed with the goal of making those errors go away. This approach to the problems of the basic writer ignores the degree to which error is not a constant feature but a marker in the development of a writer. Students who can write reasonably correct narratives may fall to pieces when faced with more unfamiliar assignments. More importantly, however, such courses fail to serve the rest of the curriculum. On every campus there is a significant number of college freshmen who require a course to introduce them to the kinds of writing that are required for a university education. Some of these students can write correct sentences and some cannot, but as a group they lack the facility other freshmen possess when they are faced with an academic writing task.

The "White Shoes" essay, for example, shows fewer sentence level errors than the "Clay Model" paper. This may well be due to the fact, however, that the writer of that paper stayed well within the safety of familiar territory. He kept himself out of trouble by doing what he could easily do. The tortuous syntax of the more advanced papers on my list is a syntax that represents a writer's struggle with a difficult and unfamiliar language, and it is a syntax that can quickly lead an inexperienced writer into trouble. The syntax and punctuation of the "Composing Songs" essay, for example, show the effort that is required when a writer works against the pressure of conventional discourse. If the prose is inelegant (although I'll confess I admire those dense sentences), it is still correct. This writer has a command of the linguistic and stylistic resources (the highly embedded sentences, the use of parentheses and quotation marks) required to complete the act of writing. It is easy to imagine the possible pitfalls for a writer working without this facility.

There was no camera trained on the "Clay Model" writer while he was writing, and I have no protocol of what was going through his mind, but it is possible to speculate that the syntactic difficulties of sentences like the following are the result of an attempt to use an unusual vocabulary and to extend his sentences beyond the boundaries that would be "normal" in his speech or writing:

> In the past time I thought that an incident was creative was when I had to make a clay model of the earth, but not of the classical or your everyday model of the earth which consists of the two cores, the mantle and the crust. I thought of these things in a dimension of which it would be unique, but easy to comprehend.

There is reason to believe, that is, that the problem is with this kind of sentence, in this context. If the problem of the last sentence is a problem of holding together these units — "I thought," "dimension," "unique," and "easy to comprehend" — then the linguistic problem is not a simple matter of sentence construction.

I am arguing, then, that such sentences fall apart not because the writer lacks the necessary syntax to glue the pieces together but because he lacks the full statement within which these key words are already operating. While writing, and in the thrust of his need to complete the sentence, he has the key words but not the utterance. (And to recover the utterance, I suspect, he will need to do more than revise the sentence.) The invisible conventions, the prepared phrases remain too distant for the statement to be completed. The writer must get inside of a discourse he can only partially imagine. The act of constructing a sentence, then, becomes something like an act of transcription, where the voice on the tape unexpectedly fades away and becomes inaudible.

Mina Shaughnessy speaks of the advanced writer as a writer with a more facile but still incomplete possession of this prior discourse. In the case of the advanced writer, the evidence of a problem is the presence of dissonant, redundant, or imprecise language, as in a sentence such as this: "No education can be *total*, it must be *continuous*." Such a student, Shaughnessy says, could be said to hear the "melody of formal English" while still unable to make precise or exact distinctions. And, she says, the prepackaging feature of language, the possibility of taking over phrases and whole sentences without much thought about them, threatens the writer now as before. The writer, as we have said, inherits the language out of which he must fabricate his own messages. He is therefore in a constant tangle with the language, obliged to recognize its public, communal nature and yet driven to invent out of this language his own statements (19).

For the unskilled writer, the problem is different in degree and not in kind. The inexperienced writer is left with a more fragmentary record of the comings and goings of academic discourse. Or, as I said above, he often has the key words without the complete statements within which they are already operating.

It may very well be that some students will need to learn to crudely mimic the "distinctive register" of academic discourse before they are prepared to actually and legitimately do the work of the discourse, and before they are sophisticated enough with the refinements of tone and texture to do it with grace or elegance. To say this, however, is to say that our students must be our students. Their initial progress will be marked by their abilities to take on the role of privilege, by their abilities to establish authority. From this point of view, the student who wrote about constructing the clay model of the earth is better prepared for his education than the student who wrote about playing football in white shoes, even though the "White Shoes" paper was relatively error-free and the "Clay Model" paper was not. It will be hard to pry the writer of the "White Shoes" paper loose from the tidy, pat discourse that allows him to dispose of the question of creativity in such a quick and efficient manner. He will have to be convinced that it is better to write sentences he might not so easily control, and he will have to be convinced that it is better to write muddier and more confusing prose (in order that it may sound like ours), and this will be harder than convincing the "Clay Model" writer to continue what he has begun.[6]

NOTES

[1] David Olson has made a similar observation about school-related problems of language learning in younger children. Here is his conclusion: "Depending upon whether children assumed language was primarily suitable for making assertions and conjectures or primarily for making direct or indirect commands, they will either find school texts easy or difficult" (107).

[2] For Aristotle there were both general and specific commonplaces. A speaker, says Aristotle, has a "stock of arguments to which he may turn for a particular need."

> If he knows the *topic* (regions, places, lines of argument)–and a skilled speaker will know them—he will know where to find what he wants for a special case. The general topics, or *common*places, are regions containing arguments that are common to all branches of knowledge....But there are also special topics (regions, places, *loci*) in which one looks for arguments appertaining to particular branches of knowledge, special sciences, such as ethics or politics. (154–55)

And, he says "The topics or places, then; may be indifferently thought of as in the science that is concerned, or in the mind of the speaker." But the question of location is "indifferent" *only* if the mind of the speaker is in line with set opinion, general assumption. For the speaker (or writer) who is not situated so comfortably in the privileged public realm, this is indeed not an indifferent matter at all. If he does not have the commonplace at hand, he will not, in Aristotle's terms, know where to go at all.

[3] See especially Bartholomae and Rose for articles on curricula designed to move students into university discourse. The movement to extend writing "across the curriculum" is evidence of a general concern for locating students within the work of the university: see especially Bizzell or Maimon et al. For longer works directed specifically at basic writing, see Ponsoc and Deen, and Shaughnessy. For a book describing a course for more advanced students, see Coles.

[4] See especially Bizzell, and Bizzell and Herzberg. My debt to Bizzell's work should be evident everywhere in this essay.

[5] In support of my argument that this is the kind of writing that does the work of the academy, let me offer the following excerpt from a recent essay by Wayne Booth ("The Company We Keep: Self-Making in Imaginative Art, Old and New"):

> I can remember making up songs of my own, no doubt borrowed from favorites like "Hello, Central, Give Me Heaven," "You Can't Holler Down My Rain Barrel," and one about the ancient story of a sweet little "babe in the woods" who lay down and died, with her brother.
>
> I asked my mother, in a burst of creative egotism, why nobody ever learned to sing my songs, since after all I was more than willing to learn *theirs*. I can't remember her answer, and I can barely remember snatches of two of "my" songs. But I can remember dozens of theirs, and when I sing them, even now, I sometimes feel again the emotions, and see the images, that they aroused then. Thus who I am now — the very shape of my soul — was to a surprising degree molded by the works of "art" that came my way.
>
> I set "art" in quotation marks, because much that I experienced in those early books and songs would not be classed as are according to most definitions. But for the purposes of appraising the effects of "art" on "life" or "culture," and especially for the purposes of thinking about the effects of the "media," we surely must include every kind of artificial experience that we provide for one another....
>
> In this sense of the word, all of us are from the earliest years fed a steady diet of art.... (58-59)

While there are similarities in the paraphrasable content of Booth's arguments and my student's, what I am interested in is each writer's method. Both appropriate terms from a common discourse (about *art* and *inspiration*) in order to push against an established way of talking (about tradition and the individual). This effort of opposition clears a space for each writer's argument and enables the writers to establish their own "sense" of the key words in the discourse.

[6] Preparation of this manuscript was supported by the Learning Research and Development Center of the University of Pittsburgh, which is supported in part by the National Institute of Education. I am grateful also to Mike Rose, who pushed and pulled at this paper at a time when it needed it.

WORKS CITED

Aristotle. *The Rhetoric of Aristotle*. Trans. L. Cooper. Englewood Cliffs: Prentice, 1932.

Bartholomae, D. "Writing Assignments: Where Writing Begins." *Forum*. Ed. P. Stock. Montclair: Boynton/Cook, 1983. 300-12.

Bizzell, P. "The Ethos of Academic Discourse." *College Composition and Communication* 29 (1978): 351-55.

_____. "Cognition, Convention, and Certainty: What We Need to Know about Writing." *Pre/text* 3 (1982): 213-44.

_____. "College Composition: Initiation into the Academic Discourse Community." *Curriculum Inquiry* 12 (1982): 191-207.

Bizzell, P., and B. Herzberg. "'Inherent' Ideology, 'Universal' History, 'Empirical' Evidence, and 'Context-Free' Writing: Some problems with E. D. Hirsch's *The Philosophy of Composition*." *Modern Language Notes* 95 (1980): 1181-1202.

Coles, W. E., Jr. *The Plural I.* New York: Holt, 1978.

Flower, Linda S. "Revising Writer-Based Prose." *Journal of Basic Writing* 3 (1981): 62–74.

Maimon, E. P., G. L. Belcher, G. W. Hearn, B. F. Nodine, and F. X. O'Connor. *Writing in the Arts and Sciences.* Cambridge: Winthrop, 1981.

Olson, D. R. "Writing: The Divorce of the Author from the Text." *Exploring Speaking-Writing Relationships: Connections and Contrasts.* Ed. B. M. Kroll and R. J. Vann. Urbana: National Council of Teachers of English, 1981.

Ponsot, M., and R. Deen. *Beat Not the Poor Desk.* Montclair: Boynton/Cook, 1982.

Rose, M. "Remedial Writing Courses: A Critique and a Proposal." *College English* 45 (1983): 109–28.

Shaughnessy, Mina. *Errors and Expectations.* New York: Oxford UP, 1977.

Mike Rose

The Language of Exclusion: Writing Instruction at the University

"How many 'minor errors' are acceptable?"
  "We must try to isolate and define those further skills in composition . . ."
  ". . . we should provide a short remedial course to patch up any deficiencies."
  "Perhaps the most striking feature of this campus' siege against illiteracy . . ."
  "One might hope that, after a number of years, standards might be set in the
high schools which would allow us to abandon our own defensive program."

These snippets come from University of California and California state legisla-
tive memos, reports, and position papers and from documents produced during a recent debate in UCLA's Academic Senate over whether a course in our
freshman writing sequence was remedial. Though these quotations — and a
half dozen others I will use in this essay — are local, they represent a kind of
institutional language about writing instruction in American higher education. There are five ideas about writing implicit in these comments: Writing
ability is judged in terms of the presence of error and can thus be quantified.
Writing is a skill or a tool rather than a discipline. A number of our students
lack this skill and must be remediated. In fact, some percentage of our students are, for all intents and purposes, illiterate. Our remedial efforts, while
currently necessary, can be phased out once the literacy crisis is solved in other
segments of the educational system.

This kind of thinking and talking is so common that we often fail to notice
that it reveals a reductive, fundamentally behaviorist model of the development and use of written language, a problematic definition of writing, and an
inaccurate assessment of student ability and need. This way of talking about
writing abilities and instruction is woven throughout discussions of program
and curriculum development, course credit, instructional evaluation, and
resource allocation. And, in various ways, it keeps writing instruction at the
periphery of the curriculum.

It is certainly true that many faculty and administrators would take issue
with one or more of the above notions. And those of us in writing would bring
current thinking in rhetoric and composition studies into the conversation.
(Though we often — perhaps uncomfortably — rely on terms like "skill" and
"remediation.") Sometimes we successfully challenge this language or set up
sensible programs in spite of it. But all too often we can do neither. The

This article is reprinted from *College English* 47.4 (Apr. 1985): 341–59.

language represented in the headnotes of this essay reveals deeply held beliefs. It has a tradition and a style, and it plays off the fundamental tension between the general education and the research missions of the American university. The more I think about this language and recall the contexts in which I've heard it used, the more I realize how caught up we all are in a political-semantic web that restricts the way we think about the place of writing in the academy. The opinions I have been describing are certainly not the only ones to be heard. But they are strong. Influential. Rhetorically effective. And profoundly exclusionary. Until we seriously rethink it, we will misrepresent the nature of writing, misjudge our students' problems, and miss any chance to effect a true curricular change that will situate writing firmly in the under-graduate curriculum.

Let us consider the college writing course for a moment. Freshman compo-sition originated in 1874 as a Harvard response to the poor writing of *upper*-classmen, spread rapidly, and became and remained the most consistently required course in the American curriculum. Upper division writing courses have a briefer and much less expansive history, but they are currently receiving a good deal of institutional energy and support. It would be hard to think of an ability more desired than the ability to write. Yet, though writing courses are highly valued, even enjoying a boom, they are also viewed with curious eyes. Administrators fund them — often generously — but academic senates worry that the boundaries between high school and college are eroding, and worry as well that the considerable investment of resources in such courses will drain money from the research enterprise. They deny some of the courses curricular status by tagging them remedial, and their members secretly or not-so-secretly wish the courses could be moved to community colleges. Scientists and social scientists underscore the importance of effective writing, yet find it difficult — if not impossible — to restructure their own courses of study to encourage and support writing. More than a few humanists express such difficulty as well. English departments hold onto writing courses but consider the work intellec-tually second-class. The people who teach writing are more often than not tem-porary hires; their courses are robbed of curricular continuity and of the status that comes with tenured faculty involvement. And the instructors? Well, they're just robbed.

The writing course holds a very strange position in the American curriculum. It is within this setting that composition specialists must debate and defend and interminably evaluate what they do. And how untenable such activity becomes if the very terms of the defense undercut both the nature of writing and the teaching of writing, and exclude it in various metaphorical ways from the curriculum. We end up arguing with words that sabotage our argument. The first step in resolving such a mess is to consider the language institutions use when they discuss writing. What I want to do in this essay is to look at each of the five notions presented earlier, examine briefly the conditions that shaped their use, and speculate on how it is that they misrepresent and exclude. I will conclude by entertaining a less reductive and exclusionary way to think — and talk — about writing in the academy.

BEHAVIORISM, QUANTIFICATION, AND WRITING

A great deal of current work in fields as diverse as rhetoric, composition studies, psycholinguistics, and cognitive development has underscored the importance of engaging young writers in rich, natural language use. And the movements of the last four decades that have most influenced the teaching of writing — life adjustment, liberal studies, and writing as process — have each, in their very different ways, placed writing pedagogy in the context of broad concerns: personal development and adjustment, a rhetorical-literary tradition, the psychology of composing. It is somewhat curious, then, that a behaviorist approach to writing, one that took its fullest shape in the 1930s and has been variously and severely challenged by the movements that followed it, remains with us as vigorously as it does. It is atomistic, focusing on isolated bits of discourse, error centered, and linguistically reductive. It has a style and a series of techniques that influence pedagogy, assessment, and evaluation. We currently see its influence in workbooks, programmed instruction, and many formulations of behavioral objectives, and it gets most of its airplay in remedial courses. It has staying power. Perhaps we can better understand its resilience if we briefly survey the history that gives it its current shape.

When turn-of-the-century educational psychologists like E. L. Thorndike began to study the teaching of writing, they found a Latin and Greek influenced school grammar that was primarily a set of prescriptions for conducting socially acceptable discourse, a list of the arcane do's and don'ts of usage for the ever-increasing numbers of children — many from lower classes and immigrant groups — entering the educational system. Thorndike and his colleagues also found reports like those issuing from the Harvard faculty in the 1890s which called attention to the presence of errors in handwriting, spelling, and grammar in the writing of the university's entering freshmen. The twentieth-century writing curriculum, then, was focused on the particulars of usage, grammar, and mechanics. Correctness became, in James Berlin's words, the era's "most significant measure of accomplished prose" (*Writing Instruction in Nineteenth-Century American Colleges* [Carbondale: Southern Illinois University Press, 1984], p. 73).

Such particulars suited educational psychology's model of language quite well: a mechanistic paradigm that studied language by reducing it to discrete behaviors and that defined language growth as the accretion of these particulars. The stress, of course, was on quantification and measurement. ("Whatever exists at all exists in some amount," proclaimed Thorndike.[1]) The focus on error — which is eminently measurable — found justification in a model of mind that was ascending in American academic psychology. Educators embraced the late Victorian faith in science.

Thorndike and company would champion individualized instruction and insist on language practice rather than the rote memorization of rules of grammar that characterized nineteenth-century pedagogy. But they conducted their work within a model of language that was tremendously limited, and this model was further supported and advanced by what Raymond Callahan has called "the cult of efficiency," a strong push to apply to education the principles of industrial scientific management (*Education and the Cult of Efficiency* [Chicago: University of Chicago Press, 1962]). Educational gains were defined as products, and the output of products could be measured. Pedagogical effectiveness — which meant cost-effectiveness — could be determined with "scientific" accuracy. This was the era of the educational efficiency expert. (NCTE even had a Committee on Economy of Time in English.) The combination of positivism, efficiency, and skittishness about correct grammar would have a profound influence on pedagogy and research.

This was the time when workbooks and "practice pads" first became big business. Their success could at least partly be attributed to the fact that they were supported by scientific reasoning. Educational psychologists had demonstrated that simply memorizing rules of grammar and usage had no discernible effect on the quality of student writing. What was needed was application of those rules through practice provided by drills and exercises. The theoretical underpinning was expressed in terms of "habit formation" and "habit strength," the behaviorist equivalent of learning — the resilience of an "acquired response" being dependent on the power and number of reinforcements. The logic was neat: specify a desired linguistic behavior as precisely as possible (e.g., the proper use of the pronouns "he" and "him") and construct opportunities to practice it. The more practice, the more the linguistic habit will take hold. Textbooks as well as workbooks shared this penchant for precision. One textbook for teachers presented a unit on the colon.[2] A text for students devoted seven pages to the use of a capital letter to indicate a proper noun.[3] This was also the time when objective tests — which had been around since 1890 — enjoyed a sudden rebirth as "new type" tests. And they, of course, were precision incarnate. The tests generated great enthusiasm among educators who saw in them a scientific means accurately and fairly to assess student achievement in language arts as well as in social studies and mathematics. Ellwood Cubberley, the dean of the School of Education at Stanford, called the development of these "new type" tests "one of the most significant movements in all our educational history."[4] Cubberley and his colleagues felt they were on the threshold of a new era.

Research too focused on the particulars of language, especially on listing and tabulating error. One rarely finds consideration of the social context of error, or of its cognitive-developmental meaning — that is, no interpretation of its significance in the growth of the writer. Instead one finds W. S. Guiler tallying the percentages of 350 students who, in misspelling "mortgage," erred by omitting the "t" vs. those who dropped the initial "g."[5] And one reads Grace Ransom's study of students' "vocabularies of errors" — a popular notion that any given student has a more or less stable set of errors he or she commits. Ransom showed that with drill and practice, students ceased making many of the errors that appeared on pretests (though, unfortunately for the theory, a large number of new errors appeared in their posttests).[6] One also reads Luella Cole Pressey's assertion that "everything needed for about 90 per cent of the writing students do...appears to involve only some 44 different rules of English composition." And therefore, if mastery of the rules is divided up and allocated to grades 2 through 12, "there is an average of 4.4 rules to be mastered per year."[7]

Such research and pedagogy was enacted to good purpose, a purpose stated well by H. J. Arnold, Director of Special Schools at Wittenberg College:

> [Students'] disabilities are specific. The more exactly they can be located, the more promptly they can be removed.... It seems reasonably safe to predict that the elimination of the above mentioned disabilities through adequate remedial drill will do much to remove students' handicaps in certain college courses. ("Diagnostic and Remedial Techniques for College Freshmen," *Association of American Colleges Bulletin,* 16 [1930], pp. 271–272).

The trouble, of course, is that such work is built on a set of highly questionable assumptions: that a writer has a relatively fixed repository of linguistic blunders that can be pinpointed and then corrected through drill, that repetitive drill on specific linguistic features represented in isolated sentences will result in mastery of linguistic (or stylistic or rhetorical) principles, that bits of discourse bereft of rhetorical or conceptual context can form the basis of curriculum and assessment, that good writing is correct writing, and that correctness has to do with pronoun choice, verb forms, and the like.

Despite the fact that such assumptions began to be challenged by the late 30s,[8] the paraphernalia and the approach of the scientific era were destined to remain with us. I think this trend has the staying power it does for a number of reasons, the ones we saw illustrated in our brief historical overview. It gives a method — a putatively objective one — to the strong desire of our society to maintain correct language use. It is very American in its seeming efficiency. And it offers a simple, understandable view of complex linguistic problems. The trend seems to reemerge with most potency in times of crisis: when budgets crunch and accountability looms or, particularly, when "nontraditional" students flood our institutions.[9] A reduction of complexity has great appeal in institutional decision making, especially in difficult times: a scientific-atomistic approach to language, with its attendant tallies and charts, nicely fits an economic/political decision-making model. When in doubt or when scared or when pressed, count.

And something else happens. When student writing is viewed in this particularistic, pseudo-scientific way, it gets defined in very limited terms as a narrow band of inadequate behavior separate from the vastly complex composing that faculty members engage in for a living and delve into for work and for play. And such perception yields what it intends: a behavior that is stripped of its rich cognitive and rhetorical complexity. A behavior that, in fact, looks and feels basic, fundamental, atomistic. A behavior that certainly does not belong in the university.

ENGLISH AS A SKILL

As English, a relatively new course of study, moved into the second and third decades of this century, it was challenged by efficiency-obsessed administrators and legislators. Since the teaching of writing required tremendous resources, English teachers had to defend their work in utilitarian terms. One very successful defense was their characterization of English as a "skill" or "tool subject" that all students had to master in order to achieve in almost any subject and to function as productive citizens. The defense worked, and the utility of English in schooling and in adult life was confirmed for the era.

The way this defense played itself out, however, had interesting ramifications. Though a utilitarian defense of English included for many the rhetorical/conceptual as well as the mechanical/grammatical dimensions of language, the overwhelming focus of discussion in the committee reports and the journals of the 1920s and 1930s was on grammatical and mechanical error. The narrow focus was made even more narrow by a fetish for "scientific" tabulation. One could measure the degree to which students mastered their writing skill by tallying their mistakes.

We no longer use the phrase "tool subject," and we have gone a long way in the last three decades from error tabulation toward revitalizing the rhetorical dimension of writing. But the notion of writing as a skill is still central to our discussions and our defenses: we have writing skills hierarchies, writing skills assessments, and writing skills centers: And necessary as such a notion may seem to be, I think it carries with it a tremendous liability. Perhaps the problem is nowhere more clearly illustrated than in this excerpt from the UCLA academic senate's definition of a university course:

> A university course should set forth an integrated body of knowledge with primary emphasis on presenting principles and theories rather than on developing skills and techniques.

If "skills and techniques" are included, they must be taught "primarily as a means to learning, analyzing, and criticizing theories and principles." There is a lot to question in this definition, but for now let us limit ourselves to the distinction it establishes between a skill and a body of knowledge. The distinction highlights a fundamental tension in the American university: between what Laurence Veysey labels the practical-utilitarian dimension (applied, vocational, educationalist) and both the liberal culture and the research dimensions — the latter two, each in different ways, elevating appreciation and pure inquiry over application (*The Emergence of the American University* [Chicago: University of Chicago Press, 1965]). To discuss writing as a skill, then, is to place it in the realm of the technical, and in the current, research-ascendant American university, that is a kiss of death.

Now it is true that we commonly use the word *skill* in ways that suggest a complex interweaving of sophisticated activity and rich knowledge. We praise the interpretive skills of the literary critic, the diagnostic skills of the physician, the interpersonal skills of the clinical psychologist. Applied, yes, but implying a kind of competence that is more in line with obsolete definitions that equate skill with reason and understanding than with this more common definition (that of the *American Heritage Dictionary*): "An art, trade, or technique, particularly one requiring use of the hands or body." A skill, particularly in the university setting, is, well, a tool, something one develops and refines and completes in order to take on the higher-order demands of purer thought. Everyone may acknowledge the value of the skill (our senate praised our course to the skies as it removed its credit), but it is valuable as the ability to multiply or titrate a solution or use an index or draw a map is valuable. It is absolutely necessary but remains second-class. It is not "an integrated body of knowledge" but a technique, something acquired differently from the way one acquires knowledge — from drill, from practice, from procedures that conjure up the hand and the eye but not the mind. Skills are discussed as separable, distinct, circumscribable activities; thus we talk of subskills, levels of skills, sets of skills. Again writing is defined by abilities one can quantify and connect as opposed to the dynamism and organic vitality one associates with thought.

Because skills are fundamental tools, basic procedures, there is the strong expectation that they be mastered at various preparatory junctures in one's educational career and in the places where such tools are properly crafted. In the case of writing, the skills should be mastered before one enters college and takes on higher-order endeavors. And the place for such instruction — before or after entering college — is the English class. Yes, the skill can be refined, but its fundamental development is over, completed via a series of elementary and secondary school courses and perhaps one or two college courses, often designated remedial. Thus it is that so many faculty consider upper-division and especially graduate-level writing courses as de jure remedial. To view writing as a skill in the university context reduces the possibility of perceiving it as a complex ability that is continually developing as one engages in new tasks with new materials for new audiences.

If the foregoing seems a bit extreme, consider this passage from our Academic Senate's review of UCLA Writing Programs:

> . . . it seems difficult to see how *composition* — whose distinctive aspect seems to be the transformation of language from thought or speech to hard copy — represents a distinct further step in shaping cogitation. There don't seem to be persuasive grounds for abandoning the view that composition is still a *skill* attendant to the attainment of overall linguistic competence.

The author of the report, a chemist, was reacting to some of our faculty's assertions about the interweaving of thinking and writing; writing for him is more or less a transcription skill.

So to reduce writing to second-class intellectual status is to influence the way faculty, students, and society view the teaching of writing. This is a bitter pill, but we in writing may have little choice but to swallow it. For, after all, is not writing simply different from "integrated bodies of knowledge" like sociology or biology? Is it? Well, yes and no. There are aspects of writing that would fit a skills model (the graphemic aspects especially). But much current theory and research are moving us to see that writing is not simply a transcribing skill mastered in early development. Writing seems central to the shaping and directing of certain modes of cognition, is integrally involved in learning, is a means of defining the self and defining reality, is a means of representing and contextualizing information (which has enormous political as well as conceptual and archival importance), and is an activity that develops over one's lifetime. Indeed it is worth pondering whether many of the "integrated bodies of knowledge" we study, the disciplines we practice, would have ever developed in the way they did and reveal the knowledge they do if writing did not exist. Would history or philosophy or economics exist as we know them? It is not simply that the work of such disciplines is recorded in writing, but that writing is intimately involved in the nature of their inquiry. Writing is not just a skill with which one can present or analyze knowledge. It is essential to the very existence of certain kinds of knowledge.

REMEDIATION

Since the middle of the last century, American colleges have been establishing various kinds of preparatory programs and classes within their halls to maintain enrollments while bringing their entering students up to curricular par.[10] One fairly modern incarnation of this activity is the "remedial class," a designation that appears frequently in the education and language arts journals of the 1920s.[11] Since that time remedial courses have remained very much with us: we have remedial programs, remedial sections, remedial textbooks, and, of course, remedial students. Other terms with different twists (like "developmental" and "compensatory") come and go, but "remedial" has staying power. Exactly what the adjective "remedial" means, however, has never quite been clear. To remediate seems to mean to correct errors or fill in gaps in a person's knowledge. The implication is that the material being studied should have been learned during prior education but was not. Now the reasons why it was not could vary tremendously: they could rest with the student (physical impairment, motivational problems, intelligence), the family (socio-economic status, stability, the support of reading-writing activities), the school (location, sophistication of the curriculum, adequacy of elementary or secondary instruction), the culture or subculture (priority of schooling, competing expectations and demands), or some combination of such factors. What "remedial" means in terms of curriculum and pedagogy is not clear either. What is remedial for a school like UCLA might well be standard for other state or community colleges, and what is considered standard during one era might well be tagged remedial in the next.

It is hard to define such a term. The best definition of remedial I can arrive at is a highly dynamic, contextual one: The function of labelling certain material remedial in higher education is to keep in place the hard fought for, if historically and conceptually problematic and highly fluid, distinction between college and secondary work. "Remedial" gains its meaning, then, in a political more than a pedagogical universe.

And the political dimension is powerful — to be remedial is to be substandard, inadequate, and, because of the origins of the term, the inadequacy is metaphorically connected to disease and mental defect. It has been difficult to trace the educational etymology of the word "remedial," but what I have uncovered suggests this: Its origins are in law and medicine, and by the late nineteenth century the term fell pretty much in the medical domain and was soon applied to education. "Remedial" quickly generalized beyond the description of students who might have had neurological problems to those with broader, though special, educational problems and then to those normal learners who are not up to a particular set of standards in a particular era at particular institutions. Here is some history.

Most of the enlightened work in the nineteenth century with the training of special populations (the deaf, the blind, the mentally retarded) was conducted by medical people, often in medical settings. And when young people who could hear and see and were of normal intelligence but had unusual — though perhaps not devastating — difficulties began to seek help, they too were examined within a medical framework. Their difficulties had to do with reading and writing — though mostly reading — and would today be classified as learning disabilities. One of the first such difficulties to be studied was dyslexia, then labelled "congenital word blindness."

In 1896 a physician named Morgan reported in the pages of *The British Medical Journal* the case of a "bright and intelligent boy" who was having great difficulty learning to read. Though he knew the alphabet, he would spell some words in pretty unusual ways. He would reverse letters or drop them or write odd combinations of consonants and vowels. Dr. Morgan examined the boy and had him read and write. The only diagnosis that made sense was one he had to borrow and analogize from the cases of stroke victims, "word blindness," but since the child had no history of cerebral trauma, Morgan labelled his condition "*congenital* word blindness" (W. Pringle Morgan, "A Case of Congenital Word Blindness," *The British Medical Journal,* 6, Part 2 [1896], 1378). Within the next two decades a number of such cases surfaced; in fact another English physician, James Hinshelwood, published several books on congenital word blindness.[12] The explanations were for the most part strictly medical, and, it should be noted, were analogized from detectable cerebral pathology in adults to conditions with no detectable pathology in children.

In the 1920s other medical men began to advance explanations a bit different from Morgan's and Hinshelwood's. Dr. Samuel Orton, an American physician, posed what he called a "cerebral physiological" theory that directed thinking away from trauma analogues and toward functional explanations. Certain areas of the brain were not defective but underdeveloped and could be corrected through "remedial effort." But though he posed a basically educational model for dyslexia, Dr. Otton's language should not be overlooked. He spoke of "brain habit" and the "handicap" of his "physiological deviates."[13]

Though his theory was different from that of his forerunners, his language, significantly, was still medical.

As increasing access to education brought more and more children into the schools, they were met by progressive teachers and testing experts interested in assessing and responding to individual differences. Other sorts of reading and writing problems, not just dyslexia, were surfacing, and increasing numbers of teachers, not just medical people, were working with the special students. But the medical vocabulary — with its implied medical model — remained dominant. People tried to *diagnose* various *disabilities, defects, deficits, deficiencies,* and *handicaps,* and then tried to *remedy* them.[14] So one starts to see all sorts of reading/writing problems clustered together and addressed with this language. For example, William S. Gray's important monograph, *Remedial Cases in Reading: Their Diagnosis and Treatment* (Chicago: University of Chicago Press, 1922), listed as "specific causes of failure in reading" inferior learning capacity, congenital word blindness, poor auditory memory, defective vision, a narrow span of recognition, ineffective eye movements, inadequate training in phonetics, inadequate attention to the content, an inadequate speaking vocabulary, a small meaning vocabulary, speech defects, lack of interest, and timidity. The remedial paradigm was beginning to include those who had troubles as varied as bad eyes, second language interference, and shyness.[15]

It is likely that the appeal of medical-remedial language had much to do with its associations with scientific objectivity and accuracy — powerful currency in the efficiency-minded 1920s and 30s. A nice illustration of this interaction of influences appeared in Albert Lang's 1930 textbook, *Modern Methods in Written Examinations* (Boston: Houghton Mifflin, 1930). The medical model is quite explicit:

> teaching bears a resemblance to the practice of medicine. Like a successful physician, the good teacher must be something of a diagnostician. The physician by means of a general examination singles out the individuals whose physical defects require a more thorough testing. He critically scrutinizes the special cases until he recognizes the specific troubles. After a careful diagnosis he is able to prescribe intelligently the best remedial or corrective measures. (p. 38)

By the 1930s the language of remediation could be found throughout the pages of publications like *English Journal,* applied now to writing (as well as reading and mathematics) and to high school and college students who had in fact learned to write but were doing so with a degree of error thought unacceptable. These were students — large numbers of them — who were not unlike the students who currently populate our "remedial" courses: students from backgrounds that did not provide optimal environmental and educational opportunities, students who erred as they tried to write the prose they thought the academy required, second-language students. The semantic net of "remedial" was expanding and expanding.

There was much to applaud in this focus on writing. It came from a progressive era desire to help *all* students progress through the educational system. But the theoretical and pedagogical model that was available for "corrective teaching" led educators to view writing problems within a medical-remedial paradigm. Thus they set out to diagnose as precisely as possible the errors (defects) in a student's paper — which they saw as symptomatic of equally isolable defects in the student's linguistic capacity — and devise drills and exercises to remedy them. (One of the 1930s nicknames for remedial sections was "sick sections." During the next decade they would be tagged "hospital sections.") Such corrective teaching was, in the words of H. J. Arnold, "the most logical as well as the most scientific method" ("Diagnostic and Remedial Techniques for College Freshmen," p. 276).

These then are the origins of the term, remediation. And though we have, over the last fifty years, moved very far away from the conditions of its origins and have developed a richer understanding of reading and writing difficulties, the term is still with us. A recent letter from the senate of a local liberal arts college is sitting on my desk. It discusses a "program in remedial writing for... [those] entering freshmen suffering from severe writing handicaps." We seem entrapped by this language, this view of students and learning. Dr. Morgan has long since left his office, but we still talk of writers as suffering from specifiable, locatable defects, deficits, and handicaps that can be localized, circumscribed, and remedied. Such talk reveals an atomistic, mechanistic-medical model of language that few contemporary students of the use of language, from educators to literary theorists, would support. Furthermore, the notion of remediation, carrying with it as it does the etymological wisps and traces of disease, serves to exclude from the academic community those who are so labelled. They sit in scholastic quarantine until their disease can be diagnosed and remedied.

ILLITERACY

In a recent meeting on graduation requirements, a UCLA dean referred to students in remedial English as "the truly illiterate among us." Another administrator, in a memorandum on the potential benefits of increasing the number of composition offerings, concluded sadly that the increase "would not provide any assurance of universal literacy at UCLA." This sort of talk about illiteracy is common. We hear it from college presidents, educational foundations, pop grammarians, and scores of college professors like the one who cried to me after a recent senate meeting, "All I want is a student who can write a simple declarative sentence!" We in the academy like to talk this way.[16] It is dramatic and urgent, and, given the current concerns about illiteracy in the United States, it is topical. The trouble is, it is wrong. Perhaps we can better understand the problems with such labelling if we leave our colleagues momentarily and consider what it is that literacy means.

To be literate means to be acquainted with letters or writings. But exactly how such acquaintance translates into behavior varies a good deal over time and place. During the last century this country's Census Bureau defined as literate anyone who could write his or her name. These days the government requires that one be able to read and write at a sixth-grade level to be *functionally* literate: that is, to be able to meet — to a minimal degree — society's reading and writing demands. Things get a bit more complex if we consider the other meanings "literacy" has acquired. There are some specialized uses of the term, all fairly new: computer literacy, mathematical literacy, visual literacy, and so on. Literacy here refers to an acquaintance with the "letters" or elements of a particular field or domain. And there are also some very general uses of the term. Cultural literacy, another new construction, is hard to define because it is so broad and so variously used, but it most often refers to an acquaintance with the humanistic, scientific, and social scientific achievements of one's dominant culture. Another general use of the term, a more traditional one, refers to the attainment of a liberal education, particularly in belles-lettres. Such literacy, of course, is quite advanced and involves not only an acquaintance with a literary tradition but interpretive sophistication as well.

Going back over these definitions, we can begin by dismissing the newer, specialized uses of "literacy." Computer literacy and other such literacies are usually not the focus of the general outcries we have been considering. How about the fundamental definition as it is currently established? This does not seem applicable either, for though many of the students entering American universities write prose that is grammatically and organizationally flawed, with very few exceptions they can read and write at a sixth-grade level. A sixth-grade proficiency is, of course, absurdly inadequate to do the work of higher education, but the definition still stands. By the most common measure the vast majority of students in college are literate. When academics talk about illiteracy they are saying that our students are "without letters" and cannot "write a simple declarative sentence." And such talk, for most students in most segments of higher education, is inaccurate and misleading.

One could argue that though our students are literate by common definition, a significant percentage of them might not be if we shift to the cultural and belletristic definitions of literacy or to a truly functional-contextual definition: that is, given the sophisticated, specialized reading and writing demands of the university — and the general knowledge they require — then it might be appropriate to talk of a kind of cultural illiteracy among some percentage of the student body. These students lack knowledge of the achievements of a tradition and are not at home with the ways we academics write about them. Perhaps this use of illiteracy is more warranted than the earlier talk about simple declarative sentences, but I would still advise caution. It is my experience that American college students tend to have learned more about western culture through their twelve years of schooling than their papers or pressured classroom responses demonstrate. (And, of course, our immigrant students bring with them a different cultural knowledge that we might not tap at all.) The problem is that the knowledge these students possess is often incomplete and fragmented and is not organized in ways that they can readily use in academic writing situations. But to say this is not to say that their minds are cultural blank slates.

There is another reason to be concerned about inappropriate claims of illiteracy. The term illiteracy comes to us with a good deal of semantic baggage, so that while an appropriately modified use of the term may accurately denote, it can still misrepresent by what it suggests, by the traces it carries from earlier eras. The social historian and anthropologist Shirley Brice Heath points out that from the mid-nineteenth century on, American school-based literacy was identified with "character, intellect, morality, and good taste...literacy skills co-occurred with moral patriotic character."[17] To be literate is to be honorable and intelligent. Tag some group illiterate, and you've gone beyond letters; you've judged their morals and their minds.

Please understand, it is not my purpose here to whitewash the very real limitations a disheartening number of our students bring with them. I dearly wish that more of them were more at home with composing and could write critically better than they do. I wish they enjoyed struggling for graceful written language more than many seem to. I wish they possessed more knowledge about humanities and the sciences so they could write with more authority than they usually do. And I wish to God that more of them read novels and poems for pleasure. But it is simply wrong to leap from these unrequited desires to claims of illiteracy. Reading and writing, as any ethnographic study would show, are woven throughout our students' lives. They write letters; some keep diaries. They read about what interests them, and those interests range from rock and roll to computer graphics to black holes. Reading, for many, is part of religious observation. They carry out a number of reading and writing acts in their jobs and in their interactions with various segments of society. Their college preparatory curriculum in high school, admittedly, to widely varying degrees, is built on reading, and even the most beleaguered schools require some kind of writing. And many of these students read and even write in languages other than English. No, these students are not illiterate, by common definition, and if the more sophisticated definitions apply, they sacrifice their accuracy by all they imply.

Illiteracy is a problematic term. I suppose that academics use it because it is rhetorically effective (evoking the specter of illiteracy to an audience of peers, legislators, or taxpayers can be awfully persuasive) or because it is emotionally satisfying. It gives expression to the frustration and disappointment in teaching students who do not share one's passions. As well, it affirms the faculty's membership in the society of the literate. One reader of this essay suggested to me that academics realize the hyperbole in their illiteracy talk, do not really mean it to be taken, well, literally. Were this invariably true, I would still voice concern over such exaggeration, for, as with any emotionally propelled utterance, it might well be revealing deeply held attitudes and beliefs, perhaps not unlike those discussed by Heath. And, deeply felt or not, such talk in certain political and decision-making settings can dramatically influence the outcomes of deliberation.

The fact remains that cries of illiteracy substitute a fast quip for careful analysis. Definitional accuracy here is important, for if our students are in fact adult illiterates, then a particular, very special curriculum is needed. If they are literate but do not read much for pleasure, or lack general knowledge that is central to academic inquiry, or need to write more than they do and pay more attention to it than they are inclined to, well, then these are very different problems. They bring with them quite different institutional commitments and pedagogies, and they locate the student in a very different place in the social-political makeup of the academy. Determining that place is crucial, for where but in the academy would being "without letters" be so stigmatizing?

THE MYTH OF TRANSIENCE

I have before me a report from the California Postsecondary Education Commission called *Promises to Keep*. It is a comprehensive and fair-minded assessment of remedial instruction in the three segments of California's public college and university system. As all such reports do, *Promises to Keep* presents data on instruction and expenses, discusses the implications of the data, and calls for reform. What makes the report unusual is its inclusion of an historical overview of preparatory instruction in the United States. It acknowledges the fact that such instruction in some guise has always been with us. In spite of its acknowledgment, the report ends on a note of optimism characteristic of similar documents with less historical wisdom. It calls for all three segments of the higher education system to "implement...plans to reduce remediation" within five years and voices the hope that if secondary education can be improved, "within a very few years, the state and its institutions should be rewarded by... lower costs for remediation as the need for remediation declines." This optimism in the face of a disconfirming historical survey attests to the power of what I will call the myth of transience. Despite the accretion of crisis reports, the belief persists in the American university that if we can just do *x* or *y*, the problem will be solved—in five years, ten years, or a generation—and higher education will be able to return to its real work. But entertain with me the possibility that such peaceful reform is a chimera.

Each generation of academicians facing the characteristic American shifts in demographics and accessibility sees the problem anew, laments it in the terms of the era, and optimistically notes its impermanence. No one seems to say that this scenario has gone on for so long that it might not be temporary. That, in fact, there will probably *always* be a significant percentage of students who do not meet some standard. (It was in 1841, not 1985 that the president of Brown complained, "Students frequently enter college almost wholly unacquainted with English grammar..." [Frederick Rudolph, *Curriculum: A History of the American Undergraduate Course of Study* (San Francisco: Jossey-Bass, 1978), p. 88].) The American higher educational system is constantly under pressure to expand, to redefine its boundaries, admitting, in turn, the sons of the middle class, and later the daughters, and then the American poor, the immigrant poor, veterans, the racially segregated, the disenfranchised. Because of the social and educational conditions these groups experienced, their preparation for college will, of course, be varied. Add to this the fact that disciplines change and society's needs change, and the ways society determines what it means to be educated change.

All this works itself rather slowly into the pre-collegiate curriculum. Thus there will always be a percentage of students who will be tagged substandard. And though many insist that this continued opening of doors will sacrifice excellence in the name of democracy, there are too many economic, political, and ethical drives in American culture to restrict higher education to a select minority. (And, make no mistake, the history of the American college and university from the early nineteenth century on could also be read as a history of changes in admissions, curriculum, and public image in order to keep enrollments high and institutions solvent.[18] The research institution as we know it is made possible by robust undergraduate enrollments.) Like it or not, the story of American education has been and will in all likelihood continue to be a story of increasing access. University of Nashville President Philip Lindsley's 1825 call echoes back and forth across our history: "The farmer, the mechanic, the manufacturer, the merchant, the sailor, the soldier...must be educated" (Frederick Rudolph, *The American College and University: A History* [New York: Vintage, 1962] p. 117).

Why begrudge academics their transience myth? After all, each generation's problems are new to those who face them, and people faced with a problem need some sense that they can solve it. Fair enough. But it seems to me that this myth brings with it a powerful liability. It blinds faculty members to historical reality and to the dynamic and fluid nature of the educational system that employs them. Like any golden age or utopian myth, the myth of transience assures its believers that the past was better or that the future will be.[19] The turmoil they are currently in will pass. The source of the problem is elsewhere; thus it can be ignored or temporarily dealt with until the tutors or academies or grammar schools or high schools or families make the changes they must make. The myth, then, serves to keep certain fundamental recognitions and thus certain fundamental changes at bay. It is ultimately a conservative gesture, a way of preserving administrative and curricular status quo.

And the myth plays itself out against complex social-political dynamics. One force in these dynamics is the ongoing struggle to establish admissions requirements that would protect the college curriculum, that would, in fact, define its difference from the high school course of study. Another is the related struggle to influence, even determine, the nature of the high school curriculum, "academize" it, shape it to the needs of the college (and the converse struggle of the high school to declare its multiplicity of purposes, college preparation being only one of its mandates). Yet another is the tension between the undergraduate, general education function of the university vs. its graduate, research function. To challenge the myth is to vibrate these complex dynamics; thus it is that it is so hard to dispel. But I would suggest that it must be challenged, for though some temporary "remedial" measures are excellent and generously funded, the presence of the myth does not allow them to be thought through in terms of the whole curriculum and does not allow the information they reveal to reciprocally influence the curriculum. Basic modifications in educational philosophy, institutional purpose, and professional training are rarely considered. They do not need to be if the problem is temporary. The myth allows the final exclusionary gesture: The problem is not ours in any fundamental way; we can embrace it if we must, but with surgical gloves on our hands.

There may be little anyone can do to change the fundamental tension in the American university between the general educational mission and the research mission, or to remove the stigma attached to application. But there is something those of us involved in writing can do about the language that has formed the field on which institutional discussions of writing and its teaching take place.

We can begin by affirming a rich model of written language development and production. The model we advance must honor the cognitive and emotional and situational dimensions of language, be psycholinguistic as well as literary and rhetorical in its focus, and aid us in understanding what we can observe as well as what we can only infer. When discussions and debates reveal a more reductive model of language, we must call time out and reestablish the terms of the argument. But we must also rigorously examine our own teaching and see what model of language lies beneath it. What linguistic assumptions are cued when we face freshman writers? Are they compatible with the assumptions that are cued when we think about our own writing or the writing of those we read for pleasure? Do we too operate with the bifurcated mind that for too long characterized the teaching of "remedial" students and that is still reflected in the language of our institutions?

Remediation. It is time to abandon this troublesome metaphor. To do so will not blind us to the fact that many entering students are not adequately prepared to take on the demands of university work. In fact, it will help us perceive these young people and the work they do in ways that foster appropriate notions about language development and use, that establish a framework for more rigorous and comprehensive analysis of their difficulties, and that do not perpetuate the raree [sic] show of allowing them entrance to the academy while, in various symbolic ways, denying them full participation.

Mina Shaughnessy got us to see that even the most error-ridden prose arises from the confrontation of inexperienced student writers with the complex linguistic and rhetorical expectations of the academy. She reminded us that to properly teach writing to such students is to understand "the intelligence of their mistakes."[20] She told us to interpret errors rather than circle them, and to guide these students, gradually and with wisdom, to be more capable participants within the world of these conventions. If we fully appreciate her message, we see how inadequate and limiting the remedial model is. Instead we need to define our work as transitional or as initiatory, orienting, or socializing to what David Bartholomae and Patricia Bizzell call the academic discourse community.[21] This redefinition is not just semantic sleight-of-hand. If truly adopted, it would require us to reject a medical deficit model of language, to acknowledge the rightful place of all freshmen in the academy, and once and for all to replace loose talk about illiteracy with more precise and pedagogically fruitful analysis. We would move from a mechanistic focus on error toward a demanding curriculum that encourages the full play of language activity and that opens out onto the academic community rather than sequestering students from it.

A much harder issue to address is the common designation of writing as a skill. We might begin by considering more fitting terms. Jerome Bruner's "enabling discipline" comes to mind. It does not separate skill from discipline and implies something more than a "tool subject" in that to enable means to make possible. But such changes in diction might be little more than cosmetic.

If the skills designation proves to be resistant to change, then we must insist that writing is a very unique skill, not really a tool but an ability fundamental to academic inquiry, an ability whose development is not fixed but ongoing. If it is possible to go beyond the skills model, we could see a contesting of the fundamental academic distinction between integrated bodies of knowledge and skills and techniques. While that distinction makes sense in many cases, it may blur where writing is concerned. Do students really *know* history when they learn a "body" of facts, even theories, or when they act like historians, thinking in certain ways with those facts and theories? Most historians would say the latter. And the academic historian (vs. the chronicler or the balladeer) conducts inquiry through writing; it is not just an implement but is part of the very way of doing history.

It is in this context that we should ponder the myth of transience. The myth's liability is that it limits the faculty's ability to consider the writing problems of their students in dynamic and historical terms. Each academic generation considers standards and assesses the preparation of its students but seems to do this in ways that do not call the nature of the curriculum of the time into question. The problem ultimately lies outside the academy. But might not these difficulties with writing suggest the need for possible far-ranging changes within the curriculum as well, changes that *are* the proper concern of the university? One of the things I think the myth of transience currently does is to keep faculty from seeing the multiple possibilities that exist for incorporating writing throughout their courses of study. Profound reform could occur in the much-criticized lower-division curriculum if writing were not seen as only a technique and the teaching of it as by and large a remedial enterprise.

The transmission of a discipline, especially on the lower-division level, has become very much a matter of comprehending information, committing it to memory, recalling it, and displaying it in various kinds of "objective" or short-answer tests. When essay exams are required, the prose all too often becomes nothing more than a net in which the catch of individual bits of knowledge lie. Graders pick through the essay and tally up the presence of key phrases. Such activity trivializes a discipline; it reduces its methodology, grounds it in a limited theory of knowledge, and encourages students to operate with a restricted range of their cognitive abilities. Writing, on the other hand, assumes a richer epistemology and demands fuller participation. It requires a complete, active, struggling engagement with the facts and principles of a discipline, an encounter with the discipline's texts and the incorporation of them into one's own work, the framing of one's knowledge within the myriad conventions that help define a discipline, the persuading of other investigators that one's knowledge is legitimate. So to consider the relationship between writing and disciplinary inquiry may help us decide what is central to a discipline and how best to teach it. The university's research and educational missions would intersect.

Such reform will be difficult. True, there is growing interest in writing adjuncts and discipline-specific writing courses, and those involved in writing-across-the-curriculum are continually encouraging faculty members to evaluate the place of writing in their individual curricula. But wide-ranging change will occur only if the academy redefines writing for itself, changes the terms of the argument, sees instruction in writing as one of its central concerns.

Academic senates often defend the labelling of a writing course as remedial by saying that they are defending the integrity of the baccalaureate, and they are sending a message to the high schools. The schools, of course, are so beleaguered that they can barely hear those few units ping into the bucket. Consider, though, the message that would be sent to the schools and to the society at large if the university embraced — not just financially but conceptually — the teaching of writing: if we gave it full status, championed its rich relationship with inquiry, insisted on the importance of craft and grace, incorporated it into the heart of our curriculum. What an extraordinary message that would be. It would affect the teaching of writing as no other message could.

Author's note: I wish to thank Arthur Applebee, Robert Connors, Carol Hartzog, and William Schaefer for reading and generously commenting on an earlier version of this essay. Connors and Hartzog also helped me revise that version. Bill Richey provided research assistance of remarkably high caliber, and Tom Bean, Kenyon Chan, Patricia Donahue, Jack Kolb, and Bob Schwegler offered advice and encouragement. Finally, a word of thanks to Richard Lanham for urging me to think of our current problem in broader contexts.

NOTES

[1] Quoted in Lawrence A. Cremin, *The Transformation of the School: Progressivism in American Education* (New York: Alfred A. Knopf, 1961), p. 185.

[2] Arthur N. Applebee, *Tradition and Reform in the Teaching of English: A History* (Urbana. Ill.: National Council of Teachers of English, 1974), pp. 93–94.

[3] P. C. Perrin, "The Remedial Racket," *English Journal,* 22 (1993), 383.

[4] From Cubberley's introduction to Albert R. Lang, *Modern Methods in Written Examinations* (Boston: Houghton Mifflin, 1930), p. vii.

[5] "Background Deficiencies," *Journal of Higher Education*, 3 (1932), 371.

[6] "Remedial Methods in English Composition," *English Journal*, 22 (1933), 749–75.

[7] "Freshmen Needs in Written English," *English Journal*, 19 (1930), 706.

[8] I would mislead if I did not point out that there were cautionary voices being raised all along, though until the late 1930s they were very much in the minority. For two early appraisals, see R. L. Lyman, *Summary of Investigations Relating to Grammar, Language, 2nd Composition* (Chicago: University of Chicago Press, 1924), and especially P. C. Perrin, "The Remedial Racket," *English Journal*, 22 (1933), 382–388.

[9] Two quotations. The first offers the sort of humanist battle cry that often accompanies reductive drill, and the second documents the results of such an approach. Both from NCTE publications.

"I think...that the chief objective of freshman English (at least for the first semester and low or middle — but not high — sections) should be ceaseless, brutal drill on mechanics with exercises and themes. Never mind imagination, the soul, literature, for at least one semester, but pray for literacy and fight for it" (A University of Nebraska professor quoted with approval in Oscar James Campbell, *The Teaching of College English* [New York: Appleton Century, 1934], pp. 36–37).

"Members of the Task Force saw in many classes extensive work in traditional schoolroom grammar and traditional formal English usage. They commonly found students with poor reading skills being taught the difference between *shall* and *will* or pupils with serious difficulties in speech diagramming sentences. Interestingly, observations by the Task Force reveal far more extensive teaching of traditional grammar in this study of language programs for the disadvantaged than observers saw in the National Study of High School English Programs, a survey of comprehensive high schools known to be achieving important results in English with college-bound students able to comprehend the abstractions of such grammar" (Richard Corbin and Muriel Crosby, *Language Programs for the Disadvantaged* [Urbana Ill.: NCTE, 1965], pp. 121–122).

[10] In 1894, for example, over 40% of entering freshmen came from the preparatory divisions of the institutions that enrolled them. And as late as 1915 — a time when the quantity and quality of secondary schools had risen sufficiently to make preparatory divisions less necessary — 350 American colleges still maintained their programs. See John S. Brubacher and Willis Rudy, *Higher Education in Transition: A History of American Colleges and Universities, 1636–1976*, 3rd ed. (New York: Harper and Row, 1976), pp. 241 ff., and Arthur Levine, *Handbook on Undergraduate Curriculum* (San Francisco: Jossey-Bass, 1981), pp. 54 ff.

[11] Several writers point to a study habits course initiated at Wellesley in 1894 as the first modern remedial course in higher education (K. Patricia Cross, *Accent on Learning* [San Francisco: Jossey-Bass, 1979], and Arthur Levine, *Handbook on Undergraduate Curriculum*). In fact, the word "remedial" did not appear in the course's title and the course was different in kind from the courses actually designated "remedial" that would emerge in the 1920s and 30s. (See Cross, pp. 24–25, for a brief discussion of early study skills courses.) The first use of the term "remedial" in the context I am discussing was most likely in a 1916 article on the use of reading tests to plan "remedial work" (Nila Banton Smith, *American Reading Instruction* [Newark, Delaware: International Reading Association, 1965]. p. 191). The first elementary and secondary level remedial courses in reading were offered in the early 1920s; remedial courses in college would not appear until the late 20s.

[12] *Letter, Word, and Mind-Blindness* (London: Lewis, 1902); *Congenital Word Blindness* (London: Lewis, 1917).

[13] "The 'Sight Reading' Method of Teaching Reading, as a Source of Reading Disability," *Journal of Educational Psychology*, 20 (1929), 135–143.

[14] There were, of course, some theorists and practitioners who questioned medical-physiological models, Arthur Gates of Columbia Teacher's College foremost among them. But even those who questioned such models — with the exception of Gates — tended to retain medical language.

[15] There is another layer to this terminological and conceptual confusion. At the same time that remediation language was being used ever more broadly by some educators, it maintained its strictly medical usage in other educational fields. For example, Annie Dolman Inskeep has only one discussion of "remedial work" in her book *Teaching Dull and Retarded Children* (New York: Macmillan, 1926), and that discussion has to do with treatment for children needing health care: "Children who have poor teeth, who do not hear well, or who hold a book when reading nearer than eight inches to the eyes or further away than sixteen.... Nervous children, those showing continuous fatigue symptoms, those under weight, and those who are making no apparent bodily growth" (p. 271).

[16] For a sometimes humorous but more often distressing catalogue of such outcries, see Harvey A. Daniels, *Famous Last Words* (Carbondale: Southern Illinois University Press, 1983), especially pp. 31–58.

[17] "Toward an Ethnohistory of Writing in American Education," in Marcia Farr Whiteman, ed., *Writing: The Nature, Development, and Teaching of Written Communication,* Vol. 1 (Hillsdale, N.J.: Erlbaum, 1981), 35–36.

[18] Of turn-of-the-century institutions, Laurence Veysey writes: "Everywhere the size of enrollments was closely tied to admission standards. In order to assure themselves of enough students to make a notable "splash," new institutions often opened with a welcome to nearly all corners, no matter how ill prepared; this occurred at Cornell, Stanford, and (to a lesser degree) at Chicago" (*The Emergence of the American University,* p. 357).

[19] An appropriate observation here comes from Daniel P. and Lauren B. Resnick's critical survey of reading instruction and standards of literacy: "there is little to go back to in terms of pedagogical method, curriculum, or school organization. The old tried and true approaches, which nostalgia prompts us to believe might solve current problems, were designed neither to achieve the literacy standard sought today nor to assure successful literacy for everyone... there is no simple past to which we can return" ("The Nature of Literacy: An Historical Exploration," *Harvard Educational Review,* 47 [1977], 385).

[20] *Errors and Expectations* (New York: Oxford University Press, 1977), p. 11.

[21] David Bartholomae, "Inventing the University," in Mike Rose, ed., *When a Writer Can't Write: Studies in Writer's Block and Other Composing Process Problems* (New York: Guilford, 1985); Patricia Bizzell, "College Composition: Initiation into the Academic Discourse Community," *Curriculum Inquiry,* 12 (1982), 191–207.

Beverly J. Moss and Keith Walters

Rethinking Diversity: Axes of Difference in the Writing Classroom

Few issues on campus in recent memory have sparked the debate, argument, and some would contend uncivil behavior by students and faculty that have accompanied the topic of diversity. From our perspective, the topic represents the latest attempt to deal with long-standing issues — many would say problems — in the academy and the larger society. Yet given the social, economic, and political contexts in which the topic has been raised, it represents far more than a trendy relabeling of another problem that simply will not go away. As citizens and educators, we are faced with the fact that large numbers of students — mostly African Americans, Hispanics, Native Americans, Appalachians, and other poor Americans of European roots — are not succeeding in our schools and universities or in the workplace. At the same time, these institutions have begun to confront a major demographic shift in the populations they serve, the ultimate result of which is that no single ethnic group will constitute the majority of Americans: instead, the majority will soon be composed of various groups of ethnic minorities that have traditionally been underrepresented in these same institutions.

Although many would reduce discussions of diversity to questions of the changing demographics of this society and issues of ethnicity and social class, we contend that a serious analysis of diversity in American writing classrooms encompasses far more — especially in higher education.

DIVERSITY AND HOW WE TEACH

One can approach teaching from many perspectives. One can see it as transferring information, coaching (or something akin to it), or assuming the role of master craftsperson in a process of apprenticeship. Similarly, but perhaps less obviously, one can think about teaching as a speech event, an activity or aspects of an activity "directly governed by rules or norms for the use of speech" (Hymes 52). From this sociolinguistic perspective, teaching involves participants — minimally, a teacher and students, although assistants, observers, or visitors may be part of the event. Likewise, it involves rules for speaking or remaining silent as well as norms for evaluating both linguistic and nonlinguistic behavior.

This article has been excerpted with the kind permission of the authors. It was originally published in *Theory and Practice in the Teaching of Writing: Rethinking the Discipline,* ed. Lee Odell (Carbondale: Southern Illinois UP, 1993).

As is usually the case with social phenomena, the rules and norms usually go unstated: they are assumed to be shared and are noted only when violated.

From this perspective, the focus of teaching, even the teaching of writing, becomes spoken language and the ways in which spoken language is used for a host of purposes. Thus, a discussion of how we teach focuses our attention on the very complex, unfolding world of the pedagogical conversation,[1] whether in the classroom, the office, the hallway, or some other setting, in which we can never be sure that our norms or motives for interacting will automatically be shared by our interlocutors. Increasingly, we are learning to ask questions about misunderstandings between teachers and students and coming to realize that many axes of difference can interfere with what at one level seems like such a simple task: helping students develop the skills they already have in order to progress as writers and thinkers.

Last year, Keith had a problem involving a Pakistani-American student who clearly had different rules from those that Keith expected for asking questions of the teacher. For instance, in class discussion, the student sometimes asked what he believed to be an information question and received what Keith believed to be an adequate reply. Then, when asking a follow-up question, the student began by restating the assumption that led to the original question as if to reconstruct his position and perhaps to rehearse all of the steps of argumentation in whatever was being discussed. Perceiving that the student had ignored (or at least failed to acknowledge) the answer that he had just given the student, Keith believed that his authority was being baldly challenged. From discussions with the student, Keith knew that the student perceived his own behavior to be neither overly insistent nor rude, yet given Keith's own assumptions about questions and how they should be asked in the classroom, Keith perceived the behavior to be rude and even belligerent. Did the student have a problem because Keith and some of his other professors perceived that he challenged them to an excessive degree in class? Did Keith have a problem because his assumptions were not shared by all of his students? Or did the student and his teachers share a problem because they seem to be operating with different assumptions about the rules and norms for the use of speech in classroom settings? What are the consequences of assigning the "problem" to the student or teacher alone, or to the student and his teachers?

Similar questions arise for Beverly and other teachers with respect to issues of age difference in the classroom. Although many teachers lament that they and their eighteen- and nineteen-year-old undergraduates inhabit different worlds, we rarely examine seriously the role of age differences as a source of misunderstanding in the classroom. Beverly, because she looks as young as some of her undergraduates and is younger than many of her graduate students, finds herself in the position of dealing with possible conflicts resulting from age differences. She frequently finds herself questioning how she deals with older students who, Beverly feels, at times seem to challenge her authority in the classroom. Yet these older students appear to think they treat her the way they treat all of their professors. Are there assumptions that members of our culture make about cross-age face-to-face interaction that might lead to misunderstandings between a younger professor and an older student or an older professor and a younger student? The sorts of misunderstandings related to assumptions about language and language use extend far beyond students' asking questions in what teachers might feel are inappropriate ways or differences of age between teacher and student.

For example, Sarah Michaels and Susan Philips have examined the nature of misunderstandings that can occur between teachers and students from different cultural and linguistic backgrounds. In the first-grade class that she studied, Michaels found that the black children were more likely to be interrupted and "corrected" by the white teacher than were the white children during sharing-time (sometimes referred to as "Show and Tell," when first graders shared stories with their classmates while all sat on a rug at the front of the classroom). An analysis of the discourse patterns used by black and white children during sharing-time revealed that the white children's discourse patterns, labeled topic-centered, more closely matched those of the white teacher and more closely resembled an academic notion of a narrative than did those of the black children. Yet the black children's discourse patterns — moving from one event to another and assuming that context or listeners' knowledge would establish connections among these events — were the norm in their home communities, where to be explicit about the links between episodes of a narrative is to insult the listener by assuming that he or she is not intelligent or interested enough to deduce the connections. The well-meaning teacher assumed that the black children did not know how to tell stories properly and sought to "help" them by interjecting questions as they talked. At least some of the black students, however, perceived these questions as frustrating interruptions. As Michaels clearly demonstrates, sharing-time is not just about telling stories — the characterization that both teacher and students might initially offer; rather, it is really about a student's co-narrating a story with the teacher, who, through questions and comments, creates a scaffolding of sorts that the student, through responses, fills in. When teacher and student share this schema for storytelling and for teacher/student interaction, the stories are acceptable to the teacher — and by extension the academy. But when teacher and student begin with different notions of what a good story is or how one co-narrates a story with a social superior, the mismatch may well have grave repercussions for not only sharing-time but later instruction and achievement in speaking and writing as well.[2]

Working in the Warm Springs Indian community, Philips found that the cultural expectations brought into the classroom by Anglos were very often in direct conflict with rules for communicative behavior native to the reservation community. Like others who have worked in Native American communities, she found that the preferred response patterns of the Indian children did not match the patterns of white, middle-class students and were often unacceptable to the non-Indian teachers. Because, for example, the Native American children would not respond to direct questions and sought to avoid going to the blackboard, the Anglo teachers perceived the students to be uncooperative or unintelligent. As Philips pointed out, what the teachers did not understand (and therefore could not appreciate) was that in this Native American community, as in many, direct questions are rarely posed because the person who tries to answer but answers incorrectly loses face. Similarly, individuals in this community are rarely forced into public situations—like going to the blackboard—in which they could fail before their peers and superiors or in which they might be forced as individuals to excel, thereby distinguishing themselves from other members of the group. Rather than seeking to demonstrate individual competence or mastery—so much a goal of mainstream schooling—these students were much happier working in groups with no appointed leader or "helping" the teacher solve a problem. Thus, Philips concluded that "in the structuring of attention, and in the regulation of talk, there are differences between Anglos and Warm Springs Indians that result in miscommunication between students and teacher in the Indian classrooms" (127). Certainly, research such as that of Michaels and Philips has encouraged us to see that no methodology or pedagogy is culture free or culture neutral.

Traditionally, teachers at the college and university level have favored the lecture method as a teaching tool, and those who teach large classes may feel they need to rely on a classroom format that involves the teacher holding the floor and speaking all (or nearly all) of the time. In such cases, the goal is transmitting a body of knowledge organized and presented (some might say broadcast) by the teacher. Writing teachers, however, have long held such methods in disdain, arguing instead for small-group activities or discussions that students participated in or led. Of course, organizing classroom time so that students talk to the teacher or to one another represents a shift in goal: the focus is no longer the monologic transmission of knowledge but creating (or, more accurately, cocreating) it through dialogue or polylogue. These methods are not without controversy. They are not value free; rather, they entail assumptions about using spoken and written language that may not be shared by everyone who enters the classroom door.

As demonstrated in the following sections, "Diversity and What We Teach" and "Diversity and Whom We Teach," teachers of writing, like all educators, find themselves in a fix. Unhappy with the lecture method that informed most of our own educations and all too acquainted with its limitations for many students, we seek alternative methods of teaching and interacting with students. Yet we understand little about the ways in which various teaching techniques or methods constrain or shape students' possibilities for displaying knowledge (cf. Freeman; Janda; Sperling; and Walters "'It's Like Playing Password'"). In his research on classroom interaction, Hugh Mehan has pointed out that the competent student must not only possess the requisite information, but he or she must also display it in an acceptable fashion. With respect to diversity, it is this issue of display, the complex problem of finding acceptable packaging, that we believe to be especially crucial. In a very important sense, each display of knowledge is a possible locus—a point in real time and social space—at which diversity may play itself out before our eyes.

Our goal here is to point out that if we are committed to broadening our repertoire of pedagogical strategies and widening our methods of sampling and evaluating student ability, knowledge, and achievement, we can begin in our own classrooms, usually without waiting for administratively sanctioned curricular change.

From our perspective, how we teach — our assumptions as well as our actions — reflect the extent to which we accommodate diversity, whether we use it as an integral part of learning, merely acknowledge it, or, perhaps, at worst, teach to an ideal student who may bear little resemblance to those who actually occupy the seats in our classrooms.

DIVERSITY AND WHAT WE TEACH

Teachers of writing at the college and university level are teachers of language and of advanced literacy skills. In this section, we deal with a basic part of what we teach, language and, more particularly, Standard English as it relates to other varieties of English. In a very real sense, our discussion of what we teach spills over into the next section, "Diversity and Whom We Teach," in which we consider the related but broader topic of home literacies and language use as they sometimes contrast with what Ron Scollon and Suzanne Scollon term the *essayist literacy* of the academy. Although the topics of language and literacy are closely related, we have chosen to separate them in order to highlight the constellations of issues surrounding each. As noted in the introduction, we see the topic of language as a very important one because our assumptions about language ultimately influence nearly everything we say and do. Certainly, nearly all of the spoken or written language that is produced in the context of writing classes is in some sense language about how to use written language effectively. Equally important, because writing teachers insist that students use Standard English, it is important for teachers to have as rich as possible an understanding of that variety and the nature of standard languages in general.

If asked to define what Standard English is, most students and many teachers would reply that it is "good grammar" or "correct language that doesn't break any rules" — characterizations they learned from teachers and textbooks. There would be no comment about where this variety of language came from, who makes up the rules, or where we might find them.

In fact, defining what the standard is and is not constitutes a very complex task because we are dealing with several notions of the standard at once. In one instance, we might think of the *descriptive standard,* the variety of American English that corresponds to the definitions of standard languages that most sociolinguists and language planners might give. Such definitions usually note that a standard variety is the one used by people with social, political, and economic power and influence — "a dialect with an army and a navy," as some put it. It is also the variety taught to native and nonnative speakers of the language and used in the various media in its spoken and written forms.

Such a descriptive standard is much broader than the *prescriptive standard,* which corresponds to the written variety the rules of which are inscribed in handbooks of the sort that are used in writing classes. Most of the marks that are made in the margins of student papers — frag, dm, split inf., diction — represent efforts to get students to respect, use, and internalize the rules of this prescriptive standard. Of course, handbooks differ, and pronouncements about usage change. Most important, careful readers frequently find "violations" of these prescriptive rules in the speaking of the socially, politically, and economically powerful and in such written texts as *The New York Times,* textbooks, and professional journals. In other words, teachers of writing ultimately must acknowledge that these speakers and writers do not seem to be following the sets of rules inscribed in the handbooks used in our classes. Additionally, those of us with prescriptivist tendencies should acknowledge that many of the students who currently suffer our marginal comments are soon likely to wield far more economic, social, or political power than we ever will; consequently, their speaking and writing will help determine the descriptive standard for the coming generation. In earlier periods when our profession sought to acknowledge and deal with linguistic diversity, considerations such as these were frequently marshaled by those trained in linguistics in order to argue against the existence of something called Standard English. For example, these sorts of arguments favored prominently in the discussions and debates surrounding the "Students' Right to Their Own Language" statement issued in 1976.

In addition to the descriptive and prescriptive standards, we also find what we might term the *perceived standard,* that is, what speakers and writers believe Standard English to be. Here, we find such myths as "Never start a sentence with *and,*" and "Never end a sentence with a preposition," as well as patterns of conscious analysis that lead writers to mispunctuate dependent clauses beginning with "whereas" or "which is to say" as if they were sentences. Thus, the perceived standard is what language users, whether students, graduates, or teachers, ultimately invoke when evaluating their own language and that of others or when called upon to justify their judgments or behaviors. And for many speakers, this perceived standard contains inconsistencies or logical contradictions.

Because a component of the *perceived standard* involves judging the behavior of the self and the other, whatever is different from one's own behavior becomes part of that "everything else." There, unsavory things like regional, social, and ethnic dialects exist along with all of the "ill's," "un's," and "non's," of the society: illiteracy, illegitimacy, unemployment, underachievement, and nonstandard language. In these cases, "different from the standard" really means "inferior" because what is being judged is not simply language but a host of personal and cultural attributes that members of the society associate with varieties of language and, by extension, their users. It is not acceptable for most Americans to label someone inferior because of his or her skin color; far more acceptable, however, is the sort of claim made by a white American on *The Oprah Winfrey Show* during a discussion of Black English when he asserted that the use of "good English," which he assumed he spoke and wrote, was a question of self-discipline. In his eyes, speakers of Black English simply lacked self-discipline—because their speech did not resemble his. This speaker, like most, clearly associates the use of what he perceives to be Standard English with particular moral virtues. His comments remind us that the issues involved in discussions of standard language extend far beyond the question of the nature of Standard English as a linguistic variety.

As our discussion has demonstrated, there is variability even within what is usually termed *Standard English.* More specifically, it in no way represents the fact that educated Americans are far more tolerant of a speaker's maintaining his or her native regional accent while speaking Standard English than they are of his or her retaining grammatical features of a regional dialect when speaking or writing. It is fine to sound like a Southerner, a New Yorker, or a Californian, as long as one sounds educated—that is, as long as one's "grammar" stays within the range acceptable to speakers of Standard English. Equally important, the figure does not capture other observations that any speaker of English who has lived in this country for any length of time realizes: as one goes up the social ladder, one finds less variation among dialects. In other words, it is from lesser-educated individuals that one most frequently hears forms labeled nonstandard. In contrast, the more that people become educated, the more likely they are to have learned to bleach their speech and writing of markers that reveal their native regional and social dialect, especially if these dialects are considered nonstandard by society at large. Such a common-sense observation is, of course, an admission that access to Standard English is related to issues of social class and social mobility.

Speakers of stigmatized regional and social dialects have, literally, a longer way to go as they move from their native variety to Standard English. Of course, the same is true for speakers of Black English. Their ability to style-shift from African-American English toward Standard English will depend on their life circumstances. Speakers who live, work, and relax in communities where African-American English is the most commonly used variety of American English will probably be most comfortable using that variety. On the other hand, African Americans who live, work, and relax in communities where Black English is rarely or never used may not even be able to speak Black English. Their native variety of American English may be one that is close to the regional and social variety of the community in which they live, work, and relax. Most African Americans will find themselves somewhere between these two extremes.

Interestingly, a number of African-American students at the University of Texas at Austin who come from racially integrated, middle-class communities and who attended public high schools in Texas report that they are exposed to and use Black English more now that they are at UT than at any previous time in their lives. Because African Americans constitute a very small minority at UT and because they perceive that the university is hostile to their presence, they turn to other African Americans for support and hence spend a great deal of time in the presence of African Americans from a variety of social backgrounds.

Thus, some African-American students who grew up not speaking Black English make a conscious effort to acquire and use it while at UT in order to be accepted as members of the African-American community there. These are the kinds of forces that are likely to influence the linguistic behavior of speakers of highly stigmatized social or regional dialects across their lifetimes.

Writing teachers talk about language and its use a great deal of the time, and most of their comments on student papers represent efforts to persuade students to develop certain kinds of strategies for using written language in particular ways in particular contexts. All of this talk about writing is based on some sort of model — however implicit, however inchoate, however unexamined — of language and the relationship of the standard to other varieties. And the less accurate and less rich the model of language that informs a teacher's comments and commentary, the more likely his or her students will not reach everyone's goal: mastery of Standard English for use when it is appropriate. Talking about "correct" or "incorrect," for example, assumes one model of language; talking about "appropriate" and "inappropriate" in this or that context assumes a very different model. Over the years, Keith has discovered in his own teaching that replacing a model of language based on correctness with one based on appropriateness is a very challenging task because it forces him to think constantly about *why* a particular usage should be labeled inappropriate or appropriate in a given context. Marking things "wrong" is much simpler than thinking seriously about context and appropriateness, but the consequences of the former view seem to be overwhelmingly negative. Certainly if writing teachers talked about language as if diversity were an integral part of it — if we admitted that the standard language itself continues to change and that the notion of standard is itself problematic — we would have to move away from the view of language correctness and spend more time examining our own linguistic assumptions and educating ourselves about the actual nature of language.

In this section, we have tried to outline productive ways of thinking about one of the major things that we teach — language and specifically the standard language. Rejecting the society's ideology about the nature of Standard English, we have provided alternative ways of representing the relationship between the standard variety and other varieties of English. For us, a view of language and human behavior — one that attempts to describe what speakers and writers do as they use language strategically to create and maintain individual and group identities — is far more likely to help us value and appreciate linguistic diversity in its many forms than a view of language that *ab initio* labels some varieties and users of language deficient.

DIVERSITY AND WHOM WE TEACH

At least since the time of Aristotle, teachers of rhetoric have taught their students that one persuades different audiences in different ways and that the successful rhetor knows a great deal about the characteristics of his or her listeners. As our student audience becomes increasingly diverse, we as writing teachers need to consider the possible axes of difference we may encounter in our classroom and our potential responses to these kinds of difference. In this section, we look at several axes of difference that our experience has led us to conclude influence the ways various segments of our increasingly diverse student population respond in the writing class. These variables include language and literacy practices of the home community, first language, age, sex or gender, and sexual orientation.

Home Literacies and Language Use

Although thinkers like E. D. Hirsch, Jr., argue for a monolithic approach to issues of literacy, language, and knowledge (cf. Walters, "Whose Culture?"), we find such an approach seriously lacking when we consider the challenges we face in the classroom or the challenges our students face during their lives as they become part of an increasingly interdependent world economy. At the heart of this monolithic approach is the notion that only one kind of literacy — academic literacy — exists. In contrast, we argue that academic literacy is but one of many literacies, albeit a powerful and important one. Associated with this literacy (as with all others) is a particular belief system, which includes beliefs about how language — oral and written — should be learned and used. Even though the notion of academic literacy has been most closely associated with school literacy, it has also become the standard for judging literacy and language practices outside of school.

It is easy to see why schools in this culture and around the world succeed admirably in the task of educating children from middle-class backgrounds: they arrive at school bringing with them the very assumptions about using language and literacy that the school seeks to inculcate and most frequently rewards. The greater challenge — and one we have yet to meet in this country — involves those who arrive with expectations that are no less rational, no less systematic, no less grounded in social practice, but that differ from those assumed by the school. Thus far, however, schools have had little room for difference, preferring a pedagogy that has often guaranteed near exclusion for many of the very groups most in need of assistance.

One of the many ways to help us rethink our traditional ways of thinking about language and literacy is to consider work in such fields as anthropology, sociolinguistics, and education about linguistically and culturally diverse populations. Although a quick survey of a few of these studies provides teachers with information about the linguistic and cultural backgrounds of particular groups of students, it more importantly suggests the kinds of issues teachers might begin considering when thinking about issues of diversity in the classroom.

Probably the best-known research in home literacy and language practices is Shirley Brice Heath's work, which has challenged many teachers to ask questions about the literacy and language practices in the home communities of their students. From Heath, we learn about functions and uses of literacy in three Piedmont Carolina communities in the late 1970s. Heath concludes that

> the patterns of language use of the children of Roadville [a blue-collar white community] and Trackton [a blue-collar black community] before they go to school stand in sharp contrast to each other and to those of the youngsters from [middle-class] townspeople families. Though parents in all three communities want to "get ahead," their constructions of the social activities the children must engage in for access to language, oral or written, vary greatly. The sequence of habits Trackton children develop in learning language, telling stories, making metaphors, and seeing patterns across items and events do not fit the developmental patterns of either linguistic or cognitive growth reported in the research literature on mainstream children. Roadville children, on the other hand, seem to have developed many of the cognitive and linguistic patterns equated with readiness for school, yet they seem not to move outward from these basics to the integrative types of skills necessary for sustained academic success. (343)

Like Heath, Scollon and Scollon also point out differences between the practices of a non-mainstream group, the Athabaskan, a group of Alaskan Native Americans, and mainstream practices. For example, as they grow up, Athabaskan children are taught not to take the initiative in speaking to a person they do not know. Scollon and Scollon note that "where the relationship of the communicants is unknown [in face-to-face interaction]...the Athabaskan prefer silence" (*Narrative* 53). Yet, in mainstream schools, these students are expected to write to an unknown audience on a consistent basis, a practice that conflicts with the norms governing interaction in their home community. Using examples like this one, Scollon and Scollon conclude that "where the interethnic communication patterns produce social conflict between [Athabaskan and non-Athabaskan] speakers, these same patterns produce internal conflict for an Athabaskan writer." Continuing, they contend that "it is this internal conflict that explains much of the problem of native literacy programs as well as problems with English literacy in the public school systems of Alaska and Canada" (53). The examples from the work of Heath and that of Scollon and Scollon should remind us of the potential for conflict between home community patterns for using language and literacy and those of the school. Although some students may be relatively successful in moving between the two, that success often comes at a great price as these students seek to create identities that will allow them to belong to the communities of both home and school. Traditionally, however, school has set up a false dichotomy, forcing non-mainstream students to choose one — the "correctness" of the school and its practices — or the other — the "ignorance" of native and natural ways of using language and literacy (Walters, "Whose Culture").

Among the barriers we as teachers face in understanding, learning about, and then building upon the growing diversity in our classrooms is a lack of information about groups to which we do not natively belong. Important complicating factors are the myths and false information — which we often treat as fact — that we have about the practices of those who are different from the mainstream "ideal" student. As the passage from Heath cited above makes unequivocally clear, the shared goal of families in many communities—ensuring a better life for their children—does not entail using spoken or written language in ways that the school expects, supports, encourages, or rewards or in ways familiar to many of us. From our perspective, ethnographic research about the patterns of language and literacy use across communities can become the basis for building bridges between home communities and schools, a necessary step if educators are to move from being merely curious about linguistic and cultural diversity to using such diversity as a resource.[3]

Beverly's own research (Moss 1988), an ethnographically oriented study of literacy in African-American worship services in Chicago, grew out of her desire to build such bridges between the academic and home communities of African-American students. From her own experience, she knew that a great deal of literate behavior took place in black churches among the very people who were often labeled illiterate by schools and other institutions and that schools seemed to be unable to capitalize on the kinds of literacy and literate behavior used in black churches and black homes. In conducting her fieldwork, Beverly learned a great deal about the kinds of texts and literacy people are exposed to as they grow up in this community; she also observed that the nature of the major literacy events in this community differ markedly from that of the major literacy events in school. Additionally, although she found some literacy practices that are similar to those in the academy, the function and uses of these events and the values attached to those practices are complicated and probably unique to the African-American church. One of the more interesting and complex literate texts, for example, was the church bulletin. In most churches, bulletins include the order of service and a few church-related announcements. Generally, they are printed on two to three 8½-by-11-inch sheets folded in half to comprise four to six pages of information. In the largest church that Beverly observed, however, the Sunday bulletin averaged fifteen letter-sized pages with print on both the front and back of each sheet. In addition to the traditional order of worship and church-related announcements, the bulletin of this church also included advertisements for apartments and jobs, information about upcoming plays and concerts, community-related news, as well as statements, memos, and essays from the minister. The texts written by the minister covered a range of topics, but their general function was protest. For example, one memo called for a boycott of Colgate-Palmolive products because the company was marketing a new product, Sambo toothpaste, the name of which carried negative connotations for African Americans. Another piece stated the minister's position against apartheid and P. W. Botha. A third memo railed against a local Chicago politician.

Clearly, this text fulfills the traditional roles of church bulletins in that it provides information about the day's service and related announcements. We can safely assume that the creators of such a large bulletin believe that members of the congregation have certain kinds of literacy skills that lead them to do far more than merely receive information. In fact, the text is used to connect the congregation to the church community, the local African-American community, the city, the nation, and the world. It is also a text that introduces people to and engages them in political debates. It is sometimes a document of protest. Finally, this voluminous text, read from front to back by most congregants, signals to us that print literacy is an integral part of what has traditionally been mislabeled and reduced to an oral culture. Many of our African-American students have probably been exposed to this type of multifunctional literate text. Yet, because we know little about the language and literacy practices of students from home communities like these, we remain ignorant about this complex use of a written text, the skills they might bring to our classrooms, or the ways in which we might be able to build upon their knowledge and skills.[4]

If we understand that African-American churches have historically been the community institution that African Americans have looked to not only for spiritual guidance but also for information and for models of how to use language, then we begin to appreciate the influence of this institution on language use in the community. We can recognize that the participant structures — the interweaving of text and talk during the service, the dialogic quality of the sermon, the seamlessness of the service — are the norm for interaction in the African-American community. Yet, the behaviors that are appropriate in this community setting are usually anything but appropriate outside this setting, largely because outsiders know so little about what goes on in this community that they devalue its practices. Hence, a potential resource in the classroom is lost.

In our discussion of home language and literacy practices, we have sought to demonstrate the ways in which the culture the student brings to the classroom may have a profound influence on his or her behavior there. If teachers of writing are to do any more than scratch our heads and comment "Well, the problem must have something to do with the kid's background," that is, if we are to build any sorts of bridges between the kinds of knowledge about language and literacy students bring to the classroom and the expectations of the academy, a necessary first step is learning a great deal about those kinds of knowledge. Perhaps the best way to learn about those kinds of knowledge is to examine available ethnographic research on literacy across communities (e.g., Moss, *Literacy across Communities*). Such research can provide important information about particular communities, but more important, it can help us as teachers develop a healthy respect for differences in this area and a useful perspective for considering the problems experienced by our own students.

First Language

Certainly, a major change in writing classrooms across the country over the last few decades has been the decrease in the number of classrooms made up uniquely of native speakers of English. Consequently, teachers, even those with extensive training and experience in teaching composition to native speakers, find themselves faced with new kinds of problems at many levels. Although a growing body of research deals with many of these issues, we have little understanding of the range of topics that are relevant. A tendency of many teachers is to belabor the point that speakers of certain languages have special problems with articles or the use of the perfect tenses. We do not wish to minimize the importance of mastering the code itself; however, from our perspective, focusing on patterns of fossilized errors may not be a teacher's or student's best use of time or energy. Our concerns here are those that relate to issues of rhetoric: how to develop and arrange arguments in order to persuade readers; how to select and organize material to support arguments; how to use logical, ethical, and pathetic appeals appropriately.

From his own study of Arabic, his experience teaching speakers of Arabic, and his reading of available research on the Arabic rhetorical tradition and the problems speakers of Arabic have when learning to write in English, Keith has learned some of the ways that Arabs and Americans are likely to differ when they construct, for example, an argumentative text. A native speaker of Arabic reared in an Arab country and trained in the tradition of Arab rhetoric is likely to provide far more background information than an English-speaking American reared in the United States probably would. Often, the Arab will begin at a far more abstract level of generalization than the American is likely to. Keith remembers one Arab student's essay on families that began "All over the world and in many places, we find families." In addition to what seems to be the unnecessarily obvious generalization to the American academic reader, the pair of prepositional phrases in this opening sentence illustrates the extent to which repetition with variation is highly valued among speakers and writers of Arabic, at least partly because of the ways in which the morphology and semantics of the Arabic language interact, thereby providing linguistic resources simply not available to the English-language writer. Perhaps most important, however, might be the general notion that whereas persuasion in this country is ostensibly based on carefully amassing logical arguments for a position not already held by the hearer or reader, in the Arab tradition, persuasion is based on reminding the hearer or reader of some truth that he or she already shares with the speaker or writer, making way for a view of persuasion requiring logical, ethical, and pathetic appeals.[5]

Particularly important in discussions of these issues are the observations that cross-cultural and cross-linguistic differences exist and that they can create problems for members of either group who are trying to use the other language to persuade. For example, when Keith has attempted to write something in Arabic, he has had to work very hard to keep from falling back on what seemed like his perfectly good American strategies, which do not get him very far. What seemed like such an obvious, straight line to him was evaluated as being far too short and dotted by his Arab readers in much the same way that their English-language texts represent lines that are far too long, doubling back on themselves far too often. Thus, other cultures have conventionalized ways of selecting, organizing, and presenting information; even if we as researchers or classroom teachers have a very incomplete grasp of what those ways may be, we can begin to acknowledge the existence of differences and to realize that our preferred ways of structuring texts are themselves conventional, standing at the intersection of English as a linguistic system, the Western rhetorical tradition, the teaching of writing in American schools, and a host of other influences. Such a rethinking of our own position, such a decentering, reminds us again of the limitations of our own knowledge of our tradition and the traditions of others; it also demonstrates the need for models of teaching and learning based on mutual respect through collaboration and cooperation.

Age

In addition to the increase in the number of students from diverse ethnic backgrounds who will attend college in the coming years, the average age of students attending college will continue to rise, a tendency already clear in many schools. Consequently, no longer can we expect our first-year writing courses to be made up of eighteen- and nineteen-year-old students fresh out of high school. Our older students may include wives, husbands, single parents, military veterans, full-time workers, and part-timers of many sorts. These "nontraditional" older students bring life and work experiences into our classes that affect the way they value school and many of its practices. With these experiences come knowledge, expectations, and skills that we might not normally associate with the typical eighteen-year-old first-year student who may be away from home for the first time. Although we know of no research concerning the ways in which the presence of this population might affect the writing classroom, we know from personal experience that these students have different kinds of goals and different strategies for reaching them than their younger classmates. Beverly has noticed, for example, that older women returning to school often prefer to rely on their own life experiences and those of their friends rather than simply citing secondary sources when arguing a point. Beverly welcomes this source for authority and the concomitant personal narratives that are woven into otherwise academic papers, but she also recognizes that the academy traditionally values citations from scholarly works far more highly than it values narratives of personal experience. She has also observed that these older women's classmates are sometimes enthralled by the women's argumentative strategies; other times, however, they are baffled by them.

And because many of these students are older than we are, patterns of face-to-face interaction shift as we find ourselves speaking with people who are our elders even though we may be their teachers and vested with the authority to evaluate their work and assign them grades. Additionally, for these students, responsibilities outside school often have to take priority over schoolwork. Therefore, helping older students balance their schoolwork and personal lives will bring us new challenges. While we view the different perspectives that older students bring as resources, teaching them well will likely require that we rethink our notion of whom we teach and our assumptions about them. Having older students may ultimately affect our assignment-making, class discussions, and dynamics inside and outside the classroom just as having students from a variety of linguistic and ethnic backgrounds often does.

Sex/Gender

The last two decades have seen a great deal of research devoted to male and female differences in language use. With rare exception, researchers have assigned subjects to categories according to biological sex (or, more accurately, apparent or reported biological sex), although their real interest has been gender, the complex set of cultural beliefs, norms, and behaviors associated with appropriate behavior for males and females or assumptions about the nature of masculinity and femininity. Even distinguishing between sex and gender in this fashion does not automatically make the relationship between sex, gender, and language transparent in any way. When researchers discuss sex- or gender-related patterns of language use in English, they are usually concerned with what Sally McConnell-Ginet in "Language and Gender" terms *gender markers,* ways of using language associated with, but by no means exclusive to, members of one sex or the other (80–81), although they often seem to rely heavily and unreflectively on gender stereotypes or gender norms, even in discussion and interpretation of empirical data.[6]

Among the most important findings to emerge from the research on sex- or gender-related patterns of language use in this society is the observation that males and females may well use language in different ways because they have different sorts of interactional goals (e.g., Tannen, *You Just Don't Understand*) and because they were socialized in different ways as children (e.g., Maltz and Borker). Male children tend to grow up playing in hierarchical groups, whereas female children seem to prefer to have a "best friend" who may change frequently. Researchers such as Penelope Eckert, who conducted ethnographic fieldwork in a Detroit high school as part of a study of linguistic variation and language change in progress, points out that the reputation of male adolescents seems to depend on what they do, but the reputation of female adolescents seems to depend on "the whole woman": "Girls in high school are more socially constrained than boys. Not only do they monitor their own behavior and that of others more closely, but they maintain more rigid social boundaries" ("The Whole Woman" 258).

Given these differences in life experience and perception of the self and the Other (as well as the self in contrast to the Other), should we be surprised that females and males might use language in different ways to different ends? Females, it appears, are often concerned with watching the group interaction and paying attention to both what is said and how it is said — the affective dimensions of the interaction. Borrowing Eckert's language, in general, females seem to monitor carefully the interactions in which they are involved in ways that most males do not. Based on these sorts of observations, Pamela Fishman has contended that most, if not all, of the "shitwork" in interactions falls to females. Males, on the other hand, appear to be less attuned to the affective aspects of messages. As Deborah Tannen ("Teachers' Classroom Strategies") points out, in class discussions, for example, males may feel it is their responsibility to contribute by speaking, even if they seem to dominate, whereas females may see their responsibility as being sure that they do not speak too often lest others not have the opportunity. Similar situations occur and recur in our classrooms. Not surprisingly, researchers investigating language and sex or gender frequently talk about issues of power.

In "Teachers' Classroom Strategies Should Recognize That Men and Women Use Language Differently," Tannen reminds university professors that such differences in using language have implications for what happens in the classroom. Professors who rely uniquely on one style of interaction should not be surprised to find that males or females as a group may be uncomfortable — or perhaps even alienated — by what occurs or fails to occur. Because large-group discussions are in many ways "public" forums, males may feel more comfortable contributing to them than females; similarly, males may be more comfortable than females with interactions that resemble debate or argument. Yet, as earlier research (Hall and Sandler as well as references cited in Kramerae et al.) reminds us, both male and female teachers tend to give male students more eye contact and verbal feedback than their female counterparts; similarly, teachers tend to reward uses of language that resemble "essayist literacy" as discussed above, practices that some have associated with male ways of using language (cf. Tannen's discussion of Ong's *Fighting for Life* in "Teachers' Classroom Strategies").

Such studies and observations are sometimes seen as indictments of the particular teacher whose behavior is analyzed or evidence of a societal conspiracy to silence females or to eradicate certain styles of interaction. Yet, as researchers such as Tannen remind us, sex and gender interact with culturally influenced conversational style and individual personality in complex ways. Our point in discussing this body of research is to remind ourselves and our readers that sex or, perhaps more accurately, interactional styles traditionally associated with male and female socialization in this culture constitute one additional axis of diversity that is likely to manifest itself in the classroom. Related work such as that of Cynthia Selfe and Paul Meyer, on the one hand, and Elizabeth Flynn, on the other, on the behavior of female writers and readers reminds us again of how much we have to learn about the ways that sex and gender may influence the production or comprehension of written language.

Sexual Orientation

We know very little about the ways in which sexual orientation can be an issue in educational settings or more specifically writing classes. First, as Sarah Sloane, in "Invisible Diversity: Gay and Lesbian Students Writing Our Way into the Academy," reminds us, "the gay and lesbian community...comprises a unique minority because, to a large extent, members can choose whether or not to reveal their minority status." Because of societal homophobia and the fear it inspires in individual lesbians, gay males, and bisexuals, few should be surprised that many members of this group choose not to reveal their sexual orientation, especially when one considers the possible negative consequences of doing so. Additionally, we must acknowledge that there is little encouragement for students to be honest about these issues in the classroom. Certainly, any bisexual, lesbian, or gay student can attest to the absence of representation (except perhaps negative ones) of his or her life experience in the reading assigned for most courses. Yet teachers who have been influenced even marginally by reader-response or feminist theories of reading or by social constructionist epistemologies must logically acknowledge that because the life experiences of lesbian, bisexual, or gay students differ in significant ways from those of their strictly heterosexual classmates, their responses to the texts they are asked to read or construct may differ. Investigating these differences is made all the more complex because college represents a time when many students are first dealing with these issues for themselves and because various institutions of our society including the university are being challenged to rethink their public and private stances on these issues.

Despite these difficulties, we can point to the findings of some research and speculate about other potential areas of interest. Sloane interviewed several gay and lesbian students at a large Midwestern university. On the basis of her research, she reminds teachers that assignments in writing classes, especially highly personal writing assignments, can put lesbian and gay students in a difficult position, leading them to engage in what she terms "omission," the silencing of parts of experience that they fear may not be safe to reveal, and "transformation," which might include such strategies as "pronoun laundering" to disguise the sex of the participants involved in an event. Deciding how to respond honestly to such assignments for gay, lesbian, and bisexual students is likely to be a different sort of choice than it is for heterosexual students, something that most professors probably have not considered.

Similarly, if teachers want bisexual, lesbian, or gay students in their classrooms to feel comfortable talking about issues related to their life experience — and we acknowledge that many teachers do not — those who do will have to let these students know that it is safe to do so.

In our discussion of whom we teach, we have considered a number of particular axes of difference for several reasons. Obviously, the easily labeled variables we have discussed do not show up in disembodied form in our classrooms. Instead, we teach individuals who may differ from their teacher along several of these axes at once. These variables are in no sense additive: to be a first-generation Asian-American lesbian is not to be merely "native language other than English + Asian-American + female + lesbian." It represents a particular way of being in the world — in this society at this time — that is similar to and different from the ways of being in the world of others who are different. Similarly, although understanding the cultural and linguistic backgrounds of our students provides teachers with great insight, we must constantly recognize that not all students from a particular cultural background are alike. Not all African Americans are alike. Not all women or Native Americans are alike. Not all bisexual, lesbian, or gay students are alike just as not all straight white males — dead or alive — are alike. Assuming that we should treat all members of a particular group the same is just as dangerous as not recognizing the differences between groups. Teachers and students who are similar in some way because society has labeled them different will often negotiate their response to such labeling in complex, contrasting ways.

Many times what emerges from efforts to deal with diversity is a well-meaning but, we believe, errant notion that recognizing and building upon diversity means developing separate pedagogies for each group — the "right" way to teach African-American students, Native Americans, women, and so on. We find such a move troubling. For example, following the work of Sarah Michaels on what she has characterized as ethnic differences in narrative style, many educators seem now tempted to assume that all (and only) African-American children use a topic-associative discourse style and that all (and only) white children use a topic-centered discourse style. We fear the day may have already arrived when students in education programs are given charts contrasting these two ways of constructing and using narratives with one column labeled black and the other labeled white. If so, the black or white child coming into a classroom for the first time will not be an individual; instead, regardless of social class background or prior life or school experience, he or she will be labeled a "topic associator" or a "topic centerer" before uttering a word. For us, the desire or need to put students into fixed categories or to lock them into our neat little boxes based on ethnicity, sex, age, first language, sexual orientation, or some other sociodemographic variable is as irresponsible as denying that diversity exists in our classrooms.

DIVERSITY AND WHO WE ARE: RETHINKING AUTHORITY IN OUR CLASSROOMS

Thus far, we have concentrated on diversity among students, who they are, what they know, and what they bring to the classroom. Yet, no discussion of diversity would be complete without a consideration of the teacher, who, we contend, is always more than simply a conduit of information. Every teacher who reads this text is an individual of a particular social class, age, sex, sexual orientation, and ethnic and social background. It is our belief that these axes of difference matter in the classroom and that they influence how all of us have learned and how we now teach in ways we can probably never understand. When we seek to understand the significance of these kinds of difference, we find ourselves confronting issues of authority, its origin, and its manifestations in our classroom.

Sometimes, the significance of one or more of these axes of difference in relation to authority is both evident and salient. Most of us, for example, would be surprised to find a male teaching a course entitled "Introduction to Women's Studies," a reaction that should remind us of our assumptions about who is mostly likely or most suited to teach certain subjects. When, for example, Keith began teaching an undergraduate course about the structure, history, and use of Black English, he was immediately faced with issues of authority. A few minutes into the course on the first day of class the first time he taught the course, a Hispanic female asked about his "background." Certain facts — that he is a sociolinguist familiar with the relevant research literature, that he had grown up in the South and taught in sub-Saharan Africa, that he had worked with many African-American students — were not obvious in the way that his ethnicity is.

Certainly, Beverly faces different issues than does Keith. Almost every time that she walks into an undergraduate English course (other than one with "African-American" in the title), students are surprised to see her, an African-American woman, stand before the class. Because she teaches at a university that attracts large numbers of white students from rural or suburban areas, many of her students, especially the first-quarter freshmen, have never had or even seen an African-American teacher. Most of what they know or think they know about African Americans comes from the media, and much of that is negative. Once many of these students get over the shock of finding out that she is the professor, many of them start to question her authority. She is asked many times if she has a PhD, where she went to school, and how old she is. And often she is challenged by students in ways that she doubts a white male or even a white female would be.[7] She remembers the day that someone observed her Freshman Honors Composition class and commented afterwards that the all-white class seemed uncomfortable with a black teacher. She also recalls that in one of the evaluations of an introductory literature and composition class, a student complained that Beverly had focused too much on "that minority literature" when actually less than twenty percent of the writers read in the course were people of color, a percentage Beverly sees as low when one considers the demographics of the English-speaking world. She wonders if the student would have complained about the syllabus had the teacher not been a woman of color. Many times when Beverly attempts to design a class in which she and the students negotiate or share authority, the students never perceive her as having any authority to begin with. She sees part of her task as teacher as helping students see that her being an African-American woman adds a positive dimension to their classroom experience as their presence contributes to her life experience. Yet she knows that students must be educated to rethink their views on diversity in the classroom (including diversity in front of the class) in the same way that teachers must be.

We contend, however, that issues of power and authority are inherent in all acts of teaching and learning and that they manifest themselves in myriad ways in all classrooms. We likewise believe that all of us need to continue thinking about these issues with respect to the teaching we do. At the same time, we do not believe we can or should tell others how to negotiate issues of authority in their classrooms. We can only point to our current understanding of our experiences, share what we think we have learned from them, and challenge others to do the same.

Traditionally, the notion of teaching culturally and linguistically diverse populations within one institution, one classroom, has often resulted in the question, "What am I supposed to do with them?" (The "them," of course, refers to those who have not been represented in large numbers in our university writing classes, and the "I" is someone whose ancestors hail most recently from Europe.) This panicked approach has traditionally been dealt with by the scholarly community through a growing number of conferences and publications on the topic. A similar attitude prevailed in the 1960s, when the advent of open admissions served as impetus for such work as Shaughnessy's *Errors and Expectations* and sometime later David Bartholomae's "Inventing the University." What this body of scholarship and most of our teaching experience have encouraged us to do is to rethink our definition of "student." We now acknowledge that there is no monolithic student; there are students who come to the classroom from various communities and bring with them much of the baggage, positive and negative, of those communities as well as their own individual idiosyncrasies and agendas. They also bring into the classroom their own discourse patterns, reflecting community values and world views. Sometimes these patterns and values match those of the teacher and others in the academic institutions; sometimes they do not. The mismatches and the ways in which teachers and those who design curricula respond to them call attention to how sensitive or insensitive we are to issues of linguistic and cultural diversity. Because we have operated for so long with an "ideal student" mentality that has not only failed to acknowledge difference but also been philosophically and ideologically opposed to building upon whatever difference might have grudgingly been acknowledged, reeducating ourselves to serve our diverse student populations represents a major task.

It is easy to see why we as teachers, even teachers of writing, have long wished to ignore diversity. Acknowledging difference, examining it, and finding creative ways to build upon it — to make it the cornerstone of individual and corporate philosophies of educational theory and classroom practice — require that we see ourselves, our beliefs, and even our actions, from a new perspective, one that forces us, as Clifford Geertz has put it, to see ourselves among others. Our preferred way of using language and of being literate becomes a way among ways rather than the single, correct way; it is appropriate in some contexts and useless in others. What seem like natural or logical ways of presenting information or evaluating knowledge no longer stand alone as the only possible alternatives or even the most expedient ones.

We have come to realize that dealing with diversity has led us to change not only how we teach but also our understanding of what constitutes "those things which are to be understood" in the first place (Augustine 7). Throughout this

process, we find ourselves having to rethink — that is, renegotiate — our authority and, consequently, our role and our practice in the classroom and in the
larger professional arena. We have come to see these sites as places where we
should assume far less common ground than we traditionally have and where
we realize we probably have more to learn than we do to teach or at least a great
deal to learn as we teach. These are lessons all good teachers no doubt know.
The need to relearn them and to think about them in new and deeper ways constitutes, we believe, a challenge of tremendous proportion, one that, if met, has
the potential of changing what it means to teach and learn in this society in
important, positive ways.

NOTES

[1] We use "conversation" metaphorically to include, as implied above, a variety of teacher/student
interactions ranging from classroom lectures during which a teacher may speak to a group of students, receiving little direct verbal feedback, to conversations between student and teacher on the
telephone or in the office to electronic exchanges between two or more parties, one of whom is
the teacher. To varying degrees, all of these kinds of interactions are based on patterns associated
with face-to-face two-party conversations; as the literature on language in the classroom reminds
us, these categories of interactions also differ crucially from one another and from "everyday conversation" in ways that are not at all transparent.

[2] Michaels's work clearly shows that the black students are quite aware of the differences between
their narrative style and that of the teacher. In "Deena's Story: The Discourse of the Other," Beth
Daniell argues that Deena's refusal to adopt the teacher's preferred strategies lest she forfeit her
own identity and autonomy constitutes an act of resistance. Deena's refusal can also be read in
light of the work of Le Page and Tabouret-Keller.

[3] For an especially interesting exchange on the possible limits of ethnographic research in effecting
educational change, see the paper by Cazden ("Can Ethnographic Research Go Beyond the Status
Quo?"), Kleinfeld's response ("First Do No Harm"), and the comments on this exchange by Amsbury,
Barnhardt, Bishop, Chandler, Greenbaum and Greenbaum, Grubis, Harrison, and Stearns as well as
the final statements of Kleinfeld ("Some of My Best Friends") and Cazden ("Response").

[4] Valerie Balester's unpublished dissertation examines some of the ways in which the rhetorical
practices of the African-American community and especially the African-American church influence the writing of students familiar with these traditions.

[5] Of course, exceptions to this generalization are plentiful. Advertising in this country rarely
focuses uniquely on logical appeals alone; in fact, Keith would contend that an interesting part of
Western rhetoric (or at least Western rhetoric as instantiated in most freshman texts) is its pretending that only logical appeals matter. In some ways, the task of the Arab rhetor might be compared to that of many Christian ministers, especially Fundamentalist ones, who, even in their
efforts to save souls, often do so by reminding the lost ones of the Truth that, at some level, they
are assumed already to know. Many of these issues are treated in a book by Barbara Johnstone
and an unpublished manuscript by Keith ("On Written Persuasive Discourse").

[6] A major intellectual problem for this field of research — like all fields involving axes of difference — is determining the extent to which its findings represent actual accounts or explanations
of phenomena rather than reifications of cultural categories, stereotypes, or norms.

[7] Interestingly, in his course about Black English, Keith wonders if his students — African-American
and non-African-American — do not question the data he presents in class (often from published
research) in ways they might not if he were black.

WORKS CITED

Amsbury, Clifton. "The Problem of Simplicity." *Anthropology and Education Quarterly* 15 (1984): 168–69.

Augustine, Saint. *On Christian Doctrine*. Trans. D. W. Robertson, Jr. Indianapolis: Bobbs-Merrill, 1978.

Balester, Valerie M. "The Social Construction of *Ethos:* A Study of the Spoken and Written Discourse of Two Black College Students." Diss. U of Texas at Austin, 1989.

Barnhardt, Ray. "Anthropology Needs No Apology." *Anthropology and Education Quarterly* 15 (1984): 179–80.

Bartholomae, David. "Inventing the University." *When a Writer Can't Write*. Ed. Mike Rose. New York: Guilford, 1985. 134–65.

Bishop, Ralph J. "Educational Failure and the Status Quo." *Anthropology and Education Quarterly* 15 (1984): 167–68.

Cazden, Courtney. "Can Ethnographic Research Go Beyond the Status Quo?" *Anthropology and Education Quarterly* 14 (1983): 33–41.

——. "Response." *Anthropology and Education Quarterly* 15 (1984): 184–85.

Chandler, Joan M. "Education Equals Change." *Anthropology and Education Quarterly* 15 (1984): 176–78.

Daniell, Beth. "Deena's Story: The Discourse of the Other." *Journal of Advanced Composition* 16 (1996): 253–64.

Eckert, Penelope. "The Whole Woman: Sex and Gender Differences in Variation." *Language Variation and Change* 1 (1989): 245–67.

Fishman, Pamela M. "Interaction: The Work Women Do." Thorne, Kramerae, and Henley 89–101.

Flynn, Elizabeth. "Gender and Reading." *Gender and Reading: Essays on Readers, Texts, and Contexts*. Ed. Elizabeth Flynn and Patrocinio Schwieckart. Baltimore: Johns Hopkins UP, 1986. 267–88.

Freedman, Sarah, ed. *The Acquisition of Written Language: Revision and Response*. Norwood, NJ: Ablex, 1985.

Geertz, Clifford. *Local Knowledge: Further Essays in the Interpretive Anthropology*. New York: Basic Books, 1983.

Greenbaum, Susan D., and Paul E. Greenbaum. "Integrating Ethnographic and Quantitative Research: A Reply to Kleinfeld with Implications for American Indian Self-Determination." *Anthropology and Education Quarterly* 15 (1984): 171–73.

Grubis, Steve. "A Teacher Perspective." *Anthropology and Education Quarterly* 15 (1984): 178–79.

Hall, Roberta M., and Bernice R. Sandler. "A Chilly Climate in the Classroom." *Beyond Sex Roles*. 2nd ed. Ed. Alice G. Sargent. St. Paul, MN: West Publishing, 1985. 503–10.

Harrison, Barbara. "Training for Cross-Cultural Teaching." *Anthropology and Education Quarterly* 15 (1984): 169–70.

Heath, Shirley Brice. *Ways with Words: Language, Life and Work in Communities and Classrooms*. Cambridge: Cambridge UP, 1983.

Hirsch, E. D., Jr., *Cultural Literacy: What Every American Needs to Know*. Boston: Houghton, 1987.

Hymes, Dell. "Models of the Interaction of Language and Social Life." *Directions in Socio-Linguistics: The Ethnography of Communication*. Ed. John G. Gumperz and Dell Hymes. New York: Holt, 1972. 35–71.

Janda, Mary Ann. "Collaboration in a Traditional Classroom Environment." *Written Communication* 7 (1990): 291–315.

Johnstone, Barbara. *Repetition in Arabic Discourse: Paradigms, Syntagms, and the Ecology of Language.* Amsterdam: John Benjamins, 1991.

Kleinfeld, Judith. "First Do No Harm: A Reply to Courtney Cazden." *Anthropology and Education Quarterly* 14 (1983): 282–87.

———. "Some of My Best Friends Are Anthropologists." *Anthropology and Education Quarterly* 15 (1984): 180–84.

Kramerae, Cheris, Barrie Thorne, and Nancy Henley. "Sex Similarities and Differences in Language, Speech, and Nonverbal Communication: An Annotated Bibliography." Thorne, Kramerae, and Henley 151–331.

Le Page, R. B., and Andrée Tabouret-Keller. *Acts of Identity: Creole-Based Approaches to Language and Ethnicity.* Cambridge: Cambridge UP, 1985.

Maltz, Daniel, and Ruth Borker. "A Cultural Approach to Male-Female Miscommunication." *Language and Social Identity.* Ed. John J. Gumperz. Cambridge: Cambridge UP, 1982. 196–216.

McConnell-Ginet, Sally. "Language and Gender." Newmeyer 75–99.

Mehan, Hugh. "The Competent Student." *Working Paper #69.* Austin, TX: Southwest Educational Development Laboratory, 1979.

Michaels, Sarah. "Sharing Time: Children's Narrative Styles and Differential Access to Literacy." *Language in Society* 10 (1981): 423–42.

Moss, Beverly J. "The Black Sermon as a Literacy Event." Diss. U of Illinois at Chicago, 1988.

———. ed. *Literacy across Communities.* Cresskill, NJ: Hampton Press, 1994.

Newmeyer, Frederick, ed. *Language: The Socio-Cultural Matrix.* Vol. 4 of *Linguistics: The Cambridge Survey.* Cambridge: Cambridge UP, 1988.

Ong, Walter. *Fighting for Life: Contest, Sexuality, and Consciousness.* Ithaca, NY: Cornell UP. 1981.

The Oprah Winfrey Show. Exec. prod. Debra DiMaio. Dir. Jim McPharlin. With Bernadette Anderson, Ronnie Carter, Gary D., Thomas Kochman, Geneva Smitherman, and Bonnie Thompson. NBC. WXAN, Austin, TX. 19 Nov. 1987.

Philips, Susan U. *The Invisible Culture: Communication in Classroom and Community on the Warm Springs Indian Reservation.* New York: Longman, 1983.

Scollon, Ron, and Suzanne B. K. Scollon. "Literacy as Focused Interaction." *Quarterly Newsletter of the Laboratory of Comparative Human Cognition* 2.2 (1986): 26–29.

———. *Narrative, Literacy and Face in Interethnic Communication.* Norwood, NJ: Ablex, 1981.

Selfe, Cynthia, and Paul Meyer. "Testing Claims for On-Line Conferences." *Written Communication* 8 (1991): 163–92.

Shaughnessy, Mina. *Errors and Expectations.* New York: Oxford UP, 1977.

Sloane, Sarah. "Invisible Diversity: Gay and Lesbian Students Writing Our Way into the Academy." *Writing Ourselves into the Story.* Ed. Laura Fontaine and Susan Hunter. Southern Illinois UP, 1993.

Sperling, Melanie. "Dialogues of Deliberation: Conversation in the Teacher-Student Writing Conference." *Written Communication* 8 (1991): 131–62.

Stearns, Robert D. "Beyond an Emic View of Anthropologists and Anthropology: An Alaskan Perspective." *Anthropology and Education Quarterly* 15 (1984): 174–76.

Students' Right to Their Own Language. Urbana, IL: NCTE, 1974.

Tannen, Deborah. "Teachers' Classroom Strategies Should Recognize That Men and Women Use Language Differently." *Chronicle of Higher Education* 19 June 1991: B1, B3.

——. *You Just Don't Understand: Women and Men in Conversation.* New York: Morrow, 1990.

Thorne, Barrie, Cheris Kramerae, and Nancy Henley, eds. *Language, Gender and Society.* Cambridge, MA: Newbury, 1975.

Walters, Keith. " 'It's Like Playing Password, Right?': Socratic Questioning and Questioning at School." *Texas Linguistics Forum* 24 (1984): 157–88.

——. "Language, Logic, and Literacy." *The Right to Literacy.* Ed. Andrea A. Lunsford, Helene Moglen, and James Slevin. New York: MLA, 1990. 173–88.

——. "On Written Persuasive Discourse in Arabic and English." Unpublished essay, University of Texas at Austin, 1987.

——. "Whose Culture? Whose Literacy?" *Diversity as Resource in the Classroom: Redefining Cultural Literacy.* Ed. Denise Murray. Alexandria, VA: TESOL, 1992.

Bruce Herzberg

Service Learning and Public Discourse

At the beginning of homeroom period on my first day of seventh grade, the teacher read a list of students and directed them to go to another room to get their class schedules. I could tell from the teacher's tone that this was a list I wanted to be on. I listened attentively for my name to be called, even after he passed my spot in the alphabet. I reasoned hopefully that if my name were not on the list, then perhaps I had misread his tone and it was a bad list rather than a good one. But my stomach stayed in a knot. After the chosen group had left, the teacher gave the rest of us our schedules, and it became clear that those who had left were in the honors track and the rest of us were not. On the way out of homeroom, I asked the teacher to check his list again. I had always been a straight-A student and had never even seen a C on my report card. What did it take to get into the honors class? But, no, my name was not there, and the teacher could do nothing about it.

I went off to my classes, all located on the bottom floor of Memorial Junior High. The rooms had high ceilings with small windows at the top of the back wall, just like a basement. The other students looked bored and some, even on the first day, spent the period with their heads on their desks. The teachers all seemed to have the same teaching style: they handed out worksheets that occupied the class for most of the period; then they announced the homework. The worksheets seemed infantile to me; the knot stayed in my stomach. I told my story to each teacher, and received from each no more than a sympathetic smile.

During lunch period, I found the assistant principal, who told me that the school got tracking assignments from central administration. She said that the school was simply not allowed to make changes but that she would contact central administration and see what had happened in my case. My mother called after school and got the same answer. In a few days, we learned that my records had not arrived from my elementary school, which was in the next state (my family had moved that summer). My mother spoke to the principal and repeated that I was an A student. The principal replied, "I believe you, but I need official documentation." I showed him my old report cards, but he said that they were not "official documents." My parents argued with the principal several times. I pleaded that the regular classes were too easy. My biggest concern was that I was losing valuable time at the beginning of the year. The honors classes, where I would surely wind up eventually, were getting ahead; and when I got there, I would be at a disadvantage. Nothing worked. The principal was kind and sympathetic but repeated that he could do nothing.

This article is reprinted from the *Journal of Advanced Composition* 20.2 (2000): 391–404.

"Listen," I begged, "what can it hurt to put me in the honors class? If I can handle the work, it will prove that I belonged there in the first place. If I fail, I'll just go back to the regular classes. Why wouldn't you agree to a request like this from any student, any student at all who wanted to try to do the harder work?" The principal assured me that he didn't doubt my ability, my mother's word, or the evidence of the report cards. He simply could not do anything until my records arrived. I don't remember if he ever answered my question.

About two weeks into the semester, I was handed a note, instructing me to see each of my teachers and show them the note; I was now reassigned to the honors track and would begin attending classes immediately. During first period, I handed the note to Mrs. Beard, who congratulated me and told me that she was sorry to see me go because I was the only one in the class who always correctly answered all the worksheet questions. (I diligently did the worksheets in the absurd hope that someone would realize that a mistake had been made.) Then, I went upstairs to Mr. Farnelli's science class. I had assumed that all the seventh grade classes were in the basement and that we would move up with each grade. But all my new classes were on the second and third floors.

I entered Mr. Farnelli's class and was literally dazzled. Floor-to-ceiling windows stretched the entire length of the side wall. Opposite the windows, glass-fronted cases held ranks of microscopes, bottles of chemicals, racks of test tubes, stacks of petri dishes, and rows of Erlenmeyer flasks (how I envied Erlenmeyer, who had such an elegant thing named for him). Instead of desks, students sat in pairs at lab tables, each with a black slate top and two gas jets. The floor was stepped from front to back like a college lecture hall, so that each set of tables was on its own level. Despite the knot in my stomach from anxiety about being the new kid and needing to catch up with the schoolwork I had missed during my time in the basement, I felt that I had ascended almost to heaven.

I sometimes tell this story to my first-year composition class while we are reading Mike Rose's *Lives on the Boundary*. Rose describes how he was one of those students who was "scuttling along at the bottom" of the school system until a teacher saw his potential and elevated him to the honors track (26). But such upward movement was a rarity. For most of the kids in his book, low-track placement was a life-sentence. For kids who don't have an exceptional teacher or parents who will advocate for them, there is no escape. As psychologist Sheila Tobias laments, "Those who test well are encouraged and expected to succeed and offered the most challenging work. Those who do not, get a watered-down curriculum that reflects the school's minimal expectations of them" (55). Thus, this diluted curriculum guarantees immobility. My own story further shows the utter paralysis of the system even in the face of a simple error.

My students easily see the significance of the windows and worksheets in my story, and some of the students have similar stories about themselves or friends who felt victimized or embarrassed or helpless in the tracking system. Tracking comes up frequently in Rose's book and in some of our other readings on education in the United States. Moreover, tracking becomes an issue for my students because they serve as tutors at a local public school through our class's service-learning project. Every year, one or two of them will choose tracking as a topic for the research paper that they write in the second semester.

In their research, students find that academic studies are virtually unanimous in condemning tracking. In principle, tracking is supposed to benefit all students, but, in practice, it focuses resources in the upper tracks. The differences in materials, teacher attitudes, and curriculum are described in both long-term studies, such as Jeannie Oakes' *Keeping Track,* and in innumerable follow-up studies in the journals of the NEA and Phi Delta Kappa. Studies confirm Jonathan Kozol's observations in *Savage Inequalities* that tracks are thoroughly divided by race (Tobias contends that tracking was in part a strategy for resegregation). Moreover, the walls between the tracks are virtually impermeable. Once a student is ensconced in a lower track, differences in curriculum (and, as Rose reveals so vividly, in attitude) make it almost impossible to move up. Finally, the different tracks come to seem like different countries. Actual ability or performance cease to matter, as my situation showed. What I lacked was a properly stamped passport. The kind of barrier that I faced is insurmountable when it is placed before children and parents who lack the resources to attack it.

My students readily find that the kind of sources I have noted and their drafts, like many of the books and articles they read, often take on a self-righteous tone as they condemn the racism and classism that characterizes tracking and as they lament the needless damage done to students by inequitable resource distribution and by the inherent evils of the system. They also find an increasing number of studies extolling the virtues of non-tracked classrooms ("heterogeneous grouping," as the jargon has it).

Part of the writing assignment that I make is, of course, to represent all of the arguments or perspectives on an issue, so the students make a real effort to find proponents of tracking. While every year they find more new sources opposing tracking, it is remarkable that every year they cite the same two or three academic defenders of tracking and can find no more. It seems as though there is hardly any other side to this debate. Still, tracking remains standard practice.

At this point, I ask the students to reconsider the focus of their research. They have been trying to say whether tracking is good or bad, and they are supporting the thesis that it is bad. I ask them to consider this key question: if it is overwhelmingly clear that tracking is a bad policy and practice, why is it that tracking not only continues to exist but continues to be the norm in public schools? Is the harm caused by tracking a new discovery? No, since sources going back many years testify to the inequities in the practice. Are the academic studies, the experiments in non-tracked classes, and the arguments of Rose and others unknown to school officials and teachers? Probably not, since such reports appear in teachers' magazines and ordinary daily newspapers. Well, then? What's the story?

Many of the other topics that students work on bring them to a similar point, at which academic knowledge and public policy are at odds — or in an odd relation. Research into prison education is a striking example. Here, too, it is almost universally found by researchers that education in prison dramatically reduces recidivism. Some eighty percent of sentenced inmates are illiterate (and, by the way, most of the illiterate are black and Hispanic). The cost of prison education is far, far less than the police and court and prison costs of recidivism. These facts seem to be well-established. Yet, prison education programs continue to be attacked and dismantled by certain citizens' groups, by legislators and governors, even by wardens. Opponents consider prison education, together with television and sports equipment and conjugal visits, to be entertainment and coddling. In this case, as in the case of tracking and so many other topics in our course, the public policy question must be asked: if the answers are so clear, why are discredited policies still in place, and why are they still defended?

My students are admirable people. They volunteer to take my yearlong first-year composition course with its required community service project. They go through a workshop for tutors. They get themselves to Boston — to the Pine Street Inn or to Waltham Middle School or to Hamilton Elementary — every week. And when they begin working on research projects investigating the conditions of education in the U.S., they bring a special passion and commitment to the issues they confront — issues such as the unequal distribution of resources to schools in different communities in the same state; the efficacy of school choice or voucher programs; the representation of minorities in school textbooks; the use of IQ testing, prison literacy programs, multicultural curricula, or tracking. They also learn how to leave campus and observe on their own — a major benefit of service learning.

The required research paper in my service-learning course attempts to take advantage of the special qualities and new abilities of these students, who are required to include field observation and personal investigation in their papers. They may visit a prison education program and talk to the inmates, teachers, and warden; they may compare two schools that are differently funded and talk to the students; they may attend school board meetings, and so on. As for their print and Internet sources, they must cite material from three different audience categories (broadly defined): professional publications by academic experts; popular works by experts, journalists, or policy makers; and public works such as newspaper articles, editorials, and Web postings.

What they find when they compare academic sources with more popular ones is not surprising. By and large, public policy follows popular, not academic, opinion. In the case of tracking, for example, despite some movement by principals and activist teachers toward heterogeneous grouping, the determining arguments time and again are either flat assertions by parents that lower-track kids will drag non-tracked classes down to their level, or statements by teachers that they would need lots of expensive training to be able to teach non-tracked classes.

For several years, I worked to move my students toward analyzing this gap between academic investigation, on the one hand, and public discourse and public policy, on the other. I hoped they could observe the ways that academic studies were used or reflected in the more popular media and that they could say which voices seemed to have the greatest effect on public policy in the spheres they studied. This was too sophisticated an assignment for them, no matter how I tried to package it. More recently, I have asked a different question: how could you — or someone who held your position on the issue you have studied and who was motivated to do so — bring your arguments effectively before the public?

This new question has been much more successful in revealing some of the boundary issues in crossing from academic to public discourse. It has also opened the classroom to discussion of producing public discourse, a move that, in a first-year composition course, caused me some trepidation.

The topics my students have chosen are serious issues of public policy, but the students have a strong and perfectly natural tendency, when writing a research paper, to adopt a formal academic approach. This is hardly surprising. They feel that they don't have the ability to contribute anything new to the academic discussion, and they cannot imagine entering public discourse. Of course, they are not wrong to recognize that they are novices, that they lack the knowledge and authority to add their voices to long-running conversations among powerful interlocutors. In addition, they know that their teachers, especially in college, expect academic papers: papers that are abstract, formal, and addressed to "everyone" in the sense of "no one"; papers that are proof of diligence and that are aids to their own learning but devoid of any other purpose. Moreover, as a teacher of composition, I myself am bound to help them learn this form of writing. As a teacher of rhetoric, however, I feel the inadequacy of the form and of the automatic move to its safety and comfort. I am not the only one.

In his 1996 Chair's address to the CCCC convention, Lester Faigley called on writing teachers and all academics to enter public discourse, not only to represent our work for ourselves but also to engage in the serious questions of public policy that affect us and about which we have knowledge to share. The week following Faigley's address, history professor Russell Jacoby made the same plea in the *Chronicle of Higher Education*. Gerald Graff has repeatedly sounded this call and has worked to heed it in his own writing. Rose, too, has shown how to straddle the line between academic analysis and public discourse.

If we wish to claim that the composition course is truly about rhetoric, about civic virtue, and about public as well as academic discourse, we must learn how to conceptualize the connections between the academy and society in ways that our students, our administrators, and we ourselves find convincing. In constructing ourselves as experts — a role we find comfortable and that society supports — we isolate ourselves, falling prey to instrumentalist justifications of our work (that is, the teaching of composition as a set of skills) and the ideological consequences that follow. Even worse, we come to view society as a research site and not as a realm of true engagement. My students' tendency to write academic papers reveals the genesis of our own identical inclination.

I must hasten to say that I do not advocate that we abandon teaching academic discourse, especially in the first-year composition course. The trepidation I mentioned earlier — my hesitation about having students write public discourse — arose chiefly from a sense of obligation to stick to the academic and not to waste students' time with hollow "letter to the editor" exercises. What I want to understand better is the practical or, more importantly, theoretical justification for teaching public-discourse writing to my class.[1]

I can think of four possibilities. First, there is the claim that students are more engaged by current issues. The *engagement* theory seems to say that we can use whatever "works," whatever stimulates student interest. If current public issues will be interesting to students, then such issues can be our source of topics. If it seems exciting to write a letter to the editor or an article for the school newspaper, then we can make the most of these venues to teach rhetoric. I do not mean to be dismissive of this pedagogy. I know teachers who do very good work using newspapers as course texts and whose students appear to learn a great deal about writing. I regard this justification, however, as theoretically weak. The "whatever works" argument can be used to justify, after the fact, any kind of reading and writing — personal narrative, fiction, journalism, literary criticism — that seems to the instructor to "work." I want to see a strong before-the-fact argument, one that goes directly to the issue: why should we teach public discourse *qua* public discourse?

A second justification is that the rhetorical immediacy of public discourse helps students understand audience and genre constraints. In fact, this view forms the basis of an important and well-established model of service learning in composition in which students write documents for community agencies. This approach does a real service for non-profit companies, providing them with manuals, newsletters, reports, and so on. Students do indeed face audience and format constraints. They must learn the appropriate professional discourse, meet deadlines, satisfy their supervisors — all valuable experiences, to be sure. I don't use this approach, mainly for practical reasons. Students have to complete sophisticated writing tasks well to serve the agencies' needs and I don't think my students can perform well enough. Also, I am not inclined to have a writing internship replace direct service, such as tutoring. I have some concern, too, that this sort of writing would overwhelm the academic research and writing part of the course.

A third justification concerns *critical pedagogy,* the goal of which is to promote social consciousness or something like a Freirean critical consciousness and, if possible, to lead students to social action. This approach thus also supports service learning (though, significantly, service learning has other sources of theoretical support). Critical pedagogy appeals to many writing teachers, including me, who have a political orientation toward teaching. While it does not *require* teaching the rhetorical forms of public discourse, critical pedagogy does provide a coherent argument for taking up public issues in the classroom — though, to be sure, its critics claim that a blatant political orientation is inappropriate and irrelevant to the main goal of improving students' writing.

The fourth, and perhaps most attractive, is the historical justification. In the history of rhetoric we have a noble tradition of education for civic leadership. This is the legacy of Isocrates, of Cicero, and of the medieval university, whose mission was to create civic and ecclesiastical leaders. Educating students to produce public discourse was the whole point! But are we justified *today* in focusing our idea of rhetoric and our composition pedagogy on civic discourse, on public policy, on citizenship? After all, our institutions of higher education are very different from the schools of Isocrates and Cicero or the universities of medieval Europe. Our colleges are technical and professional; they are no longer essentially civic in nature. Are we not presumptuous in proposing to teach about social issues, to encroach upon political science and sociology? Isn't our job (at least in required composition courses) to teach the conventions of academic discourse, the formal features of language, the strategies of college writing? If we claim that civic discourse is now the focus of rhetorical education, are we abandoning our proper role? Is this what we are being paid to do? Can we fulfill our roles as teachers of academic discourse while adopting this new role as educators for democracy?

I am not among those who criticize academic discourse or seek its demise. Although I would be happy to see some of the changes its critics propose, I will not teach my students some alternative to academic discourse that doesn't presently exist in the hope that they—mere undergraduates—will exert pressure for change. Thus, my own longstanding approach has been to assign an academic research paper that draws in various ways on the students' powerful experiences in the service project. This method produces a deep understanding of the issues, deeper than performing service and observing alone could possibly produce. It thus seems to satisfy the goals of critical pedagogy while teaching academic discourse.

Still, this approach did not lead my class into the gap between research and policy—in other words, it did not engage the issues "on the ground" (as the BBC journalists so colorfully put it). Surely, there was an opportunity here, because it should be possible in a service-learning class to construct a bridge between academic and public discourse, between technical education and education for democracy.

What I sought, in other words, was a way to move students toward a fairly traditional kind of public rhetoric that would require them not only to examine and practice public discourse forms but also to figure out how to bring their academic knowledge to bear in public argument. This path is fraught with well-documented perils. Reviewing the complexity of the public sphere, its "array of discursive practices," and its historical density, Susan Wells says, "We do not do justice to this history, this set of possibilities, when we assign students generic public writing, such as an essay on gun control, or a letter to a nonexistent editor" (328).

I put this problem to my students: "You are doing a lot of work. Your research papers are extensive. Most of you are passionate about the arguments you are making. What is going to happen to your work when you are finished? Will it go anywhere other than my desk? Can we imagine ways of going public?"

We addressed this question in stages. First, students took a week to look over the sources they had already used, to poke around the Web, and to brainstorm about ways to go public. In one class meeting, we discussed the forums for public argument. Students first offered basic forms—books, articles, and so on—as ways of going public. The power of textbooks to influence the public was pointed out. Students suggested personal appearances at particular forums—school board and PTA meetings, for example. They also suggested making phone calls. (I hadn't thought of this one, despite the amount of phone-nagging I do myself.) They suggested running for public office (another I hadn't expected to hear) and lobbying. Finally, they suggested numerous other forums—pamphlets and fliers, radio and television, interactive Web sites, specialized Web postings, email campaigns, booths at fairs, demonstrations, bumper stickers, and tee-shirts—as well as a number of activities: searching for organizations, starting organizations, engaging in community activism, and sponsoring benefit rock concerts. Step one worked well, I thought. Somewhere in there was the letter to the editor, but it hardly mattered.

In the second stage, I asked students to pick a medium or form and to figure out its rhetorical characteristics. Who uses the medium? Who is the audience? How much space or time is there to make a case? What kinds of arguments and evidence are used? I asked students to choose a way to go public that seemed appropriate for their arguments and to begin to think about how they might do it.

The discussion that followed included a letter to the editor, but it was a specific editor at a particular local newspaper in the community where the student had done part of her research. Leslie (all student names in this article are fictitious) had sample letters to this paper, an estimate of their length, and a sense that there were different approaches to be considered. She also introduced the problem of length—or rather brevity—which seemed to characterize so many of the public discourse forms. The same student also had an assessment of speaking at school committee meetings: it would be necessary, she pointed out, to yell. Jill also wanted to write to an editor—of *The Nation*, it turned out, because she liked the articles it publishes. But did it make sense, she asked, to write to a publication that you agreed with? This was a good audience question: if you want to affect public ideas, wouldn't it make more sense to find an audience who disagreed with you initially?

John liked the idea of a flier campaign and, in the third stage, produced a flier to show us how it would work. Using clip art from his computer, simple layout, and easy vocabulary, he produced a flier urging elementary school students (he targeted the kids at Hamilton Elementary, where we did our service project) to see the value of education and commit to doing better on their homework. His second flier was designed to convince kids and their parents to commit to a joint effort to improve homework. The third one urged parents to organize a campaign to get the school board to provide more money for books for the school's limited library.

Jennifer, who was writing about the Ebonics debate, wanted to sharpen her response to someone she had overheard making fun of black English, running down bilingual education, and opposing programs for immigrants. It turned out that what she reported saying was already pretty sharp, but the discussion that ensued in class — about the importance of even these individual encounters — was very worthwhile. Pat was interested in talk radio responses about his topic, prison education, which was an issue that had recently come up again in the press. In this situation, rhetorical constraints consist of how fast you had to talk, how long you might expect to go before being cut off, and what reaction you might try to provoke. Being witty was clearly desirable, and Pat certainly was.

In the third stage, I asked students to produce a sample letter, script, or Web posting that conformed to the constraints we discovered. Mike, who was also working on Ebonics, printed out a viciously racist Web page with an address for postings, plus his two-part submission — a short, punchy version of his argument, followed by the entire text of his research paper! Donna created a survey on integration and busing. The short survey included a short history and explanation of busing. Donna reasoned that people loved to answer surveys and that this one would be educational and perhaps stir up debate. There were several letters to the editor and Web postings, all with addresses and copies of the editorials or other letters to which the students were responding. David, who introduced the idea of a benefit rock concert, explained in detail how it would work. Bands would donate their services, the hall would be donated, the admission price would be low (drawing big crowds), and a record company would even produce a CD with the participating bands. David couldn't produce the concert, of course, but he did produce a set of CD liner notes that consisted primarily of his research paper, printed in a tiny font.

These efforts were not especially polished. Some of these efforts, by their nature, could not go beyond sketches. Some students did send off their letters and postings, but only a few of the efforts had the feel, to me, of a fake exercise. When I raised that possibility with the students, however, they told me that I was the only one worried about it. Several mentioned later that they liked the idea of figuring out how to make use of arguments that they worked on in their research projects.

There were other benefits, too. The focus on effective argumentation in the exercise on "going public" fed back into the research papers. So many of the public statements were refutations of other arguments that students brought new energy to what was often a perfunctory exercise in acknowledging the existence of opposing points of view. Unexpectedly, too, we wound up working at length on integrated citation style. Students wanted to avoid the clumsiness and lack of popular appeal in discourse that displayed footnotes or other academic citation forms, but they wanted to learn how to use academic style (and I wanted them to learn it) so that they could use it correctly in school papers. I found some examples of integrated forms — a style in which authors and works were fully identified in the text ("Educator Mortimer Adler, author of *The*

Paideia Proposal...") and followed by a standard academic citation as well, which was adopted by most of the students.

Looking at the differences between their academic papers and their "going public" exercises sharpened the class's understanding of the purposes of different sources. While teachers complain about students who use magazines like *Newsweek* as main sources, it's more common in my classes for students to ignore *Newsweek* altogether and stick to academic sources. These students can miss the sense that there are public debates about the issues. They may be dismissive of all popular sources. Even those students who use both academic and journalistic sources will put them side by side in jarring ways. But by examining the public policy debate as a part of the issue at hand, students can better see the rhetorical dimension of academic and public discourses. This concern increases with the use of the World Wide Web for research. Our exercise with forms of public discourse gave students the chance to get a taste of writing in popular media and helped them not only distinguish among audiences but also to see the persuasive purposes of different forms.

Furthermore, in an effort to look for a way to help students get a rhetorical grip on the organization of their research papers (which are unusually long and complicated as first-year research papers go), I recommend Quintilian's five-part scheme: introduction (*exordium*), narration (*narratio*), argument (*confirmatio*), refutation (*refutatio*), and conclusion (*peroratio*). This method of arrangement works remarkably well both for the academic research paper, and (why was I surprised by this?) for public discourse. The textbook method of organization — group related ideas and put them in logical order — founders on the ambiguity of "logical order." With a rhetorical purpose in view for "going public," we were able to see the virtue of arranging the more academic paper for rhetorical effect. I warn students that not all of their professors will be engaged by the engaging exordium (an illustration, example, revealing story, startling statistic, or other striking way to introduce the issue). However, students who use it in other courses report frequent success: it is very sophisticated when done well. So, too, with the other elements: adaptation is important, but having the basic tool makes adaptation possible. Students, too, are impressed to learn that there is an ancient art of persuasion. With their encouragement, I often introduce the three appeals and even some matters of style. And, of course, I point out the civic goals of classical rhetoric.

Susan Wells, whom I cited earlier on the vacuity of typical letter-to the-editor assignments, makes a number of important observations about teaching public discourse, observations I should consider before concluding on a triumphant note. Wells describes four ways of dedicating composition classes to public writing. The first approach is to regard the classroom itself as "a version of the public sphere" (338). She criticizes this approach for its typical lack of true exigency — the texts that students produce don't actually affect anything within the classroom. The second approach is to teach the analysis of public discourse, which aligns the class with "the powerful traditions of rhetorical study" and "mortgages composition to the analytic bias of such study" (339).

The problem here is that (if I understand Wells correctly) analysis and evaluation are not themselves forms of public discourse. The third approach aims "to produce student writing that will enter some form of public space" (339). Here, Wells appears to be referring to internship work, such as the writing-for-agencies model of service learning. Her concern is that "direct experience of the social can be a very convincing argument for the impossibility of change" (339). The fourth strategy, one she unreservedly endorses, is a class that examines the ways that different academic disciplines engage their publics, a class in which students practice producing discourses that are so addressed. This last form is necessarily an advanced course to which students bring disciplinary expertise.

Wells raises important questions about our goals in asking students to write for the public sphere. The approaches she presents reveal difficulty in creating a pedagogy that will achieve the desired aims. Her third approach — the one closest to service learning — may certainly produce resignation and doubt rather than commitment. I don't agree, however, that this risk is greater than the rewards. To be sure, service learning doesn't always work well. It requires a great deal of mere managing and arranging, and things can go terribly wrong. Many service-learning writing courses and programs do seem undertheorized; however, I believe this is often a consequence of the effort to manage details of placements and travel and oversight. In more mature courses and programs, success is typical. Students do see possibilities for change, and they can see — and teach us to see — that publics can be addressed if we are truly willing to engage them.

NOTE

[1] I want to thank Tom Deans for criticizing me for this reluctance to pursue public discourse in my class, which he does in *Writing Partnerships,* a book that offers a superb analysis of service learning in composition, both in practical and theoretical terms. His book is currently under review. I have summarized some of its main points in "Service Learning and Public Discourse."

WORKS CITED

Adler, Mortimer J. *The Paideia Proposal: An Educational Manifesto.* New York: Macmillan, 1982.

Faigley, Lester. "Literacy after the Revolution." *College Composition and Communication* 48 (1997): 30–43.

Herzberg, Bruce. "Civic Literacy and Service Learning." *Coming of Age: The Advanced Writing Curriculum.* Ed. Linda K. Shamoon, et al. Portsmouth, NH: Heinemann, 2000.

Kozol, Jonathan. *Savage Inequalities: Children in America's Schools.* New York: Harper, 1992.

Oakes, Jeannie. *Keeping Track: How Schools Structure Inequality.* New Haven: Yale UP, 1985.

Rose, Mike. *Lives on the Boundary: The Struggles and Achievements of America's Underprepared.* New York: Penguin, 1989.

Tobias, Sheila. "Tracked to Fail." *Psychology Today* 23 Sept. 1989: 54+.

Wells, Susan. "Rogue Cops and Health Care: What Do We Want from Public Writing?" *College Composition and Communication* 47 (1996): 325–41.

Andrea A. Lunsford and Cheryl Glenn

Rhetorical Theory and the Teaching of Writing

RHETORIC AND THE DYNAMIC ELEMENTS OF WRITTEN COMMUNICATION[1]

For some 2,500 years, speakers and writers have relied — often unknowingly — on rhetorical theory to achieve successful persuasion and communication or to gain cooperation. "Rhetorical theory?" — it sounds formidable, perhaps even beside the point. Yet every teacher and every student works out of rhetorical theory, a conceptual framework that guides us in the dynamic process of making meaning, sustains our classroom writing practices, and informs our textbooks.

Long the staple of communication theory, the *"communication triangle,"* comprising *sender, receiver,* and *message,* has expanded to incorporate *universe* (or *context*), the fourth component of this rhetorical set of interrelationships [see Figure 1]. These four elements of meaning not only guide teachers in their teaching choices but also guide writers in their writing choices, choices based on (1) their own values; (2) those of their receivers; (3) the possible range of messages; and (4) the nature of the universe, of reality.

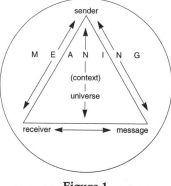

Figure 1

[1]We thank Gerald Nelms for helping with the citations and bibliography. We are also grateful to Jon Olson and Jamie Barlowe, whose sensible suggestions and supportive criticism helped us rewrite parts of the manuscript.

This article is reprinted from *On Literacy and Its Teaching,* ed. Gail Hawisher and Anna Soter (Albany: State U of New York P, 1990), 174–89.

Aristotle may have been the first to separate the rhetorical elements (the persuasive appeals) of communication when he wrote that the true constituents of the art of rhetoric are *ethos,* the appeals exerted by the speaker (the sender); *pathos,* the appeals to the emotions or values of the audience (the receiver); and *logos,* the appeals to reason of the message itself—with all appeals reflecting or affecting the *universe* (*Rhetoric,* 1.2.1356c). And his definition of *rhetoric* as "the faculty of observing in any given case the available means of persuasion" (1.2.1355b) has undergirded all rhetorical theory thenceforth, providing scholars, critics, and rhetoricians a dependable and expandable base for their own contributions to rhetorical theory and practice.

In his landmark *Theory of Discourse* (1971), James Kinneavy relates Aristotle's rhetorical triangle to fields other than rhetoric (such as literary theory, anthropology, communication, and semiotics), showing, in each case, just how *any* communication can emphasize one particular element of the triangle. Like Aristotle, who demonstrates three purposeful discourses, Kinneavy locates the variable aims of discourse in its emphatic triangulation of author, audience, universe, or in its reflexive emphasis on itself, the text.

Kinneavy refers to the work of literary theorist M. H. Abrams (310–48), whose *The Mirror and the Lamp* posits the four elements in the total situation of a work of art: the *work,* the artistic product itself; the *artist,* who produced the work; the *universe,* the subject of the work itself or from which the work is derived; and the *audience* to whom the work is addressed or made available (6–7). Although a work of artistic literature itself always implicitly assumes an author, an audience, a universe, the four coordinates of the work vary in significance according to the theory in which they occur: mimetic theories emphasize art's imitation of the *universe;* pragmatic theories propound art's effect on the *audience,* on getting things done; expressive theories center on the *artist* as cause and criterion of art; and objective theories deal with the *work of art* itself, in parts and in the mutual relations of its parts.

Kinneavy also refers to the work of anthropological linguists, who, like the literary theorists, evaluate language in terms of its aims: as verbal gesture, *interjectional;* as imitation of reality, *representational;* as a pragmatic symbol for getting things done, *utilitarian;* and as expression of the sender, poetic or *play* (51–52). The communication theorists, too, refer to language aims: informative, exploratory, instrumental, and emotive—aims that stress the importance of one rhetorical element (53–54). Communication theorists call the elements *encoder, decoder, signal,* and *reality,* and they connect informative communication with the signal or text; exploratory with reality or the universe; instrumental with the decoder or the audience; and emotive with the encoder or the author.

Eminent rhetorician Kenneth Burke extended the grammar of rhetoric to encompass five elements, expanding the rhetorical triangle to a pentad: agent (who?), action (what?), scene (where and when?), purpose (why?), and agency (how?) (*A Grammar of Motives*). Not intended as a heuristic, an aid to discovery or invention, Burke's pentad, nonetheless, supplies writers and readers with a method for establishing the focus of a written or spoken text. His theory of dramatism, focusing as it does on the ratios between the elements in the pentad, calls attention to the ways these representative terms are linked. Dramatism is a theory of action that breathes life into a text, humanizing the action. When a person's acts are to be interpreted in terms of the scene in which she is acting (as in *Robinson Crusoe, Lord of the Flies,* or *Riddley Walker,* for example), her behavior falls under the heading of a "scene-act ratio." In *Lord of the Flies,* both Ralph and Jack, leaders of opposing factions, "act" in reaction to the "scene": they are stranded on a desert island without the traditional protection of society. Yet, within the scene-act ratio falls a range of behavior that must again be evaluated according to the "agent-act ratio" — what is the correspondence between a person's character and action and between the action and the circumstances? Well-adjusted, optimistic, and athletic Ralph "naturally" acts out the desire for civilization, while Jack, the cruel and ugly bully, acts out the feral desire for mastery by intimidation and violence. Other dynamic relationships, other ratios, disclose still other features of human relations, behavior, and motives. Yet no matter how we look at texts, no matter which theorist's game we play, we always seem to swing around the poles of the original rhetorical triangle.

Like Burke, Wayne Booth also expands the notion of the rhetorical triangle. Burke uses his pentad retrospectively to analyze the motives of language (human) actions — texts or speeches — while Booth stresses the persuasive potential of his triangulated proofs: *ethos,* which is situated in the sender; *pathos,* in the receiver; and *logos,* in the text itself (*Modern Dogma and the Rhetoric of Assent* 144–64). Both their analytic frameworks can be used two ways: (1) as systems or frames on which to build a text; and (2) as systems of analysis for already completed texts. Booth's rhetorical triangle provides a framework that can be used to analyze a text, for it is the dynamic interaction of *ethos, pathos,* and *logos* that creates that text. To understand the *meaning* of an already completed text, however, Booth would examine the content, analyze the audience that is implied in the text, and recover the attitudes expressed by the implied author. The total act of communication must be examined in order to recover the *ethos*/character of the speaker, authorial attitude and intention, and voice — vital elements, resonant with attitude, that create a text. Burke, too, realized the importance of "attitude" and often talked of adding it to his dramatistic pentad (thereby transforming it into a hexad).

In "The Rhetorical Stance," Booth's message to teachers, he posits a concept of rhetoric that can support an undergraduate curriculum:

> The common ingredient that I find in all of the writing I admire...is something that I shall reluctantly call the rhetorical stance, a stance which depends on discovering and maintaining in any writing situation a proper balance among the three elements that are at work in any communicative effort: the available arguments about the subject itself, the interests and peculiarities of the audience, and the voice, the implied character, of the speaker. (27)

Like Aristotle, Booth posits a carefully balanced tripartite division of rhetorical appeals. Ever mindful of the audience being addressed, Booth would have us — as writers — strike such a balance to have a clear relationship with our reader(s) and our texts. As readers, Booth would have us keep this triangulation in mind, too, searching for and analyzing ethical, emotional, and logical appeals as we read. Otherwise, he warns, our reading of the text will be at best insensitive, at worst inaccurate. In *Lord of the Flies,* we analyze Ralph's and Jack's speeches for persuasive appeals, just as we analyze the appeals imbricating the omniscient author's narrative. Similar to Aristotle, who believed the ethical appeal to be the most effective, Booth wants speakers and writers — teachers and students alike — to examine their assumptions and to inspect the reasons for their strong commitments. Booth would like to reintroduce into education a strong concept of *ethos,* the dynamic start of persuasive communication: in balancing these three elements, the *logos* may determine how far we extend our *ethos* or what *ethos* we use or how much *pathos.* Booth goes on to say that "it is this balance, this rhetorical stance, difficult as it is to describe, that is our main goal as teachers of rhetoric" (27).

The traditional, stable, tricornered dynamics of written communication have been recently expanded. Gone is the notion of one speaker, one listener, one message — one voice. Instead, such univocal discourse has been replaced with many speakers, many listeners, many messages. In most communications, people are both speakers *and* listeners, or there is a multitude of listeners for one speaker; and the message is constantly affected by and adjusted to both speakers and listeners. To complicate communication even further, each listener interprets each speaker differently, even if only one speaker exists. Thus, just as the speaker and listener cannot be univocal, neither can the interpretation. Although the resulting icon is no longer the "rhetorical triangle," the triangular dynamics remain, for the figure becomes one of equilateral triangles with varying but concentric orientations. The familiar triangle has been embellished, but the original three key terms — speaker, listener, subject — remain.

WHAT RESEARCH TELLS US ABOUT THE ELEMENTS OF WRITTEN COMMUNICATION

The revival of rhetorical theory witnessed during the last twenty-five years has reacquainted teachers with the primary elements of the rhetorical tradition — *ethos*/audience; *logos*/text — and with the way those elements have been played out in the canon of rhetoric. Although they might not be familiar with the actual names, most teachers are familiar with concepts forming the canons of rhetoric: invention, arrangement, style, memory, and delivery. While this formulation is in some sense reductive, it nevertheless provides a useful framework for investigating the recent contributions of rhetorical theory to the teaching of writing. Close attention to the *writer* during this time has resulted in much important work that attempts essentially to answer this twofold question: where do a writer's ideas come from and how are such ideas formulated into writing? Such a question demands a new focus on *invention,* the first canon of rhetoric, and has led in two provocative and profitable directions. The first, represented in the work of Richard Young, Janice Lauer, and Richard Larson (to name only a very few), aims at deriving heuristic procedures or systematic strategies that will aid students in discovering and generating ideas about which they might write. Such strategies may be as simple as prompting students to generate ideas about a subject by asking — who, what, when, where, why, and how — the traditional "journalistic formula" mentioned above. Or they can be as complex as the nine-cell matrix presented in Young, Becker, and Pike's *Rhetoric: Discovery and Change*. Essentially, this heuristic asks student writers to look at any subject from nine different perspectives. For example, a student writing about a campus strike might look at it first as a "happening" frozen in time and space, or as the result of a complex set of causes, or as a *cause* of some other effects, or as one tiny part of a larger economic pattern. Looking at the subject in such different ways "loosens up" mental muscles and jogs writers out of unidimensional or tunnel-vision views of a subject.

We see this interest in procedural heuristics as related theoretically to the work of researchers interested in cognition. Linda Flower and coauthor John Hayes are best known for their studies of writers' talk-aloud protocols, tape-recorded documents that catch a writer's *thoughts* about writing while the writing is actually in progress. As any methodology is bound to be, such methodology is flawed, but it *has* provided a fascinating "window on writers' minds," to use Flower's descriptive phrase. Stephen Witte has recently built on the work of Flower and Hayes in order to study what he calls a writer's "pre-text," a writer's "trial locution that is produced in the mind, stored in the writer's memory, and sometimes manipulated mentally prior to being transcribed as written text" (397). Other researchers have attempted to map the relationship of affective factors to a writer's "invention": John Daly, in terms of writing apprehension, and Mike Rose, in terms of writer's block. All of this research aims to help teachers understand the rich, diverse, complex, and largely *invisible* processes student writers go through in writing.

But a renewed interest in student writers has led in another powerful direction as well, notably in the work of Ken Macrorie and, more pervasively, of Peter Elbow. Elbow is interested in how writers establish unique voices, in how they realize individual selves in discourse, and his work with students presents dramatic evidence of such activity. In a series of very influential books (*Writing without Teachers, Writing with Power, Embracing Contraries*), Elbow has focused on how writers come to know themselves — and then share those selves with others.

The researchers and teachers we have been surveying here differ in many ways, but their work is all aimed primarily at that point of the rhetorical triangle that focuses on the writer and her powers of invention. They want to know what makes writers tick — and how teachers can help writers "tick" most effectively.

If we shift the focus of our discussion from writer to *text*, we also find that rhetorical theory has much to offer the teacher of writing. Students are often puzzled when teachers do not "get the meaning" they intend. Rhetorical theory helps us explain why such miscommunication takes place and suggests powerful ways to avoid it. One of the simplest to use with students is I. A. Richards's own version of the rhetorical triangle [see Figure 2]. Richards argues that no direct relationship exists between a word — a set of black marks on a page — and its referent in the world (Ogden and Richards *The Meaning of Meaning* 10–13). That is to say, the meaning of *cat* is not inherent in the little squiggles we call letters not in the furry, purry pet we might have. Rather, meaning arises in the perceivers — in people — as they filter the linguistic signal *cat* through all their experience with both word and thing. So *cat* might well mean one thing to someone who adores cats and something quite different to someone who was, as a child, badly scratched by a cat.

Reader's idea of a "cat"

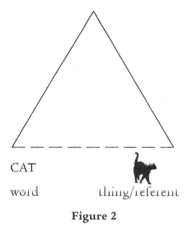

CAT

word   thing/referent

Figure 2

Richards uses another principle to help us understand how we derive meaning from texts. He calls this principle *interinanimation of words,* which simply means that any one word is strongly affected by other words around it (*Philosophy of Rhetoric* 47–66). The word *love,* for instance, suggests one meaning when connected to the words *grandparent* and *grandchild,* another when connected to *husband* and *wife,* and yet another when connected to a business tycoon and her self-image. Students can put Richards's principle to use by examining a text closely for the ways its words interinanimate one another. And teachers can use the principle of interinanimation to show students that we are all very much *what we say,* that our words work together (interinanimate) to create the people we are, with our individual values, prejudices, and so on.

Three other concepts used by modern rhetorical theorists may help students and teachers get inside the intricacies of any text. Richard Weaver provides one set, what he calls *ultimate* or *God terms* and *Devil terms,* to indicate those words or concepts that represent something we will make sacrifices for (87–112). In the 1950s, Weaver hypothesized that *Americanism, progress,* and *science* served as God terms, large concepts that most people held very dear. He went on to suggest that God or Devil terms establish hierarchical relationships in texts — that is, that many other related terms usually clustered under them. Identifying such central terms and then mapping related clusters of terms can help students get at complex meanings in texts.

Burke suggests that we look at a text (or any discourse, spoken or written) as a *terministic screen* (LSA "Terministic Screens" 59 ff). If we think of a text as a very fine-meshed screen, with every point connected to every other point, what Burke has in mind becomes apparent. The "screen" of the text directs our attention in certain ways, selecting some points for emphasis, deflecting others. And the screen is made up not of wire, but of words or *terms.* Burke challenges us to trace all the minute interstitial connections among terms in any text/screen as a means of constructing meaning.

One other key principle deserves our attention in discussing rhetorical theory and texts: *intertextuality,* which refers to a principle very similar to those we have been discussing. Most simply, intertextuality denotes the great conversation among texts, the way texts refer or allude to one another, build on or parody one another, revolve around one another. The Mel Brooks movie *Young Frankenstein,* for instance, is part of an elaborate and extensive conversation stretching back through countless other movies to Mary Shelley's novel (with its subtitle *The Modern Prometheus*) to many poems and plays and mythical accounts of Prometheus, to the creation of Adam in the Bible — or *forward* to the contemporary debate over genetic engineering and our ability to create life. Introducing students to this principle of intertextuality allows them to enter this great conversation and provides them with an effective method for probing textual meaning.

The theorists we have been discussing offer ways to see the "big picture" of a text; they deal with the macrostructure element of the second canon of rhetoric, the *arrangement* of argument. But rhetorical theory offers help on the microstructures of the "little picture" as well. This tradition of research, which focuses on organization, on the relationship between form and function, is extensive and complex. Here we will cite two rhetoricians whose work seems most helpful for the teaching of writing. Many readers of this book already might be familiar with the first, Francis Christensen. In a series of essays, Christensen demonstrated a way to map sentences and paragraphs according to levels of generality and modification. *Periodic* sentences and paragraphs are those that delay or postpone announcing the general main clause/topic until the very end, leading into the topic with supporting or modifying details ("A Generative Rhetoric of the Sentence" 155–56). This kind of structure forces a reader to hold the subject in mind until the very end and keeps syntactic tension high. In the hands of skilled writers, periodic structures can keep readers alert for what is to come and make the main idea, when it finally does appear, all the more impressive.

Although structures using various degrees of periodicity can be very effective in challenging and interesting readers, they do not constitute the most frequently used pattern in modern English. Rather, the *cumulative* structure, which adds details after the main clause or announcement of the topic, is the more dominant. Christensen writes: "The main clause, which may or may not have a sentence modifier before it, advances the discussion; but the additions move backwards, as in this clause, to modify the statement of the main clause or more often to explicate it or exemplify it, so that the sentence has a flowing and ebbing movement, advancing to a new position and then pausing to consolidate it, leaping and lingering as the popular ballad does" (156). Because the main clause/topic is presented at or near the beginning of the sentence/paragraph, cumulative structures do not require readers to hold the subject in suspense until the end. In one sense, then, these structures may be easier to read than periodic ones, yet the skillful writer can position the most important piece of information at the end. Like all sentence patterns, however, the cumulative sentence can be used effectively or, as in the following example, ineffectively: "The cumulative sentence in unskilled hands is unsteady, allowing a writer to ramble on, adding modifier after modifier, until the reader is almost overwhelmed, because the writer's central idea is lost."

Using exclusively periodic or cumulative structures, of course, would be monotonous. And so the best writers mingle structures — short and long, periodic and cumulative — although never forgetting that the most important ideas naturally deserve the most prominent positions. Our own students can easily test the structures of others' as well as their own texts, relating purpose to structure, and can learn to balance their own prose with purposeful and effective movement between general and specific information.

More recently, Richard Coe has elaborated and extended the work of Christensen, moving toward what he calls a *grammar of passages*. In his monograph by the same name, Coe takes the traditional syntactic relationships between form and function — coordinate, subordinate, and superordinate — and subdivides them further: (1) coordination: contrasting, contradicting, conjoining, and repeating on the same level of generality; (2) subordination: defining, exemplifying, giving reasons, deducing (deductive conclusion), explaining (making plain by restating more specifically), qualifying; and (3) superordination: drawing conclusions, generalizing (making an inductive inference), commenting on a previously stated proposition (32–33). Then Coe goes on to develop a system of mapping these relationships. This syntactical system has been tested extensively with student writers, in classes ranging from ESL to technical writing, to basic writing, to advanced composition, with dramatic results. Students learn to "map" their own texts and thereby have a means of deciding whether those texts are coherent, whether they "make sense."

But what of the third angle of the rhetorical triangle — that pointing to *audience* and *context*? Does rhetorical theory offer any insights into these crucial elements in communication? Of course. As a discipline, rhetoric has always been intensely interested in the effects a writer's intentions, words, texts, have *on people* in varying situations. That is to say, taking a "rhetorical stance" always places us in a full context. In this regard, rhetorical theory has helped us learn about the psychology of readers (or listeners, interpreters, responders), from Aristotle's discussion of how different types of people react to different subjects and Plato's elegant oration on souls, to contemporary persuasion theorists (Petty, Ostrom, and Brock) on the one hand and reader-oriented researchers and critics (Rosenblatt, Bleich, and Iser) on the other.

What this research tells us as teachers of writing is simply this: the processes of reading and responding to texts are at least as complex as those of writing a text; that all readers build up frameworks (called schemata), which they use to make sense as they read; that such frameworks are affected both by everything we already know and by what we are (gender, for example, exerts powerful influence on patterns of interpretation and response). As teachers, we must help students understand and theorize about their own such patterns. Doing so leads to the second major point we want to make here. That is, we can often understand our own patterns of response by seeing them *in context,* as related to others' responses and as part of a large social process aimed at negotiating and constructing meaning. If intertextuality is a coin, this is its flip side — interreaderability — the fully contextualized, multiple voices out of which we forge an understanding of texts.

PEDAGOGICAL IMPLICATIONS OF A WRITTEN COMMUNICATION

A rhetoric of written communication demands a dynamic balancing of speaker, listener, subject (of *ethos, pathos, logos*). And when a teacher introduces these elements into the writing classroom, she can expect learning to emerge. The interdependency of these elements creates galvanic tension, in terms not only of the rhetorical elements themselves, but also of the students, teacher, and texts.

The pedagogical implications for teachers are manifold, most prominent being that they must learn to share authority, thereby enabling students to experience, create, and evaluate their own and others' texts. One of the best ways teachers can share responsibility for learning is to provide "demonstrations," occasions for active learning for their students. In the terms of education researcher Frank Smith, demonstrations provide students with opportunities to become so engaged that they really teach themselves; they forget that they are learning and take an active role in their own learning.

In fact, writing teachers can most easily provide students with demonstrations by adjusting writing assignments, making them (to use an overused term) "relevant" to the students' lives. Often, meaningful writing assignments are merely those that provide students with information on their intended audience, their purpose for writing, and the context of the communication — information that encourages students to harness the dynamics of the rhetorical triangle. Other teachers provide demonstrations by building their syllabi on a theme, such as "education" (cf. Bartholomae and Petrosky; Lunsford). A teacher in an open admissions college provided his students with demonstrations by building a syllabus on "work." Urging his students to meet in small groups, to speak out, to read and respond to one another's writing, to expect concrete details and supporting observations, this teacher watched as his class of low-paid, blue-collar manual workers reinvented their daily lives, sharing their experiences, critically analyzing their situations, and writing persuasively and feelingly about their lives. No longer was learning the retrieval and transmission of static information — from the teacher's head to the students'. Rather, learning became the dynamic interactions of the students, a demonstration of their abilities to discover and create, construe and communicate their own knowledge. Once they realized their own rhetorical stance, the values and attitudes of their intended audience, and the importance of their message, their rhetorical triangles were balanced. In this case, choice of writing assignments indicated the teacher's willingness to share responsibility for classroom learning.

Hence, such a classroom transforms itself from uni- to polyvocal. The original rhetorical triangle, weighted fully on the teacher/speaker side, becomes a series of phase-shift rotations, rhetorical triangles that constantly achieve, lose, and reestablish rhetorical balance. Each shift, a fusion of rhetoric and dialectic, is determined by whose paper is being featured, who is serving as author, who is serving as audience, and how the in-draft text is being affected and effected by the speaker and audience. And ultimately, that original triangle, in recreating itself, begins to round out and resemble an expanded circular universe of discourse.

To make the polyvocal, rhetorical classroom "work," students, too, must learn to share responsibility for their learning, and to rely no longer solely on their teacher for grades, knowledge, approval, or ego gratification. What might be initially perceived as instability will soon be seen for what it is — dynamics. Once students begin to take advantage of these classroom dynamics — teacher and students alike working as sharers and evaluators — they will realize the potential for their own written communication. No longer will they be content to serve as repositories for their teacher's knowledge, to write *for* and *to* only their teachers, to remain silent. Yet often and understandably, just transferring their allegiance from their teacher to their peers is difficult, accustomed as they are to years of passive learning. Accustomed as teachers are to years of one-way teaching and nearly total responsibility for learning (and teaching), many find relief in newly shared allegiance. Students need to know that in the rhetorical classroom, their teachers are willing to share their work, their responsibility, even their authority.

In the rhetorical writing classroom, students broaden their intended audience from the teacher-evaluator to include their peers, carefully considering the responses and evaluations of those peers, perhaps more than they did those of their teachers. Many students choose to respond orally and in writing to classroom, in-draft texts and to participate in the final evaluation of themselves and their peers. Peers create an actual audience and often a reason for writing, for they provide response — what Elbow calls "the main experience that makes people want to write more" (130). In *Writing without Teachers,* Elbow writes about one student's thrill of working with her peers: "Her words got through to the readers. She sent words out into the darkness and heard someone shout back. This made her want to do it again, and this is probably the most powerful thing that makes people improve their writing" (130).

When students are involved in one another's writings, serving as senders and receivers of communication, as questioners of purpose, as judges of *ethos,* *pathos,* and *logos,* as refiners of style and tone, when they are respectfully attentive of one another's *author*-ity, when students have the opportunity to question responses to their drafts *as they draft,* when they coach as they are being coached, then they are indeed sharing the responsibility for their own learning and incorporating in their learning the dynamics of rhetorical theory.

The implications for a rhetoric of written communication go beyond those for the teacher and students, however, to affect the very physical structure of the classroom itself. Always, or so it seems, students have sat in neat rows of nailed-down desks, discouraged from making so much as eye contact with their peers, asked to write in solitude. But as teachers and students begin to use rhetorical theory, begin to see that senders need the responses of receivers, that the universe, the "out there," plays an integral part in communication, and that messages are colored by all the elements in the rhetorical triangle, they will be unable to work in the traditional classroom environment. They will want tables or moveable desks so they can sit and work together. They will want to talk on the phone or through their computers both during and after school. They need to be together. And they need time.

Gone should be the days when students are asked to complete their writing in forty-eight minutes or to evaluate the work of their groups in forty-eight minutes. Gone should be the days when one draft — the first and final — is handed in for an unchangeable grade. Many schools, in fact, are moving toward the portfolio method of evaluation, which encourages students to gather their best revisions for one end-of-the-term grade.[1] Thoughtful writing and thoughtful responding take time, time for planning, thinking, drafting, responding, revising, and polishing. Hence, classrooms themselves must be designed in response to the evolution of classroom practices as well as classroom schedules.

ISSUES RAISED BY A RHETORIC OF WRITTEN COMMUNICATION

Teachers and students committed to examining the dynamic relationship among writers, audiences, texts, and contexts will face a number of important issues, foremost among them the complex question of ethics and language use. If we are not so much what we *eat* as what we say or write, if as Jacques Derrida claims, we don't write language so much as language *writes us,* then words can never be "mere" words again. Instead words are, to use Burke's term, symbolic *acts (LSA)*; as Weaver says, a speaker's words have *consequences,* and these consequences affect other people, texts, and contexts (22 1ff). As language users, we thus must be responsible for our words, must take the responsibility for examining our own and others' language and seeing how well, how truly, it represents the speaker. We can do so playfully, through parody or spoofing, or we can do so most seriously, as in an analysis of the consequences of political doublespeak. But we — teachers and students alike — must carry out such analyses consistently and rigorously.

Once students grasp this principle of analytic responsibility, they become rhetors. They see writing and reading not as boring school-bound drills or as ways of packaging static information, but as ways of creating and recreating themselves through and with others, as a student reported during a recent evaluation of one of our courses:

> When we first started this class, I couldn't *imagine* what you meant by our being rhetoricians, getting rhetorical stances of our own. What's all this, I thought? You're the teacher. You know a whole lot of stuff, and you better just *tell* it to us. Now I know that you really do know a lot of stuff, more even than I thought. But that's not what matters. What matters is what I know. And now I know that I'm making what I know in language, forming, transforming, and reforming myself with other people. What I know is we are all of us learners in progress. Even you! So — *wish me luck.*

Teachers, of course, are the ones who develop and nurture such an atmosphere, who set the terms within which an ethos of the classroom emerges. Building such an atmosphere implies that the teacher becomes a member/participant of the class, providing questions, tasks, and situations that will allow the class to experience what it means not to *reveal* knowledge but to *construct* it, to be learners-in-progress. This role is a demanding one, far more so than traditional teacherly roles have been.

In the final analysis, a rhetorical perspective on the teaching of writing pushes us outside our private selves, beyond our solitary teacherly or writerly desks, to a realization of the ways in which we all use language to create — or destroy communities, societies, worlds. The writing classroom is one such world. Rhetorical theory provides us, together with our students, with the means of making that world, one that is rich in diversity, complex in meaning, and full of all the life our blended voices can give it.

NOTE

[1] The portfolio method of assessment has been most thoroughly documented and argued for by Peter Elbow of University of Massachusetts–Amherst. The largest school with plans to adopt a portfolio method of assessment is University of Minnesota, which, beginning in 1990, plans to use portfolios for evaluation in introductory composition as well as for promotion.

WORKS CITED

Abrams, M. H. *The Mirror and the Lamp: Romantic Theory and the Critical Tradition.* New York: Oxford UP, 1953.

Aristotle. *The Rhetoric and the Poetics of Aristotle.* Trans. W. Rhys Roberts. New York: Modern Library, 1984.

Bartholomae, David, and Anthony Petrosky. *Facts, Artifacts, and Counterfacts: Theory and Method for a Reading and Writing Course.* Upper Montclair, NJ: Boynton/Cook, 1986.

Bleich, David. *Subjective Criticism*. Baltimore, MD: Johns Hopkins UP, 1978.

____. *Readings and Feelings: An Introduction to Subjective Criticism*. Urbana, IL: National Council of Teachers of English, 1975.

____. "The Subjective Character of Critical Interpretation." *College English* 36 (1975): 739-55.

Booth, Wayne C. *Modern Dogma and the Rhetoric of Assent*. Chicago: U of Chicago P, 1974.

____. "The Rhetorical Stance." *Now Don't Try to Reason with Me: Essays and Ironics for a Credulous Age*. Chicago: U of Chicago P, 1970.

Bruffee, Kenneth. "The Brooklyn Plan: Attaining Intellectual Growth through Peer-Group Tutoring." *Liberal Education* 64 (1978): 447-69.

____. "Collaborative Learning: Some Practical Models." *College English* 34 (1973): 634-43.

Burke, Kenneth. *A Grammar of Motives*. Cleveland: World, 1962.

____. *A Rhetoric of Motives*. Cleveland: World, 1962.

____. "Terministic Screens." *Language as Symbolic Action*. Berkeley: U of California P, 1966.

Christensen, Francis. "A Generative Rhetoric of the Sentence." *College Composition and Communication* 14 (1963): 155-61.

____. "A Generative Rhetoric of the Paragraph." *College Composition and Communication* 16 (1968): 144-56.

Coe, Richard. *A Grammar of Passages*. Carbondale: Southern Illinois UP, 1987.

Daly, John. "The Effects of Writing Apprehension on Message Encoding." *Journalism Quarterly* 54 (1977): 566-72.

____. "Writing Apprehension and Writing Competency." *Journal of Educational Research* 72 (1978): 10-14.

Derrida, Jacques. *Of Grammatology*. Trans. Gayatri Chakravorty Spivak. Baltimore, Md.: Johns Hopkins UP, 1974.

Elbow, Peter. *Embracing Contraries*. New York: Oxford UP, 1986.

____. *Writing with Power*. New York: Oxford UP, 1981.

____. *Writing without Teachers*. New York: Oxford UP, 1973.

Flower, Linda, and John R. Hayes. "Uncovering Cognitive Processes in Writing: An Introduction to Protocol Analysis." *Research on Writing*. Ed. P. Mosenthal, S. Walmsley, and L. Tamor. London: Longman, 1982. 207-20.

Iser, Wolfgang. *The Act of Reading: A Theory of Aesthetic Response*. Baltimore, MD: Johns Hopkins UP, 1974.

____. *The Implied Reader*. Baltimore, MD: Johns Hopkins UP, 1975.

Kinneavy, James L. *A Theory of Discourse*. Englewood Cliffs: Prentice-Hall, 1971.

Larson, Richard L. "Discovery through Questioning: A Plan for Teaching Rhetorical Invention." *College English* 30 (1968): 126-34.

Lauer, Janice. "Heuristics and Composition." *College Composition and Communication* 21 (1970): 396-404.

Lunsford, Andrea A. "Assignments for Basic Writers: Unresolved Issues and Needed Research." *Journal of Basic Writing* 5 (1986): 87-99.

Ogden, C. K., and I. A. Richards. *The Meaning of Meaning: A Study of the Influences of Language upon Thought and of the Science of Symbolism*. New York: Harcourt, 1936.

Petty, Richard E., Thomas M. Ostrom, and Timothy Brock, eds. *Cognitive Responses in Persuasion*. Hillsdale, NJ: Erlbaum, 1981.

Richards, I. A. *The Philosophy of Rhetoric*. New York: Oxford UP, 1936.

Rose, Mike. *Writer's Block: The Cognitive Dimension*. Carbondale: Southern Illinois UP, 1984.

Rosenblatt, Louise. *Literature as Exploration.* 3d ed. New York: Barnes and Noble, 1976.
———. *The Reader, the Text, the Poem: The Transactional Theory of the Literary Work.* Carbondale: Southern Illinois UP, 1978.
Smith, Frank. "Research Update: Demonstrations, Engagements, and Sensitivity—A Revised Approach to Language Learning." *Language Arts* 68 (1981): 103–12.
Weaver, Richard M. *Language Is Sermonic: Richard M. Weaver on the Nature of Rhetoric.* Ed. Richard L. Johannesen, Rennard Strickland, and Ralph T. Eubanks. Baton Rouge: Louisiana State UP, 1970.
Witte, Stephen. "Pre-Text and Composing." *College Composition and Communication* 38 (1987): 397–425.
Young, Richard E., Alton L. Becker, and Kenneth L. Pike. *Rhetoric: Discovery and Change.* New York: Harcourt, 1970.

Peter Elbow

The Cultures of Literature and Composition: What Could Each Learn from the Other?

The history of relations between composition and literature has involved a vexed tangle of misunderstanding and hurt. Both fields would benefit if we could think through some of the vexations. That's what I'm trying to do here.

But I won't talk about the most obvious problems: political and material issues of power, money, and prestige. These matters cannot be ignored, but I will mention them quickly and pass on. Composition has been the weak spouse, the new kid, the cash cow, the oppressed majority. When writing programs are housed in English departments, as they so often are, teachers of writing are usually paid less to teach more under poorer working conditions—in order to help support literature professors to be paid more to teach less under better working conditions. I'm hoping that these material vexations might be starting to recede just a bit now— as composition gets stronger and more secure, as writing programs find they can prosper outside English departments, and as literature itself struggles because of weak support for the humanities (not to mention frequent attacks on "professors" and all of higher education). Even the virus of relying on part-timers and adjuncts is increasing in mainstream literature, too. I ask only that we not forget how hard it will be to get past the deep legacy of anger, hurt, and guilt.

I won't even address the much-discussed question of whether writing and literature should marry, stay married, or divorce. My essay could be read as an argument for maintaining the marriage; and I certainly admire the situation in many high schools and a few smaller liberal arts colleges where members don't actually feel a tension between literature and composition. But I hope my thoughts will be of use, whatever the contractual or sleeping arrangements are between literature and composition.

I turn away here from those issues and seek instead to explore what might be called—very loosely—the *cultures* or *traditions* or *identities* of literature and composition. I'm interested in the intellectual and psychological traditions of these fields—not just practices but what I sense still lurks in our minds and in the air when we experience ourselves as "literature persons" and/or "composition persons." My ultimate goal is to answer some practical professional questions: What does the tradition or culture of literature have that composition needs? What does composition have that literature needs? How could each learn from the other?

This article is reprinted from *College English* 64.5 (May 2002): 533–546.

I must confess at once that I am writing from a personal and subjective point of view. Worse yet, this essay is an exercise in large arguable generalizations (one reviewer called them "too easy") based on my "feel" or "sense" of things over the years — rather than on scholarship and research in the manner of Graff and Scholes. I present no proof; only a pudding. If my generalizations don't ring usefully true to many members of both communities, I've simply failed. Still, my subjectivity is based on forty years' teaching at six colleges or universities — and consultations, talks, and workshops at countless others.

I started full-time college teaching in 1960 and, having made it to age sixty-six, I've retired from full-time university employment. I'm continuing busy in my professional career, but this new step makes me look back. One thing I notice is my recurring sense of being torn between my identities as a literature person and as a composition person. I've long been seen as a composition person, and I've been a writing program director at two universities. But all my training was in literature, my first book was about Chaucer, and I didn't experience myself as a member of the "field of composition" till at least twenty of these past forty years had passed.

I.

I start with a sentence that makes me nervous (although I enjoy how it links the personal and professional): "I miss literature." What do I mean? First, it's just literal: I miss having works of literature central in some of my teaching. Why should I be nervous to say this? The problem is not so much sounding disloyal as being actually misleading. For when I say "I miss literature," it will sound to many as though I am voicing a whole complex of other thoughts that people in composition so often hear from people in literature: "I can't stand reading student writing." "Students have nothing of significance to write about." "No one could really get intellectually interested in student writing." "We can't teach students to write unless we give them models of good writing by good authors to imitate." How do I say, "I miss literature," without saying any of these other things that seem toxically false?

I miss the comfort and pleasure of planning a whole class around a literary text, and preparing for class by simply immersing myself in it as deeply and carefully as I can and preparing generative questions (assuming that I already possess enough background secondary knowledge). The goal in preparing is the same as the goal for the class: not just to understand but to try to get inside of and be stretched or even transformed by a text that is miraculously good.

As a teacher of writing, I focus on texts in class that are fruitful and interesting (student writing and published essays about writing and other topics), and they can stretch us — not the least, student writing. But these texts are seldom transcendent or magical the way so many works of literature are. They seldom make me choke up.

Yet since I've become a composition person, I've come to use a richer process for class planning. I plan by devising *workshop activities* designed to create *experiences:* all kinds of writing exercises, out-loud readings, and various kinds of work in peer groups or pairs. Class planning feels more like trying to manage complex activities than quiet immersion in an amazing text. This approach to teaching that I learned as a teacher of writing tends to result in classes that are more lively and active than my old literature classes: fewer dead spells, less tooth pulling, less talk from me, more learning. I know now, of course, that this difference is a historical accident. I can now teach a "product" of literature by using active, experiential workshop activities I learned as a teacher of writing — and thereby increase the chances of students' actually *experiencing* the literary work and the critical concepts we are studying. A fair number of literature teachers have learned to do the same, but I think the field of composition gets some of the credit for this. (See *When Writing Teachers Teach Literature* [Young and Fulwiler], which contains my "Breathing Life into the Text.")

Process and Product. People in composition have taken to using rubber gloves for the word "process" ("Oh, we're *way* beyond the 'process approach'!"), but an emphasis on process is ineluctably in the blood stream of composition. (Similarly, no one in literature would be caught dead identifying as a New Critic, but the profession has permanently digested that essential methodological contribution of close reading for the sake of focusing on the usually complicated relationship between what's stated and what's implied. New Criticism and the focus on writing process were surely the founding — and I dare say defining — events of the two professions as they presently exist.) Almost every literature class is about a "product," a text, and the literature teacher usually wants the students to carry away a product too — some summarizable knowledge about that text. Almost every writing class is about a process, and the writing teacher usually wants the students to carry away some increased skill in that process. Of course literature teachers seek to teach the process of reading, but I think my rough contrast is supported by a glance at two characteristic teaching practices in the two fields. In literature classes, lecturing is extremely common. It's rare or absent from writing classes. Literature exams rarely ask students to read a new text; they usually focus on works the students have already studied — and heard the teacher's conclusions about. Writing exams (if used at all) ask students to write a new text.

Still, "I miss literature" in another sense. I miss living in a culture that considers the metaphorical and imaginative uses of language basic or primal. Owen Barfield wrote a useful essay about the "invention" of literal language, arguing that metaphor came first as the default, and literal language was a late development achieved only through a complex process of mental and linguistic differentiation. I'm not saying that the culture of composition *ignores* metaphor and imaginative language altogether. People in the field usually acknowledge that such language helps essays do their discursive work; and some teachers invite students to write a story at the start of the semester. But I'm sad that the composition tradition seems to assume discursive language as the norm and imaginative, metaphorical language as somehow special or marked or additional. I'd argue that we can't harness students' strongest linguistic and even cognitive powers unless we see imaginative and metaphorical language as the norm—basic or primal.

Yet I found I was pleased and proud when I was drawn *away* from literature by my growing interest in writing. When I finally came to see myself as a composition person, I felt an enormous relief at finally feeling *useful*—as though I could make an actual difference for people. I'd never felt solidly useful trying to teach and write about literature. I'm proud that composition is the only discipline I know, outside of schools of education, where members feel their field has a built-in relationship to teaching and to students.

I fear, in fact, that the culture of literary studies still carries a bit of that traditional implication that there is something "lower" about teaching than scholarship; that the tone of a scholarly essay is reduced if there is talk about teaching; and that teaching issues are for the less able. People in literature are more likely than those in composition to make a distinction between teaching and their "real work." George Levine, introducing the new journal *Pedagogy,* meditates at length on the phrase "my work," and how people in literary studies tend to use it to mean research rather than teaching—in explicit contrast to people in composition (10). David Bartholomae points out tellingly that at the beginning of the twentieth century, when the profession of "English" was still primarily philological and not yet "literary," the teaching of writing was taken very seriously at the highest levels. But then, "Composition fell out of sight of the MLA and most of the other significant venues of professional discussion" ("Composition" 1952).

The culture of composition carries a concern not just for teaching but also for students: attention, interest, and care for them, their lives, and what's on their minds. The core activity in teaching composition is the act of reading what's on students' minds; the core activity in teaching literature is reading the literary text. ("[T]he writing of my students and the problematic relationship between their work and the work of the academy[:] these seemed to hold all of the material I needed to make a career" [Bartholomae, "Freshman" 39].) Composition teachers are more likely, when asked what they teach, to give that ornery answer: "I teach students." I'm proud that we can be a rich scholarly field and still keep these ties to teaching and students. The culture has somehow managed to build a felt value in *identifying with* students—or at least refusing to see them as "other." Writing is more of a leveler than reading: in writing more than reading, teachers and students tend to feel the same anxieties (see my "War between Reading and Writing").

And yet. I seem to be praising composition for being more "real" and practical, and for dealing more directly with the genuine needs of students (and also, by the way, with concerns felt by the public). I am. Yet I must turn again and choose a different lens for a different view. For in a genuine sense, the most real and practical use of language is for making stories, images, and even poems. Mark Turner, in *The Literary Mind,* talks of story as the primary mode of language that organizes our very minds. When we dream, we may sometimes explain or argue, but the basic language of our nightly dreams is images and stories. Imaginative language touches people most deeply; sometimes it's the only language use that gets through. When people feel the tug of wanting to write (it's too little recognized in both traditions that *most* people actually feel such a tug) — what most often tugs at them is the call to render experience in narratives, images, or poems. (On the burgeoning research on "everyday writing," see Barton, Bloome, Sheridan, and Street; Barton and Ivanic; Hamilton, Barton, and Ivanic.)

So literature is no less "real" or "useful" than composition. And yet sadly, I feel that the culture of literature misses the boat here. Most teachers of literature neglect the task of teaching students how to *use* language imaginatively — how to write stories and poems. The tradition in literature seems to declare: "Imaginative writing can't be taught — it's too mysterious" or "Only artists or geniuses create art" or "We must try to staunch the hemorrhage of second-rate writing into the world." (I sometimes sense teachers of literature trying to stamp out "bad" amateur poetry. But it's a futile effort. Huge numbers of people write it, although they usually fear to show it to most of their teachers — whether literature or composition.)

But imaginative writing *can* be taught — and taught well, even to rank novices. I'm not, by the way, thinking of the teaching in MFA programs — where faculty assume that their students have no trouble producing imaginative writing, and therefore see their task as providing "workshops" to help students "critique" better. No, I'm thinking about a small but powerful stream of teachers in the schools (and in a few undergraduate writing courses) who are helping their students in a more generative fashion to write stories and poems and other imaginative and personal pieces. This interesting tradition has many sources. I am proud of its roots in the early days of composition — back when folks were not so nervous to talk about "creativity" or "invention." But I want to pay special homage to a crucial bridge that has carried this fragile tradition of teaching imaginative writing from the early days of composition to these important school classrooms: the so-called "area writing projects" scattered all around the country that grew from the original Bay Area Writing Project. There are now some 165 National Writing Project sites every summer, and they maintain a sturdy tradition of inviting teachers themselves to do imaginative writing of their own. (Of course they sponsor academic and critical writing, too.) This tradition of imaginative writing in the schools derives in addition from some crucially generative poets like Kenneth Koch — and from some small, powerful organizations like Teachers and Writers Collaborative and Poets in the Schools.

Not only does the literary tradition neglect the teaching of imaginative *writing*, it also neglects teaching us to *read* in such a way as to help bring powerful imaginative texts most palpably into our lives. The problem I'm speaking of could be called the "distancing mode" — the tradition of "critical reading." In the tradition of New Criticism, students are urged to look at literary works as complex artifacts rather than as devices for making sense of their lives and feelings. In addition, postmodernist and deconstructive practices also function as ways to distance oneself from the text as a kind of *intellectualized* aesthetic object. In contrast, teachers in the newer and powerful tradition of cultural studies usually do try to help students use texts for making sense of their lives (and often seek texts that students feel as part of their lives already — such as popular music or TV). But even here, I often sense the tradition of distancing. The goal in cultural studies tends to be to help students read with more critical detachment — to separate themselves from felt involvement in these texts.

Thus, the culture of literary studies feels to me to work against students' impulses to involve themselves personally with literature and feel they are making personal connections with characters and authors — to feel a genuine relationship with Chaucer or Iago. I'd argue that most good readers actually *do* this — and that even good critics do it and take it for granted before they go on to their critical practices. But most students need *help* achieving this kind of personal entanglement with texts.

I imagine readers of *College English* resisting me here and arguing that the problem with students is that they *already* identify too much — that they lack the ability to question and to achieve critical distance — to read against the grain. But the validity of this objection papers over a crucial distinction. Yes, students often don't read against the grain; but that doesn't mean they are good at reading *with* the grain. Lack of critical distance is *not* the same as full, rich involvement. For all too many students, the text is a pretty "nothing" experience. Why should they be interested in learning to question or see contrary depths in a "nothing" experience? I'm not making an either-or argument against critical detachment; I'm arguing that most students need help learning how to enter into mentalities and experience points of view different from their own (see Nemerov; see also my essays about "the believing game" or "methodological belief").

We can better notice the distancing dimension in the culture of literary studies if we compare it to the work of Robert Coles. A psychoanalyst and scholar in many fields, he describes in *The Call of Stories* how he teaches literature to Harvard undergraduates and medical and business students as ways to help them work through larger ethical questions of life and work (see also O'Connor's "Words and the World at a New York Public School: Can Writing Really Matter to Inner City Children?"). I'm not suggesting that teachers of literature abandon the use of all distancing techniques; I'm suggesting the need for what is almost entirely neglected, namely "involving" techniques (as in much of Young and Fulwiler).

Speaking of distance, let me stand back now and meditate for a moment on the two essential dimensions of language use that I have been implying here: rhetoric and poetics. In one sense, *all* language is rhetorical; Wayne Booth made it clear that even literature has designs on readers — argues, does business. But the tradition from Nietzsche and I. A. Richards provides the opposite lens to help us nevertheless see that all language use is also an instance of poetics: a figurative or metaphorical structure that characteristically yields up more meaning or pleasure when we see it as a self-contained or intertextual structure—one that always means more than it purports to mean. (Deconstructive critics—wisely or perversely?—define rhetoric itself as figurative language or poetics.) Once we stand back this way, it's obvious that neither rhetoric nor poetics is better. What's sad is that a discipline devoted to understanding language use should tend to restrict itself to one lens.

I'll end Section I by summarizing what I wish the cultures of literature and composition might learn from each other:

- I wish the culture of composition would learn to give an equally central place to the imaginative and metaphorical dimensions of language. And I don't want my emphasis on stories and poems to obscure my larger emphasis on *all* languages—even if the only goal is teaching essays. Surely many of the best and most effective essays don't just make good *use* of metaphors and images; rather, they grow out of imaginative metaphorical *thinking*—out of the imagination itself. But we won't understand the craft of such essays unless we feel their roots in the imagination rather than only in clear logical thinking and language.
- I wish the culture of literature would learn more inherent attention and concern for students—their lives and what's on their minds. If it did, I think teachers of literature would give more attention to helping students read with involvement and write imaginative pieces. Even if our only goal is to get students to understand a work of literature, nothing works better than inviting students to write stories or poems that are structurally, thematically, or rhetorically related to it (see my "Breathing Life into the Text").

II.

I fear I sound hopelessly corny and naive. I hear a contrary voice even in my own mind: "But your only use for literature is in fact to *use* it—for personal therapy. You want everything to be utilitarian and pragmatic. You're just a cornball—blind to all the sophistication in the literary tradition."

Sophistication. Yes. Just as I started off saying I miss literature, so too I miss sophistication. I miss elegance and irony and indirection—qualities that composition has sometimes reacted against. My dissertation and first book were about complex or double irony in Geoffrey Chaucer. What I love about Virginia Woolf is not just that she finds words for the felt texture of human experience but that she somehow embodies mental rawness in such elegance and sophistication.

But just as loving literature has gotten itself all tangled up with a noxious tradition of failing to value students and their writing and thinking, so, too, loving sophistication is all tangled up with an equally noxious tradition of condescension, snobbery, and elitism. Let me explain.

When I was trained in literature, both as an undergraduate and as a graduate student, I felt a subtle but insidious pressure: if I wanted to be good in this field, I had to learn somehow to be a slightly different kind of person from who I was — somehow "not ordinary." I happened to have had the right gender, race, sexual orientation, and a more or less acceptable accent, but I still felt I was supposed to learn to be in some subtle internal sense *different* — somehow "higher" or "finer."

That was a long time ago. Perhaps I can be convinced that this aura is no longer in the air, but I still feel in many departments and seminar rooms today that old feeling: that training in literary study is not just learning knowledge and skills but learning to stop being "ordinary" or "regular" and instead be more sophisticated and even oblique. Close reading, highly refined perception, and fine-tuned awareness of nuance: these usually involve the ability to process texts and ideas not just with your intellect or thinking but with your self or sensibility. All this often shades over into a value system that asks aspiring graduate students to have a better sensibility or self. "Better" sometimes connotes "more cultured," slightly "higher class" — even more conservative. Sometimes it connotes something leftist or politically correct. Political correctness is strong in composition too, but somehow I don't feel in this culture the same faint pressure to *be* different or feel different as *people* — somehow faintly to improve or abandon *who* we are.

I've always sensed that this training in sensibility or taste that we get in literary studies explains why people with literary training take everything so personally — and why English departments are so remarkably rancorous: if you disagree with my reading of a text or my judgment about a theory, you aren't just criticizing my thinking, you are impugning my very self-as-sensibility. (Cathy Davidson, having moved from being a chair to being a vice provost writes: "From conversations I've had with administrators across the country I know that, relative to other departments, English departments are frequently embattled" [102].) If you fail to appreciate what's good or if you like what's bad, there is something wrong with *you* — not just your opinions. Taste is feeling and sensibility, not just thinking. What does it mean to have better taste if not to have your teeth set on edge by more things than the other person? (Is there any other discipline than English that has cast off so many subgroups that used to be integrally part of it? Speech, communication, theater, film, ethnic studies, women's studies — not to mention a professional or technical interest in the nature of language? Interestingly, literary studies now hankers for a piece of theater's turf: performance studies.)

And yet I have to turn again. I love it that I got training in a culture that asked me to develop not just my thinking skills but my ability to attune my every fiber to the text or the idea at hand. It's a common failure of rationality or intelligence to restrict the definition of rationality to the exercise of conventional reasoning. Frankly, I credit widespread literary training with the fact that so many people in composition take emotion so seriously and insist on links between feelings and cognition — and haven't allowed the powerful war against the personal dimension in writing to be won. And there's no doubt that my literary training gave rise to one of my main preoccupations and areas of research in composition: "voice" in writing. (Interestingly, I've found in linguistics the most compelling empirical evidence that humans tend to put their individual stamp on the language they use. I'm thinking of a remarkable book, *The Linguistic Individual: Self-Expression in Language and Linguistics,* by Barbara Johnstone.)

Let me briefly focus my attention on a particular thread in the larger weave of sophistication: *high.* What better word than "high" to connote all the condescension people in composition often feel from literary folk — and to connote the elitism and snobbery that so many people at large have felt in the culture of literary studies. From on high, we can look down. Yet again I turn. I can't throw away "high." I want to value it and keep it — yet peel away what's noxious. Is there not something valuable that follows from revering and even trying to live with things one experiences as "above" one — Milton? Woolf? Morrison? — from trying to get our minds around things that are miraculously good? Edward Said, no conservative, insists baldly that the word "exalted" has "a particular resonance for me" — and quotes Michael Fried on the "unshakeable conviction in the supreme achievement and absolute importance of certain works of art" (7). When we try to give full attention to such works, I think we are likely to feel the need to "give in" to them, to submit, to play the believing game. So even though I fight elitism, I still want to value "high." The problem is the temptation to feel "higher than others" if one appreciates high and subtle things they don't appreciate — whereas true awareness of the high ought to make us feel low.

Let me pull a different thread from the weave of sophistication: style. And with it, artificiality; artifice, mannerism. The culture of literary studies puts a high value on style and on not being like everyone else. I think I see more mannerism, artifice, and self-consciousness in bearing (sometimes even slightly self-conscious speech production) among literary folk than composition folk. Occasionally I resist, yet I *value* style and artifice. What could be more wonderful than the pleasure of creating or appreciating forms that are different, amazing, outlandish, useless — the opposite of ordinary, everyday, pragmatic? Every child is blessed with an effortless ability to do this: it's called play.

So I miss sophistication; and yet I fight back when people in literature condescend to composition as unsophisticated. I am proud of what I sense as a kind of *resistance* to sophistication — a kind of allergy — that I feel in the culture of composition. (The last chapter of my Chaucer book is about how he *relinquishes* irony.)

Uh oh. Does it sound as though I'm painting composition as a culture of innocent, childlike naiveté? I don't mean that; it has its share of skepticism and even corruption. Still, I'd insist that there *is* a genuine naiveté, corniness, or innocence in the world of composition, and I value it and wish more literature people could learn it. Is it not naive in the best sense to think we can truly identify with our students? Is it not corny to think we can be or can strive to be "like everyone else" or "regular"? That we can transmit the power of literacy to *everyone?* That we can be a democratic or egalitarian force to change society? These are values deep in the culture of composition.

Let me move toward my ending with another tiny meditation. Just as rhetoric and poetic are two essential dimensions of language, so sophistication and naiveté (or refusing sophistication) are two ways of being in the world: we can be complex, sophisticated, ironic, and adorn ourselves with style and artifice; or we can be naked, naive, and direct. Here again I'm trying to escape either-or thinking — escape the tired habits in which the sophisticated look down on the naive, while the naive look back down just as haughtily. There's no need for higher or lower, better or worse, with these two ways of being. We can have sophistication without snobbery, elitism, or condescension; we can have naive and open identification with everyone else, and yet not neglect intelligence, complexity, and careful thinking. And it is perfectly feasible for *both* cultures, literature and composition, to help both styles to flourish.[3]

So I wish more people in literature could learn less pretension and more acknowledgment that, really, we *are* all like one another — driven by the same basic need to be loved and heard. I wish the culture of literary studies gave more honor to the courage of just sitting with, attending to, or contemplating a text — or enacting or performing it without any striving for an interpretation. And I see signs for hope that more people in literary studies are on their way to giving more honor to being pragmatically useful in the world — for example, with the recently awakened interest in the training of teachers of English.

And what do I wish people in composition could learn from the culture of literature? More honoring of style, playfulness, fun, pleasure, humor. Better writing — and a more pervasive assumption that even in academic writing, even in prose, we can have playfulness, style, pleasure — even adornment and artifice — without being elitist snobs.

There's also a piece of *scholarly* sophistication I wish composition could learn from literary scholarship. I've noticed in composition scholarship a tacit acceptance of reductive oversimplifications about historical periods and movements (for example, claims that take the form of "Romanticism meant..." or "Romantics believed...") — and readings of important historical figures (claims that "Plato said..." or "Aristotle said...") based only on quotations from a reductive secondary source. It's almost as though people in composition insist on more care and respect for student texts than for texts from large figures from distant historical eras.

Finally, I think both cultures can learn from each other with respect to their *status as disciplines*. I have a vision of composition and literature passing each other on opposite escalators at Macy's. Just as composition is achieving disciplinary strength, literary studies is relinquishing whatever pretensions it had for disciplinary coherence — and sometimes seems in fact to be disintegrating as a discipline. Literary studies has become more and more a motley crew thrown together by history and change.

Composition, on the other hand, started out as nothing *but* a motley collection of people historically thrown together (mostly by teaching exigencies) who even now continue to call on an amazing array of disciplines: rhetoric (classical and modern), linguistics, literary studies, history, philosophy, psychology, education, and others. There is still no preferred methodology, paradigm, or point of view. Different members use historical investigation, quantitative research, qualitative/ethnographic research, and textual studies (hermeneutic and theoretical) of the sort traditionally practiced in English and philosophy. For this reason — or perhaps because the field is so tainted by its commitment to teaching — the National Endowment for the Humanities won't recognize composition as a field of scholarship: no one can take part in NEH activities or get any NEH support for scholarly work in the field of composition. When the *Chronicle of Higher Education* lists "New Scholarly Books" every week, it doesn't include books in composition. None of this goes for *rhetoric*, of course, which is old enough to see English as a recent upstart. Rhetoric is seen as coherent and untainted by teaching and is thus recognized by both the NEH and the *Chronicle*.

Composition is just as polyglot as it's always been, but it's on the up escalator. It's become ever more vigorous and impressive as a scholarly field in the last couple of decades and developed an amazingly coherent energy and esprit de corps — a sense of itself as a healthy undertaking marching down the road as a single enterprise. The contrast with literary and cultural studies couldn't be more striking. I admire how this has happened without composition closing ranks around a dominant vision or discipline or methodology. But I fear the hunger to be more impressive by becoming a "real discipline" in the old-fashioned sense of *having* a dominant vision and methodology.[4] I sense the scholarly discourse having sometimes become more competitive and divisive — as though we can't be a real discipline unless some vision or methodology or paradigm "wins" — as though one paradigm can't be right unless the others are wrong. I fear the culture of composition losing its venerable tradition of "big tent" tolerant pluralism and mutual respect toward all stances. Even in 1989, David Bartholomae saw the danger of coherence-yearning: "I am suspicious of calls for coherence. I suspect that most of the problems in academic life — problems of teaching, problems of thinking — come from disciplinary boundaries and disciplinary habits [....] The charge to this generation and the next is to keep the field open, not to close it" ("Freshman" 49).

Interestingly, I see people in literary studies beginning to develop a genuine if grudging tolerance and even respect for the deep differences that have been increasing in recent decades — learning to live productively with a wildly diverse plurality of outlooks and critical and methodological practices. People in composition have always been good at this in the past but have sometimes felt it as an accidental function of oppressed status. So I wish *both* cultures could fully accept that a discipline can be even richer and healthier if it lacks a single-vision center. A discipline based on this multiplex model can better avoid either-or thinking and better foster a spirit of productive catholic pluralism.

What would it look like, then, for the two cultures to learn from each other? Obviously — and very hopefully — it's been starting to happen. I can't do better than to quote, with deep gratitude, from Jane Danielewicz's response to an earlier draft:

Literature and composition people need to get off those diverging escalators and join forces. Not just learn from each other but live with each other — go for integration rather than separate but equal accommodations. There's lots of movement in this direction already. Interestingly, there are a number of comp people turning up as chairs of English departments. [The field of composition often attracts community minded "good citizens," and writing program administration has given lots of them good experience in tricky administration. PE] We see composition and literature people team teaching; some literature professors are retooling to teach composition while comp professors are teaching lit courses. If we consider the texts people are producing, there has been an explosion in both fields of mixed genres of writing, as well as the introduction of creative nonfiction in both fields, renewed interest in the personal and in the personal essay, and attention to writing as a force (as in feminist manifestos, regional and ethnic texts such as Caribbean and Latino literatures, cultural literatures such as gay and lesbian studies, and so on). We have a chance now and ought to run with the momentum generated by current circumstances (even negative ones such as budget cuts in the humanities) to find ways of working together.[5]

NOTES

[1] Thanks to Elizabeth Sargent for this point.

[2] Thanks to Charlie Moran for this perspectival point.

[3] Of course these are slippery matters. One of the guises of sophistication is naiveté (nakedness as high artifice), as in the genre of the pastoral. True enough; a special case, but not the whole story of plainness. I can't resist citing a piece of work that admirably defies these two categories. It's a literary essay that stakes out a stance called and even claimed as naive (insisting on treating "the speaker" in a poem as "the author"), but that enacts far more grace, sophistication, and learning than most writers who might charge it with naiveté: Clara Claiborne Park's "Talking Back to the Speaker."

[4] A large coalition of writing program administrators from across the country has pulled off an impressive job of collaboration in producing a single "outcomes statement" for first-year writing courses. Of course first-year writing is *not* the same as the large field of composition, and the administrators are *not* trying to produce a uniform curriculum. Their goal is only to clarify thinking (and I've written "A Friendly Challenge to Push the Outcomes Statement Further" for their planned book about it), but I fear the pressure of orthodoxy that such impressive unity might engender. For the outcomes statement, see the Works Cited.

[5] My deep thanks go especially to Jane Danielewicz, but also to Sheridan Blau, Joe Harris, Charlie Moran, Jean Nienkamp, Irene Papoulis, Elizabeth Sargent, and *College English* readers — and others — for helpful responses to drafts.

WORKS CITED

Barfield, Owen. "The Meaning of the Word 'Literal'." *Metaphor and Symbol*. Ed. L. C. Knights and Basil Cottle. London: Butterworths, 1960.
Bartholomae, David. "Composition, 1900-2000." *PMLA* 115 (2000): 1950-54.
____. "Freshman English, Composition, and CCCC." *CCC* 40 (1989): 38-50.

Barton, D., David Bloome, D. Sheridan, and Brian Street. *Ordinary People Writing: The Lancaster and Sussex Writing Research Projects.* Working Paper Ser. 51. Lancaster, England: Centre for Language in Social Life, Dept. of Linguistics and Modern English Language, Lancaster U, 1993.

Barton, David, and Roz Ivanic. *Writing in the Community.* Newbury Park: Sage, 1991.

Coles, Robert. *The Call of Stories: Teaching and the Moral Imagination.* Boston: Houghton, 1989.

Davidson, Cathy N. "Them versus Us (and Which One of 'Them' Is Me?)." *Profession 2000:* 97–108.

Elbow, Peter. "Breathing Life into the Text." *When Writing Teachers Teach Literature.* Ed. Art Young and Toby Fulwiler. Portsmouth: Heinemann Boynton, 1995. 193–205. Rpt. in *Everyone Can Write: Essays toward a Hopeful Theory of Writing and Teaching Writing.* Ed. Peter Elbow. New York: Oxford UP, 2000. 360–71.

———. "The Doubting Game and the Believing Game." Appendix. *Writing without Teachers.* New York: Oxford UP, 1973. 147–91.

———. "Methodological Doubting and Believing: Contraries in Inquiry." *Embracing Contraries: Explorations in Learning and Teaching.* New York: Oxford UP, 1986. 254–300.

———. "The War between Reading and Writing—and How to End It." *Rhetoric Review* 12 (Fall 1993): 5–24. Rpt. in *Everyone Can Write: Essays Toward a Hopeful Theory of Writing and Teaching Writing.* Ed. Peter Elbow. New York: Oxford UP, 2000. 281–99.

Graff, Gerald. *Professing Literature: An Institutional History.* Chicago: U of Chicago P, 1987.

Hamilton, Mary, David Barton, and Roz Ivanic. *Worlds of Literacy.* Toronto: Ontario Institute for Studies in Education, 1994.

Johnstone, Barbara. *The Linguistic Individual: Self-Expression in Language and Linguistics.* New York: Oxford UP, 1996.

Levine, George. "The Two Nations." *Pedagogy: Critical Approaches to Teaching Literature, Language, Composition, and Culture* I (Winter 2001): 7–19.

Nemerov, Howard. "Speaking Silence." *New and Selected Essays.* Carbondale: Southern Illinois UP, 1985. 49–55.

O'Connor, Stephen. "Words and the World at a New York Public School: Can Writing Really Matter to Inner City Children?" *Teachers and Writers* 32.2 (Nov.–Dec. 2000): 1–8.

"Outcomes Statement." *WPA: Writing Program Administration* 23 (1999): 59–70.

Park, Clara Claiborne. "Talking Back to the Speaker." *Hudson Review* 42.1 (1989): 21–44. Rpt. in *Landmark Essays on Voice and Writing.* Ed. Peter Elbow. Hermagoras, 1994. 139–56.

Said, Edward. "Scholarship and Commitment: Introduction." *Profession 2000:* 6–11.

Scholes, Robert E. *The Rise and Fall of English: Reconstructing English as a Discipline.* New Haven: Yale UP, 1998.

Turner, Mark. *The Literary Mind.* New York: Oxford UP, 1996.

Young, Art, and Toby Fulwiler. *When Writing Teachers Teach Literature: Bringing Writing to Reading.* Portsmouth: Heinemann Boynton, 1995.

Cynthia L. Selfe

Toward New Media Texts: Taking Up the Challenges of Visual Literacy

How can teachers of composition *begin* working with new media texts — especially when they feel less than prepared to do so? One productive route of approach, I suggest in this chapter, is through visual literacy.

It is not unusual for faculty raised on alphabetic literacy and educated to reach composition before the advent of image-capturing software, multimedia texts, and the World Wide Web to feel inadequate to the task of teaching students about new media texts and the emerging literacies associated with these texts. Many have used computers extensively in the composition instruction they offer students, but most, if not all, of the assignments they favor regularly depend on the alphabetic, demand it as a primary focus, have — in most cases — been limited to it.

In part, faculty may limit their teaching in this way because they lack familiarity with a range of new media texts that they consider appropriate for study in composition classrooms. Given their educational backgrounds and expertise, after all, most faculty remain book readers, primarily. Further, although they may have encountered some new media texts, and may even enjoy these texts in many ways, they may not be convinced that such texts are worth further study in the English composition classroom. In addition, faculty may feel that they lack the analytical skills they need to conduct serious study of these texts, an effective vocabulary and set of strategies for discussing the structure and composition of new media texts, or that they lack expertise with the software packages typically used to create such texts — Macromedia Director™ and Dreamweaver™, Adobe Photoshop™ and Premiere™, Corel Poser™ and Bryce™, among others.

Importantly, operating from these constraints, many English composition faculty realize that they can offer only limited help to students who read new media texts; and they cannot help students who want to compose such texts. And, as the work of scholars as diverse as Manuel Castells, Gail Hawisher, and The New London Group suggests, this illiteracy can be costly in terms of faculty's understanding of the ways in which communication is changing at the beginning of the 21st century. Perhaps more importantly, however, it may have a cost for the students in their classes—individuals who need to learn more about the new media literacies now being used to shape meaning and information as it is composed and exchanged.

This article is reprinted from Anne Frances Wysocki, Johndan Johnson-Eilola, Cynthia L. Selfe, and Geoffrey Sirc, *Writing New Media: Theory and Applications for Expanding the Teaching of Composition*. Logan: Utah State University Press (2004): 67–93.

To work toward a better understanding of new media texts — and to open composition classes to some of the expanded possibilities suggested by such terms — a good first step may involve focusing on visual literacy and on texts, both online and in print, that depend primarily on visual elements and materials.

My reasoning in suggesting this approach is simple, but then so, too, is my level of skill in this new area: one of the primary elements that make new media texts new for me — and at times difficult to discuss in a composition classroom — is their heavy dependence on visual communication. This is an area in which I, personally, feel less than confident as a teacher of English composition, given our profession's historical focus on alphabetic literacy and uncertainty about whether visual studies is an appropriate focus for composition classrooms (cf., George; Sean Williams). Therefore, like most of my colleagues, I have only limited ability to help students analyze the visual elements of text and even less in helping them create texts composed of such elements.

Given this context, I suspect if we can help teachers become more knowledgeable and comfortable in working with students to read, discuss, and compose texts that depend primarily on visual elements, they will also be increasingly willing and able to apply these understandings to the teaching of new media texts as well. For me, focusing on the visual in composition classrooms is a productive first step — albeit not the only route — toward the larger goal of focusing on new media texts in the same environment.

This chapter, then, seeks to provide a brief rationale and several specific strategies for integrating visual literacy into composition classrooms — both in terms of consumption and production.

SOME WORKING DEFINITIONS FOR THIS CHAPTER

Most teachers thinking about integrating visual literacy into composition classes need some definitional focus for their efforts. And although, as Diana George notes, the definitions of visual literacy — and the related terms of visual communication, visual rhetoric, and the visual — remain under formulation in our profession, it may be useful to pose a temporary working definition for some of the key terms in this chapter, while recognizing that the larger professional effort to settle on a formal acceptable definition will continue to go forward.

By visual literacy, then, I will refer to the ability to read, understand, value, and learn from visual materials (still photographs, videos, films, animations, still images, pictures, drawings, graphics) — especially as these are combined to create a text — as well as the ability to create, combine, and use visual elements (e.g., colors, forms, lines, images) and messages for the purposes of communicating (cf. Kress and van Leeuwven, *Reading Images;* Debes and Williams; *The On-line Visual Literacy Project*). And — although I understand some of the problems posed by using the lens of alphabetic literacy to understand visual literacy (Wysocki and Johnson-Eilola) — based on the work of scholars such as Brian Street, James Gee, Harvey Graff, Deborah Brandt

("Literacy Learning"), and David Barton and Mary Hamilton, for the purpose of this chapter, I will assume, further, that visual literacy (or literacies), like all literacies, are both historically and culturally situated, constructed, and valued.

By texts that depend primarily on visual elements, visual texts, and visual compositions, I will refer to communications (e.g., visual poems, visual essays, visual messages, visual arguments, collages, multimedia presentations, among other forms) that people compose/design (both online and in print environments) in which visual elements and materials assume the primary burden of communication.

I will also use the term **the visual**, to refer broadly to a focus on visual elements and materials of communication, and the term visual compositions to refer to the texts that individuals or groups design/compose, primarily of visual elements and materials, for the purposes of communicating.

Finally, I will use the term **composer/designer**, instead of "author" or "artist," for instance, to describe an individual who produces or creates a visual text and the term **design/compose** to describe the complex set of activities involved in such a creative and strategic task. To refer to the reader of visual texts, I will use the term **reader/viewer** and, for the complex set of activities associated with understanding and interpreting a visual text, I will use **reading/viewing**. Although I understand these terms have their own limitations, I believe they are suggestive of the richness of visual compositions and will provide teachers some help, even if on a temporary basis, in reading this chapter.

FOCUSING ON THE VISUAL

More About Approach and Avoidance

If focusing visual literacy may be a useful first step in approaching new media texts, it is, itself, not always an easy one for teachers of English composition.

Although we have always acknowledged, at some level, the visual appearance of alphabetic texts (their formatting, their appearance, the spatial presentation of information), both visual compositions and the new media texts on which this book focuses typically privilege such information — depend on and focus on visual images, photographs, animations, multimedia depictions in ways that print texts typically do not.

This emphasis on the visual presentation of information, as Gunther Kress (" 'English' ") has noted, is manifested broadly in our culture and represents an important "turn to the visual" (66). Alphabetic texts, Kress continues, are being challenged by texts that are more oriented toward visual elements:

> The visual is becoming more prominent in many domains of public communication. From a different perspective this is to realize that written language is being displaced from its hitherto unchallenged central position in the semiotic landscape, and that the visual is taking over many of the functions of written language. (68)

Acknowledging this turn toward the visual — which has occurred in print texts as well as new media texts — scholars have begun to re-examine the role of visual literacy and our understanding of the visual in composition studies. Wysocki and Johnson-Eilola, for instance, have pointed out the limitations of using alphabetic literacy as a lens for understanding the new — and often visually rich — compositions that students are encountering in computer-based communication environments. Geoffrey Sirc has argued that visual compositions may provide teachers a valuable "demographic" that they have, in the past, lacked, one which reveals the "form patterns" — born of poetic expression — that individuals "actually make in their lives" as they try to "live their desire" (11) in a postmodern culture. Diane Shoos and Diana George argue for much broader definition of literacy, composition, and reading, one that takes a critical, visual intertextuality into account, among other things, and that acknowledges the "relationship(s) of texts [visual ads of commercial magazines, film posters, documentaries, television fiction, essays among them] to one another and to their multiple contexts" (124). And this is only a small sampling of the recent work done in composition studies with an emphasis on the visual.

Despite this work, however, as Diana George has recently pointed out, many teachers continue to rely on impoverished approaches to teaching visual literacy in their composition classrooms, introducing visual texts as the less-important and less-intellectual sidekicks of alphabetic texts. Such approaches are deeply sedimented, not only in the cultural, linguistic, and historical practices that privilege alphabetic literacy (cf. Wysocki and Johnson-Eilola; Wysocki, "Impossibly Distinct"; Jay; Kress, "English'"), but also in the practices and approaches of our profession. As George reminds us, when English composition teachers have thought to bring visual forms into their classes — a practice which they have carried on for at least forty years — they have typically presented them as second-class texts: either as "dumbed down" (32) communications that serve as "stimuli for writing but [...] no substitute for the complexity of language" (22) or as texts related to, but certainly not on an equal footing with, the "'real' work of the course" (28).

English composition teachers have continued to privilege alphabetic texts over texts that depend on visual elements, I believe, because such texts present familiar forms, forms with which we have developed a comfortable, stable intellectual relationship. We know, for instance — from lots of previous experiences — how to approach a book or a non-fiction essay; we have developed many strategies for reading and understanding such texts, for analyzing and interpreting them, for talking about them. Indeed, we feel confident about teaching students how to compose alphabetic texts primarily because we are so familiar with those forms. Relatively few English teachers, however, feel as comfortable in approaching a visual text unless they have some training in art or design. Given this context, we remain unsure how to approach visual texts, how to explore them, how to understand them, and how to teach them. And we also feel less than competent about composing visual texts ourselves.

Part of the reason this feeling has persisted, of course, has to do with the material conditions of teaching and learning in the United States and the relations of such conditions to technologies of production and composition. Many of us, for instance, had our last art class in elementary school and have learned since that time to pin our hopes for academic and professional success on alphabetic texts. As a result, we have also learned to use and value technologies — pens, pencils, typewriters, ditto machines, books, journals, and, more recently, computers and word-processing packages — for the ease they afford us in creating alphabetic texts. It is only recently — in conjunction with the cultural turn to the visual, I believe — that increasing numbers of composition teachers have had some access to technologies which allow for the production of texts highly dependent on visual elements (color photocopiers, digital scanners; computers that contain page-layout, photo-manipulation, animation, multimedia software, etc.). Many of these technologies, however, are still expensive — and, thus unevenly distributed in schools along the axis of material resources — as well as relatively difficult to access and learn.

Finally, I would suggest, many English composition teachers have downplayed the importance of visual literacy and texts that depend primarily on visual elements because they confront us with the prospect of updating our literacies at the expense of considerable work, precious time, and a certain amount of status. Teachers continue to privilege alphabetic literacy over visual literacy, in other words, because they have already invested so heavily in writing, writing instruction and writing programs — and because we have achieved some status as practitioners and specialists of writing. Undertaking the study of literacies based in visual studies, learning to analyze and talk about and compose these texts — especially with a high degree of technological sophistication will take time and effort — may also force us to acknowledge gaps in our own literacy sets.

Recently, however, our single-minded focus on alphabetic texts in composition classes has come to seem outdated, even obdurate, in the face of practical realities. Global communications, for example — exchanged via increasingly complicated computer networks that stretch across traditional geographic and political borders and that include people from different cultures who speak different languages — increasingly involve texts that depend heavily, even primarily, on visual elements (New London Group). Moreover, with the ongoing expansion of global markets, political systems, and communication networks, such an emphasis is sure to continue, if not increase.

Given the pace and scope of changes accruing from this set of circumstances, if our profession continues to focus solely on teaching alphabetic composition — either online or in print — we run the risk of making composition studies increasingly irrelevant to students engaging in contemporary practices of communicating. Students already, as Diana George reminds us, have a "much richer imagination for what we might accomplish with the visual" than we ourselves have (12).

By continuing a single-minded focus on alphabetic literacy—and failing to give adequate attention to visual literacy—as Sean Williams points out, we not only unnecessarily limit the scope of composition studies, both intellectually and practically:

> Restricting composition to verbal media and reproducing the verbal bias in our classrooms is perilous [...] because it contradicts the critical thinking skills that we as composition teachers strive to teach.[...I]f composition's role is to help students acquire skills to lead a critically engaged life—that is to identify problems, to solve them, and to communicate with others about them—then we need to expand our view of writing instruction to include the diverse media forms that actually represent and shape the discursive reality of students. The verbal bias, then, reveals two closely interwoven perils;
>
> - a political one that reinscribes a conclusion-based rationality, and
> - a rhetorical one that ignores the possibility that different media function more or less effectively in different contexts. (25)

As Kress and van Leeuwen (*Reading Images*) put the case, then, it may be time to rethink what 'literacy' ought to include, and what should be taught under the heading of 'writing' in schools (32).

By adding a focus on visual literacy to our existing focus on alphabetic literacy, we may not only learn to pay more serious attention to the ways in which students are now ordering and making sense of the world through the production and consumption of visual images, but we may also extend the usefulness of composition studies in a changing world.

WHERE DO WE GO FROM HERE?

Individual teachers and programs, surely, will differ widely in their willingness to experiment with the challenges of visual composition, to take personal and intellectual risks as they learn to value visually-oriented texts, and to engage in composing texts that combine the visual as well as the alphabetic.

The following pages provide examples of assignments designed to provide teachers a range of approaches to visual texts, even when instructors have no formal coursework or professional preparation in this area.

1. The assignments connect what is—at least for some teachers—the less-familiar realm of visual composition with the more-familiar realm of alphabetic composition.
2. Most of the assignments deal at some level with a combination of both visual and alphabetic literacies. Most—following the lead of scholars such as Susan Hilligoss, Sean Williams, Clay Spinuzzi—use a rhetorical approach to analyzing the audience, purpose, and messages conveyed by a visual text—employing questions that many instructors already use in teaching students how to compose more conventional alphabetic texts.

3. And most of the assignments do not require teachers or students to use sophisticated computer environments as contexts for visual assignments — three of the four assignments, for example, suggest that students might want to create visual compositions on poster boards; and only the last assignment requires that students know how to create a Web page.

4. Importantly, I would add that most of the assignments involve teachers and students as co-learners in the project of paying increased attention to visual texts. As a result, they do not require teachers to begin with a great deal of information or background on visual literacy. Through the completion of the assignments, both teachers and students will acquire some basic conceptual vocabulary that they can use to discuss the reading/viewing and composing/designing of texts that rely primarily on visual elements. For those colleagues who feel more comfortable approaching such assignments with some background reading under their belts, I can suggest Kress and van Leeuwen's *Reading Images: The Grammar of Visual Design*.

The topics of the following assignments are far less important than their focus on the visual, and so teachers are also encouraged to revise them to fit specific courses. For example, the first assignment is currently designed for an undergraduate course on literacy issues. It asks students to create a visual essay that describes their general development as readers and writers over the course of their lifetimes. However, in another course focused on the American novel, the same assignment could be revised to ask students to trace a more specific line: focusing on their family's history in America. Similarly, the second assignment — currently designed for a first-year English course focused on the relationship between humans and robots/cyborgs — asks students to make a visual argument about what this relationship will look like in 2050. In a course focusing on issues of race, this same assignment could be revised to ask students to make a visual argument based on their stance toward affirmative-action programs.

Ultimately, the goal set for these assignments is both modest (in that the general process will be familiar to most teachers of composition) and exceedingly challenging (in the attempt to focus primarily — although not exclusively — on the visual), and one I hope many teachers of composition can embrace: to help students and ourselves better understand the communicative power and complexity of visual texts by reading and looking at them, by thinking seriously about these texts and analyzing their components, by talking to other people about our interpretations of them, by composing visual texts ourselves, by sharing our efforts at composing with other author/designers, and by reflecting on the compositions we create and exchange with others as complex symbolic instantiations of the human need to communicate.

ACTIVITY 1: A VISUAL ESSAY

Teachers' Notes

Goals

- To involve students in reflecting on and representing
  - the range of the literacies they have developed in their lifetimes (both online and in-print).
  - the development of these literacies.
  - their feelings about/values toward various forms of literacy.
- To help students understand how much tacit knowledge they have about visual composition.
- To provide students some basic vocabulary they can use in talking about and analyzing visual compositions.

Time Required

- one homework assignment to compose visual essay (1 week for out-of-class work).
- 30 minutes in class for viewing and reflecting on visual essays
- 30 minutes in class for discussion of successful strategies for:
  - creating overall visual coherence
  - visually identifying 2–4 of the essay's most important points
  - visually indicating pattern(s) of organization
- one homework assignment focused on comparing author/designers' reflections and audience/viewers' reflections

Sequence

1. **Creating a visual essay.** As a homework assignment, each student creates a visual essay on the range of literacies (both on and off computers) they have developed over their lifetimes and their feelings toward literacy.
2. **Viewing and Reflection Session.** In class, students form teams of three for a 30 minute *Viewing and Reflection Session.* During this session, teams do three rounds of reflection. During each round, the team views a visual essay for 10 minutes and reflects on a series of questions. Composer/designers reflect on what they tried to accomplish; readers/viewers write about what the visual essay communicates to them.
3. **Discussion.** In class, the teacher asks students to point out the successful strategies that authors/designers used in their essays to:
   1. impart visual impact
   2. create an overall sense of coherence
   3. indicate the importance of 1–4 major points
   4. create pattern(s) of organization

4. **Comparing Author/Designers' Reflections with Audience/Viewers' Reflections.** As a homework assignment, each composer/designer compares his/her own answers on the reflection questions to those provided by the audience viewers. Each author/designer will summarize areas of agreement and disagreement.

Useful Vocabulary

from Kress and van Leeuwan's *Reading Images: The Grammar of Visual Design*

- **Visual impact:** The overall effect and appeal that a visual composition has on an audience.
- **Visual coherence:** The extent to which visual elements of a composition are tied together with color, shape, image, lines of sight, theme, etc.
- **Visual salience:** Importance or prominence of a visual element.
- **Visual organization:** Pattern of arrangement that relates the elements of the visual essay to one another in a way that makes them easier for readers/viewers to comprehend.

VISUAL ESSAY

HOMEWORK

Assignment (Homework)

Objectives

- To reflect on the entire range of literacies (both online and print) you have developed over your life; the practices, understandings, and values that make up your literacies; where these practices, understandings, and values came from; how you have developed them; and who has helped you become literate.
- To represent this information as richly as possible in a visual essay.
- To provide you practice in documenting images.

Task

- Compose a visual essay that represents and reflects on

  1. the range of different literacy practices, values, and understandings you have developed over your lifetime (from birth to now)
  2. how you have developed these literacies (where, how, who helped)
  3. your feelings about these literacies

- The audience for this essay is other students in the class. The purpose is to show the range and extent of your own personal set of literacies, their development over time, and your feelings toward literacy at various points of your life.
- For the purposes of this essay, we will define literacy broadly—not only as your reading and writing skills but also the values and understandings that go along with these skills. For instance, you might (but don't have to) include, such activities as reading and writing in print contexts (books and magazines, writing stories and plays), on computers (designing Web sites, reading gaming situations, writing in chat rooms), on television (reading the texts of television programs), in church (reading the Bible, writing for your church bulletin), at home (writing letters, reading directions), in school (reading lab reports, collaborating with a group to compose a report).
- The essays should demonstrate a high degree of visual impact.
- The essay should demonstrate an overall coherence (elements of the essay should be linked by color, shape, theme, arrangement, etc.).
- The essay should identify 2-4 major points as particularly important (using strategies to make these points prominent and stand out from other elements: size, color, contrast, placement, etc.).
- Use some pattern of organization to help viewers to comprehend your essay (arrange elements along a timeline, a path, a trail, or some other

metaphor that represents your life; separate your computer and your book-based literacies or connect them if they are related).

Format

- Your essay can take any number of forms. Be creative in your thinking and representation: create your own literacy path or trail, a diagram of human development annotated with images of your literacy activities, a scrapbook with "snapshots" of your literacy development; a map of your literacy landscape; a literacy game board; a literacy Web.
- Compose this essay either on a Web page that you create online or on a poster board that you purchase at the college bookstore.
- If you create a Web page, compose your essay from images that you find or create online. Before you download an image from another Web site, carefully check to make sure the Web site does not prohibit the copying of images.
- If you use poster board, create your collage from images you cut out of magazines or from family photographs.
- Include at least 15 images in this essay.
- Document the source of each image using the formats below.

Web Essays & Documenting Images from an Online Source

- Create a Web page for your essay.
- Create a separate Web page for each image's bibliographic citation.
- Link each image in your essay to the appropriate Web page containing its bibliographic entry. Here is a model, with an example:

Artist (if given). Title of file. <Web site from which image was taken> (date on which you accessed Web site).

Example: Doe, Jane. SpottedPig.jpg. <http://www.spottedanimal/pigs/#22> (Accessed 22 June, 2002).

Poster Board Essays & Documenting Images from Print/Photographic Sources

- Create your essay. Number each image.
- Create a bibliography page. List entries in numerical order, numbering each entry to correspond to an image: [15] "Drink Milk." Time 20 September 2002: 15.
- Attach this page to the back of your essay.

Artist (if given). "Title of image" (if given). Magazine Title or Photograph Collection Day Month Year: page number (if applicable). *Example from a magazine:* [15] "Drink Milk." Time 20 September 2002: 15.

Example from a photograph: [15] Doe, John "Me and My Mother." Personal photograph collection. Taken 9 August 1978.

VISUAL ESSAY

CLASSROOM WORK

Reflection Sheet

(Composer/Designer)

Composer/designer _____

Objective

- To articulate and reflect on what you are trying to convey about your literacies, literacy development through/in your essay.
- To identify what parts of your essay worked well and what parts worked less well.
- To reflect on your attempt to create visual coherence, salience (prominence/importance), and organization in your essay.

Task

Take 10 minutes to reflect on the first three questions that follow. For homework, reflect on the last four questions and hand in this page — along with the reader/viewers' Reflection sheets from your team — at the beginning of next class. *Do not speak about or explain your visual essay to your readers/viewers.*

During Class

- What were you trying to convey about your literacies/literacy development in this essay?
- What parts of this essay worked the best? Had the most effect impact? Why?
- What parts of this essay worked less well in your opinion? Had the least effective impact? Why?

For Homework

- What specific techniques did you use to establish visual coherence in your essay?
- What specific strategies did you use to identify each of the 2–4 major points you were trying to make in this essay and to lend them visual salience (make them prominent to the reader/viewer)?

VISUAL ESSAY

CLASSROOM WORK

Reflection Sheet

(Reader/Viewer)

Essay composed/designed by _____

Essay read/viewed by _____

Objective

- To articulate what the visual essay conveyed to you as a reader/viewer.
- To reflect on what parts of the essay worked well/had great impact for you and what parts worked less well/had low impact for you.

Task

Take 10 minutes to reflect in writing on the following questions. Do not talk to the composer/designer.

- What did the essay convey to you about the composer/designer and his/her literacies? His/her development as a reader/viewer or composer/designer? List at least five impressions you got.
- What parts of the essay worked the best for you — had the highest impact?
- What parts of this essay worked least well for you — had the lowest impact?
- Below, please identify the 2-4 main points you think the composer/designer wanted to make in the essay.

VISUAL ESSAY

Sample Evaluation

Composer/designer _____

1: OVERALL EFFECT OF THE VISUAL ESSAY

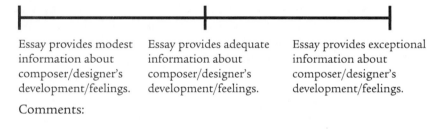

Essay's overall
impact is low &
presentation is
less than effective.

Essay has moderate
level of overall impact
and presentation is
moderately effective.

Essay has exceptional
overall impact and
presentation is highly
effective.

Comments:

2: COMPOSER/DESIGNER'S DEVELOPMENT/FEELINGS

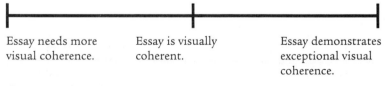

Essay provides modest
information about
composer/designer's
development/feelings.

Essay provides adequate
information about
composer/designer's
development/feelings.

Essay provides exceptional
information about
composer/designer's
development/feelings.

Comments:

3: VISUAL COHERENCE

Essay needs more
visual coherence.

Essay is visually
coherent.

Essay demonstrates
exceptional visual
coherence.

Comments:

4: VISUAL SALIENCE

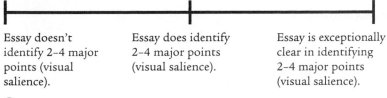

Essay doesn't identify 2–4 major points (visual salience).

Essay does identify 2–4 major points (visual salience).

Essay is exceptionally clear in identifying 2–4 major points (visual salience).

Comments:

5: ORGANIZATION OF THE ESSAY

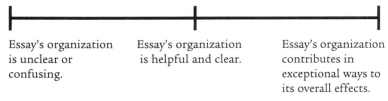

Essay's organization is unclear or confusing.

Essay's organization is helpful and clear.

Essay's organization contributes in exceptional ways to its overall effects.

Comments:

6: DOCUMENTATION OF IMAGES

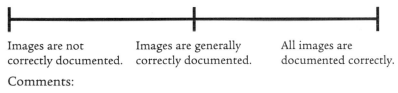

Images are not correctly documented.

Images are generally correctly documented.

All images are documented correctly.

Comments:

7: REFLECTION

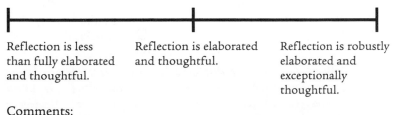

Reflection is less than fully elaborated and thoughtful.

Reflection is elaborated and thoughtful.

Reflection is robustly elaborated and exceptionally thoughtful.

Comments:

VISUAL ESSAY

CLASSROOM WORK

Sample Evaluation (a model)

Composer/designer *Michelle Sarinen*

1: OVERALL EFFECT OF THE VISUAL ESSAY

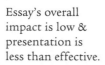

Essay's overall
impact is low &
presentation is
less than effective.

Essay has moderate
level of overall impact
and presentation is
moderately effective.

Essay has exceptional
overall impact and
presentation is highly
effective.

Comments: *Very complete rendition of literacy activities, but not designed for a*
high level of impact. All the events are shown at essentially the
same level of impact. Is this possible?

2: COMPOSER/DESIGNER'S DEVELOPMENT/FEELINGS

Essay provides
modest information
about composer/
designer's develop-
ment/feelings.

Essay provides
adequate information
about composer/
designer's development/
feelings.

Essay provides
exceptional informa-
tion about composer/
designer's development/
feelings.

Comments: *The essay doesn't give me a sense of you. It could be about almost*
anyone in this class. Can you give some visual emphasis to the
details/events that really helped you form your identity?

3: VISUAL COHERENCE

Essay needs more
visual coherence.

Essay is visually
coherent.

Essay demonstrates
exceptional visual
coherence.

Comments: *I think you could make more effective use of color and line to make*
your points and get your essay to hang together. For instance, why
not color-code the print-based events in your childhood to differenti-
ate them from the computer-based events in your adolescence?

4: VISUAL SALIENCE

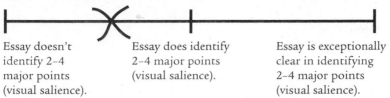

Essay doesn't
identify 2–4
major points
(visual salience).

Essay does identify
2–4 major points
(visual salience).

Essay is exceptionally
clear in identifying
2–4 major points
(visual salience).

Comments: *I really didn't get a sense of which elements/events were most important in your life . . .*

5: ORGANIZATION OF THE ESSAY

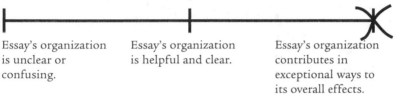

Essay's organization
is unclear or
confusing.

Essay's organization
is helpful and clear.

Essay's organization
contributes in
exceptional ways to
its overall effects.

Comments: *Yes—The organization is clear: it's chronological.*

6: DOCUMENTATION OF IMAGES

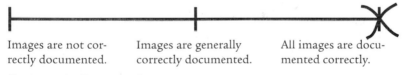

Images are not cor-
rectly documented.

Images are generally
correctly documented.

All images are docu-
mented correctly.

Comments: *Yes, complete.*

7: REFLECTION

Reflection is less than
fully elaborated and
thoughtful.

Reflection is elaborated
and thoughtful.

Reflection is robustly
elaborated and
exceptionally thoughtful.

Comments: *It doesn't seem as though you've reflected too much on what specific literacy events have shaped you as a person. Or, at least, I
can't see it . . .*

ACTIVITY 2: VISUAL ARGUMENT ASSIGNMENT*

Teachers' Notes

Goals

- Involve students in identifying effective strategies composers/designers have used in their arguments to establish visual impact, coherence, salience, and organization.
- Introduce some new vocabulary for discussing the concepts of visual impact, coherence, salience, and organization.

Below, we list some of the possible strategies that students may identify for establishing visual impact, coherence, salience, and organization. However, such strategies work differently in combination and within the context of specific arguments. Encourage students to identify unusual strategies that generate innovative and surprising effects — especially if those effects succeed.

Discussion Questions

After students have completed the assignment on the following pages, look together at all the arguments they've made. Get the class talking by asking the following questions. The questions are set up around the vocabulary from the previous assignment.

Questions About Visual Impact

VISUAL IMPACT is the overall effect and appeal that a visual composition has on an audience.

- *Which arguments that you looked at exhibited the highest overall impact/effect? Why?* Ask the team members to identify the strategies they think the particular author/designer employed to establish visual coherence. Ask students on other teams to identify additional arguments that succeed in establishing overall coherence. Encourage students to identify strategies that are unusual, unexpected; that generate surprising (and yet successful) effects; that are innovative.
- *Students might mention these strategies for creating visual impact:*
- author/designer employed an overall concept
- author/designer used images that were especially effective
- author/designer used lots of details
- author/designer used color effectively
- author/designer composed an especially creative visual design
- author/designer used elements that the audience could relate to

---

*I am indebted to Dr. Diana George for the concept of visual arguments. She describes several such arguments created by students at Michigan Technological University in her article "From Analysis to Visual Design."

Questions About Visual Coherence

VISUAL COHERENCE is the extent to which the various elements of a visual composition are tied together, represent a unified whole.

• *Which essays demonstrated an effective sense of visual coherence? Why?*
Ask the team members to identify the strategies they think the particular composer/designer employed to establish visual coherence. Ask students on other teams to identify additional essays that succeed in establishing overall coherence. Encourage students to identify strategies that are unusual, unexpected; that generate surprising (and yet successful) effects; that are innovative.
Students might mention these strategies for creating visual coherence:
  • composer/designer linked elements by using patterns or color
  • composer/designer linked elements through similar shapes
  • composer/designer created coherence with unifying pictorial graphics (lines, arrows, paths, etc.)
  • composer/designer tied elements together using proximity, overlapping, or juxtaposition
  • composer/designer tied elements together using a shared visual theme (images of books, pens, or computers)
  • composer/designer balanced major elements to create cohesion

Questions About Visual Salience

VISUAL SALIENCE is the relative prominence of an element within a visual composition. Salient elements catch viewer's eye; they are conspicuous.

• *Which arguments demonstrated an effective sense of visual salience?*
Ask the team members to identify the strategies they think the particular composer/designer employed to establish visual salience. Ask students on other teams to identify additional arguments that succeed in establishing salience. Encourage students to identify strategies that are unusual, un-expected; that generate surprising (and yet successful) effects; that are inno-vative.
Students might mention these strategies for creating visual salience:
  • composers/designers increased the size of major elements
  • composers/designers sharpened the focus for major elements
  • composers/designers increased the contrast (darker, lighter, more satu-rated colors) of major elements
  • composers/designers positioned major elements in the center
  • composers/designers positioned major elements in the foreground
  • composers/designers highlighted major elements with color
  • composers/designers used pictorial graphics (lines, arrows, etc.) to point toward major elements
  • composers/designers used/angled other elements to direct the viewer's eye toward a major element

Questions About Visual Organization

VISUAL ORGANIZATION is the pattern of arrangement that relates the elements of the visual essay to one another so that they are easier for readers/viewers to comprehend.

- *Which arguments demonstrated an effective sense of visual organization?*
  Ask the team members to identify the strategies they think the particular author/designer employed to establish effective patterns of visual organization. Ask students on other teams to identify additional arguments that succeed in establishing effective patterns of visual organization. Encourage students to identify strategies that are unusual, unexpected; that generate surprising (and yet successful) effects; that are innovative.
  Students might mention these strategies for creating visual organization:
  - composer/designer linked elements by using patterns of color
  - composer/designer linked elements through similar shapes
  - composer/designer created coherence with unifying pictorial graphics (lines, arrows, paths, etc.)
  - composer/designer tied elements together using proximity, overlapping, or juxtaposition
  - composer/designer tied elements together using a shared visual theme (images of books, pens, or computers)
  - composer/designer balanced major elements to create cohesion

VISUAL ARGUMENT

HOMEWORK

Creating a Visual Argument

Objectives

- To engage students in reflecting on the relationship between humans/ robots/cyborgs and constructing this relationship actively through visual representation.
- To provide students practice in identifying and visually representing a line of argument.
- To provide students practice in analyzing visual arguments and evaluating their effectiveness.
- To provide students practice in documenting images

Task

During this term, we have read Karel Capek's play *R.U.R.*, and Isaac Asimov's *I, Robot,* and we have watched Ridley Scott's *Bladerunner*. In discussing these works, we have asked the following questions, among others:

Are humans already cyborgs?
Can robots have a soul?
Why do humans guard intelligence so jealously?
Why do humans craft robots in their own image?
Why do humans fear robots?

With these readings and questions in mind, create a visual argument on the following topic:

By the year 2050, I think humans and robots will become more alike, become increasingly different, or should establish the following relationship: _____

- You may want your argument to address questions like these: *Will robots have a soul? Should robots have emotions? Should robots/cyborgs be able to love/marry/inherit property/become a citizen/raise children? Will most humans become cyborgs? Should humans respect robots as living beings? Will humans be able to download their brains into robots? Should such robots be considered cyborgs?*
- Your audience is a group of ordinary citizens, one of whom will be selected (by lottery) to sit on a national panel of robot/cyborg ethics that will make decisions on the kind of robot/cyborg research that can/should go on in this country. Your purpose is to persuade these individuals to adopt the most productive possible understanding of the human/robot/cyborg relationship.
- In your essay, make sure you identify the premise(s) of the argument and provide adequate evidence for the position you are representing. Choose evidence that will be persuasive to your audience.

Format

- Compose your essay either on a web page that you create online or on a poster board that you purchase at the college bookstore.
- If you create a Web page, compose your essay from images that you find or create online. Before you download an image from another Web site, carefully check to make sure the Web site does not prohibit the copying of images.
- If you use poster board, create your essay from images you cut out of magazines.
- Include at least 15 images in this essay.
- Document the source of each image using the formats below.

Web Essays & Documenting Images from an Online Source

- Create a Web page for your essay.
- Create a separate Web page for each image's bibliographic citation.
- Link each image in your essay to the appropriate Web page containing its bibliographic entry. Here are a model and a sample:

Artist (if given). Title of file. <Web site from which image was taken> (date on which you accessed Web site).

Example: Doe, Jane. SpottedPig.jpg.
<http://www.spottedanimal/pigs/#22> (Accessed 22 July, 2002).

Poster Board Essays & Documenting Images from Print/Photographic Sources

- Create your essay. Number each image.
- Create a bibliography page. List entries in numerical order, numbering each entry to correspond to an image: [15] "Drink Milk." Time 20 September 2002: 15.
- Attach this page to the back of your essay.

Artist (if given). "Title of image" (if given). Magazine Title or Photograph Collection Day Month Year: page number (if applicable).

Example from a magazine: [15] "Drink Milk." Time 20 September 2002: 15.

Example from a photograph: [15] Doe, John. "Me and My Mother." Personal photograph collection. Taken 9 August 1978.

VISUAL ARGUMENT

INCLASS WORK

Review and Reflection (Reviewers' Sheet)

Composer/designer _____

Reviewer _____

Objectives

- To give you practice in analyzing visual arguments and evaluating their effectiveness.

Task

Form Review teams of three people. For each essay in your group (two essays per person), take 10 minutes to reflect in writing on the questions that follow. *Do not ask the composers/designers to explain their essays.*

- Provide a title for this essay that speaks to the argument and the position it represents.

- In one sentence, identify the premise(s) of this essay.

- Identify the evidence that the composer/designer provides for this argument.

- Does this argument depend primarily on logos? Pathos? Ethos? Explain your answer.

- Rate the visual impact/effectiveness of this essay from 1 (least effective) to 5 (most effective). Explain the reasons for your rating with specific reference to parts of the visual essay/strategies that the author used in composing the argument.

VISUAL ARGUMENT

INCLASS WORK

Review and Reflection (Composer/Designer's Sheet)

Author/designer _____

Objective

- To involve composer/designers in reflecting on their success in presenting an argument.
- To provide students practice in analyzing visual arguments and evaluating their effectiveness.

Task

For your own essay, take 10 minutes to reflect in writing on the first five questions that follow. *Do not explain your essay to reviewers.* For homework, answer the last two questions. Hand in both the reviewers' comments on your essay and your own reflections at the beginning of the next class period.

In Class

- Provide a title for this essay that speaks to the argument and the position it represents for you.
- In one sentence, identify the premise(s) of this essay.
- Identify the evidence that you provide for this argument.
- Does your argument depend primarily on logos? Pathos? Ethos? Explain your answer.
- Rate the effectiveness of your essay from 1 (least effective) to 5 (most effective). Explain the reasons for your rating with specific reference to parts of the visual essay.

For Homework

- What are the most effective parts of your argument? Why?
- What are the least effective parts of your argument? Why?

VISUAL ARGUMENT

INCLASS WORK

Evaluation

Composer/designer _____

1: OVERALL EFFECT OF THE VISUAL ARGUMENT

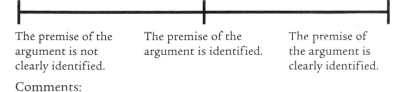

Argument's
overall impact is
low & presenta-
tion is less than
than effective.

Argument has
moderate level of
overall impact and
presentation is
moderately effective.

Argument has
exceptional overall
impact and presenta-
tion is highly effective.

Comments:

2: THE PREMISE OF THE VISUAL ARGUMENT

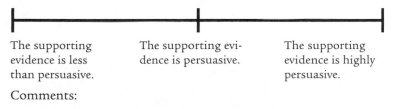

The premise of the
argument is not
clearly identified.

The premise of the
argument is identified.

The premise of
the argument is
clearly identified.

Comments:

3: SUPPORTING EVIDENCE FOR THE ARGUMENT

The supporting
evidence is less
than persuasive.

The supporting evi-
dence is persuasive.

The supporting
evidence is highly
persuasive.

Comments:

4: REFLECTION

Reflection is less
than fully elaborated
and thoughtful.

Reflection is elaborated
and thoughtful.

Reflection is
robustly elaborated
and exceptionally
thoughtful.

Comments:

5: DOCUMENTATION OF IMAGES

Images are not cor-
rectly documented.

Images are generally
correctly documented.

All images are docu-
mented correctly.

Comments:

Bruce Horner and John Trimbur

English Only and U.S. College Composition

The fact that U.S. writing instruction is conducted in English seems common-sensical. After all, though English is not the official language of the U.S., this is an English-speaking nation. As everyone from politicians and educational policymakers to non-English speaking immigrants knows, in the U.S., a knowl-edge of English is virtually required to get an education, to develop profession-ally, and to participate in civic life. As a consequence, a first-year course in written English, along with basic writing and ESL courses that point students toward fluency in written and spoken English, seems not only to make sense but to be inevitable in the design of writing programs and curriculum.

The purpose of this essay is to raise some questions about this familiar state of affairs. We argue that a tacit language policy of unidirectional English monolingualism has shaped the historical formation of U.S. writing instruc-tion and continues to influence its theory and practice in shadowy, largely unexamined ways. We are aware that for many writing teachers the very notion of language policy is likely to call up images of English Only legislation, debates about Ebonics, and the phonics wars — issues to take a position on by voting, lobbying, and calling on our professional associations to use their pow-ers of influence in public forums. To say the first-year writing course actually *embodies* a language policy that privileges English in relation to other languages may sound, in the first instance, either far-fetched or simply a statement of the obvious terms that define our work. We can imagine readers asking how it could be otherwise. For this reason, we want to make clear at the outset that we are not quarreling with the fact that writing instruction in college composition courses takes place in English. Instead we want to examine the sense of inevitability that makes it so difficult to imagine writing instruction in any language other than English. As we hope to show, a tacit language policy of unidirectional monolingualism has a history and a cultural logic that have gone largely unacknowledged in our field and that, by remaining unexamined, continues to exert a powerful influence on our teaching, our writing programs, and our impact on U.S. culture.

Histories of rhetoric and composition as an academic discipline typically consider the field's intellectual affiliations and professional identities in rela-tion to English studies, on one hand, and to speech communication, on the other, with virtually no attention to the relation of writing instruction to modern languages other than English. Writing instruction in the modern

This article is reprinted from *College Composition and Communication* 53.4 (June 2002): 594–629.

university, as many have noted, was institutionalized in the late-nineteenth and early-twentieth centuries as part of a larger modernizing initiative to replace the classical curriculum of the old-time pietistic college with a secular education in the vernacular. The question for the modernizers, as Theodore W. Hunt put it in 1884, was, "Will the classics as taught in our colleges make any concessions of their large amount of time to the modern languages?" (121). For compositionists, the history of these turf fights for space in university curricula is often invested with nostalgic regrets for the decline of rhetorical education and yet, at the same time, approval of the modernizers' struggles against the stultifying practice of teaching Greek and Latin as "mental discipline" and the restrictive premises of its underlying faculty psychology.

What has been neglected, in our view, is that the final defeat of the ancients by the moderns institutionalized not only a required first-year course in written English but also a language policy that replaced the bilingualism (in principle if not always in practice) of the classical curriculum with a unidirectional monolingualism. We are certainly not defending the justly discredited oral recitations and "translation English" of the classical curriculum, but we want to call attention to the fact that the triumph of the vernacular dramatically rearranged the relationships among languages and the roles they were slotted to play in the curriculum. After overturning the classical curriculum, the victorious moderns had, in effect, to work out a postwar settlement that allotted spheres of influence to the modern languages. As we will see, a "territorialization" of the modern languages separated them into departments — distinct academic entities defined by their national borders — where French, German, Spanish, and Italian took their place in the curriculum as reading courses to study national literatures and cultures, while English alone was assigned the task of writing instruction.

This territorialization of the modern languages, we argue, cannot be understood simply as a recognition of inevitable linguistic differences that account for the present configuration of the curriculum. Our task, as we see it, is to examine the history of the inevitable and to identify the cultural logics that produce it. In the most general sense, the settlement arranged by the moderns can be seen in terms of a chain of reifications that has settled into our own contemporary beliefs and practices as writing teachers. By "reification," we mean the treatment of something, such as spoken and written language, that is always in process, located in and subject to ongoing and varying material practice, as a fixed, idealized entity removed from the vagaries of time, place, and use. In this regard, reification is what makes things seem inevitable, givens by the fact of their being instead of their history. Here are the links in the chain of reification. First, the territorialization of languages according to national borders puts into place a reification of social identity in terms of language use: one's social identity is defined in terms of nationality, which itself is defined in terms of a single language. Next, language use itself is reified and identified with a reification of language, located most commonly in writing, so that the variety, range, and shifting nature of language in use are reduced and restricted to the canons of "proper usage" embodied in standard written English. Finally, and of great relevance to writing teachers, these reifications are used to locate individual learners on a sequence of development fixed in its order, direction, and sociopolitical significance.

This chain of reifications inflects our work as writing teachers in consequential and sometimes unsuspected ways. Our argument in the following sections has two main parts. First, we show how the tacit language policy of unidirectional monolingualism took root in the late-nineteenth century in the very formation of the U.S. first-year writing course by characterizing the other modern languages as national literatures to be read and studied but not written or spoken.[1] Second, we demonstrate the pervasiveness of a tacit unidirectional, monolingual language policy by showing how it operates today in parallel ways in debate over English Only legislation and beginning college-writing students. The pervasiveness of this tacit policy extends to recent debates in ESL scholarship on relationships among languages and between languages and social identity. Though a full discussion of these debates is well beyond the scope of this essay, we find them apposite to any rethinking of both English Only policies and the tacit monolingualism of U.S. college composition.

As might be expected, the assumptions of a unidirectional monolingual policy are rampant in arguments advocating English Only legislation and in views hostile to beginning college-writing students. More troubling is the fact that these assumptions, as we show, are also prevalent in arguments *against* English Only and *for* the interests of beginning college writing students, as well as in arguments for and against ESL. While political expediency may, at times, justify these latter arguments, we question the long-term consequences of such accommodationist rhetoric. Against such a stance, we pose an alternative way of thinking about composition programs, the language of our students, and our own language practices that holds monolingualism itself to be a problem and a limitation of U.S. culture and that argues for the benefits of an actively multilingual language policy.

LANGUAGE POLICY IN THE FORMATION OF THE MODERN CURRICULUM

The displacement of the classical languages that made room in the curriculum for the modern languages and writing instruction in the vernacular resulted from a protracted struggle more than from a single decisive battle. By 1885, when Adams Sherman Hill succeeded in institutionalizing the first-year course at Harvard, the traditional authority of the classical curriculum had already seriously eroded. As S. Michael Halloran points out, as early as the mid-eighteenth century at Harvard, English had started to replace Latin in disputations and orations, and while at first only the dullest students composed in English, eventually the brightest were doing so as well. Moreover, before the Civil War, "scientific schools" such as Sheffield at Yale, Lawrence at Harvard, and the Massachusetts

Institute of Technology granted bachelor of science and bachelor of philosophy degrees that dispensed with either Greek or both Greek and Latin as graduation requirements. In fact, by the turn of the previous century, as Laurence R. Veysey notes, "the practice of granting separate degrees...for students who lacked a background in the classics began to disappear at most major universities" (118), and many colleges and universities had abolished altogether both entrance requirements in the classical languages and required course work for graduation.

The story of how the required first-year writing course fits into the modernization of the university curriculum has been told many times before. Understandably, the interest of composition historians such as James A. Berlin, John Brereton, Robert J. Connors, Sharon Crowley, and Susan Miller has been to explain the low status of writing instruction in the modern university. The formation of the first-year course at Harvard looms emblematically in this regard. Both Hill and the four reports of the Harvard Committee on Composition and Rhetoric in the 1890s sought to establish entering students' poor preparation in written English as the grounds for a required first-year course and a downward pressure on Harvard's feeder schools to increase attention to instruction in written English. While this line of reasoning certainly helps explain why first-year English has such an ambiguous academic status, defined not so much as part of the college curriculum as a stop-gap measure until the secondary schools improved their students' preparation in writing, it was not the only means of arguing for space in the curriculum. Conservative Yale, for example, took the opposite tack from Harvard, arguing in its 1900–01 *Annual Report* that it was the *achievement* of students interested in written English, rather than their poor preparation, that justified more space in the curriculum. Two years before required Greek was abolished at Yale, we can see the rationale for a new allotment of space in the curriculum being put in place:

> Among all college studies the one which most steadily grows in public favor is English....It is chosen by students of the higher classes in constantly increasing numbers; and what is perhaps most important of all, its serious study outside the classroom is increasing year by year. The formation of reading clubs, the active competition for places in the college periodicals, and the *increased excellence of the student work* which finds its way into these periodicals, are all evidences of a general trend. (qtd. in Veysey 234, emphasis added)

But whatever arguments were made for assigning more space in the curriculum to course work in written English, the abolition of requirements in Greek and Latin marked a decisive shift away from the traditional claim of the old-time college system that the study of the classical languages provided students with cultural literacy, mental discipline, and the ability to write and speak well in English. Consequently, the deployment of language in undergraduate education changed in two major respects. First, the classical curriculum's predominantly oral and performative pedagogy of classroom recitation and rhetoricals, or exhibitions of public oratory, was replaced by an emphasis on such now standard literate practices as lectures (delivered from written texts) and student production of written texts (e.g., daily themes, note taking in lectures, written examinations, lab reports, abstracts, research papers). Second, the relationships among languages were rearranged. English was separated altogether from Greek and Latin as the vehicle of writing instruction, and the modern languages settled into their respective departments as national literatures. We look at each of these changes in turn.

The oral recitations of the classical curriculum offered an especially inviting target for the scorn of the modernizers. Recitations, to be sure, tended to be dull and mechanical exercises, as the following well-known passage by Lyman H. Bagg demonstrates. At Yale in the 1860s, Bagg says,

> In a Latin or Greek recitation one may be asked to read or scan a short passage, another to translate it, a third to answer questions as to its construction, and so on.... The reciter is expected simply to answer the questions which are put to him, but not to ask any of his instructor, or dispute his assertions. (qtd. in Russell 39)

To the contemporary observer, it is no wonder, as Edward E. Hale put it, that the "classical men made us hate Latin and Greek" (qtd. in Graff 19). Moreover, as Charles Francis Adams argues in his 1883 Phi Beta Kappa address, "A College Fetich," there is little relation in the oral recitations between means and ends and no substance to the classical theory that "a knowledge of Greek grammar, and the having puzzled through the *Anabasis* and three books of the *Iliad,* infuses into the boy's nature the imperceptible spirit of Greek literature, which will appear in the results of his subsequent work, just as manure, spread upon a field, appears in the crop which that field bears" (qtd. in Graff 30).

This relation of means and ends, or what the modernizers considered to be a lack of connection between oral recitation in Greek and Latin and the ability to write in English, is taken up in the Harvard Reports, where Adams appears again, along with E. L. Godkin and others, as one of the modernizing authors appointed by President Charles Eliot. Not surprisingly, the First Report (1892) attacks explicitly the long held theory that "the proper way to learn to write English is to translate orally Greek or Latin" (Brereton 93), and the Second Report (1895) presents a brief experiment that challenges the connection between translating Greek and Latin and the ability to compose in English. While the Fourth Report (1897) concedes the potential value of translating Greek and Latin into *written* English, the traditional *oral* method of language learning is characterized as "slovenly," "slip-shod," and "inexact," producing only "that lazy, mongrel dialect 'Translation English'" (Brereton 114). Despite the gesture toward the bilingualism of the older curriculum — and the explicit approval of the educational value of students' moving between languages by translating Greek and Latin into English — the real solution, as far as the authors are concerned, is to make more time in elementary and secondary education for instruction in written English and to replace the daily oral recitations in all classes with regular written exercises. The assumption resounds throughout the Harvard Reports that the proper preparation for the "advanced work" in college is mastery of written English. The authors quote tellingly as a typical statement of the problem the remark by an entering Harvard student: "I believe that I received [in preparatory school] far too little training in writing English, for my own good" (Brereton 117).

The issues raised in the modernizers' attacks on the recitations of the classical curriculum go well beyond the matter of identifying effective means of language learning. The moderns' characterization of the recitation as what John Franklin Genung called "a most grateful refuge to dull and perfunctory teachers" (Brereton 139) has a certain formulaic and stereotypical quality which suggests that profoundly different orientations toward language divided the modernizers of vernacular literacy from the "classical men" of the older oratorical tradition. David Russell's more balanced appraisal of the classical curriculum indicates, for example, counter to the findings of the Harvard Reports, that while the "recitation and the rhetoricals were almost always oral, they necessitated much writing as preparation for speaking" (38). Indeed, in Russell's view, the interaction of oral and written modes created a particularly language-rich environment:

> If much of the speaking and writing in recitation classes was highly structured, it was at least structured to include many kinds of activities: oral reading, note-taking on spoken and written material, translation, paraphrase, historical and philosophical commentary. Students not only manipulated language (and languages) they did so in progressively more sophisticated ways throughout their schooling, leading up to full-blown public speaking and debate. In the 1870s recitation would suffer wide attack for its sterility, routine, and lack of motivation. But in the hands of skillful teachers (and there were some), recitation was a flexible instrument for gradually developing the linguistic and, with it, intellectual facility that students needed to enter positions of authority in an oral, face-to-face culture. (40)

As Russell makes clear, the gap between the ancients and the moderns is a cultural as much as a pedagogical one — a matter of a perceived epochal and generational shift from the older nineteenth-century oratorical culture to the print culture of the modern age. According to the Fourth Harvard Report, the "old generation — the masters of the old school . . . could only in rare individual instances adapt themselves to the new order of things" (Brereton 124). For this reason, unsurprisingly, it "devolved" on Harvard to lead the "great change" into the modern era, aiming at "nothing less than elevating the study of English to the same plane of dignity which has for centuries been the peculiar attribute of the classical tongues" (Brereton 125). To put it another way, by discrediting the older oratorical tradition and the classical curriculum's belief that the study of Greek and Latin offered an effective means of learning to write in English, the modernizers at Harvard shifted the terms of work from the movement *among* languages to writing instruction in English only. In an important sense, the language policy of the modern university begins to emerge in recognizable form as writing in English is severed from its former association with the classical languages.

And this shift, in turn, is linked to the second major change in literacy education we have already noted. With the abolition of Greek and Latin requirements, the modernization of the university not only sealed the fate of the classical curriculum and the older oratorical tradition, it also created a moment of flux in which the linguistic terrain of the curriculum appeared, at least briefly, to be up for grabs. That is, to consolidate the triumph of the vernacular, the modernizers needed to reach a settlement among the modern languages by assigning them their cultural roles and spaces in the curriculum.

This territorialization of the modern languages has its own peculiar history. The Smith Chair in French and Spanish, for example, had been established at Harvard in 1816, and by 1872, just three years after Eliot arrived at Harvard, there were already departments of English, French, German, and Spanish. Still, it was not immediately agreed upon what languages should be counted as modern in the college curriculum. As Wallace Douglas observes, the "original staples of modern language study were modern only in the sense that they were not classical, . . . 'fundamental courses' such as Old and Middle English, Old Norse, Old French, Old High German, and the like" (48). Nor was it necessarily clear whether the modern languages constituted one field or many and how time should be allotted to each. As late as 1901, nearly thirty years after departments of English, German, French, Italian, and Spanish had been established at Harvard, President Eliot still referred to the modern languages, in his welcoming address to the annual MLA convention, as a single division of knowledge within the university rather than separate departments. Earlier, in the first volume of *PMLA* (1884–85), Theodore W. Hunt, one of the foremost advocates of an enlarged share of the curriculum for English, divided the curriculum into "the three great departments of Science, Philosophy, and Language and Literature" (118), recommending that the one-third time allotted to language and literature be divided equally among the major languages — Latin, Greek, French, German, and English (with English getting its fifth).

Nonetheless, Hunt's plea for an "equitable regime," where languages and literatures joined together in the curriculum "on a common ground and for a common end" (122), largely went unheard. The experience at Harvard, once again, is suggestive. In 1894, the only two courses required of all students were first-year English and a modern language. By 1897, however, the only requirement was the first-year English writing course. Instead of the increased "prominence" Hunt had recommended for English, English was elevated to preeminent status in the curriculum, and the other modern languages were, in effect, assigned their limited spheres of influence, territorialized as national literatures in their separate departments, where students encountered them as texts to be read, not living languages to be written or spoken.

This settlement of the modern curriculum, as we have already indicated, has been largely overlooked in composition histories of the first-year course. This oversight, in turn, obscures the outlines of the language policy that has long guided institutional practice in the first-year course and in the relations among the modern languages. For not only did the monolingual emphasis on written English replace the implicit bilingualism of the classical curriculum's emphasis on translation, the territorialization of the modern languages as reading courses assigned the status of a living language to English only, making it alone the primary vehicle of instruction in writing and speaking. If, in retrospect, this territorialization appears to be inevitable, we now need to consider how this sense of inevitability was articulated and codified as a standard feature of the modern curriculum. During the first two decades of the Modern Language Association, from its formation in 1883 to 1902, when *PMLA* discontinued the "Pedagogical Section" in the journal, there was a good deal of pedagogical and curricular discussion of both English and the other modern languages that offers important clues to how the languages were reconfigured in the curriculum following the demise of the classical curriculum. As we will see, faculty in the "foreign" languages played a crucial part in representing English as the "mother tongue" and the other modern languages as national literatures. Over this twenty-year period, we can identify four overlapping and mutually reinforcing strategic beliefs that shaped the settlement of the modern curriculum and the roles ascribed to English and the other languages.

1. Learning the Modern Languages as Living, Spoken Languages Is Held to Be a Nonintellectual, Feminine Activity

The Yale Report of 1828, a defense of the classics and mental discipline against advocates of a more flexible program of undergraduate study, set the tone for many years by dismissing the modern languages as subjects "to be studied, as an accomplishment, rather than as a necessary acquisition" (qtd. in Graff 36). Viewed as a social attainment and a sign of good breeding rather than proper intellectual work, the acquisition of fluency in speaking the modern languages, especially the Romance languages, was characterized as a suspiciously effeminate activity that evoked both the supposed sensuality of the Catholic Mediterranean and the lack of seriousness associated with the female academies and boarding schools, where French, Italian, and Spanish were studied instead of the ostensibly more rigorous Greek and Latin. Along these lines, in his MLA Presidential Address of 1890, James Russell Lowell, Smith Chair of French and Spanish at Harvard, caricatured the "stray Frenchman" who, after "failing as a teacher of his mother tongue... turned dancing master"—a "calling," Lowell says, which "public opinion seems to have put on the same intellectual level as the other" (5). Marked as both feminine and nonintellectual, the "mere fluency in speaking a language," E. H. Babbitt, professor of modern languages at Columbia, argues, "requires no higher order of intellect, and no more exercise of the judgment... than to play the banjo; and both can be learned equally well in 'six easy lessons'" (54).

2. The Modern Languages Are Represented Not as Living Languages but as Texts in an Archive

Babbitt's dismissal of fluency in speaking as a pedagogical goal shows the pressure to legitimize the study of the modern languages by investing it with the same kind of rigor and intellectual seriousness ascribed to study of the classics. In "How to Use Modern Languages as a Means of Mental Discipline," Babbitt says that the study of modern languages can develop the faculties of memory and judgment, just as the classical studies did, by emulating such elements of classical pedagogy as grammatical analysis, etymological identification, vocabulary development, and the appreciation of national cultures, literatures, and intellectual life. For Babbitt, a serious study of the modern languages would imitate the classic's engagement with dead, no longer spoken languages that exist solely in the form of written texts. It is only, Babbitt says, once a "pupil has acquired a good practical reading knowledge" that he can "gain the same amount of discipline as is to be obtained from classical studies" (62).

Edward J. Joynes, professor of modern languages at University of South Carolina, is even more explicit in his argument that students should encounter the modern languages as written texts and not as living languages. The "chief object of knowing [the modern languages]," Joynes says, "is to read them" (35). To clear the ground for such textual engagements, Joynes first dismisses the idea of "learning to speak in the college classroom" as "futile," "utterly wasted" exercises (38). Then he says that not only is writing in the modern languages typically begun too early, it is also "exaggerated beyond its proper importance, as though it were an end unto itself, instead of being regarded — what it really should be — as a help to easier and more accurate reading" (40). By the same token, W. T. Hewett, professor of German language and literature at Cornell, polarizes language study into "two methods...a knowledge of the literature *or* the ability to speak" (30, emphasis added) in order to show how speaking exercises divert "valuable time which should be spent in the study of the literature" and, thereby, risk leaving the student "the proud master of a few sentences, but without any literary knowledge" (31).

As we can see, the study of the modern languages is articulated along the older premises in the classical curriculum that language study promotes mental discipline and cultural literacy. As was the case in classical studies, modern language students encountered written texts drawn from an archive of literary language separated from the daily uses and common speech of the vernacular. In this sense, the modern languages were institutionalized not as living languages but as repositories of texts, embodied both in the pedagogical and curricular practices of reading the modern languages as national literatures and in the actual assembly of written texts into archives. The establishment of the Ticknor collection of Iberian Spanish texts from the fourteenth to the nineteenth century at the Boston Public Library — the life work of George Ticknor (1791-1871), first Smith Chair of French and Spanish at Harvard and the first American to receive a PhD degree from a German university — was indicative of this trend to see the modern languages exclusively in textual terms.

3. The Study of Modern Languages Figures Unidirectionally, Not as an End in Itself but as a Means to Mastering English

Along with the old classical appeals to discipline and a cultivated literary sensibility, modern language study was also justified in terms of "its influence in improving the pupil's command of his own" language (Babbitt 56). As noted earlier, the "modern" languages that Douglas lists, from the philological perspective dominant at the time, take their importance in the curriculum as linguistic antecedents to English.

This rendering of modern language study into an accessory to English comes out quite clearly, for example, in Joynes's insistence that "for this American people there is only one mother tongue, to which all other languages are alike foreign, and to be studied as such, by its norms and largely, too, for its own sake" (43). Even though he recommends the activity of translation as "not only the best test of the knowledge of both idioms" but as a work of "art," "science," and even the "conscience," Joynes evades any sense of reciprocity or mutuality in the movement among languages. "It were better," he makes plain, "that our students should never know other languages than to use them to debauch their English" (43). To find their proper place in the curriculum, the modern languages must take on the role of assisting the learning of English — the mother tongue to which they remain alien and other.

In fact, the preeminent position of English as the end of all language study figures in the modern university as the guarantor of knowledge in all fields, the living language of the academy and the ultimate warrant of understanding. As James Morgan Hart, professor of French and German at Cornell and Cincinnati and, later, of rhetoric at Cornell, asks in his revealingly titled address to MLA, "English as a Living Language," "Are you prepared to assert that a student is adequately trained in German, let us say, when he is unable to express in English the grammatical logic of a German sentence, the relation of dative and accusative, of verb and object? Do you truly believe that a student is mastering history in its sequence of cause and effect, when he is unable to express this causal sequence in phrases that have grammatical sequence?" (xv). In this sense, English has colonized the other academic fields, including the modern languages, for, as Hart says, "defective English vitiates all work in every department" (xv).

4. English in the U.S. Is Represented in Geographical Isolation from the Other Modern Languages

The subordination of the modern languages to English was reinforced by drawing linguistic borders around the continental U.S. and separating the nation's English monolingualism from a polyglot Europe. To be sure, the notion that learning to speak modern languages other than English is of some genuine practical value for commerce, diplomacy, or general culture had been acknowledged early in the nineteenth century, even by some of the classicists, as long as conversational fluency figured not as a curricular fixture but as a social attainment for those who wished or were required to travel to non-English-speaking countries. In general, however, the working assumption was that Americans, as Franklin Carter, president of Williams, says in 1886, "are not forced by geographical position...as are the French and Germans" to acquire fluency in "at least two modern languages." After all, Carter continues, "we are three thousand miles from European culture," and, besides, "England is the country which we as a rule first visit when traveling in the old world" (4)—whoever the "we" may be in this sentence. Further, Carter holds, it is "absurd...for someone living all his life in America to spend his time in mastering conversational Russian" and "certainly true," he concludes, "that most of our graduates never visit Europe nor really need a conversational use of any modern language" (5).

Carter's view of "Modern Languages in Our Higher Institutions" is remarkable not only for the way his American exceptionalism hinges on "our" differences from Europeans. It also serves to erase the modern languages that at the time *were* spoken widely within both recent immigrant and longstanding ethnic cultures in America—French, German, Spanish, Yiddish, Chinese, Italian, Polish, Hungarian, and (yes) Russian—not to mention the "foreign language" schools and presses that flourished during the nineteenth and early twentieth centuries. Moreover, as Jamie Candelaria Greene shows, even the written literate use of the Roman alphabet in North America begins not with the British colonies of the seventeenth century, where historians' Anglocentric bias has conventionally located it, but a century earlier in New Spain—and in Spanish, not English. Ironically, Carter's claim for the geographical isolation of English speakers in America appears in the same issue of *PMLA* that published the second in Alcee Fortier's series of three articles—"The French Language in Louisiana and the Negro-French Dialect," "French Literature in Louisiana," and "Bits of Louisiana Folklore"—along with A. Marshall Elliott's "Speech Mixture in French Canada, Indian and French." Apparently, Carter's "we" was not so removed from other language speakers as he made them out to be.

What Carter and the others we have cited (themselves mostly professors of the modern languages rather than of English) help us to see is that a unidirectional monolingual language policy that gives primacy of place to English in the modern curriculum is warranted as inevitable, not because English was the only living language available in North America but because the use of spoken and written English forms what Benedict Anderson calls an "imagined community" and a sense of nationhood. In relation to English, the other modern languages are unnaturalized and alien, *foreign* languages territorialized outside the U.S. by the borders that map the nation-states as discrete geopolitical entities and the modern languages as separate departments in the university curriculum. At the same time, this tacit language policy puts into place the chain of reifications we mentioned earlier that purifies the social identity of U.S. Americans as English speakers, privileges the use of language as written English, and then charts the pedagogical and curricular development of language as one that points inexorably toward mastery of written English.

Now, it should come as no surprise that such a language policy emerged in the modern university around the turn of the century, at the height of what the historian Richard Hofstadter calls the "Anglo-Saxon mystique." The modernizing wing of the old elites in Boston and New York that Eliot drew on for the Harvard Reports, along with modern language professors writing in *PMLA*, share the era's patrician fears of race mixing, mongrelization, and a loss of vigor among the better classes. But if the robust Teutonic roots of English were invoked to provide some measure of defense against the sensuality of the Catholic Mediterranean and the otherness of Eastern European Jews and Slavs, it is easy enough for us today to renounce the First World, great power chauvinism of the time. What takes more work, and to which we now turn in the next section, is the task of showing how assumptions about language that were institutionalized around the turn of the century, at a high tide of imperialism, colonial adventure, and overseas missionary societies, have become sedimented in the way we think about writing pedagogy and curriculum.

We do so by attending to the parallel assumptions underlying debate over English Only legislation and basic writers as well as ESL. We first identify the operation of reified notions of language and sociocultural identity where it is to be expected, in the arguments advocating English Only — the most obvious current embodiment of official monolingualism — and in underlying challenges found in debates about the academic legitimacy of first-year composition students. We then show what is more alarming: the parallel operation of these same notions in arguments made *against* English Only policies and *for* the rights of first-year composition students. Finally, we consider the implications of such parallels for our arguments and practices regarding English Only, composition instruction, and ESL.

ENGLISH ONLY, BASIC WRITING, AND ESL: KEEPING THE ENGLISH IN LANGUAGE INSTRUCTION AND POLICY

English Only legislation has arisen as a response to immigration to the U.S., and much of the support for English Only has been fueled by xenophobia.[2] Indeed, the debate over English Only frequently takes the form of a debate over immigrants themselves. Those arguing for English Only legislation implicitly, and sometimes explicitly, denounce current immigrants as a threat to the health of the nation's cultural, social, economic, and physical environment. A political advertisement funded by the American Immigration Control Foundation against current immigration policies that ran in the *Des Moines Register* during the 1999–2000 Iowa caucus season links language, immigrants, and culture quite explicitly. In the advertisement, a statement superimposed in bold white letters on a black-and-white photograph of a classroom full of children of apparently different ethnic backgrounds pledging allegiance reads, "Reciting the Pledge of Allegiance together isn't as easy as it used to be because many students can't speak English." Below the photograph image appears the explanation:

> "One nation; under God; indivisible" just doesn't work anymore. Because of mass immigration, we're becoming many nations. Under many gods. And very divided...[S]ome [immigrants] don't even care about our heritage. So, they don't speak our language, and they create their own countries within ours....take jobs and social services from our poorest citizens....Expand our welfare rolls. And divide our nation. (American Immigration Control Foundation)

Similar advertisements appearing during the same period and using almost identical formatting, but with their sponsorship identified as the Federation for American Immigration Reform and two organizations named Population-Environment Balance and Negative Population Growth, blamed immigrants for suburban sprawl, environmental degradation, and the corruption of politics (see Federation for American Immigration Reform, Population-Environment Balance, Negative Population Growth).

Those familiar with debates over basic writers and open-admissions students will note the parallels between the depiction of immigrants in such advertisements and representations of such students by those opposed to their admission to higher education. Borrowing on similar fears of the foreign, as a number of composition scholars have noted, those expressing opposition to the admission and teaching of beginning college-student writers traditionally excluded from college have commonly identified these students precisely as foreign — not just when referring to students who have immigrated to the U.S., or even primarily when referring to such students, but when describing students born in the U.S. whose native language is English (see, for example, Shaughnessy 2–3). Basic writers have commonly been described as immigrants and foreigners to the academy, those whose right to be there is suspect and whose presence is often seen as a threat to the culture, economy, and physical environment of the academy. Basic writers have been accused of not wanting to learn, attending classes only to stay warm, resisting assimilation to academic ways and mores, crowding out those who rightfully belong there, and taking away scarce resources from those who deserve them (see Horner, "The 'Birth'" 7–10; Lu 34–36).

More significantly, for those of us concerned with language issues, both debates invoke the same chain of reifications of language, sociocultural identity, language learning, and, ultimately, language learners we have seen in the formation of the language policy of the modern curriculum. In the English Only debate, we see such reifications in the clear distinctions assumed between the foreign and the native, the citizen and the immigrant, distinctions used to classify, simultaneously, both peoples and languages. The advertisement cited above exemplifies such assumptions: the possibility that the photograph depicts American citizens, not all of whom speak English, is not broached nor is the possibility that the students are Americans patriotically reciting the Pledge in some other language (as indeed occurs).

Such distinctions among and reifications of peoples, languages, and sociocultural identities ignore the fact that, for example, the social identity of immigrants can be described as in some ways in process: they are of no *fixed* or single national, regional, or linguistic identity nor, for that matter, are those identified as nonimmigrants. Indeed, such distinctions are arbitrary. It is not clear, for example, how many years or generations must have elapsed for an individual or family to shed "immigrant" status. And it is common for individuals to move back and forth between the land of their birth and the U.S. (and vice versa) and to identify with different nations and languages at different times.

For instance, in an essay on distinguishing among bilingual writers, Jan Frodesen and Norinne Starna describe "Alex," a "functional bilingual," as similar in background to many other students "whose families move back and forth between the United States and Mexico" (65). Alex, born and raised in Los Angeles with his family, moved at the age of five to Mexico with his mother and siblings for economic reasons, where he remained until age sixteen, when he returned to Los Angeles to live with his father and attend school (Frodesen and Starna 65–66). Yuet-Sim D. Chiang and Mary Schmida, in a study of how and with what consequences Asian-American students at UC Berkeley manage linguistic and cultural identity, report that students frequently "position themselves as *in between* worlds" (85, emphasis added). One student, for example, answered a question about being bilingual by explaining, "I'm kind of in between, I guess. I don't really speak [Chinese] that well, therefore I'm non-native Chinese. But language and culture are kind of connected, I think" (qtd. in Chiang and Schmida 86). Noting the "spectrum" of responses students give when asked to explain their native and non-native identification, Chiang and Schmida observe that such categories "force [students] to categorize their identity into an either-or sort of framework, when in fact they may not perceive it in such clear-cut distinctions" (90).

Chiang and Schmida conclude their study by challenging the efficacy of "clean cut categories such as mainstream English speaker, ESL speaker, or bilingual students" (91). While acknowledging that "categories like ESL, bilingual, and linguistic minority do indeed serve to delineate some students, these categories are inadequate when it comes to capturing the literacy journey of students whose lived realities often waver between cultural and linguistic borderslands" (94). However, these types of categories, based on reifications of language and identity, have dominated the way students are represented and programs institutionalized in both ESL and non-ESL college composition. Such categories, as several complain, overlook important differences among students. Linda Harklau, Kay Losey, and Meryl Siegal note, for example, that "ESL texts and curricula often contain an implicit assumption that international students are the normative population of college ESL classrooms, leading to certain suppositions concerning learners' backgrounds and skills," and overlooking the growing numbers of bi- or multilingual students raised in the U.S. ("Linguistically Diverse" 2). More generally, while careful not to deny the importance of acknowledging differences among students, scholars are increasingly questioning the validity, in both teaching and research, of categorizing students and their writing into native/non-native (Kachru, "Sources"; Leki; Sridhar; Valdés). Distinctions based on similar reifications of language and identity have operated in tracking students into basic writing courses. As David Bartholomae has observed,

> As a profession, we have defined basic writing (as a form or style of writing) by looking at the writing that emerges in basic writing courses. We begin, that is, with what we have been given, and our definition is predetermined by a prior distinction, by a reflex action to sort students into two groups (groups that look

"natural" or "right")....We know who basic writers are, in other words, because they are the students in classes we label "Basic Writing." (67)

To shore up the reification of an individual's national identity against one's actual, the very notion of identity is itself tied to language (as in the injunction "Speak American!") (Rodby 34). However, just as the identification of a nation and national identity with a single language is problematic, so the language identity of those named foreign, immigrant, or native is no more easily fixed than is their national identity (cf. Leung, Harris, and Rampton). Establishing a speaker's language identity is difficult for at least three reasons: first, the boundaries distinguishing the languages spoken are themselves both arbitrary and in flux (cf. Canagarajah 70-75; Rodby 33); second, the relation between the speaking of a language and one's social identification is at best tenuous; and third, a speaker's language competence, for lack of a better term, is in constant flux (Spack 772; Valdés). There is, after all, no clear point at which an individual can be said to be or not to be a speaker of a given language, just as there is no clear point at which someone can be said to have achieved literacy (Valdés 102-08; Harste et al. 69). Rather, as Pierre Bourdieu observes, linguistic competence is a political judgment about legitimacy:

> The competence adequate to produce sentences that are likely to be understood may be quite inadequate to produce sentences that are likely to be *listened to*, likely to be recognized as *acceptable* in all the situations in which there is occasion to speak. Here again, social acceptability is not reducible to mere grammaticality. Speakers lacking the legitimate competence are *de facto* excluded from the social domains in which this competence is required, or are condemned to silence. (55; cf. Schiffman *277*)

And as Bartholomae has observed,

> [Basic writers] are not the only ones who make mistakes and who present their work in ways that are inappropriate for a university. Mainstream freshmen, senior English majors, graduate students, our colleagues may all produce work that is naive, wrong, or off the track. The issue, then, is not who misses the mark but whose misses matter and why. To say this is to return attention to institutional processes of selection and exclusion. (68)

Hence we are hesitant to use the term *competence* to describe a speaker's language, since what constitutes language competence is itself arbitrary and continually subject to negotiation and redefinition.

Moreover, despite the standard hypostatization of languages by linguists, the boundaries distinguishing individual languages are at best, in Einar Haugen's term, "ragged margins" (Rodby 33; Zamel "Complicating"). What does and does not constitute English, for example, so long as it is spoken, remains subject to change, negotiation, even fracturing into different Englishes (see Canagarajah 128-29; McArthur). And finally, the speaking of a given language has no clear correspondence with how one identifies oneself, though it may be inappropriately used by others as a marker of one's social or cultural identity (see Spack; Zamel "Toward"). Chiang and Schmida find that "students' self-definition is not grounded in a clear or competent ability to speak the ethnic language; instead, it is informed by a sense of cultural identification" (85). Students "identify with their heritage language, even if they do not speak it.... It is as if by claiming the language, they claim a linguistic identity that perhaps exists in their minds, but not in their tongues" (87). Conversely, Constant Leung, Roxy Harris, and Ben Rampton suggest this last complication in noting studies that show urban youth destabilizing ethnicity through their language use, and the phenomenon of "language crossing," in which minority languages are used by ethnic "out-groups" (e.g., Panjabi spoken by African-Caribbean Britishers) (Leung et al. 548; see also Canagarajah 74–76 and studies cited there). A similar complication to linking language to national identity is suggested by the indigenization of English in a host of postcolonial polities to the point where English has come to be understood not as a foreign but a second or native language (Canagarajah 4, 129; Kachru *Alchemy;* Nayar 11).

In an apparent concession to this state of flux in language and social identity, a process of language learning is sometimes acknowledged; however, that process is imagined to develop in a fixed sequence leading, again, to an ideal, arbitrarily defined competence (Canagarajah 128; Kachru "Sources"; Sridhar). This idealized competence is often linked, again, with a distinct national identity: legally, for example, a specific competence in English is required to be granted U.S. citizenship. In what appears to be a further concession to the possibility of someone speaking a range of languages, at least in some arguments of those advocating English Only legislation, it is claimed that restrictions are to be placed only on written language or language for official occasions, meaning effectually language based in writing, whatever the medium of delivery, and not on private speech.[3] Thus, in these arguments, writing, not spoken practice, is viewed as the codification of the official language, the one that counts.

This privileging of writing as the embodiment of the standard against which other uses of language are judged marks the point where the teaching of writing and the debate over language legislation most clearly intersect. Moreover, in debates over the place of composition students in the academy, we can see comparable reifications of social identity, tied to language use; reifications of language itself, linked to writing; and the assumption of a fixed sequence of language development moving toward an ideal state of competence. We have already noted the common identification of certain groups of native-born U.S. students as foreigners to the academy in public and scholarly discourse on composition students. Such identifications use instances of these students' written language to mark them as belonging outside the academy, foreign to its ways. Significantly, that outsider status is based on the assumption of the fixed state of their language: the language evidenced in an instance of their writing, as in a written placement essay exam, is taken as evidence of their language use as a whole, which is assumed to be fixed and uniform.

Further, just as in the English Only debates, the boundaries separating one language from another are imagined as fixed, so in representations of students, the language of the academy is seen as discrete from the language of the outside, associated with students' home neighborhoods or ethnic, class, and racial identities. Finally, the composition course, or a fixed sequence of required writing courses, is charged with moving students/foreigners to the academy toward that ideal state of competence in academic English writing through a predetermined set of stages of writing development (cf. Rodby 19; Horner "Mapping" 117–25). Writing itself, like language, is understood in reified form, rather than as a set of heterogeneous and shifting practices.

Again, these parallels are perhaps most obvious, perhaps too obvious, in arguments for English Only and in arguments *opposed* or *hostile* to the admission of some students, such as those labeled basic writers, and opposed to granting the academic credit to college composition courses for these students on the grounds that the work accomplished in such courses is at best preparatory, rather than integral, to academic work generally. What we wish to address now is the degree to which that same set of parallel assumptions operates in arguments *opposed* to English Only and *for* the rights of beginning college composition students.[4] Many arguments opposing English Only legislation make the point that such legislation is unnecessary because (1) immigrants are already learning English as fast as, if not faster than, immigrants in the past, and so clearly show an awareness of the importance of knowing the language; and (2) English Only legislation ignores the difficulty of learning a second language, characteristically making no provision for helping immigrants to learn English, and so would leave many immigrants in the lurch (see, e.g., Nicolau and Valdivieso; Crawford "What's Behind" 175–77; Fishman 167). Thus, the arguments go, English Only legislation is offensive in its assumption that immigrants are so ignorant as not to be aware of the value of English, when they clearly are aware of it, and it is insensitive in failing to recognize the difficulty of learning English and in failing to assist immigrants in doing so. It is also argued that such legislation, far from providing a means of preventing cultural divisions, is itself divisive in offending and insulting immigrants.

Given current political exigencies, we are not about to forswear these arguments as unimportant. And we are certainly willing to stand behind their validity. Significant and credible evidence shows that immigrants to the U.S. are aware of the importance of English fluency and are attempting to achieve it, and that language legislation like English Only has, globally and historically, always had the effect of producing and reinforcing, rather than ameliorating, cultural strife.[5] Nonetheless, such arguments leave unchallenged several of the key assumptions made by those arguing *for* English Only.

First, and most damagingly, *the legitimacy of a primarily monolingual culture is generally accepted* (Schiffman 269; cf. Nayar 12, n. 2). Learning, maintaining, or increasing knowledge of a second language is often encouraged primarily as a means of improving one's knowledge of English. For example, in an eerie echo of E. H. Babbitt's recommendation that English-speaking students study the modern languages as a means of improving their command of English, the National Council of Teachers of English 1997 Resolution on Developing and

Maintaining Fluency in More Than One Language opens its argument by observing that "Literacy transfers across languages. Current research confirms the fact that English language learners acquire English more easily if they are literate in their native language."

In public debate over English Only, few arguments are made for the legitimacy of speaking languages other than English. At best, as in the nineteenth century, multilingualism is encouraged for the economic, trade advantages it may give states or businesses. In these arguments, what Judith Rodby terms a universalist understanding of languages, including English, is assumed: that is, languages are equated with currency (31). In such arguments, the nature of each language is assumed to be fixed, and what language is to be used is determined according to instrumentalist concerns, in terms of its exchange value. Unfortunately, this same view of language is invoked by advocates of English Only: English, they sometimes observe, just happens to be the common currency of the United States (and, increasingly, the world); therefore, foreigners had better exchange their languages for ours (see U.S. English).

Of course, as Rodby observes of discussions of ESL, "most discussions incorporate terms and occasionally even conflicting conclusions" (39). Those arguing both for and against English Only frequently adopt not just universalist but what Rodby terms ethnicist approaches to language that assume a link between a reified language and reified ethnic identity (Rodby 34).[6] So, for example, in arguments against English Only, multilingualism is also encouraged as a way of preserving ethnic diversity, on the assumption that language is the primary bond and reliable cue to ethnicity (cf. Montaner 164). Unfortunately, this assumption plays into the hands of those arguing for English Only, who, no less contradictory than their opponents, herald English as the only means of ensuring the unity of American culture and society (Schiffman 271–72), an argument invoked in the advertisement cited above.

But more commonly, in arguments opposed to English Only, the threat those advocating English Only see immigrants posing to monolingual English culture is dismissed as no threat at all: those immigrants, we are assured, are eager to become fluent monolingual English speakers just like we are, their language differences something that, with time and patience and training, will disappear (see, for example, American Civil Liberties Union). For example, the Conference on College Composition and Communication statement supporting its 1988 resolution on a National Language Policy explains that English Only is unnecessary because

> English, the global lingua franca and the language of wider communication in this country, is not threatened. For two centuries, most immigrants learned English within a generation without any laws compelling them. Current immigrants are doing the same.

While there is substantial evidence that this is true (see Veltman *Language Shift*, *The Future*), we question whether such an ideal should remain uncritiqued or form the guiding assumption of U.S. writing instruction.

Second, and in line with this, *the status of English itself as a fixed entity to be acquired or not remains in place.* As linguists have long recognized, the boundaries and, for that matter, the interior of the linguistic territory known as English are subject to change so long as it remains in use. That this is the historical norm, however, is ignored in claims that encounters with other language practices will not change what people think of as English. Located in actual practice, what is called English inevitably adjusts to changing circumstance (see Leung et al. 548; McArthur). Located, however, in the realm of the ideal associated with proper English and with writing, English either remains inviolable, in the arguments against English Only, or, in arguments for it, is at risk, either of disappearing altogether or of being debauched, as Edward Joynes worried about long ago in proscribing instruction in speaking, as opposed to reading, foreign languages.[7]

Third, in many of the arguments against as well as for English Only, it is assumed as an ideal *a single direction for language learning: by immigrants only, moving toward competence in English* (Crawford *Hold* 206-07, 256-57; Schiffman 269; Zamel "Complicating"). Aside from ignoring variations and fluctuations in English and the concomitant arbitrariness of defining competence in it, these arguments identify the problem strictly as a deficit of immigrants and differ only in how to address that deficit, rather than seeing the difficulties faced in encounters with new immigrants as providing evidence of the limitations of the monolingualism of U.S. culture. This assumption is perhaps most tellingly revealed in the labels ESL uses to name its students and their languages. For example, as Ruth Spack has noted, terms like "foreign," "international," and "other" used to identify ESL students assume specific sociocultural identities for the students and their languages and posit English, and English speakers, as "the norm against which the other, the different, is measured" (766; for responses to and replies from Spack, see Nelson et al.). Like the term "immigrant," such labels, while at times benign and even useful, can also be problematic, misleading, even politically noxious.

Fourth, in line with this acceptance of monolingual, reified English as the norm, it's often accepted *that possession of the English language by itself accounts for the socioeconomic status of ethnic groups* (Fishman 168-70; Schiffman 271-72). This is the assumption behind an Iowa state legislator's claim, in arguing for English Only legislation, that "[t]he unwritten message that [the bill] sends is, 'to realize the American dream you need to speak English'" ("English Language Bill OK'd"). But it is also the assumption opponents bank on when calling, instead, for increased funding for ESL instruction, a fact that has led proponents of English Only legislation in Iowa, for example, to cleverly link such legislation with bills offering token support for such instruction (see "Immigrants' English, Welcome Centers Eyed").[8] In other words, the focus on language ignores the degree to which language in and of itself provides no guarantee of socioeconomic advancement, operating instead in contingent relation to a host of other factors — such as race, ethnicity, gender, class, and age — in determining one's economic position.

Finally, in keeping with a reified view of language, *the material costs of achieving a multilingual, as opposed to an accommodationist monolingual, society are downplayed.* Because English Only advocates often portray immigrants as a drain on the economy — demanding health and social services, schooling, jobs, translations, housing — those opposed have denied any costs associated with the presence of non-English speakers. They emphasize, instead, that immigrants pay far more in taxes and contribute far more to the economy than they receive in benefits, and they point to the insignificance of the costs of providing translations of government documents and the like (see, for example, American Civil Liberties Union; Crawford "Canard"). Again, while we agree with this latter cost-benefit assessment, it sidesteps the more significant costs and even more significant benefits, both economic and cultural, associated with pursuit of an actively bi- or multilingual policy, such as English Plus.[9] If the aim of English Only advocates, however mean and misguided, is to protect the cultural status quo of the U.S., we should be wary of accommodating that aim in our arguments opposing such a strategy. We should refuse to accept the notion that present-day U.S. culture does not need to change, and won't be for the better, by different speakers, thinkers, and writers speaking, thinking, and writing differently.

BEYOND ENGLISH ONLY

If we are right about the limitations of those arguing against English Only in the assumptions they share with their opponents, then it behooves us to consider the possibility of parallel limitations in how compositionists think of and argue for their students and courses. For one thing, as several compositionists have argued, representations of students have been limited in problematic ways. While describing students as foreigners to the academy may have sometimes assuaged critics by assuring them that students' language differences were not evidence of cognitive deficiencies, such representations have also ignored the ways in which neither students nor teachers have ever been either fully at home in, or isolated from and foreign to, the academy (Horner "Mapping"; Soliday "The Politics of Difference"; Spack 766). As Mary Soliday has argued, "If we assume only an oppositional difference between us (the academy) and them (culturally different students), we limit the possibilities for complex relationships and various kinds of journeys for individual students." Thus, such assumptions might blind us to the identification she reports students making of "a strong continuity among themselves, their experiences, and the university" ("Politics" 270).

Reified notions of students' cultural identities and language habits have also misled teachers into attributing to the influence of a particular foreign culture particular writing practices. Ilona Leki, in an essay exploring the limitations of contrastive-rhetoric study for understanding second-language writing, warns that "the findings of contrastive-rhetoric research on a single text type (or a small number of text types) have sometimes been promulgated as discoveries about an entire cultural group's general rhetorical preferences" (236). Such overgeneralizations are especially troubling, Leki says, when much of this research bases its claims about rhetorical preferences on students' writing in a second language. "Imagine," she suggests, compositionists accepting "descriptions of English rhetorical patterns based on essays by a randomly selected group of NES [native English-speaking] freshmen writing in a language other than English" (236). While Leki defends studying difference for demonstrating the relativity of cultural norms, she notes that "it can also lead to regressive and limiting, even blinding, stereotypes and unwarranted categorical distinctions among groups" (241).

Such categorizing can also lead us to overlook direct and indirect interaction between cultures. Spack, for example, reports one researcher thinking "that the 'flowery effusions' in [a student's] writing were the product of the rhetorical traditions of [the student's] 'native' Afghani culture," but later found that they "were actually the result of [the student's] imitation of the style of the Harlequin romances she was fond of reading" (Spack 772). As Vivian Zamel observes, reified notions of students' cultural identities and language practices reinforce the idea "that each [language and culture] is separate from, even in opposition to, the other and keeps educators from understanding the complex ways in which the two intersect, mingle with, and give shape to one another." Thus they encourage "a deterministic stance and deficit orientation as to what students can accomplish in English" ("Toward" 341).

Moreover, an emphasis on the foreign character of students' language has sometimes led not simply to believing in but to attempting to teach a reified version of academic language at odds with its heterogeneity, fluctuating character, and negotiability. As Zamel has observed of ESL scholarship, the construction of both students' and academic culture as "discrete, discontinuous, and predictable — colors both the ways in which we view our students and the academic wor(l)ds [sic] they will encounter" ("Toward" 343). While Bartholomae was being ironic in suggesting that students needed to "invent" the university in their writing, there is a real sense in which students, like all the rest of us writers, do participate in *re*-inventing — not simply reproducing but potentially altering — university language in each act of writing. As Rodby has put it in arguing for ESL writers, "the writer has not only the ability but the right to 'do unheard of things with [English]'" (47; see also Canagarajah 168–69, 175).

If we grant that definitions of academic discourse and competence in it are arbitrary, then the notion of leading students through a fixed developmental sequence of stages to mastery of that language has to be rethought. While different writing courses may well appropriately focus on different aspects of all that goes into writing and different writing practices, recognition of the heterogeneity and fluctuating nature of writing, including what's called academic writing, requires that we incorporate attention to such heterogeneity and fluctuation in how we design both individual writing courses and curricular programs. Relatedly, recognition of the arbitrary and fluctuating character of writing at particular sites, including the academic, requires that we reject denials of the legitimate place of students and their work in the academy, manifested in the refusal to grant academic credit for basic writing courses and the treatment of composition courses generally as, at best, preparatory to rather than an integral part of academic work. If we reject the reification of academic language and competence in it, we cannot use instances of students' language to deny them academic citizenship. This doesn't mean the abolition of standards but the development, by students and teachers working together, of different standards, understood as contingent, local, and negotiable (cf. Boomer et al.; Fox ch. 4).

Just as in debating English Only we should not shy from confronting the material and cultural costs, and even greater benefits, of pursuing a multilingual ideal, so we should be wary of denying the material costs to the academy of pursuing the ideals we have for our composition programs. Highlighting such costs has usually been one of the chief strategies of those opposed to such programs, particularly basic writing programs, as justification for their elimination or downsizing. Such arguments assume that the integrity of the academy has already been achieved and is being threatened by such programs. But if we are to take academic mission statements at their word, we might argue that the costs of composition programs, far from threatening academic integrity, are crucial to achieving that as yet unrealized integrity. Certainly, any substantial writing program, whether basic writing or the universally required freshman composition course or some other version, can reasonably be understood to affect the work of its institution. But justifications for such programs usually define their role as strictly supplementary or preparatory to normal academic work. These justifications thus render the programs vulnerable to charges that they are remedial — efforts at mopping up after the failures of secondary schools — and, hence, that they deserve to be continually underfunded as inessential temporary add-ons. Moreover, these arguments leave unchallenged the legitimacy of the existing work of the academy as something simply to be supplemented or prepared for, rather than something in dire need of change (Horner "The 'Birth'" 6–11,16–18).

Alternatively, we might argue that composition courses and programs provide crucial opportunities for rethinking writing in the academy and elsewhere: spaces and times for students and teachers both to rethink what academic work might mean and be — who is and should be involved, the forms that work might take, the ends it might pursue, the practices that define it and which might be redefined (cf. Brannon; Trimbur). The incorporation of service learning into composition courses obviously represents one movement in this direction, as it redefines the normal mode and purpose and practices for academic work by students, teachers, even administrators. More generally, such a justification for composition would place it at the academy's center, necessary to enabling the academy to achieve its heralded ideals of student-centered, interdisciplinary learning, training for responsible citizenship, service, and the like, and, as such, deserving of increased funding and support. And as several writers have suggested, we might call on our most immediately accessible constituents, the students, for support in arguing for their own centrality (Horner "Traditions" 393–94; Soliday "Class" 739; Thompson A23).

As other writers have argued, the institutional, pedagogical, and research relationships among college composition, ESL, and other language instruction need to be rethought (see, for example, Matsuda; Muchiri et al.; Silva et al.; Valdés). For those of us who identify ourselves primarily as compositionists, this means first and foremost acknowledging the degree to which our field and our pedagogy are rooted in and tacitly perpetuate a policy of English Only and the assumptions underlying English Only in much of its research, pedagogy, and institutional arrangements. In addition to broadening the range of scholarship on which they draw in thinking about their work, compositionists need to recognize the limitations of the prevailing disciplinary division of labor Paul Kei Matsuda identifies between composition and ESL in meeting the needs and building on the strengths of both composition and ESL students (see Matsuda; Matsuda and Silva). More broadly, compositionists must learn to resist thinking of identifying students and our teaching in terms of fixed categories of language, language ability, and social identity, however natural and inevitable such categories can seem to be in our day-to-day work and in the arguments we make to the public in defense of our work. Finally, we should consider how writing programs can encourage writing in languages other than English. We might, for example, begin a dialogue with teachers of the other modern languages to identify shared concerns as well as differences in language pedagogy. And, where it makes sense, we should draw on students' interests and existing linguistic resources to design bilingual programs of study that seek to develop students' fluency in more than one written language and the possibilities of moving between the modern languages (Trimbur).

WHOSE ENGLISH, WHOSE INTERESTS?

We are, of course, trading here in ideals, and for care in how we define ideals, in our arguments about both language legislation and composition. In doing so, we don't mean to deny the significance of local historically and institutionally immediate circumstances in determining what is politically appropriate to a particular argument, or set of institutional arrangements, made in a particular set of circumstances. Nonetheless, we would urge that it is appropriate, as we make our arguments, to keep in mind the larger ideals at which we (and our opponents) aim and the assumptions we may advance in the name of politics, and that we beware of the long-term political consequences of making those assumptions for ourselves, our neighbors, and our students.

In making the case for such long-term ideals, we can benefit not only from considering the limited assumptions on which our opponents base their arguments and on which, as we have shown, compositionists themselves have sometimes relied, but also from an understanding of composition's tacit monolingual, English Only policy as an historical development. What seems both natural and inevitable must be understood instead as historical and, therefore, both the product of human agents and something subject to change. In fact, as we have shown, the historical formation of the first-year composition course is tied in tightly to a monolingual and unidirectional language policy that makes English the vehicle of writing instruction in the modern curriculum. The fact that this seems inevitable only serves to legitimate the tacit language policy.

As we have argued, this tacit language policy weighs heavily on our work studying and teaching writing. This largely unexamined language policy has made it difficult to see that U.S. college composition, from its formation to the present day, operates for the most part within national borders, at worst justifying writing instruction for reasons of economic productivity, cultural integration, and now perhaps homeland security, while at best imagining a more inclusive, pluricultural, and participatory civic life in the U.S. There is little question in our minds that U.S. college composition today is more cosmopolitan than it was, say, twenty years ago, not to mention one hundred years ago when it figured unequivocally as nationalistic instruction in an unquestioned mother tongue. There are cross-cultural and multicultural readers, syllabi with discussions of globalization, and a growing interest in how writing is taught in other countries. Still, as our review of the English Only debate indicates, despite this worldliness, many of the most progressive perspectives in composition studies locate the problem of English squarely within the confines of the United States. The task, as we see it, is to develop an internationalist perspective capable of understanding the study and teaching of written English in relation to other languages and to the dynamics of globalization. At a point when many North Americans hold it self-evident that English is already or about to be the global lingua franca, we need to ask some serious questions about the underlying sense of inevitability in this belief — and about whose English and whose interests it serves.

NOTES

[1] The history of language teaching is long, complicated, and evenly documented. In *25 Centuries of Language Teaching*, Louis G. Kelly argues that pedagogical approaches have veered back and forth between "formalism" and "activism" depending on the relative emphases placed on the three main objectives of language learning — communication, literary appreciation, and philosophical (i.e., linguistic) analysis. In the early-nineteenth century, the first two holders of the Smith Chair of French and Spanish at Harvard, George Ticknor and Henry Wadsworth Longfellow, treated the modern languages as living ones and, therefore, emphasized their spoken, idiomatic character. By the late-nineteenth century, however, the balance in U.S. college language teaching had clearly tilted toward the traditional grammar-translation model, largely ignoring or being unaware of the "direct method" proposed by reformers in France and Germany and the work of linguists such as Henry Sweet, Otto Jespersen, and Harold A. Palmer in the U.K. (see Stern 75–116; Titone; Van Essen). As late as 1929, the now infamous Coleman Report, in presenting the findings of the Modern Foreign Language Study, recommended that the main goal of language learning should be reading fluency. It was not until the postwar period that secondary and college language teaching uniformly shifted to audiolingual, immersion, and other "activist" methods of learning. This shift is conventionally attributed to the response to Sputnik in 1957 and the National Defense

Education Act of 1958, but, as Roger A. Pillet points out, the Modern Language Association had already initiated programs, funded by the Rockefeller Foundation from 1952–58, to improve language instruction.

[2] While proponents of English Only insist that they are calling not to restrict language use to English but to make English the official language of the United States, the efforts of the organizations supporting official English to ban bilingual education and to ban other languages from advertising, menus, radio and television broadcasts, books on the shelves of public libraries, and even telephone bills persuade us to continue to designate the policy as one of English Only. For an analysis of organizations that support making English the official language of the U.S. and their underlying motives, see Crawford "What's Behind." In our discussion of assumptions about language and identity in the English Only debate and parallels in composition, we draw on Horner " 'Students' Right.' "

[3] English Only legislation introduced in the state of Iowa, for example, states, "The official language of the state shall be the English language and all official proceedings, records, and publications shall be in the English language."

[4] In light of the critique we offer, it seems appropriate to note that it applies equally to arguments made against English Only legislation by one of us in his lobbying work and that the experience of such work is part of what has prompted our critique.

[5] On the desire and efforts of immigrants to the U.S. to learn English, see Crawford *Hold* 97; Fishman 166, 168; Nicolau and Valdivieso 318; Veltman *Language Shift, The Future;* American Civil Liberties Union. On the divisive effects of language legislation, see, for example, Crawford "What's Behind" 177, and *Hold* 108, 200–01; Draper and Jiménez 93; Horowitz 132–33; Inglehart and Woodward; Manogaran 46–47, 52–53; Tambiah 73–77.

[6] We can see both approaches implicit in the Teachers of English to Speakers of Other Languages Resolution on Language Rights insistence that "all individuals have the opportunity to acquire proficiency in English while maintaining their own language and culture" (Teachers). See also the National Council of Teachers of English Resolution on English as a Second Language and Bilingual Education.

[7] While debate on English Only occasionally broaches the permeability of the borders distinguishing English, or "Official English," from other languages and from expressions of unofficial language, such as "canoe," "habeus corpus," and "y'all" (see *Language Loyalties* 88), generally what constitutes English is assumed to be self-evident rather than subject to challenge or in need of definition.

[8] James Crawford reports that many of those voting in support of English Only initiatives do so in the mistaken belief that they are supporting the provision of ESL instruction to immigrants ("What's Behind" 175).

[9] English Plus policy encourages the teaching of English plus one or more additional languages to all students in the U.S. Among the many groups supporting English Plus are NCTE's Conference on College Composition and Communication, Teachers of English to Speakers of Other Languages, and the Linguistic Society of America.

WORKS CITED

American Civil Liberties Union. "The Rights of Immigrants." ACLU Briefing Paper, 1998. <http://www.aclu.org/library/pbp20.html>

American Immigration Control Foundation. "Reciting the Pledge." Political advertisement. *Des Moines Register* 4 January 2000: 5A.

Anderson, Benedict. *Imagined Communities: Reflections on the Origin and Spread of Nationalism.* Rev. ed. London: Verso, 1991.

Babbitt, E. H. "How to Use Modern Languages as a Means of Mental Discipline."
    PMLA 11 (1896): 52–63.

Bartholomae, David. "Writing on the Margins: The Concept of Literacy in Higher
    Education." *A Sourcebook for Basic Writing Teachers.* Ed. Theresa Enos. New York:
    Random, 1987. 66–83.

Boomer, Garth, Nancy Lester, Cynthia Onore, and Jonathan Cook, eds. *Negotiating the
    Curriculum: Educating for the 21st Century.* London: Falmer, 1992.

Bourdieu, Pierre. *Language and Symbolic Power.* Ed. John B. Thompson. Trans. Gino
    Raymond and Matthew Adamson. Cambridge: Harvard UP, 1991.

Brannon, Lil. "Confronting the Logic of Instrumentalism: Using Rhetoric for Social
    Change." Conference on College Composition and Communication. Phoenix, AZ,
    13 March 1997.

Brereton, John C. *The Origins of Composition Studies in the American College, 1875–1925: A
    Documentary History.* Pittsburgh: U of Pittsburgh P, 1995.

Canagarajah, A. Suresh. *Resisting Linguistic Imperialism in English Teaching.* Oxford: Oxford
    UP, 1999.

Carter, Franklin. "Study of Modern Languages in Our Higher Insitutions." *PMLA* 2
    (1887): 3–21.

Chiang, Yuet-Sim D., and Mary Schmida. "Language Identity and Language Owner-
    ship: Linguistic Conflicts of First-Year University Writing Students." Harklau et al.
    81–96.

Conference on College Composition and Communication. National Language Policy
    Statement, 1988. <http://www.ncte.org/positions/national.html>

Crawford, James. *Hold Your Tongue: Bilingualism and the Politics of "English Only."* Reading:
    Addison-Wesley, 1992.

———. "Canard: 'Multilingual Government.'" <http://ourworld.compuserve.com/
    homepages/JWCRAWFORD/can-mult.htm> 1997.

———. "What's Behind Official English?" *Language Loyalties* 171–77.

Douglas, Wallace. "Accidental Institutions: On the Origins of Modern Language
    Study." *Criticism in the University.* Ed. Gerald Graff and Reginald Gibbons. Evanston:
    Northwestern UP, 1985. 35–61.

Draper, Jamie B., and Martha Jiménez. "A Chronology of the Official English Move-
    ment." Excerpted from "Language Debates in the United States: A Decade in
    Review." *EPIC Events* 2.5 (1990): 1, 4, 7. Rpt. *Language Loyalties* 89–94.

"English Language Bill OK'd." *Des Moines Register* 18 March 1999: 1A.

Federation for American Immigration Reform. "Ten Virgin Acres. A Freshwater Stream.
    Dozens of Old-Growth Trees. What a Great Place to Build a Parking Lot for the New
    High-Rise." Political Advertisement. *Des Moines Register* 12 January 2000: 5M.

Fishman, Joshua A. "The Displaced Anxieties of Anglo-Americans." Excerpted from
    "'English Only': Its Ghosts, Myths, and Dangers." *International Journal of the Sociology
    of Language* 74 (1988): 125–40. Rpt. *Language Loyalties* 165–70.

Fox, Tom. *Defending Access: A Critique of Standards in Higher Education.* Portsmouth:
    Boynton/Cook Heinemann, 1999.

Frodesen, Jan, and Norinne Starna. "Distinguishing Incipient and Functional
    Bilingual Writers: Assessment and Instructional Insights Gained through Second-
    Language Writer Profiles." Harklau et al. 61–79.

Graff, Gerald. *Professing Literature: An Institutional History.* Chicago: U of Chicago P, 1987.

Greene, Jamie Candelaria. "Misperspectives on Literacy: A Critique of an Anglocentric
    Bias in Histories of American Literacy." *Written Communication* 11.2 (1994): 251–69.

Halloran, S. Michael. "From Rhetoric to Composition: The Teaching of Writing in America to 1900." *A Short History of Writing Instruction: From Ancient Greece to Twentieth-Century America.* Ed. James J. Murphy. Davis: Hermagoras, 1990. 151-82.

Harklau, Linda, Kay M. Losey, and Meryl Siegal, eds. *Generation 1.5 Meets College Composition: Issues in the Teaching of Writing to U.S.-Educated Learners of ESL.* Mahwah: Erlbaum, 1999.

———. "Linguistically Diverse Students and College Writing: What Is Equitable and Appropriate?" Harklau et al. 1-14.

Harste, Jerome C., Virginia A. Woodward, and Carolyn L. Burke. *Language Stories & Literacy Lessons.* Portsmouth: Heinemann, 1984.

Hart, James Morgan. "English as a Living Language." *PMLA* 1 (1884-85): xi-xviii.

Hewett, W. T. "The Aims and Methods of Collegiate Instruction in Modern Languages." *PMLA* 1 (1884-85): 25-36.

Hofstadter, Richard. *Social Darwinism in American Thought, 1860-1915.* Philadelphia: U of Pennsylvania P, 1944.

Horner, Bruce. "The 'Birth' of 'Basic Writing.'" Horner and Lu 3-29.

———. "Mapping Errors and Expectations for Basic Writing: From the 'Frontier Field' to 'Border Country.'" Horner and Lu 117-36.

———. "'Students' Right,' English Only, and Re-imagining the Politics of Language." *College English* 63 (2001): 741-58.

———. "Traditions and Professionalization: Reconceiving Work in Composition." *College Composition and Communication* 51 (2000): 366-98.

Horner, Bruce, and Min-Zhan Lu. *Representing the "Other": Basic Writers and the Teaching of Basic Writing.* Urbana: National Council of Teachers of English, 1999.

Horowitz, Donald L. *Ethnic Groups in Conflict.* Berkeley: U of California P, 1985.

Hunt, Theodore W. "The Place of English in the College Curriculum." *PMLA* 1 (1884-85). 118-32.

"Immigrants' English, Welcome Centers Eyed." *Des Moines Register* 24 February 1999: 4M.

Inglehart, Ronald F., and Margaret Woodward. "Language Conflicts and Political Community." Excerpted from *Comparative Studies in Society and History* 10 (1967): 27-45. Rpt. *Language Loyalties* 410-23.

Joynes, Edward J. "Reading in Modern Language Study." *PMLA* 5.2 (1890): 33-46.

Kachru, Braj B. *The Alchemy of English: The Spread, Functions, and Models of Non-Native Englishes.* Oxford: Pergamon, 1986.

———. "Monolingual Bias in SLA Research." *TESOL Quarterly* 28 (1994): 795-800.

Kelly, Louis G. *25 Centuries of Language Teaching: An Inquiry into the Science, Art, and Development of Language Teaching Methodology, 500 B.C.-1969.* Rowley: Newbury House, 1969.

Language Loyalties: A Source Book on the Official Language Controversy. Ed. James Crawford. U of Chicago P, 1992.

Leki, Ilona. "Cross-Talk: ESL Issues and Contrastive Rhetoric." Severino et al. 234-44.

Leung, Constant, Roxy Harris, and Ben Rampton. "The Idealised Native Speaker, Reified Ethnicities, and Classroom Realities." *TESOL Quarterly* 31.3 (1997): 543-75.

Lowell, James Russell. "Address." *PMLA* 5.1 (1890): 5-22.

Lu, Min-Zhan. "Conflict and Struggle: The Enemies or Preconditions of Basic Writing?" Horner and Lu 30-55.

Manogaran, Chelvadurai. *Ethnic Conflict and Reconciliation in Sri Lanka.* Honolulu: U of Hawaii P, 1987.

Matsuda, Paul Kei. "Composition Studies and ESL Writing: A Disciplinary Division of Labor." *College Composition and Communication* 50.4 (1999): 699–721.

Matsuda, Paul Kei, and Tony Silva. "Cross-Cultural Composition: Mediated Integration of U.S. and International Students." *Composition Studies* 27.1 (1999): 15–30.

McArthur, Tom. *The English Languages.* Cambridge UP, 1998.

Montaner, Carlos Alberto. "Talk English—You Are in the United States" ["Why Fear Spanish?"]. *Miami Herald* 25 April 1988: 14A. Rpt. *Language Loyalties* 163–65.

Muchiri, Mary N., Nshindi G. Mulamba, Greg Myers, and Deoscorous B. Ndoloi. "Importing Composition: Teaching and Researching Academic Writing beyond North America." *College Composition and Communication* 46.2 (1995): 175–98.

National Council of Teachers of English. Resolution on Developing and Maintaining Fluency in More than One Language. <http://www.ncte.org/resolutions/fluency 971997.html>

National Council of Teachers of English. Resolution on English as a Second Language and Bilingual Education. <http://www.ncte.org/resolutions/bilingual821982.html>

Nayar, P. Bhaskaran. "ESL/EFL Dichotomy Today: Language Politics or Pragmatics?" *TESOL Quarterly* 31.1 (1997): 9–37.

Negative Population Growth. "How Do You Feel about Paving over the Amber Waves of Grain, the Purple Mountain Majesties and the Fruited Plain?" Political advertisement. *Des Moines Register* 4 January 2000: 6A.

Nelson, Gayle L., Ruth Spack, and Joan G. Carson. "Comments on Ruth Spack's 'The Rhetorical Construction of Multilingual Students.'" *TESOL Quarterly* 32 (1998): 727–46.

Nicolau, Siobhan, and Rafael Valdivieso. "Spanish Language Shift: Educational Implications." *Language Loyalties* 317–22.

Pillet, Roger A. *Foreign Language Study: Perspective and Prospect.* Chicago: U of Chicago P, 1974.

Population-Environment Balance. "Mass Immigration Costs Taxpayers over $69 Billion a Year. Chicken Feed Compared to the Environmental Costs." Political advertisement. *Des Moines Register* 3 January 2000: 6M.

Rodby, Judith. *Appropriating Literacy: Writing and Reading in English as a Second Language.* Portsmouth: Boynton/Cook, 1992.

Russell, David. *Writing in the Academic Disciplines, 1870–1990.* Carbondale: Southern Illinois UP, 1991.

Schiffman, Harold. *Linguistic Culture and Language Policy.* London: Routledge, 1996.

Severino, Carol, Juan C. Guerra, and Johnella E. Butler, eds. *Writing in Multicultural Settings.* New York: Modern Language Association, 1997.

Shaughnessy, Mina P. *Errors and Expectations: A Guide for the Teacher of Basic Writing.* New York: Oxford UP, 1977.

Silva, Tony, Ilona Leki, and Joan Carson. "Broadening the Perspective of Mainstream Composition Studies: Some Thoughts from the Disciplinary Margins." *Written Communication* 14 (1997): 398–428.

Soliday, Mary. "Class Dismissed." *College English* 61 (1999): 731–41.

____. "The Politics of Difference: Toward a Pedagogy of Reciprocity." Severino et al. 261–72.

Spack, Ruth. "The Rhetorical Construction of Multilingual Students." *TESOL Quarterly* 31 (1997): 765–74.

Sridhar, S. N. "A Reality Check for SLA Theories." *TESOL Quarterly* 28 (1994): 800–5.

Stern, H. H. *Fundamental Concepts of Language Teaching.* Oxford: Oxford UP, 1983.

Tambiah, S. J. *Sri Lanka: Ethnic Fratricide and the Dismantling of Democracy.* U of Chicago P, 1986.

Teachers of English to Speakers of Other Languages. Resolution on Language Rights [1987]. Rpt. *Language Loyalties* 148–49.

Thompson, Karen. "The Ultimate Working Condition: Knowing Whether You Have a Job or Not." *College Composition and Communication Forum* Winter 1998: A19–24.

Titone, Renzone. "History: The Nineteenth Century." *Routledge Encyclopedia of Language Teaching and Learning.* Ed. Michael Byram, London: Routledge, 2000. 264–270.

Trimbur, John. "The Problem of Freshman English (Only): Toward Programs of Study in Writing." *WPA* 22.3 (1999): 9–30.

U.S. English. "In Defense of Our Common Language." Rpt. *Language Loyalties* 143–47.

Valdés, Guadalupe. "Bilingual Minorities and Language Issues in Writing." *Written Communication* 9.1 (1992): 85–136.

Van Essen, Arthur. "History from the Reform Movement to 1945." *Routledge Encyclopedia of Language Teaching and Learning.* Ed. Michael Byram. London: Routledge, 2000. 270–75.

Veltman, Calvin. *The Future of the Spanish Language in the United States.* New York and Washington, DC: Hispanic Policy Development Project, 1988.

———. *Language Shift in the United States.* The Hague: Mouton, 1983.

Veysey, Laurence R. *The Emergence of the American University.* Chicago: U of Chicago P, 1965.

Zamel, Vivian. "Complicating Perspectives on the Acquisition of Language and Literacy." Conference on College Composition and Communication. Minneapolis, MN, 13 April 2000.

———. "Toward a Model of Transculturation." *TESOL Quarterly* 31 (1997): 341–52.

Acknowledgments

David Bartholomae. "Inventing the University." From *When a Writer Can't Write,* edited by Mike Rose. Copyright © 1985. Reprinted by permission of Guilford Press.

Wendy Bishop. "Helping Peer Writing Groups Succeed." From *Teaching Lives: Essays and Stories,* by Wendy Bishop. Copyright © 1997. Reprinted by permission of Utah State University Press.

Lynn Z. Bloom. "Why I (Used To) Hate to Give Grades." From *Composition Studies as a Creative Art.* Copyright © 1998. Reprinted by permission of Utah State University Press.

Robert J. Connors and Andrea A. Lunsford. "Frequency of Formal Errors in Current College Writing, or Ma and Pa Kettle Do Research." From *College Composition and Communication,* December 1988. Copyright © 1988 by the National Council of Teachers of English. Reprinted with permission.

Edward P. J. Corbett and Robert Connors. Excerpts from *Classical Rhetoric for the Modern Student,* Fourth Edition by Edward P. J. Corbett and Robert Connors, eds. Copyright © 1965, 1971, 1990, 1999 by Oxford University Press, Inc. Used by permission of Oxford University Press, Inc.

Peter Elbow. Excerpts from appendix of *Everyone Can Write* by Peter Elbow. Copyright © 2000 by Peter Elbow. Used by permission of Oxford University Press. "The Cultures of Literature and Composition: What Could Each Learn from the Other." From *College English,* Volume 64, Number 5, May 2002. © 2002 by the National Council of Teachers of English. Reprinted with permission.

Janet Emig. "Writing as a Mode of Learning." From *College Composition and Communication,* May 1977. Copyright © 1977 by the National Council of Teachers of English. Reprinted with permission.

Patrick Hartwell. "Grammar, Grammars and the Teaching of Grammar." From *College English,* February 1985. Copyright © 1985 by the National Council of Teachers of English. Reprinted with permission.

Bruce Herzberg. "Service Learning and Public Discourse." From the *Journal of Advanced Composition* 20.2 (2002). Reprinted by permission.

Bruce Horner and John Trimbur. "English Only and U.S. College Composition." From *College Composition and Communication* 53.4, June 2002. Copyright © 2002 by the National Council of Teachers of English. Reprinted with permission.

Ilona Leki. "Meaning and Development of Academic Literacy in a Second Language." From *Multiple Literacies for the 21st Century,* by Brian Huot, Charles Bazerman, and Beth Stroble, eds. Copyright © 2004. Reprinted by permission of Hampton Press.

Andrea A. Lunsford and Cheryl Glenn. "Rhetorical Theory and the Teaching of Writing." From *On Literacy and Its Teaching: Issues in English Education,* by Gail Hawisher and Anna O. Soter, eds. © 1990 State University of New York. Reprinted by permission. All rights reserved.

Beverly J. Moss and Keith Walters. "Rethinking Diversity: Axes of Difference in the Writing Classroom." From *Theory and Practice in the Teaching of Writing: Rethinking the Discipline,* by Lee Odell, ed. Copyright © 1993 by Beverly J. Moss and Keith Walters. Reprinted by permission of the authors and Southern Illinois University Press.

Acknowledgments (continued)

"Penn State's Guide to Understanding Plagiarism" and "Penn State University's English 15 Grading Standards." Courtesy of Penn State University and PSU English Dept.

Gabriel Rico. Excerpt from pp. 36–37 in *Writing the Natural Way* by Gabriel Rico. Copyright © 1983 by Gabriel Lusser Rico. Used by permission of Jeremy P. Tarcher, an imprint of Penguin Putnam, Inc.

Mike Rose. "The Language of Exclusion: Writing Instruction at the University." From *College English* 47.4, April 1985. Copyright © 1985 by the National Council of Teachers of English. Reprinted with permission.

Jacqueline Jones Royster. "When the First Voice You Hear Is Not Your Own." From *College Composition and Communication,* February 1996. Copyright © 1996 by the National Council of Teachers of English. Reprinted by permission.

Cynthia L. Selfe. "Toward New Media Texts: Taking Up the Challenges of Visual Literacy." From *Writing New Media: Theory and Applications for Expanding the Teaching of Composition,* by Anne Frances Wysocki, Johndan Johnson-Eilola, Cynthia L. Selfe, and Geoffrey Sirc. © 2004 Utah State University Press. Reprinted by permission.

Nancy Sommers. "Responding to Student Writing." From *College Composition and Communication,* May 1982. Copyright © 1982 by the National Council of Teachers of English. Reprinted with permission.

William Steig cartoon. From *The New Yorker,* 1958. Copyright © 1958. From Cartoonbank.com. All rights reserved.

Index